3D

3D

History, Theory and Aesthetics of the Transplane Image

JENS SCHRÖTER

Translated by Brigitte Pichon and Dorian Rudnytsky, revised by Jens Schröter

International Texts in Critical Media Aesthetics

BLOOMSBURY
NEW YORK • LONDON • NEW DELHI • SYDNEY

Bloomsbury Academic
An imprint of Bloomsbury Publishing Inc

1385 Broadway
New York
NY 10018
USA

50 Bedford Square
London
WC1B 3DP
UK

www.bloomsbury.com

Bloomsbury is a registered trade mark of Bloomsbury Publishing Plc

This translation first published 2014

The translation of this work was funded by Geisterwissenschaften International – Translation Funding for Humanities and Social Sciences for Germany, a joint initiative of the Fritz Thyssen Foundation, the German Federal Foriegn office, the collecting society VG WORT and the Börsenverein des Deutschen Buchhanders (German Publishers and Booksellers Association).

ISBN: HB: 978-1-4411-9408-4
PB: 978-1-4411-6726-2
ePDF: 978-1-4411-2999-4
ePub: 978-1-4411-4816-2

Library of Congress Cataloging-in-Publication Data
Schroeter, Jens.
[3D. English]
3D: history, theory, and aesthetics of the transplane image / Jens Schröter.
pages cm. — (International texts in critical media aesthetics)
Translated from German.
Translation of: 3D
Includes bibliographical references and index.
ISBN 978-1-4411-9408-4 (hardback) — ISBN 978-1-4411-6726-2 (paperback) — ISBN 978-1-4411-4816-2 (ePub) 1. Photography—Psychological aspects 2. Three-dimensional imaging—History. 3. Imagery (Psychology) 4. Aesthetics. I. Title. II. Title: History, theory, and aesthetics of the transplane image. III. Title: Three D.
TR183.S3713 2014
006.6′93—dc23
2013034736

Typeset by RefineCatch Limited, Bungay, Suffolk
Printed and bound in the United States of America

The domain of the modern episteme *should be represented rather as a volume of space open in three dimensions.*

Michel Foucault

Historians of science 100 years from now might characterize our era by the present efforts toward better three-dimensional imaging techniques.

Takanori Okoshi

CONTENTS

PART THREE Conclusions

ACKNOWLEDGMENTS

I'd like to thank Brigitte Pichon and Dorian Rudnytsky for their excellent translation, Anja Griesbach, Leonie Häsler and Marius Meckl for assisting the translation and revising the bibliography, Jan Wagener for working on the image rights and Rosemarie Klein for checking the bibliography again. My thanks are, of course, also due to the publishers Fink in Munich and Bloomsbury Publishing (former Continuum International Publishing group), especially to Katie Gallof and Francisco J. Ricardo, Angelika Bentfeld and Nadine Albert. My thanks to Jörgen Schäfer who made the first contact with Continuum (now: Bloomsbury). Above all, I wish to thank the *Börsenverein des deutschen Buchhandels* for their generous grant in 2011 towards the cost of translation. Finally my thanks and love to my parents, my brother and, of course, to Nicola for all her patience.

Visit my website: www.multimediale-systeme.de

PART ONE

Theoretical and Methodological Considerations

CHAPTER ONE

Outline

The history of optical media and the closely related but dissimilar history of vision or visual media have been widely discussed for some time already—certainly since the *pictorial* or *iconic turn*. Nonetheless, some additional questions need to be raised.

My *first proposal* is that there is a blind spot in the existing historical studies chronicling optical or visual media. They have not adequately accounted for what I will provisionally call the history of the *technological transplane* image.[1] Starting in the nineteenth century, this history has resulted in a series of technologically very different types of images (stereoscopy, photo-sculpture, integral photography, lenticular images, holography, volumetry, and a series of sub-types and hybrids). What they all share is that they *provide more information on space or the spatial structures of objects* than the images of (analog and digital) photography do that are projected in linear perspective. But they also provide more—or a different type of—information on space or the spatial structures of objects than the serialized images of film, video and TV. In this respect, on the one hand, they also surpass the forms of computer graphics oriented on perspective, while on the other hand they are themselves incorporated into other transplane forms of images generated by the computer.

Thus, as a *second proposal*, an alternative methodical access to the problem is suggested in contrast to Jonathan Crary's widely read study *Techniques of the Observer* (see section 1.1). Crary's study seems a likely starting point since he is one of the few scholars dealing in depth with the oldest 'three-dimensional image,'[2] stereoscopy. To be more exact: He is trying to include it into a history of a variety of 'optics.' He is the only one having tried this so far. Moreover, he is the only one who has even tried to structure a history of optical media by way of optics.[3] My study follows his concept except in assuming a successive and exclusive sequence of different optics. Consequently, this history of technically generated images in the nineteenth and twentieth centuries, and thus also the history of modern vision—provided it is formed and guided by technically generated images—is conceived as layers or as a palimpsest of simultaneous and different forms of optical knowledge (see section 1.2). From these different forms of optical knowledge the optical/visual media emerge—and therefore also transplane images (see section 1.3).

In the twentieth century, transplane images have become more and more important for diverse practical uses in military aerial reconnaissance, industrial engineering and ergonomics, natural sciences and medicine precisely because they are able to provide more spatial information. Moreover, their traces can also be found in the far-reaching field of the arts since it is particularly in that realm that in modernity the new *productions of space* (Henri Lefebvre, see section 1.4) are drawn on and reflected; here, new *media aesthetics* (see section 1.5) of spatiality and their images emerge. This study will attempt to write a history of the forms of transplane images that exist only in parts—if at all—and are lacking any systematical coherence.[4] It will include their genesis, their implications, functions and aesthetics—accepting the necessary limitation that not all forms and uses can be accounted for and therefore only those will be considered which I believe to be exemplary. In section 1.6 the succession of the historical case studies will be described.

1.1 Jonathan Crary's *Techniques of the Observer*

Crary's widely read *Techniques of the Observer: On Vision and Modernity in the Nineteenth Century* was published in 1990, effectively promoting the discussions on a history of vision.[5] One of its reviewers called it a "sort of bible of critical research in perception" (Apel 2002, 38). Another termed it one of the "most powerful studies in the realm of a cultural history of perception from a discourse analytical perspective" (Stiegler 2004, 287). Not only did it almost immediately play a prominent role in the theories of the arts and media; recently several branches of literary studies also discovered Crary's concepts, using them in order to approach such different subject matters as Brockes' baroque poetry or the psychological novels by Henry James.[6]

Wherein then lies the importance of *Techniques of the Observer*? Probably in the fact that Crary has given a new impulse to theories of art since he proposed writing a critique of the long tradition of the 'grand narratives' on the one hand. On the other hand he generally offers a new approach by attempting to transcend a history of technically generated images or optical media. He makes an effort to write a history of vision with regard to a history of the observer by connecting elements of the history of art with those of a history of technology against the background of a rather generalizing characterization of modernity as a capitalist formation. His arguments, which rely mainly on Foucault and Deleuze, are as inspiring as they are problematic. Therefore I will first introduce—but also criticize—his concept, especially with regard to the programmatic introduction to *Techniques of the Observer* pointing out the perplexing problems of his approach. These problems were the reasons for motivating me to think about an alternative model of media history. Choosing Crary as a contrast in this respect is therefore not only due to his importance or his detailed reference to the stereoscope.

1.1.1 Contours of Techniques of the Observer

1.1.1.1 Introducing the rhetorics of ruptures

"This is a book about vision and its historical construction" is the opening statement of *Techniques of the Observer*. The first page leaves no doubt that the motivation of this historical study is a most profound media upheaval of the twentieth century. Referring to "computer-generated imagery," Crary lists in a kind of 'Chinese encyclopedia' "[c]omputer-aided design, synthetic holography, flight simulators, computer animation, robotic image recognition, ray tracing, texture mapping, motion control, virtual environment helmets, magnetic resonance imaging, and multispectral sensors."[7] He argues that this diffusion of manifold new forms of imagery and practices with new media make the culturally established meanings of the observer and representation obsolete. One begins noticing that Crary is using a strong rhetorics of ruptures.

1.1.1.2 Rupture around 1820: Embodying vision

Yet, *Techniques of the Observer* does not really deal with the new pictorial forms that it only mentions in the beginning. It focuses on a rupture in the first third of the nineteenth century, an upheaval that produces "crucial preconditions" (Crary 1990, 3) for today's transformations. This rupture around 1820 can neither be reduced to a historical event in technology nor to certain historical changes in art; it separates "Renaissance, or *classical* models of vision and of the observer" from a "modern and heterogeneous regime of vision"[8]—a regime in which the body of the observer plays a central role. It is as important here that the *heterogeneity* of the modern regime of vision is mentioned as it is that the author talks of classical *models* of vision in the plural. This is pointed out specifically here because later on Crary will not mention the *synchronic* plurality and heterogeneity of regimes of vision again. Instead, when continuing, he is problematically homogenizing both the classical (see Atherton 1997) and the modern regime of vision.

He assumes a "crucial systemic shift" (Crary 1990, 5) to an *embodied observer* through whom in the end both modern painting and the optical media like photography and film should emerge.[9] The rupture then is one from a "pervasive suppression of subjectivity in vision in seventeenth- and eighteenth-century thought" to "models of subjective vision" (Crary 1990, 9).

1.1.1.3 The observer as effect: Crary's references to Foucault

Crary explicitly does not see this disruptive transformation of the status of the observer as one exclusive to the realm of (visual) perception. He considers visual perception a nebulous term, particularly when it is reduced to "changing forms of artworks over time."[10] He argues in contrast that the observer is a position where vision historically materializes. The observer is seen as the effect of an "irreducibly heterogeneous system of discursive, social, technological, and institutional relations." "There is no observing subject prior to this continually shifting field."[11] Crary reveals his methodological sources in a footnote to this last sentence, Michel Foucault, whose genealogical or archaeological method can be understood as an analysis of the historical conditions for the formation of subjectivity instead of as a type of historiography that presupposes the subject.[12] This pointed reference to (a specific reading of) Foucault's approach does not remain without consequences in Crary's methodological design. He particularly refers to Foucault's book *Les mots et les choses* (1966) in which Foucault also argues using strong rhetorics of ruptures (see 1.2.2). Closely aligning himself to this, Crary diagnoses a "general break or discontinuity at the beginning of the nineteenth century" (Crary 1990, 7).

1.1.1.4 From geometrical to physiological optics

Since the modern observer supposedly is embodied, Crary characterizes this break consequently as the "passage from geometrical optics of the seventeenth and eighteenth centuries to physiological optics, which dominated both scientific and philosophical discussion of vision in the nineteenth century" (16). This is the main reason why Crary's book is so significant for the design of this study: *He attempts to deduce the history of optical media—and also of the first three-dimensional image, stereoscopy—from the history of various optics*, something that is not done by other authors.[13] Such a deduction seems useful; for example, recognizing 'physiological optics' allows for plausible conclusions since

> efficiency and rationalization in many areas of human activity depended on information about the capacities of the human eye. . . . Retinal afterimages, peripheral vision, binocular vision, and thresholds of attention all were studied in terms of determining quantifiable norms and parameters.[14]

According to Crary, some of the optical tools, which he subsequently discusses more closely, evolved within the frame of these determinations.[15] Examples are stereoscopy as a by-product of analyzing binocular vision and cinema as a consequence of the study of the 'persistence of vision.' Consequently, photography is not the optical technology that embodies most succinctly the regime of modern vision after 1820—as one could believe—but *stereoscopy* (see Crary 1990, 116). The *camera obscura*, contrarily, is assigned to the status of the observer in the seventeenth or eighteenth century.[16] It is hardly surprising then that Crary can in no way accept the customary narrative[17] according to which photography, officially introduced in 1839, developed as a direct outcome of the earlier camera obscura.

1.1.1.5 The problematic status of photography

Obviously, photography, which Crary explicitly describes as a consequence of the shift to the embodied observer (see Crary 1990, 5), does not fit into this model.[18] Photography is mainly a product of the research on light or on the effects of light on chemical substances and in no way has its origins in the systematic study of human vision. None of the inventors and tinkerers (like Niépce or Bayard) or the entrepreneurs (like Daguerre) and scientists (Talbot, Herschel) who in the nineteenth century contributed to the development of the different forms and/or concepts of photography referred to the characteristics of the viewing body[19]—or did so only independently of it. Insofar it seems that Kittler's criticism of Crary's trendy "overemphasis of the body" is valid: "Crary's thesis would therefore be more precise if he had not spoken about physiology but rather about material effects in general, which can impact on human bodies as well as on technical storage media" (Kittler 2010, 148).

Crary indeed underlines the rift between optical technology that operates with knowledge of the body (stereoscopy) and photography. The first "*preceded* the invention of photography and *in no way required* photographic procedures or even the development of mass production techniques" (Crary 1990, 17). At the same time, however, the spreading popularity of the stereoscope would have been hardly possible without the implementation of stereo *photography*.[20] Therefore, it could be more expedient to see the development of the stereoscope and of photography not as two manifestations of *one* 'modern regime of vision', but indeed as two developments that are relatively independent from each other and which *then* can also interfere with each other.[21] Crary is unable to master photography. On the one hand its role is central: "It is through the distinct but interpenetrating economies of money and photography that a *whole social world* is represented and constituted exclusively as signs" (Crary 1990, 13; my emphasis). On the other hand he maintains: "Photography, however, is not the subject of this book" (Crary 1990, 13). It seems that photography is the "structuring absence"[22] in *Techniques of the Observer:* "Photography potentially threatens to undermine Crary's entire argument" (Phillips 1993, 136).

1.1.2 The self-dissolution of Crary's approach

The whole problem is poignantly concentrated at one point.[23] It can be found at the end of the chapter in which the modern regime of vision is outlined and which is entitled "Techniques of the Observer" (like the whole book). Its extensive discussion of the stereoscope ends with the plausible question why the stereoscope as a popular medium of entertainment disappears at the end of the nineteenth century if it is, as Crary was saying, the "intersection point" of the modern regime of vision.

The first paragraph states: "So when . . . the stereoscope eventually disappeared, it was not part of a smooth process of invention and improvement, but rather because [this] earlier form . . . [was] no longer adequate to current needs and uses" (Crary 1990, 132–3). Initially one notices that Crary explains the (seeming) disappearance of the stereoscope through evolving "needs and uses." This is surprising since he accounted for the transition from classical to modern regimes of vision in exactly the same way: "By the early 1800s, however, the rigidity of the camera obscura, its linear optical system, its fixed positions, its identification of perception and object, were all too inflexible and immobile for a rapidly changing set of cultural and political requirements" (Crary 1990, 137). In other words, the camera obscura paradigm first disappears due to new demands (a so-called modernization), clearing the way for the modern regime of embodied vision which in the nineteenth century was most significantly exemplified by the stereoscope.[24] But this stereoscope will itself disappear some decades later, a victim of new 'needs and uses' (whatever these may be). However, this time these do not signalize the beginning of a new regime of vision. This is difficult to comprehend.

Crary continues: "Photography defeated the stereoscope as a mode of visual consumption as well because it recreated and perpetuated the fiction that the 'free' subject of the camera obscura was still viable" (Crary 1990, 133). He argues that photography has defeated the stereoscope because it was accompanied by the fiction that the 'free subject of the camera obscura'[25] was still (or again) possible. Does this mean that shortly after it supposedly collapsed so spectacularly and completely at the beginning of the nineteenth century the paradigm of the camera obscura has been 'recreated and perpetuated' by photography?[26] Does this mean that the new 'needs and uses' that make the stereoscope disappear are calling for the paradigm of the camera obscura? And, moreover, how and why does this paradigm revive in photography of all places—photography which Crary ostentatiously differentiates from the camera obscura in six locations of *Techniques of the Observer*[27] as he does in the passage quoted here? Obviously Crary has a problem with geometrical optics and physiological optics existing side by side and he cannot integrate this fact into his model. Crary has no convincing explanation for the victory of photography, or rather he does not convince us why the stereoscopic way of viewing photographs has disappeared from the bourgeois living rooms (see Figure 1.1).

What is still more important: Stereoscopy does not disappear around 1900. It may be possible that it disappeared as a popular medium from the living rooms because from 1889 onward one could take photographs oneself, send photo-postcards, or somewhat later go to the movies.[28] But stereoscopy does not disappear from European and American culture at all. As Crary says elsewhere: "The ambivalence with which twentieth-century *audiences* have received 3D movies and holography suggests the enduring problematic nature of such techniques" (Crary 1990, 127, n. 45; my emphasis). He is concentrating only on the use of three-dimensional image technology as popular mass media (as can be seen from his reference to 'audiences') without acknowledging their increasingly important role within the diverse scientific or military practices (see p. 40).[29]

Instead of speaking of the "collapse of the stereoscope" (Crary 1990, 127) or of its "obsolescence" (Crary 1990, 132), it has to be underlined that "new media do not make old media obsolete" but (at least mostly) assign them "other places in the system."[30] As I will show, one should use a model that is not centered on sequentiality (where one medium[31] replaces or displaces another diachronically).

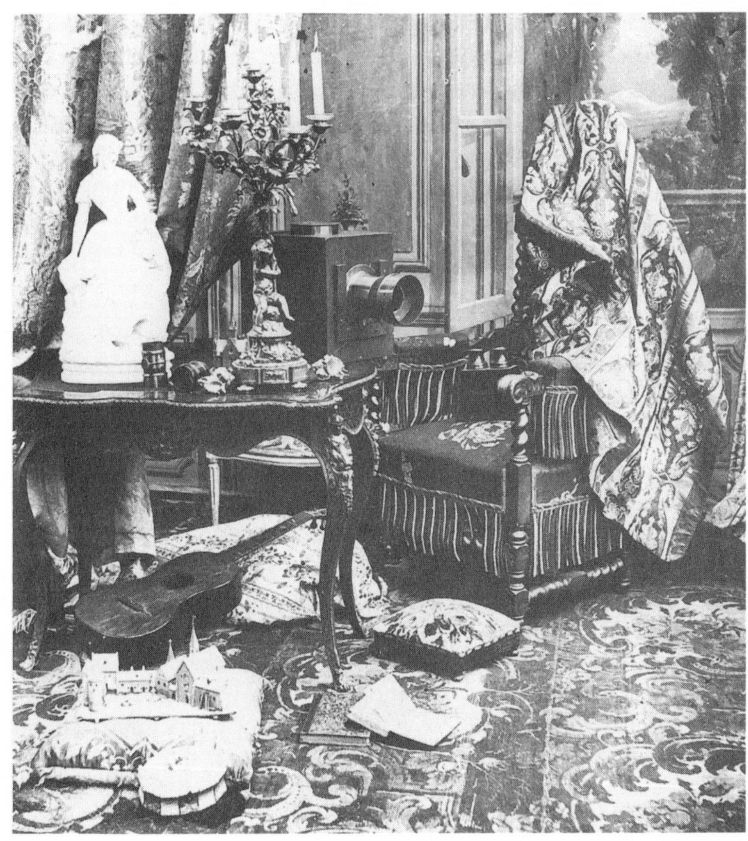

FIGURE 1.1 *Living room with stereoscope (on the armchair), in Crary (1990, 117).*

A better model would be oriented more spatially or topologically[32] (where several media are related synchronically to each other in a systemic relationship or exist and develop diachronically within a specific constellation). This allows avoiding other problems that are hinted at in the following passage:

> The prehistory of the spectacle *and* the 'pure perception' of modernism are lodged in the newly discovered territory of a fully embodied viewer but the eventual triumph of both depends on

> the denial of the body, its pulsing and phantasms, as the ground of vision. (Crary 1990, 136)

This sentence, which closes the passage discussed here and thus also constitutes the end of the chapter "Techniques of the Observer," is somewhat puzzling since with the surprising resurrection of the camera obscura paradigm in photography, the *disembodiment of the observer* is reinstated almost immediately.

1 *On the one hand* it is reinstated in photography and film as Crary writes elsewhere: "Paradoxically, the increasing hegemony of these two techniques [film and photography] helped recreate the myths that vision was incorporeal, veridical and realistic."[33]

2 *On the other hand* it is reinstated in modernism through its pursuit of the concept of disembodied, pure vision since Cézanne.[34]

The triumph of the camera obscura paradigm over its alleged successor—the modern regime of vision—is absolute.[35] It is unconditional to such an extent that precisely *the one* aspect that supposedly is constitutive for modern seeing—the embodiment—dissolves into thin air. And so, it appears that Crary's approach has conclusively deconstructed itself. But what is the reason for this "confusion" (Batchen 1993, 88) and how can the problem be approached in a different way? There seem to be three fundamental questions:

Question 1: Can one really say that a specifically '*modern regime* of vision' is following *sequentially* and quasi-free of any remnants to an earlier specifically *classical regime*?

Question 2: Can the 'modern regime of vision' really be called *a homogeneous* formation?

Question 3: What role does photography play in all this?[36]

I will anticipate the answers that I want to develop here: Questions 1 and 2 have to be answered with "No," while in opposition to Crary, photography (question 3) should be regarded as a displaced continuation of the camera obscura.[37]

1.2 Outlining an alternative

1.2.1 *Layering replacing succession*

David Phillips makes a helpful suggestion. In his concentrated analysis of *Techniques of the Observer* he comes to the hardly surprising conclusion that the "sequential narrative" (Phillips 1993, 137) of a clear-cut displacement of the classical regime of vision by a modern one is the fundamental problem. Even though Crary remarks *en passant* that "older and more familiar modes of 'seeing' will persist and coexist uneasily alongside . . . new forms" (Crary 1990, 1–2), he ultimately reduces the problem to an unambiguous sequentiality. Phillips criticizes:

> [H]e [Crary] fails adequately to take into account the persistence and durability of older modes of visuality . . . As opposed to this sequential model predicated upon an either/or model of vision . . . vision operates instead as a palimpsest which conflates many different modes of perception. (Phillips 1993, 137)

Therefore, a preliminary answer to the above Question 1 could be the following: The interesting point is not the displacement of one model by another, but possibly the addition of a new one to an older—and therefore relationally modified—model. Linda Williams argues similarly:

> Crary stresses [that . . .] the representational system symbolized by the camera obscura began to dissolve. [He] may go too far when he implies that it disappeared altogether. It seems more likely that this model survives as a rival system.[38]

Agreeing with these observations and assuming that the camera obscura paradigm does not disappear[39] but is accompanied at least since the nineteenth century by (no less than) one competing model—namely that of physiological optics—it follows: First, the model of physiological optics is no longer the 'modern' one in contrast to the classical one of the camera obscura since the latter is also part of modernity, even though it is relationally shifted.

Secondly—and that is my provisional answer to Question 2—the regime of vision in modernity cannot be taken as a homogeneous block.[40] Rather, it is a systemic coexistence characterized by changing correlations and dominances of (at least) two (there are more) different models, modes or forms,[41] correlated with different, specific types of technical images. *Obviously it is the coexistence of different types of technical images and their correlated forms of seeing that characterizes modernity.* Question 3 on the place of photography, which in Crary's approach had led to such confusion, can be answered in a preliminary way most easily as follows: Photography continues the camera obscura paradigm in a shifted way. Crary at first emphatically denies this but in the end admits to it anyway.

But this does not mean that the discontinuity underlined by Crary readily reverts into a simple continuity again. Even though the projective mechanisms in the optics of film, photography, video, digital photography and even in computer generated photorealistic images can definitely be compared with that of the camera obscura,[42] each one of them is nevertheless embedded or connected in different configurations or dispositives or constellations with different structures (for example in photochemical emulsions, quantum-electronical sensors, algorithms but also in other discourses, practices and media-aesthetic forms).

In the case of computer graphic photorealism using linear perspective, optics is itself virtual. Nevertheless it can still be regarded as the formal structure of a camera obscura.[43] Continuity and discontinuity would have to be connected systematically and in a differentiated way instead of contrasting them schematically. Crary hints at this himself: "The formal operation of a camera obscura as an abstract diagram may remain constant, but the function of the device or metaphor within an actual social or discursive[44] field has fluctuated decisively" (Crary 1990, 29). I am not denying here that the function changes; however, I do challenge the assertion that the 'formal operation' camera obscura is breaking down or disappears (as Crary repeatedly underlines in *Techniques of the Observer*). In the historical chapters of this study I will outline the manner in which the pattern of the camera obscura, i.e. geometrical optics, is being materialized in new and modified ways.

The modus involving the physical conditions of seeing (physiological optics) exists next to and together with the modus of the camera obscura. The stereoscope does not disappear at the end of the nineteenth century, as Crary maintains; it alters its "place . . .

in the system" (Kittler 1996, n.p.). Even though it leaves the area of entertainment apart from some occasional reappearances in movie theaters[45] and in playrooms (View-Master by Kodak), it becomes operative in other fields having to do with the control of space (for example aerial reconnaissance) and via that route finally becomes popularized again in 'virtual reality' (who does not know the images of data helmets and data glasses? See Figure 1.2).[46]

Another medium that is clearly a part of the 'somatic modus' (physiological optics) is cinema, since it requires the knowledge of the physiological conditions of perceiving movement.[47] By the way, as these last observations make clear, the correlation between the different modes is more or less normal: Stereoscopy in the nineteenth

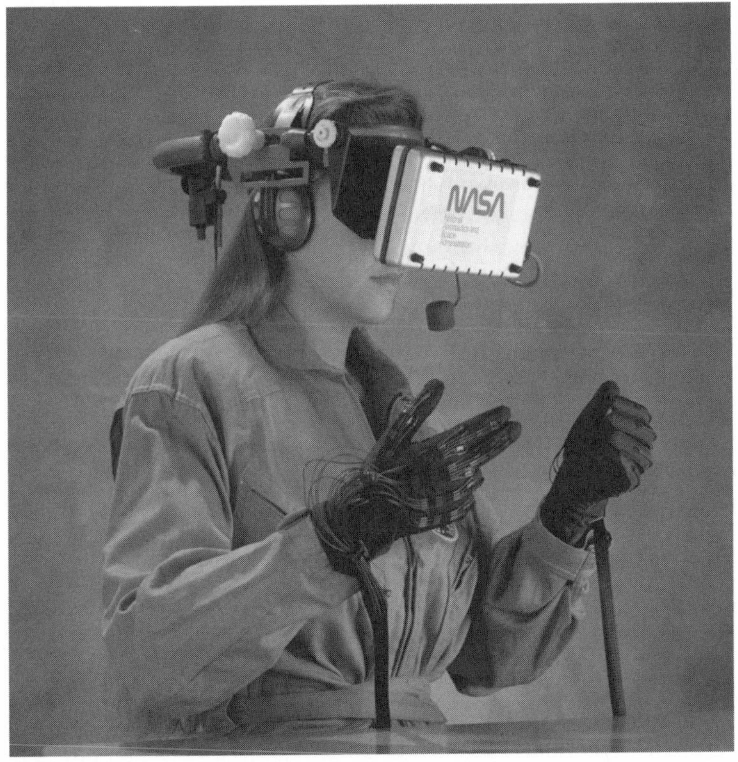

FIGURE 1.2 *Return of stereoscopy in the data glasses of virtual reality, in Bormann (1994, 80).*

century, like film, uses specific physiological characteristics of vision on the basis of images that in themselves are based on the camera obscura paradigm. It does this insofar as stereoscopy and film rely on photo-images, which is not absolutely *necessary* but which became a hegemonial correlation.[48] From this it can already be seen that a clearly separated sequential progression is a problematic model for describing the complexities of media history. Regarding optical media this would mean: The better approach is that different modes or layers of optical knowledge coexist parallel to each other. They can coalesce together with other economic and technical factors into certain optical media.[49]

In general, the methodological concern of this book is to critically assess the stories—as widely spread as they are problematic—in media historiography that proceed from 'revolutionary'[50] breaks without falling back into the equally problematic stories of teleological evolutionary developments of media.[51] I want to suggest taking the point of departure from "multi-layered temporal successions" (Koselleck 1971, 15). It remains necessary to underline that privileging layering over succession has nothing to do with the question of continuous or discontinuous processes. The only point is that there are several parallel processes of which some can be more and some less continuous.

I will now outline the question of the coexistence of discontinuity or continuity more specifically. First (1.2.2), I will examine the methodological reasoning that allows Crary to emphasize discontinuity and sequentiality. It is based in a certain reading of Michel Foucault's œuvre. We have to ask whether Foucault does not allow a different approach, which will be fundamental for the methodological design pursued here. Consequently I propose reformulating the succession of relatively homogeneous structures defined by relatively clear cuts ('the classical model' vs. 'the modern model')[52] into a more complex structure, which would be more difficult to formulate but in the end proves to be more conclusive (as Crary's problems seem to suggest). If this is done, the question remains secondly (1.2.3): Are the two following modes (which so far have hardly been delineated) either

1 the (modified) *camera obscura model* (geometrical optics), or

2 the *somatic model* (physiological optics).

Are these the only modes of optical knowledge (and the types of images correlated to them) that exist in modernity or do we have to assume more of these modes? The answer to start with is yes, there are at least two more of these modes and I will be able to describe their contours after another look at *Techniques of the Observer*.

1.2.2 Discontinuity and continuity: Which Foucault?

Let us look first at the theoretical context in which *Techniques of the Observer* is to be located. As I have mentioned already in the beginning, Crary points to Michel Foucault as a key source (see Crary 1990, 6). But *Foucault is not exactly Foucault*. His work can be differentiated into a series of different phases and steps[53] and we can legitimately ask *which* Foucault is hidden in Crary's approach. Soon enough it becomes quite clear that it is the Foucault of *Les mots et les choses* (1966; *The Order of Things*, 1994). Directly at the beginning of chapter three of *Techniques of the Observer*, "Subjective Vision and the Separation of the Senses," Crary expressly refers to *The Order of Things*. In this chapter Crary describes the (alleged) collapse of the camera obscura paradigm and the shift towards the model of embodied vision by referring both to Goethe's *Theory of Colors*[54] and to Kant. At first he quotes Foucault's comment according to which Kant's "subject-centered epistemology"[55] conflicts with the model of the transparent observer in the natural philosophy of the eighteenth century. Already here Crary sees a first and decisive step towards the model of embodied and subjective vision which was to dominate from the nineteenth century onward.[56] One page later Crary (1990, 71–2) quite extensively quotes Foucault's diagnosis for the beginning of the nineteenth century:

> [T]he site of the analysis is no longer representation but man in his finitude . . . These led to the discovery that knowledge has anatomo-physiological conditions, that it is formed gradually within the structures of the body, that it may have a privileged place within it, but that its forms cannot be dissociated from its peculiar functioning; in short, that there is a *nature* of human knowledge that determines its forms and that can at the same time be made manifest to it in its own empirical contents. (Foucault 1994, 319)

Clearly Crary has transformed Foucault's claim that the nineteenth century had discovered the physiological and anatomical conditions of knowledge into his own thesis that during exactly this same period the physiological-anatomical conditions of vision become central. Only a few pages later Crary once again repeats this explicit reference to the Foucault of *The Order of Things*:

> Physiology at this moment of the nineteenth century is one of those sciences that mark the *rupture* that Foucault poses between the eighteenth and nineteenth centuries, in which man emerges as a being in whom the transcendent is mapped onto the empirical.[57]

The Order of Things, therefore, can be called the basis of *Techniques of the Observer*; as noted previously, both books begin with a rather peculiar enumeration of heterogeneous phenomena on their opening pages (see Foucault 1994, xv; see Crary 1990, 1). And one notably rediscovers the idea of a rupture that suddenly and sequentially divides a classical from a modern regime in which the human empirical anatomy shifts to the center.[58] Crary takes over certain characteristics of Foucault's *The Order of Things*: to be precise, the (quite conventional) classification of history into several sequential, quite homogeneous large formations which Foucault calls *episteme*. But since this model becomes rather problematic for Crary's aims—as I have shown—we should ask whether there could not have been other paths with a different Foucault.[59]

Regarding the differences between *The Order of Things* (1994) and *The Archaeology of Knowledge* (1972) (which was published in France three years after *Les mots et les choses* in 1969), Bernhard Waldenfels remarks: "What appears here [in *The Order of Things*] in the form of global *epistemai* as large historical formations is divided in *The Archaeology of Knowledge* into a multiplicity of specific *discourses*" (Waldenfels 1995, 238; emphasis in the original). Indeed, in his *Archaeology* Foucault is criticizing his own approach in his *Order*: "in *The Order of Things*, the absence of methodological signposting may have given the impression that my analyses were being conducted in terms of cultural totality" (Foucault 1972, 16). This means that only three years after the publication of the *Order*, Foucault was no longer convinced that an analysis of the terminology of large historical formations would be the correct way. He writes in the *Archaeology*:

> To say that one discursive formation is substituted for another is not to say that a whole world of absolutely new objects, enunciations, concepts, and theoretical choices emerges fully armed and fully organized in a text that will place that world once and for all; it is to say that a general transformation of relations has occurred, but that it does not necessarily alter all the elements; it is to say that statements are governed by new rules of formation, it is not to say that all objects or concepts, all enunciations or all theoretical choices disappear. On the contrary, one can, on the basis of these new rules, describe and analyse phenomena of continuity, return, and repetition. (Foucault 1972, 173)

This means that one could also follow arguments by Foucault that do not force discontinuity upon us.[60] But in fact in *Techniques of the Observer* there is even an entry in the index for 'discontinuity' which points out nine references (see Crary 1990, 165) and Crary underlines, for example:

> While my discussion of the camera obscura is founded on notions of *discontinuity* and *difference*, Alpers, like many others, poses notions of both *continuity* in her lineage of the origins of photography and *identity* in her idea of an a-priori observer who has perpetual access to these free-floating and transhistorical options of seeing.[61]

In my opinion this is a reading that emphasizes discontinuity (and which accuses Alpers of advocating *continuity* and therefore *identity* even though these two aspects do not necessarily have to be identical) whereas the real question should be how the correlation between discontinuity and continuity can be understood.[62] Foucault in his *Archaeology* describes cases in which "elements . . . may remain identical . . . yet belong to different systems of dispersion" or "elements that remain throughout several distinct positivities" up to "elements that reappear after a period of desuetude, oblivion, or even invalidation."[63] His conclusion is:

> The problem for archaeology is not to deny such phenomena, nor to try to diminish their importance; but, on the contrary, to try to describe and measure them: how can such permanences or

> repetitions, such long sequences or such curves projected through time exist? (Foucault 1972, 174)

Therefore, Foucault claims that "[a]rchaeology proposes . . . (for our aim is not to accord to the discontinuous the role formerly accorded to the continuous) to play one off against the other" (Foucault 1972, 174). The result is that

> the rupture is not an undifferentiated interval . . . between two manifest phases . . . The idea of a single break suddenly, at a given moment, dividing all discursive formations, interrupting them in a single moment and reconstituting them in accordance with the same rules—*such an idea cannot be sustained*.[64]

And Foucault concludes:

> Archaeology disarticulates the synchrony of breaks, just as it destroyed the abstract unity of change and event. The *period* is neither its basic unity, nor its horizon, nor its object . . . The Classical age, which has often been mentioned in archaeological analyses, is not a temporal figure that imposes its unity and empty form on all discourses; it is the name that is given to a tangle of continuities and discontinuities. (Foucault 1972, 176; emphasis in the original)

It could not be more explicit that Foucault in no way encourages "concerning [one]self primarily with the analysis of the discontinuous."[65] I propose joining Foucault in the suggestion that the rupture that supposedly separates the model of the camera obscura from the modern regime of seeing should be replaced by a "dispersion of the discontinuities" (Foucault 1972, 175) and—it should be added—of continuities. Notably, it is the ways in which the element of the camera obscura is included into very different formations and sedimentations (see section 1.3) or in which binocular vision is therein operationalized that necessitates such an approach as much as it illustrates it. An "ever-increasing number of strata" or layers whose "specificity of their time and chronologies"[66] has to be considered. It could well prove to be that the different 'modes of seeing' or the different forms of optical knowledge and the technical images connected to them will be precisely these layers. Taking up a term by Crary, the 'modern viewer' is therefore not defined by *one* specific modern regime of seeing; rather they are characterized by being exposed to a plurality of pictorial forms or ways of seeing (and this means to the discursive practices connected with the images).[67] Consequently, this assumption asserts that *the* modern viewer does not exist at all, but rather a field of possible positions for viewers.[68]

But we have to be careful: Foucault also underlines that archaeology is not "trying to obtain a plurality of histories juxtaposed and *independent of one another*" (Foucault 1972, 10; my emphasis). Instead, something else is in effect:

> The problem that now presents itself—and which defines the task of a general history—is to determine what form of relation may be legitimately described between these different series; what *vertical system* they are capable of forming; what interplay of correlation and dominance exists between them; what may be the effect of shifts, different temporalities, and various rehandlings; in what distinct totalities certain elements may figure simultaneously. (Foucault 1972, 10; my emphasis)

The different series of optical knowledge that form the complex formation of modern vision by way of their interferences and competitions, their correlations and dominances[69] are kept together by way of (at least) one specific "vertical system"[70] (Foucault): It is the *control of space*.

However, this comment will make us pause immediately: Isn't it one of the most conspicuous characteristics of modern technical visual media to be able to show *moving images* for the first time—i.e. temporalized types of images? This is indeed true and therefore we have to understand the modern technologies of visualization as powerful methods to control space *and* time (or, since Einstein: space-time).[71] However, the *control of time* (the repeatability of operations, fast and slow motion and the inversion of the temporal axis) by way of moving images will play only a secondary role here for two reasons. First, this aspect has been extensively treated elsewhere[72] while here we are contrarily dealing with the history of *spatial control* that hitherto has hardly been analyzed. Secondly, putting images in motion (be they drawn, photographed, stereoscopic, holographic or images generated by a computer) is always a process of *serializing* the images. This process does not have anything to do with the question of the different optical series that are the basis of the (individual) technical images,[73] apart from the fact that this serializing has to presuppose a physiological-optical knowledge (or at least a similar heuristic experience) of the conditions that allow a chain of images to be perceived as a moving image.[74]

1.2.3 The four optical series

Continuing, I will deal with the question whether apart from the *geometrical-optical* series (linear perspective,[75] camera obscura, photography) and the simultaneously existing somatic—or more precisely *physiological-optical*—series (stereoscopy, cinema), any others exist in modernity. As already mentioned, the answer is yes.

A third series that Crary mentions only in passing is the series of *wave optics*, appearing as a small digression in the third chapter of *Techniques of the Observer* in which he is dealing with the shift to the embodied observer: "The physiological optics outlined by Goethe and Schopenhauer with their models of subjective vision . . . must be seen against the profound changes that took place in theories of the nature of light."[76] Crary maintains that simultaneous with the shift to the embodied observer a change in the concepts of the nature of light becomes apparent:

> The wave theory of light made obsolete the notion of a rectilinear propagation of light rays on which classical optics and, in part, *the science of perspective* was based. . . . The verisimilitude associated with perspectival construction obviously persisted into the nineteenth century, but it was severed from the scientific base that had once authorized it . . . Dominant theories of vision [before wave optics] . . . described . . . how a beam of isolated light rays traversed an optical system, with each ray taking the shortest possible route to reach its destination. The camera obscura is inextricably wedded to this point-to-point epistemological setup. (Crary 1990, 86; my emphasis)

Geometrical optics have for a long time now described the nature of light as a bundle of linear light rays.[77] However, from the beginning of the nineteenth century it was displaced by the idea of light as a transversal wave-front comparable to waves in water.[78] This happened not at all in a sudden rupture but rather slowly thanks to new experimental findings that were not compatible with geometrical optics. But Crary's conclusion, ending in the assumption that with this transition perspective[79] and the paradigm of the camera obscura (which at this point once again are named in the same breath) were somehow divested of their scientific basis and therefore obsolete, does not seem to be correct.

First, geometrical optics simply continues to exist to this day (with modifications). Geometrical optics is the knowledge of the observable regularity of light especially in the macroscopic realm. It is that field of knowledge which Crary sometimes names "classical optics" associating it with perspective and camera obscura and which indeed is connected to these two technologies. Carter states this succinctly:

> Scientific perspective, known variously as central projection, central perspective, or picture plane or Renaissance or linear or geometrical perspective, may be regarded as the scientific norm of pictorial representation. The story of its development belongs as much to the history of geometry as that of painting. It is the perspective of the pin-hole camera (and with certain reservations as regards lens distortion) of the camera obscura and the photographic camera. It derives from geometrical optics and shares with that science its basis in physics: the rectilinear propagation of light rays.[80]

In a current benchmark study on optics, geometrical optics is of course still a subcategory (see Hecht 1987, 128–241). It is clearly said: "There are many situations in which the great simplicity arising from the approximation of geometrical optics more than compensates for its inaccuracies [as compared to wave optics]" (Hecht 1987, 129). One of these situations is the calculation of optical systems. The approximation of light as a ray is operative and functional for the description of the behavior of light in lens-systems and is a given for nearly all technological images in one form or another, be they stored and/or generated in an analog or a digital way.[81] In connection with geometrical optics, the camera obscura—and its logical successor the camera—is also dealt with in the just quoted standard work: "The prototype of the modern photographic camera was a device known as the *camera obscura*, the earliest form of which was simply a dark room with a small hole in one wall" (Hecht 1987, 198). As previously repeatedly mentioned, the series of geometrical optics continues to exist together with the somatic series, i.e. physiological optics.[82]

Secondly, the latter, which is so strongly exposed by Crary in his book, has nothing to do with the question of whether light is comprehended as a bundle of rays (or particles emitted in form of rays), or as a transversal wave front. Physiological optics deals with the fact that people (in general) have two eyes and that by way of complex cognitive processes the impression of movement is generated from successively projected images and so on. And for these questions it is simply irrelevant what the nature of light is. They are simply two different series of optical knowledge—on the one hand the question is the behavior of a radiation while on the other hand it is the reaction of biological organisms to this radiation.[83]

Crary continues arguing by referring to Augustine Jean Fresnel, a significant theoretician of early wave optics:

> Fresnel's work participates in the destruction of classical mechanics, clearing the ground for the eventual dominance of modern physics. What had been a discrete domain of optics in the seventeenth and eighteenth centuries now merged with the study of other physical phenomena, i.e., electricity and magnetism. Above all, it is a moment when light loses its ontological privilege. . . . More importantly here, however, as light began to be conceived as an electromagnetic phenomenon it had less and less to do with the realm of the visible and with the description of human vision. (Crary 1990, 87–8)

The question here is no longer whether the understanding of light as a transversal wave front displaces the conception of light as a bundle of linear rays or of the flux of particles. The question, rather, is in what way light, with the beginning of modern electrodynamics, has to be conceived of as a special case of the electromagnetic spectrum (a topic that is historically connected to wave optics but is in no way identical with it).[84] It thereby would lose its 'ontological privilege' as well as its linkage to visibility. But this argument is problematic as well. Of course light becomes part of a much wider spectrum (visible light is merely the small field between wave lengths of 400–750 nm), but visible light is precisely the visible part of this spectrum. It does not become less visible because it is part of this spectrum. Nevertheless, Crary draws the following conclusion:

> So it is at this moment in the early nineteenth century that physical optics (the study of light and the forms of its propagation) merges with physics and physiological optics (the study of the eye and its sensory capacities) suddenly came to dominate the study of vision. (Crary 1990, 88)

It is also just as self-evident as it is tautological that only physiological optics[85] can describe human vision—who else could do it? The real problem lies in the fact that Crary disregards physical optics even though it is to this day fundamentally relevant both in the form of geometrical as well as wave optics. In no way *can* the history of (modern) vision only be a history of subjective vision since there are technologies based on physical optics that allow us to see images[86] which do in no way presuppose physiological attributes or the knowledge of these. Examples for that are photography (including their analog and digital-electronic successors) as noted several times, or holography – which is in no way marginal[87] in the twentieth century and which I will discuss later—not to mention the computer-generated images of *virtual optics* (see Chapter 10). Modernity cannot be reduced to one singular regime of physiological optics.[88] Wave optics is simply a genuine *series*—as Foucault would say.

On the one hand it has to be differentiated from the series of geometrical optics (perspective/camera obscura/photography) even though geometrical optics is mathematically implied by wave optics. Wave optics describes phenomena of light like diffraction, polarization and interference, which geometrical optics does not describe—and does not have to describe as a rule. Refraction and reflection suffice as descriptive categories because the structures which interact with light (mirrors, lenses, etc.) are large in relation to the wave length (λ) of light. If it were different we could look around corners since light would flow around them like waves of water (see Pirenne 1970, 11). To a certain extent this really happens; this is precisely the effect that is called diffraction. But these wave-optical phenomena appear as disturbances in the field of geometrical-optical technologies—diffraction limits the resolution of lenses.

Nevertheless, these disturbances can become starting points for new knowledge and therefore for new wave optical technologies.[89]

On the other hand wave optics has to be differentiated from the series of physiological optics as well. This becomes implicitly obvious in Stiegler:

> Even if the invention of the stereoscope cannot be directly related to the wave theory discussed by Thomas Young and experimentally established by Agustin Fresnel, it takes place at a point in time when the new theory begins to take a hold. (Stiegler 2001, 60–1)

Maybe that point in time is *approximately* the same[90]—but that is about as far as it goes. After that, wave optics is no longer talked about; even Crary mentions its most important after-effect—holography—only twice and only in passing, and moreover hardly in connection with his remarks on wave optics.[91]

Ultimately we have to reproach Crary's *rhetorics* of discontinuity and heterogeneity.[92] On the one hand he wrongly underlines discontinuity by constructing a succession of "geometrical optics of the seventeenth and eighteenth centuries to physiological optics . . . in the nineteenth century"—which is only possible because he represses the continuation of geometrical optics (up to several procedures of computer graphics; for example, ray tracing).[93] On the other hand he is still not 'heterogenistic' enough since after all he is degrading wave optics (and the optical procedures based on it) to an attendant phenomenon, despite its difference from physiological and geometrical optics. That means we have to speak of at least three series of optical knowledge:

1. *geometrical optics*
2. *wave optics*[94]
3. *physiological optics*

These three layers or series are those fields of knowledge that—cautiously stated—*are connected* with all technical visual media (see section 1.3).

1. Knowing the rules of *geometrical optics* permits the construction of (physical or virtual) systems of representation—from photography to virtual ray tracing.

2 Knowing the mathematical formulas of *wave optics* allowed Lippmann in 1891 to develop interferential color photography and Gabor in 1948 to lay the foundations of holography—ultimately leading up to virtual synthetic holography.

3 *Physiological optics*, by measuring the human eye or rather human cognition, permits precisely constructing different optical technologies that use the specific characteristics of the human senses—from stereoscopy via film up to the virtual volumetric displays.

Already these three descriptions indicate that beyond them there is still a fourth layer that stands, as one could say, in an oblique relation to these three optics. It emerges from the second half of the twentieth century onwards and repeats, reallocates and connects all different series of optics discussed so far once more.

4 This is *virtual optics* which makes all "optic modes optional," (Kittler 2001, 35) thereby connecting the different optics in a manner that until then had not been possible; it also relates them to other series (for example, by reviving the importance of the sense of touch in the so-called 'interactive images'; see Chapter 10).

1.3 Some short remarks on optics and optical media

There are four series of optical knowledge. But how can we describe the connection between optical knowledge and technologies of media accurately? Does optical knowledge precede the formation of a specific technology? There are examples: What is interesting with regard to Lippmann photography first presented in 1891 (which still needs to be discussed more closely) is among other things that Lippmann was a physicist interested in optics who explicitly aimed at developing this new photographic procedure.[95] However, the relationship can also be less unambiguous—the alternative could be that forms of knowledge can emerge inversely from media technologies. Interestingly enough the scholars at the time of the invention of photography did not quite understand precisely how the change in the photosensitive material took place (see Arago 1839, 29; see also Hagen 2002, 200). Similarly in film: Even though psycho-physiological knowledge was an (implicit) prerequisite to build movie projectors, it was back then not known exactly how the perception of movement functioned. On the contrary—cinematography prompted new questions and it became a means to study perception (see Hoffmann 2001).

Kittler observes: "From the camera obscura to the television camera, all these media have simply taken the ancient law of reflection and the modern law of refraction and poured them into hardware" (Kittler 2001, 34–5; see also Kittler 2010, 49). What does it mean to pour an optical law into hardware? It is much easier to understand how these laws, due to their mathematical structures, can themselves become computer software and therefore—as Shannon has shown (see Shannon 1938)—also digital hardware.[96] But what does this mean for technologies that are not programmable in a narrower sense?

Let us stay with Kittler's example. Since light can be mathematically described as straight and linear rays, the rules of linear perspective could be formulated[97] and technical appliances could be built that follow these rules automatically and far more accurately than the hands of a painter could.[98] In other words, photography does not create linear perspective images because the rules somehow 'emigrated' from painting into photography (as Kittler 2010, 61 seems to imply): It creates them because building lens-systems is based on the same behavioral model of light as the one that forms the basis of linear perspective (see Snyder 1980). Lens optics, then, are a different *materialization* of geometrical optics[99] rather than a *continuation* of the linear perspective as used in Renaissance images. The series of geometrical optics is a *transmedial*[100] field of knowledge that can be materialized in different materialities of media in slightly altered but sufficiently similar form in order to be compared to each other.

The status of the other optical series that are discussed here is similar. In film, television or virtual volumetric images the knowledge of the conditions for creating the impression of movements by way of serialized images—an element of physiological optics—can be materialized in different ways. Every materialization of optical knowledge is a "heterogeneous ensemble" (Foucault 1980, 194) of different discursive and non-discursive elements.

For example: The existence of lens systems[101] based on the model of geometrical optics is self-evidently a basis for the existence of photography today, but by no means fully adequate. Of course, photography only became possible with the development of materials that changed with the incidence of light and could also be fixated, i.e. with a certain chemical knowledge.[102] However, this is also true for *photograms* that are made without lens optics and were quite prevalent in the still unstable and fluctuating early phase of photography (see Figure 1.3) simply for the reason that often the

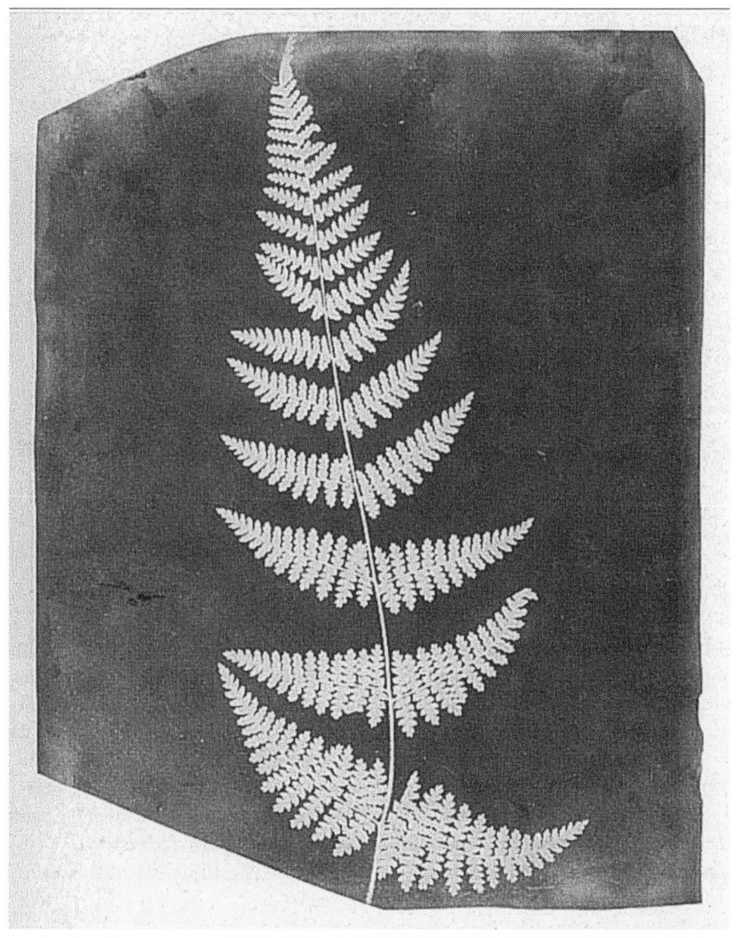

FIGURE 1.3 *Henry Fox Talbot,* Buckler Fern *(1839), Photogram, Negative, 22.1 × 17.7 cm, in Getty Museum (2002, 25).*

photochemical emulsions were not sensitive enough for an image projected through a lens (since lenses swallow light).

In his speech on July 3, 1839, Arago already talks of the use of the camera obscura for the creation of images and in the same way photography is self-evidently seen today as a geometrical-optical image projected by a lens system onto a chemical sensor—with the exception of the art system in which photograms, for example, enjoyed a certain resurgence of popularity in the 1920s (Moholy-Nagy). The two elements 'geometrical optics' and 'photochemical recording'—that in no way necessarily belong to each other—have consolidated or 'punctualized'[103] over time into a relatively stable constellation, namely photography, after they had passed through diverse photochemical procedures and different types of lens-systems.[104]

It seems that only with the introduction of quantum electronic sensors like the CCD to commercial photography in 1989 did some sort of change take place. A hectic discussion on the (alleged) loss of reference of photographic images began—however, in everyday practice like family photography digital photography is used in very similar ways as analog photography before. Shifting constellations are quite conceivable and are relatively 'normal'—therefore the excitement about the transition to digital photography seems exaggerated (see Schröter 2004a).

And by the way, reproducibility was not part of photography from the beginning—daguerreotypes were still one of a kind. It took Talbot's independently created inventions in photography based on paper that established the difference between a negative from multiple positives could be made. This development established itself from 1841 onward for a variety of reasons (commercial, legal) over daguerreotypes, which actually had a rather better quality: "Thus from an accidental discovery and invention still some new, useful, and strange things can emerge which in the beginning had not been thought of at all."[105]

The optical series on which the projection of the object onto a light-sensitive carrier is based is comparable within camera obscura, camera, film and television, as well as within digital photography and even in computer-graphic photorealism (ray tracing). In film, every frame is also projected geometrically onto a light-sensitive carrier; however, this procedure is serialized, an apparatus synchronizes the exposure and transport of pictures on an elastic ribbon (somewhat similar to industrial production, see Berz 2001, 403–96). Television cameras also project the picture geometrically onto a sensor, but it is not stored chemically there; it is electronically scanned.[106] In this way the image can be transmitted and reconstructed on the receiver's side again. Like in film, one has to presuppose the use of the knowledge from physiological optics once more, i.e. what the number of scanning lines and how fast the image buildup has to be so that the image can produce a fluid movement for human perception. It seems that optical media[107] are to be described as something like 'correlations' and 'linkings' of different and not only optical[108] series.

And so it is in stereoscopy as well. Charles Wheatstone, in his important text on the physiology of vision in which he first envisions the stereoscope, quite consciously used simple drawings very pointedly in order to avoid any other reference to depth of vision except that of binocularity.

> For the purposes of illustration I have employed only outline figures, for had either shading or colouring been introduced it might be supposed that the effect was wholly or in part due to these circumstances, whereas by leaving them out of consideration no room is left to doubt that the entire effect of relief is owing to the simultaneous perception of the two monocular projections, one on each retina. (Wheatstone 1983, 72)

This means that for Wheatstone a stereoscopic use of photography (which by the way at this point in time had not yet been officially introduced) would have been practically counterproductive.

Commercial providers discovered the potential in a fusion of stereoscopy and photography around 1851, a relationship that soon stabilized and seemed almost natural (see Schiavo 2003). This connection established itself because, as I have mentioned, when faced with increasing complexity, stereoscopic drawings quickly became hard to produce accurately whereas the rigid geometry of the camera lens automatically guaranteed the necessary synchronicity of the images. The effort to correlate the two images can be delegated to the lens. This joining of photography and stereoscopy then became 'stereoscopy'—a blunder which has left its marks until today and is also visible in Crary.[109] In around 1966 the stereoscopic scheme once again connected to new technologies and discourses; these were interactively generated images and for a

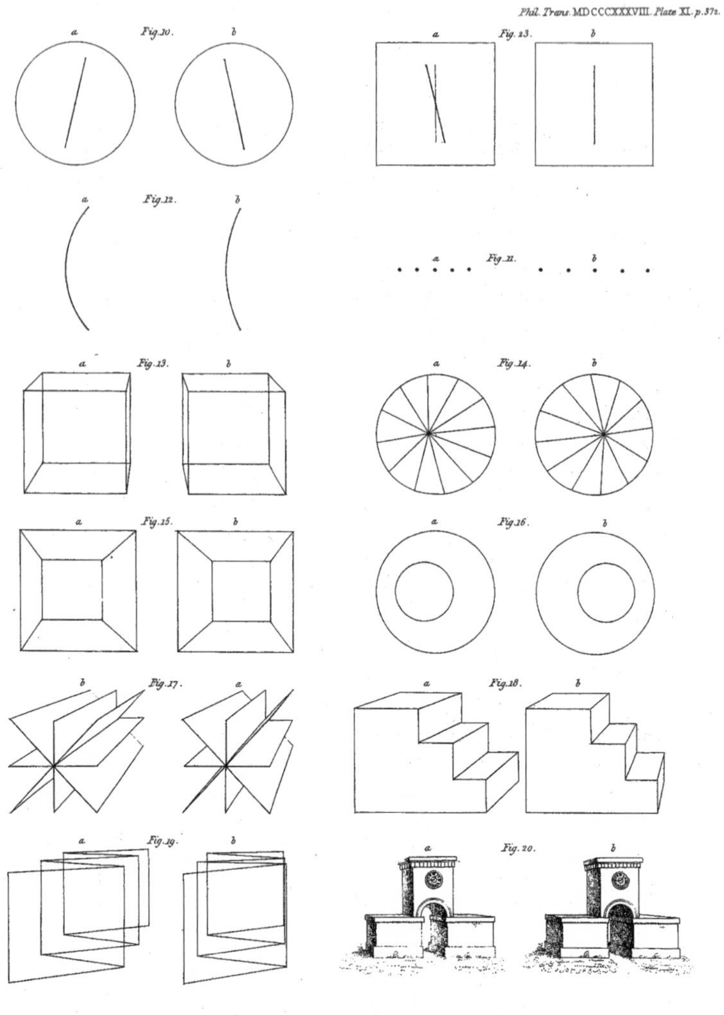

FIGURE 1.4 *Stereoscopic drawings, in Wheatstone (1983, 73).*

certain amount of time this was part of so-called 'virtual reality' with its stereoscopic data glasses.

I would like to call these processes of stabilizing a medium via tinkering and experimenting, superimposing various series, elements and materials, and by repeating certain procedures and attributions, 'sedimentation.'[110] This means that technologies never emerge monocausally from a field of knowledge (e.g. geometrical or physiological optics) or from a social practice (e.g. the natural sciences or the military);[111] it is always the result of conflicting and complex consolidations.[112] Very often "*urgent need[s]*" (Foucault 1980, 195) provide the initiation of such experiments in new technologies. If a technology has been developed as a functional prototype, it might happen that industries attempt to market this technology in areas outside of their original operational area. In most cases certain standards are established after having passed through conflicts in the beginning—the sedimentation is thus often characterized by industrial strategies (see Winston 2003, 1–15). Some of these processes in relation to technical transplane images will be described in this study.

1.4 Transplane images and the production of space (Henri Lefebvre): 3D

Evidently, there are obvious differences between the media-technological sedimentations of the four interfering optical series.

1.4.1 *First series: Geometrical optics—plane*

The aim of the projective procedures in geometrical optics (like perspective projection, camera obscura and later as its outgrowth photography) is the *projection of a three-dimensional object or several objects within space onto a two-dimensional plane.*[113] In *De pictura* (1435) Alberti defined the painted image, as an "*intersection* of the visual pyramid . . . [an intersection] reproduced with art by means of lines and colors on the given surface" (Alberti 2011, 34; my emphasis).

As I have explained, the procedure in painting to construct this section of a plane by using the intercept theorem is dissimilar from the procedures in technological optical systems, where these rules of

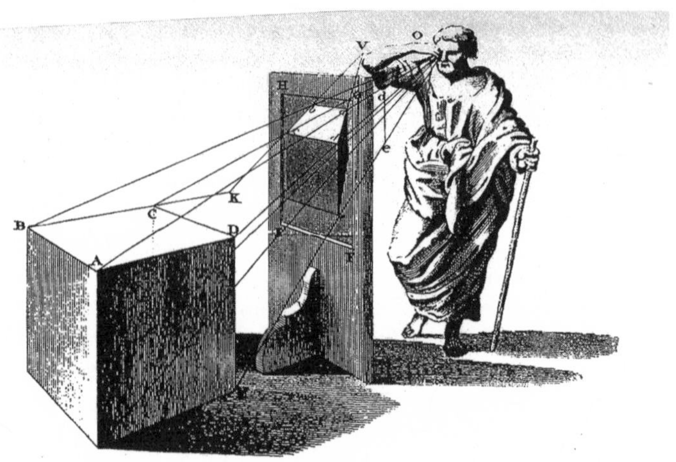

FIGURE 1.5 *Section of the visual pyramid composed of lines (Taylor 1715), in Andersen (1992, 231).*

construction have been automated, therefore separating them from the work of the human hand. Nevertheless, the element 'projection onto a plane' is central to the media based on geometrical optics to this day:

> Reflection and linear perspective, refraction and aerial perspective are the two mechanisms that have indoctrinated the Western mode of perception [on perspectival projection], all counterattacks of modern art notwithstanding. What once could be accomplished in the visual arts only manually, or, in the case of Vermeer and his *camera obscura*,[114] only semi-automatically, has now been taken over by fully automated technical media.[115]

Implicitly emphasizing the importance of the plane with regard to the concept of the image is a result of the continuing dominance of linear perspective. This is important, particularly since perspective does not necessarily demand the projection onto the plane.[116] I do not want to leave unmentioned that one of the oldest concepts of images—"So God created man in his own image, in the image of

God created he him, male and female created he them"[117]—cannot be understood as the projection of a three-dimensional object onto a plane; far more it talks of a spatial and three-dimensional replication of a supranatural entity about whose physical make-up we know next to nothing. Even though terms like 'sculptural image' or 'pictorial arts' indicate that sculptural phenomena at the very least were historically called 'images,' according to Martina Dobbe the concept of image still follows to this day the "paradigm of the composed panel painting."[118]

The consequence of these historical developments is *planocentrism*, which to this day permeates all discussions on the term 'image,' and could be understood to be similar to Derrida's term 'logocentrism' (as a critique of the displacement of the signifier's exteriority, see Derrida 1976). It is, according to Derrida, typical for Western logocentric metaphysics of presence to privilege voice over writing, i.e. presence over temporalization and spatialization. In a similar way planocentrism privileges the plane that supposedly is readily comprehensible 'at a single glance,'[119] i.e. as a presence within the awareness of an observer who is present him- or herself. In contrast to this, space can never be perceived in one swoop so that human observers are consistently thrown back onto their irreducible corporeality and perspectivity.[120]

There are numerous examples for this—I would like to briefly mention only one of the most striking and well-known ones. In 1967 the art historian and theoretician Michael Fried published a famous attack on *minimal art*, relatively new at that time. In this text, "Art and Objecthood," he first disputed the thesis of the minimalist Donald Judd who maintained that the "rectangular plane is given a life span." Fried counters by saying that the minimalists had to "give up working on a single plane in favor of three dimensions" (Fried 1968, 118; Judd quoted by Fried). Figure 1.6 shows the work *DIE* (1962) by Tony Smith.[121] The "dying" in the title could be applied to projection and plane without problems since the cube projected onto the plane in this figure is now present in space itself—without projection and without plane (apart from being projected again *here*).

This, according to Fried, necessitates that the minimalists' works have to be experienced "*in a situation*" and "one that, virtually by definition, *includes the beholder*" (Fried 1968, 125; emphasis in the original). Fried calls this situation explicitly 'theatrical.' In

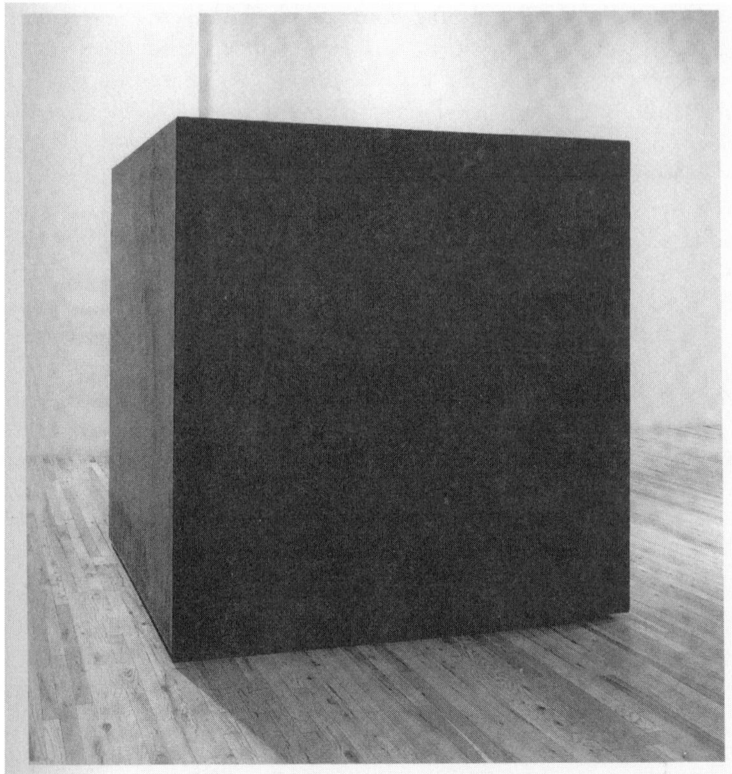

FIGURE 1.6 *Tony Smith, DIE (1962). One can see how the cube projected in Figure 1.5 now returns as a real object.*

opposition to this theatrical "*duration of the experience*" he underlines the experience of modernist art which "*has no* duration." According to him, works of this type of art are (allegedly like planes) "*at every moment wholly manifest.*" This is even "true of sculpture despite the obvious fact that, being three-dimensional, it can be seen from an infinite number of points of view" (Fried 1968, 145; emphasis in the original). This counterintuitive emphasis of "instantaneousness" (Fried 1968, 146) is symptomatic for planocentric discourse.[122]

We can see everywhere that the "transportable rectangular plane remains strangely dominant in the philosophies of the image"

(Schwarte 2004, 74). Already in 1994 Gottfried Boehm stressed: "What we encounter as an image rests on the fundamental contrast between a *tightly structured total surface area* and all that it includes as internal events" (Boehm 1994c, 29–30; my emphasis). Rehkämper and Sachs-Hombach wrote in 1999: "Images can be characterized as *plane* and clearly limited objects that as a rule within a communicative act serve as an illustrative representation of a factual situation" (Rehkämper and Sachs-Hombach 1999, 10; my emphasis). Or, as Martin Seel has specifically observed in 2003:

> The picture is a surface phenomenon that cannot be transferred into (real or imaginary) spatial relations. Where the space becomes a picture and the picture a space, we are concerned no longer with pictoriality but with a visual phenomenon that is sui generis.[123]

It obviously follows from this focus on the plane that architectural, sculptural and installative phenomena cannot easily be seen as images—if for no other reason than that they threaten to blur the borders between image and object (see Glaubitz and Schröter 2004). Alex Potts, for example, maintains that sculpture "disrupts the pervasive logic of the two-dimensional image in modern culture" (Potts 2000, ix) and thus tends to be generally devaluated. Excluding architecture, sculpture, installation and relief from the field of images is not necessarily a problem since terms like 'architecture,' 'sculpture,' 'installation' and 'relief' underline the otherness of these phenomena in comparison with the planar image, and therefore the question could be asked whether unscrupulously expanding the concept of 'image' is truly helpful. There is, however, another field of phenomena in which the strict opposition between image and space (pointedly underlined by Seel in his culmination of a long chain of arguments) leads to real problems. This is precisely the field of what are characteristically called *three-dimensional* or *3D images*.

1.4.2 Second, third and fourth series: 3D

Some (but not all) media technological sedimentations of the physiological optical, wave optical and virtual optical series break with the projection of objects onto planes. Isn't it the point of stereoscopy,[124] holography[125] and certain forms of computer graphics[126] to be talked about vaguely as '3D'[127]—thereby suggesting or signalizing the repression of plane two-dimensionality and thus encouraging a strong orientation to three-dimensional space? 3D images seem to represent a disturbing phenomenon on the border between the planar image and space. Following Seel's above-noted apodictic thesis, we should not even count them among images—and they hardly appear in any discourse of visual or media studies. It does not mean a complete renunciation if the plane in three-dimensional images is transgressed; instead it means a deferred repetition (in terms of Foucault): in the doubling of the plane in stereoscopy, in the holographic sheet as the passageway of the wave front in holography, in the virtual space presented and made accessible for navigation on the plane screen of the computer monitor and in the rotating plane in volumetry . . .

Therefore I want to talk of *transplane* images and not of *spatial images*.[128] The latter term would refer to images that are based on three-dimensional structures—for example sculptures or plastic art.[129] To be more exact: I define 'spatial image' as the comprehensive category comprising both transplane images and those that have a three-dimensional material support (like types of sculpture or, for example, globes).[130] The long and complex history of sculpture does not have to be discussed here; however, in certain specific cases I will consider how transplane images in the nineteenth and twentieth century were used in order to guide sculptural art into the age of reproduction (see more on this in Chapter 2).

It seems that technological transplane images break with the planocentric regime of geometrical optics by reconfiguring the plane. According to Crary it was exactly the "tantalizing apparition of depth" (Crary 1990, 132) that represented the fascinating quality of stereoscopy. And he continues: "There is no longer the possibility of *perspective* under such a technique of beholding" (Crary 1990, 128; my emphasis). Is there a reason for this crisis of perspective?

My thesis is that perspectival projection in modernity indeed conflicts with certain 'needs and uses' (to say it *with* Crary). Perspectival projections are not isomorphic, i.e. they do not store all information on spatial form.[131] The two-dimensional pattern on the plane could possibly correspond to very different three-dimensional configurations:

> [W]hile we can work out what the projection of a given three-dimensional object will be like on a given plane, the projection

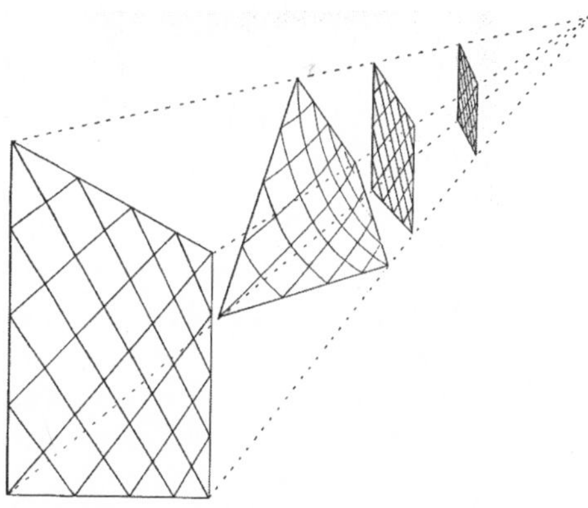

FIGURE 1.7 *Equivalent but different configurations from a certain point of view, in Gombrich (1982, 192).*

itself does not give us adequate information about the object concerned, since not one but an infinite number of related configurations would result in the same image.[132]

This limitation creates restrictions for a variety of tasks.[133] Thus, in architectural drawings or in architectural designs different types of *parallel projection* have been preferred for quite some time now since they are much better at retaining relative lengths and angles.[134] Photographic media cannot provide such alternative types of projections since photography follows the geometrical optics of light. If the source of light is very distant, then its rays arrive in an almost parallel manner and the shadow of an object would then be a quasi-parallel projection. However, a photographic medium focuses light and therefore has to project in linear perspective.[135] Only virtual optics will again provide the possibility of parallel projection.[136]

The inevitable orientation of photographic media on perspectival projections entails problems particularly in unpleasant emergency situations—for example, in war, where aerial photographs level the whole terrain into a two-dimensional plane. It then becomes no longer possible to recognize what is high, what is flat, what are mountains, what are valleys. Helmholtz already knew this in his *Treatise on Physiological Optics:*

> There is no difficulty about comprehending a perspective representation of a building or a piece of machinery, even when the details are fairly complicated. If the shading is good, it is easier still. But the most perfect drawing or even a photograph of a thing like a meteoric stone, a lump of ice, an anatomical preparation or some other irregular object of this sort hardly affords any picture at all of the material form of the body. Photographs especially of landscapes, rocks, glaciers, etc., are usually just an unintelligible medley of grey spots to the eye; and yet the same pictures combined properly in a stereoscope will be the most astonishingly faithful renditions of nature.[137]

Via stereoscopic images (each of the two planar images used in stereoscopy remains linear perspectival) and using the knowledge of binocularity, spatial information can be reconstructed from the images—for example, in WWI this was as essentially important as it is today in the production of maps (in surveys).[138] (See Figure 1.8.)

One can see very clearly here that—contrary to Crary's argument—the stereoscopic image that originally developed from the study of perception *does not disappear* at the beginning of the twentieth century precisely because *it is able to provide a heightened knowledge*

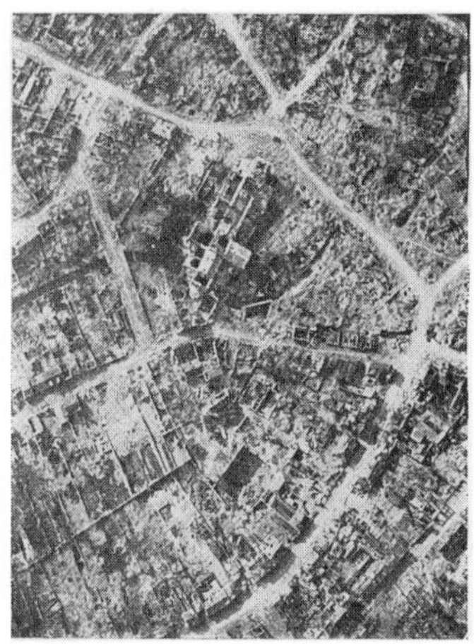
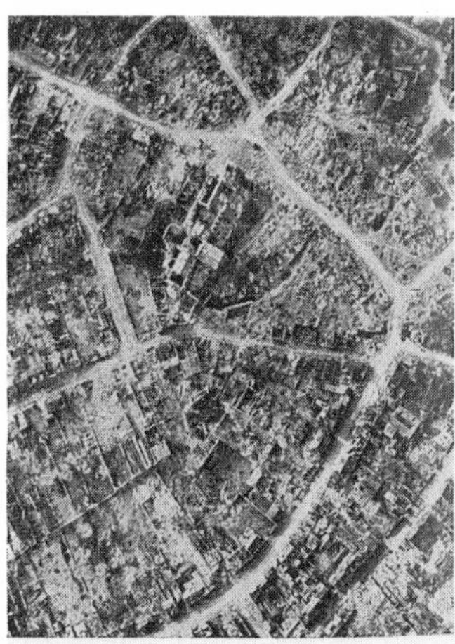

FIGURE 1.8 *Stereoscopic aerial photograph, in Judge (1926, 211 opposite page).*

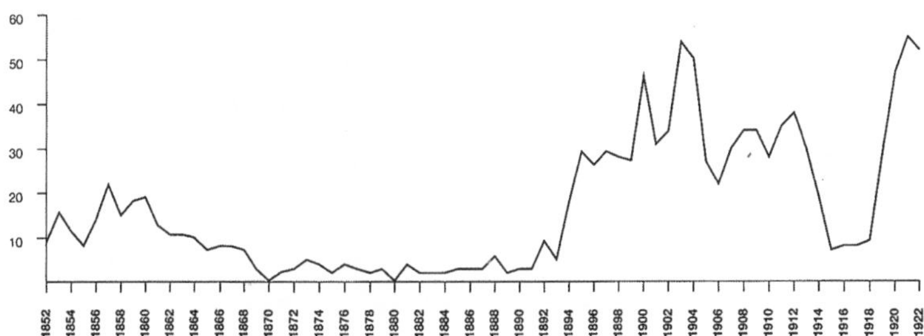

FIGURE 1.9 *Patents for 3D Processes (dominantly stereoscopy) in France. In Timby (2000, 159). A marked upsurge around 1900 is obvious.*

of space, making it more easily manageable. Timby had published a survey of the patents regarding three-dimensional inventions for France, and at the time that meant predominantly stereoscopic processes (see Timby 2000). The number of patents clearly rose around 1900 (see Figure 1.9).

This is even more true for the other technological transplane images and their diverse usage in the natural sciences,[139] industrial engineering and ergonomics (see Witte 1921, 31 and Mehrtens 2003, 51), astronautics,[140] meteorology (see Lorenz 1989), medicine (see especially Chapter 8), or engineering (see Hildebrandt 1959 and Lorenz 1987), some of which will be discussed in this book. We can contradict Bruno Latour who observes that a "simple drift from watching confusing three-dimensional objects, to inspecting two-dimensional images which have been *made less confusing*"[141] would be quite sufficient. Helmholtz's and numerous other examples show that the flat "inscriptions," as Latour calls them, sometimes have to contain more information from the original three-dimensional object in order not to be confusing. In many cases "plane photography—even if it is plastic—does not by far provide as many insights as does stereo photography."[142]

The transgression of the planocentric regime (still continuing its parallel existence) of a projection-onto-the-plane in transplane images is then of an entirely different category than the break that took place in the second half of the nineteenth century in (important parts of) modernist art and which is mentioned by Crary and other authors.[143] This period revoked the hetero-reference of painting in favor of self-reference.[144] Conceptualized as a window opening onto a visible scene (in Alberti's sense of the "finestra aperta," see Alberti 2011, 167), linear perspective always existed in a latent tension with the surface of the painting. In modernist painting the perspectival paradigm lost ground, thus the *surface plane* came to the fore. As Maurice Denis wrote in 1890: "It is well to remember that a picture—before being a battle horse, a nude woman, or some anecdote—is essentially a plane surface covered with colors assembled in a certain order."[145] A large part of modernist painting and the art history developing alongside[146] is criticizing the perspectival revocation of the 'image' in favor of a view into an illusionist, three-dimensional space:

> The 'image' characterized like this [as 'finestra aperta' organized linear perspectivally] destroys itself, in the same way as the mirror image destroys itself as an image, insofar as it loses itself in simply presenting the shown objects as such. (Boehm 1969, 30; cf. Boehm 1994b, 33–8, and Winter 1999, 17–19)

This criticism is problematic, however, for the very reason that the linear perspectival picture—unlike the objects presented—is *flat*. With the smallest movement and the clearly missing shading ('Abschattung' in the sense of Husserl) of the objects, it becomes apparent that these are not the objects themselves but a surface covered with colors.[147] This means that Boehm initially implies a completely immobile, monocular[148]—and therefore disembodied—observer. However, it is the aspect of a potential movement of the observer with regard to the spatiality of the presented objects in particular that differentiates the painting from the *mirror image* that Boehm is using as an analogy. The mirror image as a quasi-natural 3D image allows for different views of the mirrored object, depending on the movement of the observer. Mirrors (almost) completely reflect the light of the side of the objects that are turned towards them; therefore, the mirrored image contains all available spatial information. Looking into the mirror one can, for example, focus on objects at varying distances, something that will only be once again possible (partially) in holography. If we want to call the mirror image an image (in contrast to Eco 1984) then it predates sculpture as the very first three-dimensional image.[149] "Every image visible in a plane mirror is a spatial image. It is in fact the most perfect spatial image theoretically possible in the objective, physical world."[150] In this respect Boehm's equating planar image and mirror image implies a displacement of the transplane character of the latter; therefore, it is symptomatic for the dominant planocentric conception of the image.[151]

It is interesting to note that specifically the lacking 'illusionist' dimension of the plane, linear perspectival image was criticized by some so-called pioneers of technological transplane 3D image, invoking again the model of the 'image-as-window.' As Gabriel Lippmann wrote in an article in 1908:

> La plus parfaite des épreuves photographiques actuelles ne montre que l'un des aspects de la réalité; elle se réduit à une image unique fixée dans un plan ... On voit les objets dans l'espace, en vraie grandeur et en relief, et non dans un plan. ... Est-il possible de constituer une épreuve photographique de telle façon qu'elle nous représente le monde extérieur s'encadrant, en apparence, entre les bords de l'épreuve, comme si ces bords étaient ceux d'une fenêtre ouverte sur la réalité?[152]

The transplane transgression of the projection onto the plane then arises because the perspectival projection does not provide sufficiently precise information on the spatial structure of the object or the scene. It hardly makes sense to call what transplane images achieve an 'illusion,' for as a general rule whatever information might be conveyed about the structure of a given space is not an illusionist deception (that lets us confuse the representation with the thing itself—there are still at least the 'bords de l'épreuve' to keep us from that pitfall). What these transplane images do convey is an operative knowledge about space, about its structure and the arrangement of objects, possibly also on their spatial structure. It is a knowledge by way of which various discursive practices attempt to understand, control and change the things and their spatial configurations.

This expansion of knowledge about space by way of technological transplane images and the discursive practices connected to them are a central subject of this book. It mainly deals with a problem that has not been discussed in research so far: How can '3D' images be understood systematically in connection with the *production of space*—as Henri Lefebvre has called it—in modernity. To say that space itself might be something historical and produced may sound somewhat odd at first. However, if we do not conceive of 'space itself' as an empty container for all things (as physics has defined it, at least until Einstein—and even this description could already be called a form of production), then it seems convincing that space has to succumb to historical change as well. Thus, in the context of modernity or modernization as it was discussed by Crary, a lot has been talked about the annihilation of space, of its—as Marx has already said – "concentration . . . by means of communication and transport"[153]—a thesis that is known to lead to McLuhan's 'global village' (see McLuhan 1965). In contrast to the thesis of the compression or the disappearance of space (cf. Virilio 1998) within a temporalized or accelerated modernity it is far more fruitful to talk about the "formation of a new space or rather a new spatiality."[154] For example, the destruction of space, topical in the nineteenth century with the advent of the railroad, can only surface because a new spatial structure—the railroad net—crosses geographical space. Thus, with the diffusion of every new technology a new "striation of space-time" (Deleuze and Guattari 2004, 542) is taking place.

Koselleck observes that "denaturalizing a geographically predetermined space permits extending one's power, thereby increasing control."[155] Control over space, the creation of specific spaces increases in modernity in a number of areas. Contrary to the popular thesis that time had triumphed over space, Lefebvre observes:

> The capitalist mode of production . . . [tries] to master space by producing it—that is the political space of capitalism—while at the same time reducing time in order to prevent the production of new social relations. . . . The idea of *producing*, for example, today extends beyond the production of this or that thing or work to the *production of space*.[156]

Therefore, according to him, an "attribution of priority to space over time" takes place (Lefebvre 1991, 219; see Debord 2006, 95). Taking up on this, Schmid speaks of the "emergence . . . of the so far underestimated reality of the production of space."[157] Thus, in the twentieth century not only have the technological controls of space[158] increased, but also the ways in which the nature and perception of space was thought and discussed. A multiplicity of examples for this exist (Simmel, Husserl, Heidegger, Schmitt, Innis, Foucault, Lefebvre).[159]

Lefebvre differentiates three levels (or 'formants') of the production of space:

1 *Spatial practice*

2 *Representations of space*

3 *Representational spaces* (see Lefebvre 1991, 38–9)

The first level names the material spatial production, for example of buildings and streets and their given respective forms of *perception and action*, while the third and last level refers to "spaces that stand for 'something"' (Schmid 2003, 306)—and this 'something' can, for example, be something 'divine' as in cathedrals. Concerning this last point, we are then dealing with lived experience adding to the *meaning* of spaces. However, the second level is especially relevant. It concerns the representation of space, meaning the production of knowledge of space:

> *Representations of space*: conceptualized space, the space of scientists, planners, urbanists, technocratic subdividers and social engineers, as of a certain type of artist with a scientific bent. . . . *This is the dominant space in any society* (*or mode of production*). Conceptions of space tend . . . towards a system of verbal . . . signs.[160]

This is why Lefebvre demands: "We should have to study not only the history of space, but also the history of representations, along with that of their relationships—with each other, with practice, and with ideology" (Lefebvre 1991, 42). However, Lefebvre's concentration on the verbal encoding of the representations of space—which he calls only "metaphoric"[161] elsewhere—led to neglecting the really most obvious level of spatial representation, namely the level of images, although Schmid observes the following: "Representation of space consequently is a representation that *depicts* a space, thereby defining it."[162]

Lefebvre's concentration on language brings about a possibly too clear separation between the first level (*spatial practice—perception*) and the second level (*representation of space—knowledge*). Regarding images in the more narrow sense, perception and knowledge are always closely connected.[163] Even though Lefebvre concedes that "techniques, which have a great influence upon . . . the order of space are liable to change" (Lefebvre 1991, 159), he underlines that "[t]hanks to technology, the domination of space is becoming, as it were, completely dominant" (Lefebvre 1991, 164). He emphasizes further that in modernity the "logic of 'visualization' . . . now informs the entirety of social practice. . . . By the time this process is complete, space has no social existence independently of an intense, aggressive and repressive visualization" (Lefebvre 1991, 286). Nevertheless, technologies of visualization in the book appear only marginally.[164] Yet, visual representations of space or of spatial relations of objects are of central importance in at least a twofold respect:

1. They *reflect* ideas of space at a certain time—see for example the shift in painting from a space structured by theologian stipulations in medieval painting to the linear-perspectival space organized with respect to a human observer (cf. Kern 1983, 140). Thus the dominance of the linear-perspectival pictorial space[165] since the renaissance can be described as expressing anthropocentrism. Consequently thereafter the departure from perspective in painting since the nineteenth century seems to be a sign for still another shift, a shift in which the human individual is being cast out from the center and is being marginalized by the raging forces of modern technology (or of capitalism). The conservative art historian Hans Sedlmayr spoke of the 'loss of the center' also in this sense. Therefore, cubism can be seen as an expression of an industrial-technological fragmentation of space-time, as an answer to or as a result of the 'choc' (Benjamin) of modernity.

2. At the same time and maybe even primarily, pictorial representations *are producing* a 'pre'-figuration of space and are thereby permitting the operationalizing of it first of all by producing knowledge of space: "[R]epresentations of space have a practical impact, that they intervene in and modify spatial *textures* which are informed by effective knowledge and ideology" (Lefebvre 1991, 42; see Majetschak 2003, 40). Linear perspective therefore not only mirrors the epistemological recruitment of anthropocentrism—it is producing it in the first place.[166] It is the linear perspectival image that allowed for the production of spatial knowledge and therefore its control in very different areas which I cannot specify individually here. For this present context, Bruno Latour has emphasized a particularly relevant aspect for perspectival images (and other "inscriptions" as he calls them):

> They are made *flat*. There is nothing you can *dominate* as easily as a flat surface of a few square meters; there is nothing hidden or convoluted, no shadows, no "double entendre." . . . The two-dimensional character of inscriptions allows them to merge *with geometry*. As we saw for perspective, space on paper can be made continuous with three-dimensional space.[167]

Edgerton has elaborated on the connection between painting, geometrical optics, linear perspective and scientific revolutions in an impressive study out of which only one notable example will be mentioned due to its relevance for the development of technological visual media: Perspectival projection (and also different forms of parallel projection), allowing for spatially reproducing technological artifacts correctly, e.g. functional construction plans that were reproduced in large numbers and thus became a precondition for the development of modern technology and science in Europe.[168] These procedures "still provide . . . the standard pictorial conventions for the teaching of modern science" (Edgerton 1993, 22; cf. 289). And so, then—in order to underline my criticism of Crary's discontinuous model once more—geometrical optics, also in Edgerton's sense, continues to remain with us.

Another example that should be mentioned here only peripherally is the image/text hybrid *map* that cannot be valued highly enough for its importance regarding the representation of space. Farinelli (1996) even said that the "nature of modernity" was characterized by "cartographic reason."

However, in modernity the (painted) linear-perspectival image and the map find themselves plunged into a crisis regarding their operative function of spatial control[169] (among other things) because of the expansive character of wars.[170] Maps are limited because they denote or operatively represent the stable, static, and therefore *general* aspects of real space[171]—and therefore, as semiotically complex, composite signs that include different types of symbols and strata, simply have to be created in a time-consuming process.[172] With technical media that automatically create linear perspectival images, knowledge of space can be produced more quickly. However, "the satellite and aerial pictures are similar to maps, but they are not connected to any generalization" (Pápay 2005, 292). This means that these and similar images have an advantage over maps by concretely *depicting this space or the spatial structure of this object at that specific point in time* and not the respective spatial structure in general. However, aerial photographs for example need "interpretation"[173] in order to provide the necessary information that in maps is already implemented by the legend. The interpretation of the images is often nonetheless only possible by overcoming the limitations of perspectival projection. Additional and—regarding parallel projection—different spatial information has to be included in a different way, for example by using stereoscopy for aerial reconnaissance, or holography for the evaluation of events in bubble chambers, or volumetric images in processing radar or medical data. In this present work, therefore, I want to outline the functions of the *production of space* by way of transplane images in contrast to the planocentric production and reduction of space of geometrical optics. In modernity, technological transplane images have not necessarily been developed with the aim of producing and controlling space. But once they exist they will soon be used for it.

With the system of perspectival representation began that epoch of the—as was quoted above—"intense, aggressive and repressive visualization" of space that according to Lefebvre continues to increase even today. This almost forces an analysis of technological visual media and their practices to operationalize space. Lefebvre writes that

> from the Italian Renaissance to the nineteenth century . . . the representation of space tended to dominate and subordinate . . . representational space. . . . The vanishing line, the vanishing-point and the meeting of parallel lines 'at infinity' were the determinants of a representation, at once intellectual and visual, which promoted the primacy of the gaze in a kind of 'logic of visualization'. This representation . . . became enshrined . . . as the code of linear perspective. (Lefebvre 1991, 40–1)

Lefebvre underlines the central importance of linear perspectival representation (at least in Western cultures). His arguments remain conventional in this and that is also true for his rhetorics of rupture. According to him, at the beginning of the twentieth century perspectival space supposedly disappeared. Obviously this pattern resembles classical art historical narratives[174] in a surprising way. According to these, since the beginning of Renaissance the relatively unbroken dominance[175] of linear perspectival projection was

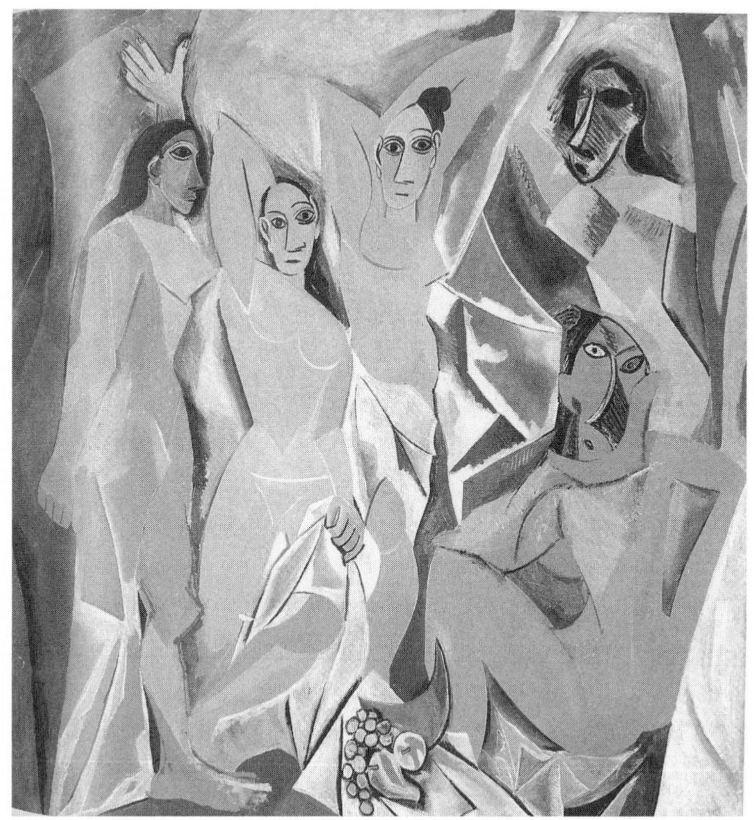

FIGURE 1.10 *Pablo Picasso,* Les Demoiselles D'Avignon *(1907).*

plunged into a crisis with the beginning of modernism (see once more Novotny 2000 and Francastel 1952). Indeed Lefebvre, who relatively rarely uses images as examples, refers to the strategies of the so-called artistic avant-garde—more precisely to Picasso and his painting *Les Demoiselles D'Avignon* (1907, Figure 1.10)—in order to characterize the allegedly fundamental break between the 'perspectival' and the significantly called 'abstract' space.

> The fact is that around 1910 a certain space was shattered. It was the space . . . of classical perspective and geometry, developed from the Renaissance onwards . . . Euclidean and perspectivist

> space have disappeared as systems of reference . . . It was at this time that Picasso discovered a new way of painting: the entire surface of the canvas was used, but there was no horizon, no background, and the surface was simply divided between the space of the painted figures and the space that surrounded them. . . . Picasso's space *heralded* the space of modernity.[176]

I will come back to the idea that artworks can register—or better yet, reflect on—the shifts in the production of space later on.[177] In any case, referring to *Les Demoiselles D'Avignon*, Lefebvre calls abstract space, which supposedly has taken the place of perspectival space, a "space at once homogeneous and broken" (Lefebvre 1991, 301). For him, on the one hand space is homogeneous because global capitalism in its never-ending expansion is linking space everywhere to its flows of communication and commodities.[178] Global space is created by globalization. On the other hand, space is cut up and dissected on very different levels by this process: On the level of spatial practice it is divided into plots and then sold (spatial practice), or barriers and divisions are established.[179] However, according to Lefebvre every science also creates its own space on the level of the representation of space (see Lefebvre 1991, 334–5). "The space that homogenizes thus has nothing homogeneous about it. After its fashion, which is polyscopic and plural, it subsumes and unites scattered fragments or elements by force."[180] By elevating (in contrast to his earlier considerations) the projection onto the plane—"space is literally flattened out, confined to a surface, to a single plane" (Lefebvre 1991, 313)—into the dominant feature of abstract space in modernity, he misses the fact that *transplane images* move alongside the series of geometrical optics with their more or less manifest planocentrism allowing for completely new representations of space.

In general, technological images—photography, film, to say nothing of transplane images—are not taken into consideration by Lefebvre at all. "Space . . . shattered into images" (Lefebvre 1991, 313) in modernity can indeed be found mainly in technological images. First of all because it is represented in extremely different ways in quantitatively immeasurable and medially quite dissimilar images, not to mention that in media such as film, video or television space is itself assembled from spatial particles. Moreover, the tendency toward abstraction and *abstract space* originates in modernist painting *also* (even though not exclusively) from the competition with photography (and soon with film).[181] This, by the way, may be one of the deeper reasons for Lefebvre's suppression of photography, film and also television. The images of these technological media can only be classified with difficulty into the asserted *general* tendency toward abstraction.[182] If one can thus agree with the idea that in modernity space becomes visual then this finding cannot adequately be expressed with rhetorics of breaks, of disappearance, or of removal and—what is often implied—of progress. This process can be described much more precisely with the model of the palimpsest or the superposition of different layers, since in the nineteenth and twentieth century the multiplication, coexistence and intermedial interconnections of the most unlike types of images clearly emerge.[183]

1.5 Spatial knowledge and media aesthetics of transplane images

Of course, my choice of examples has to be substantiated since not all transplane images can possibly be mentioned, and both *functional* and *artistic* uses have to be considered. The functional uses have their origin in scientific, military and medical practices. It will be discussed what kind of knowledge of space transplane images are basically enabling. Also, various forms of discourse or even fantasies connected to them will be considered. As an example, volumetric displays but also holography "can only be understood through the fantasies and the politics that [their] invention was responding to."[184]

In order to ask questions beyond the functional usage, I want to consider artistic explorations of possible media aesthetics of transplane images. Since the term 'media aesthetics' is freely applied nowadays in a quite inflationary way, I want to briefly define it.

In his text "Vor dem Schein kommt das Erscheinen" Martin Seel speaks of "self-referential appearance" (Seel 1993a, 781) of certain specific (but not only) artistic artifacts and asks to what extent this at least stimulates aesthetic perception. Aesthetics itself has continued discussing whether a self-referential and thus aesthetic—Seel finds the word 'reflexive' too strong in this case (see Seel 1997,

34)—perception is either a human faculty that can be used at will for any object, or whether we are dealing with a type of perception that is being provoked by certain objects, usually defined as artistic—or by these objects in a specific context (key-word: White Cube). This question has been much discussed and in my mind has not been clearly resolved by Seel either, and I venture to say that aesthetic perception—in the sense of a perception *that perceives the act of perceiving itself*—is indeed a human faculty that basically can be used for every object or situation. However, as a rule these types of perception are not supported in everyday life; they are purposefully blocked out in order, for example, to be able to pragmatically and functionally concentrate on driving a car. Any self-referential perception would immediately lead to an accident. Therefore, at least in some cultures, there are one or several fields of objects in specific institutional contexts that encourage and promote aesthetic perception. As a rule, but not obligatorily, this is called *art* (see Seel 1993b).

The analysis of the artistic use of transplane images, then, is about the question to what extent they bring into view their own medium and the ways in which they present space. Artistic usages show reflexively what forms of spatial perception they allow. This kind of use regarding transplane images means—as Bernhard Waldenfels phrased it—that they "are not only visible and do not only make something visible, but that they simultaneously make visibility as such visible as well."[185] The "paradox of the 'flat depth"' that Boehm noted as an "aspect of iconic difference" (Boehm 1994c, 33) characterizes transplane images in a singular way and is enhanced in their artistic usages. These artistic usages, then, should be first-rate objects in order to find out the guiding principles for the possible *regimes of vision*[186] that are produced and performatively enacted with the new images. Thus, the oscillation in transplane images between the plane and its spatial (possibly even sculptural) impression will be pursued.[187]

By definition, transplane images can be reproduced on the pages of a book only with difficulty. Once again it becomes clear to what extent Derrida influenced the idea of planocentrism: As the "idea of the book . . . is the encyclopedic protection . . . of logocentrism against the disruption of writing" it also performs a "logocentric repression" (Derrida 1976, 18 and 51) of transplane images insofar as everything that can enter into books has to have become plane in the first place. The only form that still can be reproduced relatively easily is stereoscopy. Therefore Crary has to be contradicted when he says: "Since it is obviously impossible to reproduce stereoscopic effects here on a printed page, it is necessary to analyze closely the nature of this illusion . . . to look through the lenses of the device itself" (Crary 1990, 124). He is of course correct in saying that one has to view the transplane images oneself. But as Figure 1.8 shows, this is readily possible with a stereoscopic pair of images. One does not need a stereo-viewer in order to see the effect. Hold the book about four to eight inches away from your eyes and fixate on a point behind it. The two images should shortly merge into each other and create a third, plastic image (see Helmholtz 1985, 299). This is quite easy to do with a little practice, although about 10 percent of those who try cannot perceive the stereo effect (see Ninio 2000, 21, n.3). The spatial appearance of holographic[188] and volumetric images can only be dissolved in photo sequences that are accompanied by detailed commentaries. It is interesting that stereoscopic reproductions are being used frequently in order to be able to reproduce at least a small part of the spatial impression of holographic or volumetric images on the printed page.[189]

In closing, a remark on the problem of the *X-ray image*. Wouldn't it also be necessary to address its discovery inasmuch as the X-radiation can see through the body (or other objects) and therefore can produce more spatial information? However, the mere scanning is not the point. When an object is being X-rayed and projected geometrically-optically (even as a 'shadow') onto a plane, then all levels of the object are placed on one image plane and thus create exactly those same problems of understanding the spatial information against which transplane images are being utilized. This was already the case in 1896 when stereoscopy was used in order to make the images of X-rays easier to understand[190] and similarly, holograms on the basis of X-rays have already been used in a variety of ways (see Jacobsen 1990). This means that it is not the X-rays and their images (radiographs) that form something like a genuine 'optical series'; X-rays are electromagnetic waves just like visible light, only they have a much smaller wavelength.[191] Depending on whether the images produced by them are being projected geometrically-optically or are stereoscopically arranged by using binocular vision (physiological optics), or are recorded holographically by using their wave characteristics (wave optics, cf. Hiort 2000), they are the results of one of the optical series mentioned here. Therefore there will be no individual chapter on radiographs.

1.6 Summary and outline

In conclusion I will briefly present an outline of this study. It would seem obvious to continue with four extensive chapters that would address each of the four optical series, unfolding their respective histories. I have considered such an outline—and I have discarded it. These are the reasons: First, it does not make sense to devote an individual chapter to the series of geometrical optics since in this present study I am dealing with the history, the use, the implications and the aesthetics of transplane images. Geometrical optics, however, is mostly planocentrically structured on the projection-onto-the-plane—with the sole exception of integral photography, which will be discussed in Chapter 5. Moreover, the other technological sedimentations of this series (conventional photography, for example) have been addressed sufficiently elsewhere. Secondly, it does not seem wise representing the three remaining optical series (physiological optics, wave optics, virtual optics) and the correlated types of transplane images in three chronologically ordered chapters. This type of presentation would have reintroduced a strong sequential moment reminiscent of Crary's successive representation criticized earlier. It makes no sense to criticize Crary's model of temporal discontinuity and then replace it with a model of 'epistemological discontinuity' in which the optical series quasi-exist parallel to each other without contact. As I have said, the *Archaeology* is in no way "trying to obtain a plurality of histories juxtaposed and independent of one another" (Foucault 1972, 10). Acknowledging the continuity of, for example, geometrical optics (also known as the camera obscura paradigm) means that when a new series emerges, the original series is transformed by the emergence of a new series; not acknowledging this shift would mean that the attempt is made to bypass the dichotomy of continuity and discontinuity. Therefore, I have chosen another form of presentation; a form that applies quasi-micrological 'drillings' crosswise through the various layers.

Therefore, I will continue with a series of smaller chapters in chronological order. In each of these chapters I will first deal with a specific example of one (or several) optical series and the resulting transplane images. Secondly, I will deal with their use for controlling, saving, measuring, producing, and commercializing space, i.e. for its specific "production" (Lefebvre) as the "vertical system" (Foucault) connecting the individual cases. Thirdly, some of these chapters will contain analyses of artistic experiments with transplane images.

Chapter 2 assesses the period around 1851. We encounter an early use of stereoscopy (as an example of the series of physiological optics) representing and archiving highly complex spatial structures, namely sculptures. Certain potentials but also limitations of stereoscopy will become visible.

Chapter 3 will begin around 1860. I will deal with different forms of photo sculpture that—even though this might sound puzzling at first—can be seen as first steps in the series of virtual optics. Certain of its procedures are still centrally relevant to this day. I will analyze works by Karin Sander and a scene from the popular film *The Matrix* in which some methods of photo sculpture are being taken up in an aesthetic manner.

Chapter 4 will discuss a technique that became public for the first time in 1891 and is almost forgotten today—interferential color photography. This procedure is the first media technology based on the wave optical series. In 1908 Gabriel Lippmann was awarded the Nobel Prize in Physics for its development. This exotic method not only has an important transplane successor—holography. It has also recently become very important in different security-related applications. The description of its genealogy is particularly interesting with regard to its intricacy—sedimentations of optical series are always complex processes.

Chapter 5 In the year he was awarded the Nobel Prize, Gabriel Lippmann published a paper in which he developed a transplane imaging technology that can be described as shifted use of the series of geometrical optics, namely integral photography. As simple and as amazing as its concept is, as difficult is its realization, it has only recently enjoyed a resurge in interest and rediscovery in the area of digital technologies. A simplified version of this procedure—lenticular images—has been known and used for quite some time. Mariko Mori, a media artist, has used a lenticular image in an important work of hers.

Chapter 6 Transplane images also appear in unexpected connections. Stereoscopy, which apart from its continual use in surveying and in military aerial photography and that, according to Crary, supposedly faded away around 1900, flourished again in 1935 within—of all places—the Third Reich. At least Hitler himself, his personal photographer, Heinrich Hoffmann, as well as Albert Speer all seem to have liked what could be done with it. The spatial image connected well with the Nazis' ideology of space. This peculiar politics of the transplane image will be looked at together with a short epilogue on Thomas Ruff's stereo works.

Chapter 7 will reflect on Marcel Duchamp in detail. The series of geometrical optics and its logics of projection as well as the series of physiological optics connected to transplane images have been major topics in the works of this artist. An analysis of some selected works by Duchamp will therefore contribute to the media aesthetics of the transplane image.

Chapter 8 will deal with the wide subject of the so-called 'volumetric images' that continue to be largely in a state of flux. These images, which emerged from the strategically important question of visualizing radar data, are created in an image volume—i.e. they are spatial themselves. The series of physiological optics is their basis, also as their own virtual double. Fundamentally connected to the spatiality of the volumetric images is the spatiality of the human body and therefore also the politics of its medical control and modification. Artists like Jenny Holzer and Olafur Eliasson have dealt with these questions.

Chapter 9 will cover a technology that—apart from stereoscopy—is conventionally associated with '3D,' namely holography. It is one of the most intriguing types of all images, shattering almost all media historical and aesthetic categories. At the same time it is currently widely used in many areas of the natural and materials sciences as well as in security-related applications. Today there are many scanning cash registers in supermarkets that couldn't operate without it; nevertheless, holography is presently known only in a quite distorted way. I want to explore this heterogeneous field.

Chapter 10 The emergence of digital computers after 1945 meant that shortly thereafter more and more and ever-faster calculating machines became available for use. Since the 1960s, anything that could be mathematically formulated in geometrical, wave, and physiological optics was converted step by step into software programs for computers. But as always, repetition invites difference as well. Thus, shifted repetitions and hitherto impossible recombinations of the existing transplane images as well as forms of interactive-transplane images became possible.[192]

Chapter 11 will provide a brief conclusion.

Notes

1 The term 'image' is generally preferred instead of the term 'picture' unless otherwise necessary.

2 As long as one does not call sculpture the first 'three-dimensional image,' as Okoshi (1976, 2) has done. However, transplane images should be differentiated from spatial images (see p. 38) and Okoshi starts his history of technical three-dimensional images with stereoscopy. Nevertheless, sculpture will continue to play a role here. Another early form of three-dimensional images might be found in the artfully designed landscape garden, see Kelsall (1983).

3 Neither Hick (1999) nor Kittler (2010) have done this systematically. Therefore I will not deal with their informative and inspiring studies extensively.

4 Cahen (1990) describes the history of some types of three-dimensional images (in some parts imprecisely) but does not develop any systematics.

5 See Crary (1990). Earlier, Crary had developed some theses in individual essays that were then combined in the book; see Crary (1985; 1988a; 1988b).

6 Some examples would be Hick (1994), one of the earliest German texts in which Crary is mentioned; also Hick (1999) essentially relies

on Crary as does Stiegler (2001). Steigerwald (2000) analyzes Brockes' "techniques of the observer" and Brosch (2000) discusses the "change of perception in the nineteenth century" with regard to Henry James' writings by more or less projecting Crary's theses onto James while Kosenina (2001) discusses "microscope and (portable) 'Zograscope' as tools and metaphors of poetry" by rather loosely connecting back to Crary.

7 Crary (1990, 1). Indeed, it doesn't seem to be a coincidence that *Techniques of the Observer* opens with such a heterogeneous list. It is heterogeneous because here methods of computer graphics ('ray tracing') appear next to technical apparatus ('flight simulators') and new fields of practice ('computer aided design'). The whole study more or less follows Foucault's *The Order of Things*, which on its first page also begins with a heterogeneous enumeration (Foucault 1966, 14) where Foucault is referring to Jorge Louis Borges' (fictitious) 'Chinese Encyclopedia.' Crary's reference to *The Order of Things* will still have to be discussed regarding its implications; see 1.2.2.

8 Crary (1990, 3). On the term "regime of vision" see Jay (1988).

9 On this criticism see Williams (1995) and Hentschel (2001).

10 This remark is directed against the concept of a 'history of vision' as it has been used in traditionally formalistic histories of art (see specifically Wölfflin 1950; see also Crary 1990, 36 critically on 'Woelfflinism') where it was seen only as a history of *artistic* images.

11 Crary (1990, 6). It should be asked whether the description of the field as "continually shifting" is consistent with assuming *one* regime of modern vision.

12 See Foucault (1984) on the term 'genealogy.' See also Paech (2003) on the term 'dispositive.'

13 See Hick (1999). Somewhat imprecisely, she adds up historical materials that in the end lead into the invention of the cinema. (For its criticism see Geimer 2000). Kittler (2010, 19–46) begins his study with a preface and a discussion of theoretical considerations. In the German text the word 'Optik' (optics) appears only once, but in the English translation of the book it is translated into 'visual,' removing Kittler's argument even more from the history of optics. Wave optics is mentioned only *en passant* and with reference to photography which is in no way essentially connected to it (Kittler 2010, 124). His study is interested in other matters such as the history of optical media as a history of escalation through military influence (Kittler 2010, 41–3; see on this Stiegler 2003, 70). See also Mann (2000) for a historical overview of other optical instruments, which also does not relate these to a history of optical knowledge.

14 Crary (1990, 16). The knowledge emerging in this way for Crary is just as fundamental regarding the shift to modern art (Crary 1990, 9). This directly makes sense for movements like pointillism insofar as, for example, Seurat had based his theories directly on the findings of physiological optics; cf. Schug (1997); see Crary (1999, 152–76).

15 Cf. also Rieger (2001, 2002, 2003); Waldenfels (1999, 169) talks of an "abstractive and normalizing corporeality" of the modern observer in Crary's book.

16 See Crary (1990, 8). On excluding the body in the camera obscura paradigm see Crary (1990, 41). Incidentally, Crary does not equate this paradigm with linear perspective (Crary 1990, 34, 41), even though he does not seem to keep rigorously to this differentiation; see for example p. 86, where he is talking of the "point-to-point epistemological setup" of the camera obscura (which corresponds exactly to linear perspective), or when his criticism of traditional narratives in the history of art and media quietly relocates their reference to perspective (Crary 1990, 3–4) into a reference to the camera obscura (Crary 1990, 26). The connection between linear perspective and the camera obscura will be discussed at a later point—here it should be mentioned only that both belong to the series of geometrical optics.

17 See for example Frizot (1998, in particular 17–18).

18 And not only photography—also holography, which will be discussed later, seems to clash with this concept, see Chapter 9.

19 See for example Schaaf (2000, 19–20) on the chemical experiments by Talbot. See Hagen (2002, 202–3) who points out that Herschel in 1839 had described "photography as the ontological medium of the physics of light." Batchen (1997, 83) reports on one exception in Talbot that nevertheless contributes very little to the development of photography. This, however, does not contradict the fact that within the field of photography in the nineteenth century specific artistic movements invoked physiological knowledge (see Stiegler 2006, 147–51). On the contrary, this discussion proves that photography was hardly associated with physiological vision in general.

20 It was indeed the use of photographs which were able to create hallucinatingly plastic images of certain 'real' spaces that popularized the stereoscope. It is very difficult to produce useful, drawn image-pairs with which the effects of the stereo can be attained—unless we refrain from simple (but effective) geometrical drawings that dominated the earliest phase of stereoscopy (see Wheatstone 1983, 73; Tortual 1842).

21 See section 1.3. An interesting point in case is the discussion stirred up by contemporaries—especially Brewster—regarding the so-called Chimenti-pair, a seemingly drawn stereo-pair from the seventeenth century by Jacopo Chimenti. Even though it was concluded after a heated discussion that the Chimenti-pair could not be seen as stereoscopic views, it becomes evident that one had indeed interpreted the principle of stereoscopy as something to be differentiated from photography; see also Wade (2003).

22 Phillips (1993, 136). Earlier he maintains: "photography has an ambiguous role and it is one that Crary never fully resolves" (130).

23 Batchen (1993, 86) remarks a "troubling contradiction" at this point whereas Phillips (1993, 135) talks of "real contradictions."

24 See Crary (1990, 116): "The most significant form of visual imagery in the nineteenth century, with the exception of photographs, was the stereoscope." The encounter between photography and stereoscopy in this quote will still prove to be a problem.

25 Crary (1990, 41) describes the subject created by the camera obscura in more detail. The observer in the dark chamber admiring the spectacle of the projection (and Crary does not distinguish between accessible and portable cameras) is described as a "disembodied witness to a mechanical and transcendental re-presentation of the objectivity of the world. . . . The camera obscura *a priori* prevents the observer from seeing his or her position as part of the representation." Provided that the observer perceives the representation as differentiated from themself, Crary can declare them a 'free' subject.

26 By the way: to be recreated and to be perpetuated are in no way the same processes.

27 See Crary (1990, 13, 27, 31, 32, 36, 57, 118). See also Crary (1988b, 3 n.2): "Thus I contend that the camera obscura and photography, as historical objects, are radically dissimilar."

28 Cf. Wedel (2007) who underlines to what extent stereoscopy influenced early cinema. Similarly see also Gosser (1977).

29 See Phillips (1993, 137) who assesses Crary's references to physiological research in *Techniques of the Observer* as a mere "backdrop" that obstructs a more profound discussion of the history of science.

30 Kittler (1996, n.p.). But there are also media that really disappear, see on this http://www.deadmedia.org [last accessed September 2, 2013].

31 The tiresome question of what a medium 'really' is cannot and will not be discussed here (see Winkler 2004a). Heuristically, I agree with

Kittler (1993, 8) who defines media as techniques that serve "to transfer, to save and to process [I would add: 'and to present,'] information". Three-dimensional images, then, would be media insofar as they save and transfer information on spatial structures and as they can virtually also process and finally present this information (see Chapter 10).

32 In the sense in which Steiner (1992, 85) has suggested to speak of Foucault's approach rather as topology than of archeology.

33 Crary (1988a, 43). But apart from the problems discussed above, the effortless association of photography and film with a *disembodied* way of seeing (in pornography?) and a *realistic* one (what about fictionality?) can be called problematic.

34 Here Crary is referring to the works of Rosalind Krauss (1986, 1988, 1990) who describes in detail the "modernist fetishization of sight" (Krauss 1986, 147). It should be mentioned in passing that the art of the twentieth century never relies solely on disembodied vision. It is true that for example 'opticality' in American high modernism after 1945 had again attained a place of central importance. However, in *minimal art* which followed around 1965 the embodied observer became important. See Krauss (1987, 61) on the observer in modernist art as "abstracted from his bodily presence" and as "pure optical ray" in contrast to the observer implied in minimalism as a "bodied . . . corporeal . . . subject" (Krauss 1987, 63).

35 Especially if it is taken into consideration that the earliest testimonials of successful attempts in photography took place even before the invention of stereoscopy (the earliest instance of photography reported is the one made by Joseph Nicéphore Niépce in 1826).

36 If it is allowed to assemble the manifold photographic procedures (especially of the nineteenth century) into the term 'photography.'

37 Paech (1998, 19) or Kittler (2010, 61 and 133) see it similarly. See Adelmann (2003): "While Crary in his discourse analysis establishes an epistemological break between the models of the camera obscura and photography, Kittler views photography . . . as the perfection of the camera obscura. This is where in my mind the really exciting discussion should be taking place, which Kittler, however, somehow avoids." It is really quite striking that all 'pioneers' of photography took it quite for granted that photography served the recording of the image of the camera obscura. See already Wedgwood and Davy (1980, 16), Arago (1839, 9–10), Janin (1839, 146), Talbot (1980, 24; 1969, 61) and many others. See also Rohr (1925, 2) who underlines

that "from the portable dark chamber used as a drawing aid after 1839 emerged today's hand- or static camera." See Batchen (1997, 78–90). It is hard to believe that the continuity between camera obscura and photo camera is only an invention of some later photo historiographies. One example given by Crary (1990, 31) is Eder (1978, 36–45).

38 Williams (1995, 8–9). See also Lummerding (1998, 56).

39 Interestingly, Hammond (1981, 104) observes: "There is little doubt that during the nineteenth century the camera obscura reached the height of its popularity." Cf. also Rohr (1925) and Phillips (1993, 136): "The actual presence of the camera obscura (as apparatus) may have disappeared by the early nineteenth century but its ghost was clearly alive and well." The same of course applies to the role which it takes on as a metaphor in the works of Karl Marx and later Sigmund Freud; see on this Kofman (1973). Crary (1990, 29) also addresses these metaphors, but he assesses their mostly negative appropriation in the nineteenth century (for example by Marx) as a sign for the disappearance of the classical and the appearance of the modern regime of vision. But one could ask whether the metaphors of the camera obscura don't indeed allow concluding that the paradigm continues to exist—even if in a shifted form—instead of disappearing.

40 Neither was the classical model such a homogeneous block, something that Crary incidentally mentions (1990, 30 and 138 on "sfumato" as "counter-practice to the dominance of geometrical optics"). On "sfumato" see also Wellmann (2005, 73–95).

41 Allow me to continue using these terms relatively openly next to each other. After my discussion of Foucault I will replace them with the term "series."

42 See Snyder (1980, 512) who refers to Alberti's linear perspective.

43 See Potmesil and Chakravarty (1982, 85) who in an important text observe on the simulation of photo lenses in computer graphics that the algorithms "for realistic rendering of complex three-dimensional (3D) scenes . . . have continued to use the *pinhole camera* [!] projection geometry." (Emphasis in original.)

44 And I should add: technological.

45 See Hayes (1989). Since space in the movies is already constituted narratively (see Bordwell 1985, 99-146; Winkler 1992), the additional stereoscopic information on space is superfluous (apart from occasional thrusts in the increase of spectacularity). Apart from the diverse technical difficulties, this may be the reason why stereoscopy did not succeed in the movies; see Paul (1993) and also

Milner (2006, 29). Even the contemporary boom of 3D cinema might in the long run just lead to a differentiation of cinematic presentation instead of all films becoming stereoscopic.

46 On stereoscopy and virtual reality see Schröter (2004c, 239–60).

47 This is true for the perception of movement, which according to Paech (2005, 87–90) presupposes the recognition of the controlled differences between the individual images and therefore a whole series of complex cognitive processes; it is also true for the perception of different frames as a continuum that has to be differentiated from them (since it also is true for freeze-frames); see Hochberg (1989; Hochberg and Brooks 1996). This amalgamation can in no way be reduced to the so called 'persistence of vision' as Paech has underlined. Nichols and Lederman (1980) point out that there is a "critical fusion-frequency" from the point of which the human eye can perceive the successive still images in film only as a unified movement. This characteristic of the human body had to be understood by the pioneers of film, even though its deeper reasons were not yet known in the nineteenth century.

48 Animations, or more precisely animated cartoons are interesting especially because they preserve the memory that film is a "movement-image" (Deleuze) in the first place and only secondly a photographic image (this knowledge returns increasingly in the context of computer animated film today); see Thompson (1980, 106). Paech (1998) precisely discusses the contingent interdependence of photography and film and their intermediality in specific films.

49 See section 1.3. The perspective outlined here touches on the assumption in Schröter (2004d), where intermediality predates the so-called individual media.

50 On the criticism of the "revolutionary turning point" see Eco (1986a, 255) for which I have to thank Peter Gendolla.

51 Regarding the much discussed differentiation between analog and digital, I have already shown that the popular narrative asserting that at some point the digital media arrived out of the blue *after* the analog ones ('digital revolution'), which then disappear, is somewhat problematic (see Schröter 2004b). But here I do not aspire to the grand aim to write a theory of media change as such (see Engell 2001; Rusch 2007). I want to be much more modest and name only minimal conditions for a less reductionist historical narrative of the optical/visual media.

52 Or in other contexts, 'the analog media' vs. 'the digital media'; 'literate culture' vs. 'image culture' and so on and so forth.

53 See Fink-Eitel (1989, 10) who mentions that "one could take Foucault's different works for the works of different authors unless one knew that they were written by the same author."

54 See Chapter 4 for the question of what we are dealing with and why there are also problems hidden in this reference.

55 Crary (1990, 70). On the transparency of the classical episteme he is quoting Foucault (1994, 132). See also Crary (1988b, 5).

56 Even through it might seem somewhat forced to compel a merging of Kant's philosophy of the transcendental conditions of experience and the concrete analysis of the bodily conditions of cognition and perception from the nineteenth century onward, there are indeed already in Kant some traces that indicate a paving of the way. A case of particular interest is Kant's indecisiveness in his *Critique of Judgment* whether color should be grouped with beauty or merely with pleasantness. By referring to "our body", Kant even questions his own thought that the perception of color as beautiful may possibly result from the fact that the perceiving subject could somehow become aware of the light waves; see on this Schröter (2000, 146). Crary (1990, 74) simplifies Kant's position into a "devaluation of colour" again referring to Foucault (1994, 133).

57 Crary (1990, 79; my emphasis). In a footnote he is referring to Foucault (1994, 318–20).

58 See for example Foucault (1994, 217): "The last years of the eighteenth century are broken by a discontinuity similar to that which destroyed Renaissance thought at the beginning of the seventeenth."

59 Crary (1990, 6–7) discusses the question himself "of how one can pose such large generalities . . . as 'the observer in the nineteenth century'." And he answers it in a (quite self-ruinous) manner that lets the concentration on a break between two large, relatively homogeneous formations appear even less conclusive: "[T]here are no such things as continuities and discontinuities in history, only in historical explanation. So my broad temporalizing is not in the interest of a 'true history,' or of restoring to the record 'what actually happened.' The stakes are quite different: how one periodizes and where one locates ruptures or denies them are all political choices that determine the construction of the present." See Mitchell (1994, 22–3) criticizing Crary's reading of Foucault. See also Gronemeyer (2004) on a history of visual media in early modernity that is oriented on the same classification of historical epochs of *The Order of Things*.

60 This is what Foucault (1972, 8–9) seems to suggest at the beginning of the *Archaeology*.

61 Crary (1990, 36; emphasis in the original). He is referring to Alpers (1983).

62 See Batchen (1991; 1993, 92; 1997, 184–7). See Luhmann (1976, 294) who from a quite different theoretical point of view observes "continuity and discontinuity have to be made possible simultaneously within the same system. Therefore, confrontation and play-off of these two terms do not offer any solution, and not even an appropriate frame of reference to discuss the problem." See in a fundamental manner Baumgartner (1972). See lately the media-historical focus in Schüttpelz (2006, 108–10).

63 Foucault (1972, 173/174). This terminology could be applied, for example, to the recurring disappearance and reappearance of the stereoscopic principle.

64 Foucault (1972, 175; my emphasis). Cf. also Deleuze (2011, 19) about Foucault: "and when a new formation appears, with new rules and series, it never comes all at once, in a single phrase or act of creation, but emerges like a series of 'building blocks,' with gaps, traces and reactivations of former elements that survive under the new rules."

65 Foucault (1972, 174). Foucault uses the quoted phrase in order to point to the criticism of his approach accusing him of privileging exactly this. By attempting to invalidate this criticism he underlines that he is precisely *not* solely concerned with the analysis of the discontinuous.

66 As Foucault (1972, 8) states in a phrasing that evokes Koselleck (1971; 2003). Characteristically Foucault coins this beautiful phrase directly in connection with the question of the "development of a particular technique" (1972, 8).

67 Crary has leanings in this direction himself. In his study *Suspensions of Perception* published nine years after *Techniques of the Observer*, he writes: "If vision can be said to have any enduring characteristic within the twentieth century, it is that it has no enduring features. Rather it is embedded in a pattern of adaptability to new technological relations, social configurations, and economic imperatives" (Crary 1999, 13). The question, therefore, is whether this flexibility can correspond to only *one* modern regime of vision (how could vision then have "no enduring features"?) or rather whether it consists in a plurality of overlapping series. My present study argues into this direction.

68 See Phillips (1993, 137) who is pointing out that possibly it is exactly the oscillation of the viewers through the different modes of perception that are experienced as enjoyable and attractive. Cf.

Williams (1995, 37) who also argues for a plurality of viewing (or observing). Fiorentini (2004, 65), for example, states that the subject implied by the camera lucida, popular in the nineteenth century (cf. Chevalier 1839; Hammond and Austin 1987) cannot be unequivocally classified within 'objective' (classical model, camera obscura as central technology) or 'subjective' (modern model, stereoscopy as central technology) vision.

69 See Rheinberger (1997, 182) on the "differential reproductions of serial lines."

70 On the term "vertical system" in Foucault see Frank (1989, 174).

71 This idea goes back to Innis (1991).

72 See Becker (2004) on the history and theory of fast and slow motion. On the specific aspect of the use of photography and film in the practices of controlling the body in *scientific management* see Lalvani (1996). See also Kittler (1990) on the inversion of the temporal axis. Vilém Flusser (1993, 155) has gotten to the heart of the matter: "The film-maker can do what god cannot do; he can redirect the course of events into temporal directions outside of radial linearity."

73 On my terminology: The term 'series' used here and taken from Foucault refers to different forms of optical knowledge; 'serializing' signifies the simple fact that moving images are chains of still images that succeed each other so fast that the human eye can only see a moving image.

74 See also section 1.3. However, mobilizing the images may also irritate the perspectival structure of the individual images; see on this Decordova (1990) regarding the example of early films.

75 On my terminology: Below I will talk of linear perspective (in brief: perspective) when I mean the form developed during the Renaissance of projecting a three-dimensional object onto the intersection of the visual pyramid consisting of straight (therefore: linear) visual or light rays. The term central perspective means a specific form of linear perspective with just one vanishing point.

76 Crary (1990, 85–6). Crary here alludes to the experiments by Goethe in his *Theory of Colors* with afterimages. See Chapter 4.

77 In a more ancient model of vision the lines of sight emerge from the eyes ("beams of vision") and illuminate the objects, see Simon (1992, 29–66). This model reappears sometimes in treatises on perspective when the eye-point seems to be the source of the lines of sight. It seems even to survive in today's concepts of 'ray tracing' in computer graphics.

78 See Buchwald (1989). It was already recognized in the seventeenth century that the classical interpretation of light as a bundle of linear

rays (be they individual waves or particles) had to be incomplete. Diffraction and interference cannot be explained like this. On the history of wave optics see briefly Chapter 9.

79 See Alberti (2011, 26), who in his groundbreaking treatise on perspective describes light rays as "certain extremely fine threads, connected as straight as they can [be] in a single extremity." See on this also Lindberg (1981).

80 Carter (1970, 840). See also Gombrich (1960, 250–1). Tsuji (1990) shows in what way the origin of linear perspective in Brunelleschi around 1425 could possibly be closely connected to the use of a camera obscura. As far as the central perspective follows the rules of geometrical optics, it is not only to be viewed as a mere convention, cf. Rehkämper (2002).

81 Holography, based on wave optics (see Chapter 9) is the great exception here. The break with the 'point-to-point epistemological setup' (Crary) of geometrical optics is often underlined, separating holography from photography that is governed by just this scheme (cf. Françon 1974, 39). This geometry is independent of the fact whether the image is stored analogically or digitally; see Schröter (2004g).

82 Bringing in another instance, Veltman states that in the twentieth century "more books have been published on the question of perspective than during the fifteenth, sixteenth, and seventeenth centuries together" (Veltman 1995, 26). He therefore is even talking of a "renaissance of perspective" in the twentieth century. But of course more books have also absolutely appeared during this period.

83 Alberti (2011, 28) already knew this in his treatise on perspective: "But at this point it is much less necessary to consider all functions of the eye in relation to vision." Alberti of course did not refer to the stereoscopic image, but to the fact that for understanding perspective projection it is quite unnecessary to know how the eyes operate (see on this Edgerton 1975, 64). For just this reason, Lacan has criticized Alberti's ontology of light as lines: "Now, the light is propagated, as one says, in a straight line, this much is certain" (Lacan 1978, 93). Because as far as the projection is modeled according to the image of palpable threads "[s]uch optics are within the grasp of the blind" (Lacan 1978, 92). Interestingly, Lacan counters this by using metaphors ("floods", "fills") that allude to water thereby seemingly implying the wave characteristics of light: "Light may travel in a straight line, but it is refracted, diffused, it floods, it fills . . . The relation of the subject with that which is strictly concerned with light seems, then, to be already somewhat ambiguous" (Lacan 1978, 94).

84 Only in 1864—long after the double-slit experiment by Young in 1802 and Fresnel's theoretical considerations in the 1820s—and therefore also long after the rupture claimed by Crary, James Clerk Maxwell has found a valid description of visible light as a minuscule fraction of the electromagnetic spectrum. On the connection between wave optics and electrodynamics see Silliman (1974).

85 . . . and its further developments like ophthalmological optics.

86 See Deleuze (2011, 50) who underlines that "visibilities are inseparable from machines." One general remark has to be made: Of course all images are in a sense related to human perception because they are made to be viewed (in photography, for example, the chemical emulsions are made to be sensitive to visible light). But insofar as this is true for every image it is a useless truism. One can still differentiate between images which are based on physical knowledge about light and those which are based on knowledge of perception in the strict sense.

87 . . . looking at its role in material control, scanning cash registers, security technologies and even in the arts and its proliferating use of metaphors; see Chapter 9.

88 See Köhnen (2009), who unfortunately does not systematically differentiate the various forms of optical knowledge because he concentrates on the 'eye.' For example wave optics are not discussed at all.

89 On this dialectics of disruption see Geimer (2002). On the constitutive functions of disruption see also the important volume edited by Kümmel and Schüttpelz (2003).

90 Cf. Buchwald (1989, 296–302) where the 1830s is specified as the decade in which wave theory is established. And Sir David Brewster was indeed taking part in this discussion and partly followed the wave theory (Buchwald 1989, 254–60). But this has nothing whatsoever to do with the later invention of the so-called Brewster stereoscope. Crary (1985, 38) also mentioned that Brewster here and there talks skeptically about wave optics—it is significant that this suggestion is no longer in *Techniques of the Observer*.

91 See Crary (1990, 1 and 127n). When he first mentions it, Crary moreover refers to "synthetic holography" thereby completely leaving out the whole history of holography in favor of its digital simulation, see Chapter 10.

92 See Mitchell (1994, 21): "The rhetoric of rupture and discontinuity forces him [Crary] to make arguments that *appear* in the guise of historical particularity and resistance to 'homogeneity' and

'totality' but actually wind up producing exactly what they want to avoid."

93 In—characteristically called—ray tracing (see Watt 2000, 342–69) the virtual light of simulation (Chapter 10) is to this day treated as a recursive implementation of an "infinitely thin ray of light" (Kittler 2001, 38). Descartes's geometrical optics (which is pointed out in Kittler (2001, 37/38) and in Watt (2000, 131–3) is still with us—and therefore also linear perspective which in today's photorealistic computer graphics is indispensable (see Schröter 2003). Crary (1990, 1) mentions ray tracing without realizing its explosive force for his model of discontinuity.

94 Strictly speaking, wave optics that includes geometrical optics (as I have said before) is only a sub-phenomenon of *quantum optics* (founded by Einstein in 1905; cf. Fox 2006; see Saleh and Teich 1991, 385, who additionally mention electro-magnetic optics as a level between wave and quantum optics that is unnecessary to my argument here). The fact that quantum optics does not play a role here has one simple reason, formulated by Axel Zweck (in Reuscher and Holtmannspötter 2004, n.p.): "The quantum nature of the light used has hardly played a role in the development of optical technologies so far."

Two exceptions exist: "Until the beginning of the 1980s spontaneous emission has been the only phenomenon which needed to be taken into consideration for the description of quantization of the radiation field" (Reuscher and Holtmannspötter 2004, 2). This does not only hold true for the spontaneous emission but also for the stimulated one; again Einstein submitted the first theories on this and its description has been the foundation for the invention of the maser and then later the laser around 1960 (see Hecht 1987, 577–93). The laser is one of the important requirements for the use of holography as a medium for images; strictly speaking, holography goes back to both wave and quantum optical series. Strikingly, however, in the pertinent publications on holography, quantum optics (see for example Klein 1970, 13) is usually not considered independently and this is another reason for postponing the discussion of quantum optics. The second exception is the transformation of light into electrical energy in CCDs, i.e. those elements that are the foundation of digital and video cameras (see Hagen 2002).

95 See Connes (1987, 157). The author underlines the difference between wave optics and physiological optics, remarking on Lippmann's research: "The vagaries of human vision . . . are not even considered" (158). See Chapters 4 and 5.

96 The best current example is the way in which linear perspective projection (far from disappearing) returns in the form of the hardware of graphic boards in commercial computers because the 3D representation in computer games is currently extremely valued, see Vollmer (2007).

97 On the mathematics of perspective in detail see Aitken (1986).

98 See the many examples of modifications often made consciously and in a well-directed way by some painters in Elkins (1994, 117–80). See also White (1987, 189–201; 286); Edgerton (1975, 53–4).

99 See Kittler (2010, 148), who talks of the transition of the geometrical model of optics to a materialistic one. See also Kittler (2010, 72) describing how the "technology of lenses forced physical light itself . . . into the perspective that was invented only theoretically in the Renaissance."

100 On the term 'transmediality' see Schröter (2012, 20–6).

101 Including holes that function like lenses—as for example in the camera obscura.

102 See for example Schaaf (2000, 19–20) on the various attempts by Talbot to fixate his photo-sensitive paper. The thiosulfates described by Herschel in 1819 gradually proved to be the best fixing agents (ammonium thiosulfate is still used today when making chemical black and white photography).

103 The term "punctualise" is taken from Law (1992, 384–5). See Batchen (1997) who seems to claim that it is the "desire to photograph" which is responsible for the fact that photography stabilized. It seems to me that this additional conjecture is unnecessary.

104 It is hard to believe today, when at least in the realm of amateurs a few processes have completely stabilized, how diverse the photographic processes were in the nineteenth century, see Eder (1978) and Knodt (1999).

105 Arago (1839, 21) in a very lucid statement. See also Geimer (2001, 135): "What historians of photography can read retrospectively as an invention began as a photochemical experiment with uncertain results."

106 See Hagen (2005, 631): "Let us firstly keep in mind that the television image was based on the technical construction of a third image when it was born in 1939—a third image as a pure construction of electric effects and therefore not a camera obscura. The light entering the camera, the image entering does not come out again and neither does it cast any light onto anything in an exposing

sense." Hagen challenges the continuity between the camera obscura and the television camera. But the type of storage and transmission, however, does not say anything about the projection-geometry of the image. As an example: very often when watching soccer, anamorphotically warped (i.e. according to the rules of linear perspective) advertising slogans next to the goals are placed on the lawn and only look correct when seen through the television camera—clearly the rules of geometrical optics are in effect here.

107 This is true for all other media as well but here I am focusing on the optical ones.

108 Electronic or chemical, etc. ones as well.

109 The blunder is as grave as it is because photography and stereoscopy belong to two very different registers. The first is a way of recording light, the second is a way of ordering images.

110 The term 'sedimentation' has been tested elsewhere, see Schröter (2004c; 2004d; 2005a). It connects motives from Foucault's *Archaeology* with Winkler's (2000) ideas, as well as with impulses of the Actor/Network Theory (also inspired by Foucault); see among others Akrich (1992), Bijker (1990) and Latour (1991). See also Rheinberger (1997, 28–30; Rheinberger here speaks of "embed[ding]").

111 Especially the military is named by some authors as the central source of all media technologies. In my opinion, it is of course correct that in the case of war, foundational research on new technologies can attain a specific urgency. But this neither explains the emergence of all media technologies, nor does it make evident to what extent the military molding of a specific technology continues to characterize this technology in later usage; for the example of the internet see Schröter (2004f).

112 See Kittler (2010, 153): "Technical media are never the inventions of individual geniuses, but rather they are a chain of assemblages that are sometimes shot down and that sometimes crystallize (to quote Stendhal)."

113 On my terminology: By 'projection' I understand the controlled (using linear perspective or parallel perspective) representation of a three-dimensional object in the medium of a two-dimensional plane—and not projection in the sense of film- or slide-projection or in the sense of psychoanalysis. See Müller-Tamm (2005) on the important role of the projection metaphor, even in the late nineteenth century. This once more contradicts Crary's diagnosis of the disappearance of the camera obscura. See also Païni's art historical considerations on projection (Païni 2004).

114 Kittler is quoting Wheelock (1995) who attempts to show how Vermeer used a camera obscura to compose his paintings. See on this also Schwarz (1966), Fink (1971), and Steadman (2001).

115 Kittler (2001, 35; emphasis mine). The remark concerning perspectival projection was added with regard to the German version of the text. See also Kittler (1997b, 15) and (2004, 196–7). I will address the "counter attacks of modern art" below.

116 Of course, a projection onto an arched plane is possible as well, see Rehkämper (2002, 47). This often happens for frescoes in churches. On the historical genesis of planarity see Schapiro (1972). I will show in Chapter 5 that there is a marginal technology that creates transplane images by way of geometrical optics—integral photography.

117 Gen. 1.26–7 and 10.6; here Gen. 1.27. See on this Bauch (1994, 275–9) who underlines that "the most 'original' meaning of the word 'image' [Bild] continues to live in the German words 'Bildhauer' [sculptor], 'Bildschnitzer' [wood carver] . . . 'Standbild' [statue], 'Bildsäule' [ornamented column], 'Bildstock' [wayside shrine], 'Reiterbild' [equestrian portrait]", which specifically are not based on the plane. [Translators' note: In the German language, as becomes visible above, remains of the term 'image' can be found in the description of sculptural phenomena as well. Unfortunately they cannot be transferred into English]. See also Schulz (2007, 286n).

118 Dobbe (2003, 260). Cf. Boehm (2005, 32) who speaks of "discursive abstinence regarding space."

119 Even this is of course a myth as the discovery of the saccades has shown.

120 It is interesting that Derrida in Brunette and Wills (1994, 10) mentions, "Obviously, because we are starting an interview on the 'visual arts', the general question of the spatial arts is given prominence, for it is within a certain experience of spacing, of space, that resistance to philosophical authority can be produced. In other words, resistance to logocentrism has a better chance of appearing in these types of art." See also Glaubitz and Schröter (2004) on corporeality and spatial imagery.

121 The works by Tony Smith are not always counted within the canon of minimal art; see Potts (2000, 19) whearas Didi-Huberman (1999) regards Smith's works as paradigmatically minimalistic.

122 With the example of Heinrich Wölfflin we will meet with a remotely similar subsumption of the sculptural under the plane in Chapter 2.

123 Seel (2005, 181). What Seel might mean when he says that the image "cannot be transferred into imaginary spatial relations" can hardly be understood when we think of the historically dominant role of the perspectival representation of space.

124 See Selle (1971) who has entitled his commendable bibliography on stereoscopy "3D mirrored in books."

125 Benyon (1973, 4) misleadingly wrote, "Put simply, a hologram is a 3D photograph." See on holography as '3D photography' also Johnston (2006b).

126 Already Watt (2000) uses the term *3D Computer Graphics* in his title.

127 See Reynaud, Tambrun and Timby (2000). In this beautiful catalogue entitled *Paris in 3D* different types of technical-transplane images are addressed side by side.

128 Early on, in German one finds the term 'spatial image' (Raumbild) for stereoscopy, in the English translations it is usually translated as "stereoscopic image" see Helmholtz (1985, 317). For art history and relating to sculptures see, for example, Wölfflin (1946b, 93).

129 On the pictoriality of sculpture see Winter (1985) and the contributions in Winter, Schröter and Spies (2006). Sculpture can be mainly differentiated from transplane images in that in given spatial information they do not allow for a reduction of data and mass, except in the case of a change of scale. Another special case would be the photo-sculptural images discussed in Chapter 3.

130 On the category of the spatial image see Winter, Schröter and Barck (2009). Architecture, sculpture and installation are discussed here in terms of 'spatial images.'

131 Therefore it seems to be a symptom of planocentric discourse when Latour (1986, 7) mentions, "In a linear perspective, no matter from what distance and angle an object is seen, it is always possible to transfer it—to translate it—and to obtain the same object at a different size as seen from another position." If this statement only refers to size relating to distance, it is correct; it is not correct, however, if we are talking about a view of the object from a different perspective. Some pages later, Latour admits as much: "But perspective still depended on the observer's position, so the objects could not really be moved every which way without corruption" (Latour 1986, 27).

132 Gombrich (1982, 191); see also (1960, 249–57). Incidentally, the limitations of linear perspective do not in principle contradict the possibilities of photogrammetry (which will be repeatedly discussed later)—which, however, is only possible on the basis of sufficient information: "Photogrammetry in principle is nearly as old as perspective itself. We saw . . . that Leonardo da Vinci showed how to deduce true information from a perspective drawing given *certain information*. Given just a photograph one can deduce nothing." (Booker 1963, 222). See Carter (1970, 841): "In order that a three-dimensional object be correctly presented to the beholder he must know what the object is."

133 Manovich (1996a, 236–8), for example, speaks about the question to what extent perspective today has become an obstacle for "computer vision." See also Lacan (1978, 96) who observes that something "was elided in the geometral relation—the depth of field."

134 See Bois (1981) and Evans (1989). See also quite concisely Schudeisky (1918).

135 It is interesting that Bordwell (1985, 107–11) argues differently. He is right insofar as some telephoto lenses produce images that come close to parallel projections, but in general photography produces images in linear perspective. In photogrammetry the case of orthophotography exists. As a rule, it consists of aerial photographs in which the geometrical distortion of the landscape's topographic structure is subtracted out—today digitally. This, however, presupposes that a 3D model of topography already exists, which as a rule is being created by stereoscopic procedures. In other words, the possibility of the parallel projected orthophotography requires the use of transplane technologies. See Real (1972). Also in so-called 'photomacrography' images are produced photographically which resemble parallel projections. See Root (1985).

136 See Krikke (2000, 10): "Visual computing doesn't rely on a camera. It doesn't have to play by the optical rules of clair-obscure and linear perspective." The author later on demonstrates the usefulness of axonometric and isometric projections for computer graphics. See Beil and Schröter (2011) discussing parallel projections in digitally generated images.

137 Helmholtz (1985, 285). See also Jensen (1871) with examples from the representation of brains.

138 Historically, on photogrammetry see Eder (1978, 398–403) and Konecny (1985, 925), who interestingly remarks that the use of stereoscopy for the production of maps "was the first wide-spread use of stereoscopy, which around the turn of the century [!] was introduced as a measurement principle for stereo-photogrammetry." Arago's speech before the French Chamber of Deputies during

which he officially introduced photography on July 3, 1839 (he had already previously informed the Academy of Science on January 7) explicitly points out this possibility; see Arago (1839, 14). Helmholtz (1985, 283) already knew how important spatial information could be for "military purposes." See Babington-Smith (1985, 78). On the role of stereophotogrammetry for the creation of maps see Judge (1926, 210–26), Gierloff-Emden (1957) and Burkhardt (1989). Geometrical-optical procedures of calculation and those of physiological-optical evaluation thereby are superimposed, see also Aschenbrenner (1952a; 1952b). See on this in general Pulfrich (1923). On the historical role which the military played (especially during WWI) for the development of these processes see also Collier (2002).

139 On the techniques of visualization in particle physics, Grab (1993, 201) observes: "The representation of three-dimensional information is particularly important. Spatially far apart objects can be positioned close to each other in a two-dimensional projection, thereby easily leading to wrong interpretations." On the use of stereoscopic images in electron microscopy see among others Nankivell (1963). On holography see Chapter 9.

140 For the example of the *Mars Pathfinder* see Smith (1998).

141 Latour (1986, 16). This critique of Latour's emphasis on the 'flat' character of 'immutable mobiles' does not mean simultaneously that I am also criticizing his support of an ontologically 'flat' sociology (see Latour 1996, xi; 2005, 171–2). These are two categorically different levels.

142 Wolf-Czapek (1911 and later, 112). See Merritt (1984) on "tasks virtually impossible without 3-D."

143 See Crary (1990, 4) on the "narrative of the end of perspectival space" as "myth of modernist rupture." Crary is certainly alluding to Novotny (2000) here who had argued that with Cézanne the end of perspective had arrived. See also Francastel (1952) and Kemp (1978).

144 I would like to add, however, that abstract painting in the era before 1945 (e.g. Kandinsky or Malevich) was still burdened by quite a bit of semantic surplus. The pure concentration on self-reference can be attributed to this movement only with difficulty, see Wyss (1996). Many painters of high modernism such as Barnett Newman or Cy Twombly flirted with mythological semantics. It has to be added that painting before modernity also exhibited self-referentiality as Stoichita (1997) has shown.

145 Denis (1996, 94). In the twentieth century, this movement culminates in the USA after 1945 in the abstract painting of high modernism. Its mastermind Clement Greenberg (1978, 200) therefore underlined that it was "the stressing, however, of the ineluctable flatness of the support that remained most fundamental in the processes by which pictorial art criticized and defined itself under Modernism."

146 This seems true at least for that history of art that was oriented towards a formal intrinsic logic of the image (see Wiesing 1997) and does not apply in the same way to the semantically oriented movements like iconography or iconology.

147 Helmholtz (1985, 296) has clearly labeled this point: "The effect of every movement is to bring out instantly the difference in visual appearance between the original and the copy." 'Original' here means the real object and 'copy' its pictorial representation. Of course, framing a painting (or another type of image) strongly denotes the difference from the object of reference.

148 In his important Text "Bildsinn und Sinnesorgane," Boehm (1980, 131n) writes the following: "As a general rule, perceiving simultaneously demands an unmoving and rigid eye of the viewer," adding somewhat undecidedly: "Binocularity might be important here as well." See contrary to this Helmholtz (1985, 298): "On the other hand, in looking at a flat drawing or painting, the retinal images in the two eyes are practically the same, except for the perspective distortions that may possibly be produced by the plane of the painting itself in the images on the two retinas. But the object that is portrayed in the image, unless it too happened to be flat, would necessarily produce different retinal images in the two eyes. Here again, therefore, in the direct apperception of the sense of sight there is something that indicates a difference between the view of a solid object of three dimensions and the view of a flat picture of this same object."

149 Halle (1997, 59) writes: "Mirrors, semi-silvered or not, are perhaps the most effective (and cost-effective) *three-dimensional* displays used in theme parks today." Also Lippmann (1908, 824) refers to mirrors.

150 Hesse (1954, 114). See also Claus (1985, 81) on the "three-dimensional mirror-world facing us through a mirror."

151 Hartmut Winkler in his book *Diskursökonomie* in a similar way—even though he comes from a completely different theoretical context—repeatedly opposes the "3D-solid reality" (Winkler 2004b, 242), the "3-dimensional world" (93), or the "3D-solid world of things" (70; see also 200) with the "symbolic" (93), which for Winkler is the realm of signs (writing, images, etc.); see also Winkler (2004b, 204–5). Thus, spatiality (therefore the '3D' reference?) is bracketed out of the sphere of the semiotic (and therefore the pictorial). There are cases, however, in which the "3D-solid reality [takes over] the role of signifiers" (Winkler 2004b, 242). On "three-dimensional semiotics" see Bunn (1981, 47–75). See on the history of the displacement of spatiality from concepts of the image Glaubitz and Schröter (2004).

152 Lippmann (1908, 305–6): "The most perfect of the current photographs shows only one aspect of reality; it is reduced to a single, fixed image on a plane. . . . [In normal vision] [o]ne sees the objects in space, in their true size and in their spatial dimensions and not on a plane. . . . Is it possible to make a photographic image in such a way that it shows us the exterior world in a frame, as an appearance within the borders of the copy, as if these frames were those of a window opening up to reality?" On this see also Chapter 5.

153 Marx (1901, 36). See also Marx (1981, 524): "Capital by its nature drives beyond every spatial barrier. Thus the creation of the physical conditions of exchange – of the means of communication and transport – the annihilation of space by time – becomes an extraordinary necessity for it."

154 Balke (2002, 119). See Simons (2007) who describes the cultural reactions to the shifted spatial paradigms of modernity in detail.

155 Koselleck (2003, 94). See also Debord (2006, 94): "Capitalist production has unified space." On the deconstruction of the naturalized terms for space see Tholen (2007).

156 Lefebvre (1991, 219). See also p. 95: "With the advent of modernity time has vanished from social space. . . . Economic space subordinates time to itself; political space expels it as threatening and dangerous (to power). The primacy of the economic and above all of the political implies the supremacy of space over time." On space as 'force of production,' see Gottdiener (1987). This is in line with the fact that according to Jantzen (1938) the term 'space' plays a role in art history only since the late nineteenth century.

157 Schmid (2003, 257). See Lange (2001, 9) on the fact that in modernity "spatial concepts stand out as constructed."

158 For example also radar (see Guerlac 1987); see on this Chapters 8 and 9.

159 Consequentially, at the end of the twentieth century a "spatial turn" was proclaimed, see Döring and Thielmann (2008) who in their introduction (7–45) stress the importance of Henri Lefebvre. Therefore he takes on a central position in this book. See also Günzel (2007).

160 Lefebvre (1991, 39; my emphasis). See Lefebvre 1991, 45 on his concept of representation.

161 Lefebvre (1991, 286). Schmid (2003, 220) is pointing out that Lefebvre "takes language as a model for his theory."

162 Schmid (2003, 306; my emphasis). Of course a depiction does not necessarily have to be visual or figurative, as the respective terms for depiction in mathematics show (see http://en.wikipedia.org/wiki/Image_(mathematics) [last accessed September 2, 2013]). Nevertheless, the term 'depict' at least suggests pictoriality in terms of visual representation.

163 See on the specific meaning of images Boehm (1980) and the knowledge specifically opened up through the pictorial, especially the contributions by Boehm, Imdahl and Waldenfels in Boehm 1994a.

164 See Lefebvre (1991, 298) in which he mentions the "space of images and photographs, as of drawings and plans" in brackets. In other places, technological images are connected from a cultural-critical point of view only with "error and illusion" (97). But at least he mentions the "non-verbal signifying sets" (62). See also Kirsch (1995) who criticizes Lefebvre's lack of analyzing the role of technology in the production of space—without, however, mentioning the role of technological optical and visual media.

165 See White (1987) and Damisch (1987). See also Belting (2008) on the Arab roots of perspective which are often overlooked.

166 See Panofsky (1991, 72) who in connection with perspective talks of the formation of a "modern 'anthropocracy'." Thus perspectival projection has left deep traces in 'occidental' epistemology; see the example of Descartes's *cogito* as the 'vanishing point' (Goux 1985). See also Lüdemann (1999) with Luhmann as an example.

167 See Latour (1986, 21 and 22). See already Adorno (1990, 57): "It is no coincidence that [in German] the term 'plate' is used without any modification and with the same meaning in both photography and phonography. It designates the two-dimensional model of a reality that can be multiplied without limit, displaced both spatially and temporally, and traded on the open market. This, at the price of sacrificing its third dimension: its height and its abyss."

168 See Edgerton (1993, 1–22 and 148–92). See also Ivins (1975, 12), Booker (1963) and Kittler (1997b, 13–15; 2010, 80–2). Edgerton (1993, 7) also mentions the isometric projection (as a form of the parallel projection mentioned above) that to this day is valued by engineers. It had been developed by William Farish in 1822 and is

better suited for technical drawings than linear perspective. Edgerton maintains—to my mind wrongly—that "isometric *scale* drawing is . . . a further Euclidian modification of linear perspective developed to make it more amenable to the needs of science and technology" (1993, 7–8).

169 See also Veltman (1979) on the central role of linear-perspectival (and axonometric or isometric, i.e. parallel) projections for the military.

170 Regarding the orientation of space in modern wars see Kittler (2000, 222), who observes: "Technical wars destroy the spaces in which living beings could at all have been living beings."

171 See Pápay (2005, 288–93). To be more exact, maps connect general and individual aspects. Lefebvre (1991, 84) only mentions the role of maps very incidentally.

172 On the complex semiotics of maps see Freitag (1992); Koch (1998); Kowanda (1997); Nöth (1998); Robinson and Petchenik (1976) and Schmauks (1998).

173 Pápay (2005, 292). See Gombrich (1982, 172–214) on the difference of photographs and maps. See on aerial photography generally Newhall (1969) and on the specific, in particular military demands on interpretation, Sekula (1975). For example Major Edward Steichen (1919, 359) reports about his experiences: "The average vertical aerial photographic print is upon first acquaintance as uninteresting and unimpressive a picture as can be imagined. Without considerable experience and study it is more difficult to read than a map, for it badly represents nature from an angle we do not know."

174 Narrations that were first criticized by Crary, but then covertly reintroduced again (by maintaining that geometrical optics was superseded).

175 This shows that for Lefebvre a new mode of production does not necessarily always create a new space, quite contrary to what he sometimes seems to suggest. Perspectival space obviously overlaps different modes of production (feudalism, capitalism) and he underlines this himself elsewhere, see Lefebvre (1978, 285). De Chapeaurouge (1975) has elaborated that the dominance of perspective was often only relative. And Elkins (1994) has underlined to what extent the narratives of the dominance of perspective have used idealizations and homogenizations in varied ways.

176 Lefebvre (1991, 25, 301–2). See also Lefebvre (1978, 285): "C'est une erreur de penser encore en termes d'espace perspectif puisque dès 1910 la peinture de Kandinsky, celle de Klee et celle du cubisme analytique, nous avertissent qu'il y a une rupture de l'espace perspectif." (We should not make the mistake of continuing to think in terms of perspectival space, since from 1910 on the paintings of Kandinsky, Klee and of analytical cubism have shown us that perspectival space has been fractured.)

177 See section 1.5. See Lefebvre (1991, 304 and 308). Lefebvre also underlines there that he does not want to suggest that the artists were inventing new spaces.

178 See Lefebvre (1991, 306–8). Already in the nineteenth century an expansive 'imperialist' tendency of European capitalism was noticeable. At this point the influence of non-European, 'primitivist' art on Picasso should be discussed, but here isn't the space to go deeper into this; see Rubin (1984), Barkan and Bush (1995) and Lemke (1998).

179 An example of barriers are the fences around the 'fortress Europe' as they became visible in the dramatic events concerning the refugees in the summer of 2005 on the borders of the Spanish exclaves in Morocco. Another example is of course the barrier that separates Mexico from the US.

180 Lefebvre (1991, 308). His term 'polyscopic' is interesting because it seems to match my model developed here (in contrast to Crary's) very well.

181 Admittedly, this relationship is much more complex than the overly simplifying thesis that photography had forced painting into abstraction suggests. Of course, many painters of the nineteenth century have also used photographs as models for figurative painting (Degas for example), and especially in the second half of the twentieth century movements like pop or hyperrealism testify that the reference to photography by no means had to force painting into abstraction; see, in general, to this day Scharf (1975). The fact that painting became abstract at the beginning of the twentieth century can also be traced back to the influence of 'esoteric' and 'spiritistic' movements, see Wyss (1996). Also the role of modern sciences (especially physics) should not be underestimated.

182 For it was the 'realism' of representation in particular that impressed the contemporaries of the invention of photography (see Kemp 1980, 31; Galison 1998). Something similar occurred in the reception of film or television—the latter in the 1950s was also entitled as a "window to the world" in a curious analogy to the definition of paintings in Alberti (2011, 167), see Winter (1999, 17).

183 See on this the informative publication by Paech (1994).

184 As Kittler (2010, 22) has formulated in a quite 'unkittlerian' way; see Chapter 8.

185 Waldenfels (1994, 238). His thesis is connected with the modernist thesis that art should necessarily reflect its own medium. See also Seel (2005, 170).

186 See Waldenfels (1994, 241) who underlines that "the regime of vision is not given as material or as form *before vision and forming*, but emerges simultaneously *with vision and forming*."

187 Regarding the spatially oriented aesthetics of relief and sculpture see among others Volkmann (1903, 78–132); Arnheim (1948); Heidegger (2009); Boehm (1977); Winter (1985). See also my analysis of sculptural or, more precisely, installative works by Karin Sander in Chapter 3 and by Jenny Holzer and Olafur Eliasson in Chapter 8.

188 In the case of holograms the non-reproducibility is exploited itself—we must only think of the small holograms on credit cards or banknotes (see Chapter 4). Nevertheless, it should be specifically noted that it would be quite easy to integrate simple white-light reflection holograms into books; however, these will then not be reproduced in the book but will be simply glued into it—which is quite cost-intensive for large editions.

189 See for example Traub (1967, 1086) where the three-dimensional image produced by a volumetric display on the basis of varifocal mirrors is reproduced (partially) using a stereoscopic pair of images (see Chapter 8).

190 See Mach (1896) and Thomson (1896). See on the history of the use of transplane images in medical visualization also van Tiggelen (2002, esp. 266), where the author justifies the necessity of three-dimensional images: "The radiographic image is the sum of the shadows of all the objects located between the radiation tube and the photographic film. It is thus the bidimensional projection of a tridimensional volume. Interpretation of such an image is sometimes uneasy as the level at which the shadows are located cannot be determined." See also Chapter 8.

191 10^{-8} to 10^{-12} m.

192 See also my preparatory work on digital media Schröter (2003; 2004a; 2004c, 194–205; 2004e; 2006c; 2007b).

PART TWO

Case Studies

CHAPTER TWO

1851: Sir David Brewster and the stereoscopic reproduction of sculptures

On the Series of Physiological Optics 1

Coloured on a flat: yes, that's right. Flat I see, then think distance, near, far, flat I see, east, back. Ah, see now: Falls back suddenly, frozen in stereoscope.

JAMES JOYCE (1992, 69)

The planocentric discourse can be found in many locations—among them also in Walter Benjamin's texts. As his very well known diagnosis states, today's works of art are shaped by the age of technological reproduction. He believes that the aura of originals is dissolving since reproductions have replaced originals almost equivalently. Benjamin is not only talking about paintings, drawings or printed graphic works alone; he speaks of architecture or sculpture as well. For example, he writes the following on the era in which photographic reproduction already exists: "The *cathedral* leaves its locale to be received in the studio of a lover of art" (Benjamin 1978, 221; my emphasis). And regarding the time before the beginning of photographic reproduction he observes: "The Greeks knew only two procedures of technically reproducing works of art: founding and stamping. Bronzes, terra cottas, and coins were the only art works which they could produce in quantity" (Benjamin 1978, 218). It was through founding and stamping then that the Greeks were able to reproduce sculptural objects—bronzes—in an analogous format, and nowadays photography makes the minimized reproduction of sculptural structures possible that would have been much too large for reproduction (e.g. cathedrals) by casting. However, Benjamin withholds (or suppresses) the fact that the step from founding to photographic reproduction (to stay within Benjamin's examples) is exactly the step from a truly three-dimensional reproduction of a three-dimensional object to the projection of a three-dimensional object onto a plane. At first, this would seem to be a truism since every photograph is the fixation of *one* view of different "aspects of the original."[1] But this specific limitation of photographic reproduction means that not "all transmitted works of art" (Benjamin 1978, 219) can be adequately reproduced in their entirety. Architectural and sculptural works of art or those in the form of reliefs or installations obviously cannot be reproduced as photographs without losing one of their central characteristics—namely that they are *not plane*. In short, the substitution of the original by photographic reproduction seems to work only for works of art that themselves are plane, like paintings. Benjamin himself has underlined that "the manner in which human sense perception is organized, the medium in which it is accomplished, is determined not only by nature but by historical circumstances as well" (Benjamin 1978, 222). This means that even Benjamin is committed to the persistently hegemonial medium of pictoriality despite its many breaks and shifts, namely to the projection of three-dimensional objects onto a two-dimensional plane. As the following example will show, long before Benjamin's essay there had been attempts to avoid or to surpass the limitations of the reproduction of a three-dimensional object in the form of a two-dimensional plane. The practice of the plaster cast, which was widely spread in the nineteenth century, or the industrially created minimized copies of sculptures (see p. 94) that had been made possible with the invention of Watt's "sculpture machine" (Dickinson 1929, 14–15) in 1804 are examples that Benjamin did not name: Even though he referred to "founding" (Benjamin 1978, 218) in passing, he located it only in antiquity without pointing to these methods.[2]

After 1839, the plaster cast—as well as ekphrastic descriptions or engravings—had to face photography as a serious competitor in the reproduction of sculptural artworks.[3] By relying on Benjamin, Malraux and others, we might justifiably say that *archiving* and *allocating* artifacts were the primary characteristic functions of photography in the modern practice of art history. Photography guarantees the continued survival of works that were destroyed by wars but mainly it allows conquering distances of space and time; for example, works of art from Paris and Florence and from the nineteenth and the fourth century can now be simultaneously displayed in one place—see André Malraux's *Musée Imaginaire* (Malraux 1978). By way of photographic reproduction, the stylistic and iconographic/iconological comparisons of artistic works are at the very least facilitated and expedited (see Roetting 2000). However, until recently obligatory art-historical practice of the double projection of slides of architectural objects or sculptures led to a problem since in reality sculptures are perceived as non-planar. This means that viewing sculptures requires movements of the viewer. From this *process* of successive viewing from different locations, photography captures only one specific moment. After all, approximately forty-five (or fifteen) years before Benjamin published his famous text (the 1939 version), Heinrich Wölfflin had already written three essays (1895, 1896, and 1925) criticizing that most of the photographic reproductions of sculptures were in no way satisfactory.

Attempting to eliminate the viewer from the process of imaging in photographic practice[4]—for example as applied (at least temporarily) in the natural sciences—is not feasible when photographing sculpture. The photographer has to decide from which location to photograph the object and how he wants the light to fall on it. In Henry Fox Talbot's *The Pencil of Nature* from 1844–46 (Talbot 1969), one of the first-ever published books containing photographs, two photos of a bust of Patroclus are shown from different points of view (see Figures 2.1a and 2.1b).

Talbot, who had placed the bust on a turntable and put it in motion himself, observed about the potential photographs: "These delineations are susceptible of an almost unlimited variety . . . the directness or obliquity of the illumination causing of course an immense difference in effect" (Talbot 1969, Plate V). Different possibilities, like for example changing the distance of the camera

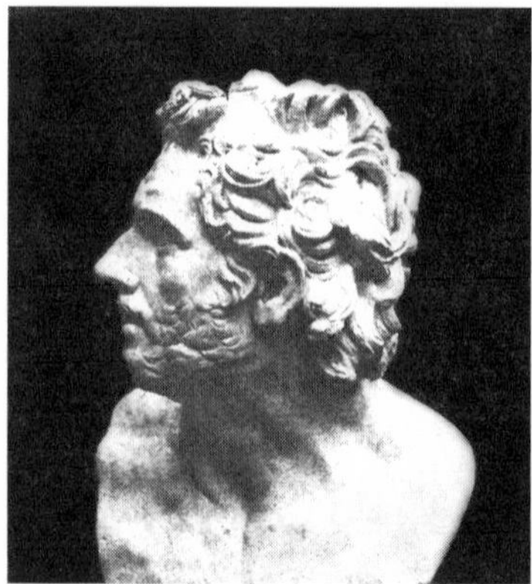
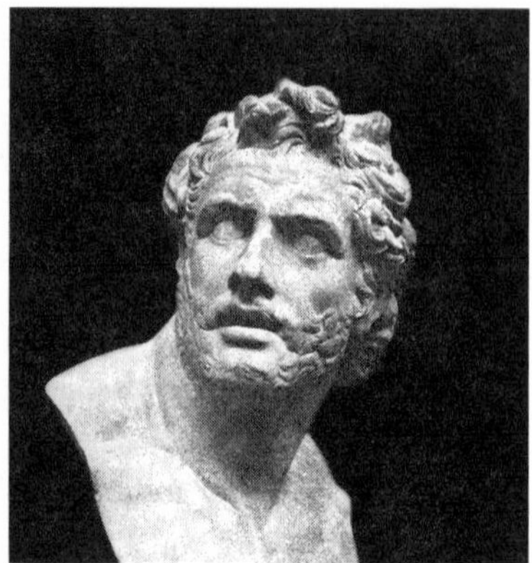

FIGURES 2.1(a) and 2.1(b) *Henry Fox Talbot,* Bust of Patroclus. *(a) Plate V and (b) Plate XVII, in Talbot (1969)*

obscura from the sculptural object, exist. Talbot writes that "it becomes evident how very great a number of different effects may be obtained from a single specimen of sculpture."[5]

Thus, it is impossible to leave this to an automatic process of technical reproduction since it has to be decided first of all from which viewpoint the sculpture should be photographed—at least if there is no alternative to projecting the object from one point of view onto a plane. Do we then *have to* agree to *any* kind of haphazard subjective decision whatsoever? Or does photographing sculptures necessitate a previous interpretation by the photographer? The latter was quite decidedly underlined by Wölfflin in 1896 in the first part of his essay on the question "how one should photograph sculptures":

> [I]t seems to be the widely held opinion that sculptural artworks can be photographed from any side, and it is left totally to the discretion of the photographer at which angle to the figure to set up his machine. (Wölfflin 2013, 53; see also Dobbe 2000b)

Wölfflin demands leaving the viewing of the sculpture not to the "uncultivated" or the "layman's eye," but to the "educated eye" (Wölfflin 2013, 53–4). The viewer/photographer should not withdraw from the process of imaging; the judgment he makes should only be guided by the knowledge of the aesthetics of sculptures. After all, sculptural objects are created for the viewer – as is any art; they specify a principle view (or several central ones)—but simultaneously also reflect on their own structures.[6]

Thus, as Peter Galison has aptly phrased it in a different context, when photographing sculptures, the aim is to already include "interpretation into the very fabric of the image" (Galison 1998, 352). Only by way of a judgment that structures the process of picturing is the possible flood of "unfortunately distorted" views (Wölfflin 2013, 58) reduced to the most likely correct answer. Only then it will become possible to find out what characterizes the sculpture as a sculpture in a media-specific way:

> When coming face to face with the original, however, one will find a particular relish in moving from the inferior view [contrasted to unsuccessful photographs] to the completely convincing [view], and one does not tire, when repeating the experiment, of allowing from inadequate appearances the purified image to emerge which stands calm and clear . . . This is a pleasure that painting cannot give us. (Wölfflin 2013, 59; [view] added by the translator Geraldine A. Johnson)

Specifically *because* photographic reproduction can reproduce the spatial structures of the sculptural object only in a projected way, it is possible to provide the knowledge that is supposed to direct the view and to instruct the eye. Photography can provide *successful experiments*. It can show an ideal case (or ideal cases) of 'perfect' views. Because photographic reproduction of sculptural objects was able to do this, it asserted itself against other types of reproduction, especially against the bulky, non-transportable plaster cast copies that could be used for mass education only with difficulty. "It would be many decades before the rehabilitation of the three-dimensional copy could begin" (Fawcett 1987, 21).

At the threshold to modernity the trend had been to subordinate even sculpture to planocentrism. This was visible in the normative demand that sculptures should be concentrated on a planocentric main view. Wölfflin explicitly advocates the "law of planar sculpture" (Wölfflin 2013, 60), thereby relying on his friend Adolf von Hildebrand who created reliefs himself. In his subsequently very influential publication *The Problem of Form in Painting and*

Sculpture, Hildebrand called for a planar sculpture that was meant to prevent the viewer from being restlessly "driven all around" (Hildebrand 1907, 95) the object. He differentiated "kinesthetic ideas"—in form of successive perceptions from short distances—from the "visual impression"—in form of a simultaneous overview from an adequate distance as "distance picture". The latter permits a "visual perception at a glance with the eye at rest" that provides three-dimensional forms only by viewing them two-dimensionally. According to Hildebrand, the perception of space requires that we "imagine ourselves as changing our point of view and as getting merely a succession of disconnected shifting views of the object." This succession, however, is "unsatisfactory ... as its unity is spoiled by its demands for shifting." In other words "[i]t is only in the visual projection that these demands cease, and permit the unitary plane picture to produce its full effect unspoiled" (Hildebrand 1907, 22–31; see also 36). Therefore it should hardly be surprising that Hildebrand ultimately advocates subordinating sculptures to the regime of the plane: "Unified, from its principal points of view, in one common plane, the figure gives the same feeling of repose and visibility that we obtain in the case of a clear impression received at a distance." Thus, in a way the distanced picture "appears equally unified" so that "even from near by, the appearance is that of a plane picture" (Hildebrand 1907, 92). It follows that "[i]f a figure in a representation must be arranged so as to appear unified in a plane layer, then the spectator must choose his point of view with reference to such a plane."

But even regarding sculptures with several intended views, there will "always be one [view] that dominates. This one is representative of the total plastic nature of the object, and, like a picture or relief, expresses it all in a single two-dimensional impression" (Hildebrand 1907, 94). As a consequence, Hildebrand demands that "ultimately the entire richness of a figure's form stands before us as ... one simple plane ... It is only when the figure, though in reality a solid, gains its effect as a plane picture, that it attains artistic form" (Hildebrand 1907, 95–6; see also 83–4).

Obviously this symptomatic media aesthetics of the sculpture-as-plane[7] (inspired by photography?) is the requirement for Wölfflin's assumption that there should be a single point from which a sculpture can be photographed *pars pro toto*. Even though there are many sculptures with only one satisfactory major perspective (see

Larsson 1974), one might prefer to also reproduce their other possible views. In any case there are numerous other sculptures that present more than just one interesting view, the variety of which could be represented only in a photo sequence, a film or in more current types of transplane reproduction. There are also many sculptures where it is controversial whether there is only one or several views. The decision on this question becomes even more difficult if the reproductions already predetermine the interpretation, thereby denying Wölfflin's 'experiment' of the viewer's independent transition from the 'lesser' to the 'correct' view. When the orientation on the plane is emphatically rejected in the arts, as is the case in minimalism[8] or in installations, photographic reproductions seem to become ambivalent at the very least.[9]

Above all, the media-specific "pleasure that painting cannot give us" (Wölfflin 2013, 59) cannot be provided by a photograph either (unlike a plaster-copy), since the 'experiment' has always been carried out already—and by the way this also holds true for cinematic takes which are able to record spatial complexity by re-coding it into temporal sequentiality.[10]

For didactic aims it would be optimal to find a reproductive mode in which the easy availability and mobility of photography could be connected to an improved spatiality, especially if it could be explored by the viewer on their own. And indeed, attempts to reproduce the spatial structures of a sculpture in a different way than by recasting it in plaster existed earlier than Fawcett assumed. This took place outside of the art historical context (which at the time was hardly established) by means of stereoscopy.[11] Benjamin hardly ever mentions stereoscopy[12] although the inventors of this method had already underlined its potential for the reproduction of sculptural objects. Indeed, stereoscopy, which emerged from the series of physiological optics in the nineteenth century (and outside of art history), was frequently used for the reproduction of sculptures.[13] The three-dimensional impression of stereoscopic images permitted even to modify the topos connected with the beginnings of photography, namely that nature painted itself (in the sense of Talbot 1980). According to the enthusiastic Auguste Belloc (1858),

> [p]hotography is not limited to reproducing lines and surfaces. It has found its complement in the stereoscope, which gives to a design the most irresistible appearance of relief and roundness,

> insomuch, that nature is no longer content to reproduce her superficially, she gives, in addition, the complete idea of projections and contours; she is not merely a painter but a sculptor.[14]

Sir David Brewster, besides Wheatstone—the second important nineteenth-century scientist in the area of stereoscopy, had already published an article in 1851 entitled "Account of a binocular camera, and of a method of obtaining drawings of full length and colossal statues, and of living bodies, which can be exhibited as solids by the stereoscope."[15] There he identifies the representation of statues as the most interesting field of application for stereoscopy.

Brewster describes in detail how a sculpture should be correctly reproduced by stereoscopy. In order to substantiate this, he starts out with fundamental considerations on the perception "of a building or a full-length or colossal statue" (Brewster in Wade 1983, 219). Despite commencing by viewing with just one eye, he underlines the difference between viewing from close up and from afar. This means that he differentiates—similarly to Hildebrand—between a close-up and a view from a distance. This connection between the ideas of Hildebrand and those of Brewster concerning perception is in no way accidental since Hildebrand bases his thoughts on the existence and effect of sculptures on the insights of his time regarding the physiology of perception. (See Figure 2.2.)

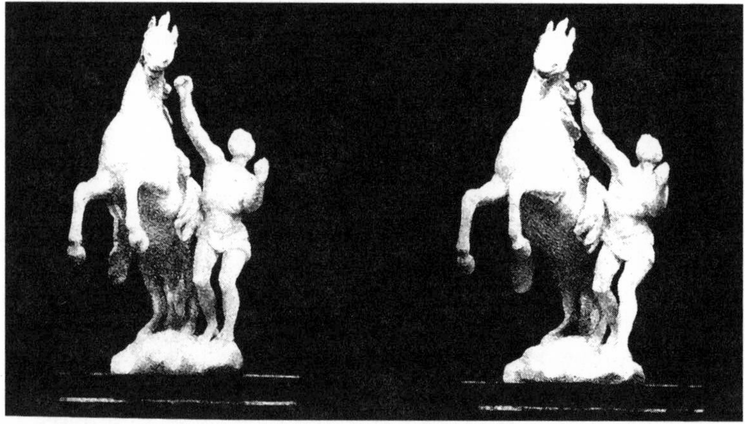

FIGURE 2.2 *Stereoscopic image of a sculpture, Brewster's* Account, *in Wade (1983, 223).*

These were insights on which the construction of the stereoscope had also been based. As different as they might be, Brewster's and Hildebrand's considerations have their roots in the series of physiological optics.[16]

Since Wheatstone's essay, from 1838 the conviction was that it was the difference between the two different images that each eye receives that made for the spatial impression, since he strikingly confirmed his theses by constructing the stereoscope[17]—despite the fact that the image seen with the stereoscope makes a curious impression of stage settings,[18] thereby clearly differentiating itself from the 'natural' perception of space. According to Wheatstone, the simple reason for the dominance of a planar impression at a distance is that the eyes' visual axes only converge when the objects are near, i.e. when each eye provides different views, whereas the visual axes run almost parallel when objects are viewed from farther away, i.e. when the views become more and more similar to each other, which is exactly what Hildebrand had repeatedly underlined in his book *The Problem of Form in Painting and Sculpture*.[19] Therefore, in stereoscopic images spatiality will be particularly noticeable in those elements that seem to be fairly close to the viewer while more distant elements will seem to be rather two-dimensional. All the same, Brewster underlines that this produces a problem for the stereoscopic reproduction of sculptures:

> It is obvious, however, from observations previously made, that even this camera will only be applicable to statues of small dimensions, which have a high enough relief, from the eyes seeing, as it were, well around them, to give sufficiently dissimilar pictures for the stereoscope. As we cannot increase the distance between our eyes, and thus obtain a higher degree of relief for bodies of large dimensions, how are we to proceed in order to obtain drawings of such bodies of the requisite relief?[20]

Thus, the problem with big statues is that one has to stand at a greater distance in order to be able to photograph the sculpture as a whole. But then the spatial impression shrinks, because the visual axes become increasingly parallel. However, if the camera is placed in front of the sculpture at such a close distance that a three-dimensional effect is created—i.e. that a close up is being photographed—then one can only see a small part of the sculpture.

Thus, there is only one solution for making stereoscopic images of sculptures:

> Let us suppose the statue to be colossal, and *ten* feet wide, and that dissimilar drawings of it about *three* inches high are required for the stereoscope. These drawings are *forty* times narrower than the statue, and must be taken at such a distance that, with a binocular camera having its semilenses 2 1/2 inches distant, the relief would be almost evanescent. We must, therefore, suppose the statue to be reduced *n* times, and place the semilenses of the binocular camera at the distance n × 2 1/2 inches. If n = 10, the statue will be reduced to or to 1 foot, and n × 2 1/2, or the distance of the semilenses will be 25 inches. If the semilenses are placed at this distance, and dissimilar pictures of the colossal statue taken, they will reproduce by their union a statue one foot high, which will have exactly the same appearance and relief as if we had viewed the colossal statue with eyes 25 inches distant. But the reproduced statue will have also the same appearance and relief as a statue a foot high, reduced from the colossal one with mathematical precision, and therefore it will be a better and a more relieved representation of the work of art than if we had viewed the colossal original with our own eyes, either under a greater, an equal, or a less [*sic*] angle of apparent magnitude.[21]

The question "whether or not a reduced copy of a statue, of precisely the same form in all its parts, will give us, either by monocular or binocular vision, a better view of it as a work of art" can be quite unequivocally answered with Brewster's view that "its relief or third dimension in space, must be much greater in the reduced copy" (Brewster, in Wade 1983, 219). Brewster then suggests stereoscoping a downscaled copy of the statue;[22] such a reproduction has even *more relief* than one of the original. Even though the stereoscopic reproduction of a "colossal"—i.e. gigantic—statue is also possible by increasing the distance between the two points of recording (for example to 25" on a statue of 10"), this might risk that the stereoscopic rendition looks distorted. For example, there is this opinion in a handbook from 1859:

> It is now obvious that the greater the distance of the eyes from each other the more noticeable and obvious the corporeality of

> the objects would seem to us. . . . The further away an object of which the photographer wants to create a stereoscopic view is, the further apart he has to place the two camera obscuras; the distance between them when photographing a landscape has to amount to ten, twenty and often more steps. However, one has to be careful not to make the distance too far since otherwise once the view is set stereoscopically, the stereoscopic effect seems overdone, i.e., the protruding elements of the object, for example the nose of a statue and similar parts project too far out and thus the object seems distorted and caricatured.[23]

A better solution might well be reproducing a minimized copy of the original sculpture true to scale, although today's viewers might ask themselves why one does not use the minimized copy of sculptures straightaway instead of creating stereoscopic representations. Be that as it may, in Brewster's times minimized reproductions of sculptures were available in any case; they were even widely used and quite popular. In 1828 Cheverton in Great Britain and in 1837 Collas in France introduced practicable methods to minimize sculptures that were soon used commercially. Figure 1.1 not only shows a stereoscope on the armchair but also a small statue on the table of a bourgeois living room.[24] An explanation that clarifies the curiously isolated character of the sculptures in Figure 2.2 is that it concerns less the case described by Snyder, namely that the sculptures in the reproductions of the nineteenth century often had their original backgrounds removed after the fact,[25] leaving them free in the foreground, but that it is (very likely) more due to their being considerably smaller models. Each one was placed on a table (the lines at the lower edge of the illustration are quite noticeable) and were stereoscoped before a dark background for an increased contrast, which was advisable given the relative insensitivity of the photographic materials of the time.

One can support the assumption that in the nineteenth century stereoscopes of sculptures would have been stereoscopes of smaller copies. From Brewster's collection of 190 photographs compiled between 1839 and 1850—the so-called Brewster-Album—two images are worth specially mentioning: photograph No. 15 and photograph No. 126, both made by Henry Fox Talbot. Both of them clearly show that for photographers like Brewster or Talbot it had been certainly taken for granted to use smaller copies of sculptures (see Figure 2.3 and 2.4).[26]

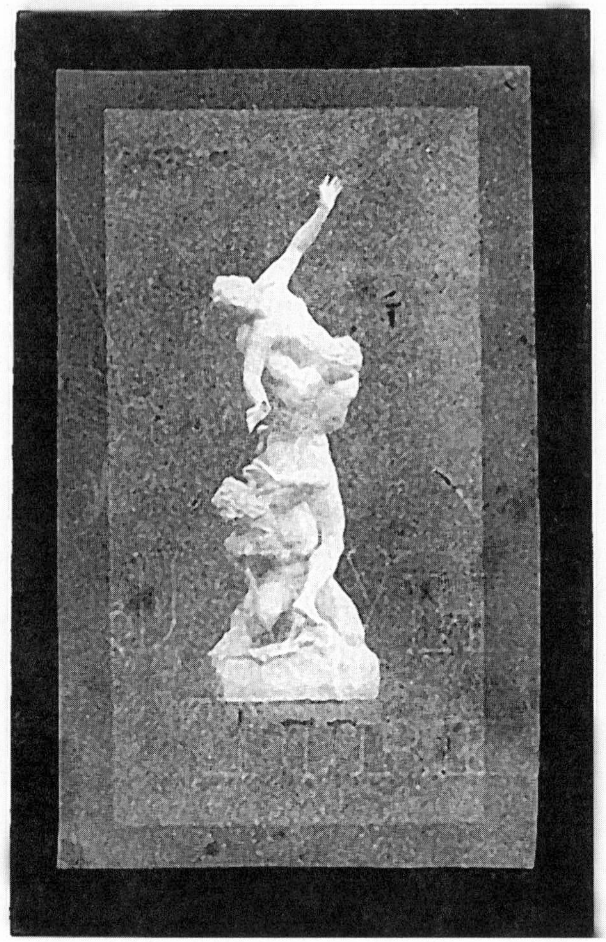

FIGURE 2.3 *William Henry Fox Talbot, Statuette of The Rape of the Sabines (Brewster's copy of a Talbot print), in Smith (1990, 129).*

The stereoscopic reproduction of sculptures thus suggests reproducing copies rather than the original. As I have underlined before, Brewster's contemporaries were fascinated by the documentary value of photographic images, although the danger was that resorting to copies endangered exactly their documentary value. This might be

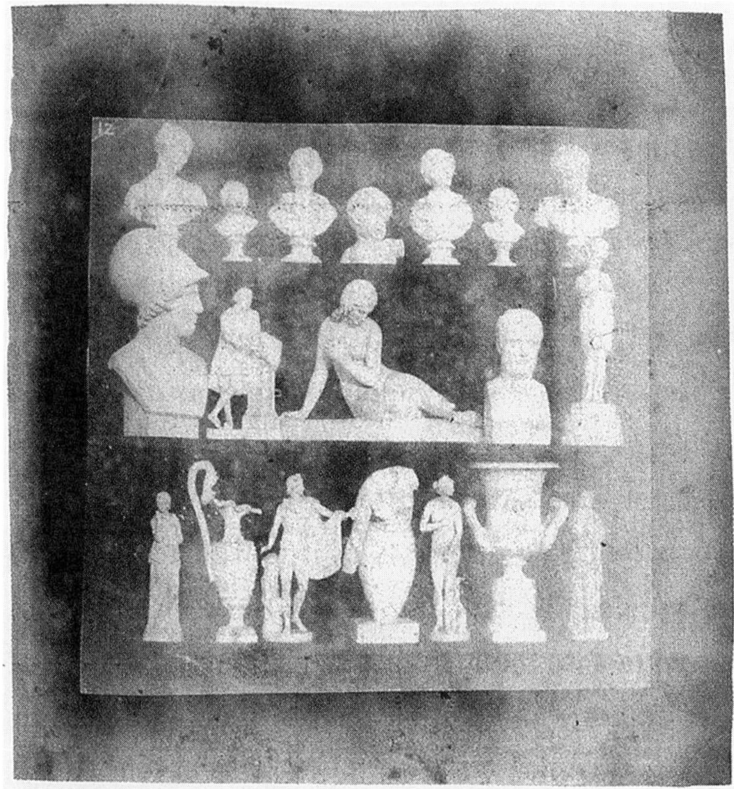

FIGURE 2.4 *Casts on Three Shelves, in the Courtyard of Lacock Abbey, in Smith (1990, 148).*

the reason why the stereoscopic reproduction of sculptures was not really successful. It could also be because a certain percentage of the populace is not capable of perceiving the stereoscopic effect (Ninio 2000, 21 n.3); moreover, perceiving this effect requires a certain amount of practice.

Anyway, an advantage of a stereoscopic reproduction may be the more precise representation of the arrangement of the elements in space. Transplane images provide more information on spatial relationships. In order to use this advantage, however, sculptures should be photographed best in such a way that one part (an arm, for example) is angled out of the plane into the direction of the viewer, since the contrast between the closer parts and those further away underlines the stereoscopic effect. Such a positioning does not necessarily have to correspond to the best view of the sculpture.[27] Moreover, in making such images, excessive separation between the lenses can lead to serious distortions, as has been pointed out previously. The sculptural effect of stereoscopic images is also peculiar and clearly different from the 'real' experience of space or sculpture in space. Objects in different levels of depth appear like flat parts of a stage set, placed one behind the other. Therefore, stereoscopic objects tend to lose their curvature and their massiveness. And when they are produced by using smaller copies in front of a dark background, the sculptures are changed into isolated apparitions; this, then, may potentially contradict both the intended effect of the mass values inherent in the design of the sculptural object and/or its (possible) integration into a spatial-architectonic ensemble.

However, stereoscopy along with photography and film still deny the media-specific joy of experimentation to bring out the 'correct' view (in the sense of Wölfflin) by way of one's own movements since stereoscopic images of course demand that the stereo-photographer determines the point of view. The view chosen can be unsatisfying, just like in conventional photographs; the rest of the statue (its hidden sides) would not be reproduced and this could mean that the stereoscopic effect of spatiality proves hardly useful or it might even prove disturbing. Brewster was nevertheless enthusiastic about his own idea in 1851[28] and therefore the text ends with a passage that is as euphoric as it is clear-sighted:

> The art which we have now described cannot fail to be regarded as of inestimable value to the sculptor, the painter, and the mechanist, whatever may be the nature of his production in three dimensions. . . . Superficial forms will stand before him [the sculptor] in three dimensions, and while he summons into view the living realities from which they were taken, he may avail himself of the labours of all his predecessors, of Pericles as well as of Canova; and he may virtually [!] carry in his portfolio the mighty lions and bulls of Nineveh, – the gigantic Sphinxes of Egypt, – the Apollos and Venuses of Grecian art, – and all the statuary and sculpture which adorn the galleries and museums of civilised nations. (Brewster in Wade 1983, 221)

This passage in Brewster's text is interesting in various ways: First, the central role of one type of technological transplane image in modernity is indicated: stereoscopy is not only interesting for artists but also for the "mechanist, whatever may be the nature of his production in three dimensions." Secondly, Brewster is sketching an archive of three-dimensional forms—a thought that will repeatedly play a role in the discussions on holographic (and virtual) reproductions of sculptures (see Chapter 9). Thirdly, in the quoted passage the ominous word 'virtually'[29] already appears, to which I will return later.

Notes

1 Benjamin (1978, 220). The use of the plural ("aspects") points to the spatial structure of the original. See also Arago already in 1839, who talks of the "plane on which Daguerre operates" (19).

2 On the plaster cast see Berchtold (1987); on other techniques of sculptural material reproduction in the nineteenth century see Fawcett (1987).

3 On ekphrasis see Boehm and Pfotenhauer (1995); on drawings and different printing methods see Fawcett (1986).

4 Snyder (1998b), in referring to Marey's graphic recording techniques as well as his chronophotography, underlines that "observers disappear from much of Marey's work" (382) since his methods do not record anything that one could even perceive without them. Daston and Galison (1992) have quite precisely pointed out that eliminating the viewer was only constitutive for visualization in the natural sciences for a certain time period. In relation to this approach Galison (1998, 331) speaks of "removing oneself from the picturing process."

5 Talbot (1969, Plate V). See Johnson (1995, 2) who points out still earlier examples of photographs of statues.

6 See Larsson (1974) and some of the essays in Winter, Schröter and Spies (2006).

7 A phenomenological critique of subordinating sculpture under the plane is provided later by Martin (1976).

8 See for example the quite decided opinion of the minimal artist Donald Judd, particularly in the following sentence: "The main thing wrong with painting is that it is a rectangular plane placed flat against the wall" (Judd 1987, 116).

9 See Potts (1998, 183) where he talks of the "minimalist view of three-dimensional art as something that has to be experienced in real space and time, which bred a deep distrust of photography." See on earlier developments in this direction Rowell (1979a). See Chapter 7.

10 See the example of the French cinema of the sixties in Liandrat-Guigues (2002); see on the representation of sculptures in television Dobbe (2000a).

11 On the history of stereoscopy see Layer (1979) and Hick (1999, 275–86). On the various different methods like anaglyphic (red/green) stereoscopy, stereoscopy via polarization, or stereoscopy by way of time-division multiplexing (TDM, better known as shutter glasses) see Benton (2001a, 111–221). On autostereoscopic methods (including parallax barriers), i.e. those that also use the binocularity of vision without additional glasses see (Benton 2001a, 225–88; the term autostereoscopy probably goes back to Estanave's patent of 1908b). The random dot stereograms, popular for some time as "magic eye" should be counted among stereoscopy, see Julesz (1960). See chapters 5 and 10.

12 In his texts on photography it does not appear, as far as I could verify. He mentions the "Imperial Panorama," a circular device for viewing stereoscopic views for twelve viewers that had been a popular attraction around the turn of the century before last (see Benjamin 2006, 42–4). It is interesting to note that Benjamin does not mention the sculptural impression of the stereoscopic views with one word.

13 See Snyder (1998a, 30): "Stereoscopic views, including those of many Classical, medieval, and Renaissance sculptures were produced by the millions starting in the late 1850s and were advertised as educational resources for the entire family." See also Crary (1990, 125).

14 Belloc (1858, 13). See also Damisch (2001, 49), who mentions that the sculptural "spell" of stereoscopy "s'impose avec une force parfois surprenante (au point que la référence soit de règle à la sculpture, à laquelle l'imagerie stéréoscopique n'aura pas manqué de payer tribut)" (imposes itself with a sometimes surprising force—to such an extent that sculpture as a rule is being used as reference, sculpture, to which stereoscopic imagery actually has been paying tribute).

15 In Wade (1983, 218–22); see also Brewster's notes (1971, 183–6).

16 See also Helmholtz (1985, 307), who remarks in his *Handbuch der physiologischen Optik:* "The stereoscopic capacity for discriminating distances diminishes rapidly for more distant objects." See also Wölfflin (1946a, 106) who had pointed out Hildebrand's interest in the works of Helmholtz, whom he also knew; see also Braunfels-Esche (1981) and Trotter (2004, 40–1) as well as Boehm (2005, 34).

17 See Wheatstone (1983). See currently Koenderink's criticism (1998) and see also Joseph (1984).

18 Cf. Crary (1990, 125–6) referring to Krauss (1982). However, this staging characteristic apparently was neither noticed in the nineteenth century (cf. Fohrmann 2001) nor far into the twentieth by the countless authors writing about stereoscopy—with one exception, namely McKay (1944, 37) who is quoting another author with the remark: "Stereoscopic photography . . . can never rank with conventional photography. Perhaps the reason for this is that it inevitably disrupts any attempt at design through its violent separation of planes." Apart from this, the perfect 'realism' of the image is always underlined. Helmholtz (1985, 303) has already remarked: "These stereoscopic photographs are so true to nature and so life-like in their portrayals of material things, that after viewing such a picture and recognizing in it some object like a house, for instance, we get the impression, when we actually do see this object, that we have already seen it before and are more or less familiar with it. In cases of this kind, the actual view of the thing itself does not add anything new or more accurate to the previous apperception we got from the picture, so far at least as mere form relations are concerned." See Soulas's (1978) critique of the alleged realism of stereoscopy.

19 See Hildebrand (1907, 21–2): "Let the observer's distance be so far removed that his eyes no longer make an angle of convergence on the object, but gaze parallel into the distance; thereupon the two retinal images become identical. The idea of a three-dimensional object which the observer continues to hold . . . is now produced by factors which have only two dimensions." This also explains the question of why Hildebrand's statement has its origin in the series of physiological optics but still can be planocentric: Hildebrand demands such a distanced position of the viewer of a sculpture that the binocularity of vision no longer plays a role. And more than that: what he calls in a significant metaphor "stereoscopic vision" he criticizes for provoking a mingling of close up and distanced image. By this he understands the normal vision with two eyes and demands: "When we close one eye it is as though we threw the object into a greater distance, i.e. we have then only one picture instead of two different ones. The simple, two-dimensional picture thus obtained we shall hereafter term a visual projection [Fernbild = distance picture]" (Hildebrand 1907, 28). Hildebrand's planocentrism thus does not only lead to *conceive the sculpture as a plane, but also to consider binocular vision as a* '*combination*' [In German the term "unrein" = *unclean* is used]. Without doubt and despite his recourse to the theories of perception of his time, he

would have rejected stereoscopic images. At another point, he critically refers to the panorama, which was tremendously popular in the nineteenth century: "The brutality [!] of such means [the panorama] lies in the fact that a sensitive observer discovers the lack of harmony between his muscular sensations of accommodation and convergence and his spatial judgments which are based on the purely visual part of his perception" (Hildebrand 1907, 56).

20 Brewster in Wade (1983, 220). By "camera" he refers to a camera with two lenses "at the distance of 2½ inches, which is the average distance of the eyes in man" (Brewster in Wade (1983, 220)), which he had described earlier. By "drawings" in the above quote he refers to photographic reproduction. Henry Fox Talbot, for example, had called the photographic method he designed in 1834 "photogenic drawing," see Snyder (1998a, 23–6).

21 Brewster in Wade (1983, 220–1). By "semilenses" is meant that Brewster divided one lens into two for the stereoscopic method—only like this could he ensure an exact geometrical-optical match between the two lenses; see Rohr (1920, 57).

22 In the nineteenth century, stereoscopic views of miniatures were quite customary. Other examples can be found in Pellerin (1995, 75, 83, 84).

23 Quoted in Stenger (1937, 102). The quirky 'hyperstereoscopic' effect of a too great or a too small distance of the focal point is wonderfully described in Mach (1986, 82–5).

24 See Frieß (1993, 210, 212): "Around 1850 hardly any English porcelain factory exists that does not manufacture copies of antique or current sculptures meeting the Victorian taste. . . . Now, thanks to mass fabrication, everyone is able to place a copy of the *Venus de Milo* into his living room. The customer can choose four different sizes."

25 See Snyder (1998a, 29–30). Incidentally, the nineteenth century also experimented with colors regarding stereoscopic views of sculptures, cf. Anonymous (1870, 211): "One can produce a strange effect by coloring the images of the stereograph with different transparent colors. . . . The colors mix in the eye and the resulting color is exactly the same as if it had been mixed by the painter and had been applied to the image . . . We have seen French stereoscope images of statues that clearly explain this principle. One of the images was colored green and the other yellow and the mix of the two was produced in the eye and resulted exactly as bronze."

26 Regarding photo no. 126 see also Getty Museum (2002, 58): "The image was itself a rendition of a reproduction, a small plaster statuette of Giambologna's famous sculpture in Florence" and (Getty Museum 2002, 132) where Larry J. Schaaf underlines that Talbot had

a large collection of such statues. Professor Nicholas Wade (Dundee) in an email sent to me on March 1, 2005 confirmed that Brewster used smaller copies of sculptures. Significantly, the first stereo image in the chapter on "Stereoscopic Photography" in Eder's seminal *History of Photography* (at least in the German version) is one of a sculptural object. With the same isolated representation of the sculpture before a dark background the image strongly resembles Figure 2.2; see Eder (1979, 534).

27 In Hildebrand's sense of a 'planar' perception this is actually downright wrong.

28 Still in 1935 Kurt Lothar Tank (1935a, 101) would write in *Das Raumbild. Monatszeitschrift für die gesamte Stereoskopie und ihre Grenzgebiete* on photographic reproductions of Rodin's sculptures: "Are these really sculptures, he will ask, these pale, plane images that reveal nothing about the power of these works? . . . But we can revive a true memory of the original experience, or—if we have not yet seen the work—a foreshadowing of the beauty of the original when we behold a good spatial picture. What is true for the sculptural work is just as true (or maybe even more so) for the spatial building." Tank in 1942 took the responsibility for an "album of spatial images" with one hundred and thirty-five stereo images of German sculptures. The preface was written by Albert Speer (see Chapter 6). See also Thinius (1937, 44): "The spatial image is absolutely predestined also for the study of the art of sculpture."

29 'Virtually' is first of all a very normal term in English. However, already in Brewster's era a further meaning of the term was also implied as pertinent dictionaries reveal: "In respect of essence or effect, apart from actual form or specific manner; as far as essential qualities or facts are concerned" (*OED*). This meaning is accentuated when technological media like stereoscopy and holography and finally virtual optics set in.

CHAPTER THREE

Since 1860: Photo sculpture

On the Series of Virtual Optics 1

Media Aesthetics of the Transplane Image 1: Karin Sander: People 1:10 *(1998–2001)*

Media Aesthetics of the Transplane Image 2: The Matrix *(1999)*

The picture can represent every reality whose form it has. The spatial picture, everything spatial, the coloured, everything coloured, etc.

LUDWIG WITTGENSTEIN (1955, § 2.171)

As I have stated in the Introduction, the geometrical-optical, linear-perspectival projection of three-dimensional objects onto a two-dimensional plane incurs a loss of information. And as I have shown in the last chapter, even stereoscopy proves to be not really a great help in reproducing objects that perhaps should be seen from a 'back side' as well. It is therefore quite notable that in the nineteenth century there was a peculiar attempt to overcome the limitations imposed by the photograph's linear perspective by way of *sculpture*.[1] I am talking of François Willème's method of photo sculpture, patented on August 14, 1860.[2]

Since 1860: Willème's photo sculpture

The aim was not so much at producing information about the spatial structure of an object or of a spatial segment; rather, Willème's photo sculpture was aimed at representations intended for the bourgeoisie via the possibility of having a bust or a sculpture in the round made without having to spend a lot of time or money. "Willème . . . wanted to create art for the people or at least for the bourgeoisie. Therefore, photo sculpture reveals certain democratic tendencies of that time" (Drost 2005, 383). While numerous technical, historical, sociological and aesthetic aspects of the different methods of photo sculpture have already been discussed in literature,[3] nobody as of yet has addressed the fact that the fundamental idea of photo sculpture is not simply a "technical curiosity"[4] that has disappeared, but that it exists to the present day (see 'rapid prototyping' below). One Walter Schlör put it in a nutshell in 1926:

> The photographic image of spatial objects is flat and without relief. Even though it is possible via stereoscopic methods to simulate three-dimensionality in an image for an observer one was not content with this pseudo-three-dimensionality and methods were developed that were able to represent the spatiality of an object in sculptural material photographically. (Schlör 1926, 718)

Photo sculpture is an attempt to reverse the process of projecting a three-dimensional object onto a plane. Thus, this does not create a proper transplane image, even though Drost speaks of "three-dimensional photography."[5] The different methods of creating photo sculptures allowed reconstructing spatial information from two-dimensional planar images in different ways with more or less success.

However, as I have mentioned before, from any *single* photograph only parts of the spatial structure of the objects or the scene represented can be reconstructed, even if there is a lot of contextual knowledge. Willème attempted to solve the problem by multiplying the plane. Eduard Kuchinka has succinctly described the production process in 1926. Permit me an extensive quote from this description:

Willème's study . . . consisted of a circular room of 10 meters diameter covered by a glass dome. . . . At the center of the room a small wooden pedestal was placed on which the person to be represented was positioned. In order to make sure that the person was exactly in the middle of the room, a lead plumb line was dropped from the center of the dome that would pass through the center of the wooden platform if lengthened. The wall around the study was only a few meters high serving as a support for the iron construction of the dome. Within the wall there were twenty-four circular openings through which just as many objectives were directed to the center of the room, i.e., to the model positioned there. The cameras had been placed in a hallway which circled the whole recording room and that was simultaneously used as a dark room. The circular platform on which the person was standing also had twenty-four sections like the room. They corresponded with the twenty-four objectives and glass plates, so that the partial images could not be mixed up. Several persons prepared the plates for photographing, filled the cassettes and placed them into the cameras. Then the model positioned itself on the wooden platform and after a certain sign, all twenty-four plates were simultaneously exposed by lifting all slides in the cassettes at the same time by way of a special mechanism. After a second sign from the room, all cassettes were closed in the same manner. Thus twenty-four images were taken all together but from different points of view. A special clarity of the negatives was not important, however, because the work was not done directly with these images of roughly the size of a thumbnail image on a visiting card since they were enlarged with a projection device. One of these little images was enlarged with this device onto a white screen (a matt screen or similar) and close to the image a pantograph was placed that was handled by two workers in such a way that the one guided the end of the pantograph onto a transparent wall and the second transferred the reproducing end onto a cylindrical mass of clay, cutting the clay in the form of any contour. The clay was then placed on a circular foot stand (a hub) that was divided and numbered in exactly the way as the wooden platform and that could be easily turned around its vertical axis, as well as being moved with a screw forwards and backwards. Once the first photograph was transferred to the clay, one continued with the next plate until all twenty-four negatives, whose outlines had to be clearly silhouetted against the background, were transferred onto the clay. For the purpose of greater precision, above the foot stand with the block of clay another plumb line was dropped. In all cases the number of images had to be divisible by four by always transferring the corresponding photographs one after the other which were taken at an angle of 90°—for example first the front and the right profile, then the back and the left profile. Afterwards the next corresponding four neighboring images had to be always formed onto the clay. As soon as the twenty-four original images were constructed and shaped, the sculpture was roughly completed and only needed to be refined. . . . The individual images were again enlarged one after the other but now the workers, mostly sculptors or modelers, not only paid attention to the outline but also to the shadows and lights, to the folds of the garments and the finer details. When this touch up was accomplished and in the end once more small uneven spots had been smoothed down, the sculptural image was finished. Since photo sculpture only provides a certain number of images of the outline by way of light sections, a reworking of the acquired shapes by a sculptor cannot be avoided. (Kuchinka 1926, 4–6; see Figure 3.1)

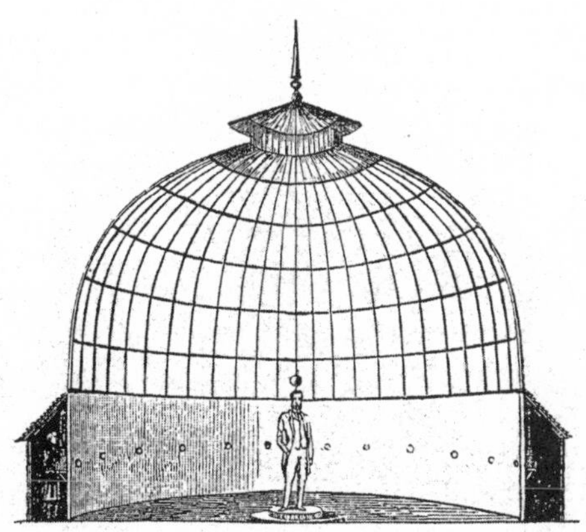

FIGURE 3.1 *Willème's photo-sculpture studio, in Kümmel (2006, 194).*

The last sentence substantiates that Willème's photo sculpture is at best a half technological method. An enormous amount of touch ups were necessary and therefore it was debatable for a long time whether photo sculpture could lay claim to artistic validity, despite its technological character. However, at this point I do not want to follow up on this discussion centering on contrasting handicraft versus technology, which I will take up below (see Drost 1986 and Winter 2006).

First of all, one thing is important—photo sculpture allows reconstructing the spatial structure of the object by multiplying the image planes, i.e. the points of view of the three-dimensional object. The reconstruction is only possible through the use of a certain "violence of decomposition" (Gall 1997, n.p.). The photographed object has to be fragmented into a series of views in order to be reconstructed again. This is a first hint at how the different methods of producing photo sculptures can be integrated into the history of the overlapping and interlocking optical series or more precisely into the history of transplane images. Even though this may sound somewhat startling at first—*photo sculpture is an early manifestation of the series of virtual*[6] *optics*. Fragmenting the whole into parts, reconstructing these parts and subsequently touching up the sculpture (see Figure 3.2 showing a rough photo sculpture before it was smoothed down) clearly reminds us of today's frequently used

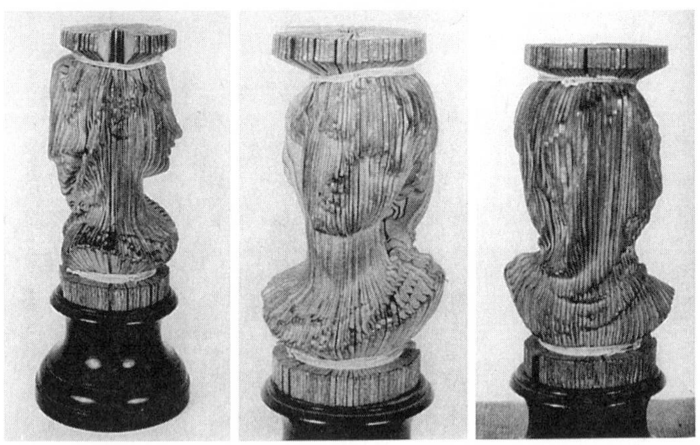

FIGURE 3.2 *Not yet touched up photo sculpture (Sorel 2000, 81).*[7]

methods of digitizing signals, reconstructing them and minimizing those glitches that occur during the process of reconstruction ('aliasing').

Digitizing or the digital are far from being identical with the binary system operative today in computers, even though nowadays the two are often considered one and the same.[8] Initially, digital only means that a discrete code is being used (defined in this way, the alphabet is digital),[9] or that a signal is being changed into discrete sample values.[10] Even though the terminology in the nineteenth century did not yet play a role, there were already certain media functioning along lines that have to be regarded as digital or as analog/digital-hybrids: the telegraph, certain forms of photo telegraphy (see Schneider and Berz 2002), or even film. Kittler for example has underlined that the principle of discrete sampling had already been anticipated by the "24 film exposures per second"[11] (strangely enough, Willème also used twenty-four samples—even though spatially and not temporally). Of course these technologies were not yet binary-digital by today's definition. They were not, because the input signals were not being measured and transferred into a mathematical and calculable code. But they were already working with fragmenting and reconstructing—and insofar encoding—information.[12] In photo sculpture, the "whole process of transcribing the series of two-dimensional photographs into a three-dimensional sculpture is only possible as a sequence of discrete steps" (Kümmel 2006, 206). Even though Willème's luxurious studio for the creation of photo sculptures financially failed in 1867, we cannot assume—similar to stereoscopy and Lippmann photography dealt with in the next chapter—that the *methods* of reconstructing spatial information by way of a (proto-)digital fragmentation had vanished.

Since 1890: From photo sculpture to rapid prototyping

Approximately in 1890 the interest in photo sculpture was awakened again, in all probability connected to the incipient boom of amateur photography. The names repeatedly connected to it are H. Pötschke, W. Reissig and W. Selke. The common bond between the methods developed by these hobbyists was that they attempted to avoid the drawbacks of Willème's method—the complexity of the undertaking and the necessarily elaborate manual touch ups[13]—in order to produce more reasonably priced products. I do not want to introduce all the methods in detail—the respective studies do this extensively (see Beckmann 1991, 5–10 and Drost 1986, 336–43). One interesting approach, however, has been described in a patent of September 26, 1893 by W. Reissig.

The most remarkable element of his outline was the attempt "to replace the mechanical work of reproduction with a mechanical impact of light" (Reissig 1893, 1). Even though Reissig's method did not succeed commercially either, it nevertheless shows even more clearly to what extent photo sculpture was a first step in the series of virtual optics, since it was Reissig who attempted transferring the principle of *rasterization* (known at the time from Jacquard looms and subsequently from certain forms of photo telegraphy) onto the reproduction of spatial structures.[14] As can be seen from the drawing shown in Figure 3.3, Reissig projected the light onto the object through a grid. The shadow of the grid appeared on the object in a deformed way, depending on the concave or convex surface forms of the object.

> Imagining for example the head of a bust or a person hit by parallel grid-lines while remaining still, these markings will create contours or lines on its surface. Depending on the distances of the lines from each other, they will have a different but specific form contingent on the spatial proportions of the object (Reissig 1893, 1).

Could we then say that a certain type of *digitizing* of spatial information exists here? Yes and No. First the deformation of the projected patterns by the object is a predecessor of today's so-called 'structured light' methods through which spatial structures can be measured and virtually reproduced with the help of computers.[15] Currently, these methods are of central importance in *computer* or *machine vision* or also in the automatic reconstruction of the three-dimensional structure of objects (see below). Secondly, however, Reissig does not at all measure the curves and distortions of the lines or of the grid in order to reconstruct the spatial information from them, all of which in 1893—and this means

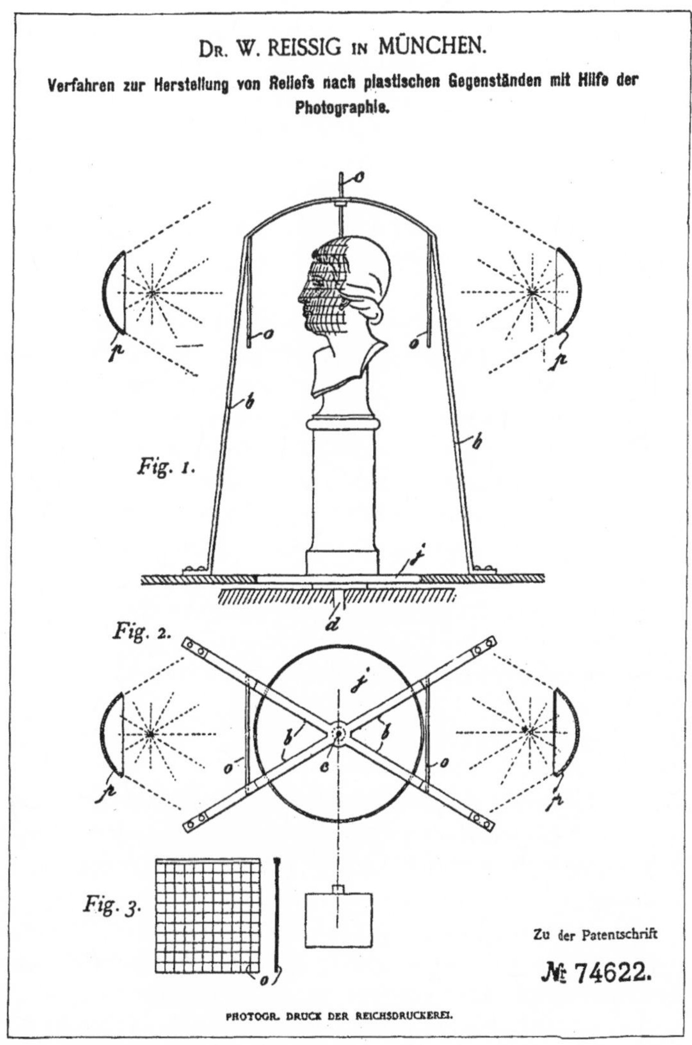

FIGURE 3.3 *Drawing showing W. Reissig's method from his patent, in Reissig (1893, 4).*

without a computer—was hardly possible.[16] Only after 1945, when the use of the computer expanded, could the methods of virtually reconstructing spatial structures be operatively used (see Chapter 10).

Even though the object is "dissected into zones," it has to be colored manually again. The object "is being colored lighter or darker with minor photo-chemically effective agents (like red ferric oxide) from one zone to the next and then photographed perpendicularly to the sectional planes" (Kuchinka 1926, 16). The reason for this unusual procedure—which is practically impossible to do with living persons and therefore has to be seen independently of questions of democratizing portrait busts[17]—is that Reissig used a new photographic method, namely chromate gelatin. Henry Fox Talbot had already patented a method on October 29, 1852 in which the photosensitive material used was a mixture of gelatin and potassium dichromate ($K_2Cr_2O_7$) that loses its "capacity of swelling in cold water"[18] "depending on the intensity with which the light operates."[19] The different colorations of the object to be represented photo sculpturally that Reissig was using then led to differences in the strength of light reflection, i.e. in the exposure of the chromate gelatin.[20] Since it swells more or less according to the strength of the light exposure, it results in a relief of the object to be represented. (This, by the way, shows clearly that Reissig no longer held on to Willème's idea of representing the object as a sculpture in the round). In his patent, Reissig explains:

> The object illuminated with the parallel lines . . . from the light plates and thereby divided into zones is correspondingly covered with the applicable mix of colors progressing from the highest point (the vertical zone which is closest to the viewer or the photographic camera) that is kept purely white, down to the lowest parts (the vertical zone that is the furthest away from the viewer or the camera). The network plate is taken away before the photograph is taken. (Reissig 1893, 2)

The last sentence clarifies that the projected grid only serves to control the process of coloring. The information that is provided by the distortions of the grid is not being photographed. Reconstructing the spatial structure of an object by way of the distortions produced by this same object from the patterns projected onto it was an idea not yet developed at the time; it surfaced later, as was already pointed out. In 1926, Kuchinka writes in his comprehensive review of *photo sculpture*:

> The method of the pointing machine used by stone sculptors . . . can be used in photo sculpture. The extraction of guiding points . . . can be achieved . . . by projecting a system of parallel or crossing lines during the exposure, alternatively light and dark, or a spiral of lines, or any other pattern with the help of a projecting machine onto the object that is to be represented three-dimensionally. (Kuchinka 1926, 19; somewhat abbreviated)

His suggestion of the "method of the pointing machine used by stone sculptors" is interesting since formalizing methods of measuring three-dimensional objects were already available during Renaissance times. No less a figure than Leon Battista Alberti, who—regarding linear perspective—had suggested a mathematically formalizable method of projection onto a plane (by way of the theorem of intersecting lines)[21] in his famous treatise *De Pictura*, had also developed suggestions for "measuring a sculpture" (Bätschmann and Schäublin 2000, 36). His treatise *De Statua*, which was very likely written before 1435 and first appeared in print in 1547 mixed with other texts, was first independently printed in 1877 (in Latin) and does not at all deal with what we would probably call an *aesthetics* of sculpture from the times of Baumgarten or Hegel. It deals with—in today's jargon—engineering questions such as how to "measure solids and statues with the help of three newly defined measuring devices like the proportional decrease or increase of a model and the compilation of a table of the ideal human proportions" (Bätschmann and Schäublin 2000, 37). In his fifth paragraph Alberti discusses these—in his opinion—two main motives of sculptors coming to the conclusion that two methods, "*dimensio* and *finitio*" (Alberti 1972b, 125) would be adequate. The measuring instruments developed by Alberti were *Exempeda, Finitiorum* and *Norma* (see Figure 3.4).

I will not go into details about these procedures.[22] But it is most significant that Alberti attempted to measure sculptures (as did Leonardo) in order to find models that could mathematically describe sculptural objects, models that would enable the reproduction of sculptures in another place and another time. This would then mean that it is

> more amazing . . . that, if you liked, you could hew out and make half the statue on the island of Paros and the other half in the

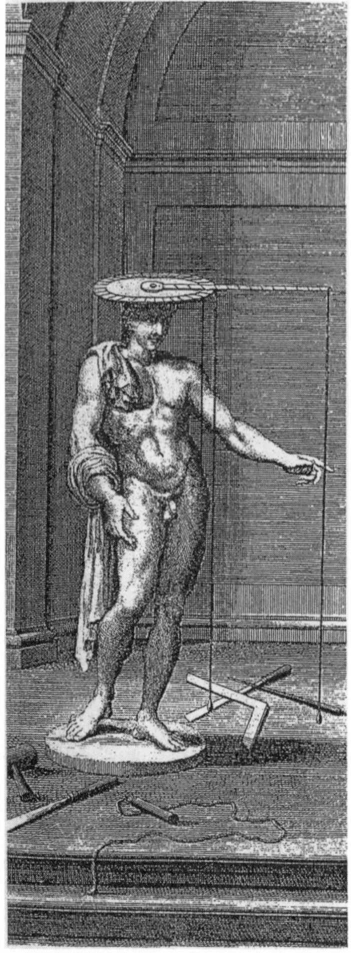

FIGURE 3.4 *Alberti: Implementation of* Exempeda, Finitiorum *and* Norma, *in Alberti (2000, 43).*

> Lunigiana, in such a way that the joints and connecting points of all the parts will fit together to make the complete figure and correspond to the models used. (Alberti 1972b, 125)

It is quite striking how Alberti's suggestion of the *transferability* of his formalized model is reminiscent of the currently quite self-evident idea of being able to send mathematical descriptions of objects—and consequently also sculptures—to any desired place. Alberti's point is that "*Dimensio* is the accurate and constant recording of measurements, whereby the state and correspondence of the parts is observed and numerically represented, one in relation to another and each to the whole length of the body" (Alberti 1972b, 125). Indeed, to be able to express any specifics—and this includes sculptures—in numbers is exactly what today characterizes virtualization.[23] Thus, Alberti decidedly demands that "our sculptors [should have] properly understood the structure of any limb, the proportions within it and of other limbs to it, and those of all of them to the form of the whole body" (Alberti 1972b, 129) and ultimately in *De Statua* Alberti offers a series of tables with physical dimensions (with regard to proportionality): "By this same means also which we have described, you could, as we said, if you wished, make one half of the statue in the Lunigiana and the other half on Paros" (Alberti 1972b, 133). It is not without reason that he repeats what he undoubtedly considered the "amazing and almost unbelievable" (Alberti 1972b, 123) discovery that the formalization of the measuring system of a sculptural object makes it possible to reproduce and transfer it. Without any doubt, Alberti and Leonardo would have enthusiastically welcomed the possibility to have all the mathematical processes performed by machines (computers) and to have their mathematical models transferred by remote transmission (internet).[24] But they were too far ahead of their time. Ultimately "Alberti's *Finitiorum* proved as impractical for working stone or wood as was later the pointing machine invented by Leonardo."[25] It still needed centuries until these kinds of formalizations could become operative in machines—and one of the requirements for machines to be able to process such descriptions of spatial objects is that first of all they receive the necessary information.

Before we arrive at a method that was developed in the 1920s and which clearly pointed to our current methods of virtually acquiring and reconstructing spatial information, I would like to have a look at what is possibly the most functional photo-sculptural method from which we can gather another quasi-digitalization *without* formalization—the photo sculpture method developed by Willy Selke (see Figure 3.5).

Between July 2, 1897 and April 19, 1911 Selke filed for no less than eight patents for the "plastic reproduction of physical objects"

No. 675,417.

W. A. C. SELKE.
PHOTOSCULPTURE APPARATUS.
(Application filed Jan. 20, 1898.)

(No Model.)

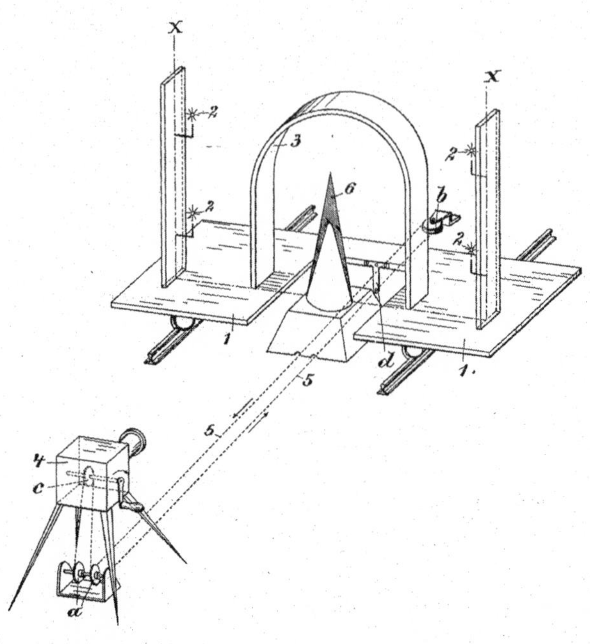

Witnesses:

Inventor:

Willy Alfred Carl Selke

THE NORRIS PETERS CO., PHOTO-LITHO., WASHINGTON, D. C.

FIGURE 3.5 *Schematic representation of Willy Selke's early method: Construction of the photo sculpture apparatus, in Selke (1898a).*

(Selke 1897, 1). The last three of these patents in 1907, 1909 and 1911 are explicitly referring to pointing machines (Selke 1907, 1). In this sense it is correct that Selke was inspired by "scientific surveying techniques."[26] However, this is not true for his earlier patents that are based far more on Reissig's method of light-sections.[27]

In 1900 a detailed description of Selke's early method was printed in the periodical *Die Umschau*:

> During the exposure the model is placed on a podium and is surrounded by a semicircular canopy. . . . The lighting system is placed in the latter, which is necessary for lighting from all sides and consisting of a number of arc lamps; their glaring light is somewhat tempered by front-loaded plates of blue glass. . . . Between this lighting system and the model a belt made of several sections is placed whose hard shadow allows the relief to stand out in a glaring light. This belt is connected to the photographic apparatus and is moving towards the camera by several millimeters between two moments of cinematographic exposure, while the model sits quite still. Since by moving the belt forward the model is shadowed more and more until the highest and last points disappear in the darkness. Thus, the individual exposures each create a silhouette of the points positioned on the same level of illumination—provided there is a steady illumination. While then the first image of the whole series contains the biggest outline of the profile, the second image already shows a smaller outline of the profile and so forth until slowly the lower parts of the relief like nose, eye, mouth, etc. (provided an image of a profile is taken) disappear and only the higher parts of the face (which therefore are exposed for a longer time) like cheeks, ear and hair are visible. Thus one obtains forty to fifty images of the same object. Each one of them is different, depending on the advancing hard shadow—however in such a way that the individual images create vertical cuts through the profile and each one of them contains the points located on the same level of illumination. All these images now are enlarged in the same scale up to life-size. Then they are cut out of heavy cardboard and glued one on top of the other so that one attains a relief with stepped edges that already in this state shows a close resemblance to the original. (Rohwaldt 2002, 59–60)

This means that at this point in time, Selke used the brand new methods of cinematography[28] in order to take such a high number of images in a short time which would be acceptable for a human model.[29] The ready cuts of the photographed object, which were glued on top of each other, reveal a view that to a certain extent is reminiscent of cartographic elevation maps (see Figure 3.6).

The relief with stepped edges that is pointed out by the commentator is important since it proves that photo sculpture belongs to the predecessors of the series of virtual optics. In digitalization, the reconstructed signal is stepped according to the rate of the sampling frequency;[30] the higher its rate the smaller the steps and the closer the reconstructed signal to the original one. If Selke had significantly raised the number of images used and therefore also of the stepped edges—as some later inventors did—the steps would have become smaller and the relief would have

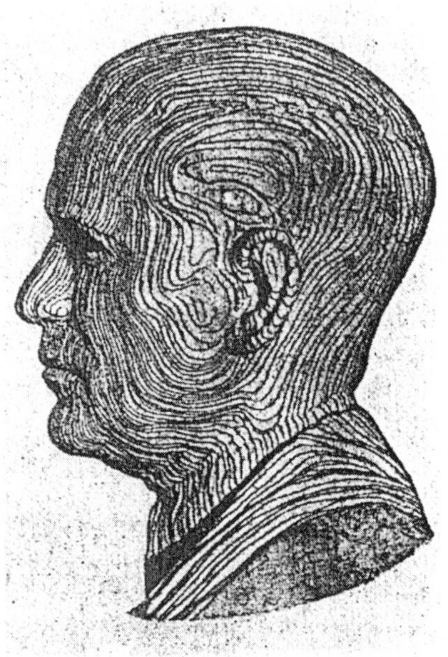

FIGURE 3.6 *Rough state of a photo sculpture by Selke, in Straub (2005, 61).*

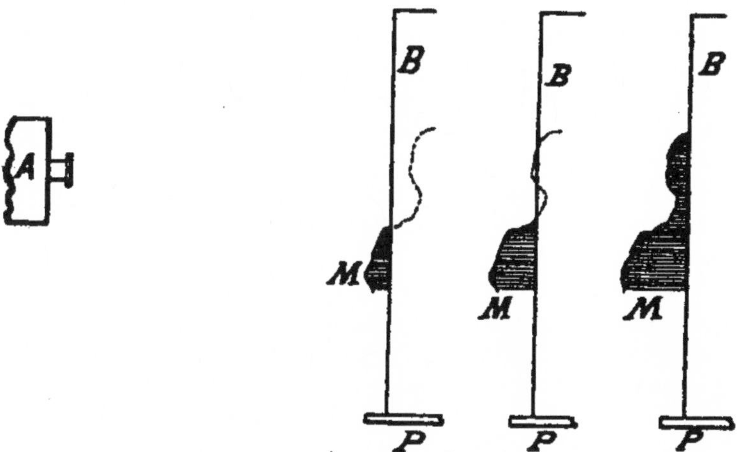

FIGURE 3.7 *Schematized representation of Selke's method of photo sculpture: advancing shadow; in Rohwaldt (2002, 60).*

achieved a *higher definition*.[31] Even though Selke's method already needed less manual post-processing, the glued levels nevertheless were touched up in order to achieve that higher definition.[32]

Selke's invention attracted a lot of interest since it was relatively practical (cf. Gaedicke 1900). It is still represented in a drawing by Schlör in his text from 1926 mentioned earlier: "His [Selke's] procedure fundamentally takes place in a similar form as the creation of a microscopic planar model" (Schlör 1926, 720). This somewhat puzzling phrase points exactly to the connection between photo sculpture and the modern methods of acquiring spatial information for virtual reproduction. In Selke's method the object is dissected into a series of clearly outlined profiles by way of the advancing hard shadow (see Figure 3.7).

Schlör had precisely this use of light in mind when pointing out the "microscopic planar model." And, indeed, in 1932 a certain Gustav Schmaltz published a text that to this day is discussed as one of the earliest concerned with the development of *structured light* (cf. for example Daley et al. 1995, 396). It deals with the "microscopic calculation of the shape of rough surfaces":

> Looking in the direction of the plane from a very pointed angle its structure appears quite fuzzy at first since all elements lying within the realm of the depth of field of the microscope are being represented simultaneously; they overlap in an unclear manner and are being overlaid by the higher and lower parts of the plane creating diffraction circles. (Schmaltz 1932, 315)

First of all the limits of the lens system based on the series of geometrical optics are being criticized.[33] However—'all is clear to the engineer':

> But if one creates a sharp image of a . . . slit by way of an optical system . . . oriented vertically towards the plane, and if this is brought [into focus], the limits of the shadow take on the shape of the plane's profile curves . . . By shifting the microscope and the lighting system fastened to it into the direction of its optical axis, a whole collection of such profile curves can be created one after the other and thus the shape of the whole plane can be represented. (Schmaltz 1932, 315–16)

This is not only Selke's method; it also represents the basic idea of today's *structured light* methods.

However, Schlör's text from 1926 is not only important in that it is anticipating today's connection between photo-sculptural techniques as substantiated here and current methods of the *acquisition of spatial information*. It also points to the methods of *formalizing* this information that has only become possible with computers. After explaining Selke's photo sculpture, Schlör elaborates on another method somewhat abruptly:

> Currently the London based Cameograph Co. has also undertaken to manufacture photo sculptures with the principle of projecting stick shadows. According to the information provided by M. Edmunds, the shadow of a series of thin threads is projected onto the object, then one takes stereoscopic images of the object including the shadows with the help of two apparatuses and then reconstructs the model based on the deviation of the shadows from the straight line with the help of a milling machine created for this purpose. (Schlör 1926, 721)

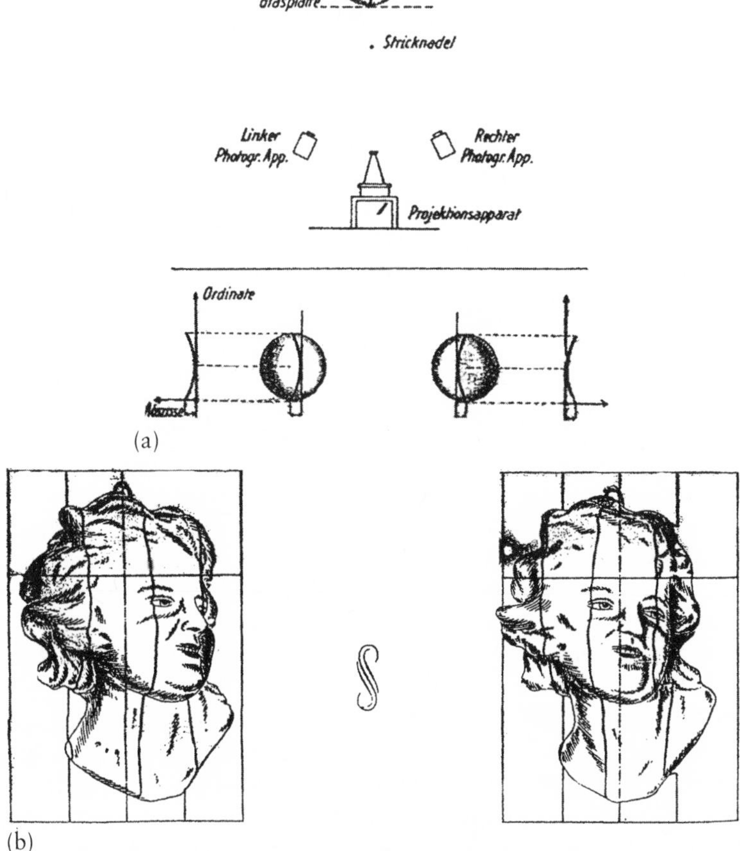

FIGURE 3.8 *(a) Figure 1 and (b) Figure 2 in Schlör (1926, 718).*

Obviously, the company works with structured light (and with stereoscopy) in this model as well.[34] Nothing new then. However, Schlör adds some remarks that directly point to the mathematical description of the deviation of the projected pattern:

> The physical basis of this process can be understood from the simple test arrangement of Illustration 1 [Figures 3.8(a) and 3.8(b)]. The light beam of a projector is directed towards a globe and a knitting needle is placed into the light beam from the

> projector throwing its shadow onto the globe. To the right and the left of the projector a camera is each placed photographing the globe with its knitting needle's shadow. Illustration 1 shows the images taken with the cameras as well as to their left and right the entry of the needle's shadow in a coordinate system. The deviation of the curve of that shadow from the ordinate axis now is exactly proportional to the distance of the related shadow point of the globe from an imagined tangential plane placed at the foremost point of the globe (in the central illustration called glass plate). In other words: the deviation of the shadow's curve from the straight line is proportional to the spatial curvature of the shadow. (Schlör 1926, 721)

Here, Schlör develops an equation with which one can infer the spatial curvature of the globe's surface from the curvature of the projecting needle's shadow. But of course he does not follow up on this idea since an automatic retroactive calculation of this curvature during his time was out of the question, particularly when dealing with more complex objects. He instead explains how the deviation of the needle's shadows can be very simply transferred analogically and mechanically by way of a milling machine.[35] However, the basic premise of all current *structured light* methods is the consideration that the measured deviations of the projected structure should be mathematically calculated retroactively in order to infer the spatial structure of the photographed object. The reversal of the perspectival principle as it is operative in photo sculpture and its successors shows decidedly and clearly here. Already in 1435 Alberti used the grid ("velum") in order to facilitate the projection of the object onto the plane: his grid remained rigid and unmovable in order to distort the object—precisely in order to project it onto the plane.[36] The *structured light* method is exactly the opposite: the grid is being distorted and one can reconstruct the spatial structure of the object from it.

Figure 3.9 shows a current example of this. It is an image from a whole series of images of *David* (here the back of his head) by Gianlorenzo Bernini (1622/23).[37] The grid that we already know from Reissig but which he used in a different way is clearly recognizable, being projected by a special flash onto the sculpture during the exposure. Under exactly calibrated conditions software can reconstruct the spatial structure of the detailed element. Thus it

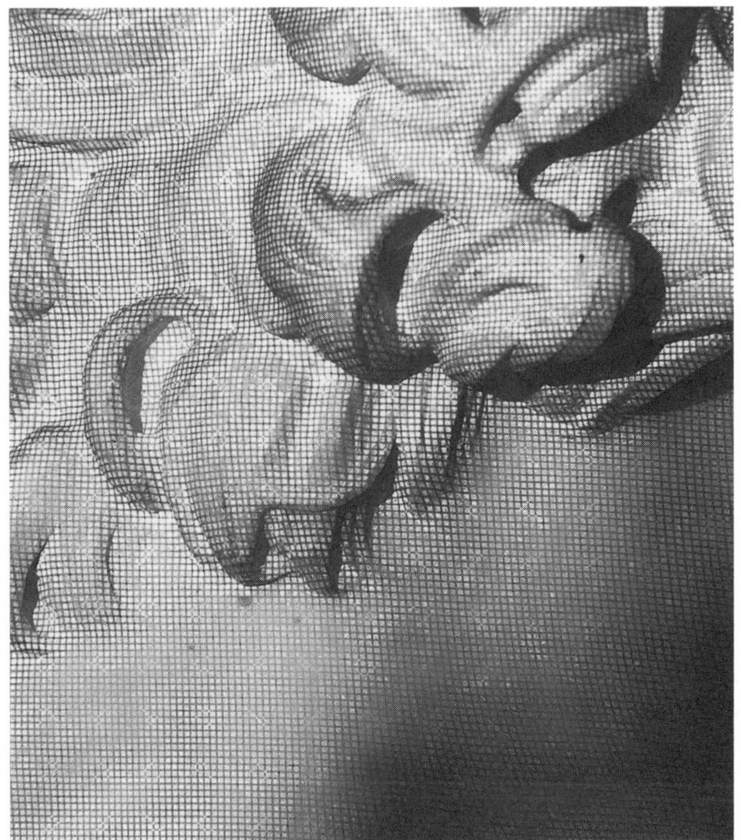

FIGURE 3.9 *Detail, back of head of Gianlorenzo Bernini's* David, *with grid, structured light-method of reconstruction.*

is possible to obtain step by step a virtual, i.e. mathematically described, model of *David* (on virtuality, see Chapter 10).

The different, at times somewhat odd, experiments with photo sculpture in the nineteenth and early twentieth century contributed to acquiring spatial information on the basis of photographic methods.[38] Thus, current approaches attempting to gain information on the spatial structure of objects and their processing by computers can only be explained as a connection of mathematical methods of formalizing information on the one hand and on the other, photographic methods of acquiring information. Or to say it differently: Alberti and Leonardo had had an idea that during their time could not be implemented, namely formalizing the spatial structure of objects; Willème, Reissig, Selke and others invented quite different procedures much later independently from each other that could not be aimed at information to be formalized yet but that provided initial attempts at obtaining information (mechanically and by way of light) which needed to be formalized.[39] Together, after the invention of the computer in the second half of the twentieth century, these methods culminated in a wide panoply of procedures for *machine vision* and for the mechanical virtualization of spatial objects, i.e. for the implementations of virtual optics.[40]

The final aim of photo sculptural methods to be able to generate a three-dimensional sculpture from transplane images is currently topical again, especially when we look at common methods like rapid prototyping or fabbing in industrial manufacturing. There, sculptural objects are created mechanically and automatically with the help of special methods like the directed removal or application of suitable materials or via pressure or other similar methods.[41] In this way it is possible in principle to create a statue of Bernini's *David* from the just mentioned virtual model. And indeed, a group of researchers at the *Fraunhofer Institute for Manufacturing Technology and Advanced Materials (IFAM)* in Bremen is working on just these methods.[42]

The three-dimensional image then would be almost completely realized and this is where we will get to a set of problems already discussed in my introduction. The image is so close to the original (at least in the case in which a sculpture is represented in the shape of a molded sculpture)—it is not flat any longer but is itself a spatial object—that the question then has to be posed whether it is still an 'image' at all.[43] Saint Augustine already suggested to keep in mind that two objects that are arbitrarily alike (two eggs, for example) cannot be seen as each other's images. Therefore, the pictorial relationship has to be established in another way (cf. Scholz 1991, 20–1). However, since in the case of the methods described here we are not dealing with two eggs that are causally unrelated but with a causal relationship, the re-manifestation that has emerged from the sampling and measuring of the original object can hardly be called anything other than a sort of imaging.[44] Unlike in sculpture—that of course can sculpt completely fictitious objects and persons in stone and that is more closely related to classical art like painting—

in photo sculpture an object is represented indexically. The situation shifts again in rapid prototyping, since virtual computer models are the templates that do not necessarily have to emerge from the sampling of real objects as in the Bremen example.[45] However, the point is that in the end real and functional products should be the result—and these are, let's say, images with an inverted temporal axis.[46] In all these cases the types of images are obviously no longer subject to a planocentric scheme of projecting onto the plane. Either three-dimensional 'images' are created from planes, as in photo sculpture, or from mathematical three-dimensional virtual models as in rapid prototyping.

Media aesthetics of photo sculpture

Now that the path taken from photo sculpture to rapid prototyping has been reconstructed, the question has to be asked what kind of descriptive categories of media aesthetics can be found with which we can grasp those types of images. As I have suggested in my introduction, there must at least exist the likelihood that the media aesthetic parameters can be described by analyzing the reflexive use of photo sculpture or of rapid prototyping.[47] Since their imaging results have sculptural characteristics, a comparison to aesthetics of sculpture makes sense.

However, in a recently published debate on photo sculpture, Gundolf Winter denies the possibility that photo sculpture could be used as a form of artistically reflexive imaging. He contrasts portrait busts created with Willème's method with those that Gianlorenzo Bernini had created of cardinal Borghese (two versions, both from 1632). No wonder that such a comparison can hardly be not in favor of the complex baroque sculptures, and not only art historically. It is a classical argument. The busts created with Willème's procedure not only aimed at a perfect and therefore quite boring reproduction of the model; they also ensured it by way of the largely automated methods of recording and representation. Therefore there was no possibility to intervene with the "genius" (a somewhat dated term from which Winter does not shy away; see Winter 2006, 21)—this enigmatic agency that gives its power to art works in the first place. By referring to Theophile Gautier's criticism of photo sculpture from January 1, 1864, Winter is taking up arguments of the nineteenth century aimed against the worthiness of photography to be called art.[48] Photography—and therefore photo sculpture—cannot create aesthetically valuable images since they create them technically and automatically. And indeed, the examples made from bisque porcelain pointed out by Winter are truly badly made—wooden, stiff and expressionless works—although this could all have been quite different especially if created via Willème's method embracing the essentially required manual touch-ups.[49] But nevertheless Winter is generalizing when he maintains that "[a]pparently there are not supposed to be images of something made from something, but the image should function in an illusionistic way" (Winter 2006, 19).

Winter is criticizing the lack of distinction between imaging and the imaged—if difference is lacking there is no intrinsic logic to the image—which, however, is something only underlined since modernism. The image according to Winter annuls itself in the iconoclastic illusion. Nonetheless, it has to be argued that this difference of course always exists—even in the wax figure (cf. Siegert 2004), the most illusionist film,[50] in the most immersive virtual reality[51] or in the best tricolored holography (see Chapter 9). Otherwise the image would be the object itself and could not claim to be in the category of image at all.[52] Thus, the art historically popular criticism of illusionism ("*In extremis* the image *completely* negates itself as image in order to achieve the *perfect* representation of an object"—Boehm 1994c, 34; my emphasis) is therefore problematic since it suggests an extreme case of representation (that is hardly possible anyway) in which the self-assumed difference of image and object would collapse.[53] Contrary to this, we would need more precisely differentiated criteria for the degrees and forms of illusionism. Does it have to be a visual 'realism'? And what does this mean? Or do we need to address several of the senses? What role do narrativity, interactivity and immersion play? How do we rate prior knowledge and context?[54]

Once again: If there were images that receded behind the represented object completely, one could not even complain about any lacks or differences—one would simply be up against another instance of the object. And indeed the copies of sculptures created by rapid prototyping are interesting because they might be one of the very few cases in which the permanently deplored illusionism is finally approximated.

But even if the criticism of the lack of difference between object and image is rejected, there is a further argument to be found in Winter's text:

> Photo sculpture fails the imaging quality as a decisive co-reality of sculpture since it defalcates the process of imagining as a visual event, or differently said, because it negates the difference of medium and image (form), i.e., because it revokes iconic difference.[55]

This is not a matter of the difference between object and image but that of medium/form of the image. As previously quoted, Boehm defines iconic difference as the "fundamental contrast between a tightly structured total surface area and all that it includes as internal events" (Boehm 1994c, 30). If we take this definition seriously—initially irrespective of its character that is centered on the plane[56]—then we are dealing with the internal logic of the image,[57] quite independently of the question of whether it represents something or what it represents or whether it refers to any model. Only by way of this immanent logic can the "attitude of the viewer be influenced by the sculpture," as Winter writes (2006, 19). Only then does the sculpture 'communicate' with the viewer, locating him at a certain distance,[58] specifying a series of partial views (thinking of the above mentioned Wölfflin; see Chapter 2) that will possibly lead to the *one*, conclusive aspect. Along these lines and in an impressive and detailed formal analysis, Winter shows the inner structure, the intrinsic logic of Bernini's busts (cf. Winter 2006, 21–6) that cannot have anything to do with the difference between object and image anyway, since there are hardly any other testimonies on how the cardinal looked than these sculptures. Photo sculpture on the other hand allows the viewer to walk around it "without being able to discern any clues, any reading, any concept" (Winter 2006, 23).

However, the problem of the interior logic of the image cannot really have anything to do with the question of whether the image has been created automatically or manually or in any mixed way. The possibility that certain tensions between the totality and the individual elements of an image are formed in technical media cannot be excluded a priori. And in all probability Winter does not make such a strict antithesis between technology and the artistic genius because somewhere else he allows for photography to enter the realm of art.[59] Here as well he is able to refer to Boehm who is also criticizing that the "modern reproduction industry" favored the "image as representation, as a double of reality" at first. For him the "electronic techniques of simulation augmented representation into a perfect 'As-If.' "[60] Nevertheless, Boehm concedes that even "with reproductive—or simulating—technologies of imaging . . . strong images could be created." It would be necessary

> to use these new technologies in order to strengthen the iconicity of the images. Admittedly, a prerequisite would have to be to build up the iconic tension in a controlled way in order to make it visible for the viewer. A strong image lives from just this double truth: to show something, to even pretend something and at the same time to demonstrate criteria and premises of just that experience.[61]

Clearly, Winter thinks it also possible that with the new technologies of photo sculpture or rapid prototyping, "strong images" can be created despite them being technological. In a footnote he implies this: "In comparison, in a revival of photo sculpture with the most current technological achievements by Karin Sander, these 'mistakes' are blatantly underlined in order to make the iconic difference quite distinct." The sentence to which this footnote is attached is the following:

> Indeed, the grooves and fissures that are first visible [see Figures 3.2 and 3.6] might document the margins of the image, and thus images could seemingly be inscribed into the medium of clay . . . but these grooves and fissures are not consciously made; they are being treated as imperfections that are expunged during the touch up. (Winter 2006, 19)

Boehm's "double truth" of the "strong image" then again contracts into a deviation of the illusionist reproduction of the original model. Let me put it somewhat bluntly: If we then allowed the incomplete elements, the 'mistakes' in Figures 3.2 and 3.6 to survive, then already the leap from a 'mere' to a 'strong' image would have succeeded. However, that would have the bewildering consequence that every faulty image—even those created by technical mishaps—would be a 'strong image.' Therefore, probably a formal, coherent strategy would have to be developed—and this certainly is the consequence of Winter's precise description and analysis of Bernini's baroque sculptures—that also represents the "criteria and premises" of imaging itself while being simultaneously an image of the original model.

The example of Karin Sander given by Winter is indeed well suited. In her work *People 1:10* (1998–2001) she aligns herself with the basic principle of photo sculpture by way of the contemporary method of rapid prototyping (Figure 3.10). With laser light from a body scanner by *Tecmath*, people were scanned for about twelve seconds. The data sets were then again additively printed by an extruder (a rapid prototyping technology) by *Glatz Engineering*[62] into figurines in a scale of 1:10. In thirty hours each and in layers of 0.2 mm, the machine then formed the contours made of a thin stream of melted ABS-plastic[63] with a precise computerized control system. The rifts between the layers (and these are what Winter refers to in his footnote) were not smoothed. An airbrush-specialist colored the work.

An author, who characterized Sander's work as a "'passage' from perspective back to the layout of the things themselves" (Inboden

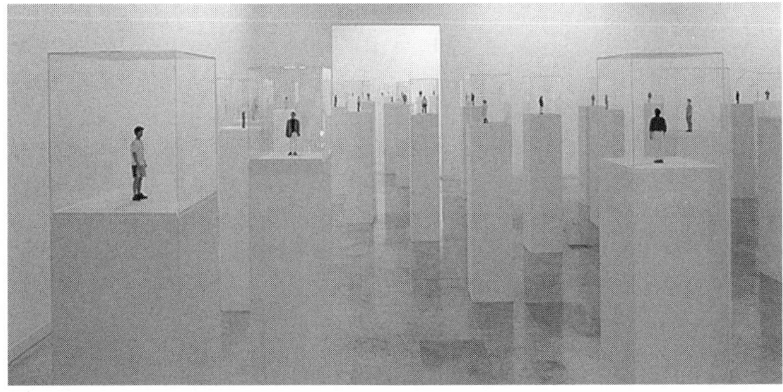

FIGURE 3.10 *Karin Sander,* People 1:10, *1998–2001, Galería Helga de Alvear, Madrid, December 1, 1999–January 22, 2000, 3D body scans of living persons, FDM (fused deposition modeling), ABS (acrylonitrile-butadiene-styrene), airbrush Scale 1:10; height: each c. 18 cm. Photo: Studio Karin Sander. Courtesy Galería Helga de Alvear, Madrid.*

2002, 22) is correct. The artist reverts to procedures that transgress the projection of geometrical optics in order to arrive at a three-dimensional 'image' again. The images represent the people from every side. At first one can't help thinking that this is a perfect example of a work that misses the quality of imaging (in Winter's sense), because it is based on perfect, illusionistic images. *On the one hand*, Sander's technique not to smooth the grooves between the individual sprayed layers does not seem to be an argument for artistically exposing the image as image since the manual touch-up is given up in favor of a purely mechanical process of transfer. *On the other hand*, it is exactly this mechanical character that is being exhibited—and this is very likely what Winter is proposing. Not only because the stepped ledges, as we already know them from photo sculpture, determine the definition thereby allowing the viewer to easily follow which technical process the machine has gone through in order to build the small sculptures.[64] The sculptures thereby also become somewhat sedimented and crystalline, intimating an opposition between the impression of the inorganic on the one hand and the realism (particularly regarding color) of representing the human—all too human—models on the other hand. Thus, not only is the manufacturing process by a machine being exhibited but also the fact that the portrayed models become objects.[65] The first of these small sculptures was created in 1996 for the *Seventh Triennial for Small Sculptures* (1997) in Fellbach, Germany, where Sander exhibited—of all people—Werner Meyer, the curator of this exhibition, in a scale of 1:10. Thus, the (professional) *viewer* of art becomes an *object* of art himself, and possibly her intention was to purposely alienate the position of the viewer. In the era of the post-human eye *machine vision* (that for example works with *structured light*), the viewer realizes that they could (possibly) be someone who is being observed (as evidenced by the ever-present surveillance cameras) and monitored.[66] People become objects of the machine gaze of virtual optics. A commentator who later was himself represented as a small sculpture reports with slight concern:

> Being scanned also includes one further dimension . . . After Karin Sander's event I had a feeling that I believe could be generalized as having left behind a first physical imprint in the data universe; a primitive precursor of what it may mean when

> one day in whatever way, not only the anatomic and genetic data of one single person, but also his/her mental ones can be entirely transformed into digital information; then the emigration of humanity from its biological carbon shell into silicone or plastic will begin. (Harry Walter, quoted in Schmidt 2001, 115)

Deleuze once wrote: "The superman . . . is in charge of the very rocks, or inorganic matter (the domain of silicon)" (Deleuze 2011, 109). By this he means that the human being defines itself through the outward powers with which it is in contact: "The forces within man enter into a relation with forces from the outside, those of silicon which supersedes carbon."[67] 'Superman' is Deleuze's word for that human being that optimizes itself cybernetically (and genetically—catchword: 'posthumanism'), therefore coming after the human being in the classical sense. The "potential of silicon in third-generation machines"[68] of course refers to the computer; they are specifically the basis for scanners and later rapid prototyping technologies. Viewed in this light, the tension between the crystalline, inorganic impression of the small sculptures and their realism coupled with the fact that the (potential) viewers become objects reflect the methods of virtual optics that ultimately go back to photo sculpture. The commentator continues:

> Being scanned is something completely different from being photographed. The sensation of being registered from all sides at once made me, at least, feel very uncertain as to the representative zones of my body. For the first time I had to imagine how I looked from behind and from above. And even between my legs. Although I was clothed, for 10 intense seconds while the laser camera ran down my body, I felt as though I was being deeply caressed. If there is such a thing as an aura, I thought to myself, it would be detectable by this device and no other. (Harry Walter, quotation given by Studio Karin Sander, email March 4, 2013)

The scanned commentator is thus asking himself how he might look from above, from the back, from below, or from many different angles. One becomes acutely aware of the spatiality of one's own body and is at the same time reminded of the mechanical glare of surveillance that keeps a constant eye on individuals, taking its point of departure from the interests of police and military institutions (see the current discussions regarding full-body scanners in airports).

Both hold true not only for the process of scanning but especially for the viewer of the installation as well. The viewer moves through a field of white square pedestals covered by cubical shells made from acrylic glass. Under each of these covers, one of the small sculptures is placed at the center with the name of the person added. Many professions, genders and generations are represented. The small sculpture is Everyman. Looking at the whimsical small persons in their transparent cages the viewer finds himself in a zoo. At some point, the contemporary clothes will look dated, resembling August Sanders' famous photo series *Face of Our Time* from 1929; (cf. Meschede 2002, 74). Sanders literally created a profile of his time by taking images of representatives of professions and labeling them with the respective term for the profession. By contrast Karin Sander's small sculptures are not labeled with the term for the profession but with the names of each person. Thus, the social or sociological attribution seems to be less important than the representation of the individual person, as it is suggested by the title of the work *People 1:10*. It is fitting that Karin Sander also calls to mind a curious use of photo sculpture in the nineteenth century, that of the miniaturized portrait busts ("bustes cartes") analogous to the visiting cards ("cartes de visite") which were in use for a short time (cf. Sorel 2000, 85). The insecurity of the commentator regarding his "representative zones" then is also the insecurity of a private person having to present themself to the public.[69]

But if it is less about a person as a public representative, as an example of a profession, but rather about a concrete being in space and time, then that which is almost never noticed in August Sanders' flat and ultimately de-personalized photographs forces itself instantly upon you here; the extremely apparent fact of the completely changed scale. This shift of the "formal category of proportion and dimension in the medium sculpture" is a very important element of the work. "The departure from the representation of reality in a scale of 1:1 is the precondition for a self-referential concept of art" (Meschede 2002, 76). The viewer can see each miniaturized Everyman from all sides. They quickly realize that we see ourselves only partially, that we can become aware of our own spatiality only proprioceptively. At the same time one also becomes aware of one's own size in comparison to the small sculptures which one knows are miniaturized representations of (persons like) ourselves.[70] Becoming aware of their own spatiality, the viewers are also instantly interrelated with the space surrounding them through which they need to move in order to view all the figurines on their pedestals, since these are placed in such a way that the viewers have to move in order to see one after the other at least from the front. This reference is underlined by the mirroring in the acrylic glass covers reflecting the viewers themselves and the space surrounding them, overlapping with the view of the small sculptures. This emphasizes the relationship between the different levels of space and in this respect this installation remains conceptually consistent with other works by Karin Sander:

> 'Space as material' implies the challenge to realize an idea in such a way that spatial concepts as expressions of three-dimensionality become conscious in such a way that changes become casually accessible to every viewer in an instant—as long as s/he permits her/himself to have this experience.[71]

Thus the artist not only addresses the shifts in the visual field as soon as it is submitted to the post-human and controlling gaze of virtual optics; she also addresses the spatiality of space which—as Lefebvre had shown (see section 1.4)—has become the true problem in modernity. In this respect, *People 1:10* takes up the "criteria and premises" (Boehm 1994c, 35) of imaging and in this case the imaging by way of a transplane rapid prototyping technology in the tradition of photo sculpture. It focuses on the question of how the sculptural objects in space relate to the moving viewers and their spatial structure.

It is not only in the narrower sense in the field of the arts that transplane methods of visualization are applied within the tradition of photo sculpture; they also exist in popular cinema. Shortly after the appearance of Karin Sander's first small sculpture, the extremely popular film *The Matrix* (USA 1999, Dir. Andy and Larry Wachowski) was released. It depicts the war between humans and more advanced artificial intelligence beings (AIs), a war long won by the latter now in complete control of Earth. Human beings serve only as an energy source. They vegetate in liquid-filled pods connected by tubes to systems that keep their vegetative functions alive within a gigantic simulation system (the Matrix) that simulates a normal life in the late twentieth century with all its delights and trials. The protagonist, Thomas Anderson (Keanu Reeves), called Neo, knows nothing—like most people—about the fact that the AIs now rule the earth. Eventually a mysterious underground organization led by the equally mysterious Morpheus (Lawrence Fishburne) contacts him, awakening Neo from his make-believe state. The underground movement then takes up the fight.

The film was not only extremely successful; it also created a tidal wave of, at times, rather peculiar philosophical affiliations, but I do not want to tackle the certainly important questions of the reality of reality or similar issues here. Instead, I would like to address only one *special effect* more closely that has contributed at least as much as the (actually not so original)[72] plot and the whole design of the film to its prominence and success.

In the first scene of the film, the protagonist Trinity (Carrie Ann Moss) is sitting in a dark room in front of a laptop. Police burst into the room. The woman is surrounded and there seems to be no way out. However, she suddenly rises with superhuman speed and overcomes the police like a post-human Kung-Fu fighter. Seeing it for the first time the scene simply takes your breath away. Trinity jumps into the air and suddenly the movement is frozen—nothing new there—but then the *camera moves around the frozen figure*. Schmidt describes it thus:

> In the second half of the 1990s the seemingly impossible effect of moving around a three-dimensional figure frozen in time caused quite a sensation in pop-videos and advertisement spots. The visual effect technique is as follows: Individual photographic units are grouped around one scene. At a certain point of a movement, all units are triggered in the same moment. Subsequently the individual images are united into a film that creates the effect described when seen on a screen.[73]

The similarity to Willème is obvious. By multiplying the focal points, additional information on space is stored. However, in the case of *The Matrix* it is not being used to reconstruct a three-dimensional figure but to spatialize a freeze-frame that itself is planar.

In the essay quoted here, Schmidt has related the relationship between Willème's model and the bullet-time effect more generally to a dispositive of modernity. He has related it to a structure in which human beings are placed center stage, but that does not—like in a panorama—look at the periphery, as it is being observed from there. This model, which he calls *centroramatic*, is for him a central method of universal supervision and control in the Foucauldian sense of the "technology of individuals" (cf. Schmidt 2002, 184–9).[74] This ties Willème and *The Matrix* together with Karin Sander, for whom the question is also one of a "visual regulation" (Schmidt 2002, 178) of human beings. The author continues writing about *The Matrix*:

> The visual effect is doubly encoded since on the narrative level it creates a meaning, but at the same time it flirts with the fact that it is an example of media technological gimmickry. It literally provokes the question: How was this done? ... Now the transformative power of media technology becomes visible. The imaging work that projects the image of a realistic form of expression now is being alienated from realistic illusionism. (Schmidt 2002, 190–1)

The sequence shows the movement around a person temporally frozen in action—the time of the represented and the time of representation not only fall apart (as would be the case in every elliptic narrative), they contradict each other radically. As Schmidt correctly says, the sequence automatically directs the attention to the technology behind it and thus self-referentially points to the plot of the film which depicts nothing but the power of technology. By addressing technology, *People 1:10* by Karin Sander and the photo sculptural bullet-time effect in *The Matrix* resemble each other.

This effect is also a simple display of the technological potentialities of current creators of special effects, an advertisement for effect technology. As such, one could say that the bullet-time effect makes technology visible not in order to reveal its possibly problematic implications but in order to make room for being euphoric about technology. While on the level of what is being represented a warning is given against an overpowering technology, on the level of representation the brilliant technological performance precisely contradicts this. One can also connect another idea with this thought. According to Lefebvre (1991, 286), the production of space in modernism is characterized by an aggressive visualization. Would it be too much to say that the bullet-time effect in *The Matrix* is also a procedure of visualizing space aggressively in order to transform it into a *spectacle* in Debord's sense,[75] to whom Lefebvre is explicitly referring in the quote? This means that transplane imaging technologies not only have a function for rendering information on space in order to make it controllable and manageable, they can also serve to transform space into a spectacle and thus make it commercially viable. Ultimately this is how transplane images are in reality most familiarly known—we only have to think of the often rekindled attempts to celebrate 3D cinema as an example of spectacular mass entertainment.[76] Also Crary in *Techniques of the Observer* refers to the stereoscope as a popular mass medium of the nineteenth century living from its "tantalizing apparition of depth." "The content of the images is far less important than the inexhaustible routine of moving from one [stereo] card to the next and producing the same effect, repeatedly, mechanically" (Crary 1990, 132). This is similar in *The Matrix*. The effect in the film is repeatedly used in order to spectacularly celebrate again and again the wondrous appearance of space amidst the two-dimensional freeze frame of the cinematic image.

Notes

1 The almost simultaneous appearance of photo sculpture, stereoscopy and also panorama (for the latter see Hick 1999, 235–61) in the nineteenth century could be assessed as evidence for Lefebvre's observation (1991, 95 and 219) that in modernity space takes precedence over time. Beckmann (1991, 3) writes in connection to photo sculpture about a "wish for detailed, realistic *and* three-dimensional representations." Whether it is helpful to speak of "wish" must be left undecided. However, these procedures must at least be considered more closely along with the cinema that was always distinguished as an example for temporalization.

2 On the patent see Willème (1861). It is notable that at this time only *one* method of photo sculpture was patented—others would follow (see below).

3 See Sobieszek (1980); Bogart (1981); Drost (2005 and 1986); Beckmann (1991); Gall (1997); Sorel (2000); Kümmel (2006); Winter (2006).

4 See the commentary in Rohwaldt (2002, 61).

5 Drost (1986, 330). It is interesting to note that the different methods of photo sculpture do not appear at all in the otherwise very elaborate standard reference on the history of photography by Eder (1978). Could this be a symptom for the perception that the results of these methods were already too 'sculptural' in order to be still regarded as images? Would this not again be an evidence for the planocentric displacement of spatiality from the discourse on imagery?

6 The exact definition of the term 'virtual' will be provided only at a later stage of reconstructing the series of virtual optics; see Chapter 10.

7 Even though this photo sculpture is by Willème, it is obviously done in a somewhat different method—there are many more than twenty-four ridges.

8 In general, on the history and changing conceptualization of the differences between analog and digital see Schröter (2004b).

9 The word digital initially comes from the Latin word for finger, *digitus*. Fingers themselves are discrete since there is no third one between two neighboring fingers.

10 See Haugeland (1981) on the differences between analog and digital concerning the criteria continuous vs. discontinuous or discrete.

11 Kittler (1996, n.p.); see also (2010, 208–9 and 225).

12 On fragmenting and reconstructing see Schröter (2006a).

13 Kuchinka (1926, 9), for example, does not fail to mention that quite often "dissimilarities were produced by bending the clay block with the knife of the pantograph." Drost (1986, 336), however, mentions that Willème was already forgotten by 1890 or thereabouts and none of the innovators explicitly referred to him. Analyzing the respective patents confirms this.

14 Cf. Schneider and Berz (2002, 200): "What was later done by scanning, namely automatically fragmenting and digitizing, was still done by human agents earlier who used key punching; [in the case of Jacquard looms] they first transferred the pattern into the cartridge and then into the key code—the basic principle, however, is the same."

15 Cf. Will and Pennington (1971) who talk about "grid coding" when they say: "It is also possible to consider recording the full 3-D

information of a scene by grid coding the image" (327). Cf. also Pennington and Will (1970).

16 Cf. Beckmann (1991, 7): "The variance from the regular quadrature practically defined the spatial specifics of the object. Reissig does not explain how to decode this encoded information on the height and depth of the template when transferring it into a photo relief."

17 Mainly referring to Reissig (1893), Selke wrote in 1897 that shortcomings of the by then existing photo sculptural methods "consist in that they can only be used for the plastic rendition of live models with difficulty" (Selke 1897, 1).

18 Eder (1978, 553). Eder is still using the term "potassium bichromate" which is no longer customary today. For a more detailed explanation of the chemical process see Eder (1880); cf. also Kuchinka (1926, 25–50). It is interesting to note that dichromate gelatin was also used for some time in the early developments of photo telegraphy, see Korn (1923, 91–8). On a general description of photographic reliefs see Smith (1968).

19 Reissig (1893, 2); cf. Kuchinka (1926, 17) and earlier Vogel (1892, 226–9).

20 The painting is necessary since "the density value of a photographic pixel does not necessarily always [match] the spatial position of the respective object point."

21 See Kittler (2010, 61–5).

22 See Bätschmann and Schäublin (2000, 36–50).

23 See Kittler (2010, 62), who with regard to Alberti talks of virtualization.

24 Cf. Gombrich (1982, 193) who after all comments on Leonardo: "how he would have relished the stereoscope and holograph!" Of course, stereoscopy and holography do not provide mathematical formalizations; Gombrich is only pointing out Leonardo's interest in more information on space.

25 Bätschmann and Schäublin (2000, 48). The 'pointing box' was Leonardo's approach for formalizing sculpture; cf. Ulmann (1984, 16–19).

26 Beckmann (1991, 7). Selke (1909, 1) talks of methods to create "maps and plans."

27 Selke (1897, 1) and Selke (1901, 1) refer to Reissig's patent No. 74622.

28 Selke (1897, 1) still called it a "series apparatus."

29 His method should then be described as 'cinemato-sculpture'; on another method based on cinematography see Bossel (1909). Later

Selke completes his method in such a way that by using several machines for taking images he can improve the "avoidance of overlapping" (Selke 1898b, 1).

30 According to Shannon and Nyquist, a sampling frequency that doubles the highest frequency of the sampled signal is sufficient to reconstruct it.

31 As Willème had already said in 1861: "Plus le nombre de ces objectifs est grand, plus la sculpture acquiert de fini" (Willème 1861, 34). (The higher the number of these objectives, the more the sculpture will look finished).

32 Selke replaces the process of gluing the cutout silhouettes on top of each other by projecting them as shadows "onto one and the same spot of a photosensitive film: In this way you get a combination image whose individual zones are exposed for different lengths of time." The variably exposed combination image then can "be transformed by way of swelling into a relief" (Selke 1899, 1). Selke resorts to the dichromate-gelatin process only in 1899.

33 It is interesting to note that the central example for a transplane image emerging from the series of wave optics, holography, will surface from Dennis Gabor's initial attempts to circumvent the limitations of electron lenses in an electron microscope. Microscopes are excellent devices for observing the limitations of geometrical optics. See Chapter 9.

34 Selke later also worked with stereoscopy (1907; 1909).

35 Kuchinka (1926, 24) describes the method of the Cameograph Co. somewhat differently from Schlör (the deviations from the shape of a projected spiral define the spatial structure); however, he is also only interested in the process of an analog and mechanical transfer: "Depending on how the line on the guiding plate deviates from the correct shape of the spiral, the stick will move the drill or something like it further forward or backward so that the drill works on the material proportionally to this deviation."

36 See Alberti (1972a, 66–9, esp. 68—the Latin text makes it quite clear): "Id istiusmodi est: velum filo tenuissimo et rare textum quovis colore pertinctum filis grossioribus in parallelas portiones quadras quot libeat distinctum telarioque distentum." Cf. Bätschmann and Schäublin (2000, 69–72).

37 The image is one of many thousands that were made in Rome with the aim in mind to reconstruct Bernini's *David* virtually. This reconstruction (as well as other groups of figures by Bernini) and their art and media historical research and use took place between 2002 to 2009 at the DFG Research Project "Virtualizing Sculptures.

Reconstruction, Installation, Presentation" (directed by Professor Gundolf Winter and Manfred Bogen at the FK 615 "Media Upheavals" at Siegen University).

38 This is how we can also read the commentary to a recent reprint of an early text: With photo sculpture "objects become those 'immutable mobiles' (Bruno Latour) that characterize the enormous success of European science and technology: they become randomly movable, randomly reproducible" (in Rohwaldt 2002, 61). Latour's (1986), "immutable mobiles" then—contrary to his own comments—do not in any way always have to be 'flat.'

39 Cf. Engelmann (1956) for a relatively late, purely analog method of photo sculpture.

40 A general overview of these methods can be found in Aggarwal and Chien (1989) with the significant title *3-D Structures from 2-D Images* and in Besl (1989). See also DePiero and Trivedi (1996). In their survey of the current state of research on *3-D Computer Vision*, DePiero and Trivedi (1996) seem to agree with my thesis that the function of transplane imaging consists in the "loss of information associated with the perspective mapping of a 3-D scene onto a 2-D image" (244). See similarly Manovich (1996a, 238): "Perspective, this first step towards the rationalization of sight (Ivins), has eventually become a limit to its total rationalization—the development of computer vision."

41 See Schwerzel et al. (1984); Gershenfeld (2005) and the interesting book by Neef, Burmeister and Krempel (2005).

42 Cf. the information of the institute at http://www.ifam.fraunhofer.de/content/dam/ifam/de/documents/IFAM-Bremen/2801/rapid-product-development/projekte/ecomarble/ecomarble.pdf [last accessed August 8, 2013].

43 However (as I have mentioned before), one of the oldest concepts of images—"So God created mankind in his own image, in the image of God he created them" (New International Version of Bible, Gen. 1.26–7 and 9.6, here 1.27)—has indeed nothing to do with the projection of a three-dimensional object onto the plane; it is dealing with the creation of a supranatural entity's image that itself is sculptural, i.e. a human being.

44 Whereby I do not want to imply that the relation of being an image of something can be reduced to a causal relationship, see Scholz (1991, 64–81).

45 This is the main point of certain currents in "Virtual Sculpture-Art," see http://www.sculpture.org/redesign/mag.shtml [last accessed August 8, 2013].

46 Computer-simulative imaging sometimes exhibits temporal modes directed towards the future, see Schröter (2004e).

47 See Ganis (2004) for a relatively current survey on the approaches of rapid prototyping sculpture

48 Cf. Winter (2006, 20–1). See on the parallels in the criticism on photography and photo sculpture Drost (1986).

49 See Drost (1986, 334): "A certain coolness can also be felt in some of the bisque porcelain sculptures created by artists. A photo sculpture made from bisque porcelain therefore cannot so easily be differentiated from a traditional one and possibly many a 'piece of art' will turn out to be a product of *art industriel*."

50 The much-quoted panic of the viewers when a train arrived in an early film of the brothers Lumière (which according to Hollywood criteria was not illusionist at all) could be taken as proof for the self-annulment of the image. This event, however, never actually took place in that manner, see Loiperdinger (2004) and in a more differentiated way Bottomore (1999).

51 Even though it has always been a phantasma of virtual reality that it could abolish the difference between image and object, both in principle and practically this is out of the question.

52 Cf. the critique of Boehm's equation of the perspectival image and mirror in section 1.4.

53 As Pizzanelli (1992) remarks with the example of holography, from this kind of criticism one can infer interesting ideas about the wish for illusion among the critics of illusionism.

54 Many of these questions have been addressed by Gombrich (1960). Also see his remarks (1973, 195) on the origin of the term 'illusionism' in Franz Wickhoff's works on the Vienna genesis: "The idea that anyone should have confused the illustrations of the manuscript with reality obviously did not enter his mind." Originally the term illusionism did not mean that "the image completely negates itself as image in order to achieve the perfect representation of an object."

55 Winter (2006, 19). With the term 'iconic difference' Winter is referring to Boehm (1994c, 29–36).

56 However, Boehm, who has already worked on sculptures for a long time (see Boehm 1977), has more recently been talking of "plastic images" (Boehm 2004, 40). See also Boehm (2005, 38).

57 In this discussion, Boehm leaves many paths open in which iconic difference can be constituted. See Müller (1997) who is studying different ways in which iconic difference can be actualized.

58 See for this central concept in the aesthetics of sculpture Winter (1985).

59 For example, the architectural photographs of the Bechers which were often called sculptural, see Winter (1999, 21–2).

60 Boehm (1994c, 35), where he is using the argument of illusionism.

61 Boehm (1994c, 35). Here Boehm is combining photography, film, video and presumably also 'digital images' somewhat imprecisely into one term ('the electronic techniques of simulation').

62 See http://www.glatz-engineering.de [last accessed September 2, 2013]. Unfortunately, the company does not exist any longer.

63 ABS = Acrylonitrile butadiene styrene.

64 Schmidt (2002, 190) remarks: "In Sander's work, technology arrives in the shape of an extensive legend: 'Werner Meyer, 1:10, 3D-Body-Scan of the living original, 1998, Fused Deposition Modelling (FDM), Acryl-Nitryl-Butadien-Styrol (ABS) and Airbrush."' Characteristically, artistic works contrarily often attempt to expose technology, while functional approaches, for example François Willème, tried to hide technology in their products; see Kümmel (2006, 195).

65 Cf. Schmidt (2002, 178): "By widening the relationship of technology and object she not only immanently comments on the genre of sculpture, she is also pointing out the history of the reification of life by media. Without fail the question arises to which perceptive disposition and media adjustment human beings are being led."

66 See Lacan (1978, 106) who has possibly already felt this: "What determines me, at the most profound level, in the visible, is the gaze that is outside. It is through the gaze that I enter light and it is from the gaze that I receive its effects. Hence it comes about that the gaze is the instrument through which *light is embodied* and through which—if you will allow me to use a word, as I often do, in a fragmented form—I am *photo-graphed*." (Apart from the last one all emphases are mine.)

67 Deleuze (2011, 109). Additional forces "from the outside" named by Deleuze are those of "genetic components which supersede the organism, or agrammaticalities which supersede the signifier."

68 Deleuze (2011, 109). On the same page Deleuze explicitly speaks of "cybernetics and information technology."

69 This is exacerbated for those persons who verily see themselves represented. Harry Walter, as quoted in Schmidt (2001, 112) had at first assumed that he would be represented by Karin Sander in a scale of 1:1 and had been "somewhat appalled imagining to be exhibited

in a gallery as a life-size, colored plastic mass and to be subjected to the very strident glances of the art public."

70 This is what differentiates Sander's figurines from the miniaturized sculptures that were popular in the nineteenth century and which I have mentioned in Chapter 2.

71 Meschede (2002, 70). Due to the narrative implications (Who are the persons? What do they do professionally?), the break of *People 1:10* from Sander's earlier works, as underlined by Meschede, does not seem to be so relevant in this context.

72 The idea of a "total simulation" on which the film is based has a long and complex history, see Schröter (2004c, 152–276).

73 Schmidt (2002, 177). See also further reference to the history of the procedure in this essay.

74 And of course it has a quite problematic gendered tradition: The peep show.

75 See Debord (2006). By the way: On p. 12 Debord writes a sentence which quite stunningly anticipates *The Matrix*: "The spectacle is the bad dream of a modern society in chains and ultimately expresses nothing more than its wish for sleep. The spectacle is the guardian of that sleep."

76 Above I have already mentioned the reasons for this failure: Films—and especially those that (largely) follow the "Hollywood mode of narration"—live from a coherent narrative that constructs a coherent space as well (see Bordwell 1985, 99–146 and 156–204). Additional information on space is not necessary—quite irrespective of the technological and receptive problems of the stereoscopic (or even holographic) cinema. On the problem of the stereoscopic film see Arnheim (1933, 236–9). In general see Hayes (1989).

CHAPTER FOUR

1891: Lippmann photography

The Series of Wave Optics 1

waves of light which would rush through the film at an enormous speed and get away into space without leaving any impression, were stopped by some special kind of film and went surging up and down in confinement – making strata . . . 'supairposeetion of strata' . . . no Englishman could move his hands with that smoothness, making you see. 'Violet subchloride of silver.' . . . When the colour photographs came, Miriam was too happy for thought.

DOROTHY RICHARDSON (1979, 106–7)[1]

The subject of this chapter—Lippmann photography—does not create three-dimensional (transplane) images nor has it survived in media history and it is hardly mentioned in the standard references of the history of photography[2] or the history of optical media.[3] Why then a chapter of its own?

First of all, Lippmann photography is a direct predecessor of holography (see Chapter 9); it is the first sedimentation of the series of wave optics, already appearing in the nineteenth century.

Secondly, this means that its emergence and its functions simply had nothing to do with any shift to physiological optics. Lippmann photography substantiates that we should accept parallel (and not one-dimensional successively) existing optical series, and furthermore, it serves as an additional item of evidence that not necessarily all recent imaging technologies must emerge from the knowledge of physiological conditions of vision. Interferential color photography, the technical term for Lippmann's method, should be better understood as a materialization of geometrical and wave optics. But this method in the end lost the competition with several other procedures and the winner was a process based on a sedimentation of physiological optics, namely the autochrome method of the brothers Lumière.[4] This seems to strengthen Crary's approach. Using Lippmann photography as an example, another concrete assessment of the media historical model suggested here becomes possible.

Thirdly, one more peculiarity becomes visible which also holds true for holography, even though in a different way. Technological media by no means always allow for reproduction (as Benjamin 1978 seemed to suggest), and this can be a considerable hindrance for their establishment in the marketplace. One of the central reasons for the disappearance of Lippmann photography may well have been the fact that it was not reproducible (another example is the daguerreotype).[5] In recent decades, however, it was just this feature that became very important again.

Regarding points one and two: Crary substantiates the alleged transition from geometrical to physiological optics with a passage from Goethe's *Theory of Colors* published in 1810 (see Crary 1990, 67–71):

> Let a room be made as dark as possible; let there be a circular opening in the window-shutter about three inches in diameter, which may be closed or not at pleasure. The sun being suffered to shine through this on a white surface, let the spectator from some little distance fix his eye on the bright circle thus admitted. The hole being then closed, let him look towards the darkest part of the room; a circular image will now be seen to float before him. (Goethe 2000, 16)

Goethe meticulously measures the following afterimages with a clock:

> I looked on the bright circle five seconds, and then, having closed the aperture, saw the colored visionary circle floating

> before me. After thirteen seconds it was altogether red; twentynine [*sic*] seconds next elapsed till the whole was blue. (Goethe 2000, 17)

And so on. Crary argues that this is a striking proof for his claim. The opening in a dark room through which the light is falling—indicating the camera obscura dispositive—is suddenly shut by Goethe in order to focus his attention to the emerging after-images of changing colors flowing into each other. The paradigm of the camera obscura ends here and now the attention focuses on the exactly measured physical elements of vision—physiological optics. *Quod erat demonstrandum*.[6]

But it seems that Crary's invocation of Goethe simplifies too much. A single glance at the table of contents of the *Theory of Colors* will show that the "physiological colors" are only one section. In other chapters, Goethe also turns to chemical and physical processes and the color effects created by them. As a general overview suggests, for Goethe several forms of knowledge coincide and overlap[7] so that one cannot really talk of a clear transition to a discourse that centers on the body. There is one passage in particular not quoted by Crary which can be found in the section "Statt des versprochenen supplementaren Teils" (In place of the promised supplementary part) in the second volume of the *Theory of Colors* published in 1810; it presents a historical survey of the different theoretical positions on color. The passage is not by Goethe himself but from the physicist Thomas Johann Seebeck (1770–1831) with whom Goethe maintained an intense friendship.[8] Goethe introduces Seebeck's contribution of about twenty pages with the following words:

> Even though for the reasons mentioned above we are refraining from reflecting upon all that has happened in the last twenty years in our field, we should not ignore the most important point that Herschel once again reminded us of, and by that we mean the effect of colored lights on glow stones, metallic oxides and plants—a chapter that we have only sketchily presented in our design but that has to become increasingly more important in chemistry. We cannot fulfill our duty in a better way than by inserting an extensive essay by Dr. *Seebeck* from Jena. (Goethe 1989, 927)

Even though this addition is obviously not by Goethe himself, he nevertheless agrees with it completely. The passage I am referring to can be found in the subsection "On the chemical activities of light and of colored illumination."

> It is one of the most important discoveries of modern times that with the exterior changes of the body through sunlight, which we have known about for a long time, quite often an interior change is also connected to it, a change in the chemical components. . . . One of the most sensitive substances reacting to sunlight is horn silver [i.e. silver chloride (AgCl)]; as is well known it is white when in a precipitate state and turns grey quite quickly and finally black, losing the biggest part of its acidity, if not all of it.[9]

Obviously Seebeck experimented with silver halides, or to be more exact with silver chloride, i.e. one of those substances that only a few years later would be used for the development of (black and white) photography. It has to do with light-effects on chemicals and therefore it cannot be a question of physiological optics. In his experiments with horn silver, Seebeck made an astonishing observation:

> When I let the spectral colors of a fault-free prism fall . . . onto white, still damp horn silver spread onto paper, keeping it in the same place for fifteen to twenty minutes by way of an appropriate apparatus I found the horn silver in the following changed state. It had become reddish-brown in the violet realm (at times more violet, at times more blue) and this coloring even extended beyond the limits of the violet indicated earlier, but it was not stronger than in the violet. In the blue realm of the spectrum the horn silver had become a pure blue and this color extended into the green, diminishing and becoming lighter. In the yellow the horn silver for the most part seemed almost unchanged, in some cases it seemed somewhat more yellow than before; in the red, however, and in several cases even beyond the red, it had taken on mostly a red of roses or hydrangeas. In some of the prisms (those in which the strongest warming had taken place outside of the red) this reddening fell completely outside of the red realm of the spectrum.[10]

One has to closely examine what is happening here: Seebeck obtains *colors* even though he has covered the paper with horn silver only, i.e. silver chloride. No colorants and therefore no three-color processes, as required by color film as it was used in the twentieth century, are involved (and even today's digital cameras rely on three-color separation). This observation appearing of all places for the first time in the second part of Goethe's *Theory of Colors* that was presented by Crary as evidence for the transition to physiological optics was still being made in various other areas in the nineteenth century. In the celebrated talk on August 19, 1839 before the Chamber of Deputies, Arago referred to Seebeck's observations, to similar findings by Nicéphore Niépce (cf. Niépce 1839, 43–4), as well as to experiments by Sir John F.W. Herschel (cf. Arago 1839, 36). In a paper received by the Royal Society in 1840, Herschel[11] reports on an experiment of July 9, 1839:

> A highly concentrated spectrum was therefore formed, by receiving the rays after emergence from the prism . . . on a large crown lens, and receiving the focus on paper prepared as in Art. 31. The result was equally striking and unexpected. A very intense photographic impression of the spectrum was rapidly formed, which, when withdrawn and viewed in moderate daylight, was found to be coloured with sombre, but unequivocal tints, imitating those of the spectrum itself.[12]

Herschel had also made a table in which he recorded the results (see Figure 4.1). Nevertheless he has to concede, "I have not succeeded in fixing these tints" (Herschel 1840, 19). Also Henry Fox Talbot occasionally observed during his photographic experiments that especially the blue sky would be reproduced in blue.[13] The best examples of these "chemical colour photographs," as Connes (1987, 154) translates the German word 'Photochromie' (sometimes also called 'Heliochromie') were produced by Becquerel and Niépce de Saint Victor (see Figure 4.2).[14] Instead of paper soaked with silver chloride, they used chlorinated silver plates (i.e. a similar method to Daguerre's).[15] At least one of Becquerel's chemical color photographs representing a parrot was shown in Paris at the *Exposition Universelle* in 1855: It was presented in a dark tent, lit only with candles. "The most pleasing photochromes made on silver plates

1. Colours of the luminous spectrum.	2. Colours impressed on the paper.
Extreme red†	None.
Mean red	None:
Orange	Faint brick-red.
Orange-yellow	Brick-red, pretty strong.
Yellow	Undecided; red passing into green.
Yellow-green	Dull bottle-green.
Green	Dull bottle-green, passing into blueish.
Blue-green	Very sombre blue, almost black.
Blue	Black, but when the exposure was long continued, metallic yellow, like an imperfect gilding.
Violet	Black, passing into the same metallic yellow by long exposure in the less refrangible portions of the violet ray.
Beyond the violet	Violet-black, or purplish-black.

FIGURE 4.1 *Sir John F. W. Herschel, Table correlating colored light and coloring of a paper soaked with AgCl, in Herschel (1840, 18). By 'extreme red' he means infrared.*

FIGURE 4.2 *Facsimile reproduction of a direct chemical color photograph on a chlorinated silver plate by Niépce de Saint Victor (exhibited at the world fair in 1867), in Eder 1905: plate XII. See color plate 1.*

are the work of Niépce de Saint-Victor, who exhibited them at the Paris Expositions of 1862 and 1867."[16] But neither Becquerel nor Niépce de Saint Victor succeeded in fixating the chemical color photographs. To this day some safely protected specimens exist. They are stable in a dark environment but very quickly dissolve as soon as they are in contact with light.

These color phenomena cannot be explained by tracing them back to physiological optics. Initially, there was no explanation for them at all. An attempt at an explanation first appeared in 1868 by a certain Wilhelm Zenker in his *Lehrbuch der Photochromie*:

> The matter looks quite different if the penetrating rays are met by rays of the same kind that issue from it. . . . Then two wave systems of the same kind meet and create a similar effect as one calls 'standing waves' in water. . . . Contrary to 'advancing waves' the variation of quiescent and maximum points is a peculiarity of the 'standing waves' also of water. They emerge at the point at which waves break vertically on bulwarks, walls and similar structures. . . . But how do these chemical effects distribute themselves? We should not expect to find them at the quiescent points. . . . From this combination of the approaching and the reflected rays we obtain small silver points arranged in a system of layers whose reciprocal distance is half a wave length of the respective color. This means that of all the colors that are contained in white light, the only one that remains is the one whose wave length coincides with the wave length of that light ray that has created the layers of silver points. . . . It seems to me that this is how one can very simply explain how identical colors emerge from the laws of the theory of waves. (Zenker 1868, 117–21)

Thus, Zenker is attempting to use the concept of *standing light waves* that are produced during the exposure of Becquerel plates in the emulsion to explain their colorful appearance. This concept originally comes from acoustics[17] (and also hydraulics) and was transferred to optics by Wilhelm Zenker. Without the acoustic knowledge of his time, he would not have been able to change optical knowledge. Zenker's "fundamental contribution to wave optics" surfaced for the first time in 1867 "in a most unexpected place and about the most unsuitable problem" (Connes 1987, 151) when he published his idea in a text on *physiological optics* in which he attempted to explain the perception of colors by way of standing light waves in the eyeball.[18] This mingling of physiological and wave optics created problems for the propagation of the concept: "Needless to say, physiologists did not take the Zenker theory seriously, while no optician seems to have ever read his paper" (Connes 1987, 151).

The concept of standing light waves was accepted and became widely known only after Otto Wiener successfully demonstrated the standing light waves experimentally in 1889 (see Wiener 1890). In 1895 Wiener also published his essay on "Farbenphotographie durch Körperfarben und mechanische Farbenanpassung in der Natur." He posed the fundamental question: "Are the colors emerging using the old procedures [i.e. Seebeck to Becquerel] pseudo-colors or body colors, i.e., do they emerge by way of interference or by absorption?" (Wiener 1895, 228). Analyzing plates of the Becquerel–Niépce de Saint Victor type and also papers à la Seebeck and Herschel, he was able to find out that Zenker's explanation was only partially true for the first and not at all for the latter. While the former type of plates (Becquerel–Niépce de Saint Victor) vary the color slightly with the visual angle, thereby showing *iridescence* (an effect that appears both with Lippmann photography and holography), this is not the case when working with paper.[19] The colors appearing in Seebeck's and Herschel's (and partially in Becquerel's) images are not owed to the formation of the interferences of standing waves. They occur during specific chemical processes in which specific compounds of silver halide (which Carey Lea had already called 'photosalts' in 1887)[20] are created in the emulsion by way of light influence. Ultimately, they are again corroded by light, but they reflect the colors contained in white light differently. On the spot where a paper of the Herschel-type is exposed to a red light (for example, in a spectrum produced by a prism), only the photo salts remain, reflecting red light best. Therefore the paper at this spot will appear as red when illuminated with white light. However, white light of course also contains light in other colors; when illuminated for a longer time, the red area will lose its color due to the chemical decomposition of the photo salt. This is also true for all other colors, and so "it seems clear that the inability to be fixated is fundamentally connected to the way in which these colors are formed since the ability to render colors is connected to their decomposability in light."[21] Thus, this media historical branch[22] of chemical color photographs (in German: 'Photochromie') had no future.

Therefore Zenker's application of the wave optical concept of standing light waves was not the right explanation for Seebeck's colors or Becquerel's chemical color photographs.[23] However, his attempt to explain them preceded Gabriel Lippmann's method by eighteen years. According to his biographers, Lippmann had already found the exact mathematical formulation of a possible use of standing waves for the reproduction of color with black and white material for photography and had presented it in his lectures in 1886 (without the knowledge of Zenker's approach). He *began with wave optical theory* in an interesting contradistinction to the invention of photography as such or to chemical color photography. A commentator called it "Mathematics conquer[s] Photography."[24] Ergo, Lippmann photography in the original sense of the word is a sedimentation of the wave optical series.[25] But this sedimentation was not a simple process; Lippmann researched for years (later also together with the brothers Lumière)[26] in order to produce the high resolution emulsions necessary for realizing the concept that had to be extremely transparent and grainless (see Connes 1987, 157). He was finally able to introduce his new procedure to the French Academy of Science on February 2, 1891 (see Lippmann 1891).

It works like this: The light of the object (in the diagram of a rose) is focused onto the photographic plate by means of a lens. Up to this point, this is a completely normal linear perspectival projection, i.e. it is the series of geometrical optics (that has in no way disappeared). Lippmann himself says:

> On peut fixer l'image de la *chambre noire*, avec son modelé et ses couleurs, en employant une couche sensible transparente et continue, d'epaisseur suffisamment grande, adossée pendant la pose à une surface réfléchissante qu'il est commode de constituer par une couche de mercure.[27]

As can be seen from the quote, the photo plate is not an ordinary one. Behind the glass plate there is a thin layer[28] of special emulsions behind which is another strongly reflecting layer. Since silver could not be used because of possible chemical reactions, Lippmann was using a layer of mercury. Once the image of the object is projected onto the plate, the injected light is mirrored on the surface of the mercury. The injected and the reflected light interfere so that they form standing waves in the emulsion.[29] Their maxima can each be

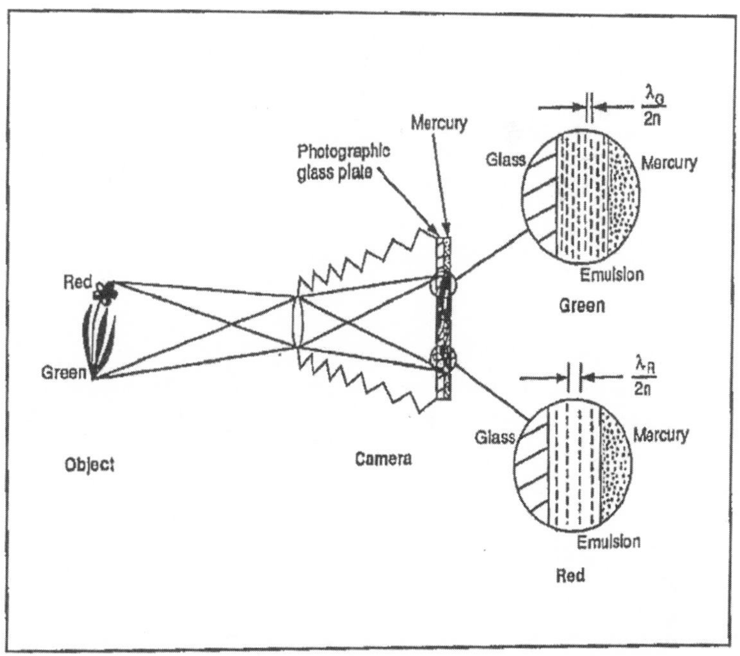

FIGURE 4.3 *Diagram of Lippmann photography, in Bjelkhagen (1999b, 56).*

found midway on the wavelength of light—from this stems the term $\lambda/2n$ specified in Figure 4.3 designating λ as the wave length of the respective light and n as the refractive index of the emulsion. At the maximum points, ultra thin silver lamellas form within the emulsion since the light corrodes the silver halide contained in the emulsion into silver and the halide ions absorbed by the emulsion, as in a normal black and white photograph.[30] When white light is directed onto the plate at a certain angle after the developing process, the original image appears in color since the lamellas void all colors contained in the white light that do not correspond to the original color via destructive interference.[31] As an answer to various criticisms, Lippmann published a group of integrals in 1894 clearly describing what kind of selective reflection is being created by what frequency within the emulsion. For the extreme mathematical elegance of his method—if for nothing else—Lippmann was awarded the Nobel Prize in Physics for his invention in 1908 (see Figure 4.4).

$$X = \frac{1}{Z}\int_A^B \int_0^Z f(\lambda)\,\varphi\left(\sin^2\frac{2\pi z}{\lambda}\right)\cos\frac{2\pi z}{\lambda'}\,d\lambda\,dz,$$

$$Y = \frac{1}{Z}\int_A^B \int_0^Z f(\lambda)\,\varphi\left(\sin^2\frac{2\pi z}{\lambda}\right)\sin\frac{2\pi z}{\lambda'}\,d\lambda\,dz.$$

FIGURE 4.4 *Lippmann's Integral, in Lippmann (1894, 104).*

Lippmann photography is a sedimentation of the wave optical series (regarding the color) connected to the geometrical optical series (regarding the geometrical projection of the scene).[32] According to his mathematical description of the process, which he based on Fourier, this is the truest process for representing color physically.[33]

Despite the peerless wave optical elegance, a "Revenge of Physiology" (Connes 1987, 163) soon took place since Lippmann photographs did not succeed in the marketplace. The high resolution of the almost grainless emulsions requires long exposure times that do not permit snap shots—the parrot in Figure 4.5 is stuffed![34]

Every Lippmann photograph is unique and cannot be reproduced since every reproduction or color copy results in the disappearance of its peculiar effect of *iridescence*, as I mentioned above. On the mirroring surface, the image can only be seen from one specific angle, and then from another converts into its complementary colors; apparently the relationship of the image as plane and the viewer is being reconfigured.[35] This iridescence also means that such an image can only be projected with difficulty[36] and can therefore only be seen by a few people at a time. In 1907, even before Lippmann was awarded the Nobel Prize in 1908, the first autochrome plates of the brothers Lumière, who had in the meantime discarded the commercially insecure Lippmann method, appeared commercially with sweeping success.

> The autochrome plates carry on a glass plate mixed red, green and blue starch grains, on which a thin film of panchromatic gelatine emulsion is applied. The exposure takes place through the glass and the color grain base. (Eder 1978, 661–2)

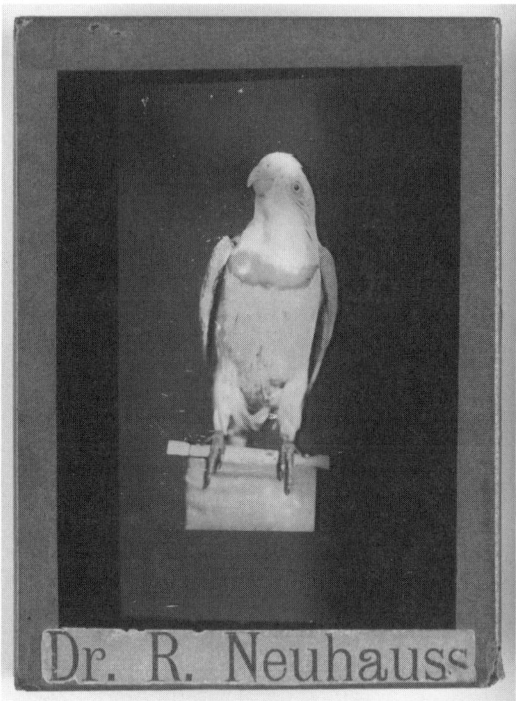

FIGURE 4.5 *A Lippmann photograph of a parrot, in Coe (1979, 27). It is not possible to reproduce the appearance of a Lippmann photograph here. See color plate 2.*

Obviously, the autochrome method is based on the three-color process used to this day "based on the physiological characteristics of human colour vision,"[37] i.e. on splitting the light into the three basic colors that are then perceived again as the secondary colors.[38] Even though Lippmann photographs in principle surpass today's three-color method by far—not only in their representation of color but also in their durability (see Fournier and Burnett 1994) because no pigment is being used—today's three-color method prevailed in the end. It was theoretically first conceived and experimentally tested by James Clerk Maxwell in 1861 (see Figure 4.6).[39]

My historical reconstruction shows that in the nineteenth century three fundamentally different methods of color photography existed and that only the one based on physiological optics prevailed. This confirms my assumption that the existent technologies considered

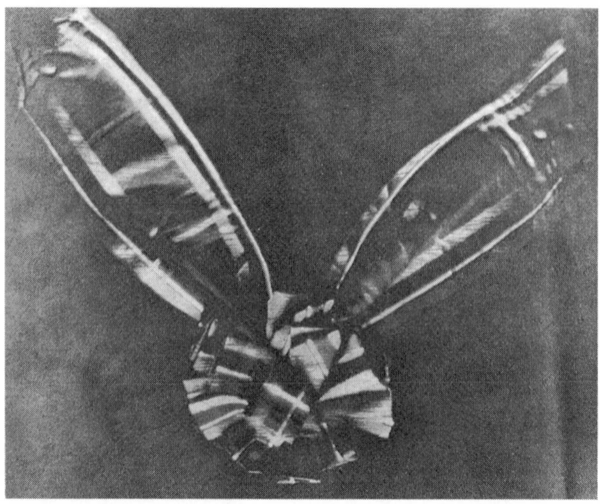

FIGURE 4.6 *First three-color photograph by Maxwell (1861) in Bellone and Fellot (1981, 88). See color plate 3.*

'normal' today are in no way the only possible or 'best' ones (whatever this may mean); they are simply those that prevailed for various historical reasons.[40] This is actually a truism and in connection with my arguments another point is more important: Is it possible that the implementation of the variant based on physiological optics is ultimately proof for Crary's thesis that physiological optics became dominant around 1820?

Even if we concede that the other series continue to exist, it might indeed be possible to imagine that at least with three-color photography and the cinema those technologies prevailed that were based on physiological optics. However, this argument does not hold. First, black and white photography on paper negatives also prevailed, even though it is not part of physiological optics (Crary's biggest problem; see section 1.1.2). Secondly, wave optics in the twentieth century had another and much more important appearance with holography. With its unique property of three-dimensional representation, with special reference to the wave-optical representation of geometrical-optical systems present in many scanners in the supermarket, in material control, in the sciences and in safety engineering, it has become indispensable (see Chapter 9). Obviously imaging technologies that are not physiological also can prevail (even though they are not part of the mass-medial phenomena that so often receive most of the focus of attention).

Thirdly, for some time already it is specifically in the area of safety engineering that precisely those particular characteristics of Lippmann photography that had originally been responsible for the fact that his method did not come out on top are appreciated again. The reproducibility that Walter Benjamin declared as the main characteristics of all technological media in his famous essay "The Work of Art in the Age of Mechanical Reproduction" (in distinction to "auratic art" as he calls painting), giving photography and the mass medium film as the only examples, is in no way the main feature of all technical media (for example daguerreotypes are not reproducible). Reproducibility indeed is a problem for capitalist societies. It is not entirely coincidental that Benjamin starts his essay by taking recourse to Marx in order to end with the thesis: "War and war only can set a goal for mass movements on the largest scale while respecting the traditional property system" (Benjamin 1978, 241). While I cannot discuss Benjamin's relationship to Marxism or the general validity of his theses here, it is a matter of his point that reproducibility not only threatens to subvert the "aura" of the work of art but also first *the copyright law*.[41] At present, the clamor about black-market copies of CDs and DVDs or illegal downloads of music or movies has been overwhelming since reproducibility has been vastly augmented with digital media.[42] In order to preserve the commodity form, namely the "traditional property system," the reproducibility of digital media absolutely requires restrictions, either by draconian threats of punishment or by the addition and application of technological protections against copying (or both). But the restriction against copying or reproducing is not only necessary in order to maintain the copyright or the profit rates of the media industry; it is secondly also necessary in order to secure the genuineness of certain entities, i.e. the differentiation between original and copy. Regarding these concerns about security, one must mention mainly *the* central medium of commodity-producing societies, i.e. money (including bank and credit cards, see Figure 4.7) as well as documents of governmental administration and control, such as, for example, identity cards. It is in these cases that imaging technologies based on the wave optical series are increasingly being used, among others also

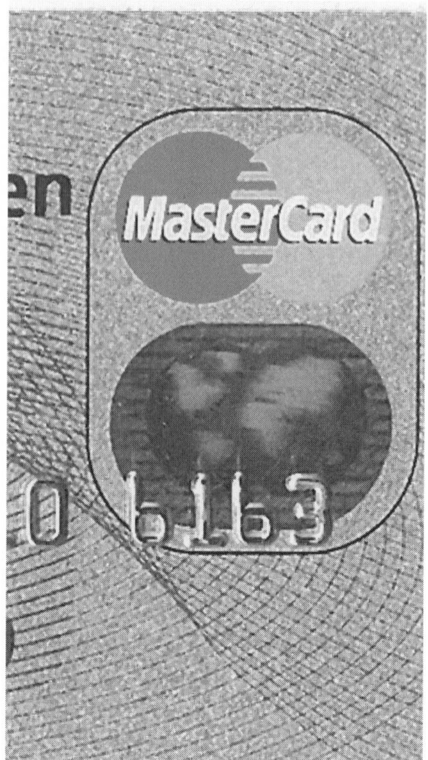

FIGURE 4.7 *Extract of the author's credit card, on the right the security hologram. The effects of a hologram cannot be reproduced here. Instead of the script 'Mastercard' that appears in all colors depending on the light angle and that seems to lie behind the slightly convex image of a double terrestrial globe oscillating in the colors of the rainbow, one can only see spatially flat and blurred streaks.*

because the technology of copying machines as geometrical-optical technologies of reproduction have continually advanced.[43]

This is precisely because using the interference of light waves creates images that cannot be copied with geometrical-optical and/or physiological-optical methods. A normal three-color photograph can be copied very well on a very good color copying machine. With an iridescent (and, in a hologram, transplane) image this is at least difficult: "The limitations of the Lippmann technique . . . which made this type of color photography impractical, have now become important advantages."[44] The question, whether an experimental method can become a usable technology then in the end depends on whether there are issues for which the method can be an answer (see Winston 2003, 5–9). Thus, Bjelkhagen (1999b, 58–60) explains that Lippmann photographs are better suited for certain security applications than holograms[45] since it is even more difficult to copy them. The reason is that in Lippmann photographs the pattern of interference is stored three-dimensionally in the volume of the emulsion, while in many types of holograms it lies superposed flat on its surface. Therefore, since the 1980s holograms can be copied industrially with certain methods of embossing—otherwise they would not exist on so many credit cards or banknotes.[46]

However, this does not mean that the average citizen can copy these holograms (for example, with a copying machine). Reproducibility is not an attribute that either exists or does not exist; instead, it is distributed on a variety of levels and in various ways. For this reason only, many citizens all over the world carry the so terribly marginalized hologram very close to their hearts—namely, on the banknotes, on their identity and credit cards in their wallets (see Schröter 2009).[47]

Notes

1 Spelling according to the original. In all probability this passage contains the only mention of the Lippmann method in literature. My thanks go to Nicola Glaubitz for the reference to this text.

2 The only exception is Eder (1978, 668–72); in Frizot (1998, 413–14) there is hardly more than one paragraph.

3 Hick (1999) and Kittler (2010) do not mention the method at all.

4 Who simply did not only 'invent' film—and we will encounter them a few more times.

5 See Eder (1978, 316): "Daguerreotypy suffered from a fundamental disadvantage. It could furnish in the camera only a single photographic image, which was not capable of multiplication by simple photographic printing methods." Daguerreotype did not prevail against the reproducible methods with paper (first introduced by Henry Fox Talbot) despite its much higher resolution.

6 Additional witnesses named by Crary are Maine de Biran and Schopenhauer, see Crary (1990, 72–9).

7 By the way, this is also true for color in Immanuel Kant whom Crary (1990, 74) opposes to Goethe; see Schröter (2000).

8 On Goethe and Seebeck see Nielsen (1989; 1990).

9 Seebeck in Goethe (1989, 936). It was Johann Heinrich Schulze who made the discovery of the light sensitivity of silver salts in 1727.

10 Seebeck in Goethe (1989, 937). The last sentence points to infrared rays. Later, Seebeck reports on several variations of this experiment. See also Eder (1978, 153–5).

11 Herschel, by the way, was the inventor of the term 'photography' (March 14, 1839; see also Eder 1978, 258–9) as well as the discoverer of the basically still used fixative sodium thiosulfate ($Na_2S_2O_3$; see Eder 1978, 319–20) and also was the first user of the terms 'negative' and 'positive' (see Herschel 1840, 3) in use throughout the photographic process of chemical photography in the twentieth century.

12 Herschel (1840, 18–19). In the 'Art. 31' (p. 10) mentioned in the quote, the preparation of a silver chloride solution is being described. Again, only silver chloride is used but no colorants.

13 See Talbot (1851, 627): "Il y a cependant une exception, c'est la couleur du ciel, qui s'est reproduite plusieurs fois dans mes expériences d'un azur très-naturel."

14 The nephew of Nicéphore Niépce and the inventor of the albumen process, see Eder (1978, 339–42).

15 For details of their chemical procedures see Eder (1978, 665).

16 Eder (1978, 665–6). See Becquerel (1848a; 1848b); De Saint Victor (1855).

17 See Connes (1987, 150–1). For the comparison of light and sound see Young (1804, 12).

18 See Zenker (1867, 252): "Thus we can see the elements of the retina as a system of planes on which the arriving light waves break almost vertically and from which they are also thrown back almost vertically. In doing so, standing waves must emerge, that specific form of interferences that is being produced by wave systems meeting each other."

19 See Wiener (1895, 246–53), particularly p. 249 on the "dependence of colors from the entry angle and the necessity to be viewed in mirrored light" in Lippmann photography.

20 See Carey Lea (1887, 352). For the details on the chemistry of chemical color photography see Valenta (1894, 1–6). In this chapter's motto from Dorothy Richardson a "violet subchloride of silver" is mentioned—this seems to allude to the photochemical phenomena

discussed here. See Eder and Pizzighelli (1881, 40) on "violet subchloride of silver."

21 Wiener (1895, 233). See Carey Lea (1887, 349). See Geimer (2002, 320): "The appearance and the disappearance of photographic images have always been located close to each other."

22 In a current standard work on the history of photography, chemical color photography only appears marginally, see Frizot (1998, 413–14).

23 Ives (1908, 325) is of a different opinion.

24 Connes (1987, 157). Therefore, Lippmann photography can be excellently represented in computer simulation (see Chapter 10); see Nareid and Pedersen 1991.

25 As if he wanted to underline his distance from Crary who centers on the series of physiological optics, Connes (1987, 158) remarks: "The vagaries of human vision . . . are not even considered."

26 The brothers Lumière "introduced very fine-grained silver-halide gelatine [*sic*] emulsions [which] became the main recording material for Lippmann photography" (Bjelkhagen 1999a, 275); see Lumière and Lumière (1893). In 1893 they incidentally also created the first portrait on the basis of the Lippmann method. See Lehmann (1907; 1908) on later, faster emulsions.

27 Lippmann (1894, 97; my emphasis): "One can fixate a *camera obscura* image with its shapes and colors by using a permanent transparent light-sensitive coating of sufficient thickness, which during the exposure time is placed on a reflecting surface that should preferably be made of a layer of mercury." See Becquerel, "De l'image photochromatique du spectre solaire, et des images colorées obtenues dans la *chambre obscure*" (1848a, 483; my emphasis). This last quotation shows again the ongoing usage of the *chambre obscure*.

28 The thickness of the emulsion coating depends on whether one wants to record only monochromatic (as in a sun spectrum) or polychromatic light (as in a normal scene); see Ives (1908) and Bjelkhagen, Jeong and Ro (1998, 76).

29 For the development of the wave optical concept of interference in the first half of the nineteenth century, see Buchwald (1989) and Chapter 9 of this book. It is interesting that many scholars who contributed to the research of the different photographic methods have done intensive work on wave optical questions.

30 But Lippmann did not make his first photographs on the basis of silver halides but on that of bichromate gelatin, see Valenta (1894, 76).

31 Valenta (1894, 30–6) and Denisyuk (1984, 36–49) provide quite lucid explanations. Also, by the way, the intense colors that one can

see on the surface of soap bubbles emerge in a similar way; see Rood (1880, 47–50).

32 See Phillips, Heyworth and Hare (1984, 168) who talk of a "complex mixture of geometrical and physical optics" (do not confuse 'physical' with 'physiological', read as wave optics). See Fournier and Burnett (1994, 508). Holograms (Chapter 9) do not resort to lenses in order to geometrically project a scene. Therefore they are purely wave optical images (regarding the laser light used they are wave-quantum optical hybrids).

33 See Nareid (1988). Mentioning in passing, Heidegger remarked in his essay "The Origin of the Work of Art" (1993, 172): "Color shines and wants only to shine. When we analyze it in rational terms by measuring its wavelengths, it is gone. It shows itself only when it remains undisclosed and unexplained." Kittler (1997a, 91) already countered this by saying that with computers and its peripheries the frequencies could become colors again. Thanks to Lippmann's wave-optical method and his mathematical descriptions of numbers of oscillations it was then possible to let colors shine again for roughly forty-four years before Heidegger's essay. Flusser's (2000, 43–4) thoughts on color photographs do not consider Lippmann photography insofar as color in photography is only referred back to a "chemical concept."

34 Is it a coincidence that this image shows a parrot like one of the early chemical color photographs by Becquerel? Certainly, no semantic charge is intended. It seems rather than the colorfulness of the parrot is only supposed to demonstrate that Lippmann photography can show color. See for similar events in the history of holography chapter 9.1.

35 This reconfiguration occurs in an even stronger way in three-dimensional images. See Chapter 9.4.

36 See Valenta (1894, 77–9) on the projection of a Lippmann photograph by Louis Lumière on August 22, 1893.

37 Nareid (1988, 141). The context of the quote is the following: "Three-colour processes rely on a coding of the spectral distribution of the recording and reconstructing light into three primary colours. The results achieved by means of this method are, however, based on the physiological characteristics of human colour vision. There is no guarantee that the reproduction is physically accurate, even though the visual match may be excellent. There are also colour reproduction situations where a visual match cannot easily be achieved by the three-colour method, a fact of which all experienced colour printers are aware." Unlike Lippmann photographs, today's normal RGB

monitors (just like TVs) that are also based on the three-color process cannot represent all possible colors (see Kittler 2001, 32).

38 Since the artists did not use only the basic colors for the pixels of their images this physiological-optical concept *in a transformed way* is the basis for simultaneous artistic currents like pointillism, see Schug (1997).

39 See Maxwell (1861). See Evans (1961) on the fact that Maxwell was actually able to create color photographs despite the fact that during his time photographic materials were mainly sensitive to blue light. On the history of three-color photography see Eder (1978, 639–64). It is strange that Crary (1990) does not mention Maxwell's color photography since it would support his thesis.

40 These reasons can be manifold. The concerted activities of different industries may establish an—actually 'worse'—technology as it happened for the VHS format, for example (see http://de.wikipedia.org/wiki/Video_Home _System [last accessed September 2, 2013]): "VHS had been developed systematically for the private market and offered relatively low-priced and simply constructed equipment. Many see this as the decisive reason why VHS was able to win large shares in the market. Another aspect underrated by Sony's VHS competitor Betamax was the power of the porno-industry. While Sony (and thus Betamax) turned their backs on the porno-industry, the first pornographic film appeared on VHS. Shortly after, the first video rental stores opened offering exclusively pornographic material on VHS cassettes."

41 In the nineteenth century, particularly in France, the photograph represented a challenge for copyright laws; see Edelman (1979).

42 Regarding these problems, Winkler (2004b, 29) observes: "Almost reminding us of Marx' contradictory terms of productive forces and relations of production, in this case the technological potential of technological reproduction and its social organization—the copyright—exactly oppose each other."

43 As I have mentioned above, stereoscopy was already used at the time in order to perform authentication (or at least there was the idea to do so), see Holmes (1861, 15); Helmholtz (1985, 304–6), Bith (1938) and Stenger (1950, 161; 1958, 202). On the use of holography on credit cards see Colgate (1994). On the history of photocopying see Mort (1989).

44 See the research done by Bjelkhagen (1999b, 55) who attempts to describe possible security implementations of the Lippmann method.

45 On holography see Chapter 9. On the alleged and real deficiencies of holograms as a security technology against copying see Pizzanelli (1998).

46 Johnston (2006a, 386–92) names techniques for copying holograms used at an early stage by counterfeiters, as well as the industry's development of more and more refined methods against copying.

47 The security technologies used on German passports and identity documents are officially named "identigram"; see on this the comments made by the Federal Printing Office (and its reference to holograms) to be found at http://www.bundesdruckerei.de/de/kunden/kunden_government/governm_persPass/persPass_identigram.html [last accessed September 2, 2013].

CHAPTER FIVE

Since 1908: Integral photography/lenticular images

Applications and Alterations of the Series of Geometrical Optics.

Media Aesthetics of the Transplane Image 3: Mariko Mori Birth of a Star (1995)

Tota in minimis existit natura.

GABRIEL LIPPMANN (2001, 309)

In the same year in which Gabriel Lippmann was awarded the Nobel prize in physics (1908), his essay "Épreuves réversibles. Photographies intégrales" was published in the magazine *Comptes Rendus Hebdomadaires des Séances de L'Académie des Sciences.* He conceived a genuine type of the transplane image in this paper, namely integral photography, the underlying idea of which has nothing to do with his interference photography. By referring to Alberti's well-known metaphor of the window, he writes in the beginning of the essay:

> Est-il possible de constituer une épreuve photographique de telle façon qu'elle nous représente le monde extérieur s'encadrant, en apparence, entre les bords de l'épreuve, comme si ces bords étaient ceux d'une fenêtre ouverte sur la réalité?[1]

And he proposes the following method:

> Supposons un film comme ceux qu'on emploie couramment, formé d'une pellicule transparente de celluloïd ou de collodion enduite sur l'une de ses faces d'une émulsion sensible à la lumière. Avant de coucher l'émulsion sur la pellicule, supposons que celle-ci ait été pressée à chaud dans une sorte de machine à gaufrer, de manière à faire naître sur chacune de ses faces un grand nombre de petites saillies en forme de segments sphériques. Chacune des saillies dont est couverte la face antérieure de la pellicule, celle qui restera nue, est destinée à faire office de lentille convergente. Chacune des saillies de la face postérieure est enduite d'émulsion sensible, et elle est destinée à recevoir l'image formée par une des petites lentilles de la face antérieure.[2]

His idea is applying a grid of minuscule lenses to the photosensitive layer.[3] Then the object is placed before the plate prepared in this way and is exposed. An additional camera is not necessary.

> La première propriété d'un pareil système est de donner des images photographiques sans qu'on l'ait introduit dans une chambre noire. Il suffit de le présenter en pleine lumière devant les objets à représenter. L'emploi d'une chambre noire est inutile, parce que chaque cellule du film est elle-même une chambre noire.[4] (See Figure 5.1)

Initially, we can note that integral photography is an interesting example of the (inventive) applications and alterations optical series can be subjected to, since we continue dealing with the series of geometrical optics (that obviously has not disappeared). The paradigm of the camera obscura continues to remain in the foreground, but it is being shifted. It is not a macro-image that is projected by way of a camera obscura (with or without a lens) onto the plane; rather, myriads of minuscule lenses (or "black chambers" as Lippmann calls them) project a network of micro-images: "Le

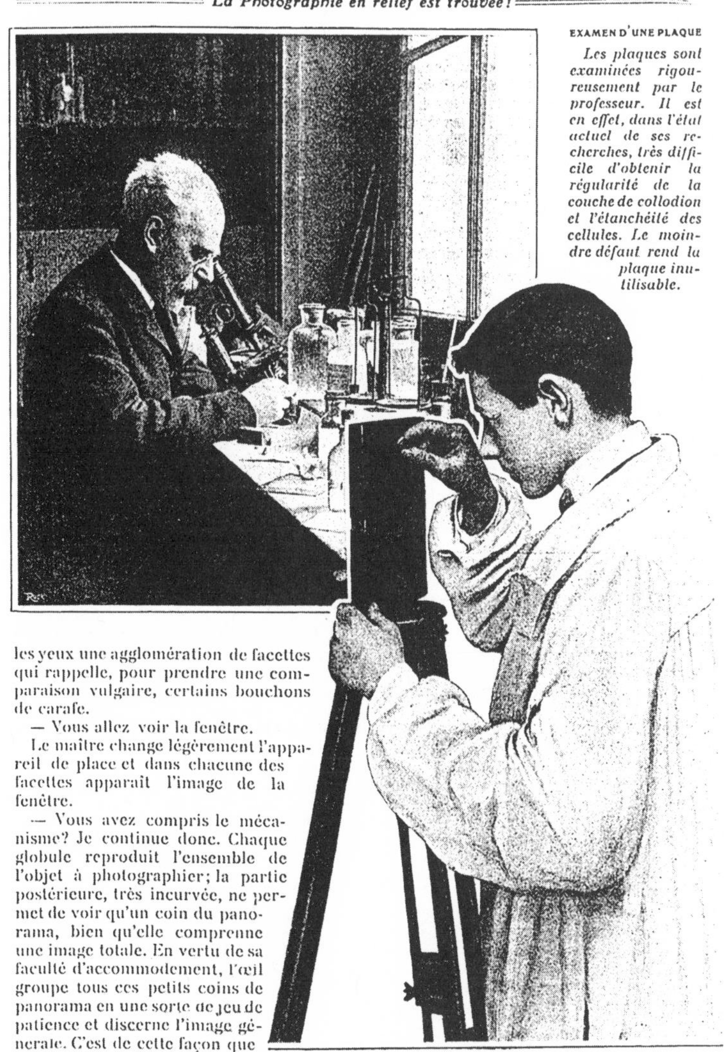

La Photographie en relief est trouvée !

EXAMEN D'UNE PLAQUE

Les plaques sont examinées rigoureusement par le professeur. Il est en effet, dans l'état actuel de ses recherches, très difficile d'obtenir la régularité de la couche de collodion et l'étanchéité des cellules. Le moindre défaut rend la plaque inutilisable.

les yeux une agglomération de facettes qui rappelle, pour prendre une comparaison vulgaire, certains bouchons de carafe.

— Vous allez voir la fenêtre.

Le maître change légèrement l'appareil de place et dans chacune des facettes apparaît l'image de la fenêtre.

— Vous avez compris le mécanisme? Je continue donc. Chaque globule reproduit l'ensemble de l'objet à photographier; la partie postérieure, très incurvée, ne permet de voir qu'un coin du panorama, bien qu'elle comprenne une image totale. En vertu de sa faculté d'accommodement, l'œil groupe tous ces petits coins de panorama en une sorte de jeu de patience et discerne l'image générale. C'est de cette façon que j'obtiens le relief et les changements de perspectives.

Chaque globule enserre hermétiquement son image, dont

L'OPÉRATION PHOTOGRAPHIQUE

Rien n'est plus simple : pas d'appareil ; on met la plaque dans un châssis ordinaire, on dispose le châssis devant ce que l'on veut obtenir, on l'ouvre, on le ferme : c'est fait.

547

FIGURE 5.1 *Lippmann inspects an integral photo plate with a microscope; an assistant exposes the plate without another camera, in Anonymous (1908, 547).*

résultat de ces opérations est une série des petites images microscopiques fixées chacune sur la rétine d'une des cellules."[5]

Viewing it, the lens is not missing as in a normal photograph; the plate is being illuminated from the back after having been developed quite conventionally and then again viewed through exactly the same network of lenses. Thus, the camera obscura is multiplied and becomes part of the reception process:

> Observées du côté de la couche sensible, ces images ne pourraient être distinguées à l'œil nu, et donneraient l'impression d'une couche grise uniforme. Par contre, supposons l'œil placé du côté antérieur, et l'épreuve éclairée par transparence en lumière diffuse, comme celle que fournirait un papier blanc appliqué contre la pellicule. L'œil verra alors, à la place du système des petites images, *une seule image résultante projetée dans l'espace, en vraie grandeur*.[6]

Instead of individual micro-images we see a three-dimensional, 'real image'[7] that seems to float between plate and viewer. In another publication from 1908, Lippmann has represented a schema that explains the effect quite plausibly: see Figure 5.2.

Originating from an object point 'A,' bundles of light-rays—and this means that here we are in the field of geometrical optics—are being focused via a micro-lens into one focal point 'a.' When the

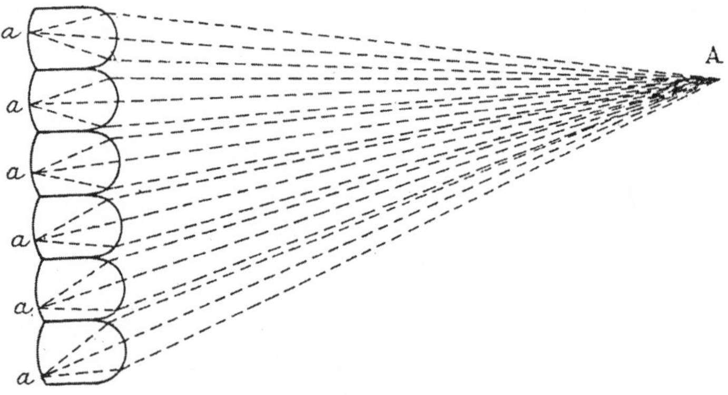

FIGURE 5.2 *Diagram of integral photography, in Lippmann (1908, 823).*

whole is being illuminated from the back, the bundle of light rays emanating from each focal point 'a' converges in point 'A' by way of the lens. This applies to each of the different points 'a^1' to 'a^n' that are each created by one lens of 'A' and of course also for every object point 'B,' 'C,' 'D' to 'n':

> Ainsi, grâce à la propriété de la réversibilité, que possède la chambre noire, que possède par suite un système de chambres noires solidaires entres elles, il suffit d'éclairer par derrière ce système pour projeter dans l'espace une image réelle qui occupe la place du point A qui a posé. Il en est de même pour les autres points B, C, D, du sujet photographié. Tous ces points se trouvent reconstitués sous la forme d'images aériennes.[8]

Lippmann also noted that after taking the image it was necessary to make an adjustment and not only to make a positive out of a negative: "De plus l'image est géometriquement renversée, le haut en bas, la droite à gauche."[9] But what he obviously had not noticed and what he possibly could not notice since he was not able to create a truly functional example for integral photography (see below), was that the image was *pseudoscopic*, i.e. that it was turned inside out, the highest points in the image, in the example of a portrait: the nose, becoming the rearmost points and vice versa, as in a mask looked at from the backside.[10] Herbert E. Ives has described this phenomenon in detail. Only the second of the methods of adjustment described by Lippmann is functional.

> In conclusion it is proper to emphasize that the method of making copies suggested by Lippmann, namely, setting up a second screen [supplied with a micro lens network] in front of the first at some distance and exposing without the interposition of any lens is valid. For a pseudoscopic copy of a pseudoscopic picture, becomes, by virtue of the double reversal, a picture in correct relief.[11]

The Lippmann method then has to be implemented in two steps. A second integral photograph has to be made from the first one so that a correct image is created, although with a certain loss of quality of the image.[12] That's it.

However, as simple and compelling as the theoretical concept is, conversely difficult is its practical realization. Optical knowledge does not transfer into the technology of optical media without laborious work and the detours of sedimentation; therefore the latter (technology) should never be reduced to the former (knowledge). "Si la théorie de la plaque r[é]versible est très simple, en revanche sa construction présente des difficultés techniques sérieuses."[13] It is extremely difficult manufacturing small enough lenses with adequately precise optical properties (since all lenses have to focus the light of the object-points on the same level).[14] Lippmann himself made "a crude test of the screen made with a number of glass rods with spherical ends" (Ives 2001, 315). Despite its elegance in principle and despite some further experiments, the method was hardly noted or used for other purposes.[15] It is therefore quite unsatisfactory to see Lippmann solely as the 'inventor' of integral photography. Some histories of media sometimes argue in this vein, particularly when an inaugural event (often in the context of military research) is being (archeologically—in a Foucauldian sense) dug out and then abruptly annexed to the most current developments.[16] Thus, the many steps of mediation and the shifts contained therein disappear. Of course, as far as it can be verified, the idea of using a micro-lens network goes back to Lippmann. However, until his death in 1921 he was only able to create such a system rudimentarily and he had also failed to see the problem of pseudoscopy. Only after WWII with the availability of new polymeric materials could a realization have become practicable.[17] With De Montebello's "Integram" method,[18] a form of integral photography was created in the 1970s that overcame the difficulties and produced excellent images. "This technology, however, has not triggered a large social demand because it is fairly expensive and so far has met with difficulty in finding appropriate applications" (Okoshi 1976, 551). Here again one of the central peculiarities of transplane imaging technologies can be seen. The additional information on space can only be provided using additional technical and financial investment. Therefore, even though these technologies are employed in 'space-intensive' and also highly cost intensive uses (like for example in certain scientific or military fields), they do not succeed in public areas like the arts or entertainment,[19] although more recently we can observe a certain return to integral photography in the form of 'integral imaging' connected to the emergence of digital procedures:

> Today's [2006] rapid progress of digital capture and display technology opened the possibility to proceed toward non-compromising, easy-to-use 3-D imaging techniques. This technology progress prompted the revival of integral imaging . . . technique. . . . [Integral Imaging] is a promising technology because: 1) It produces auto-stereoscopic images, thus not requiring special viewing devices; 2) it provides the observer images with full parallax and continuous viewing points; 3) it is passive; i.e., it does not require special illumination of the scene; 4) it can operate with regular incoherent daylight; 5) its system configuration is compact; 6) its implementation is relatively simple.[20]

Only the historically contingent linking of the geometrical-optical principle of integral photography with, first, software that has already been geared to virtually modeling geometrical-optical phenomena (ray tracing)[21] for quite some time and, secondly, with the potential need of 3D displays[22] for visualizing digital data (for example for the extremely popular computer game),[23] makes integral photography interesting again. It is specifically being considered as an alternative to holography since it does not need coherent light, is able to generate color photographs without problems, and needs a lot less computation when using it as a display.[24] However, these methods are still in an experimental state at this time despite increased research.

Theoretically, integral photography is of special interest since it illustrates the complexity of the history of optical media all at once.[25] Initially, as I have mentioned before, it is a return to the paradigm of the camera obscura, of geometrical optics. At first it seems astonishing that a technology born of geometrical optics can provide a transplane image. But this is not fundamentally different in the case of stereoscopy. The controlled *double* photograph of an object—every single image is geometrical-optically projected—allows for the use of the binocularity of the eyes. Transplane images are called 'transplane' precisely because they do not completely give up the plane, but multiply and transform it in a controlled way, mobilizing and changing it in order to supply more spatial information than perspectival projection. Thus, integral photography is a *different* sedimentation of geometrical optics. As I have suggested, there are two central differences to a linear perspectival projection: First, the number of cameras and therefore the projection surface is multiplied and secondly, the rendition of the image is also a form of projection. However, the classification of integral photography is difficult. Most authors group it with stereoscopy while others set it apart.[26] Benton justifies his classification of integral photography into stereoscopy by suggesting that integral photography is also based on the "presentation of distinct perspective views to our two eyes" (Benton 2001b, xxi). Certainly, every single lens presents a perspectivally projected micro-image. However, unlike in stereoscopy it is not the presentation of two images, but (ideally) of so many images as there are pixels. Lippmann had already remarked: "Si chaque cellule est un œil simple, leur ensemble rappelle l'œil composé des insectes."[27] The anthropomorphic doubling of the image in stereoscopy gives way to a non-anthropomorphic multiplication of eyes. Integral photography, then, is not an *extension of man* (in McLuhan's sense, 1965) but rather an *extension of fly*. Unlike in stereoscopy, in integral photography it is not the average distance between human eyes that has to be taken into account in order to prevent hyper-stereoscopic effects.[28] To a certain extent, the multiplication of the projection is an approximation of the wavefront of light. The micro-projection that is taking place at each pixel can be described as "sampling probes acting on the individual wavefronts."[29] If the individual cameras were punctiform,[30] a recording would be close to a wavefront as such. Just as geometrical optics is a special case of wave optics for macroscopic structures, the microfication of geometrical-optical media in integral photography in certain aspects approaches holography, which is based on the wave optical series:

> [S]ince each lenslet [micro-lense] plots behind it information about all of the object points, integral photography achieves more-or-less uniform distribution of subject information over the record in a manner similar to that achieved by holography of diffuse subjects.[31]

From other points of view, the two types of images remain different from each other. For example, while holograms have to be taken with coherent laser light, integral photographs can be created with incoherent white light,[32] i.e. color is no problem for the latter. In return, holograms have a much higher resolution. I have added these remarks only in order to explain that the differences between the various optical technologies can also be understood as effects of *multiplication* and *scaling*. If one doubles geometrical-optical images one can use the effects of physiological optics (as it is done in stereoscopy). If the multiplication is increased while at the same time microfying, one approaches the series of wave optics.

A method related to integral photography but one that is more easily realized was developed early on, today generally referred to as the field of 'lenticular images.' The 'lenticular images' belong to the most well-known forms of transplane images. They are those rippled 'wiggle pics' and/or 3D images often available in the form of postcards. Benton observes: "One might assume that Lippmann's invention of integral photography, using an array of tiny spherical lenslets, subsumes [lenticular photographs], but the intent and repercussions of the two developments are entirely different."[33]

The differences between the two methods pointed at in this remark can perhaps most easily be summarized in the thesis that the lenticular images are closer to stereoscopy than to integral photography, even though their basic principle seems to be quite similar. The decisive difference lies in the fact that by using cylindrical lenticular grids only the horizontal parallax is retained conforming to the arrangement of human eyes. The vertical parallax is discarded. Therefore, in Walter Hess's's[34] patent specification from 1915 that basically drafts the lenticular method for the first time (see Figure 5.3), it is simply called "stereoscopic picture."[35] Hess does not refer to Lippmann in any way whatsoever.

Instead, he first describes how in previous stereoscopic methods two different images were presented to the respective eyes. In Hess's method as well "two ordinary stereoscopic negatives are used" (Hess 2001, 291). The two stereoscopically related images are used in order to expose a film on which the layer made by cylindrical lenses is positioned (*Fig. 1* in Figure 5.3 as plane view; *Fig. 2* shows the layer as cross section; d shows the cylindrical structure). *Fig. 2* shows how two bundles of light f are focused through each cylindrical lens onto two pixels g. The two bundles of light rays f correspond to the two images of the stereoscopic photo pair (*Fig. 6* shows a suggestion for a recording-apparatus; the two photos are

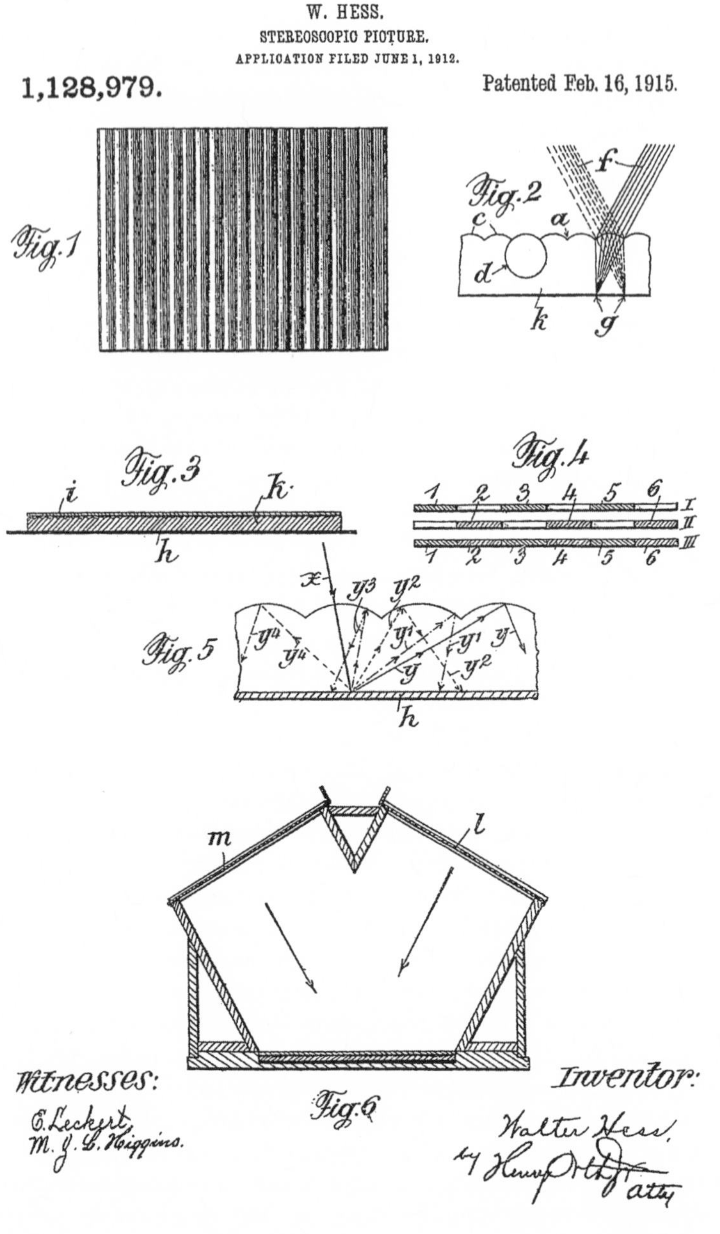

W. HESS.

STEREOSCOPIC PICTURE.

APPLICATION FILED JUNE 1, 1912.

1,128,979. Patented Feb. 16, 1915.

Witnesses:

E. Leckert,
M. J. L. Higgins.

Inventor:

Walter Hess,
by Henry Orth Jr atty

FIGURE 5.3 *Drawing from a patent for lenticular images. The lenticular grid can be seen as planar view and as sectional view, in Hess (2001, 294).*

mounted at the points m and l). As *Fig. 4* shows, the result is that on the photosensitive layer the two different images of the stereoscopic image pair are recorded in the form of adjoining 'image-strips.' *Fig. 4.I* shows the strips corresponding to one of the images; *Fig. 4.II* shows the strips corresponding to the other image. *Fig. 4.III* shows both. In viewing the lenticular image, the image-strips of each image are channeled to the corresponding eye and a stereoscopic impression of the photo is created without the necessity of additional eyeglasses. Therefore, with regard to lenticular images one also talks of auto-stereoscopic images.

> Thus, the novel product of my novel process or method consists of a picture subdivided by alternating portions of stereoscopic images III, Fig. 4, viewed through a subdivided lens surface *k* corresponding to the subdivisions of the picture, and preferably connected to or combined with such surface *k* so that no stereoscope, stereoscopic spectacles or separate light filters are necessary. Each lens element *c* of the plate *k* will therefore be common to two adjacent subdivisions of the picture, one subdivision pertaining to one stereoscopic view and the other subdivision to the other stereoscopic view. (Hess 2001, 292)

Of course it is not necessary to use a stereo-pair for the creation of the two photo strips—one can simply take two different images so that one image flips into another when the viewer moves.[36] It is also possible to take two images showing two phases of a movement; in moving before the picture (or in moving the lenticular image) the impression is created that the lenticular image represents motion. All these possibilities can be combined if one makes more than two images into strips, a method that was soon developed. The advantage of the lenticular method was that it indeed had similarities to the parallax stereogram, a method already developed in 1902 by H. E. Ives. This was a similar method insofar as two (or more) strips are drawn as a striped pattern—yet, it is not a lenticular grid that is being used, but rather a reproductive plate provided with fine opaque and transparent stripes (therefore, it is called the parallax barrier method).[37] The knowledge gained in the studies of these techniques[38] could now be used for the development of the somewhat different lenticular method. In the 1920s and 1930s, studies were done with lenticular techniques and their refinement for specific purposes.[39] And here as well, as happens so often, interesting applications and alterations can be found:

> When a lenticular array is coated with a film emulsion at its focal plane and exposed to light rays from a particular angle, once developed it will redirect the light rays in the same approximate direction as the recording angle. This unique property found its first successful commercial application not as a tool for 3D photography but as a means for producing color motion picture film as the original Kodak Kodacolor process introduced in 1928. Instead of individual stereo images being exposed behind the lenticular screen, individual stripe images relating to red, green, and blue aspects of a single view were recorded and re-combined through a special projection system into a full color image using only black and white emulsion. The process, using a very thin and fine screen of 600 lenses per inch on 16 millimeter film, ran for a number of years with considerable success, and the Eastman Kodak company as recently as 1951 was offering an improved version for the 35mm format. (Roberts 2003)

It is striking that apparently with the use of the lenticular principle it seemed more important to add color to film than enhancing the sense of space. One could speculate that those kinds of decisions expose elements of an archaeology of the medium's 'realism;' i.e. what was it that became an important indication for 'realism' and when and why? Once again the answer is that in narrative cinema space is built by narration and an additional lenticular-stereoscopic impression of space is not necessary. Moreover, a lenticular movie screen has only a relatively limited viewing field within which the spatial effect is produced. Therefore, this method was in all probability discarded as impractical for the big commercial theaters.[40] Color, on the other hand, supports the visual presence in such a way that it can hardly be substituted by narration and therefore was possibly the reason it proved more successful.

Nevertheless, the use of lenticular methods for creating non-cinematographic transplane images bloomed, in particular in France. Maurice Bonnet's developments "still stand as the zenith of this technology" (Benton 2001b, xx). In 1937 Bonnet founded his company *La Relièphographie*. His success was based on the spectacular quality of his lenticular images, which were owed to his own methods that he also had patented (cf. Frizot 2000a). Bonnet made portraits of numerous celebrities[41] as well as remarkable advertising panels (among others for the fashion industry). This connection to the commercially important use of photographs for advertising was relevant: In the USA these images triggered a small boom when the well-known magazine *Look* added a postcard-size lenticular image of a bust sculpture of Thomas Alva Edison to its edition of February 25, 1964. The method was modified in various ways and spread; lenticular postcards with or without 3D effects, with or without animation, can still be frequently found today, and small lenticular images can currently be found on the wrappings of breakfast cereals and similar things. The artist Andrew Hurle, also working with lenticular images, sighed: "Like many innovations in 3D imaging, it [lenticular images] was hailed as a major leap forward in pictorial representation before failing to develop into anything much more than a novel element in advertising and packaging."[42] Again we have to ask ourselves once more whether this is a characteristic of transplane images. It seems that their media aesthetic peculiarities are well suited for the creation of spectacular effects that can attract attention. But for developing their own aesthetics they are rarely being used.[43]

This being said, it is striking that in today's art a remarkable media aesthetic use of the lenticular image exists, namely in Mariko Mori's multimedia work *Birth of a Star* (see Figure 5.4).

One sees a girl, Mori herself, in a shrill costume. The image quotes not only the widespread fashion of 'girlism' in the 1990s but also borrows from manga comics and their futurist aesthetics—note the non-human eyes of the figure. *Birth of a Star* is accompanied by pop-music which is just as shrill, and its rhythm strangely contrasts the frozen pose of the figure. In its left hand it carries an odd tool that is probably supposed to be some sort of microphone. Initially, one could interpret the work as a sort of parody of the star cult of pop stars and starlets in the culture industry: A star is born—born by way of its spectacular and attention-grabbing presentation in mass media. In this sense the use of a lenticular image is consistent. Mori-the-pop-star reaches an enormous, bewitching presence through the three-dimensional, life-sized representation. First, the three-dimensionality is underlined by the extremely vividly colored balls.[44] Secondly, the boundaries of the pictorial space are systematically dissolved. This already happens on the level of

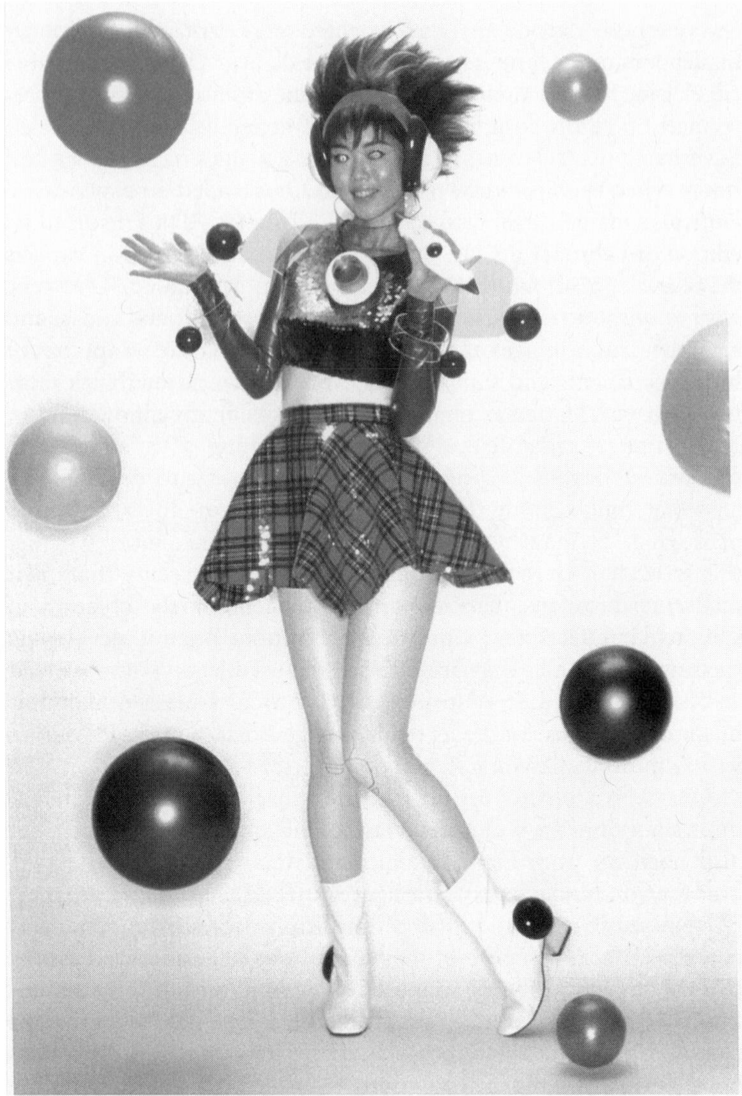

FIGURE 5.4 *Mariko Mori,* Birth of a Star *(1995), 3-D duratrans, acrylic, light box, and audio CD; 70 3/16 × 45 1/4 × 4 1/4 in. (178.3 × 114.9 × 10.8 cm), Museum of Contemporary Art, Chicago. (Unfortunately, the effect of the lenticular image cannot be recreated here). See color plate 4.*

composition—the image is structured by two diagonals. Once by the red ball on the upper left above the bent arm, then over the right edge of the little plaid skirt continuing to the black ball on the right; secondly by the yellow ball on the left, paralleling her bent leg to the small blue ball on the lower right. As these diagonals point sideways beyond the frame of the image, the vivid three-dimensional impression bursts out of the frontal boundary of the image. And this is thirdly underlined by the fact that the red, the two yellow and the black balls somehow appear to lie in the foreground—as if they were flying towards us, sent out from the figure (from which at this moment four more small blue balls seem to be ejected). The image seems to burst out of its frame, as evidenced by the cut off yellow ball on the right, and it aggressively infringes on the viewers.

This means that the effects of being caught by surprise in modern marketing are being quoted in a lenticular image that therefore represents all the other lenticular images that are being used in advertisement for some time now in order to grab attention.[45] The functional uses of transplane images, whose difference from the planocentric regime of geometrical optics is usually being perceived only as a spectacular and short-lived special effect, can now be reflected. This reflection doubles the status of art in postmodernism that tends to be attention grabbing. It is not for nothing that the artist presents herself as a pop star in *contrapposto*, thus quoting the history of the traditional artistic representation of such figures, successfully entering the art market by appearing in such a spectacular manner. *Birth of a Star* was one of the earliest works by Mori through which she became known. This merciless self-diagnosis is once more underlined by the 'girlie-look' quoted by Mori since 'girlism' at first had been a sort of neo-feminist movement which was quickly functionalized by the fashion industry as a new look,[46] the same fashion industry for which Mori had been working as a model in the 1980s. The whole work does not accidentally look like a particularly shrill fashion photograph with its glossy technical perfection and vociferating colors (cf. Bryson 1998b, 76). The lenticular image is enclosed in a circle of commerce and spectacularization here. This corresponds to Mori's "strategy ... to mime the capitalist production/consumption" (Bryson 1998b, 80).

But transplane images do not only appear in the capitalist culture industry as sensation-seeking special effects; they also appear as the promise of an uninterrupted advance of technological progress (see Mori 2000, 38). There is hardly a science-fiction film in which (fictitious) transplane images are not supposed to represent the futuricity of future.[47] Mori's reference to the ideology of technical progress in the discourse on transplane images is created by the peculiar robot-like appearance of the figure with its technical gadgets. On closer observation, the pop star appears to be merely a wind-up doll that blares some kind of pop song once you press a button—what other possible function would the light blue button on its breast have—just like the CD that accompanies the image does. The contrast between the stiff figure and the constantly unimpeded blaring of the music underlines the synthetic impression of this post human, always happy—never marked by drug or similar problems—ideal pop star of the future. The robot-like look is not only created by the clearly changed, strange eyes, but also by the light reflections on the clothes. The clothes and the balls confirm—visible by the excessively white highlights—that they are made of synthetic materials. Since polymers are literally synthetic materials that do not exist in nature, the most excessive artificiality possible is connoted; even the cheeks of the figure show noticeable white highlights.[48] Mori is in no way suggesting that her star had become a star because of its 'natural talents'[49]—which is an ideological naturalization quite common in commercial discourse, for example in the music industry (cf. Schröter 1996). Rather, the birth of a star is an artificial strategy of culture industry through and through.[50]

At the same time, the materiality of the lenticular image is made thematic by underlining the polymers and this image can only be produced on the basis of polymers—especially in this size. The defamiliarized eyes of the figure underline this thematization of the lenticular image. We see *two* (strange) eyes, underlining binocular vision—that binocular vision that also lies at the basis of the stereoscopic concept of the lenticular image. Norman Bryson writes about Mori: "She uses her body as a lens that captures the light of the contemporary image-stream, and through certain enhancements and exaggerations makes it clear what the image-stream really wants of us" (Bryson 1998b, 78). Simultaneously reflecting the materiality of the lenticular image and its discursive functionalizing within the capitalist culture industry makes Lippmann's demand of a "fenêtre ouverte sur la réalité" ironic—what kind of a 'reality' do we see through the window of the transplane image? Mori clarifies that the view through the window lets us see a spectacle. The space behind the window is only a production (Lefebvre) of the culture industry. Or, as Deleuze has remarked in a curiously sculptural metaphor: "behind the curtain there is nothing to see, but it was all the more important each time to describe the curtain, or the base, since there was nothing either behind or beneath it" (Deleuze 2011, 47).

Notes

1 Lippmann (2001, 306): "Is it possible to create a photo print in such a way that it represents the exterior world seemingly framed by the edges of the print, the edges like a window frame opening up to reality?"

2 Lippmann (2001, 306): "And let us assume a film like those that one makes in today's times created from a transparent celluloid or collodion film coated on one of its sides with a light sensitive emulsion. Before the emulsion is laminated onto the film let us assume that it had been pressed beforehand in a sort of hot waffle iron in such a way that on each of its sides a great number of small bulges in spherical form emerge. Each of these bulges with which the whole front side of the film is covered—the one which remains naked—is designed to serve as a convergent lens. Each of the bulges on the back side is covered with a sensitive emulsion and it is designed to receive the image that was formed by one of the small lenses of the front side." See Eder (1978, 669) and Okoshi (1976, 21–5) on the Lippmann method.

3 See De Montebello (2001, 317) who speak of "spherilenticular network."

4 Lippmann (2001, 307): "The first property of such a system is providing photographic images without having to go through a dark chamber [of the camera obscura]. It should suffice to expose it to full light in front of the objects one wants to represent. The use of a dark chamber is unnecessary because each film cell is itself a dark chamber."

5 Lippmann (2001, 307): "The result of these operations is a series of microscopic images that are fixed onto the retina of one of the cells."

6 Lippmann (2001, 307; emphasis in the original): "When looking at it from the light sensitive side, these images could not be distinguished by the naked eye; they would give the impression of a uniform grey

surface. On the other hand let us assume that the eye is placed on the front side and the print is lit by way of a transparency in dim light (like that which a white paper would give us if it were placed before the film). Instead of the system of small images as a result one then would see *one image only which would be projected outward into space in its true size.*"

7 See Hecht (1987, 131) on the differentiation between real and virtual images.

8 Lippmann (1908, 823): "Consequently, thanks to the reversible nature of the camera obscura, which thus is also true for a system of several individual other camerae obscure, it is enough to light up this system from the back in order to project a real image into space that takes over the place of point A having served as a model. It is the same for the other points B, C, D of the object that was photographed. All these points will be reconstructed as images floating in the air."

9 Lippmann (2001, 308): "Moreover, the image is geometrically reversed—from top to bottom and from right to left."

10 Cf. already Helmholtz (1985, 308–10) on the pseudoscopic image that emerges in stereoscopy when the right/left attribution of images is switched.

11 Ives (2001, 316). Interesting to note and quite symptomatic as well for the early history of new technological procedures is Ives' critique of Estanave (1930), who had claimed that Lippmann's original procedure functioned without any problems while never at all pointing out the problem of the pseudoscopic character of the images. It becomes visible from these instances to what extent the meanings and potentials of new technological procedures are being 'negotiated.' Several of Estanave's patents in the area of parallax-barrier procedures had been approved earlier; see Estanave (1906; 1908a; 1908b).

12 But see De Montebello (2001, 317) on the problems of Lippmann's suggestion.

13 Lippmann (1908, 824; 1911, 69): "While the theory of the reversible plate is very simple, its construction presents serious technical difficulties." In the same place we also can read that in 1911 Lippmann attained no more than twelve lens elements at most. See also De Montebello (1977, 86) on the extreme elegance of Lippmann's procedure: "A dream. Unfortunately, this is just what it was. And to realize this beautiful dream an enormously more elaborate and exacting technology had to be woven around the pure concept."

14 On the geometrical effects of imprecisely arranged microlens networks see Arai et al. (2004).

15 Eder (1978, 672–3) observes that the procedure was used in an altered form for creating three-color film.

16 See critically Schröter (2004f) with the example of the 'well known military origin' of the internet.

17 See Okoshi (1980, 549). On the history of polymers see Kohlepp (2005). He makes it evident that around the middle of the twentieth century new materials emerged in quick succession. See also Roberts and Smith (n.d.) on the different attempts at experimenting with integral photography in the twentieth century.

18 See De Montebello (2001, 319) where the author specifies the material from which the micro-lens network is formed as "polystyrene or more preferably a transparent polyester resin having a refractive index of n=1.56 or more."

19 See Winston (2003, 5–9) on the problem of technologies where no "supervening social necessity" spurs on development and distribution. Significantly, using the example of transplane holography he underlines that "the real diffusion question is whether or not holography will acquire movement and thereby emerge as an entertainment medium" (339). This means that according to Winston we can only speak of a successful acceptance when a new technology can be established in the area of entertainment.

20 Stern and Javidi (2006, 591). This text provides a survey of the lately increased research done on integral images in the area of computer graphics. Roberts and Smith (n.d.) see the beginnings of studying computer generated integral photography with Collier (1968) and Igarashi et al. (1978). We can place the beginning of studying 3D scans on the basis of integral methods with Okano et al. in 1997. In Weiss (2007), a current development is introduced. The most noticeable element of this article is that it completely leaves out the history of integral photography and that the method is advertised as the latest invention. Lately, so called 'light field cameras' based on Lippmann's ideas were developed, see Georgiev and Intwala (2003).

21 See quintessentially Athineos et al. (2006). See also Chapter 10 on ray tracing.

22 On the research done on 3D displays for visualization through computers see generally McAllister (1993).

23 See Stern and Javidi (2006, 593). Apart from '3-D video games' also '3-D television . . . interactive shopping, interior design' and other elements are listed as possible applications of integral imaging.

24 Collier (1968, 63) has underlined the advantages of integral photography compared to holography (Chapter 9) for purposes of imaging.

25 It is all the more problematic that it does not appear in the history of optical media (see for example Kittler 2010).

26 McCrickerd and George (1968, 10) or De Montebello (2001) group it with stereoscopy. But only recently in contrast Takada, Suyama and Date (2006, 429) have differentiated stereoscopy, integral photography, volumetric display (see Chapter 8) and holography (see Chapter 9) as the four basic approaches to the field of three-dimensional images. This means that stereoscopy and integral photography are clearly being differentiated. It should be underlined, however, that the division into four categories suggested by the authors is not congruent with the four optical series discussed here.

27 Lippmann (2001, 306): "When every cell is like a simple eye, their ensemble reminds us of the compound eyes of insects." To this day the term 'fly's eye' is a much used description of integral photography, see McCrickerd (1972).

28 See Hesse (1954, 114) who explicitly underlines the difference of integral-photographic methods from the series of physiological optics: "In my studies on the realization of spatial images that already date twenty years back I used a very different path than Wheatstone. At first I did not at all deal with the psychological-physical [?] problem of spatial vision and did not take my point of departure from the human eye but from the object in space! I was looking for a purely physical-optical solution." In this, the author recognized "that indeed one can succeed in an experimentally feasible spatial transmission even though one does not at all worry about binocular vision."

29 Pole (1967, 22). Is the term the author uses—'sampling'—a possible suggestion that integral photography has to be counted among the series of virtual optics? No, since here it is not elements of images but elementary images that are being recorded.

30 Of course, this is not possible practically. Not only is the production of very small elements extremely difficult; from a certain diminution downward the effects of diffraction come into play and moreover the dissolution of the photo emulsion limits the process.

31 Collier (1968, 61–2). See De Montebello (1977, 78).

32 Therefore, for creating holograms from objects with white light, Pole (1967) has suggested a procedure in two steps. The first step is to take an integral photograph (to which Pole—who does not refer to

Lippmann at all—significantly gives a different name: "Holocoder"). The second one consists in creating a hologram from the real image created via integral photography.

33 Benton (2001b, xx). Nevertheless, Okoshi (1976, 60–124) deals with lenticular images and integral photography in one context. From this contradiction between Benton and Okoshi, it can be seen again that it is not easy to classify integral photography. It seems to me that neither an identity nor a fundamental difference between the two methods—integral photography and lenticular images—should be assumed. It is rather a gradual differentiation, which nevertheless is not an insignificant one. After all, Lippmann (2001) also refers to stereoscopy, even though in a negative way which is not constitutive for his approach: "Comme, de plus, les deux yeux occupent des positions différentes, ils aperçoivent des perspectives correspondantes: les conditions de la perception du relief par la vision binoculaire se trouvent remplies, sans l'emploi d'un stéréoscope" (Lippmann 2001, 308: "Moreover, as the two eyes take on two different positions they perceive corresponding perspectives: the conditions of perceiving a relief by way of binocular vision without using a stereoscope are being fulfilled.") See also the remarks by Lippmann in Anonymous (1908, 546) and Lippmann (1911, 69).

34 I was not able to ascertain whether the man is called "Hess" or "Hesse" (as he is named in later publications).

35 See Hess (2001). Benton (2001b, xx) remarks: "Many improvements in optical plastics, the design of the single refracting surface available, and fabrication technologies have greatly improved the performance of the simple lenticular sheet, although the basic principle remains as Hess described it."

36 According to Oster (1959) the French painter G.A. Bois-Clair already had this idea in 1692—without lenticular lenses of course—by painting two images in strips onto the corresponding sides of triangular moldings. In passing by a first image changed into a second one.

37 See Ives (1902). Despite the differences Okoshi (1976, 27) sees Ives' paper as the very beginning of lenticular images. Basically on the theory of parallax barriers see Kaplan (1952). See also Frizot (2000b).

38 See Ives (1930; 1931; 1932) among others.

39 See mainly Kanolt's important patent from 1918 (see Kanolt 2001).

40 In this regard it is very interesting to see that lenticular methods were already used in the Soviet Union in some movie theaters for the creation of a stereoscopic impression in the beginning of the 1940s

see Anonymous (1948); Eisenstein (1949); Selle (1953a; 1953b) and Iwanow (1954). The exact reasons for the varying success of lenticular cinema in different cultural contexts would have to be assessed separately.

41 The fact that Bonnet highlights the portrait to such an extent has a specific technical reason, namely that in portraits one does not notice the limitations of the lenticular image; see Mahler (1954, 87).

42 http://www.andrewhurle.com/28/28.html [last accessed September 2, 2013].

43 See McCauley (2000). I will come back to this question in section 9.4, where I will be dealing with the problems that the artistic attempts based on holography have in the art market.

44 It is interesting to see that Hildebrand (1907, 31) has already used the sphere as a prototypical example for spatial perception: "We are, for instance, able to conceive the three-dimensional form of a sphere, but hardly a clear visual impression of it. Our idea of a sphere is rather that of a two-dimensional circular line, plus an idea of movement by which this circle is repeated equally in all directions."

45 Touchmore GmbH is advertising for its lenticular images with the catchphrase "SuperMotion", see http://www.touchmore.de/supermotion-high-definition-lenticular [last accessed August 30, 2013].

46 See Kailer and Bierbaum (2002). See also Mori herself (2000, 40) on her criticism of traditional feminism. And see Bryson (1998b, 80) on sexuality in Mori that "constantly moves toward the infantile—where the infantile is also the cute."

47 The most important example, which we will still encounter several times, is the projected princess Leia in *Star Wars* (USA 1977, Dir. George Lucas). See section 9.4.

48 Synthetic material produces white highlights; in metals, for example, the highlights have the same color as the object. Insofar as in early computer graphics (phong shading) all highlights were white, all rendered objects looked as if they were made from plastic (see Mitchell 1992, 144–5).

49 See Bryson (1998b, 80) who underlines that Mori "completely abandoned . . . the idea of the body as creatural, as flesh and blood."

50 See Magnan (1996, 67) on "Mori's critique of the mythmaking and manipulation involved in wooing popular culture's audience with such media generated personas."

CHAPTER SIX

1935–1945: 'People without space'—people with spatial images

Stereoscopy in the Third Reich

The Series of Physiological Optics.

The Politics of Transplane Images 1

Media Aesthetics of the Transplane Image 4: Thomas Ruff, Ruhrgebiet (1996)

It is otherwise that the Faustian world-feeling experiences depth. Here the sum of true Being appears as pure efficient Space, which is *being.*

OSWALD SPENGLER (1926, VOL. I, 398)

It is the Faustian experience of space that comes alive again when viewing the aerial "Raumbild" (spatial image) presented here.

H. MADER (1938, 9)

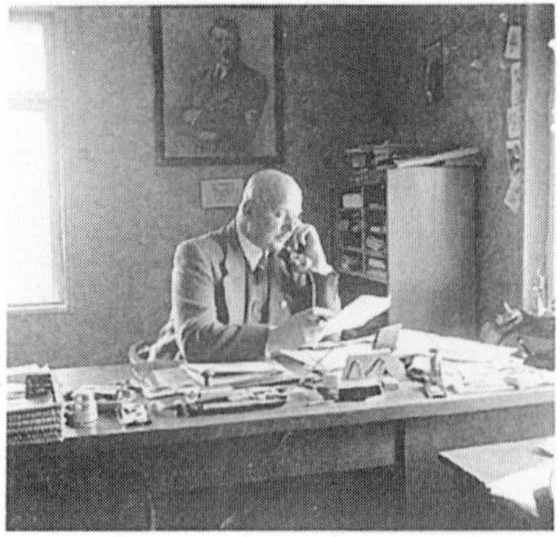
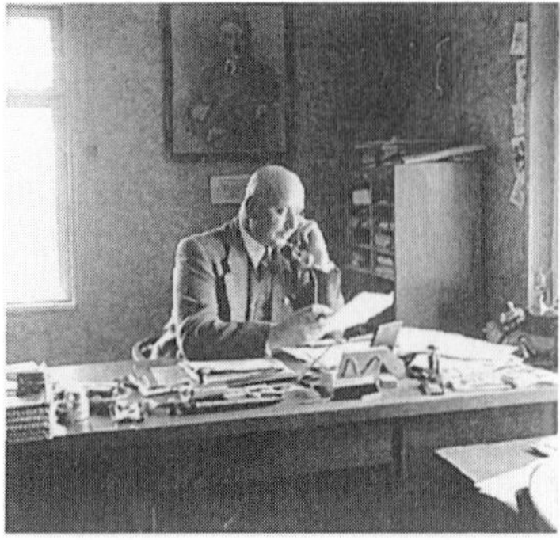

FIGURE 6.1 *Stereoscopy: Otto Schönstein, founder of Raumbild publishers, in his office, in Lorenz (2001, 2).*

Contrary to Crary's opinion stereoscopy did not disappear after 1900. It did not disappear from practices like cartography and surveys measuring the space of territories, changing them into "immutable mobiles" (Latour 1986) like maps, thus preparing them for example for later wars and other forms of domination.[1] In light of this kind of operationalization of space through stereoscopy, it is worth noting that once again it proved widely popular in the Third Reich. The publishing company, Raumbild (i.e. "spatial image"), by Otto Schönstein in Dießen (Bavaria) was founded on January 14, 1935 (see Figure 6.1).[2]

The first issue of the magazine *Das Raumbild* ("The spatial image") was published on January 15, 1935.[3] In the same year, the illustrated book *Venedig—ein Raumerlebnis* (Venice—a spatial experience) with sixty stereo illustrations of the city appeared on the market. The images could be looked at with a stereo viewer added to the book. However, the book did not prove to be an economic success for Otto Schönstein and it would certainly be an overstatement to speak of a stereo boom in the Third Reich.[4] Nevertheless, the publishing company re-energized when Schönstein began doing business with no less a personage than Heinrich Hoffmann, the main journalist commentator of the NSDAP and private photographer of Adolf Hitler.[5] Hoffmann had had the idea to take stereoscopic images of the Olympic games in Berlin in 1936 and to publish a stereoscopic photo album on this basis. It appeared in 1937 (see Figure 6.2).

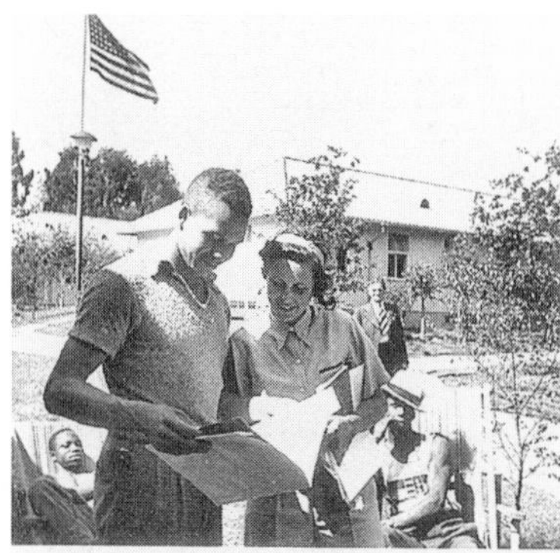
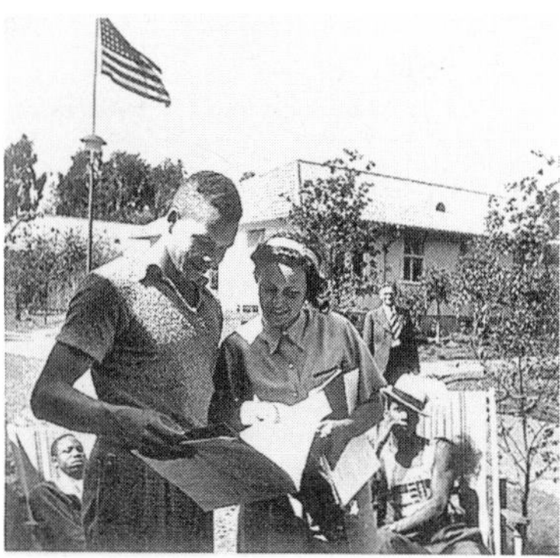

FIGURE 6.2 *Stereoscopy of Leni Riefenstahl while filming the Olympic Games in 1936. Photographer Hugo Jäger, in Lorenz (2001, 35).*

In 1938 the "Reichsstelle zur Förderung des deutschen Schrifttums" (The Reich's Department for the promotion of German literature) published a report that recommended the financial support of the publication of a stereoscopic image album entitled *Deutsche Gaue* (German counties). (See Figure 6.3)

The advantages of stereoscopic images were expressly highlighted in comparison with the two-dimensional image—in particular the three-dimensional appearance of the images. Altogether, twenty-four stereoscopic image albums appeared, often with images solely by Heinrich Hoffmann on subjects like *Reichsparteitag der Ehre; München* (The Reich's party convention of honor; Munich). *Hauptstadt der Bewegung* (Capital of the movement); *Hitler – Mussolini. Der Staatsbesuch des Führers in Italien* (The state visit of the Fuehrer in Italy); *Großdeutschlands Wiedergeburt* (The rebirth of greater Germany); *Die Soldaten des Führers im Felde* (The Fuehrer's soldiers in action) etc. (Lorenz 2001, 52–3; see Figure 6.4).

Incidentally, the *Raumbild* publishing company was also selling an unusual appliance for viewing stereo slides without glasses, the 'photoplasticon.'[6] In all probability this was one of the few cases in history in which an autostereoscopic (cf. Chapter 5) technology for images was sold commercially (at least until the very recent development of autostereoscopic TV sets by Toshiba and other companies). Its principle was that both slides of the stereo-image were projected onto a semi-permeable beam splitter through lenses behind them. In front of the appliance there was a viewing zone within which

Reichsstelle
zur Förderung des deutschen Schrifttums

Berlin C 2, 8. Juni 1938
Oranienburger Str. 79
Fernruf: 42 52 56

Sg.

Gutachten für Verleger

Alfons von C z i b u l k a .

Deutsche Gaue

Raumbild-Verlag Otto Schönstein, Diessen am Ammersee. 1938
29 921

Das Wesentliche an dem Buch sind die Bilder. Grundsätzlich sind nur Raum- (stereoskopische)bilder verwendet. Der beigegebene gute Betrachter ermöglicht es leicht, das Nebeneinander der Flachbilder in das Hintereinander der Wirklichkeit aufzulösen. Ganz zweifellos verdient es das Raumbild, dem Flachbild und dem Film vorgezogen zu werden, es hat den Vorteil der Körperhaftigkeit und ermöglicht eine ruhige Betrachtung. Frühere Raumbilder und ihre Betrachter waren für den Gebrauch in der Schulklasse viel zu gross und umständlich. Die vom Raumbild-Verlag verwendete Grösse erleichtert ganz wesentlich die Benutzung.

Die Ausstattung des Buches ist ausserordentlich zweckentsprechend und gut. Der Text gibt eine knappe, allgemein verständliche Einführung in das Wesen der deutschen Gaue (ohne Österreich). Sehr geschickt ist die räumliche Gliederung: Das Deutschland des frühen Mittelalters, das Gebiet der ersten Eindeutschung, der Ostraum jenseits der Oder. Es liegt hier ein Werk vor, das uneingeschränkte Empfehlung und weitgehende Förderung verdient.

F.d.R.
i.A.

REICHSSTELLE ZUR FÖRDERUNG DES DEUTSCHEN SCHRIFTTUMS

Dieses Gutachten ist bei Veröffentlichung seitens des Verlages mit einer Gebühr in Höhe des fünffachen Ladenpreises des gebundenen Buches verknüpft. Auslassungen, Zusätze und Abänderungen sind nicht gestattet. Bei Veröffentlichung ist das Datum des Gutachtens anzuführen.

FIGURE 6.3 *Report of the "Reichsstelle zur Förderung des deutschen Schrifttums" of June 8, 1938 on the support of the stereoscopic image album Deutsche Gaue, in Lorenz (2001, 4).*

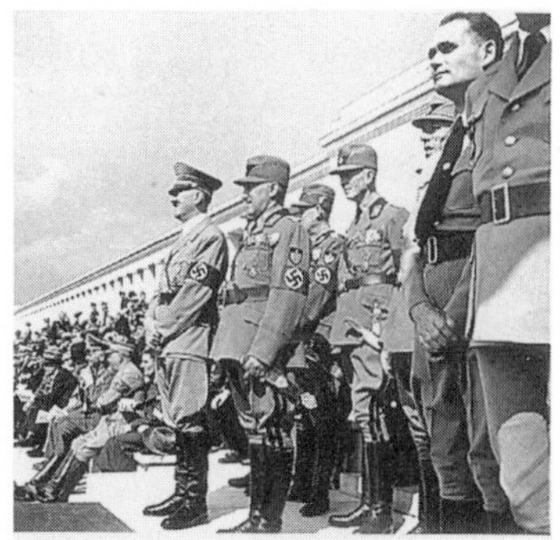
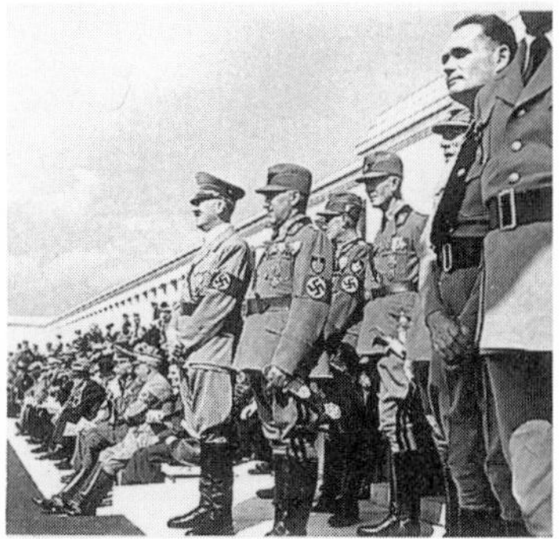

FIGURE 6.4 *Stereoscopic image of the Reichsparteitag NSDAP in Nuremberg in 1937. Photographer Hugo Jäger, in Lorenz (2001, 33).*

the image rays focused on the right and left eyes could be viewed, thereby creating a spatial impression. (See Figures 6.5 and 6.6.)

Heinrich Hoffmann soon became a partner in the publishing company. But the relationship between Schönstein and Hoffmann was hardly tension-free. Already beginning in 1937, Hoffmann demanded that Schönstein should withdraw to a subordinate, more technical position, but the real conflict emerged when Hoffmann advanced from a silent partnership to managing director in 1939. Schönstein could not do anything against it because of Hoffmann's prominent position. This was also the year in which the July edition

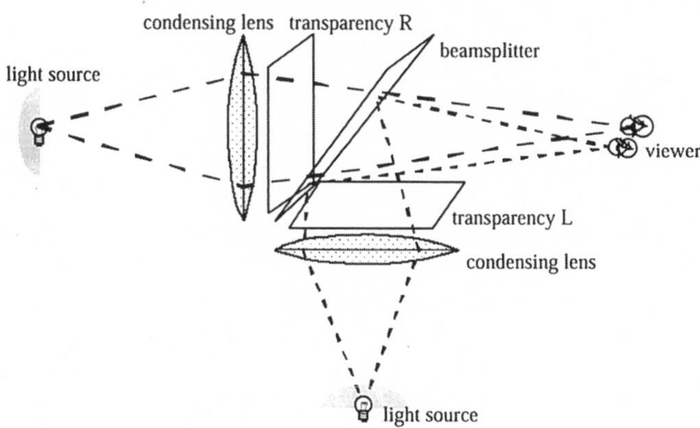

FIGURE 6.5 *Technique of the Photoplasticon, in Benton et al. (1999, 2).*

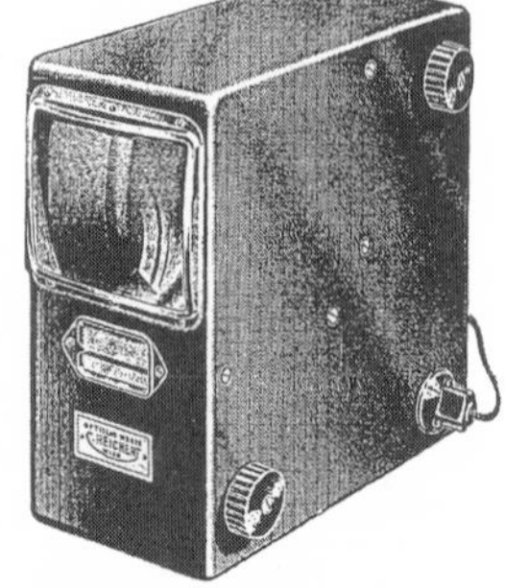

FIGURE 6.6 *Advertising for the Photoplasticon, in Benton (2001a, 235).*

of the publication contained an article entitled "The Fuehrer visits the Raumbild-Verlag" (cf. Gern 1939), a visit that took place on July 1, 1939 on the occasion of the centenary celebrations of the invention of photography. It was underlined

> to what extent the Fuehrer was personally interested in the work of the company. . . . Professor Heinrich Hoffmann had at one point been commissioned by him to pay particular attention to this branch of modern photojournalism. (Gern 1939, 145)

Hitler supposedly said during his visit: "I am convinced that stereoscopic artworks will have a great future" (Gern 1939, 146). Some of the stereoscopic albums were examined by the Führer:

> His hands held the viewer and picked ten individual ones from the many images, but his eyes, knowing the experience of space as one of the finest feelings, were closely scrutinizing the works. (Gern 1939, 147–8; see Figure 6.7)

And finally we find some concluding remarks on the 'Raumbild'—i.e. the transplane image of stereoscopy:

> Regarding international photography we can talk here of a typically German style of presentation that does not settle for recording space on mere aesthetic grounds; instead it searches within the spatial image for a powerful message in the first place, its most distinguished task to highlight the nature of the spatial experience and its inner dynamics. The publisher and its friends consider it their new mission to pave the way for this task. In

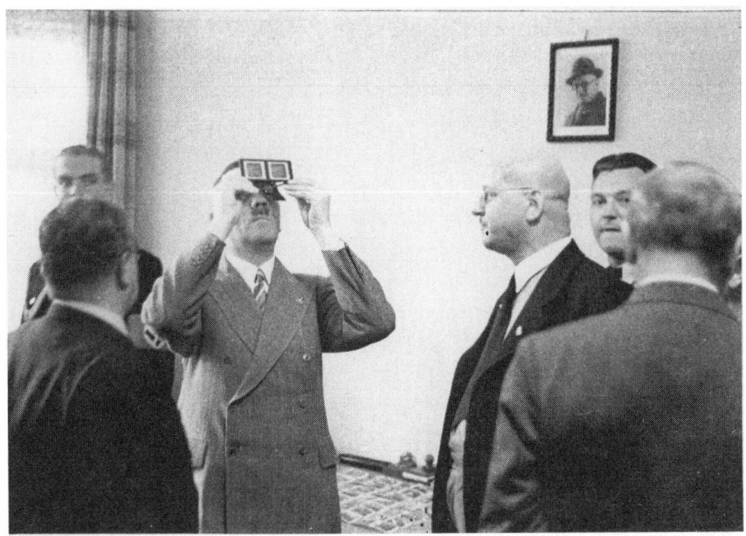

FIGURE 6.7 *Hitler viewing images through a stereo viewer, one section can be found in Gern (1939, 147). The whole image can be seen here; Heinrich Hoffmann at the left foreground (viewed from behind), and to Hitler's l;eft the baldheaded Otto Schönstein. Source: Bayerische Staatsbibliothek München/Fotoarchiv Hoffmann (Image No. hoff-26107). With my thanks to Angelika Betz.*

> order to fulfill this mission it will be necessary that additional forces take part in these works so that the stereoscopic artworks will do justice to the conviction of the Führer and accomplish what it has begun: a documentation of German magnitude and German culture. (Gern 1939, 148–9)

In calling the 'experience of space one of the finest feelings' and the fabrication and distribution of stereoscopic views for highlighting the 'nature of spatial experience' 'the most distinguished task', the question arises as to how the relationship between the spatial image of stereoscopy and the discourse on space in National Socialism can be described, especially given the fact that this question was not asked before in the literature on the Schönstein publishing company (however little even existed).[7] It is actually remarkable that National Socialism does not appear in Lefebvre's above-mentioned thoughts on the production of space (cf. section 1.4), since it was in the National Socialist ideology that the central role that space had already played semantically since the end of the nineteenth century in germanophone countries culminated. And most notably so when we begin to realize that this emphasis on space had very concrete results. Since, allegedly, the German people were a "people without space,"[8] National Socialism felt entitled to lead a war of aggression and of extermination against Eastern Europe and the USSR.

One cannot say that stereoscopy was a *critical* factor regarding the "cult of space" (Köster 2002, 12). But after WWII Gerhard Storz illustrated the "bad and dreadful magic" (quoted in Köster 2002, 7) that this phrase had had. Thus, space was so prevailing a term that the expression 'spatial image' cannot have remained neutral and unloaded. My assumption is that the NSDAP's support for the *spatial image* was indeed fueled by the prevalent ideology of space. The Raumbild publishing company after all was classified a *Wehrwirtschaftsbetrieb*, a company to assist the war economy, and some of its employees were categorized as 'indispensable,' i.e. they were deferred from military service and did not have to fight in the war. When shortly afterwards Munich was increasingly bombarded, the publishing company was even classified as strategically important.

In the editorial of *Das Raumbild* from December 15, 1936, the 'cult of space' and stereoscopy were explicitly connected to each other:

> Despite all individual interests and individual studies of stereoscopy one should not forget one thing, namely the present sense of space and the attitudes towards it. The formation of space is a formation of life. Questions of space are questions of fate. Today, this becomes more and more visible in Germany. Spatial arrangements for the development of economy and defense; illustrative [anschauliche] spatial concepts regarding political history and cultural philosophy; new attitudes regarding space and its structuring in the arts and architecture; aspirations regarding spatial films [!][9]; the conquest of space in sports and technology . . . It is not a coincidence that the idea of and research in the spatial image finds support from governmental agencies.

To use Goebbels' words—it became a program of public enlightenment: "It is the highest aim of this publication to reawaken the correct way of viewing space, to inspire the experience of space, to deepen the knowledge of space and to enable a new attitude towards space, which is the basis for the political, technical, and artistic creation of space."[10]

It could hardly be said more clearly that the transplane image of stereoscopy is to be taken over in order to create new attitudes towards space. Numerous articles in *Das Raumbild* repeatedly underlined the role played by the viewing of transplane images for the correct attitude towards space[11] and for the experience of immediate clarity ("Anschaulichkeit").[12]

Media aesthetics of the transplane image turn into politics insofar as the "ideologically dominant horizon of the significance" of space "can also be found in the aesthetic discourse . . . of art criticism."[13] I would like to underline to what extent the transplane character of stereoscopy was ideologically filled with only one, although very exemplary, case in point.

As a prototypical example a Raumbild-album from 1942 entitled *Deutsche Plastik unserer Zeit* (German sculpture of our time) stands out. It contains 135 stereo images of 'German'—i.e. conforming to NS-ideology (Breker, Thorak etc.)[14]—sculptures and statuary art and a respective stereo viewer made of solid metal including a compact user's manual (see Figure 6.8 and Figure 6.9).

The volume is a good example because first of all it connects back to Brewster's stereoscopic reproduction of sculptures, clearly showing that these attempts have not disappeared at the end of

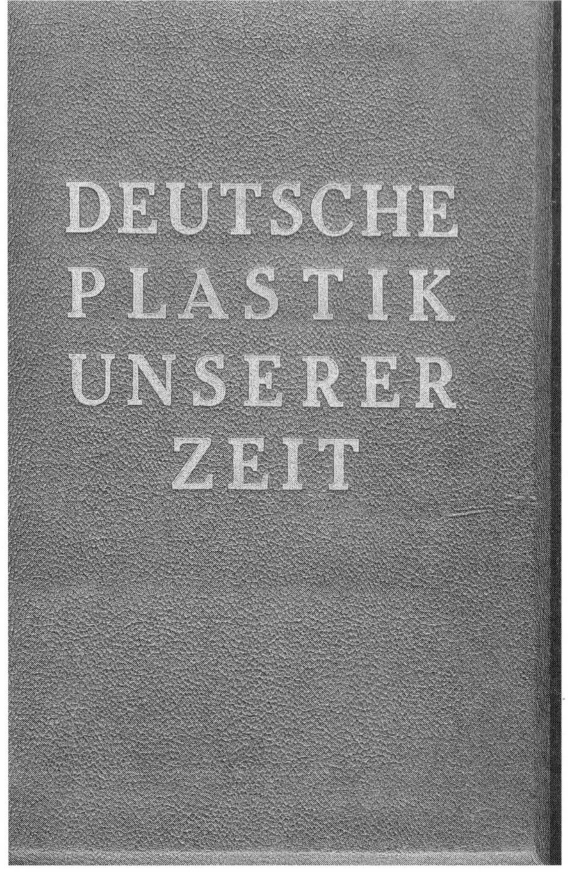

FIGURE 6.8 *Cover of* Deutsche Plastik unserer Zeit, *Tank (1942).*

the nineteenth century. Apart from this, it contains texts that connect sculptures with spatial images. I will briefly read these texts in order to show that in the aesthetic discourse and in art criticism as well, one can—not surprisingly—find National Socialist ideology concerning space and in what way these were related to the stereoscopic image.

Another example of the evidence for the surprising attention that was given to the three-dimensional image, at least by some of the higher functionaries of the Third Reich, is the foreword of the volume by none less than the *Reichsminister*, Albert Speer. A stereoscopic reproduction of Breker's sculptures in front of the

Neue Reichskanzlei designed by Speer can also be found in this volume (see Figure 6.10).

Speer writes:

> The artist today speaks intuitively through his work. He does not ponder his creation; he does not torment himself searching for reflective phrases about what he feels compelled to create artistically from an inner mandate. This means that his works also do not contain the brooding and tormented character of the arts in recent times. Art today has found its way back to classical simplicity and naturalness and therefore back to truth and beauty. Thus, and in order to let all fellow Germans actively participate in this art, no difficult words of explanation are necessary. The immediate clarity [Anschaulichkeit] of artistic works is always more important than any explanatory word. The new stereoscopic presentation will contribute in a magnificent way to allow the individual to understand and comprehend and therefore to appreciate the sculptures. (Albert Speer in Tank 1942, 5)

Clearly, elements of a National Socialist discourse are revealed here. Initially 'pondering' and 'reflective phrases' are rejected and instead an 'intuitive' process is welcomed. Unlike 'tormented' art, 'German' art is 'natural.' As compared to reflection, a spontaneous, almost mystically operating process of perception generated from an 'inner mandate' is being privileged. The same goes for the pedagogical task of the book. Instead of 'difficult words of explanation' and 'explanatory words' (it is actually strange that there are any explanatory texts in the book at all), it is the 'immediate clarity'[15] of the artwork that is frequently invoked, which is supposed to impart what it means to 'grasp'[16] the 'truth' and 'beauty' of sculpture to 'all fellow Germans.' This is where the transplane image of stereoscopy has found its place. It is able to convey the spatial structure of sculpture and thus the heroic self-image of the regime in a seemingly 'unmediated' way.[17] By way of its paradoxical unmediated mediation, stereoscopy permits forming the mythical "fellowship of Germans" (*Volksgemeinschaft*) within the scope of the visual. Since there appears to be no mediation, no differing readings can ensue that might be a result of a different level of education, regardless of any class variations, and due to the workings of this clarity, it seems as if all educational differences tend to be transcended. And this mystical union between viewer and image is equivalent to the

Bitte zuerst zu lesen!

Gebrauchsanweisung

für die Benützung des Raumbildbetrachters 6:13 cm · DRGM

Jedem Raumbildwerk DRGM liegt in dem Aufbewahrungsfach im Vorderdeckel eines jeden Werkes ein **zusammenschiebbarer** Raumbildbetrachter zum Betrachten der Raumbilder (Stereobilder) im Format 6:13 cm bei. Er besteht aus

1. der Brille (Vorderteil), 2. dem Bildhalter (Hinterteil).

Wie nimmt man den Raumbildbetrachter aus dem Aufbewahrungsfach heraus?

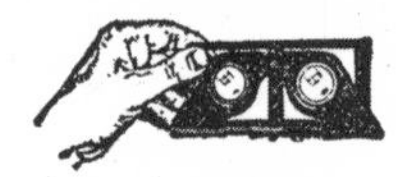

Abb. 1

Die **linke** Hand legt

1. den **Daumen** in die Nasenwölbung des Raumbildbetrachters,
2. den **Mittelfinger** in die Ausbuchtung des Aufbewahrungsfaches und hebt Raumbildbetrachter etwas hoch und zieht ihn nach links heraus.

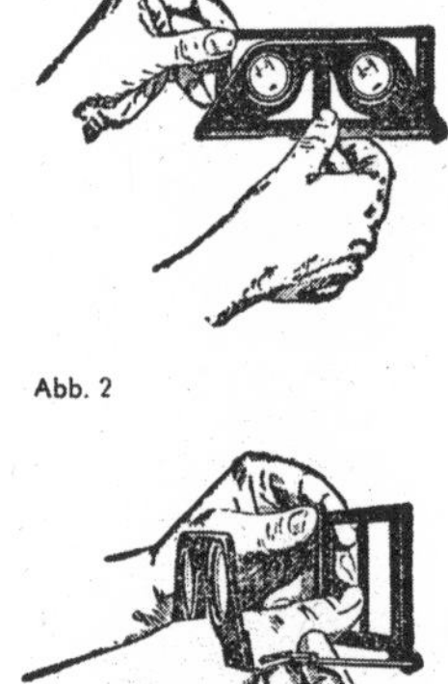

Abb. 2

Abb. 3

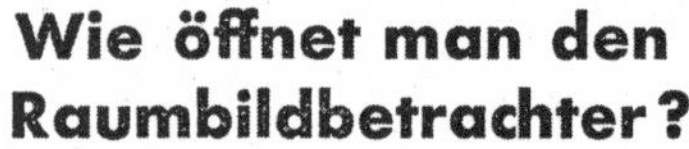

Wie öffnet man den Raumbildbetrachter?

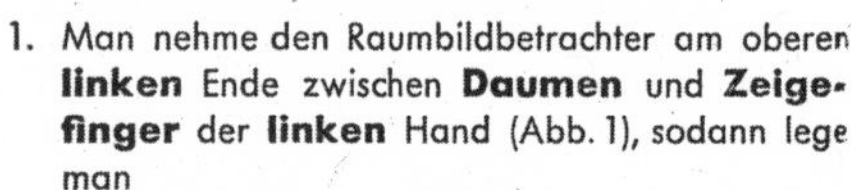

1. Man nehme den Raumbildbetrachter am oberen **linken** Ende zwischen **Daumen** und **Zeigefinger** der **linken** Hand (Abb. 1), sodann lege man
2. den **Daumen** der **rechten** Hand zwischen die Nasenwölbung der Brille an den Steg des Bildhalters (Abb. 2) und schiebe
3. sodann mit dem **Zeigefinger** der **rechten** Hand die zusammengeschobenen Brillenspreizen (unterhalb des Bildhalters sichtbar) durch einen leichten Druck solange nach vorn, bis der Raumbildbetrachter vollkommen geöffnet ist. Ein Zerren und Reißen ist unbedingt zu vermeiden (Abb. 3).

Wenden!

FIGURE 6.9 *User's Manual for the Use of the Stereo viewer (a) Front and (b) Back Cover. Supplement to Tank (1942).*

Wie betrachtet man die Raumbilder durch den Raumbildbetrachter?

1. Die Raumbilder (Stereobilder) schiebe man so in den Bildhalter (das ist der hintere Teil des Raumbildbetrachters) ein, daß diese mit ihrer **Unterkante** am Bildhalter **gut** und **gerade** aufliegen.
2. Den Raumbildbetrachter führe man so vor die Augen, als würde man eine Brille aufsetzen. – Wer Augengläser trägt, soll, **ohne diese abzunehmen,** durch den Raumbildbetrachter sehen.
3. Mit beiden Augen ruhig durch den Raumbildbetrachter sehen und sich auf eine markante Stelle des Bildes konzentrieren. Die beiden Bilder des Raumbildes müssen alsdann als ein einziges **plastisches** Gesamtbild erscheinen.
4. Wer nicht sofort das volle plastische Bild erreicht, kann durch Verschieben der Brillenspreizen die für seine Sehschärfe notwendige Entfernung einstellen.
5. Um den vollen Genuß des Raumbildes zu erreichen, läßt man das Licht **von vorne schattenlos** auf das Raumbild fallen. Je stärker das Licht auf das Raumbild fällt, desto schöner die Plastik.
6. Beim Betrachten der in einzelnen Büchern **festgeklebten** Raumbilder richtet man zuerst den Raumbildbetrachter auf die entsprechende Entfernung ein, sodann stellt man ihn so auf das zu betrachtende Raumbild, daß die beiden Bildhälften desselben im Rahmen des Raumbildbetrachters erscheinen. Hierbei läßt man wiederum das Licht **schattenlos** auf das Bild fallen.

Raumbild-Verlag
Otto Schönstein
K.-G.
München 23

FIGURE 6.9 (*Continued.*)

mystical union between the fellowship of all Germans with their Führer. In 1937 a certain Carl Thinius had already written down similar thoughts: "With the introduction of stereoscopy . . . and through its optical three-dimensional influence it might be possible to knock all great and powerful matters into the heads of our people" (Thinius 1937, 42).

In his "Introduction to Contemporary Sculpture" by *Ministerialrat* Wilfrid [*sic*] Bade that follows Speer's preface, Bade wants to shed a light on "our contemporary understanding—not only of the essence of sculpture" (Tank 1942, 9). He starts out with a praise of the Raumbild album, saying: "It is quite simply not only the first of

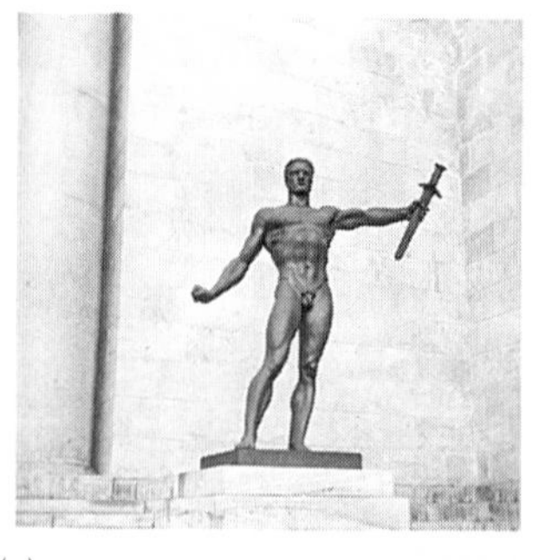

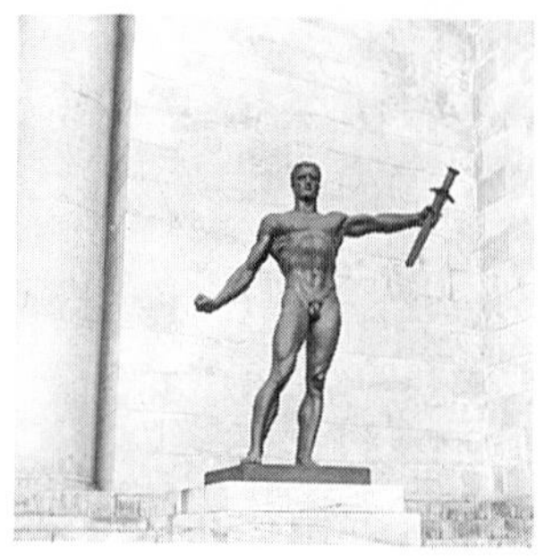

(a)

„DEUTSCHE PLASTIK UNSERER ZEIT"

Bild-Nr. 118

« Wehrmacht » Monumentalplastik im Ehrenhof der Neuen Reichskanzlei in Berlin.
BILDHAUER ARNO BREKER.

Aufnahme : E. Schlumberger, Berlin.

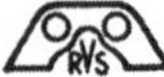

Raumbild-Verlag Otto Schönstein K. G., München 23
Alle Rechte vorbehalten

PI 16492 Pa

(b)

FIGURE 6.10 Stereoscopic image: *(a) Arno Breker's sculpture* Die Wehrmacht *in front of the former* Neue Reichskanzlei *(Architect Albert Speer) in Berlin; and (b) view of the back of the stereoscopic picture.*

its kind in the realm of representing sculptural art; it is the only one at all that can claim to represent sculpture correctly—namely three-dimensionally. Therefore, this work stands at the entryway to a new era in representing sculptural art."[18] A statement follows that is hardly surprising:

> The fact that [this book] appears at a time when sculpture is rightfully seen again as the essential expression of its spirit, its sentiments and its strengths prove that the technical means emerge whenever the times need and demand them. An era that does not experience space and form in the same way as ours does and that does not understand the expressive element that is

> suitable for it will not feel the critical lack that is felt when three-dimensional art can only be seen represented in a two-dimensional way. (Bade in Tank 1942, 9)

Initially, then, the author is suggesting that sculpture is the appropriate expression of the 'times,' i.e. those of National Socialist Germany.[19] Together with this central role of sculpture, the 'spatial image' is also assigned a central function. Bade very openly admits that it is especially due to the orientation to space in the National Socialist era that the planocentric projection of spatial objects onto the plane is perceived as lacking.[20] The author also suggests the same thing in the sentence that "the technical means emerge whenever the times need and demand them." He obviously maintains that National Socialism demanded and needed transplane images. It would be wrong, of course, to claim that National Socialism had invented the transplane image of stereoscopy, but stereoscopy can obviously be exceedingly well connected to the National Socialist discourse and its purposeful and deliberate use of space. In this respect this passage of the text is revealing since it shows to what extent technical elements have to be relatable to semantic elements in order to be potentially implemented. As soon as there is a 'cult of space' then the positive assessment and the financial support for 'spatial images' is not quite so far fetched. This meant that stereoscopy, which had no central place in public and was used mainly in scientific and military applications,[21] could once again be promoted and supported by government agencies.[22] "It is our time in particular that demands the spatial image! . . . These times demand the spatial image" (Lüscher 1936, 43). The central role played by sculpture in National Socialism mentioned by Bade continues in the same vein: architecture, sculpture and drama for him are the oldest and most important ways of expression as long as they present "a new and objective reality" (Bade in Tank 1942, 10). With this he refers to the observation that in almost all creation myths "God as a sculptor or carver has created humans in his own image." As an analogy to this, "human creativity" becomes visible "most evidently in sculpture." He continues maintaining—a claim which cannot be fit easily in agreement with the historical facts, at least not in the way in which they present themselves today—that only after the most ancient arts that created reality, those arts emerged that 'praise reality,' namely those of 'representation' like painting, epic writings and dance. According to Bade those arts that 'herald essences,' namely music, poetry and historiography appear last. In principle, here the author follows a Hegelian teleology. In his lectures on *Aesthetics* published for the first time in 1835, Hegel develops a history of art as a sequence of de-materializing, temporalizing and spiritualizing steps correlated to respective steps of civilization (or to be more exact: steps of the objectivation of the world spirit). Here, sculpture corresponds to the unfolding of ideal beauty in antique Greece.[23] Bade invokes this topos in his work *Deutsche Plastik unserer Zeit* as well. Even though his proximity to Hegel cannot be ignored, Bade does not see the highest forms of the spirit in poetry and philosophy.[24] Lastly, his model is less owed to a dialectical unfolding but more so to a morphology of different, relatively unconnected phases à la Spengler. At any rate, for the era of National Socialism the following held true: "Our time commits again to immediate creativity. Therefore, it perceives sculpture, architecture and drama as those forms of expression that characterize it best" (Bade in Tank 1942, 11). After a short digression on the question to what extent the sculpture of National Socialism is an art equivalent to and a 'soul mate' of the art of antiquity, Bade comes back to the subject of space:

> The basic experience of creativity is space and therefore form. . . . Space is the only thing that really exists. . . . By capturing movement in such a way that it remains recognizable—i.e., by representing the calm but not the stagnation—sculpture (and in its culmination architecture) is the most perfect element of existence altogether. (Tank 1942, 13)

After having made it clear again that sculpture (and architecture) are the most important of the arts in the National Socialist art system, the text inevitably mentions a problem that today might perhaps be counted as representational intermediality (see Schröter 2012):

> Every sculpture and every building by their very nature elude being represented in any other form of art that lacks spatiality. . . . Every two-dimensional representation, whether it is a drawing, a painting or a photograph deprives the sculpture or the building of precisely that, which is its essential being . . . It is for this

> reason that it has not yet been possible to view Greece's sculpture and architecture anywhere else but at their original places. (Bade in Tank 1942, 14)

Therefore it stands to reason that now the author once again invokes the transplane image of stereoscopy:

> Only this possibility [i.e. stereoscopy] has created the prerequisite that allows every person to experience sculpture in any possible place in a truly three-dimensional way. Only now the great works of the past or the present, no matter where they are located, can be represented as they really are. With the spatial image we have this possibility at our disposal. (Bade in Tank 1942, 14–15)

Thus the circle closes. In an odd way, amazingly resembling Benjamin's ideas, the three-dimensional image permits making the spatial impression *reproducible*; thereby, according to National Socialist ideology, enabling every viewer to experience the most perfect of sculptural art. Sculpture and spatial image are connected in an intermedial ensemble aiming at conveying the correct 'spatial attitude' by way of 'immediate clarity.'[25]

With the end of National Socialism in 1945 the 'cult of space' found its end as well. Otto Schönstein's publishing company—that in 1942 had been moved to Oberaudorf/Inn after it had been declared a strategically important company—unsuccessfully attempted to become established again after 1945 (for details see Lorenz 2001, 5–7). Stereoscopy played a role appropriate for the new times as a US technology named Viewmaster; its great advantage was that it was based on color film that had just been invented and therefore was able to add the dimension of color to the illusion of spatiality. It had originally been intended as an educational tool for the military but ultimately it was mostly used for children's entertainment:

> Initially it was intended that the View-Master be an educational tool, primarily aimed at adults, but as time developed the appeal of the View-Master soon spread to other areas, one of the more notable being children's entertainment. The US Military were keen advocates of the View-Master and had specially commissioned sets of reels produced to aid with artillery spotting

> and aircraft identification during World War II. They purchased many millions of reels for this purpose, together with 10s of thousands of Model B viewers.[26]

In the 1950s the Viewmaster and a few movies precipitated another short-lived 3D boom, mainly in the US (cf. Hayes 1989); afterwards, however, stereoscopy disappeared from the public and was used only in some special applications in the natural sciences and in playrooms.[27] The production of space was no longer a core value of the state or a central ideological term as it had been in the Third Reich, and Otto Schönstein passed away in 1958.[28]

By way of an epilogue, the alliance of stereoscopy and space in WW II had another, quite different connotation: "All photographs from the airplanes of our *Wehrmacht* are being taken as stereoscopic views" (Lüscher 1936, 43). This was true for the allied forces as well.[29] With the help of stereoscopic images, high and low mountains and valleys became distinguishable even from great heights and therefore the embattled terrain could be better understood. The spatial impression from great heights can only be accomplished by widening the distance of the eyes between the two stereo images so that slightly hyperstereoscopic effects appear in which the differences in height have a strongly exaggerated effect.[30]

Summing up, I would like to mention one after-effect of this history in the artistic realm. The well-known German photographer Thomas Ruff had taken a series of stereoscopic images that were aimed at such effects between 1994 and 1996 (some even a little later).

> With stereoscopic photography, it's obvious that our perception has less to do with what we see than with what our brain does with that information. If you look at the two flat images, nothing much happens; but look at them at just the right angle and the images become one – and it's three-dimensional. We may look with our eyes, but our brain constructs the images. My idea was to make these 3-D interiors look even more artificial by altering the distance between the stereoscopic camera's lenses, which are normally set apart about the same distance as a person's eyes. To take stereo h.t.b. 06, 2000 [the title of a particular work] . . . I used two cameras set about ten inches apart, which creates a perceptual transformation: The viewer becomes a twelve-foot-tall giant peering into a dollhouse-size interior. (Quoted in Jones 2001)

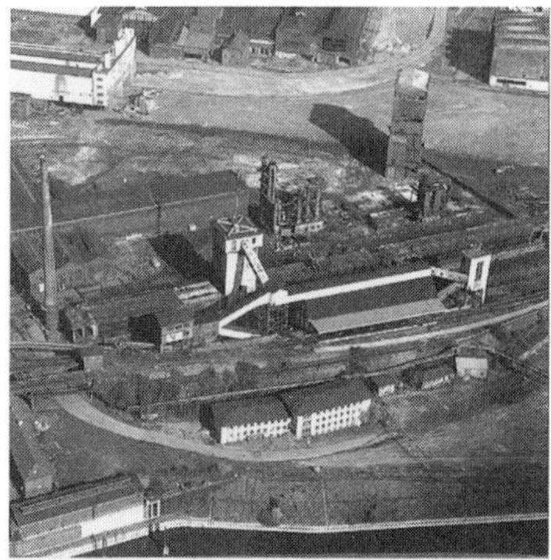
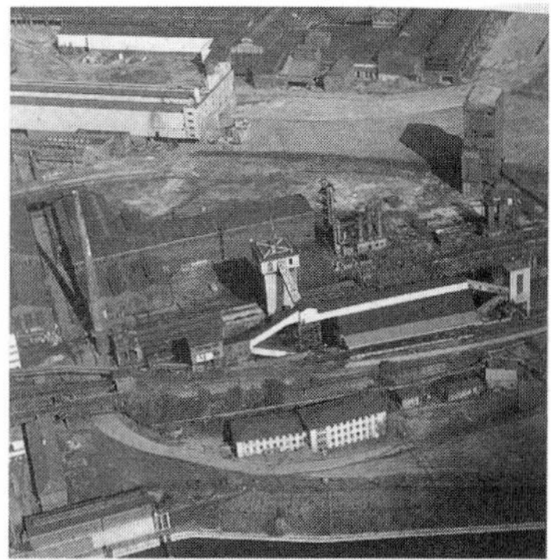

FIGURE 6.11 *Thomas Ruff,* Ruhrgebiet I *(1996), in Bätzner, Nekes and Schmidt (2008: 142)*

In one set of Ruff's works, the stereoscopic pair of images is presented in a case, the two images guided towards the eyes of the viewers by way of mirrors placed between them (almost as in Wheatstone's very first stereoscope). When looking into the mirrors from above, views of a town become visible as three-dimensional miniatures; one believes it is possible to break the little skyscrapers apart with one finger (see Figure 6.11).[31]

A commentator remarks on *Ruhrgebiet I* (1996): "The industrial facility in *Ruhrgebiet I, 1996* presents itself as open, freely explorable and unprotected to the view from above, thereby the thematic, structural and technical characteristics connect the image with military reconnaissance images" (Urban 2000, 112).

And indeed, the *Ruhrgebiet*[32] was one of the most heavily bombed areas in the Third Reich by the allied forces. The spatial image that had been hyped (at least by some National Socialists) into a school for a "Faustian attitude towards space" returned with devastating ferociousness. Ruff is quoting the stereoscopic view of aerial reconnaissance that spies on industrial facilities, which are later destroyed if necessary. His aesthetics of the stereoscopic image include invoking stereoscopy as the technique of operationalizing spatial control as it is encoded in its history. Even though it has emerged from analyzing human vision—i.e. from the series of physiological optics—hyperstereoscopy in the first place shifts the scale of the human. In Ruff's work the viewers appear gigantic in comparison with the architecture. Secondly, the technologies that emerged from the research done on human vision can be used in order to destroy human lives. With these references, Ruff is quite decidedly breaking away from his teachers, the Bechers.[33] They repeatedly photographed isolated industrial plants (also from the Ruhr district) from various set points of view, arranging them and their 'execution' into serial typologies. *On the one hand* they quasi-archeologically documented the individual facilities for posterity, while *on the other hand* they created trans-individual morphologies by isolating the individual buildings and simultaneously serializing them. It is this latter operation that notably foregrounds the "sculptural characteristics" (Winter 1999, 21) of the industrial facilities and therefore it is not surprising that in 1969 the title of a Becher exhibition was *Anonyme Skulpturen*. Ruff, in contrast, does not record individual parts of the facility for archival or formal reasons. He shows the spatial location of the plants. They are not isolated; they remain locally situated—and thus also historically. This localization is underlined by spatializing the image so that an overview is created that at the same time puts the viewer into the position of an 'oversubject' who believes he or she could, as I have previously mentioned, smash the rendered architecture with the wave of a finger; the annihilating power of the stereoscopically armed military perspective can be experienced. Ruff thus makes his subject that which the Bechers had been opposed to with their gigantic work of archiving: i.e. those destructive powers that annihilate industrial facilities (and human beings who in most cases see with two eyes, i.e. binocularly), thereby erasing them from history. Buchloh underlines the "archival structure" of the Bechers' works. He strongly criticizes their attempt to connect to the "New Objectivity" of the Weimar Republic by underlining their craftsmanship. Despite the "visible desire of the Bechers to function within a historically neutral and geopolitically objective historical realm (the area of objective, universally valid conditions of industrial production), their work is ultimately situated in a historically highly charged sphere." Buchloh especially underlines the "share (of responsibility) . . . that industrial production . . . in the world-historical catastrophe of German fascism" had (Buchloh 1998, 56–7). In his eyes, the Bechers repress what in my eyes Ruff evokes in his stereoscopic views of the Ruhr district.

Notes

1 See in general Pulfrich (1923); Gierloff-Emden (1957) and Burkhardt (1989).

2 See for the following Lorenz 2001. According to Stenger (1958, 199) the translation of the notion 'stereoscopy' into the German term 'Raumbild' supposedly happened in WW I (on the utilization of stereoscopy during this war see Seiling 1935 and for the French side Goussot 1923, 35–6). The term, however, can already be found in the German version of Helmholtz (1985) from 1867.

3 The publication appeared from 1935 to September 1939. From January 1939 onward, after Heinrich Hoffmann had seized power of the publishing house and had replaced Otto Schönstein as publisher (see below), the publication changed its title from *Das Raumbild. Monatszeitschrift für die gesamte Stereoskopie und ihre Grenzgebiete* to *Das Raumbild. Stereoskopisches Magazin für Zeit und Raum*. On the background of this see also Lorenz (1983, 214).

4 As Barsy (1943, 5) wrote: "It is all the more strange that today we have reached the lowest point in the use of stereoscopy."

5 On Hoffmann see Herz (1994).

6 See the patent by Mahler (2001); see also Mahler (1954).

7 Apart from Lorenz (1983; 2001) see only Ryder (1988; 1990). See lately Fitzner (2008) who independently arrived at similar conclusions to mine.

8 See the detailed study by Wagner (1992) for this syntagma, which was coined in Hans Grimm's novel of the same title in 1926 and which subsequently became highly influential. See also Lattmann (1969) and Zimmermann (1976).

9 See Hesse (1939) for a contemporary example of the attempts made at creating spatial films—interestingly enough on the basis of the parallax barrier or integral photography.

10 Editorial (1936, 266). Various essays in *Raumbild* attempted to inspire the advertisement for stereoscopy; see Anonymous (1935).

11 Schoepf (1937, 5) for example muses on the "education regarding imagining and perceiving space." Laber (1937, 22) in an article entitled "Books that make you experience space," writes: "Schönstein's work means nothing less than educating our generation that was used to seeing two-dimensionally into perceiving spatial images, three-dimensionally: this is a re-education that will certainly awaken a lot of creative power." According to the author, this will be

necessary "because we modern people who are used to thinking in concepts have forgotten that all real understanding has to start with viewing." Hansen (1937) discusses the role of stereoscopy serving the people's education which was again enhanced by Kahlau (1936, 218) with the following statement: "With a clear view to the importance that the spatial image has for politically educating youth towards a National Socialist world view, the *Reichsbildberichterstatter* [editor-at-large for photography of the Reich] of the NSDAP, Mr. Heinrich Hoffmann, will take care of the field of stereoscopy in close connection with the *Raumbild* publishing company. This move of our greatest political photographer is fundamentally symptomatic. Mr. Hoffmann unequivocally displays the extent of our state's and its leaders' consistent activities when purposefully recruiting even a seemingly unimportant medium like the spatial image for the great historical task of educating our people as pillars of the Third Reich." See also Wallburger (1937) and Thinius (1937).

12 'Immediate clarity' (Anschaulichkeit) was a positive criterion for the NS-ideology. It was, for example, mobilized in 'German physics' against the 'abstract Jewish' physics; see Richter (1980, 119 and 124–5). See also Tank (1935b, 11) on the question how "the spatial image allows for a vivid comparison of things."

13 Köster (2002, 11). Unfortunately he does not pursue this question any further. It is quite striking that Jantzen (1938) asks the question about the concept of space in art history in Munich precisely in 1938.

14 The extensive discussions on National Socialist sculpture cannot and will not be presented here. See among others Bussmann (1974); Damus (1981, especially 13–21 and 51–61); Bushart (1983); Adam (1992, 175–205).

15 See also Metzner (1936, 169): "There can be no doubt about it today that it is indeed visual perception that is the foundation on which every successful instruction has to be and can only be built."

16 See Schnapka (1936, 49): "What a joy and what enthusiasm erupts from the viewing of a stereoscopic view [Raumbild]. Why, that is fabulous, everything is within one's grasp!"

17 Although the image space of stereoscopy looks strangely like a stage setting (in which the characters look like cardboard cutouts and the space between them is eerily empty; see for example Figure 6.4 in stereoscopic view) it is emphasized repeatedly that "only the spatial image that is taken with two lenses is capable of revealing what is visible on land and sea one hundred percent true to nature" (Stanke 1938, 21).

18 Wilfrid [*sic*] Bade in Tank (1942, 9). On the role of photographic representation of sculpture in National Socialism see also Bressa (2001, 231–47).

19 See Damus (1981, 55) on the fact that following architecture, sculpture had the second highest rank in the aesthetic discourse of National Socialism. See also Adam (1992, 172).

20 It is noteworthy to what extent opinions changed since the days of Hildebrand and Wölfflin (see Chapter 2). They had still followed a planocentric conception of sculpture and in particular Hildebrand (1907, 96) had continued to deplore the "disturbing problem of cubic form," especially in free-standing sculptures (see Glaubitz and Schröter 2004, 44–50). In comparison—and strangely enough—the three-dimensionality of sculpture (or the sculpturality of sculpture) in National Socialism can be found in the tradition of such authors as Carl Einstein and Daniel Henry Kahnweiler (see Glaubitz and Schröter, 2004, 56–9; on Einstein see also Zeidler 2004), who should rather be grouped with classical modernism. To a certain extent the problem of the spatiality of sculpture (and thus also of the 'spatial image' i.e. the 'Raumbild') brings to light uncanny connections between the classical avant-garde and National Socialism; on the 'aesthetic mentality of modernism' and the connections between avant-garde and totalitarianism see Wyss (1996).

21 It is maybe not by accident that stereoscopy already appears around 1929 in Ernst Jünger's work; see Prümm (2004, 356): "With stereoscopy, an optical installation from the nineteenth century through which the illusion of photographic representation was considerably augmented, Jünger [in 1929] models his theory of perception in *Das abenteuerliche Herz* [The adventurous heart] which he then elevates into the fundamental principle of his poetics."

22 See Aufschnaiter (1935, 78): "It is hardly an accident that this broad subject of the spatial image . . . has been somewhat forgotten in the last twenty to thirty years since nothing has proven to be as expressive and capable of development for the dynamics and upheavals of the last twenty years as the planar image, the 35mm film, the snapshot and the movies." The author suggests that the planar image is relatable to the turbulent times of the Weimar Republic that was condemned by the National Socialists. See in a similar way Tank (1935b, 8–9), who underlines that "from the world image of an era" one can "surmise its perception of space with no great effort." Subsequently to this "theory of space", he interprets futurism as an expression of "spatial bedlam" caused by relativism, and he defines relativism unambiguously relating it to the Weimar

Republic: "In the political sphere: atomizing of parties and interests; in the sciences: theory of relativity and analyses of drives; in music: atonality; in writing: the stream-of-consciousness novel; in painting: futurism." In contrast, "youth today" (1935) discovers "a newly structured and ordered, de-complicated world. In this world space is of central significance."

23 On Hegel's theory of sculpture and its placement within his teleological model see Larfouilloux (1999, 249–389).

24 Apart from this his placement of dance and historiography into his quasi-Hegelian scheme is somewhat forced.

25 The short analysis of a different way in which National Socialism functionalized stereoscopy, namely in spatial images of mushrooms, can be found in Schröter (2005b).

26 http://www.viewmaster.co.uk/htm/history.asp [last accessed August 9, 2013]. On the "Viewmaster" see Selle (1952a; 1952b).

27 From the 1960s onward, stereoscopy will return in the head-mounted display as its virtual-optical double; see Chapter 10.

28 His archive of stereoscopic images can be found today in the Deutsches Historisches Museum in Berlin. See Lorenz (2001, 8–10)

29 See for example Katz (1948, 607 in particular) on the USA.

30 See Newhall (1969, 49 and 53). He underlines to what extent the "unrealistically" exaggerated hyperstereoscopic effects of heights and depths were able to furnish the operative knowledge of the spatial structure of the scene. See also Treece (1955).

31 See Helmholtz (1985, 312): through hyperstereoscopic effects "it will seem as if the observer were looking not at the natural landscape itself, but at a very exquisite and exact model of it, reduced in scale."

32 The *Ruhrgebiet* (Ruhr district or region) is the most densely populated and largest urban conglomeration in Germany, the fifth largest in Europe. Thanks to the building of the first German railway in 1787, it slowly developed into a highly industrialized region since the late eighteenth century due to its coal mining and later with the development of heavy industry from the middle of the nineteenth century onward. From WWI to WWII the *Ruhrgebiet* was the location of Germany's weapons industry; after the war all munitions factories were abolished and later, due to economic crises, the steel and coal industry also went into decline. Today, the Ruhrgebiet has shifted to service industries and high technology, regaining its former blooming landscapes and reducing air and land pollution to a minimum. [Translators' note]

33 Bernd and Hilla Becher, a married couple, were German photographers working together mainly in the 1960s and 1970s. They are best known for their series of photographs on industrial buildings as well as typologies of half-timbered houses. [Translators' note]

CHAPTER SEVEN

1918–1935: Marcel Duchamp: From projection to rotorelief

Media Aesthetics of the Transplane Image 5

It can be the case that an image does not conflict visually with anything (e.g., a stereoscopic image), that nothing is there in visual perception that either inclines one against it or inclines one in favor of it. But is this a meaningful possibility?

EDMUND HUSSERL (2005, 444)

This chapter will deal with some of the works by Marcel Duchamp. Even though his works were repeatedly connected with the knowledge of optics,[1] the complex constellation of modernity regarding optical media (e.g. the layering of four optical series—geometrical optics, wave optics, physiological optics and virtual optics) was never linked with his work.

A sequence of Duchamp's works from 1918 to 1935 is based on different optical series and on transplane optical media. The period from 1918 to 1935 was purposefully chosen since its beginning and its end are defined by two works with which Duchamp's systematic involvement can be clearly delineated. Moreover, it ends in the year in which the Raumbild publishing company was founded, as I have described in the previous chapter. My aim is to describe a *different* debate of the implications of the transplane image. And as a final point, his *Rotoreliefs* (1935) will connect to the next chapter in which I will discuss the *volumetric image* developed from 1946 onward. Duchamp is well suited as an example since his works demonstrate a reflexive involvement with the new (certainly also scientific and military) "productions of space" (Lefebvre); he seems even better suited than Picasso and his *Les Demoiselles D'Avignon* (1907), favored by Lefebvre.[2]

Two preliminary remarks: First, one of the central problems of Lefebvre's rather cursory reference to *Les Demoiselles D'Avignon* is the fact that he does not contextualize the painting but sees it only with regard to his thesis that space becomes abstract in modernity. The technological images like photography and film hardly play a role, even though he himself says that "abstract space . . . is . . . an ensemble of images, signs and symbols" (Lefebvre 1991, 288). This may be due to the fact that apart from exotic exceptions like the 'absolute film,' they hardly fit the proclaimed mould of 'abstraction.' But since Lefebvre defines the *representations of space* as the most important element of the production of space,[3] then not only the better known technical images should be used as examples[4] but also the transplane images, which are not even mentioned by him.

It seems to me that some additional selected works of Duchamp should be analyzed as well, stressing the developmental *sequence* of different works and not only *one* isolated work, an irritating fact in Lefebvre's study.[5] This hopefully will make the analysis less arbitrary than Lefebvre's analysis of *Les Demoiselles D'Avignon*.

Secondly, it will be necessary to examine once again, albeit in a selective and abbreviated way, the development of European art in modernity. In section 1.4 I have underlined that a large part of modern painting had initiated a break with perspective, emphasizing the self-referentiality of the painted plane.[6] This led unsurprisingly to abstraction in classical modernism and later to the accentuation of 'flatness' (Greenberg) in American abstract painting after the war. But this is not the only development. Even before WWI, as an outcome of the emphasis on the plane, in many cases a tendency in painting re-emerged that abandoned the flat surface in favor of an object-oriented spatiality of forms.[7]

In an essay for a catalogue, Margit Rowell observes on these "extensions of the picture plane into the space in front of the wall"[8] between 1912 and 1932: "The earliest objects presented here evolved as a direct consequence of Cézanne's reassessment of the painted surface" (Rowell 1979a, 10). Figure 7.1 shows an example. It is a work from 1926 that clearly shows the sculptural elements in the oblique view.

How did this development come about?

(a) *Materiality:* Initially it can be stated that emphasizing the materiality of the image plane leads to analyzing and studying the materiality and spatial reference of the 'picture-thing' (Husserl) as well; thus the transition from the accentuation on the plane in painting after Cézanne to three-dimensional objects is not all that surprising.[9] Greenberg, for example, made the following comments on cubist collage that in Picasso directly precedes his object-like works: "By pasting a piece of newspaper lettering to the canvas one called attention to the physical reality of the work of art and made that reality the same as the art."[10]

(b) *Reproducibility*: The transition to three-dimensional objects could also be an explicit or implicit and unwitting reaction to the emergence of the technical media of reproduction and this means to the frequently invoked status of the "Work of Art in the Age of Mechanical Reproduction" by Benjamin (1978).

As has been underlined several times, one of the pivotal problems of photographic reproduction is the fact that it has to project a view of an object onto a plane thereby fundamentally reducing the spatial structure of the reproduced object. Paintings (often) have an irregular, relief-like, pastose surface characterized by the painterly gesture that disappears in photographic reproduction since technological images in comparison to paintings are very smooth in the very sense of the word.[11] This loss of spatial information can be coped with normally. It takes on a different dimension, however, when the work to be reproduced contains sculptural structures itself.[12]

Doesn't it, therefore, stand to reason for an artistic avant-garde to strengthen that aspect of non-reproducibility in a work by reinforcing its spatiality? By no means have all artists of the avant-garde cultivated the idea of the singular and original work—quite

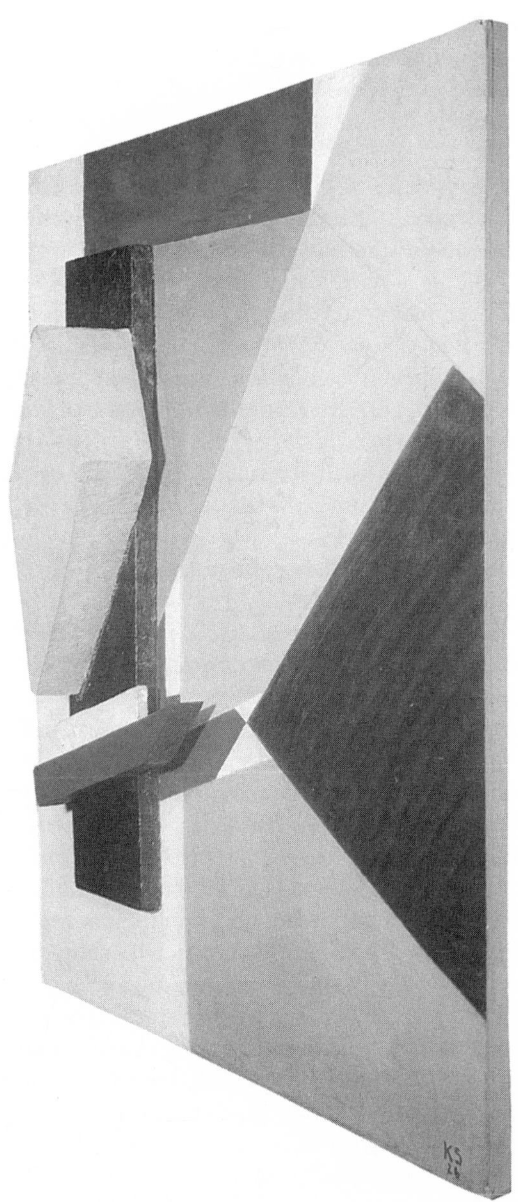

FIGURE 7.1 *Kurt Schwitters,* Merzbild mit gelbem Block *(1926), Painted Wood, 65 × 56 cm, View from the side, in Rowell (1979b, 113).*

often the contrary is true. However, even if artists embrace the photographic logic of reproducibility,[13] they can emphasize the limits of the medium photography[14] on another level by strengthening the spatial aspects of their works.

(c) *Spatiality in modernism*: On the tendency of creating object- and relief-like configurations since 1912 or so, Rowell observes that "[s]pace was the substance of the new art."[15] This seems to coincide with Lefebvre's assumption that in modernity an "attribution of priority to space over time" (Lefebvre 1991, 219) seems to emerge. And Rowell's first example is—of all painters—Pablo Picasso, who since 1912 had begun to make "experiments in actual space" (Rowell 1979a, 10), only five years after *Les Demoiselles D'Avignon*, so highly rated by Lefebvre.

Quite unexpectedly then Rowell's observation of the tendency towards spatiality in painting connects back to Lefebvre's (hardly explicit) thesis that it was Picasso who had expressed and declaimed the new formation of space. In spite of this it appears that Picasso's experimental spatial constructions can fulfill this task in a better way than the painting of *Les Demoiselles D'Avignon*[16] with its rhythmized character that is closer to *temporal* forms of art (like montage in film).[17]

It is quite striking that Rowell's descriptions of the new spatial constructions resemble the descriptions of technical-transplane images in an almost vexing way: "[W]hile none of these works may be defined as strictly two-dimensional, all are constituted of two-dimensional components or planes" (Rowell 1979a, 9). A vast majority of the artists who developed these spatial constructions saw themselves as painters who, after having concentrated on the plane in painting, now took just this plane and shifted it into space. This means that we are dealing with a complex linking of plane *and* space and it is precisely that which characterizes the transplane images of stereoscopy, holography and volumetry. Holography (see Chapter 9) in particular allows one of the most astounding experiences of vision when one approaches an inconspicuous grey plane on the wall and all of a sudden a (usually) monochrome, sculptural image jumps out at you. It really seems to stand or to float behind (and sometimes in front of) the plane, and then with another movement in front of the image, it can possibly disappear altogether. Of course, Rowell does not refer to such phenomena and the artists of the time between 1912 and 1932 could refer to it even less. Nevertheless, the analogy is there:

> Whether pinned to the wall or standing free in space, they [the artistic spatial constructions] are not intended to be viewed from all sides. Yet, despite this implicit dependence on a wall as 'ground', they exist in real space. . . . [T]he three-dimensional configuration described by these planar components was, in fact, an integrated spatial image. (Rowell 1979a, 11; my emphasis)

Can this analogy be understood in such a way that these artists reacted consciously or unwittingly to the modern "production of space" as Lefebvre claims of Picasso's *Les Demoiselles D'Avignon*? Even though Lefebvre doesn't mention it, the transplane images are very much a central element of this production of space. It might be possible that without direct causal connections, and without direct influence, similar "representations of space" (Lefebvre) occur. Crary's arguments are similar. In his paragraphs on stereoscopy he moves on to painting in the nineteenth century after having described the aggregate pictorial space of the stereoscopic image resembling a stage set:

> A range of nineteenth-century painting also manifests some of these features of stereoscopic imagery. Courbet's *Ladies of the Village* (1851), with its much-noted discontinuity of groups and planes, suggests the aggregate space of the stereoscope, as do similar elements of *The Meeting (Bonjour, M. Courbet)* (1854). . . . I am certainly not proposing a causal relation of *any* sort between these two forms, and I would be dismayed if I prompted anyone to determine if Courbet owned a stereoscope. Instead I am suggesting that *both* the 'realism' of the stereoscope and the 'experiments' of certain painters were equally bound up in a much broader transformation of the observer that allowed the emergence of this *new optically constructed space*. The stereoscope and Cézanne have far more in common than one might assume.[18]

This argumentation is quite understandable remembering Crary's use of Foucault's discourse analysis. Foucault in the *Archéologie du Savoir* envisions in passing an archaeological analysis of painting. Compared to approaches that wanted to extract the "implicit philosophy" or the "view of the world" of the painter or the "opinions of the period" from an image,

> [a]rchaeological analysis would have another aim: it would try to discover whether space, distance, depth, color, light, proportions, volumes, and contours were not, at the periods in question, considered, named, enunciated, and conceptualized in a discursive practice; and whether the knowledge that this discursive practice gives rise to was not embodied perhaps in theories and speculations, in forms of teaching and codes of practice ["recettes" in the original], but also in processes, techniques, and even in the very gesture of the painter.[19]

Foucault argues that the knowledge of a certain discursive practice can be "embodied in techniques and effects" (Foucault 1972, 194). In a similar way I argued that the knowledge of geometrical optics is sedimented in different ways in the linear perspective of the painter or in the optics of photographic media. And it could be argued that the knowledge of physiological optics—according to Crary—can be sedimented both in stereoscopy and—modified—in certain compositional strategies of painting in the nineteenth century.[20]

In order to plausibly approach the media aesthetic questions of modern productions of space, I have chosen artistic works as examples that most explicitly reflect these questions. Duchamp's works lend themselves to this as a continuation of the trend described by Rowell in which the planarity of painting has been recognized and is then left behind in favor of more spatial creations. Duchamp's works at first resist the alleged tendency toward abstraction, as did the technological visual media not mentioned by Lefebvre:

> It is paradoxical to observe that while an entire major trend of present art up to Pollock, Newman and their successors has persisted in making the picture an a-focal flat area—the notion of the picture as a material support—Marcel Duchamp thought only of going against the grain of all this 'modernity' asserting the notion of the picture as a transparent plane.[21]

Therefore, his works quite openly refer to methods of geometrical (and later also physiological) optics—Duchamp was the prototype of the "certain type of artist" whom Lefebvre (1991, 39) labeled (in a slightly disparaging way) having "a scientific bent." In my eyes, some of Duchamp's works between say 1918 and 1935 can hardly be seen in another way than as a complex and differentiated study of these developments in optics.[22] Therefore, they are eminently well-suited for collecting elements of a media aesthetics of transplane images, even though the series of wave and virtual optics play no important role for Duchamp. Henderson observes: "From his study of physics, Duchamp understood the behavior of light waves and phenomena such as reflection, refraction, diffraction, interference and polarization" (Henderson 1998, 208)—clearly pointing to the series of wave optics. Nevertheless, Duchamp did not create artistic works that directly used wave effects; at best they allude to them. Only five years before Duchamp passed away, holography was developed as a visual medium (see Chapter 9)—if he had lived longer, he certainly would have dealt with it. Likewise, the methods of computer graphics were still in their early stages (see Chapter 10).

Duchamp also commenced with painting.[23] Starting around 1911, he became interested in cubism and his first ready-mades were created circa 1913. These hardly correspond to Rowell's description of the tendency toward shifting from the plane into spatial dimensions while at the same time still maintaining the reference to the plane. This is all the more interesting, as in 1918 Duchamp still painted one more painting, his last one, which I will discuss as his first work: *Tu m'* (see Figure 7.2).

Rosalind Krauss has described *Tu m'* as "a panorama of the index" (Krauss 1985a, 198), with the 'index' meaning a sign operating by causality. The painting represents the shadows of two ready-mades by Duchamp[24] and of a corkscrew. Shadows are indexical signs because they are determined by the objects that cast a shadow and by the source of the light. Krauss also mentions the illusionistically painted pointing finger (painted, by the way, by a certain A. Klang). The finger is an indexical sign as well because the object pointed at by the gesture of the sign (e.g. 'this' corkscrew) has to be present in the same context as the gesture and therefore has to be causally connected to the gesture in order for it to make sense at all. The same is true for the shifters named in the title *Tu m'* or the personal pronouns Tu/moi (You/me) whose signified changes depending on who speaks.[25] Krauss is arguing that from this recourse to the different types of indexical signs it is possible to

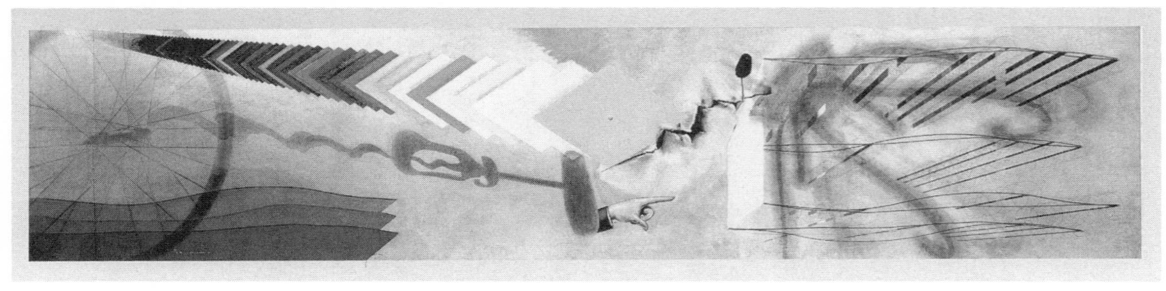

FIGURE 7.2 *Marcel Duchamp* Tu m' *(1918), 70 × 313 cm, in Gerstner (2003, 6). See color plate 5.*

read the effect which the indexical medium of photography has had on visual arts (see Krauss 2002, 192). Seen in this light, the recourse to the index in *Tu m'* following the first ready-mades (1913) is quite consistent—Krauss had already made a connection between Duchamp's ready-mades and photography, insofar as both are cutting out objects from their context.[26]

I will now supplement and expand on Krauss's detailed description to a certain extent. Referring to the index goes back to her idea that modernist art (be it painting or sculpture) is fundamentally formed by photography, which brings forth indexical signs (as Peirce had already remarked).[27] With photography—or better yet with the photographic—Krauss first associates the logic of the index and secondly the logic of reproducibility (even though she never relates the latter to *Tu m'* but rather to the works of Rodin).[28] However, she overlooks that photography (at least in its dominantly established form) is also the technological automation of geometrical optics and its *logic of projection*.

One cannot justify this exclusion by attempting to maintain that including the logic of projection in the heterogeneous ensemble of photography is accidental—contrary to the essential status of the logic of the index and the logic of reproducibility. It is true that photography is possible without the projecting optical system (e.g. photograms), but there are also photographic methods that do not follow the logic of reproducibility (daguerreotype, Lippmann photography, Polaroid, certain forms of holography). In this respect, the logic of reproducibility would also be contingent and only the logic of the index would be essential. If the contingent logic of reproducibility is called a characteristic of photography, it is therefore not understandable why the contingent logic of projection should be excluded. This logic and its shifts would then have to be taken into account when analyzing the "structural change of art" (Wolf 2000, 11) that according to Krauss was induced by photography. I have already pointed out above how artists can pit the logic of projection against the logic of reproducibility by spatializing their art.

Therefore I would like to show that the theme in *Tu m'* with its shadows of ready-mades is not only the index but mainly the *projection* of given spatial circumstances onto the normally almost-quadratic (but here strongly laterally rectangular) plane. This is in no way a marginal difference. While the index refers to the *causal* impression of real objects, stressing the projection emphasizes the *dimensional reduction* by way of which three-dimensional spatial objects—even if they do not exist at all in reality—are represented on a two-dimensional plane. Krauss herself speaks of the " 'fixated' shadows that were *projected* onto the surface of the canvas" (Krauss 1998, 81; my emphasis). Duchamp himself says of *Tu m'*:

> In that painting, I executed the cast shadow of the bicycle wheel, the cast shadow of the hatrack, ... and [that] shadow of a corkscrew. I had found a sort of projector which made shadows rather well enough, and I projected each shadow, which I traced by hand, onto the canvas. (Duchamp, quoted in Cabanne 1971, 60)

In the context of *Le Grand Verre*, Duchamp also speaks of projection

> Simply, I thought of the idea of a projection, of an invisible fourth dimension, something you couldn't see with your eyes. Since I found that one could make a cast shadow from a three-dimensional thing, any object whatsoever—just as the projecting of the sun on the earth makes two dimensions—I thought that, by simple intellectual analogy, the fourth dimension could project an object of three dimensions, or, to put it another way, any three dimensional object, which we see dispassionately, is a projection of something four-dimensional, something we're not familiar with.[29]

As can be seen, Duchamp generalizes the principle of projection to such an extent that even normal reality is understood as the projection of a higher, four dimensional level.[30]

Considering this aspect, those elements of *Tu m'* that Krauss does not discuss especially catch the eye. In the right-hand third of the painting, a bottle-brush is standing on the surface at a right angle that in the customary photographic reproductions of *Tu m'* (see also in Krauss 1985a, 199) becomes barely visible.[31] Duchamp introduces a three-dimensional element which not only resembles the above-mentioned divergence from the plane into spatial dimensions in many artistic approaches from the early twentieth century; it also illustrates once again that the leveling perspectival projection (under specific conditions) will lead to the loss of spatial information. Of course, the picture can be photographed from the side in order to highlight the brush—but then the rest of the picture cannot be viewed correctly any longer (see Figure 7.3).

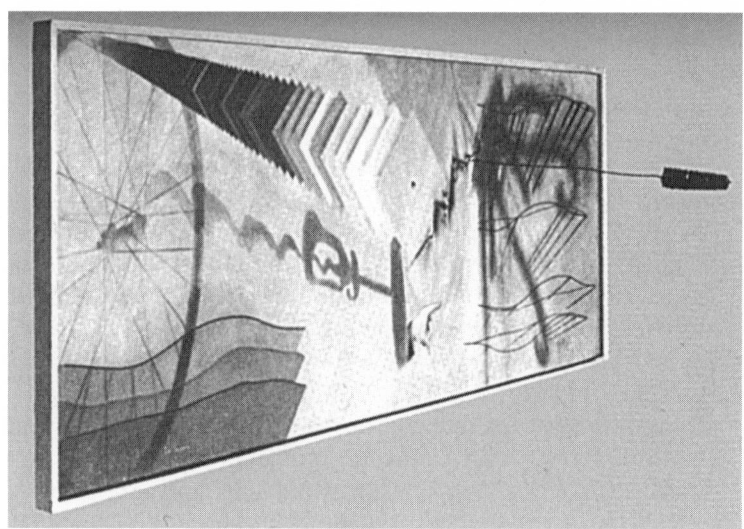

FIGURE 7.3 Tu m' *seen from the side, in Gerstner (2003, 22).*

Duchamp develops a quite complex meditation in *Tu m'*. On the one hand the brush subverts the logic of projection while itself—depending on the light conditions—throwing a shadow onto the surface of the painting on the other hand.[32] Of course the shadow cast is only the most primitive form of a geometrical-optical projection but the logic of projection (and not only the logic of the index) is clearly underlined. For directly underneath the bottle-brush is a white rectangular object (like an empty canvas) that can be viewed as foreshortened, that is receding perspectively into depth or as *seemingly* protruding from the surface of the image like the bottle-brush.[33] As a foreshortened white rectangle whose vanishing point falls directly on the edge of *Tu m'* (see Gerstner 2003, 14)—i.e. onto the margins of the plane—the form alludes to the method of perspectival projection onto the empty plane (in particular since the foreshortened white rectangle cannot be explained by taking recourse to the logic of the index). The veristically painted finger is pointing exactly to this white rectangle.[34] Not only is the white rectangle emphasized by that; yet another level of reflection is added since the reference from the tip of the finger to the rectangle is quasi-running parallel to the image while the rectangle is (seemingly) located laterally to the image area. This means that the tension between the planar image and the laterally located bottle-brush is repeated once again. In connection with *Tu m'* Krauss speaks of a "system of doubled perspective in which two competing points of view—a frontal one and a lateral one—influence each other reciprocally" (Krauss 1998, 83).

There is no need to read into Duchamp's works that he was interested in the methods and limits of perspectival projection; perspective was an important subject for this artist. Jean Clair has published a detailed study showing to what extent Marcel Duchamp comprehensively referred to the traditions of the publications on perspective in the most important work of that period, his *The Bride Stripped Bare By Her Bachelors, Even*, also known as *The Large Glass* (1915–23; see Figure 7.6).[35]

Proceeding from the function of the three-dimensional element of the bottle-brush, we have so far interpreted the logic of projection as the focus of *Tu m'*. Many other details of the artwork can be integrated into this interpretation without problems. As an example: Almost precisely at the point at which the brush handle is stuck into the canvas, a rip in the surface is painted as a *trompe l'œil*, touching the handle. This contact between handle and rip is indeed important since by indicating the role of perspective, there is the danger to put Duchamp's work in a line of tradition of the "diagrammatic mastery of a reality *disincarnated* into what has been called the 'purely ideal' status of the perspective image"[36] as Krauss has rightfully criticized. Referring to Lyotard she observes later, "[t]he visuality Duchamp proposes . . . is carnal, not conceptual" (Krauss 1993, 119). The fact that the body plays an important role for Duchamp can be seen in some of his later works (see below) in his recourse to physiological optics. Thus, bottle-brush and rip can be interpreted as allusions to male and female sexual characteristics and so in *Tu m'* they already imply the presence of the body.[37]

The seeming rip is held together with two real safety pins—again pointing to physicality with their stabbing character. Additionally, the picture's surface is being addressed and therefore also the tension between the two-dimensional representation and the three-dimensional objects. This tension is again repeated in the relationship between the spatial bottle-brush and the projected cork-screw that are held together by their semantic reference to the bottle. The series of colored squares works in a similar manner. The last yellow square contains a real screw at its center—it seems to be attached with it. This again reflects the relationship between surface and the illusion of depth (the series of squares is perspectively receding into depth). The viewer is forced into a series of back and forth *movements* in order to find out which elements are spatial and which ones have been projected. Thus the viewer is coerced to differentiate between 2D and 3D.[38]

We can therefore say: The painting is extensively discussing the logic of projection and thus comments on the fundamental elements of the series of geometrical optics and its limits.[39] To be more precise it is the analysis *both* of the logic of projection *and* of the logic of the index, as Rosalind Krauss has rightfully pointed out regarding *Tu m'*. The point is *precisely the connection of these two logics.*[40]

If you relate *Tu m'* to the indexical character of the photographic image, as Rosalind Krauss does, then one has to additionally note that today's dominant form of photography (and of course also during Duchamp's times)[41] represents the historically contingent connection of the logic of the index with the logic of projection. In the sixth paragraph of her *Notes on the Index, Part 1*, Krauss is referring to *Tu m'* for the first time; however, in reference to Man Ray's variant of photograms, the so called 'Rayogram,' she maintains that

> the photogram only forces, or makes explicit, what is the case of *all* photography. Every photograph is the result of a physical imprint transferred by light reflections onto a sensitive surface. The photograph is thus a type of icon, or visual likeness, which bears an indexical relationship to its object. (Krauss 1985a, 203)

Does this mean that indeed the subject of *Tu m'* is *only* the logic of the index and not *also* the logic of projection since photograms are not projected linear perspectivally?

I would like to argue that we should take those media technologies that are dominant at a given historical time seriously—for reasons that can be determined genealogically—as *heterogeneous sedimentations* instead of reducing them to an ahistorical essence (see section 1.3). Seen from this point of view, Krauss's argument is not unproblematic. Of course it is true that Man Ray was a good friend of Duchamp's and that the two worked together frequently. There is for example a photograph from 1920 showing the "seasoned" dust on the surface of the *Large Glass* signed by both of them (see Figure 7.4).

According to Krauss, the "accumulation of dust is a kind of physical index for the passage of time" (Krauss 1985a, 202–3). But

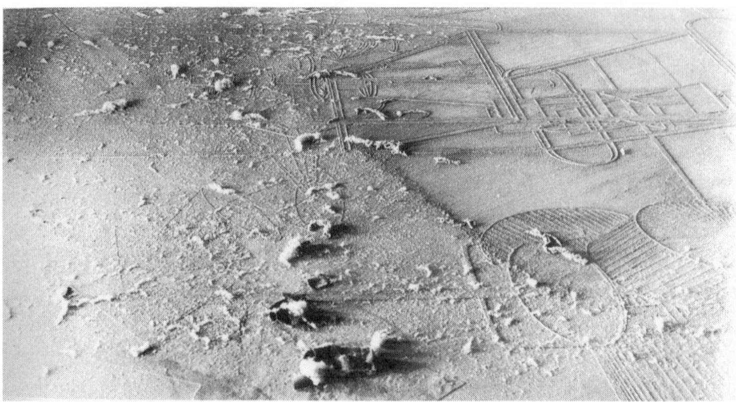

FIGURE 7.4 *Marcel Duchamp,* Dust Breeding, *(1920; Photography by Man Ray).*[42]

the picture of this "accumulation of dust" (contrary to the dust pile itself) is not *only* an index; it is *also* a *projection* (of the accumulation of dust through the optics of a lens onto a light sensitive film). As her argument progresses it becomes still more apparent that the aspect of projection in comparison with the index as the (alleged) 'essence of photography' should be considered more closely. For Krauss continues to relate the logic of the index to two utterances by Marcel Duchamp from his introduction to *The Large Glass*: "[F]or the instantaneous state of rest = bring in the term: extra-rapid;" and "We shall determine the conditions of [the] best exposure of the extra-rapid State of Rest [of the extra-rapid exposure]." And she adds: "This language of rapid exposures which produce a state of rest, an isolated sign, is of course the language of photography" (1985a, 205; square brackets, except for the first, are also in Duchamp's original quote in the source). This is correct. But is this language—and he later returns to rapid exposure effects (Duchamp, quoted in Krauss 1985a, 206)—also the language of the photogram reduced to an index? Hardly likely, since the term "rapid exposure" can be related to photograms only with difficulty. What could the photogram of a quickly moving object be? One could indeed imagine photograms that are exposed for a very short time only but this does not really make any sense since the object creating the shadow is lying motionless on the paper anyway. In contrast, the meaning of rapid exposure is to create sharp pictures of rapidly moving objects by way of very short exposure times. The term rapid exposure to my mind makes sense both in principle and historically[43] only with regard to the (then and now) dominant form of photography that connects the logic of the index with the logic of projection.

Moreover, this dominant form is connected to the logic of reproducibility,[44] which Krauss herself has repeatedly underlined. It is reflected in *Tu m'* in the series of the colored squares or rhombuses receding into depth; they were painted by Duchamp's ex-wife Yvonne Chastel and can be understood as replicas of each other: To a certain extent, Duchamp is then countering the difficult reproducibility of *Tu m'* by alluding to the logic of reproducibility. The fact that they are colored differently[45] is no counter argument. Not even two prints of the same negative are ever completely identical. If one wants to relate *Tu m'* to photography one could say that the work is referring to "photography"[46] *as a complex sedimentation of different, heterogeneous series*—projection (series of geometrical optics), index and reproducibility.[47] *Tu m'* illustrates how geometrical optics is being materialized in a specific historical technology.

It would only have been logical if Duchamp had also dealt with the series of physiological optics after he reflected in such a complex manner on geometrical optics, its limitations and its concrete materialization in this heterogeneous ensemble called photography. And this is indeed the case.[48] Shortly after *Tu m'* Duchamp created his *Handmade Stereopticon Slide* (see Figure 7.5).

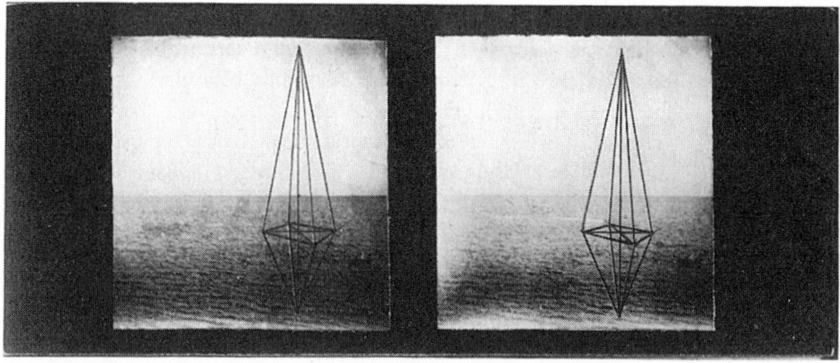

FIGURE 7.5 *Marcel Duchamp* Handmade Stereopticon Slide *(1918/1919), in Krauss (1993, 131).*

One can see a stereo picture of a calm ocean horizon in front of which hovers a peculiar geometrical figure. Duchamp bought the stereo picture and then added the drawing—the work is an *Assisted Ready Made*. At first one is puzzled about the motif of the stereo picture (the horizon of the sea), since only objects close enough to the eyes show enough difference of the parallax in order to appear as a spatial object in the stereo picture (see Chapter 2). It is Duchamp who *produces* the spatial impression of the stereo picture by including the "closer" geometrical figure into the picture.[49] First, this figure alludes to the earliest history of stereoscopy in which—still before photography—drawings of geometrical figures were used. As I have mentioned before, notably Wheatstone used drawings and therefore one can say that the drawing of a stereo-figure suggests that stereoscopy originates in the series of physiological optics (insofar as Wheatstone was a scientist researching binocular vision; Wheatstone 1983, 73). Secondly, this figure, of all things, is itself the *outline of perspectival projection*. It is a picture plane, a point from which the visual lines radiate (four rays from the corners and the centric ray which was already emphasized by Alberti)[50] and on the other end of the picture area the visual lines meet again at the vanishing point. Viewed in this light we could take the surprising motif of the horizon of the sea as a suggestion of the line of the horizon in perspectival painting (see Edgerton 1975, 43–5)—and this, too, could be underlined once more.

The separation of the seascape into an upper, somewhat higher and a lower, somewhat narrower half mirrors exactly the proportionate segmentation of *The Large Glass*[51] into an upper and a lower half (see Figure 7.6). According to Jean Clair it is itself derived from similar segmentations of respective representations in historical essays on perspective that Duchamp studied at the library Saint Geneviève during 1913–14 (see Figure 7.7).[52]

The *Handmade Stereopticon Slide* is a complex meditation on the relationship of perspective and stereoscopy. The work demonstrates that stereoscopy is capable of representing more spatial information—ironically, it does this with the model of perspectival projection itself.[53] Similarly to *Tu m'*, Duchamp addresses the contingent connection of different given entities: the work *literally* shows that geometrical-optical photographic pictures and the schema of stereoscopy (originating in the series of physiological optics) exist parallel to each other. Thus, the *Handmade Stereopticon Slide* confirms one of the central

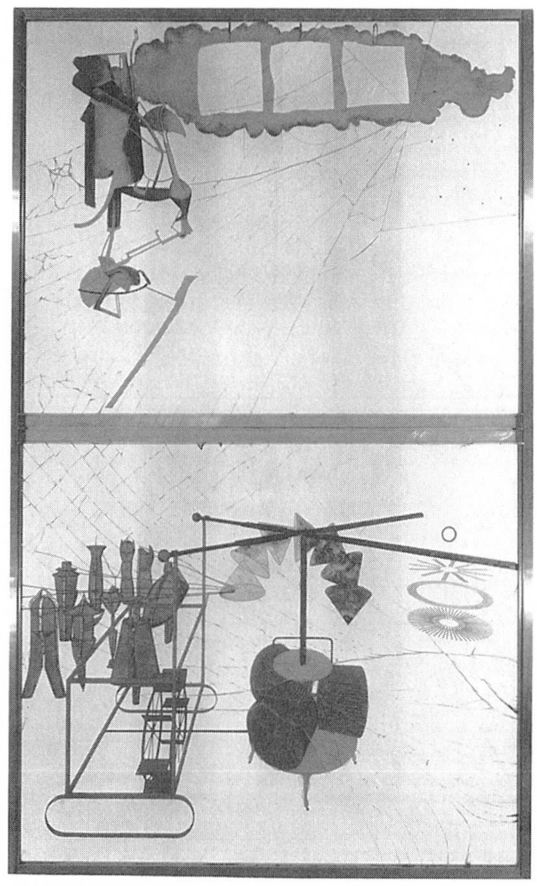

FIGURE 7.6 *Marcel Duchamp:* The Bride Stripped Bare By Her Bachelors, Even, *aka* The Large Glass *(1915–23), in Krauss (1993, 121).*

propositions of this book, namely that the regime of physiological optics does not simply supersede or displace that of geometrical optics,[54] but *that modern vision always consists in the parallel coexistence of different optical series.*[55]

Duchamp has also addressed stereoscopy in other works, in particular with the anaglyphic form of stereoscopy, i.e. that which works with the contrast of red and green.[56] Within the context addressed here, it is particularly interesting that Duchamp and Man Ray had themselves attempted to capture Duchamp's work *Rotary*

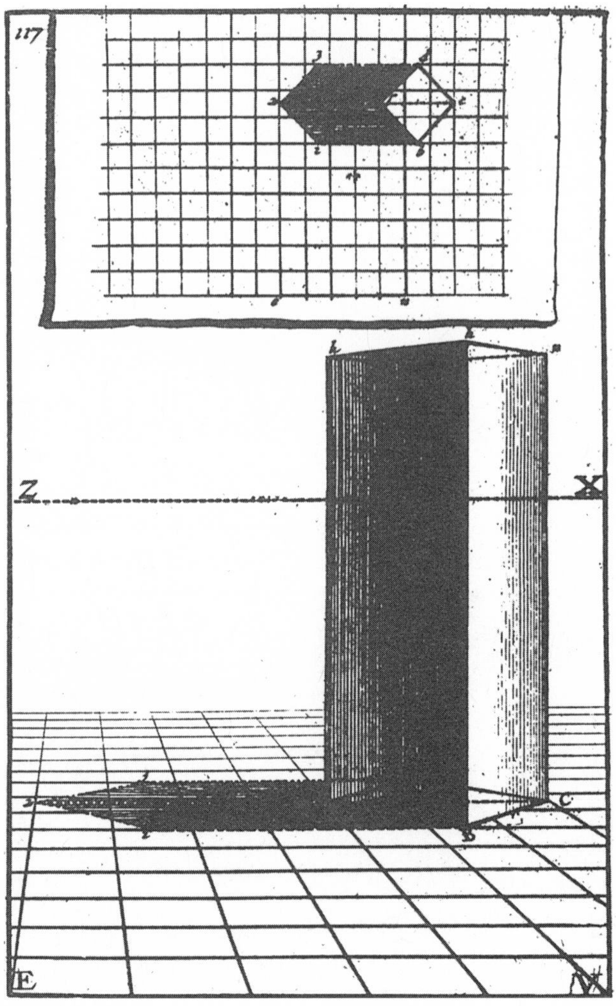

FIGURE 7.7 *From the "Essay on Perspective", in Bosse (1987, 175).*

Demisphere (Precision Optics) and the spatial effects of perception provoked by this apparatus in an anaglyphic stereo-film, a joint film-project in 1925 that unfortunately neither succeeded nor was preserved (see Figure 7.8).

With his works based on rotating discs—sometimes also fittingly called "Precision Optics"—Duchamp enlarges and refines his

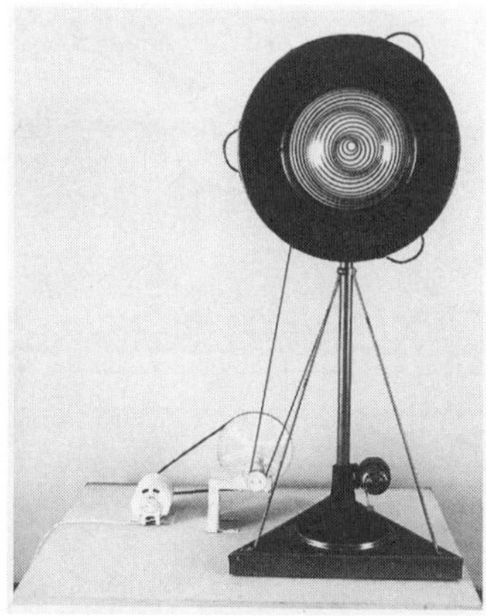

FIGURE 7.8 *Marcel Duchamp,* Rotary Demisphere (Precision Optics) *(1925), in Krauss (1993, 129).*

involvement with the series of physiological optics: "In his Precision Optics . . . Duchamp's focus was the creation of virtual relief using motion as a dimension-creating entity and an alternative to the effects of the anaglyph or stereoscopic photograph that also interested him."[57] In the *Rotary Demisphere (Precision Optics)* and also the *Rotoreliefs* that he used in 1926 in his film *Anemic Cinema* but which were originally conceived as individual works, Duchamp creates a spatial effect without having to use stereo glasses, which were necessary for anaglyphic images in particular. By rotating the colored plates on a device such as a record player, a strong effect of spatial depth is created, oscillating between pushing outward and inward, especially when viewed with *only one eye* (see Figure 7.9).

Obviously it is not the use of *binocular vision* that lies at the center of the *Rotoreliefs* but a phenomenon which physiological optics would call the *kinetic depth effect*.[58] Supposedly this effect was discovered in 1921 by the psychologist Vittorio Benussi. For the first time in 1924 a text on this effect was published by Cesare Musatti.[59] Some of the *Rotoreliefs* resemble Musatti's experimental discs (see Figure 7.10).

One of the *Rotoreliefs* even more closely resembles a disc that Ogden N. Rood used in 1879 (and that had previously already been used by Helmholtz) in order to prove how human perception autonomously creates colors (see also Rood 1880). Once the black and white disc is rotated, the viewer will see colors (Figure 7.11).

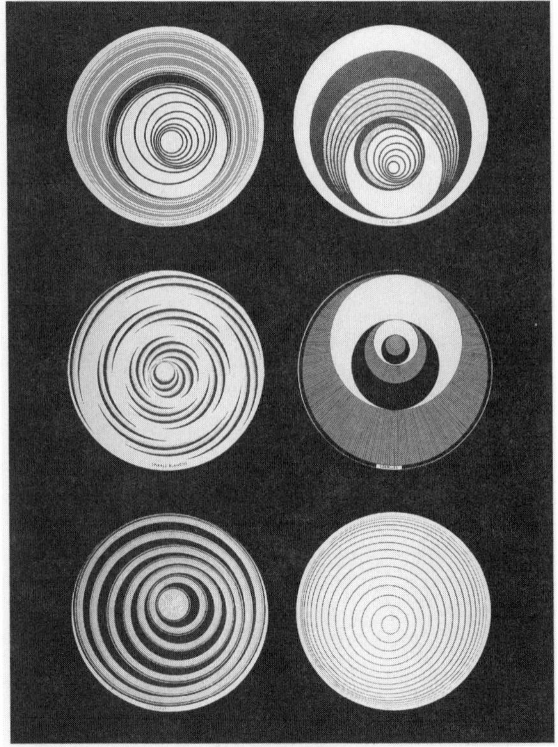

FIGURE 7.9 *Marcel Duchamp,* Rotoreliefs *(1935), in Duchamp (2002, 117).*

Clearly, then, the *Rotoreliefs* belong to the tradition of the series of physiological optics. In his interview with Pierre Cabanne, Duchamp comments:

> CABANNE: Toward 1924–25, you made some new projects for optical machines.
>
> DUCHAMP: Yes. At that time, I felt a small attraction toward the optical. Without really ever calling it that. I made a little thing that turned, that visually gave a corkscrew effect, and this attracted me; it was amusing. . . . Later, using the same procedure, I found a way of getting objects in relief. . . . What interested me most was that it was a scientific phenomenon which existed in another way than when I had found it.[60]

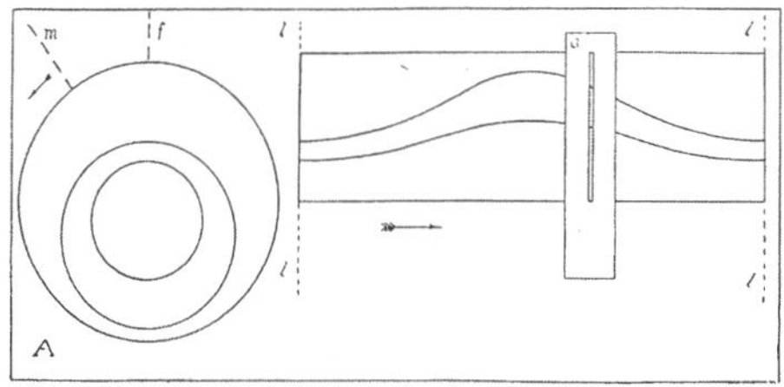

FIGURE 7.10 *Fig. 2, in Musatti (1924, 109).*

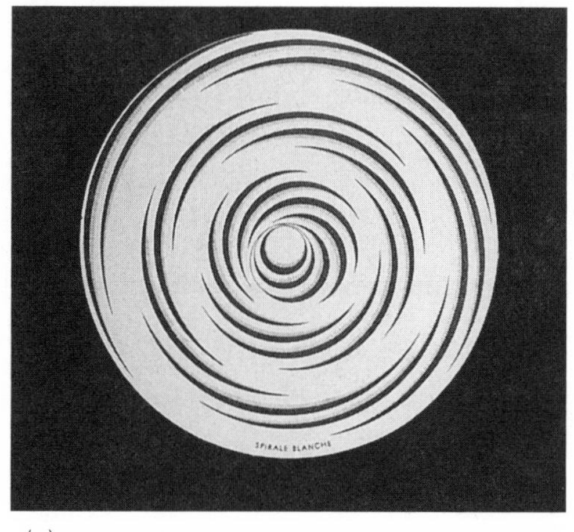

(a)

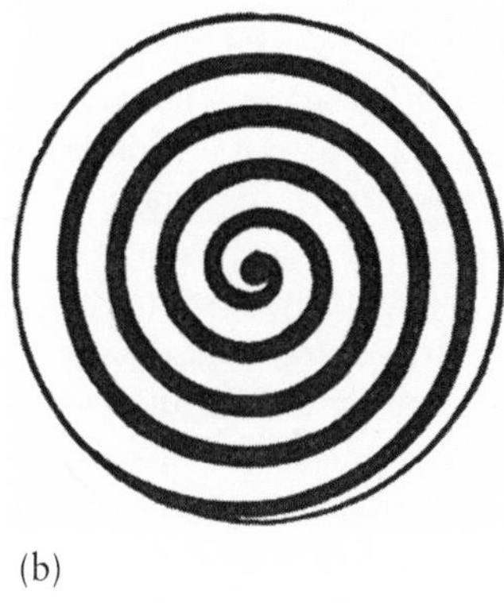

(b)

FIGURE 7.11 *Marcel Duchamp,* Rotorelief Spiral Blanche *(a) and* Testing Disc *(b), in Rood (1973, 139).*

What "interested" the artist "most" will be the most interesting here as well. Duchamp is taking up the series of geometrical and physiological optics again, which indeed had also been used "in another way." These forms of knowledge are "embodied in techniques and effects" (Foucault 1972, 194). Allan Sekula has pointed out this tension-filled relationship between the functional and the aesthetic use of technological visual media, using the example of the photo-portrait: "every proper portrait has its lurking, objectifying inverse in the files of the police."[61] It is this tension that Duchamp is facing. For example, while stereoscopy for the Nazi *Raumbild* publishing company had been a means to create a perception of space that would blindside the viewer (see Chapter 6), Duchamp exhibits the requirements and the artificiality of this spatial perception by simply adding the effect of spatiality to the stereo slide by way of the drawing.

The term "precision optics" used by Duchamp is subject to this tension as well. *On the one hand*, it signifies highly precise optical instruments for use in research and war. For example, it can already be found in a text on "precision optics" by an American Major named Fred E. Wright in 1919, complaining that with the beginning of WWI the supply of premium-quality optical instruments made by the enemy Germany had broken off. Here the connection to the functions of spatial control of (transplane) visual technology can be found. As Major Wright says: "The gunner who cannot see to aim correctly is unable to place his shots effectively and is at a serious disadvantage in the presence of the enemy" (Wright 1919, 2). In Duchamp, *on the other hand*, precision optics is a purposeless, self-referential game of optical *illusions*, thus making the purpose of precision optics absurd. With this in mind, Duchamp defamiliarizes, ridicules and analyses optical media and in particular the optical knowledge at their basis that is structuring the modern production of space, at least on the level of the "representation of space" (Lefebvre). One can also analyze Duchamp's *Rotoreliefs* in exactly this same way.

But prior to doing that, some remarks on the term "Rotorelief." With this term Duchamp refers to an artistic genre that can be located precisely between the two-dimensional picture of painting (or photography)[62] and the three-dimensional image/object of sculpture.[63] In a pertinent encyclopedia of art, the *relief* is described concisely as "a synthesis of optical and tactile values, a connection between solid figure and plane."[64] Therefore, for a media-aesthetic description of reliefs, a vocabulary could be helpful that connects elements for describing two-dimensional images with those of describing sculpture or other objects of plastic art. Trying to describe the relief in terms of planar logic alone does not meet the specifics of the relief nor will the (too strong) term 'viewpoint' since there are no main and no secondary views as in sculptures. The relief connects a (single viewpoint) arrangement of the plane with three-dimensional elements that cast changing shadows, creating an additional level of spatiality when viewed from different angles dependent on the movement of the viewers.[65] Therefore, a media-aesthetic analysis of the relief would have to resolve the question how the logic of the shadow (which is dependent on the movement of the viewer and/or the source of light) is related to the formal structures of the plane.

But exactly this does *not* apply to Duchamp's *Rotoreliefs*. The viewer can remain static and spatiality is achieved through the movement of the disc. Duchamp's reliefs do not use the effects of light and shadow, i.e. they do not refer to projection (geometrical optics) but specifically to the series of physiological optics (since the impression of shadowing and space is only created *in* the viewer through the rotation). The *Rotoreliefs* thus break with the tradition of the relief and therefore also from a media-aesthetic point of view belong to the new field of transplane pictures.[66]

And so it is questionable whether a description and an analysis of the planar logic of the *Rotoreliefs* in the classic sense are possible. In paintings or reliefs the directions are clearly defined: above and below, to the right and to the left. It is easy to describe the planar logic in relation to the rigid square of the frame. Rotating discs, however, continually interchange above and below, right and left. Of course, the images on the discs and the internal relation of their parts could be easily described; however, whether an element of the picture like a line leads 'upward' or 'downward' will depend on the actual position of the disc in the course of the rotation. By using physiological-optical knowledge, the order of the plane can thus be shifted, and will become a reason for producing specific effects of perception rather than suggesting a more or less closed, autonomous logic.[67] It might be possible that the often unsatisfactory impression left by the artistic use of transplane pictures is based on this conflict between the demands of a formal, planar logic and those of the effects of perception that are possible to achieve.

Finally, I would like to address the question already touched upon when asking which "functional doubles" (Sekula) exist for the

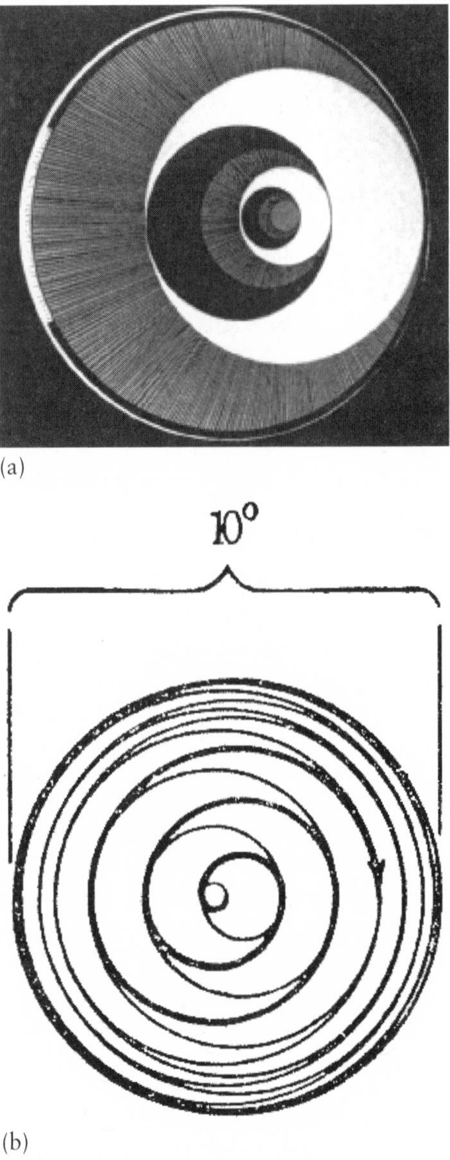

FIGURES 7.12 *(a)* Marcel Duchamp: Rotorelief Corolle, *in Duchamp (2002, 117) and (b)* Spiral Scan Pattern, *in Parker and Wallis (1948, 372).*

Rotoreliefs. Whatever else may be connected with Duchamp's rotating discs and their spatial effect,[68] here it is decisive that the idea of creating a spatial image by way of rotation would prove to have existed "in another way;" to say it more accurately, that it would in fact be used about thirteen years after the *Rotoreliefs*—namely with the technology of the volumetric display as a method of visualizing radar data, indeed very much in the tradition of Major Wright's "precision optics." Therefore, in conclusion to this chapter and bridging into the next one, I would like to contrast a *Rotorelief* with a similar picture from one of the earliest essays on volumetric 3D displays: Figures 7.12a and 7.12b).

Notes

1 See for example Clair (1978a; 1978b); Krauss (1991, 1993) or Henderson (1998).

2 See Lefebvre (1991, section 1.4). Lefebvre's main work *La production de l'espace* does not even mention Duchamp.

3 See Lefebvre (1991: 39): "Representations of space: . . . This is the dominant space in any society (or mode of production)" (my emphasis).

4 Since photography and film are usually seen in connection with a new 'production of time' (as one could say for fixating the moment in photography and for moving images and manipulation of the timeline in film). Duchamp has himself repeatedly admitted that he has, for example, borrowed the idea for his painting *Nu descendant un escalier* (1912) from chronophotography, see Duchamp quoted in Stauffer (1992, 154): "These chronophotographies gave me the idea on how to put movement into a painting, like for example in *Nu descendant un escalier*." Here he does not speak explicitly of transplane images (but which he is indeed using, see below), but he clearly illustrates his openness towards technical media in general, see Rowell (1975).

5 On the problem of succession in the history of Duchamp's works see Crary (1977, 96).

6 See Foucault (2009) on the example of Manet.

7 Of course there are also other tendencies; for example, in surrealist painting. However, I will discuss only those aspects that can be related to questions of 3D.

8 Rowell (1979a, 9). See also Boehm (1992, 16) on these "phenomena of transition between painting and sculpture, between sculpture and relief, between relief and painting."

9 Interestingly enough, this is a movement that repeats itself after 1945 under very different conditions and in a different way. It is first of all Clement Greenberg (1992) who demands a program of self-reflection and self-reduction in painting regarding its "flatness" (1978, 200) and color; it is a development that pivotally characterized American painting after the war with abstract painting dominating it. At the beginning of the 1960s, however, it is just this reduction that changes into a movement directed at three-dimensionality (e.g., in minimal art, but also in combine painting, environments, and installations); see in detail De Duve (1996, 199–280).

10 Greenberg (1988b, 260). See on Picasso particularly Bois (1990, 69–79). On Duchamp and cubism see De Duve (1991, 71–5).

11 The materiality of the surface is mainly important in the material-iconographic history of the arts. See on the problem of *impasto* and photographic reproduction in French painting of the nineteenth century Krüger (2007, 249, 250 and 357).

12 The question first raised in Chapter 2 that repeatedly rises again asking about the possibility of transplane reproductions of sculptures clearly originates from this problem; see on this also Schröter (2006b).

13 Krauss (1985b, 153) for example speaks of an "ethos of mechanical reproduction" with regard to Rodin.

14 The demand for geometrical-optical media of reproduction is to be found often, in particular in their early developmental stages, for example when Janin (1839, 146) exclaims about photography: "A cette heure, vous direz aux tours de Notre-Dame: Placez-vous là, et les tours obéiront." (You can now say to the towers of Notre-Dame: Place yourselves there, and the towers will obey). He seems to think that one can now *order* space to become plane. This triumphal demand of technological reproduction to my mind literally incites counter strategies of artistic avant-gardes.

15 Rowell (1979a, 31); she, however, also points out that these were often "brief and occasionally uncharacteristic incursions" (Rowell 1979a, 9).

16 See Greenberg (1988b, 260–1): "By 1912 Picasso was venturing into a kind of bas-relief construction in works that laid the foundation of constructivism, and indeed of all radically modern sculpture since Brancusi and Lipchitz. The picture had now attained to the full and declared three-dimensionality we automatically attribute to the notion . . . 'object'."

17 See Aumont (1992, 87) on cubism and montage in film.

18 Crary (1990, 126; last emphasis mine). Nevertheless I mentioned already in Chapter 2 that no one in the nineteenth century seemed to

have taken notice of the stage-like space of the stereoscopic picture. I couldn't find any sources for that. For examples where art was influenced by stereoscopy see Clausberg (1999, 57–79).

19 Foucault (1972, 193–4; my emphasis). The connection of Foucault's demand to his famous analysis of *Las Meñinas* by Diego Velazquez (1656) (Foucault 1994, 3–16) is not immediately evident.

20 There are also other examples for the effects of the series of physiological optics. The knowledge of the composability of colors from individual color particles or elements is manifested both in certain procedures of color reproduction in photography (see Eder 1978, 660–2) or in the monitors of television and computers and in pointillism (for example, in Seurat, see De Duve 1991, 172, who calls Seurat a "digitalized photographic plate"). The example of Seurat advises us to respect historical accuracy since Seurat did not exclusively use the three basic colors of subtractive color mixing in physiological-optical media technologies, even though his painting was close to a printing method that was widely used in the 1880s; see Broude (1978). The fact that Duchamp admired Seurat despite his dislike of painting may go back to their shared interest in physiological optics, see De Duve (1996, 172–80).

21 Clair (1978a, 48). Duchamp himself (quoted in Cabanne 1971, 18) observed on *Le Grand Verre*: "The 'Glass' saved me, by virtue of its transparency." See also on Duchamp's biting criticism of abstraction (Cabanne 1971, 43).

22 In Cabanne (1971, 116) Duchamp is said to have made "optical experiments." Of course this does not mean that the numerous other aspects of his work that are otherwise being discussed in the extensive literature—for example, the psychosexual and therefore somewhat autobiographic connotations (see for example in Krauss 1998)—are not just as important. However, they cannot be taken into account here. I will only analyze some works in the present context in a selective way according to the guiding questions of this book. Any other approach cannot be an option considering the obvious overabundance of literature on Duchamp.

23 His model, however, was never Cezanne, as it was for many other painters of his time; see De Duve (1991, 23–4; 76–81).

24 They are the shadows of the *Bicycle Wheel* (1916; but without the stool) and of the *Hat Rack* (1917; annual details according to Duchamp 2002). There also exists a photograph of the shadows of different ready-mades created by Duchamp in 1918.

25 Literature discusses the title *Tu m'* in different ways, since the verb that should follow is missing. In French the expression Tu m' is often

short for 'tu m'emmerdes', meaning 'you piss me off' or 'you are boring me.' This reference has often been connected with Duchamp's rejection of painting, which nevertheless he is doing here one last time. However, connections to the American collector Katherine S. Dreier, the person contracting the painting who had ordered it for a place above a book shelf (the reason for the pronounced horizontal format), have also been assumed because the relationship between Duchamp and Dreier was sometimes contentious.

26 On Duchamp and the index see Krauss (1985a, 204–6, particularly 206 on the parallel of ready-made and photograph) and Krauss (2002, 195). See also De Duve (1977).

27 See Peirce (1998, 380).

28 Wolf (2000) discusses Krauss's concept of the photographic, the logic of the index and that of reproducibility and their deconstructive effects on the art system.

29 Duchamp, quoted in Cabanne (1971, 40). See also Duchamp quoted in Stauffer (1992, 80).

30 On this strange reference by Duchamp to the idea of an additional spatial dimension see Adcock (1983) and Henderson (1983, 117–63).

31 See Bensmann (1989, 84). On viewing the painting for the first time, the brush is the most conspicuous element; it 'strikes the eye' (see De Duve 1991, 41). Therefore, it seems justified to start the analysis at this point.

32 See Gerstner (2003, 23). This casting of a shadow and the tracing of the shadows by the ready-mades can also be understood as a reference to the mythical origin of painting according to Plinius; see on this Dubois (1998, 108–128).

33 The red-blue line connected to the 'rear' upper corner of the plane demonstrates this as its beginning is covered by the plane. However, the painted shadow of the *Hat Rack* falls 'onto' the white rectangle, as if it were in front of it. This clearly is pointing to what Boehm (1994c, 33) has called the "paradox of the plane depth" paradigmatic for iconic difference.

34 Incidentally, at this point one could locate an even deeper *mise en abyme*. In a classical way, the hand is contrasted as a literal sign of painting to 'automatic' photography. The title of *Tu m'* already somewhat hints at Duchamp's own rejection of painting and his later venting against the 'retina' is underlined here by an emphatic *rejection of the hand* (see De Duve 1991, 173), where a quote is given in which Duchamp saw his hand as an enemy already in 1912; this rejection of the hand, by the way, also connected Duchamp with Seurat, see De Duve 1996, 174–5). The situation is very complex: In

Tu m'—which is so indexical and therefore 'antagonistic to the hand'—a *hand* is represented, and conspicuously in a realistic manner of painting that contains no individual touch of a hand (of another painter than Duchamp himself), which in turn is pointing indexically to an empty plane that is still waiting to be painted on by a hand (we are still in the realm of the medium painting).

35 See Clair (1978a). Duchamp observes on *The Large Glass*: "In addition, perspective was very important;" quoted in Cabanne (1971, 38).

36 Krauss (1993, 111; my emphasis). See De Duve (1991, 40) on Clair's somewhat overstated integration of Duchamp into the conservative camp.

37 The sexual implications of *Tu m'* could again be seen as references to Duchamp's cross-dressing experiments staged for the medium of photography.

38 See Anonymous (1984, 233) on *Tu m'*: "Everything about the painting demands that the viewer shift back and forth between two dimensions and three." It is almost as if Duchamp wanted to refer to Helmholtz (1985, 296) ironically: "The effect of every movement is to bring out instantly the difference in visual appearance between the original and the copy." By 'original' and 'copy' Helmholtz means here an object and its pictorial, two-dimensional representation.

39 And it cannot even be reduced to the logic of linear perspectival projection. This becomes visible from the representation of three different shades of brown in Duchamp's own work *Stoppages Étalon* (1913/1914) at the lower left corner of *Tu m'*. As Gerstner (2003, 16) observes: "The *Stoppages Étalon* are positioned in the lower left-hand corner, arranged one behind the other and not oriented toward a vanishing point but presented in parallel perspective – without perspective distortion. Here, Duchamp used a rudimentary construction prior to Brunelleschi's invention. If we move the white rectangle to the right-hand ends of the threads (the dotted lines are mine), we also obtain an imaginary solid body in parallel perspective. *Tu m'* is a mixed composition consisting of different approaches to the representation of spatial perspective."

40 To a certain extent one can find this connection of different logics also in *Tu m'* reflected once again. The series of colored squares recedes into the depth of the left upper corner of the painting; thus it is again pointing to the method of perspectival projection. However, this series has a vanishing point other than the white square. Under the shadow of the *Bicycle Wheel* on the left side there is additionally a hardly visible netting of red lines that strictly in linear perspective also runs towards a vanishing point at the center of the series of

colored squares. This means that there is no coherent perspectival space but a juxtaposition of different, intrinsically homogeneous perspectives—and this can also be understood metaphorically.

41 For example, think of Man Ray's photo portraits of Marcel Duchamp in drag as Rrose Sélavy.

42 Taken from http://www.metmuseum.org/toah/works-of-art/69.521 [last accessed September 2, 2013].

43 Thus there is no example for a 'rapid exposure-photogram' in historical practice.

44 However, the logic of reproducibility is in no way connected as compellingly with the 'rapid exposure' as is the projection.

45 The series of the colored squares could also be read as "color samples" (Henderson 1998, 208). This is relevant insofar as Duchamp has called all of painting itself a ready-made since it is using industrial colors in tubes that are advertised in catalogues with just these color samples. Thus, the colored squares are also a critical reference to painting itself. See for this De Duve (1991, 119–63, notably 134 on *Tu m'*; 1996, 147–98).

46 See Henderson (1998, 210) on *Tu m'*: Duchamp "had pushed painting as far as possible in the direction of the impersonal, indexical registering of the photograph or the scientific instrument."

47 Even the fact that *Tu m'* represents three of Duchamp's works (two ready-mades and the *Stoppages Étalon*) and thus is operating as a sort of archive of Duchamp's works could make us connect it to the *Logic of the Archive* that has often been associated with photography. As a survey of photography and archive see Schröter (2006c; including further references). See also Duchamp quoted in Cabanne (1971, 60).

48 This does not contradict the anti-retinal position (see Cabanne 1971, 39) as Krauss (1993, 123–5) has shown. See also Krauss (1991, 442) why one should take note of the "presence of physiological optics at work within Duchamp's thinking and production" despite "Duchamp's vehement and insistent rejection of the 'retinal.' "

49 See Deleuze and Guattari (2004) in the chapter on the "problem of the sea" as a "smooth space par excellence" (529) in which "the smooth space is directional rather than dimensional" (528). "A *dimensionality* that subordinated *directionally*, or superimposed itself upon it, became increasingly entrenched" (529)—like in Duchamp's *Handmade Stereopticon Slide*.

50 See Alberti (2011, 29): "And for what concerns this centric ray, it is certainly true that it is the most vigorous and lively of all rays."

51 I cannot expand on the countless other readings of *The Large Glass* in this context. However, already the fact that the painting is on glass can be seen as a hidden reference to Alberti's definition of the picture as a window; see Alberti (2011, 39). See also Duchamp, quoted in Cabanne (1971, 41): "The glass, being transparent, was able to give its maximum effectiveness to the rigidity of perspective."

52 See Clair (1978a). But as I have verified, this comparison holds only for some of the representations in the essay referred to by Clair. Some of the other representations do not at all match the ratio of the upper and lower half in *The Large Glass* (see e.g. Bosse 1987, 141).

53 Clair (1978b, 108) refers to Lacan (1978) who—coinciding with my suggestions in Chapter 1—maintains that "[t]his is something that introduces what was elided in the geometral relation [of the series of geometrical optics]—the depth of field with all its ambiguity and variability, which is in no way mastered by me" (96).

54 As I have shown in Chapter 1 it is specifically photography that is resisting this model.

55 With this in mind I would contradict Krauss's (1993, 134) reading of the *Handmade Stereopticon Slide*. Explicitly referring to Crary (1990, 128) this reading associates it with the (assumed) *successive break* between physiological and geometrical optics.

56 See Clair (1978b, 104–6). Duchamp's very last drawing *Anaglyphic Chimney* (1968) is also anaglyphic, see Clair (1978b, 109).

57 Henderson (1998, 212; capitalization in the original). On precision optics in Duchamp see Blunck (2008).

58 From the abundant literature on this subject see Wallach and O'Connell (1953, 206 in particular). The authors are pointing out that movement is able to give the impression of three-dimensionality, even if one views only with one eye.

59 See Musatti (1924). The first sentence in this text is: "Per fenomeni stereocinetici intendiamo le trasformazioni percettive di un complesso di figure aderenti ad un piano ed in movimento relativo, reale od apparente, su quel piano, in un complesso di figure disposte in profondità, le quali possono: o essere ancora in movimento relativo fra di loro, oppure costituire un tutto solido che si muove soltanto relativamente all'osservatore. Si possono perciò distinguere due tipi di fenomeni stereocinetici." (Stereokinetic phenomena [or depth effects] can be understood as the sensually perceivable transformation of a group of figures adhering to a plane, seemingly real or as an illusion in relative motion; they are positioned at a certain depth, either moving towards each other or forming a solid whole only moving relative to the perspective of the viewer.

Therefore, two types of stereokinetic phenomena can be differentiated.)

60 See Duchamp in Cabanne (1971, 72–3). Interestingly enough, the shadow of the corkscrew in *Tu m'* seems to anticipate the "corkscrew-effects" highly valued by Duchamp at a later time.

61 Sekula (1989, 346). See also Sekula (2004, 124). See in connection with Sekula Schröter (2006c) on Walker Evans' settling of this tension, particularly in his work *Many are Called*. On criminological photography see Regener (1999).

62 Referring back to Chapter 3 and reminding of the fact that chromatogelatine can also be used to create photographic reliefs.

63 See Kricke-Güse and Güse (1981, 18) who label the *Rotoreliefs* "kinetic reliefs".

64 See the lemma "relief" in Alscher et al. (1983, 85). On reliefs Hauck (1885) continues to be a reference.

65 On shadow and light in reliefs see Deecke (1981).

66 As I will show, not all transplane pictures follow this media-aesthetic scheme. Holography, for example, indeed resembles the aesthetics of reliefs inasmuch as it takes into account the movements of the viewers; see section 9.4.

67 This reminds me of an observation by Crary (1990, 124): "Pronounced stereoscopic effects depend on the presence of objects or obtrusive forms in the near or middle ground." Often in stereoscopic images some objects are placed directly in the foreground—not because this has to satisfy a compositional logic but because it heightens the three-dimensional effect of the picture. One can find nice examples of this in film, for example in Alfred Hitchcock's *Dial M for Murder* (USA 1954). There are some takes in which, for example, a vase can be seen in the foreground, quite obviously and without compositional motivation. But one can easily understand these compositional anomalies: The film originally had been filmed for a stereoscopic 3D presentation.

68 See for example Mussman (1967, 153) who believes there are sexual innuendoes to female sexual organs and sexual acts to be seen in the optical illusions of the discs (in *Anemic Cinema*) that are pulsating forward and backward. See also Krauss (1993, 96–7). Michelson (1973) on the other hand sees a reference to autism in the film. Many more interpretational suggestions have been made.

Plate 1 *Facsimile reproduction of a direct chemical color photograph on a chlorinated silver plate by Niépce de Saint Victor (exhibited at the world fair in 1867), in Eder 1905: plate XII.*

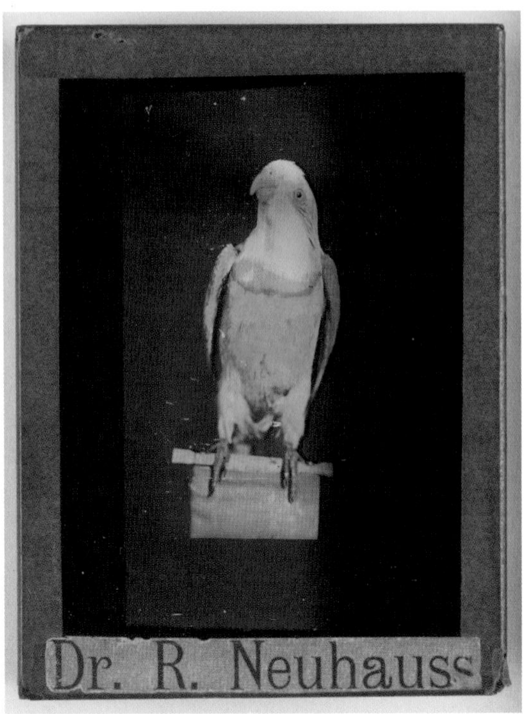

Plate 2 *A Lippmann photograph of a parrot, in Coe (1979, 27). It is not possible to reproduce the appearance of a Lippmann photograph here.*

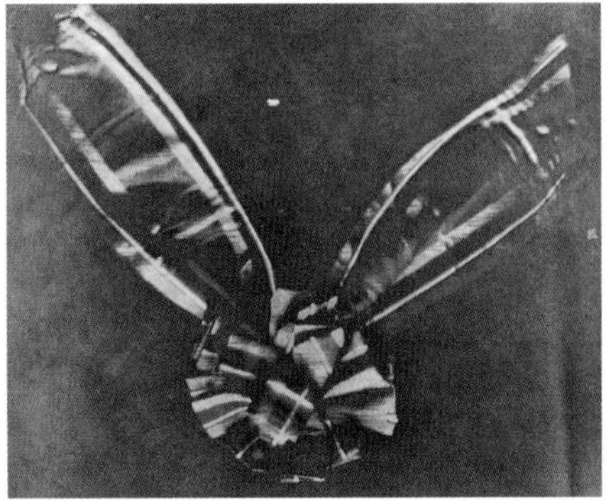

Plate 3 *First three-color photograph by Maxwell (1861) in Bellone and Fellot (1981, 88).*

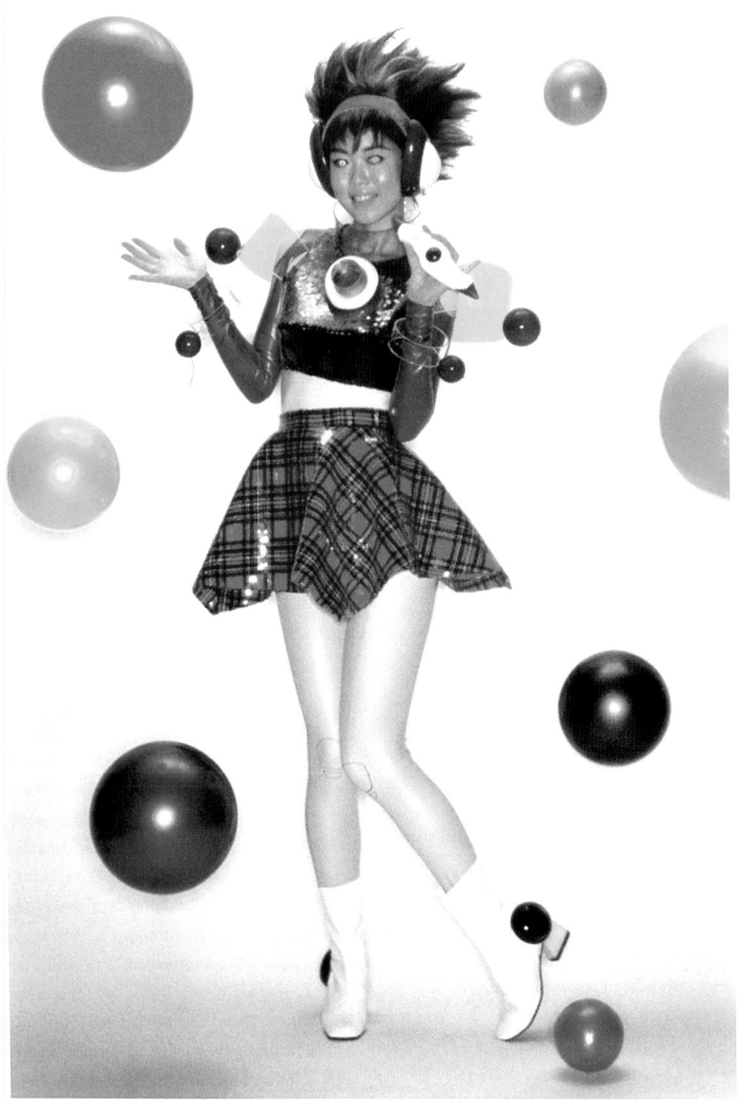

Plate 4 *Mariko Mori,* Birth of a Star *(1995), 3-D duratrans, acrylic, light box, and audio CD; 70³⁄₁₆ × 45¼ × 4¼ in. (178.3 × 114.9 × 10.8 cm), Museum of Contemporary Art, Chicago. (Unfortunately, the effect of the lenticular image cannot be recreated here).*

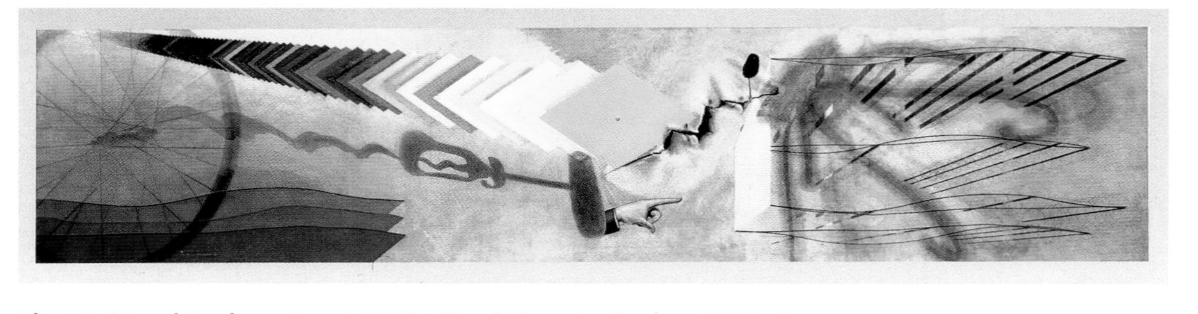

Plate 5 *Marcel Duchamp* Tu m' *(1918), 70 × 313 cm, in Gerstner (2003, 6).*

CHAPTER EIGHT

Since 1948: The volumetric display

The Series of Physiological Optics 3
The Series of Virtual Optics 2
The Politics of the Transplane Image 2
Media Aesthetics of the Transplane Image 6 and 7: Jenny Holzer, Lustmord *(1993–96) and Olafur Eliasson,* Convex/Concave *(1995/2000)*

Some data are perishable. If not understood quickly, perishable data become useless. . . . The important information must be easy to understand within a meaningful time interval, a virtue not always appreciated. In this case the perhaps unexpected benefit of adding a third spatial dimension is that less time may be needed for understanding a set of data.

LAWRENCE D. SHER (1993, 212)

Any display system able to provide an observer with the sensation of depth can greatly enhance the impact and qualitative understanding of 3-D information.

BARRY BLUNDELL AND ADAM SCHWARZ (2000, 17)

My example at the end of the previous chapter—*Spiral Scan Pattern*—originates from a text published in 1948. The accompanying text reads as follows:

> In this case, the scan of the 1° aerial beam covers a circular cone of space. Although there are many ways of producing such a scan, we shall consider one generated by an epicyclic or hypercyclic mechanism, combining two steady circular motions at different speeds.[1]

The goal is to create a certain scanning pattern with an aerial beam. The beam in question is a radar beam, radar being one of the most important methods in the twentieth century for controlling spaces. It was developed and employed in WWII (see Guerlac 1987 among others). The essay quoted here is entitled "Three-Dimensional Cathode-Ray Tube Displays" and it continues:

> Since the screen of a c.r. tube [= cathode ray tube] is only two-dimensional, only two coordinates of the object's position can be thus directly displayed. This has until relatively recently been adequate, the radar set being called upon to scan in only a single angular coordinate, usually with a 'fan beam', but the modern set may scan in two angular co-ordinates with a 'pencil beam'. It is with these volume-scanning radar sets, where the object's position in three coordinates is derivable, that we are concerned here. (Parker and Wallis 1948, 371)

Obviously, the concern here is representing three-dimensional spatial information and—since we are dealing with radar—how to do this as fast as possible in critical situations in which decisions have to be made *quickly*. "When a human operator is involved in the loop, however, all the n channels have to pass simultaneously through the bottleneck of his senses, consciousness and movements."[2] The slow "human operator" thus has to get optimal information on space. This can also be seen in a paper published in 1963, regarded as an important early text:

> A real need exists for a three-dimensional display in almost any spatial navigation problem, whether it is through water, air, or outer space. Faster and faster vehicle velocities have outmoded

> visual navigation, even when direct visual observations are possible. ... The navigator's ability to react should not be limited by his position display. (Ketchpel 1963, 324)

This means that visual 'realism' is in demand. This is the goal that Parker and Wallis have in mind for their "true three-dimensional display" and they contrast it with stereoscopic radar displays that are said to have been already developed in Great Britain around 1942–43:

> It is unfortunate that the radar picture is frequently rather flickering and indistinct, as such conditions are not conducive to stereoscopic vision. This, and the great variations in operators' vision, has in the past made stereoscopic radar displays of somewhat speculative use. (Parker and Wallis 1948, 376)

Even though the authors concede that the stereoscopic displays can be enhanced in the future, the last problem mentioned above remains. Not all potential human operators can manage stereoscopic information equally well. This might mean that the solution could be to develop a three-dimensional display that avoids just that problem: "A truly three-dimensional display is one in which the echoes appear as bright spots in an actual volume of light, at points representing the spatial positions of the corresponding objects."[3] This is the decisive point in volumetric displays. The image is not being created *on* a plane, nor on two, as in stereoscopy; it is created *in a volume*. As a result the image is perceived as spatial.[4] How can this be done? According to the authors,

> [t]he echoes are displayed in the volume of light as bright spots, by an intensity modulation of the c.r.t. spot. The deflections must be suitably synchronized with the scan of the aerial beam, in order that the echoes may appear consistently at points representing the objects' spatial positions. The deflection produced mechanically can be either 'real' or 'apparent'. An example of the former would be obtained if the c.r. tube itself were moved axially. This is, for mechanical reasons, undesirable. A similar effect can be obtained, however, by projecting the c.r.t. picture on to a moving screen. An 'apparent' deflection can be obtained, for example, by observing the c.r.t. picture in a mirror which is moved in a suitable manner[5] [see Figure 8.1].

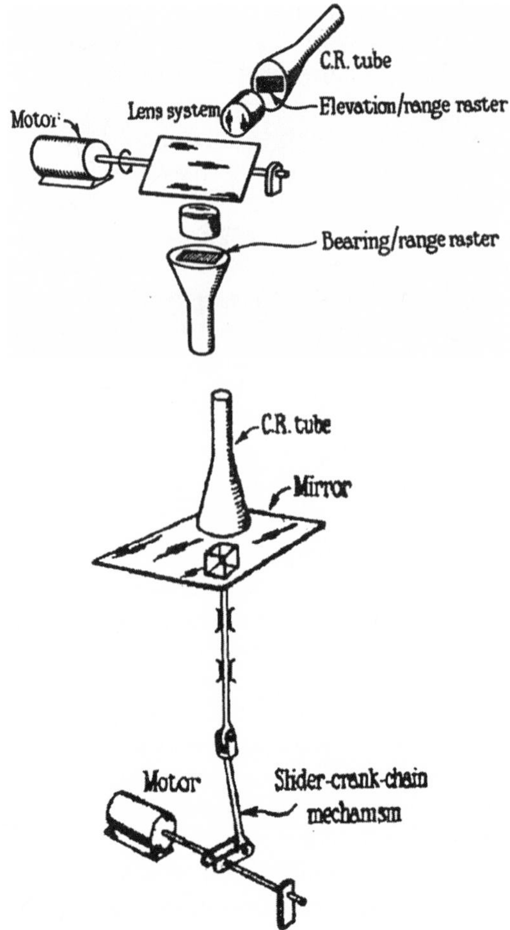

FIGURE 8.1 *Early diagrams for: (a) a "Moving Screen" and (b) a "Moving Mirror" display, two fundamental forms of volumetric display of the "swept volume"-type (see below), in Parker and Wallis (1948, 373).*

Here, Parker and Wallis are describing two fundamental types of the class of volumetric displays that create the volume of the image with movable parts ("swept volume"). In the first case the screen is rotating and the light-points are projected onto it. In the second case the plane is multiplied into a volume through a translational moving mirror.[6] This means that similar to film, volumetric displays function on the basis of the series of physiological optics with the addition of the third dimension. Human perception visualizes a three-dimensional image produced by the fast succession of projections onto the rapidly moving planes.[7] It can (in principle) be viewed from all sides without additional glasses. Contrasted to geometrical optics, this plane is being moved, thereby becoming transplane. The image then appears in the volume, described by many authors as *image-space* or *image-volume*. Therefore in studies of volumetric displays the term pixel (short for picture element) has been replaced by voxel (short for volume element; see Blundell and Schwarz 2000, 31–3). Since the volumetric display in an ideal case is really three-dimensional, it can instantly provide information on the spatial structure and the situatedness of objects. It has one limitation insofar as the images are transparent, i.e, parts of the image are unable to obscure each other[8] and thus, the depth marker of occlusion cannot be used. Parker and Wallis already knew this, as can be seen from the end of their early, clear-sighted essay:

> The displays have a limitation, in that they appear always as a 'transparency'. Light is radiated from each point in the display without regard to the radiation from other points 'between' it and the observer. This would make its direct application to a television system awkward . . . For television, a direct stereoscopic presentation using two or more cameras is more suitable. The application of three-dimensional displays to X-ray work for medical and other purposes would be assisted, however, by this transparency. It is conceivable that their application to this field might lead to advances in diagnostic and therapeutic medicine. (Parker and Wallis 1948, 384)

And this is indeed what happened. As I will discuss later, volumetric displays (especially of the type 'varifocal mirror') were at least experimentally used in medical imaging. Because of the transparent character of the images produced by them, their use is difficult to imagine in mass media; for example, in a narrative film. In reverse, one can say that every history of optical or visual media[9] or every discussion in visual studies that continues focusing on mass media and/or on artistically used visual technologies will possibly overlook the use of different, e.g. structurally transparent,[10] types of images.

In general, the problem of displays with rapidly moving discs is that the high rotational velocity of the moving parts places a heavy demand on the mechanical elements and that therefore the size of such a display is limited. As a result, solutions were attempted that create the image in a static volume (solid state displays), either by activating special materials point-wise with laser light or by combining larger quantities of very small diodes into an image-volume and then individually activating the diodes.[11] Here the image area is definitely abandoned in favor of a volume.

Even though different authors have varied in their opinion, holographic images (see Chapter 9) are not counted among the volumetric images in this context since in holography one is dealing with a wavefront construction and not with the creation of an image by activating three-dimensional image points (voxels, see above and below). Volumetric displays are preferred to holograms in many areas of application. The first reason is that "volume displays offer similar information content to digital holograms with orders-of-magnitude fewer computations" (Batchko 1992, 8). Directly connected to this is the second reason: "Holography can provide 3-D displays, but in a hologram motion is usually frozen. Real-time movement in a hologram is possible in theory, but exceedingly difficult in practice" (Brinkmann 1983, 55). Figure 8.2 outlines the different ramifications, the "bewildering variety"[12] of the developments of volumetric displays, arranged in the two main categories.

I cannot describe the individual details of the technical or genealogical developments here.[13] Most of the procedures are experimental prototypes that never left the laboratories. The few appliances that can be bought commercially[14] are quite expensive and are generally used in the natural sciences for experiments, in particular in medicine and in the military, i.e. in discursive practices in which a "production of space" (Lefebvre) is the dominant concern.

Though (or maybe because) volumetric images are used mainly in highly financed specialized areas, phantasmagorical ideas surround this topic even in concrete research projects.[15] To start with, I would like to consider these phantasmatics first. In a recent text on volumetric displays we read:

> The motivation for this work is the dream of realizing real stereovision images in space. Most of us remember the scene in

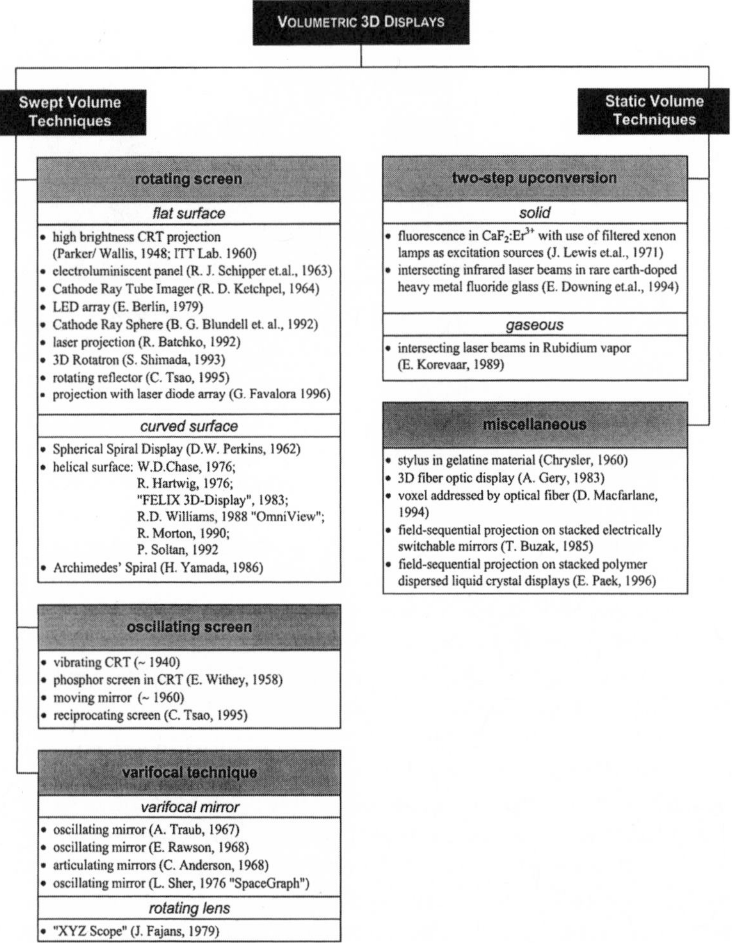

FIGURE 8.2 *Overview of the different types of volumetric displays.*[16]

the 1977 movie 'STAR WARS' in which the robot R2-D2 projects a three-dimensional image of Princess Leia, who begs Obi-Wan Kenobi for help. Besides 'STAR WARS', there have been many movies that contain scenes in which holograms appear . . . These films indicate a desire or a premonition in many of us to see this kind of technology brought to life.[17]

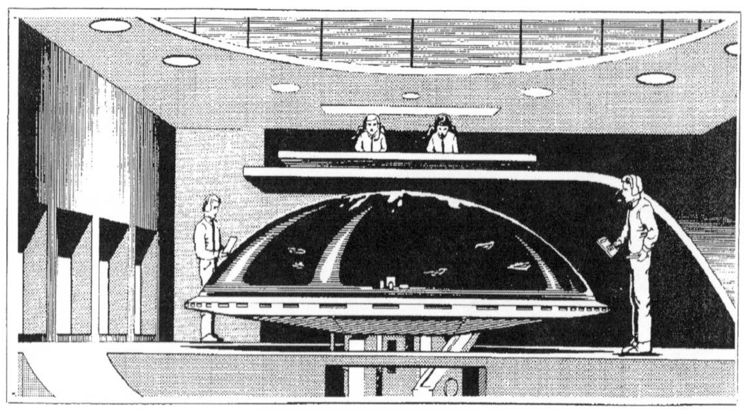

FIGURE 8.3 *Fictitious volumetric display used in a sort of traffic control system, in Williams and Garcia (1989, 9).*

Though the dream of 3D does not have to be hyped into an anthropological constant, it seems that it is an actor in this matter. In Figure 8.3 one can see a (fictional) representation of a volumetric display from a text published in 1989, remarkably similar to representations of futuristic displays in *Star Wars Episode III – Revenge of the Sith* (USA 2005, Dir. George Lucas) or *Avatar* (USA 2009, Dir. James Cameron).

Volumetric display technologies were developed concretely in connection with radar technology. Therefore it is not too far-fetched connecting ideas of control and surveillance with them.[18] The two examples already imply that it is a matter of controlling territories and the collective processes that are taking place there. Insofar as volumetric displays allow for three-dimensional representations that can be watched by any number of people from any angle without specialized glasses or any other gear, they allow for a viewing by groups that need to make decisions based on just these representations—and this is one of the *predominant advantages*. Figure 8.3 shows a sort of centralized traffic control area. Seen from this perspective, volumetric displays serve as "repressive visualization" (Lefebvre 1991, 286). Specific institutions subject a distant place to analysis and bring it under control with the help of volumetric displays. Bruno Latour has argued that the "simple drift from watching confusing three-dimensional objects, to inspecting two-dimensional images which have been *made less confusing*" is a central technique of producing knowledge.

> No matter what they [the scientists, but one could also say: the military] talk about, they start talking with some degree of confidence and being believed by colleagues, only once they point at simple geometrized two-dimensional shapes. (Latour 1986, 16)

However, research with volumetric displays has shown that this pointing, the discussions and the decision-making connected with it are in some cases more successful with three-dimensional representations proper. Through these display technologies space or spatial constellations themselves become immutable mobiles, in the sense of Latour. In this way a spatial situation is opened up to discussions and control.

The comprehensive literature on volumetric displays can be discussed here only in an exemplary way; in these texts one can find repeatedly commentaries on the viability and necessity of volumetric display technologies:

> With vendors lowering the barrier to adoption by providing compatibility with new and legacy applications, volumetric displays are poised to assume a commanding role in fields as diverse as medical imaging, mechanical computer-aided design, and military visualization. (Favalora 2005, 37)

There are two fields of applications that are named often: the military[19] and medical visualization. At all times, then, the aim is the control of spaces filled with people or the control of the human body itself. The means of control is a god's-eye view which either watches that space from outside or is able to effortlessly penetrate the body.

> In the case of all volumetric display systems known to the authors, the generation of images occurs within a containing vessel from which the [observer] is excluded. Volumetric systems therefore provide a 'God's-eye' view of any image scene. (Blundell and Schwarz 2000, 4)

Foucault has discussed the medical gaze in modernity: "The anatomo-clinician's gaze has *to map a volume*; it deals with the complexity of spatial data which for the first time in medicine are three-dimensional" (Foucault 1975, 163; emphasis in the original). This means that the medical profession needs visual technology that can unequivocally represent the volume of the body in an assessable manner. The abstract of a pertinent text expresses this in the following way:

> Today, converting the 2-D data of conventional medical images into useful 3-D clinical information requires mentally integrating the data into a 3-D image. The transformation, however, is frequently difficult even for experienced radiologists. Even with the Magnetic Resonance Imaging (MRI) device, and its remarkably sophisticated imaging, the end product image is only a 2-D presentation of 3-D. The same can be said for all ultrasound imaging devices employed throughout hospitals and in clinical laboratories. (Soltan et al. 1995, 349)

Again the point is that the human operator—in this case the experienced radiologist—has limitations that can at least be minimized with the respective information added. The authors then continue by explaining the technological details of the display to be used. It is a volumetric display that projects a transplane image onto a rotating plane in the form of a helix (see Figure 8.4).

Subsequently, possible usages of this display are again being discussed: "A logical application for the 3D volumetric display is for control and management of air traffic in a volume of aerospace for the FAA, Air Force, or Navy" (Soltan et al. 1995, 356; see Figure 8.5).

It should be noted that in this military setting only men are watching the display and thereby direct their controlling gaze on the target, although women are not excluded from the military in the USA. Figure 8.6 shows a similar situation.

The corresponding text explains:

> The Department of Defense Science and Technology Initiative identifies seven thrust areas. One of these is Global Surveillance and Communications, a capability that can focus on a trouble spot and be responsive to the needs of the commander. A

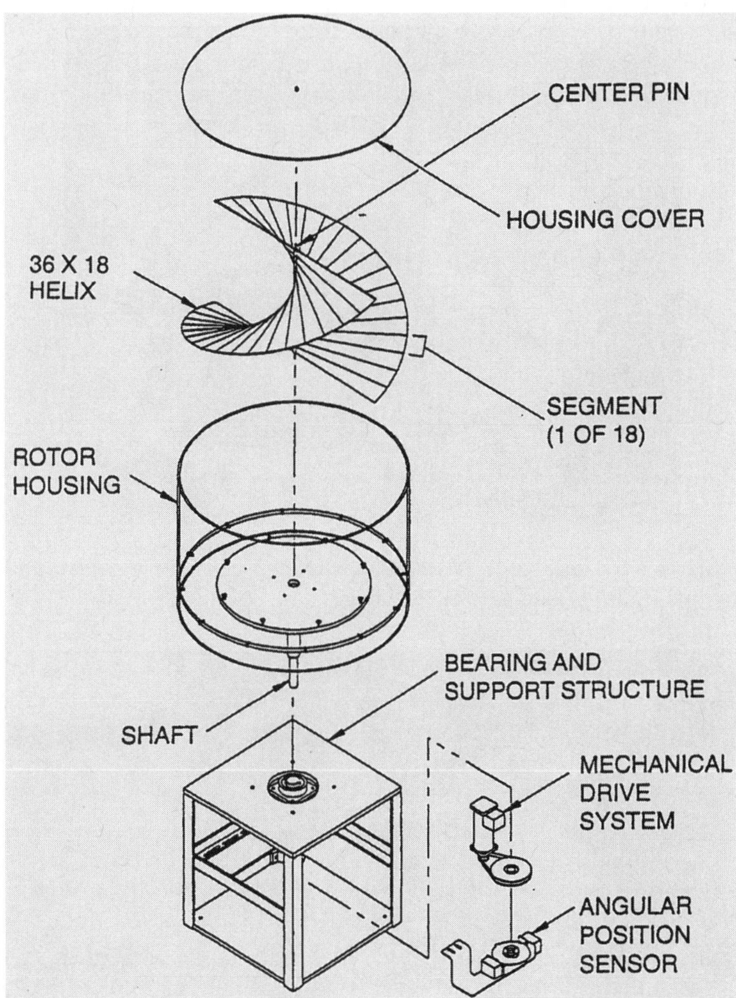

FIGURE 8.4 *Volumetric Display, in Soltan et al. (1995, 352.1).*[20]

three-dimensional display of the battle area – such as the LaserBased 3-D Volumetric Display System – will greatly facilitate this capability. Tactical data collected for command review can be translated and displayed as 3-D images. The perspective gained will contribute to quicker and more accurate

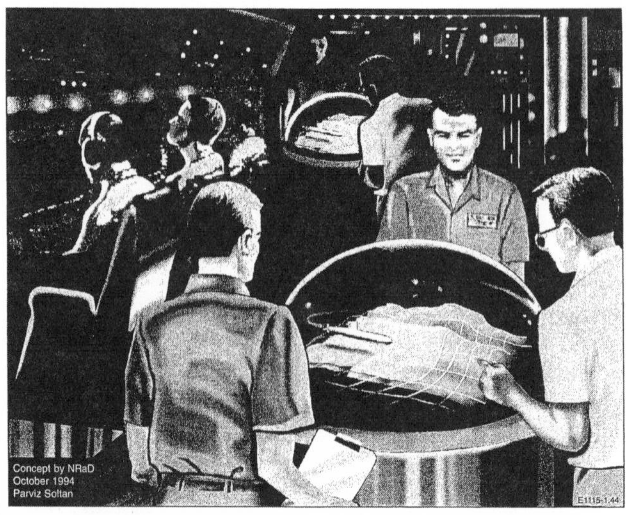

FIGURE 8.5 *Usage of a (fictitious) volumetric display for underwater control, in Soltan et al. (1996, 16).*

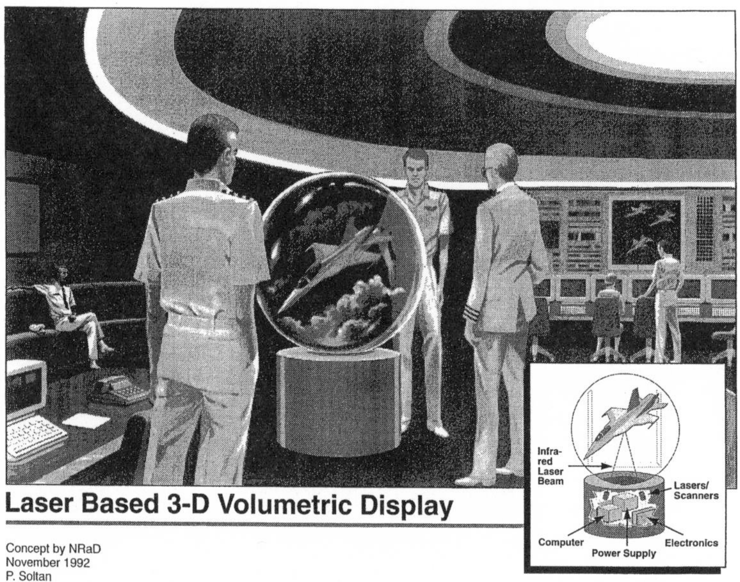

FIGURE 8.6 *Usage of a (fictitious) volumetric display for a command-and-control situation, in Soltan et al. (1996, 18).*

> decision-making regarding deployment and management of battle resources. (Soltan et al. 1996, 17)

Again we see only men watching the display with a controlling gaze.[21] The following Figure 8.7 shows this even more clearly. Here it is a woman who is at the center—but in this case she is the *object* of the medical gaze via the volumetric display.

> Employing the fully developed high-resolution images of the 3-D Volumetric Medical Display . . . all the soft tissues of the body can be monitored in 3-D color and in real time. These tissues include such major organs as the heart, lungs, and liver. Even the unborn baby can be observed in 3-D, while in the birth canal. (Soltan et al. 1996, 17)

At least in this case the androcentric politics of the transplane gaze connecting the eye and the phallus is obvious in its aggressive

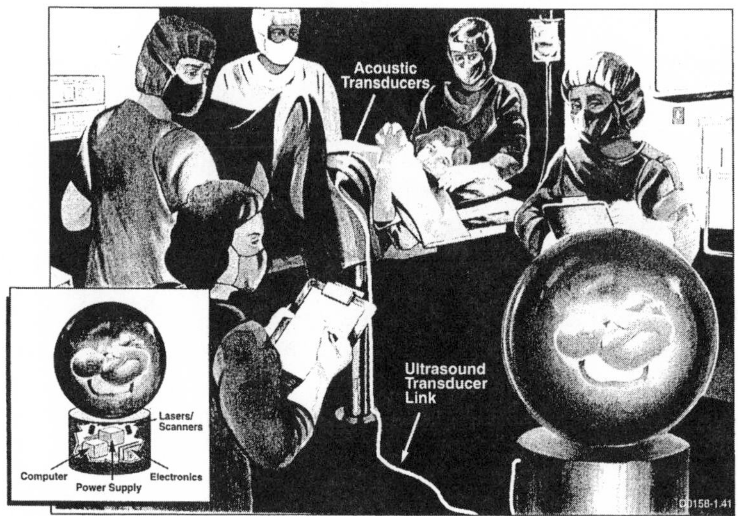

FIGURE 8.7 *Usage of a (fictitious) volumetric display for the control of a female body during birth, in Soltan et al. (1996, 20).*

visualization (see Lefebvre 1991, 302). Clearly the volumetric display is to be found in the tradition of other technologies of screening the body. As Foucault observes more precisely:

> But the absolute eye of knowledge has already confiscated, and re-absorbed into its geometry of lines, surfaces, and volumes, raucous or shrill voices, whistlings, palpitations, rough, tender skin, cries—a suzerainty of the visible, and one all the more imperious in that it associates with it power and death. That which hides and envelops, the curtain of night over truth, is, paradoxically, life; and death, on the contrary, opens up to the light of day the black coffer of the body: obscure life, limpid death, the oldest imaginary values of the Western world are crossed here in a strange misconstruction that is the very meaning of pathological anatomy. (Foucault 1975, 166)

Even outside of medicine a practice of 'mediated transparent stereoscopic images' is starting with Ernst Mach in 1866 and his "transparent stereoscopic images" (Wolf 1998, 119 and 79; see also Mach 1896) of the human cranium. It would continue with the discovery of roentgen rays in 1895 and their use in medicine that quickly follows. For a long time the roentgen rays remained the only way of scanning the body. CT (computerized tomography), which is still based on the roentgen rays, was discovered by Hounsfield and Cormack independently from each other and would be used increasingly after 1974. With the MRI (magnetic resonance imaging) suggested for the first time by Lauterbur and Mansfield, a different imaging technology emerges which only spread in the 1980s. In contrast to x-rays and CTs, it can make the tender and fluid parts of the body visible. The transplane visual technology of the volumetric display widens these visualizations regarding the physicality of the body. A group of authors, for example, writes on the possibilities of how the limitations of the tomographic visualization via three-dimensional displays can be dealt with:

> Three-dimensional displays of stacks of tomographic images, utilizing a varifocal mirror display system [a specific type of volumetric display, see below], addresses the fundamental dilemma that while tomographic images contain no superposition, they also contain no three-dimensional information even though

> comprehending three-dimensional shapes and/or spatial relationships is often desirable, if not vital. For example, an image of an oblique section may, on one hand, provide an unambiguous view of a slice through an organ but still be completely useless if the viewer does not understand the orientation of the slice with respect to structures of interest.[22]

On the one hand, the different methods of acquiring and visualizing data can be regarded as being in line with Foucault's analyses insofar as they can be understood as the continuation of the penetrating gaze bringing the inside of the body to light. On the other hand, they represent its technologically induced shift. X-rays, and the MRI[23] even more so, make for a finer and more precise view into the body *without* having to open up a corpse by force. These technologies then no longer turn the relationship of life and death upside down; they make both present simultaneously. The volumetric display is able to show the inside together with the closed living body—and even as a *spatial* phenomenon (see again Figure 8.7). To say it with Foucault, the human being can become a carnal-transplane duplicate via the three-dimensionally armed medical gaze. And it is this medical gaze that is intimately related with the military gaze that is scanning space, searching for strategic constellations and potential victims. And one could intensify the argument by saying: What is being wreaked by the military gaze has to be repaired by the medical one. Freely adapted from Kracauer, as the basis of social reality, the hieroglyph of the spatial volumetric display presents the reality of a disciplinary society based on control of the body.[24]

Even though volumetric displays continue to be experimental technologies, in some cases they are applied artistically as well. I do not want to overemphasize these instances—one can hardly construe a media aesthetics of volumetric displays from such a small number of cases. But in discussing them one can show that the reference to the human body and its annihilation, its training, and its adaptation inherent in the genealogy of volumetric displays is being reflected in the artistic works.

1. In the work *Lustmord* conceived from 1993 to 1996 by the well-known North American media artist Jenny Holzer a volumetric display is being used. The central theme of the work is violence against women, mainly during the war in Bosnia.

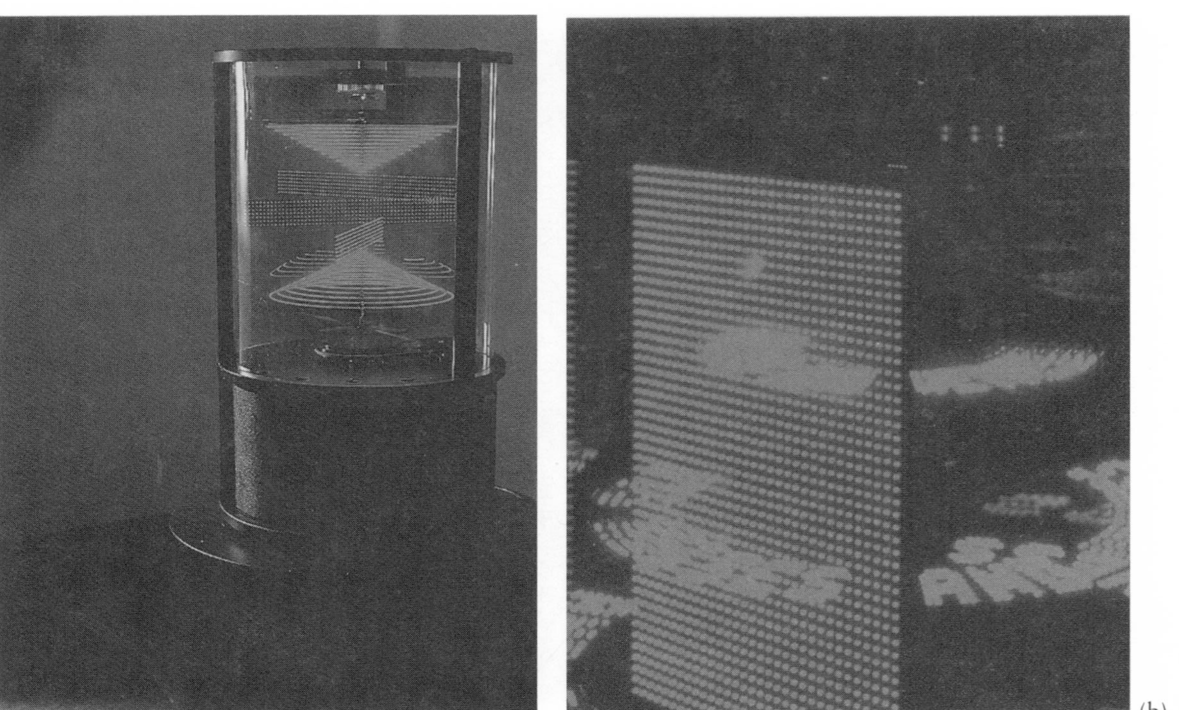

(a) (b)

FIGURE 8.8 Volumetric Display in Jenny Holzer's *Lustmord* (1993–96), (a) installed at the Bergen Museum of Art, Bergen (1994); and (b) detail from Holzer (1996, 99, 102).

First of all, the volumetric display turns out to be part of an installation. It stands to reason that transplane images can connect or contrast the spatial impressions generated by them with other spatial values, for example in order to let the viewers reflect on their perception of spatiality. In *Lustmord* Jenny Holzer is using the possibilities of a *Holoverse Volumetric Matrix Imager Model 200* to spatialize the texts in the form of LED-signs,[25] well-known from her earlier works: The LED-signs were used by Holzer in several other installations to intervene in existing spatial structures by moving along walls or facades, thereby both highlighting and hiding their structures. In *Lustmord* they move in a circle in the volumetric display as a sort of sculptural event. One could say that here a media-aesthetic potential of volumetric visual media is being suggested: namely, the possibility to vest volatile signs and images, especially computer generated ones,[26] with real spatial, even bodily qualities, thereby connecting them with sculpture, installation and architecture. The ever so 'immaterial' images and signs created by the computer could thus be directly related to the physical movement of the viewers.

Secondly, it is remarkable that Holzer is using the volumetric display precisely in connection with the issue of violence against women. This seems almost as if she were taking up the script inscribed[27] in the genealogy of volumetric imaging. This script is the gaze that penetrates the body (of women, as the examples above suggest). By connecting it to military violence against bodies this script is made explicit and is criticized. From this point of view it seems to me that a critique of *Lustmord* from 1994 that expressly mentions the "texts spinning in a glass-dome," while at the same time asking "how its heavy technological artillery relates to the abuse of women is not clear" overlooks the genealogy of the volumetric display. Holzer's "direct address of the body" (Cotter 1994, n.p.) finds an adequate medium (that itself mainly stems from medical imaging) for appropriately reflecting the body and the threats to it in the volumetric display, especially since the volumetric display uses the effects of *physiological* optics in order to generate a spatialized image.

2. There is another artistic item addressing (among other things) the physicality of vision by using techniques of the volumetric display. Olafur Eliasson, the Danish-Icelandic artist, has often been involved with the different optical series. Regarding Eliasson's installation *Your Colour Memory* (2004), Jonathan Crary, not

surprisingly, has underlined that “[h]e is self-consciously working with luminous duration and intensity so as to bring into play the subjective features of human vision associated with after images” (Crary 2005, 220).

Figure 8.9 shows another example; it is a work with the quite explicit title *Your Blue Afterimage Exposed* (2000). A square, orange light spot is projected onto a wall. The light gets stronger and stronger and suddenly snaps off. Instead of the light spot the viewers then see a square in its complementary color, becoming the projector themselves, as the artist once remarked (quoted in Grynsztejn et al. 2004, 21).

Quite in line with his assumption that modernity is characterized by the “passage from geometrical optics . . . to physiological optics,” Crary (1990, 16) argues that Eliasson refers to the series of physiological optics. He underlines: “If after-images preoccupy him, it is in part as a strategy of challenging and displacing perceptual

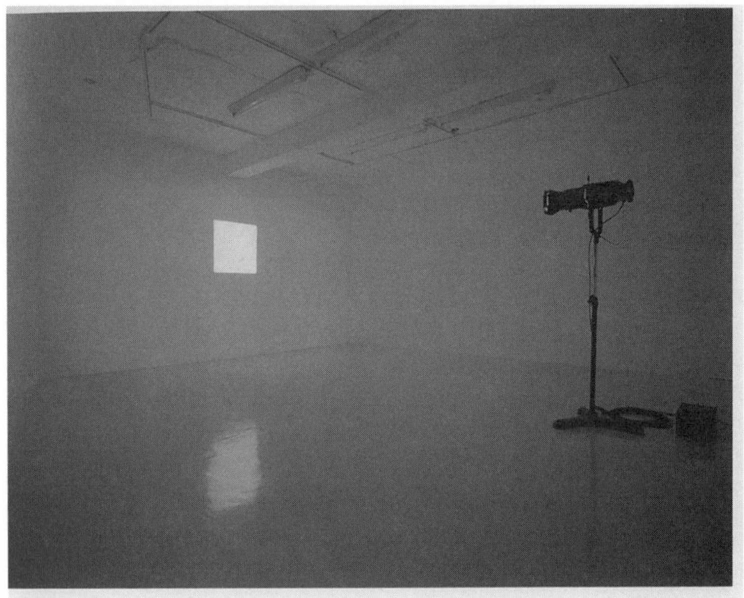

FIGURE 8.9 *Olafur Eliasson,* Your Blue Afterimage Exposed *(2000). Private collection, © Olafur Eliasson.*

habits imposed by dominant features of contemporary technological culture" (Crary 2005, 222). I agree with this analysis and will accentuate and expand on it below. However, Crary reduces Eliasson's work too much to the series of physiological optics, disregarding the numerous other works in which the artist has addressed the series of geometrical optics. In particular his work *Camera Obscura* (Figure 8.10) has to be named here. From the outside a finely ribbed

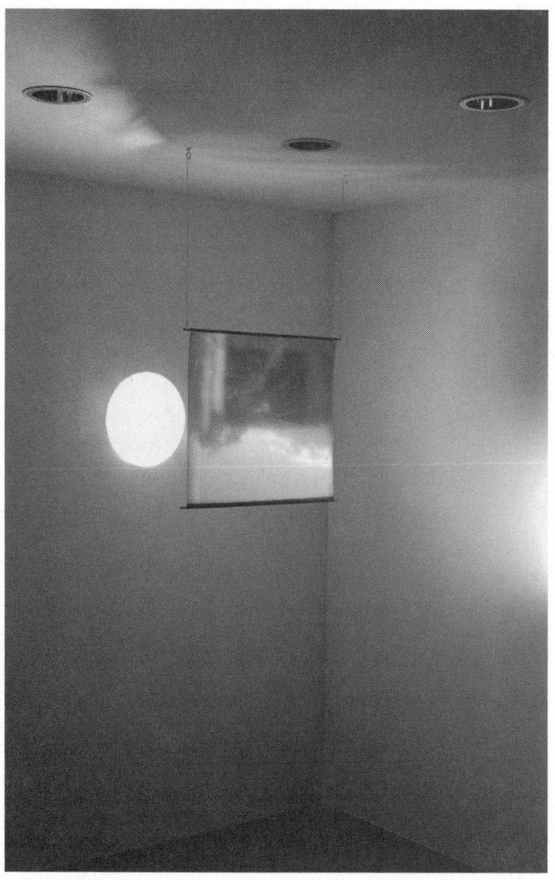

FIGURE 8.10 *Olafur Eliasson,* Camera Obscura *(1999), installation View: Dundee Contemporary Arts, Scotland (1999), Photo: Colin Ruscoe, © Olafur Eliasson and Dundee Contemporary Arts.*

plastic sheet hanging in the air is lit through a hole in a plate made of plywood. On this sheet a geometrical-optical image is created that is quite blurred because of the structure of the sheet.

Eliasson's work in particular refers to the different and irreducible optical series. Crary's tendency to reduce the heterogeneous coexistence of the different optical series into a succession is mirrored in his analysis of Eliasson's works.[28]

Even if we only concentrate on the works addressing the series of physiological optics, it becomes noticeable that Crary—echoing Henri Bergson—emphasizes mainly the "flexible and reversible temporalities" (Crary 2005, 224) of perception. And even though he underlines that Eliasson's concern is not the "currently fashionable image of Bergson as the anticipator of cinematic time" (Crary 2005, 225), he nevertheless directs his argument regarding Eliasson's work on perception more pointedly at temporal components so that the spatial ones remain too much on the sidelines (see in contrast Lehmann 2004, 362–7). Effects of perception like afterimages and stroboscopic effects are repeatedly connected to film (also noted by Crary) or lately also to television and computer monitors, i.e. to the reproduction of temporal succession like moving images. The history of the volumetric display, however, shows that stroboscopic effects can be used in order to produce transplane spatial images. Indeed, we can reduce Eliasson's work to the temporality of perception in favor of diminishing its spatiality as little as we can reduce it to physiological optics in contrast to geometrical ones. This becomes quite clear from another work of his, *Convex/Concave* (Figure 8.11).

The mirror visible here is a strongly reflecting foil in a circular mounting. The foil is alternately inflated or deflated. Depending on this, the mirror is either convex or concave—thus the work's title. These convex or concave mirrors were developed in the early sixties; they have varying focal points (see Muirhead 1961) and quite soon were used for volumetric three-dimensional displays.[29] This "most elegant" (Halle 1997, 59) method for creating a three-dimensional volumetric image is shown schematically in the Figure 8.12.

With this type of volumetric image the viewer sees a vibrating mirror showing synchronized images produced by (in this case) a 2D-cathode ray tube. Depending on the curvature of the mirror,

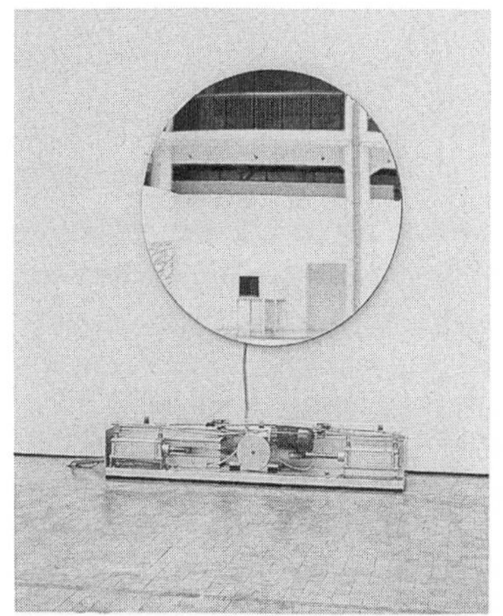
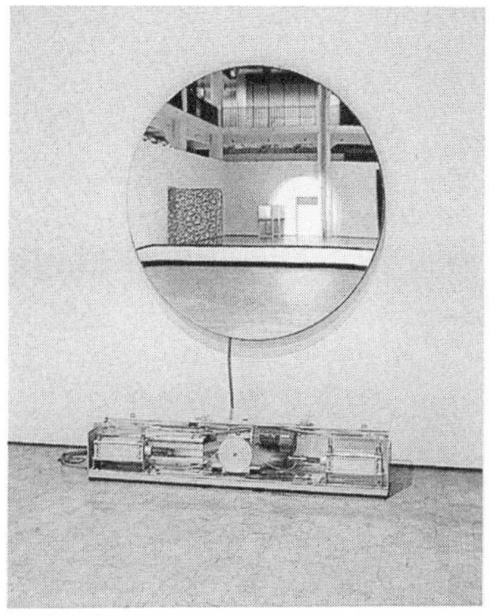

FIGURE 8.11 Olafur Eliasson, *Convex/Concave* (1995/2000), installation View: ZKM, Karlsruhe, Germany, Photo: Franz Wamhof, © Olafur Eliasson.

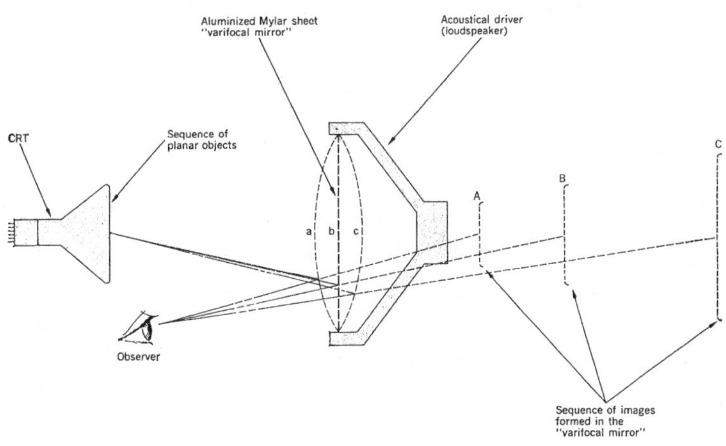

FIGURE 8.12 *Principle of varifocal mirror imaging, in Rawson (1969, 39).*

different parts of the image are mirrored in different (virtual) depths. If this is done fast enough, human perception makes out spatial depth. Compliant with the geometrical-optical equation for spherical mirrors (see Hecht 1987, 161), the amplitude for the movement of the image will typically be fifteen to thirty times bigger than the respective amplitude of the mirror's oscillation: "This allows wide flexibility in the image depth range" (Rawson 1969, 39). In this way a three-dimensional image can be created even though one cannot walk around it as in the case of swept-volume or solid-state volumetric displays; but it really is a three-dimensional image that can be viewed without any glasses: "[T]he depth effect is convincing and has readily been perceived as such by many untrained observers."[30] "The greatest difficulty with varifocal mirror displays is building a high quality varifocal optic that can be oscillated at high frequencies" (Halle 1997, 59). Because of its comparatively easy basic principle, this technology is being tested mainly in medical imaging.[31]

In this case, however, Eliasson is not using this technology in order to show computerized data revealing the inside of bodies in a visually plausible manner. The mirror reflects the environment of the exhibition hall and the viewers standing in front of it instead, i.e. it shows the exterior of the bodies. Since the curvature of the mirror is constantly changing, so does the mirror image. The varifocal mirror distorts and defamiliarizes the totally customary perception of the mirror as the first three-dimensional image. It is precisely that reflection of the body that in the well-known Lacanian argument projects an—imaginary—stable self which now is becoming shaky. Whereas the medical use of varifocal mirrors serves to normalize the body, i.e. reconstitutes its undamaged whole, here the only possible way of seeing oneself (almost) as a whole is being destabilized (see Lehmann 2004, 356–62). Seen like this, we have to agree with Crary that Eliasson is turning against "any mechanistic appropriation of the eye" (Crary 2005, 224).

At the same time the perception of space becomes self-referential. The visible environment of the bodies getting smaller and bigger becomes narrower and wider in the mirror; it seems to approach and to recede. One's own position in space becomes unstable and if one looks at the pulsating reflection for any length of time one gets dizzy. Therefore, in contrast to the functional usage of these technologies, the point is not to make space more controllable and the operator-in-the-loop more effective.[32] Apart from that and unlike in functionally used displays based on varifocal mirrors where the noise of the installation propelling the mirror and its rapid oscillation is a considerable problem because it can only be muffled with difficulty (see Sher 1993, 204–5), here the pumping facility itself is displayed. This use of a pump is a change in the conventional architecture of varifocal mirrors. These are not inflated and deflated again since that would take too long; they are made to oscillate by way of a loudspeaker creating sounds of about 25 to 33 Hz (see again Figure 8.12). In this way, Eliasson not only addresses the mechanical basis of his installation, which would be a not particularly original gesture of self-reflexivity; rather, he assigns a breathing, organic quality to the pumping mirror. As described by a commentator, the pump "breathed noisily in an effortful rhythm" (in Grynsztejn et al. 2004, 46). This "interpenetration of machinic and natural elements" (Crary 2005, 221) destabilizes the border between the animate and the inanimate body. This threefold shift in *Convex/Concave* of the physical self-image in the mirror, of the space–body relationship and of the border between the animate and the inanimate body is at least hinting at a second variation of a possible media aesthetics of volumetric displays; one could almost say that the media-aesthetic characteristics of volumetric displays *formally* consists in the fact that the images created by them do not feature "any area that can be surveyed" (Boehm 1994c, 30) since they are not two-dimensional but three-dimensional themselves. It is possible to walk around specific types of these images (not all) and to view them like sculptures, but they are not objects themselves located in the same space like the viewers; they appear in a shell instead, comparable to a new type of three-dimensional way of framing.[33] They differ from sculptures by the fact that they are transparent and moving images (sometimes even interactive). Due to their transparency, the volumetric images do not partially conceal each other like opaque sculptural objects do, neither can they be surveyed as a whole like two-dimensional images. And even though they have volume they do not imply massiveness for the viewers. Volumetric displays create images that can't easily be pigeonholed in any known category of images.[34] It seems to me that volumetric images have not yet been taken note of sufficiently in art and media historical discourse because of their generally envisioned use *outside of* the artistic sphere or in mass media.[35] This might lead to a problematic status of the existing histories and theories of optical and visual media since these are based on a too limited selection of types of images. But this criticism has to be made with caution. The history of the different forms of volumetric displays described in brief here is still unfinished—in reality it hasn't even been started yet. Blundell and Schwarz summarized the research in the year 2000 maintaining that volumetric displays "could give rise to commercial products in the not too distant future" (121). And whether and to what extent volumetric images will still proliferate, whether or not they will be used in mass media or in the arts in a more expanded form cannot be answered at this point in time.

However, precisely the fact that the development of volumetric images has not yet been solidified in certain technological and, concomitantly, in pictorial standards[36] (as one can see from the "bewildering variety" of methods), permits asking the question in conclusion, how new visual technologies develop.

The present chapter commenced rather abruptly with the essay by Parker and Wallis published in 1948 that today is regarded as pivotal. Are there really no predecessors for the idea that an image can appear not only on one (or two) plane(s) but in a volume? Yes, they do exist. But it becomes clear from the differences between the predecessors and the essay from 1948 that overly homogenizing histories of media lead to problems of all sorts. Apart from the French patent from 1912 in which a solid-state volumetric display is pondered, which at the time could not yet be realized and was never completed in this form (see Luzy and Dupuis 1912), a method indeed existed that was suggested and realized by Louis Lumière.[37] Again Lumière! As if it weren't enough that the brothers Lumière can be called the inventors of cinema and of the first commercial three-color photographic method. No, now their genius also seems to have created the beginning of the history of volumetric images. In 1920 an essay by Louis Lumière was published under the title "Représentation photographique d'un solide dans l'espace. Photo-stéréo-synthèse." The idea is relatively simple:

> Si l'on prend, à une échelle fixe, des négatifs photographiques d'une série de plans parallèles, équidistants ou non, d'un objet, en réalisant cette condition que chaque image ne représente que

> l'intersection de l'objet par le plan correspondant, on pourra, en superposant les positifs tirés des négatifs obtenus, reconstituer dans l'espace l'apparence de l'objet photographié.[38]

A series of photographs is taken of the object; each photograph represents a sharply focused image of exactly one level of the object.[39] If the photographs are now exposed onto transparent plates, one can put these on top of each other (usually six were used) and expose the whole from behind thereby creating an astonishingly spatial image of the object. The point, then, is the creation of a three-dimensional image in an image volume consisting of the different photographic plates. Figure 8.13 shows a sequence of these photographs.

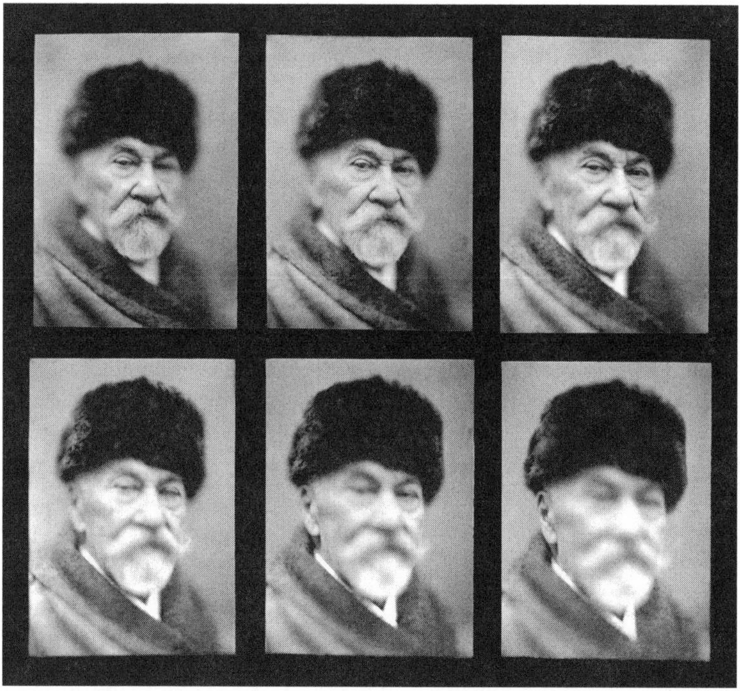

FIGURE 8.13 *Louis Lumière:* Portraits of Pierre Bellingard, *6 plates component of a photo-stéréo-synthèse (c. 1921), Collection Institut Lumière/Fonds Lumière © Institut Lumière.*

Photostereosynthesis can be regarded as another interesting but vanished branch of the history of visual media[40] because to a certain extent this method is a link between the photo sculpture discussed above (see Chapter 3) and the volumetric image. The same idea of segmenting the object into different levels can also be found in photo sculpture. However, in photostereosynthesis no image of the object is reconstructed from the different photos in a stable matter (like clay); the images themselves are assembled into a spatial object, into an image volume.

All of the surviving twelve photostereosynthetic images are portraits. But what exactly does a portrait gain by adding another dimension, even though it is surprisingly realistic and three-dimensional? The portrait photograph is supposed to re-present an absent person and additional spatiality seems to be less necessary for that than the indexical character of the photographic image that guarantees that the (beloved?) person in fact sat or stood in front of the lens.[41] The photostereosynthetic method was too lavish and expensive in the end and disappeared again. There was no imperative, no "supervening social necessity" (Winston 2003, 6) that would have been worth the expenditure and the effort.

When the idea of creating an image within an image-volume resurfaced in 1948, it happened in a completely different context. WWII had just ended and it had become clear that additional spatial information could accelerate the reaction of the radar operators. Consequently, the goal was not to take portrait photographs of absent persons but to capture radar signals of distant airplanes. The image therefore had to be animated and refreshed in real time. While Lumière's method was working with a multiplication of the plane in a shifted geometrical-optical manner, the volumetric moving image required the series of physiological optics. Nevertheless, Lumière's approach succeeded in something that is no longer there in any of the later volumetric displays: "Because the photographic layers incorporated opacity as well as reflectivity, they overcame the loss of occlusion" (Benton 2001b, xxii). This means that the photostereosynthetic image was not transparent. But the lack of occlusion in later volumetric displays is not necessarily a drawback; it facilitates the representation of computerized data (see Rawson 1969, 41) and at any rate—as I have shown earlier—the representation of medical data. Therefore the different volumetric displays are being tested and sometimes utilized for these data. Currently those applications clearly predominate—unlike the approach of Parker and Wallis[42]—that visualize digitally processed data.[43] If one disregards the strictly analog beginnings, the volumetric display then has to be attributed to the series of virtual-physiological optics and is hardly related to photo sculpture any longer. In short, only the idea of the image volume connects Lumière, Parker and Wallis and finally the later attempts; as to the rest the discontinuities clearly predominate.

The heterogeneous history of volumetric displays is not yet closed and stabilized in *the one* black box called "volumetric image." Once such a sedimentation were to be finalized at one point, some of the earlier technologies would be declared predecessors in a series of "*[r]ecurrent redistributions*" (Foucault 1972, 5) while others (with other characteristics of the images produced) would disappear from all history books. Blundell and Schwarz precisely justify their first overview, published in 2000, of the diverse developments in volumetric images with exactly this:

> The fascinating history of the research undertaken on volumetric display systems is outlined, perhaps for the first time, in this book. . . . Unfortunately, scientists and engineers working on the development of volumetric systems have tended to work in isolation. This has led to a major duplication of effort and a failure to adopt standardized terminology. The situation is reflected in scientific publications and patents where even the most basic components in display systems are often referred by different names. (Blundell and Schwarz 2000, 1–2)[44]

Maybe one day their book will be recognized as an important step in standardizing and stabilizing the volumetric image.

Notes

1 Parker and Wallis (1948, 372). Insofar as two consistent movements are overlapping here, one could also describe the "Spiral Scan Pattern" mathematically as a Lissajous curve (see Blundell and Schwarz 2000, 98; see generally Himstedt, 1884; this latter publication facilitates understanding complex Lissajous curves with stereoscopic illustrations). Another evidence for Duchamp's interest in mathematics is the fact that one of his *Rotoreliefs* nearly shows

such a Lissajous figure. Mathematics then would be the element that Duchamp possibly is using playfully whereas it is functionally used in radar scans.

2 Parker and Wallis (1948, 379). In the discussion following the presentation of their paper this idea was criticized. It may be indeed difficult to reorganize one's perception to three-dimensionality if people have been used to seeing objects on planes in perspectival representation. "It seems to me that, because we do not think easily in three dimensions, we have all the information in the quasi-three-dimensional display very simply portrayed and without the complications of a truly three-dimensional display" (J. L. Coales, in Parker and Wallis 1948, 388–9).

3 Parker and Wallis (1948, 372). See Perkins (1962, 67) who compares the different ways—symbolized-perspectival, stereoscopic, volumetric—of presenting radar data (and the information on space to be obtained from them).

4 See Blundell, Schwarz and Horrell (1994, 180): "The images are thus placed within the physical world of the observer, in comparison to virtual reality systems where the observer is placed within the virtual environment of the nonphysical image space."

5 Parker and Wallis (1948, 372). See also Blundell and Schwarz (2000, 96) who underline that Parker and Wallis had intended synchronizing the radar scan directly analog with the image volume. Therefore Parker and Wallis also suggest a different display structure for each of the two different scan patterns.

6 These methods were developed later into "varifocal mirror displays" (see e.g. Traub 1967): sometimes they are differentiated from volumetric displays, depending on the question whether the volume is real or virtual (see Blundell and Schwarz 2000, 5). Below I will come back to these types of displays, which I am counting among the volumetric displays in Benton's (2001b, xxii) sense.

7 The projection and the rotational or translational movement of the screen or the mirror have to be synchronized quite carefully; otherwise the three-dimensional image cannot be created.

8 On the limitations ("dead zones") of volumetric displays with rotating screen see Blundell and Schwarz (1994).

9 On this difference see section 9.3.

10 See Blundell and Schwarz (2000, 247–8). Only volumetric displays of the solid-state-type on the basis of photochrome or thermochrome materials (178–82) could possibly generate volumetric images. But these technologies have not yet been sufficiently developed.

11 See Blundell and Schwarz (2000, 134–89). It is interesting to note that a French patent already existed in 1912 launching research in this direction, see Luzy and Dupuis (1912) But this method never seems to have been realized. Blundell and Schwarz (2000, 250) are pointing out an analogy to the history of early television. Just as the solutions with rotating Nipkow-discs were superseded by electronic methods because of their mechanical problems, possibly the future will belong to the solid state volumetric images (based on electronic methods).

12 Blundell and Schwarz (2000, 26). There exist a large number of patents dealing with the development of these volumetric displays.

13 See Blundell and Schwarz (2000) and their excellent, detailed overview, including a very helpful glossary. See also Blundell and Schwarz (2002).

14 See as one example the often-mentioned "Perspecta System": http://inition.co.uk/3D-Technologies/actuality-systems-perspecta-volumetric-3d-display [last accessed September 2, 2013].

15 Blundell and Schwarz (2000, 92) in their chapter on the volumetric displays of the swept-volume type argue in a similar vein: "In preparing this chapter, it has been necessary to review many publications relating to swept-volume systems, and unfortunately, it has sometimes been difficult to differentiate between systems that were simply conceptualized and those that were actually constructed."

16 Image taken from http://www.blohm.onlinehome.de/files/paper_pw_98 [last accessed September 2, 2013].

17 Otsuka, Hoshino and Horry (2004, 187). The scene from *Star Wars* (USA 1977, Dir. George Lucas) mentioned in this quote will also play a role in section 9.4. Please keep in mind that in this quote holography and volumetric displays are mentioned in the same breath even though these are two different technologies.

18 By the way: In episode one, season four of the television series *Crime Scene Investigation: New York* a volumetric display showing a human skull can be seen in the forensic lab. In the context of this forensic police procedural the volumetric display is used to signify the high tech-equipment used by the police. Thereby the display becomes an ideological figure representing the incorruptible state, equipped with the most advanced technology, always bringing the right ones to justice.

19 See also the aims of Zebra-Imaging producing advanced holographic images at http://www.zebraimaging.com/defense [last accessed

August 12, 2013]. See also Coddington and Schipper—even in this early text on a solid-state volumetric display system it is of course considered of prime importance integrating it "in the Naval Tactical Defense System (NTDS) or Semi-Automatic Ground Environment (SAGE) System" (Coddington and Schipper 1962, 177).

20 Incidentally, it may be interesting that the volumetric display is itself represented here in an axonometric projection and not in linear perspective.

21 The woman sitting at a terminal in the background does not disturb this impression.

22 Harris et al. (1986, 67). See only a few of many other examples of volumetric visualization in medical research (Simon 1969; Szilard 1974; Littfeld, Heiland and Macedonia 1996).

23 On MRI see also Joyce (2005); Prasad (2007); Burri (2008).

24 On Kracauer's concept of the spatial image see Döring (2009).

25 For an overview of the texts used for her possibly most well-known installation *Truisms* (1979); see http://mfx.dasburo.com/art/truisms.html [last accessed August 12, 2013].

26 As the term 'volumetric display' suggests, these technologies are being used today for visualizing data from the computer; for example, connected to medical imaging. The beginnings by Parker and Wallis discussed had still been purely analog technologies.

27 In terms of Akrich (1992).

28 In an earlier text on Eliasson, Crary is writing himself: "Some of the most compelling aesthetic and conceptual thinking today, such as the work in this exhibition, comes out of an understanding of the patchwork, hybrid consistency of contemporary perceptual experience" (Crary 1997, n.p.)

29 See Traub (1967, 1085): "[A] varifocal membrane mirror . . . is formed by stretching a metallized plastic film tightly over a circular frame so that it forms a round, plane mirror of fairly good optical quality. It can be made *convex or concave* by the application of pressure or suction within a cavity behind it" (my emphasis). The potentials of the new type of three-dimensional display are demonstrated with a "simulated air traffic control." See also Sher (1993) providing an overview until 1993.

30 Traub (1967, 1087). However, the author is also pointing out that the perspective in varifocal mirrors is "anormal"—objects approaching the viewer become smaller and not bigger. The 2D images projected onto the mirror therefore have to be pre-distorted.

31 See once more Harris et al. (1986). Numerous sources on the use of volumetric displays on the basis of varifocal mirror for imaging tomographic data can be found there.

32 However, Eliasson's application and alterations of the mirror is not completely original. Robert Whitman had used varifocal mirrors already in 1969 in his installation *Pond* at the *Jewish Museum* in New York (see Whitman 2003, 210). Sponsored by "Experiments in Art and Technology" he collaborated with Eric G. Fawson of Bell Laboratories who at the time was working intensely on volumetric displays on the basis of varifocal mirrors. At least in this case there is a direct connection between the research done with these displays and the artistic use of varifocal mirrors. In an essay on the use of varifocal mirrors for 3D displays, Rawson (1969, 43) briefly described the installation (calling it "light sculpture") and its connection to vibrating varifocal mirrors with strobe lights: "The strobe light frequency is adjusted to within about 1 Hz of the fundamental mirror frequency, resulting in the observer's reflected image moving back and forth along the depth axis at the difference frequency, about 1 Hz. Due to the large size of the mirrors, many high-order vibrational modes are excited, resulting in complex undulations of the reflected images." Similar to Eliasson, the varifocal mirrors are used precisely not to generate an easily understandable spatial image. They rather destabilize the physical image of the viewers and their relationship to their environment.

33 The only exception seems to be a procedure—the Xyzscope—operating with a rotating lens (see Fajans 1992, 25–6): "A planar light source, e.g. a CRT or LED array, is projected by a rotating lens into a display volume which has no enclosure. Physical objects can easily be combined with the display and easily removed." The possible uses are described as well: "Areas for applications of the xyzscope are air traffic monitoring, CAD, medical imaging, and entertainment" which are supplemented with "[a]dditional possibilities [like] dynamic sculptures in light, games, and advertising." As far as I can see, this interesting concept—a volumetric image that can be connected to real objects since it is not placed in an enclosure—has not yet been significantly further developed.

34 Resembling holography which I will discuss in Chapter 9.

35 With the exceptions named here.

36 The different approaches create image spaces with different characteristics; see Blundell and Schwarz (2000, 250–58).

37 Benton (2001b, xxii) names Lumière's essay among the predecessors of volumetric images, counting it among "Slice-Stacking Displays."

38 Lumière (1920, 891): "If you take negatives of a series of parallel planes of an object set on a fixed scale—whether they are equidistant or not—while making sure from the corresponding plane that each image represents only the intersection of this object, then it is possible to recreate the appearance of the object that has been photographed in space by superposing the positives taken from the negatives which you have obtained." See Kuchinka (1926, 67) who compares the photo-stereo synthesis with the "effect of the stage set at the theater," a comparison that Crary relates to stereoscopy, as is known.

39 The question is how one can arrange for having only one object level sharply focused while all levels in front or behind it are sufficiently unfocused. Lumière (1920, 895) developed a special camera in which first of all for each of the six or seven image planes to be taken, the camera could be advanced to a certain extent and secondly the image plane and the lens were moving in a vertical circle synchronously during each image taken. By way of this rotation the pixels that were focused on the respective image plane were not touched while all pixels that were out of focus became even more blurred so that an adequate separation of the focused and unfocused levels inside each image plane was guaranteed; see also Frizot (2000c).

40 Neither in Eder (1978), Frizot (1998), Hick (1999) nor in Kittler (2010) can any sentence or word be found on this method.

41 This at least is Barthes's (1982) argument.

42 See Blundell and Schwarz (2000, 95) on Parker and Wallis: "Since electronic digital computer systems were in their infancy when this work was undertaken, information processing was carried out by analog computation." The point for Parker and Wallis was a strictly analog depiction of the signals.

43 See Halle (1997). Blundell and Schwarz are pointing out that the heyday of the development and production of cathode ray tubes took place above all in the 1950s and early 1960s and that during this time on this basis volumetric displays had been suggested (see Ketchpel 1963). But the development of computers was still in its early stages as Blundell and Schwarz (2000, 99) point out: "Had our present computational systems (and associated visualization requirements) been available during this period, it is likely that volumetric display systems would have gained widespread acceptance."

44 And it may not be accidental that the volumetric images on the basis of varifocal mirrors are disappearing from Blundell's and Schwarz's '[r]ecurrent redistributions' (as Foucault would say).

CHAPTER NINE

Since 1948: Holography

The Series of Wave Optics 2

[W]hat seems to me the most exciting value of this technique . . . has to do with the three-dimensionality. When I first had occasion to see Dr. Wuerker's holograms I was bowled over just by the aesthetic view of the engineering information and its three-dimensional display, and the extent to which one can peruse at length this stored bit of three-dimensional information; this is most dramatic.

ROBERT L. POWELL (1970, 128–9)

Then, as in the case of the sectional plane of two optical media, patterns and moirés emerge: myths, fictions of science, oracles.

FRIEDRICH KITTLER[1]

My previous remarks showed that in Crary's eyes the primal scene of the break-like transition from geometrical to physiological optics seems to be this scene from Goethe's *Theory of Colors*:

> Let a room be made as dark as possible; let there be a circular opening in the window-shutter about three inches in diameter, which may be closed or not at pleasure. The sun being suffered to

> shine through this on a white surface, let the spectator from some little distance fix his eyes on the bright circle thus admitted. The hole being then closed, let him look towards the darkest part of the room; a circular image will now be seen to float before him.[2]

Goethe closes the opening of the dark room; thus he cancels the paradigm of the camera obscura in order to address the afterimage effects of physiological optics. So much for that.[3] But almost simultaneously with the *Theory of Colors*, published for the first time in 1810, a similar primal scene existed that in its effects, however, was quite different. It is the double slit experiment made first by the British scientist Thomas Young in 1802:

> I made a small hole in a window-shutter and covered it with a piece of thick paper, which I perforated with a fine needle. . . . I brought into the sunbeam a slip of card, about one-thirtieth of an inch in breadth, and observed its shadow, either on the wall or on other cards held at different distances. (Young 1804, 2)

Another dark room, another opening through which light comes in. The opening in the shutter is again closed—however, this time not in order to watch the afterimages in the dark. The cover is perforated, making a small opening in order to let in a very fine sunbeam. Young holds a very narrow piece of carton into the light and his discovery is amazing:

> Besides the fringes of colours on each side of the shadow, the shadow itself was divided by similar parallel fringes, of smaller dimensions, differing in number, according to the distance at which the shadow was observed, but leaving the middle of the shadow always white. Now these fringes were the joint effects of the portions of light passing on each side of the slip of the card, and inflected, or rather *diffracted*, into the shadow. (Young 1804, 2; my emphasis)

In analogy to sound waves, the interference pattern[4] of the diffracted light waves shows the wave character of light, or, as Young concisely describes it: "[T]here must be some strong resemblance between the nature of sound and that of light" (Young 1804, 12. See also Young 1807, 457–71).

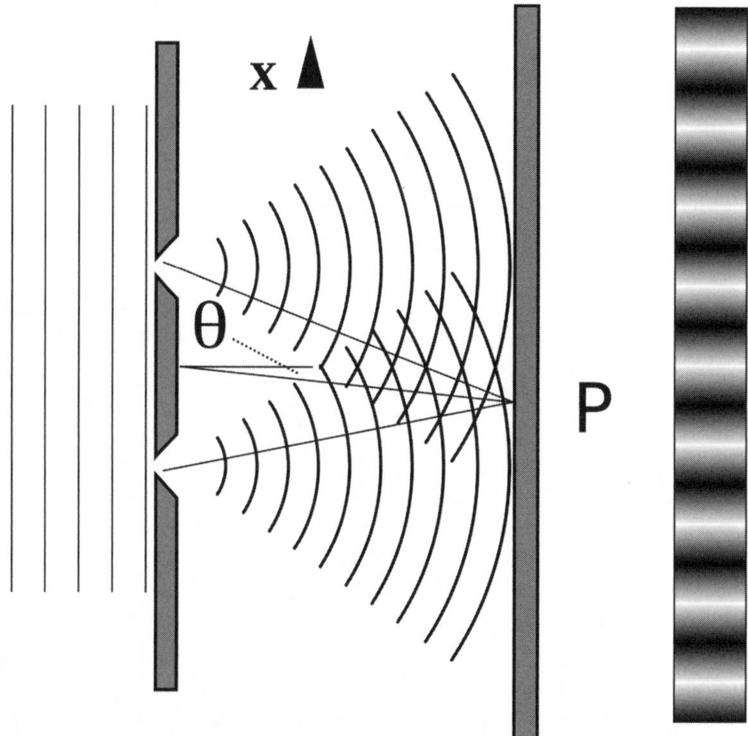

FIGURE 9.1 *Double slit experiment according to Young. Interference of light waves into an interference pattern, http://en.wikipedia.org/wiki/File:Doubleslit.svg* [last accessed September 2 , 2013].

Diffraction had already been observed by Francesco Maria Grimaldi in his publication *Physico Mathesis de Lumine, Coloribus et Iride* (1665). Grimaldi considered it his unique discovery that next to direct transmission, reflection and refraction another characteristic of light existed.[5] His first experiment begins with the scene of the dark room into which light is admitted and in which the effects of diffraction are being observed. Here already the "aperto in fenestra" (Grimaldi 1665, 2) that is symptomatic for the emergence of the series of wave optics replaces Alberti's "finestra aperta" (see Alberti 2011, 167) of geometrical optics. Grimaldi had already assumed that light should be imagined as a sort of "fluidum" or like an oscillation within it (see Grimaldi 1665, 12–13 and Neurath 1915, 378–9). Shortly afterwards, in 1678, Huygens in his *Abhandlung über das Licht* (Treatise on light) had postulated the wave nature of light without directly referring to Grimaldi.[6]

The time was wrong for the modeling of the light as a *wavefront* to assert itself against the power of the Newtonian corpuscular theory. Despite Young's experiments the rediscovered concept of the wave nature of light was not really accepted for quite some time to come.[7] Only after Augustin-Jean Fresnel experimented successfully with interference again in 1815 did the concept gain acceptance (see Silliman 1974, Kipnis 1991 and Mollon 2002). I cannot present a history of the series of wave optics in detail here (see for this Buchwald 1989). For the context presented here, it is only decisive that parallel to the strengthening of physiological optics at the beginning of the nineteenth century wave optics were also (re) discovered, which—as I have mentioned above—is brought up by Crary only briefly and to my mind inaccurately.[8]

Up to the present day wave optics is considered the valid description of light, including geometrical optics as the border case of vanishing wavelength.[9] This epistemic inclusion of the geometrical-optical series by the wave optical one means that holograms are virtually able to simulate the effects of geometrical-optical technologies like mirrors, lenses and so on (see section 9.3). But as I have already said in Chapter 1, this does not mean that wave optics supersedes geometrical optics in the sense that the latter disappears. Geometrical optics remains an essential component of all textbooks on optics (see for example Hecht 1987, 128–241) simply because it is quite sufficient as a description of the behavior of light on a macroscopic scale; for example, for lens systems.

However, the modeling of light as a wave[10] also allows for understanding interference, polarization and diffraction and not only refraction, shadow effects and reflection as in geometrical optics. This means that this knowledge is not only the basis for Lippmann photography (see Chapter 4) but also that of holography. Both methods can be described as different recordings of interference patterns, like the 'moirés' that Kittler mentions in passing (see below).[11] Significantly, for the first time in 1901 the physicist Aimé Cotton, who succeeded Gabriel Lippmann on the chair for physics at the Sorbonne in 1922, suggested recording the interference patterns *without* using *a lens*.

> Dans les expériences dont il communique les premiers résultats, M. Cotton s'est proposé d'obtenir des réseaux par la photographie de franges [d'interférence] mais cette fois *sans employer d'objectif*. . . . Un écran ou une plaque photographique dont la surface est *plane* est alors recouvert par une série de franges rectilignes et équidistantes formant un réseau dont l'intervalle a une valeur qui peut être fixée à l'avance.[12]

Even though Lippmann had already been using the stored interferences in the depth of the photo emulsion in order to reconstruct the color (i.e. the wave length) of light, the image was nevertheless projected in the traditional way, namely geometrically-optically onto the plane. Cotton, on the other hand, was already forecasting the (wave optical) departure from the lens that would be so characteristic for holography in the future. For this he was using an "arc au mercure" (Cotton 1901b, 10), i.e. a similar light source as Dennis Gabor would be using fifty years later in his experiments. Cotton, however, did not yet have the idea of using the interference pattern in order to reconstruct the original wave front.

In this chapter I will not describe the whole history of holography and the great variety of its different forms and uses since this is neither possible here nor is it necessary.[13]

In section 9.1 I will explain the basic principles of holography, some important stations of its genesis and some of its media-historical assessments to date.

Section 9.2 will describe holo-interferometry. It allows particular possibilities of analyzing spatial structures in keeping with the basic thesis of this present work, namely that transplane images are able to mediate more and different knowledge on space.

Section 9.3 will analyze the phenomenon that the transplane holographic image also includes the representational potentials of geometrical optics. This makes new optics possible like those that ensure the optimized flow of goods and payment at many scanning cash registers of supermarkets today. And inversely, holograms are not reproducible by technologies based on geometrical optics—for this reason holograms are to be found, for example, on banknotes and on credit cards.

Section 9.4 will initially deal with an aspect of holography that has been at the center of various popular (and often misleading) representations of holography: The spectacular presentation of space as a sensational, 'illusionist' effect. Subsequently, holographic pictoriality will be considered media-aesthetically since for each media-aesthetic strategy the 'illusionism' or 'realism' that is repeatedly attested to when talking of the holographic image is a serious problem. How is it possible to ensure the aesthetic "self-referential appearance" (Seel 1993a, 781) of an image if it seems to *almost coincide* with the represented object? Maybe here we can find an answer to the question why holography was unable to establish itself within the mainstream of the arts.

9.1 Principles, genesis and theory of holography

Dennis Gabor is considered the 'real' inventor of holography. His first publication on the subject was published in the same year as the first essay on volumetric displays (see Parker and Wallis 1948; see also Chapter 8). This seems to be a curious coincidence—or maybe it attests to the fact that in the twentieth century it was of central importance to gain additional information on space by way of transplane images and that these attempts were made in different places and in different ways. Initially, Gabor was looking for a very specific type of spatial information. From 1947 onward the inventor, who was finally awarded the Nobel Prize in 1971, had been looking for a way to improve the *resolution of electron microscopes*:

> It is known that the spherical aberration of electron lenses sets a limit to the resolving power of electron microscopes at about 5 Å. [5×10^{-10} m] . . . The new microscopic principle described below offers a way around this difficulty, as it allows one to dispense altogether with electron objectives. (Gabor 1948, 777)

The decisive point of the new type of representation—which in this first text was still called "interference diagram" (Gabor 1948, 778)—is that the *lens*[14] (provided that it is supposed to collimate electrons or light rays for representation on a carrier) can be omitted. This means that the distortions and limitations of the depth of field produced by the lens can be avoided.[15] Retrospectively, as he remembers, Gabor's earliest ideas on the problem had already been explicitly guided by an attempt to overcome the projection onto the plane:

> I asked myself a question . . . "When we take a photograph, the image appears in the plane of the plate. But by Huygens' Principle the information which goes into the image must be there in *every* plane before the plate, also in the plane before the lens. . . . Why can we not extract it [i.e. the information]?" (Quoted in Johnston 2006a, 23)

In a detailed elaboration of his method published in 1949, the term 'hologram' appears for the first time: "The name 'hologram' is not unjustified, as the photograph contains the total information required for reconstructing the object."[16]

The peculiar uniqueness of a hologram consists in the fact that—unlike in photographs—the light reflected by the referent during its formation is not recorded *after being collimated and focused by a lens*. Rather, it is the interference pattern (created by the interference of the light diffracted by the illuminated object when meeting the non-diffracted light) that is stored on the photographic plate:

> If a diffraction diagram of an object is taken with coherent illumination, and a coherent background is added to the diffracted wave, the photograph will contain the full information on the modifications the illuminating wave has suffered in traversing the object. (Gabor 1949b, 455)

As we can see from the quote ("coherent illumination" and "coherent background"), the light has to be adequately *coherent*[17]; otherwise no (or at least no sufficiently precise) phenomena of interference would appear (see Figure 9.2).[18] The holographic plate, then, does not show the image of an object but an extremely fine pattern of light and dark zones. This means that the resolution of the holographic materials has to be extremely high (see Nassenstein et al. 1970; see also Johnston 2006a, 220–7).

If the light of the same type used during the recording is directed through this pattern again (this is why holograms are either based

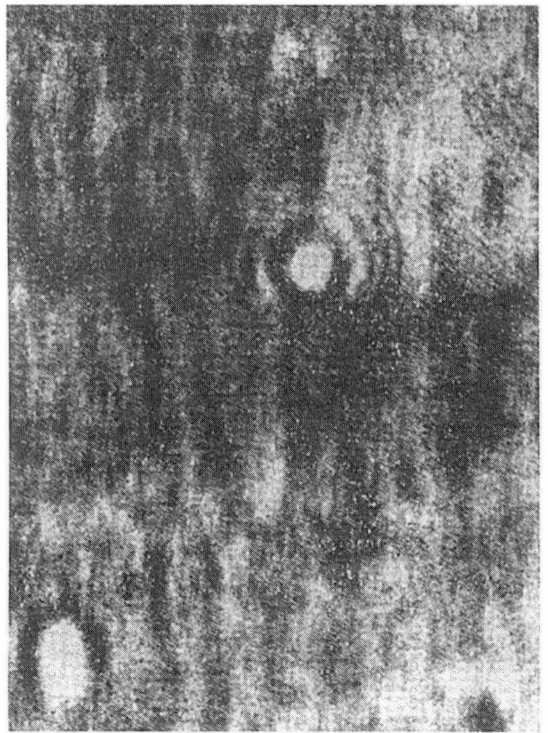

FIGURE 9.2 *Enlarged illustration of the interference pattern in a hologram, in Johnston (2006a, 102).*

on transparent or on reflective carrier materials), it will be diffracted at the minuscule transparent or non-transparent spots,[19] *exactly reconstructing the wave front* originally created by the object. An image appears that (unlike 'illusionist' representations of the object) is not a 'phantasm' of what we want to, are supposed to, or have to *believe* is the object—like in photography according to Roland Barthes (1982, 82). *The wave front is exactly the one that we would see if we were to see the object itself* (however, usually with the exclusion of color since the light has to be monochromatic).[20]

For his new method, Gabor first tested a *slide* on which—almost self-reflexively and in a way reminding of media art—the names

Christiaan Huygens, Thomas Young and Jean-Augustin Fresnel were depicted, those scientists who had founded wave optics.[21] Gabor wanted to correct the flaws of the electron lenses in the electron microscope (which are much worse than the lenses for visible light) by means of conventional lens systems. The interference pattern created by the interference of the electron rays with themselves[22] thus should be reconstructed in a magnified size by way of visible light.[23] By trying not to avoid the lens but to improve it, Gabor initially developed holography as a method of *magnification*. The light used by Gabor came from a high-pressure mercury arc lamp, similar to Cotton's. This had two drawbacks: First of all it was only moderately coherent, i.e. the holograms created by it were quite blurred. Secondly, it only featured a very minor coherence length. This means that the light of the mercury arc lamp could only keep the coherence that was required for the recording, or—as here—for the reconstruction of the interference pattern over a minute distance (around 0.1 mm; see Johnston 2006a, 25). Since the coherence length was so short, Gabor could only record and reconstruct a very small and approximately *two-dimensional* object—the obviously *flat* slide measured only 2 mm^2. Nevertheless, he had already suggested in 1948: "Moreover three-dimensional objects may be recorded in one photograph, hence the suggested name 'holoscope', which means 'entire' or 'whole' vision" (quoted in Johnston 2006a, 29), and in the first published paper on this subject he underlined that "[i]t is a striking property of these diagrams that they constitute records of three-dimensional as well as of plane objects."[24] Nonetheless, a three-dimensional image in the macroscopic realm could not yet be thought of—and this is the delimited realm of which we talk when speaking of optical or visual media[25] in media and art historical scholarship. His idea was hardly noticed and only specialists in electron microscopy were interested in it.[26]

Several years later, holography was again discovered by Emmeth Leith. Initially he had done research in the direction of holography for other reasons and without knowledge of Lippmann, Cotton or Gabor.[27] Since the middle of the 1950s he had been involved with the development and improvement of so-called "synthetic aperture radar" systems, an important technology of the cold war.[28] Similar to the volumetric display discussed above (see Chapter 8), one of the roots of the transplane image—holography—can be found in the spatial control technique that is radar (see Guerlac 1987). In 1965, two authors would quite explicitly establish the analogy: "A hologram may be likened to a radar system where the photographic plate corresponds to a two-dimensional phased array antenna" (Haines and Hildebrand 1965, 10). Leith was particularly involved with the theoretical development of optical processing methods in which coherent radiation was already being used.[29] Thus, in 1955 he established that the recordings of radar signals made by way of interference permitted reconstructing the original wave field:

> To make a fairly long story short, in the process of developing the theory of coherent optical processing of SAR [Synthetic Aperture Radar] data, and of the way the coherent light beam interacted with the raw data, which we planned to record on photographic film, I was struck by what I thought was a most astonishing observation: when the recorded data was illuminated with coherent light, the transmitted light was an optical regeneration of the original field that would be recorded by the airborne radar antenna as it was carried along the aircraft flight path. The process recreated in miniature the original microwave field, scaled down in both linear dimensions and in wavelength—1000 feet of flight path was scaled down to about 20 mm on the signal record, and the microwave wavelength was scaled down from about a centimeter to about 500 nm, the wavelength of the light illuminating the record. (Leith 2003, 432)

Similarly to Gabor, by using radiation of a different wavelength for the reconstruction, a change in scaling occurs. But Leith only learned later about Gabor's research through a paper by Kirkpatrick and El-Sum (see Kirkpatrick and El-Sum 1956). He began to pursue the problem of reconstructing wave fronts and worked in this field together with his colleague Juris Upatnieks. Based on Leith's experiences with synthetic aperture radar, i.e. the separation into an 'information' signal and a 'reference' signal,[30] they developed a structural change of the process of producing a hologram (see Leith and Upatnieks 1961 and 1962) that evades two problems that Gabor had in his in-line arrangement (see Figure 9.3). First of all, Gabor could only 'holograph'[31] partially transparent objects (like slides) and secondly during his experiments a second,

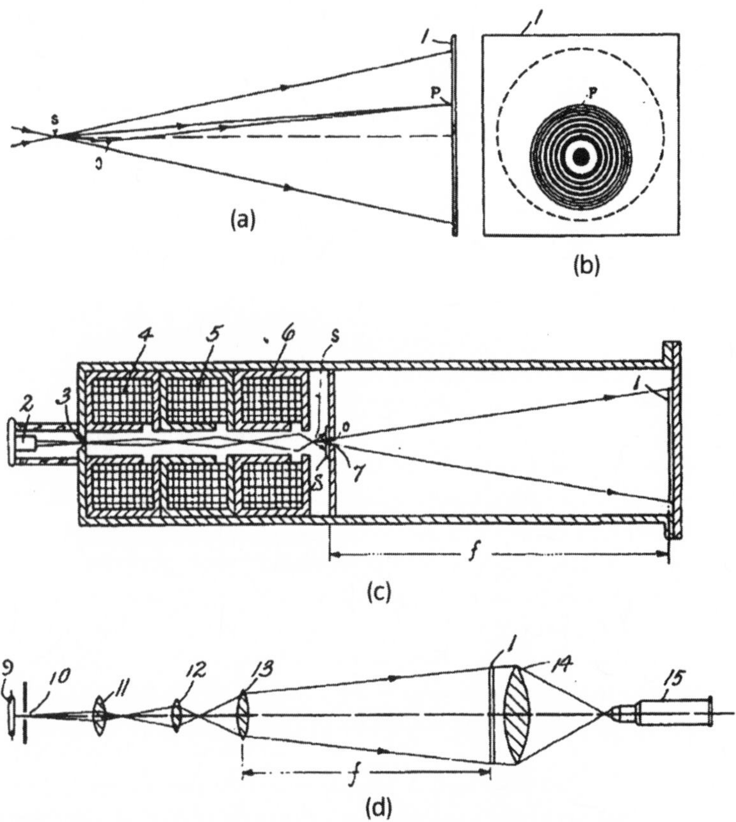

FIGURE 9.3 *Gabor's in-line arrangement, in Johnston (2006a, 28).*

pseudoscopic image emerged (the so-called 'real' image) in the line of sight of the desired 'virtual' image which blurred the latter.[32] Even though a real image emerges in the off-axis arrangement of Leith and Upatnieks, it does not appear in the line of sight of the virtual image.[33]

In this historical description it is important to underline that Leith could not simply transfer concepts from the realm of radar to the field of (holographic) optics without problems. When he applied optical concepts to the theory of synthetic aperture radar, he was hardly taken seriously in the beginning (see Leith 1996, 9). Conversely, the transfer of the concept of a separate reference signal

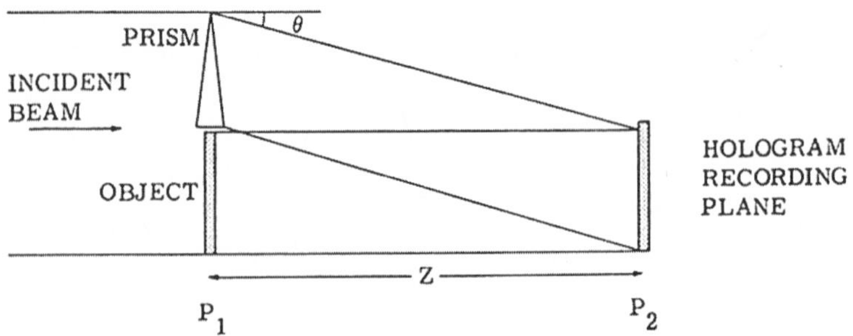

FIGURE 9.4 *Off-axis hologram; early arrangement for recording a slide, in Leith and Upatnieks (1963b, 1377). It is evident that the object to be holographed has to be diaphanous.*

to optics in the beginning was also unusual: "What was natural and easy to do with electronic signals did not readily carry over to optics" (Leith 1996, 15; see Leith 1996, 9). The results that retrospectively seem so evident crystallized only in the course of a long lasting and tentative process of trial and error. As Gabor had done, initially Leith and Upatnieks holographed two-dimensional slides containing simple patterns (see Figure 9.4).[34]

However, they soon had the idea that they could also make attempts with photographs in shades of grey, i.e. with objects that were no longer transparent but at least partially opaque (see Figure 9.5).

This means that the goal was the reconstruction of photographs (still slides). First, this shows the epistemic inclusion of geometrical optics into wave optics, which I will discuss later (see section 9.3). Secondly, and more importantly, it was in no way directly evident that it was possible to create transplane images. By quoting Marshall McLuhan's by now clichéd dictum that the content of a medium is always another one, one would rather cover up the tedious process in which the series of wave optics separated from geometrical optics.[35] Remember, Gabor's early postulation that holography can produce three-dimensional images demanded quite specific features of the light to be used. In 1964 Leith and Upatnieks wrote:

> In making a hologram of a scene in reflected light, two conditions must be met which do not arise when the object is a transparency.

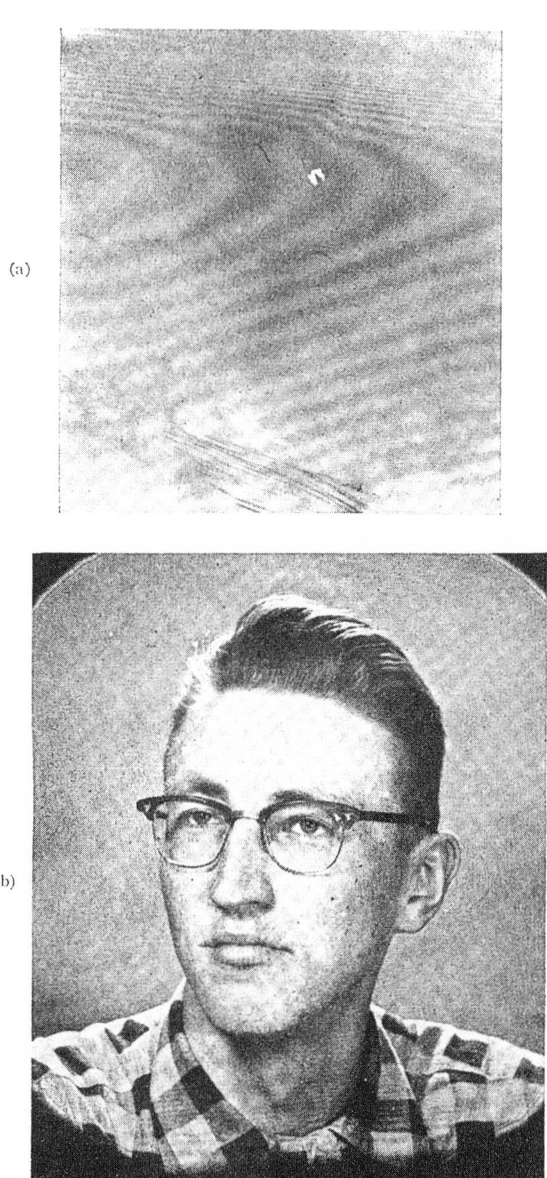

FIGURE 9.5 *Hologram of a photograph with the corresponding reconstruction, in Leith and Upatnieks (1963b, 1380).*

> First, the coherence length of the source must be greater than the maximum difference in light path between the reference beam and the object beam. Thus, the depth of the scene cannot be greater than the coherence length of the light source. (Leith and Upatnieks 1964, 1300)

For all scenarios that contain only a little more depth than a two-dimensional slide only the *laser light*, which had been developed around 1960 quite independently of the different experiments concerning holography, was able to fulfill this demand.[36] If this relatively contingent meeting of laser light and wave front reconstruction had not occurred there would be no three-dimensional holography to this day. Already early on, Leith and Upatnieks were using such a device[37] that provided a stronger light than the mercury arc lamp and that first of all contained a much greater length of coherence. However, the use of the laser instead of the mercury arc lamp, still preferred until then, was not necessarily promising from the beginning:

> [W]hen the laser was tried in place of the Hg [mercury] source, the results were utterly distressing. The light in the recording plane was enormously brighter than before, the images a bit crisper, but the noise was abominable. The images, engulfed in this massive noise, were most unappealing. (Leith 1996, 21)

The smallest impurities will cause image interferences because of the high coherence of the laser light. A retrospective success story would describe the meeting of wave front reconstruction and laser as a contingent but fortunate one all the same. On closer inspection, however, one notices that a massively detailed work was necessary beforehand in order to attain an acceptable result: "One by one, these noise sources were discovered and either eliminated or reduced. Eventually, the noise was reduced to tolerable levels" (Leith 1996, 21). But even when these problems had finally begun to be resolved, reconstructing two-dimensional images was continued, as was comparing this process with quite conventional methods of reproduction.[38] Thus, in an early report on the new "lensless photography" in the *Wall Street Journal* the possibility of three-dimensional imaging was not mentioned at all.[39] The above mentioned comparison at first offered the advantage to connect the wave front reconstruction with better known phenomena: "Wavefront reconstruction was no longer just a work-around for dissatisfied microscopists or a convenient way of decoding radar data: it was about *pictures*" (Johnston 2006a, 101). Gradually the potentials of three-dimensional representation emerged.[40] (See Figures 9.6 and 9.7.)

As always, retrospectively everything looked quite consistent. In 1964 a series of now legendary three-dimensional images of a toy train and of other smaller objects were created (see Figure 9.8).

Regarding Figure 9.8, the art historian Thomas Hensel asked me some time ago which "iconological program" was hiding behind this choice of objects. The idea of the mythical beginning of the movies with the film by the brothers Lumière *L'arrivée d'un train à La Ciotat* (F 1895, screened for the first time on January 6, 1896) instantly comes to mind. Supposedly the viewers panicked when they saw the first image of an arriving train (see Figure 9.9).

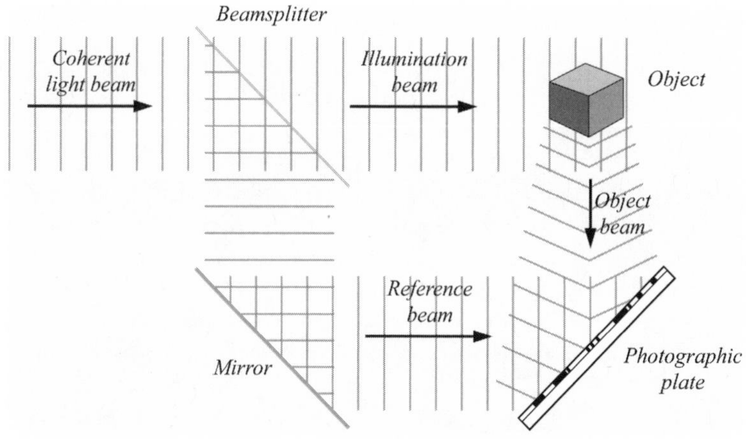

FIGURE 9.6 *Off-axis hologram scheme of generating images as per Leith and Upatnieks. This somewhat changed arrangement can not only 'transilluminate' at least partially or half transparent objects but can also illuminate solid ones; http://upload.wikimedia.org/wikipedia/commons/thumb/7/77/Holograph-record.svg/2000px-Holograph-record.svg.png* [last accessed September 2, 2013].[41]

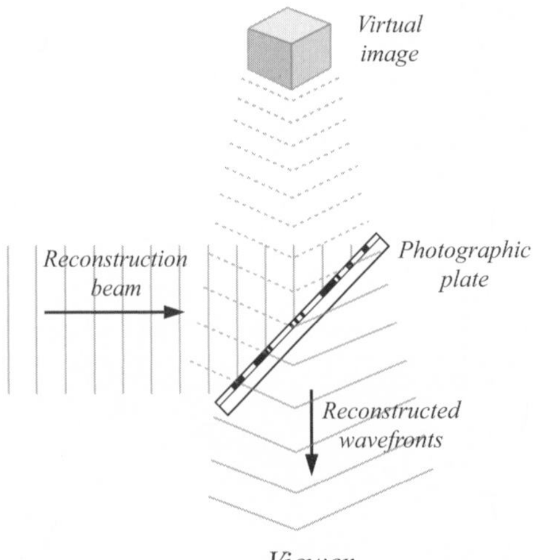

FIGURE 9.7 *View of a hologram as per Leith and Upatnieks; http://upload.wikimedia.org/wikipedia/commons/thumb/a/a0/Holography-reconstruct.svg/2000px-Holography-reconstruct.svg.png* [last accessed September 2, 2013].

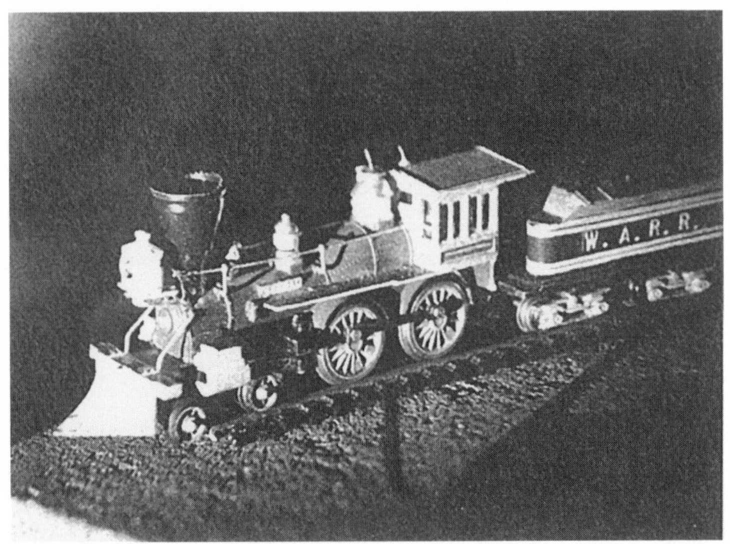

FIGURE 9.8 *One of the first holographic images by Leith and Upatnieks, in Johnston (2006a, 114). The holographic image cannot be reproduced here.*

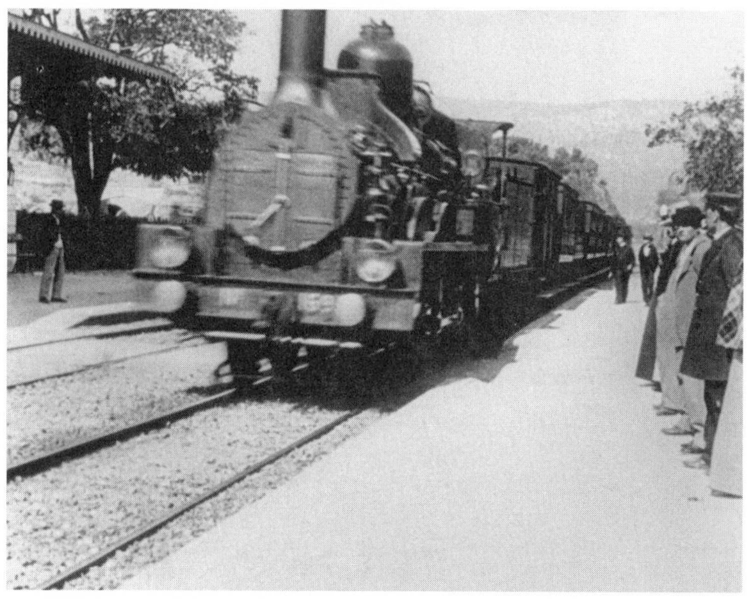

FIGURE 9.9 *Still from L'arrivée d'un train à La Ciotat (F 1895).*

It seems as if the first traces of holography are quoting the first traces of film on purpose (especially since the direction of the train is roughly the same) and are therefore reflecting the effects of new illusionist imaging overwhelming the public. Quite fittingly, the first public presentation of a version of this first really three-dimensional hologram supposedly provoked bewildered and dismayed reactions in the viewers.

> Many of the specialists were disbelieving or confused. The toy train appeared perfectly real and yet could not be touched behind the photographic plate. Several questioned where it was hidden or sought the mirrors that had produced the illusion. One feared that his eyes had been damaged by the laser light. (Johnston 2006a, 115; see also Leith 1983, 3)

But nevertheless there is no conscious, media-reflexive, iconological program in the first holograms. When asking from an art-historical point of view about the intention behind this design one will fail since the only reason for the choice of the objects was that they are three-dimensional, that they are sufficiently small, and that they were spontaneously available at the laboratory (see Johnston 2006a, 110). The fact that the first holographic image by Leith and Upatnieks depicted a train, a toy train to be more exact, is simply a *coincidence*.[42] In freely adapting McLuhan one could say: The medium is never as much message as it is at its beginning. The *appearance* of the medium in its early stages is different from its *co-appearance* in artistic, media-aesthetic strategies. The latter have to presuppose a repertoire of self-referential forms, i.e. a medium that is already established.[43] The first holographic image is not supposed to inform its viewers of the compositional intentions of Leith and Upatnieks. It is supposed to let us know that through the tinkering[44] and through the disruptions,[45] which at the beginning of the use of laser amply existed, a new medium for possible future creative intentions (with artistic or non-artistic purposes) has emerged. As Leith later wrote:

> Our first holograms of 3-D, reflecting objects were made in November, 1963. Then, as now, the first major problem was to find suitable objects; such objects had to be both photogenic and hologenic. The hologenic requirements included object stability, some interesting 3-D characteristics, some good parallax, and some interpositions, so that the viewer could look around something and see what was hidden behind. For our first attempt the best object scene we could produce was a pile of junk retrieved from odd corners of the laboratory. (Leith 1983, 2)

But when interlinking laser, optical knowledge about wave front constructions and the debris in the hidden corners of a laboratory, a perplexing image may be created that is able to stand for holography metonymically. The attention that was initiated by this *emergence event*,[46] as one could almost call it (i.e. the presentation of that one image exhibited by Leith and Upatnieks), unleashed a strongly increased interest. Since they had demonstrated that there was a stabilized entity, further attempts were made to develop it for further potential creations. Therefore, increasingly improved high-definition photographic plates were developed. A wide field of holography opened up with course books and manuals and soon with separate institutes at universities and sections in exhibitions as well.[47] Almost utopian fantastic speculations emerged (see section 9.3) with rapid advancements and further developments following; holographic methods were differentiated and—interestingly enough—not all of them wanted to address the human eye as I will show in sections 9.2 and 9.3. And it should also be noted in passing that holography was repeatedly taken into consideration as a storage medium for data.[48]

At any rate, the history of holography can be described successfully with the model outlined in section 1.3. The development of an optical technology does not necessarily emerge from optical knowledge—its *sedimentation* is rather a contingent and heterogeneous process of detours. However, once the technology was adequately established, retrospectively—already by using the one term holography—homogeneity was suggested. A homogeneity that in the beginning did not really exist—terms like holoscopy (Gabor); lensless photography (Leith and Upatnieks) and wave photography (Yuri Denisyuk, see p. 323) were used at first.

By now we can at least infer that despite the fact that holography is based on photochemical emulsions, it is not three-dimensional photography (something that one could at most say of stereoscopy or photo sculpture).[49] This is already obvious on the level of what one can see: Generally speaking, holography is monochrome since it has to be created with coherent, that is monochromatic light.[50] Holography usually presents isolated objects in a dark environment since the image has to be taken in absolute darkness in order to avoid disturbing the interference pattern with stray light. In principle, holographic negatives do not exist; the images are always positives since an inversion of the interference patterns does not change anything in its diffraction characteristics. By slightly altering the frequency of the coherent light or by changing the angle of incidence one can store an arbitrary number of images that do not interfere with each other on every holographic plate. Precisely this property has been for decades the point of departure in the discussion of the potential uses of holograms as storage media. The objects to be represented have to stay immovable since the slightest movement leads to a strong disturbance or complete destruction of the pattern. But this vulnerability to noise and disturbance in the recording process is simultaneously the starting point of one of the most important applications of holography (see section 9.2). However, since the end of the 1960s it has also been possible to take images of moving objects like live people by way of bright and short-pulsed laser light.

Reconstructing any hologram creates a *virtual and a real image.* The latter—because of its remarkable characteristic of appearing *in front of* the hologram surface and also because it is pseudoscopic (i.e. upended)[51]—also underlines the difference of holography vs. the series of physiological optics. “The real image can be observed visually, but the observer may have some initial difficulty in coordinating his eyes when so doing, for reasons possibly having their origin in physiological optics” (Leith and Upatnieks 1964, 1300). The three-dimensionally reconstructed image of holography can be photographed like the real object and one can also focus on different parts of the holographic image (see Leith and Upatnieks 1964, 1300). The holographic image is simply *not part of geometrical or of perspectival projection* and their 1:1 correlation of image- and object-points—as is dominant in analog and digital photography, in film and video and even in today’s leading (photorealist) forms of computer graphics.[52] Instead, in holography, every object point is correlated with each image point.

This creates another, quite peculiar phenomenon. Every shard of a broken hologram plate contains the whole image, even though with a proportionally smaller resolution to the partial size (see Françon 1974, 39). This means that the informational content of holographic recordings is enormous. It is exactly this characteristic of the interference moirés that led to the “myths, fictions of science, oracles” evoked by Kittler in the motto at the beginning of this chapter. This characteristic repeatedly gave rise to more or less strange speculations that our brain or even the whole universe could be something like a hologram.[53]

Since the holographic image is *not subject to geometrical optics or perspectival projection*, this also means that holography does not need a lens for *projecting the object.*[54] Therefore it does not suffer from the problem of a decreasing depth of field;[55] it can show only objects that match the size of the plates (depending on the distance) since without a lens one can neither reduce nor enlarge.[56] To a certain extent a hologram is itself a highly complex lens. As normal lenses focus light, the hologram diffracts the light in order to reconstruct the wave front. To this effect, with regard to the slides reconstructed by Gabor or in the beginning by Leith and Upatnieks, one can say: “It was almost as if . . . slide (image information) and lens (focusing device) were one and the same thing!" (Klein 1970, 67–8). This means that the hologram plate itself is not an image; it is only the necessity for reconstructing the wave front.[57] The obvious counter argument—of saying that videotapes, if one looks at the tape itself, also do not show the images—is not sound. Videos are about the recoding of the images into electronic signals which are then stored. Video is not an optical medium, it is a visual one. Holography, by contrast, is an optical medium but not necessarily a visual one (see section 9.2. on this difference). This constitutes a *major* potential of provocation for media history and theory.

This is why holography is not present in the pertinent literature.[58] If one can find it in the art- and media-historical literature at all, then it pops up in completely surprising connections presenting strange assessments, thereby symptomatically underlining its strangeness. I would like to discuss three different examples:

1. The art historian Norman Bryson in his work *Vision and Painting. The Logic of the Gaze* (1983, 89) maintains:

> [P]hotography is the product of a chemical process occurring in the same spatial and temporal vicinity as the event it records: the silver crystals react continuously to the luminous field; a continuity that is controlled temporally in the case of holography and both temporally and spatially in the case of photography.

The last sentence is somewhat unclear. What does it mean that the continual (analog) change of light-sensitive materials is temporal in the case of holography and temporal and spatial in the case of photography? The only possible interpretation seems to be that photography is cutting out a moment from the duration of the photographed phenomenon while reducing its spatiality to the plane, while holography is cutting out a temporal moment (at least when using pulse lasers) without reducing the spatial information to the plane. This is plausible. It is, however, strange that in a book on painting, holography is mentioned quite marginally and without any compelling reason; as in a Freudian slip,[59] it suddenly appears quite unexpectedly. Significantly, it is not mentioned anywhere else in the whole book[60] and its principle is not explained either. Its principle distinguishes it fundamentally from photography, even though Bryson is suggesting in the quote (which starts with photography) that it is something like a subspecies of photography. Even though this is true regarding the recording on (as a rule) halide emulsion, the differences are so significant that the fact that Bryson is mentioning it can only be seen as reintroducing phantom-like what had been repressed by planocentrism.

It is no accident that Bryson's book deals with the fact that the perspectival methods of projecting objects onto the plane, established in occidental painting since Renaissance times, have displaced exactly that surface area of painting themselves: "through much of the Western tradition oil paint is treated primarily as an *erasive* medium. What it must first erase is the surface of the picture-plane" (Bryson 1983, 92). Critically contrasting this, Bryson wants to show the surface as the place into which the painter's body deictically or indexically inscribes itself as an area of semiotic processes: "Western painting is predicated on the *disavowal of deictic reference*, on the disappearance of the body as site of the image" (Bryson 1983, 89). With this in mind, his discourse is markedly planocentric—insofar as he explicitly focuses on the picture plane—and it is all the more strange that all of a sudden the transplane visual medium holography appears. Even though by way of its indexical quality (a characteristic it shares with photography) it serves Bryson as a counter example to the pictorial surface of occidental painting that in Bryson's eyes negates its own causal origin in the hand of the painter, the argument does not quite succeed. One can describe the surface of the hologram as a place into which certain conditions are indexically inscribed creating an illusionist image during the process of reconstruction. But the surface of the hologram is nevertheless not the surface of the holographic image—in the case of the real image it can even appear *in front of* the hologram. As I have said, the hologram is not a picture but a complex lens formed by light itself. The 'surface' of the three-dimensional image and that of the material hologram fall apart in a way that is different from all other pictures. (See Fahle 2009a; 2009b; see also section 9.4)

2. In the otherwise trailblazing text on the role of photographs for the practice of pornography by Linda Williams (in which she also addresses Crary's approach in detail), holography appears as significantly as it does unexpectedly in a footnote:

> there now seems good reason to question the underlying notion that the entire prehistory of cinema from the camera obscura to the holograph [*sic*] represents a continuous line of the Western metaphysical ideology of the visible. (1995, 38–9, n. 6)

In this note dealing with the so-called apparatus debate,[61] holography turns up as part of the prehistory of cinema, a statement that is neither historically nor systematically correct. Williams places holography in a timeline between camera obscura and cinema, i.e. she considers it, as does Bryson, as part of the series of geometrical and moreover of physiological optics. Can this again be understood as a symptom of the planocentric discourse? The deformed return of (suppressed) holography both in Bryson and Williams can be seen as further proof for the fact that in modernity one obviously cannot talk of a disappearance of the paradigm of geometrical optics or—as Crary calls it—that of the camera obscura. The paradigm of geometrical optics obviously seems to be so overpowering in theory that holography can only be understood as a modification of photography or of cinema.

3. Even the well-known philosopher and urban planner Paul Virilio cannot avoid mentioning holography. In the German translation of his work *La machine de vision* (entitled in German *Die Sehmaschine*), holography appears prominently on the back cover (see Figure 9.10).

Also, in the listing of the University of Siegen's library of the original French publication, the third noted tag is after all the term holography (see Figure 9.11).

Therefore, what can Paul Virilio contribute to the assessment of holography in 1988 (and 1995 in the English translation)? According to the blurb of the German edition (1989), holography belongs within the frame of the "paradoxical logic of images," together with "videography" and "infography." Since holography appears only three more times in this whole work (apart from the blurb), I explicitly want to quote all references:

> The age of the image's *formal logic* was the age of painting, engraving and etching, architecture; it ended with the eighteenth century. The age of *dialectic logic* is the age of photography and film or, if you like, the frame of the nineteenth century. The age of *paradoxical logic* begins with the invention of video recording,

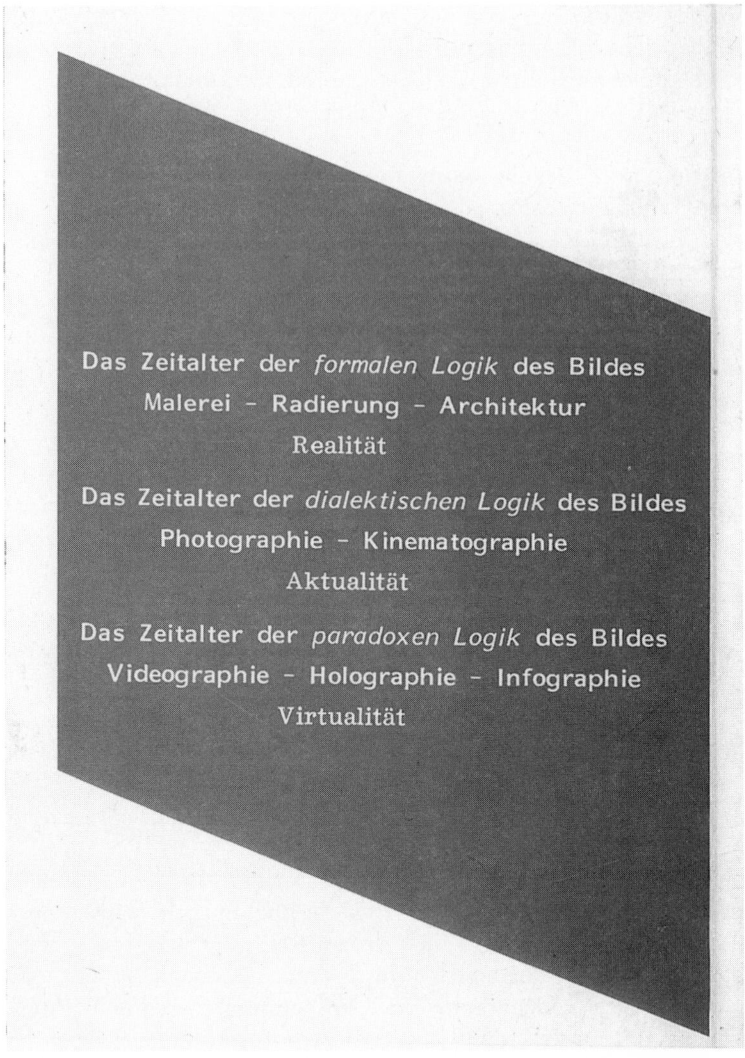

FIGURE 9.10 *Back cover of Virilio (1989).*

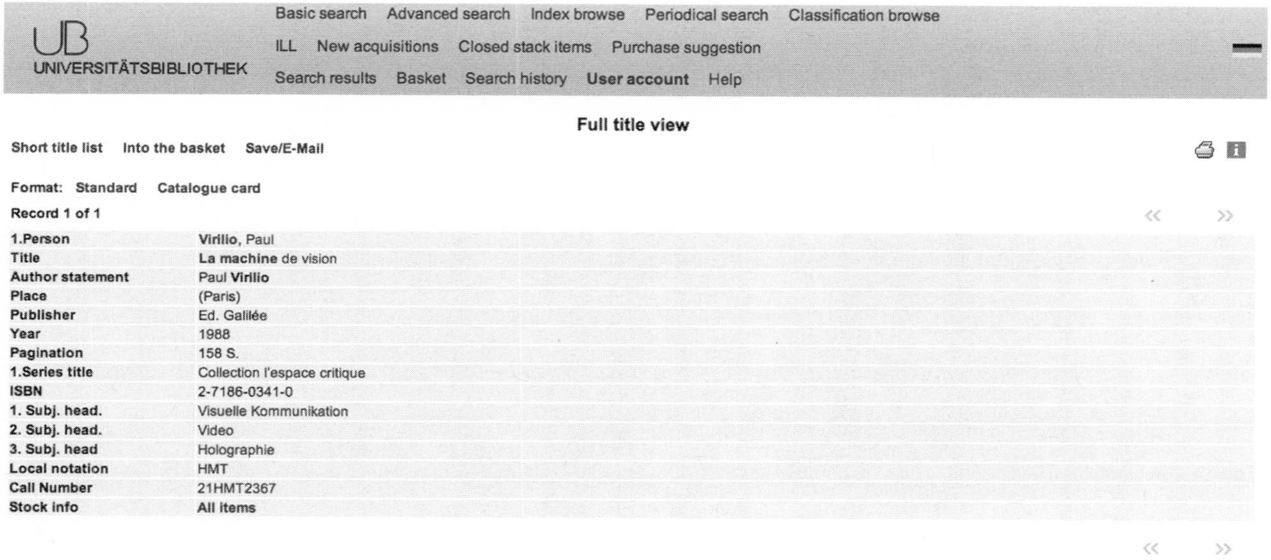

UB
UNIVERSITÄTSBIBLIOTHEK

Basic search   Advanced search   Index browse   Periodical search   Classification browse
ILL   New acquisitions   Closed stack items   Purchase suggestion
Search results   Basket   Search history   **User account**   Help

Full title view

Short title list   **Into the basket**   **Save/E-Mail**

Format: **Standard**   **Catalogue card**

Record 1 of 1   « »

1.Person	**Virilio**, Paul
Title	**La machine** de vision
Author statement	Paul **Virilio**
Place	(Paris)
Publisher	Ed. Galilée
Year	1988
Pagination	158 S.
1.Series title	Collection l'espace critique
ISBN	2-7186-0341-0
1. Subj. head.	Visuelle Kommunikation
2. Subj. head.	Video
3. Subj. head	Holographie
Local notation	HMT
Call Number	21HMT2367
Stock info	**All items**

« »

FIGURE 9.11 *Listing of Virilio (1989) at the university library Siegen. Third tag: holography (1989).*

> holography [first reference] and computer graphics . . . as though, at the close of the twentieth century, the end of modernity were itself marked by the end of a logic of public representation. Now, although we may be comfortable with the *reality* of the formal logic of traditional pictorial representation and, to a lesser degree, the *actuality* of the dialectical logic governing photographic and cinematic representation, we still cannot seem to get a grip on the *virtualities* of the paradoxical logic of the videogram, the hologram [second reference][62] or digital imagery. (Virilio 1995, 63; emphasis and punctuation in the original; see also Virilio 1988, 133–4)

Holography (or the hologram) is then regarded as belonging to the "paradoxical logic" of the image that is simultaneously connected with the term "virtuality." One page later, Virilio states:

> With paradoxical logic, what gets decisively *resolved* is the reality of the object's *real-time* presence. In the previous age of dialectical logic, it was only the delayed-time presence, the presence of the past, that lastingly impressed plate and film. The paradoxical image thus acquires a status something like that of surprise, or more precisely, of an 'accidental transfer.' (Virilio 1995, 64; emphasis in the original)

The "paradoxical logic" to which the hologram supposedly belongs is thus attributed to a resolution of "real-time presence." It is differentiated from the "dialectical logic" of the image," clearly only dealing with the "presence of the past" which "lastingly impressed" "plates" (e.g. photographic plates). Obviously this in no way applies to holography. Holography is a method for the creation of images that—in contrast to most of the methods of photography prevalent today (mostly digital)—is based on high-resolution photo plates. The holographic image has a temporal mode similar to that of photography insofar as it connects the 'here and now' of the object with its 'has been' (see Barthes 1982, 76). Indeed the presence of the object that 'has been' at one point is more intense, more sculptural, and more entrancing than in a photograph; the object is able to appear *in front of* the plate, detached from the recording, as it were.[63] The 'here and now' seems to overpower the 'has-been'—but this has nothing to do with 'real time' (if something like the live-principle is meant). One might suspect that Virilio is somehow mistaking holography for three-dimensional computer graphics created in real time. And indeed, some pages later he says:

> [It is] as though the chronology of the invention of cinema were being relived in a mirror, the age of the magic lantern giving way once more to the age of the recording camera, in anticipation of digital holography [third and last reference]. (Virilio 1995, 70; punctuation as in the original. See Virilio 1988, 147)

It becomes obvious that Virilio is mixing up holography in a rather unclear way with what he calls 'infography.' He seems to understand holography as another name for computer generated images—and that is simply wrong. Of course, in the late 1960s there already existed (at least in an early state) 'digital holography', i.e. computer generated holograms (see Tricoles 1987). Yet, if he really meant those then they would only be a sub-form of what he calls the 'infographic image' (or as I am suggesting terminologically: the series of virtual optics).[64] But I am quite sure that Virilio does not mean this series—at least nothing is pointing out that the difference between optical and virtual-optical (computer-generated) holograms is known to him.

In fact, it is not clear what he wants to say *at all* with his three or four references to *holography* (including the blurb), pigeonholing it with *videography* and *infography*. These three types of images simply cannot be put together into the *one* category of the 'paradoxical logic of the image.' It is Virilio's attempt to lump together three completely different phenomena:

1 Video: the analog-electronic image transmission (probably for this reason he is talking of 'real time') and also storage.

2 Holography: Apart from the laser light source, holography is not at all electronic but analog-optical and in addition also not geometrically- but wave-optically generated. Apart from that, it emerged and is being created mostly on less sensitive photo plates; therefore one cannot talk at all of real time.

3 'Infography', i.e. probably computer graphics. This is categorically different from the first and the second category. It belongs to the series of virtual optics. This means that the

> aim is generating images on the basis of mathematical processes in modern digital computers. This can also include geometrical-, physiological- and wave-optical phenomena as long as they can be formulated mathematically (and don't need too much computing resources).

To a certain extent Virilio errs on a similar level to Crary. He believes that from the fact that video, holography and infography to a certain degree emerged simultaneously in the 1960s, he must draw the conclusion that a new 'epoch' has started, namely (as if he were quoting a quasi-Hegelian triad) that after the epoch of the 'formal' and the 'dialectic,' now the epoch of the 'paradoxical' pictorial logic appears (the design on the back cover underlines this, see Figure 9.10). Like Crary, Virilio thinks successionistically—one epoch follows the next.[65] Completely different phenomena are forced into one category only in order to be able to keep within the frame of this logic. It would be much simpler and more cohesive to assume that there are different series that exist relatively independently, parallel to each other yet that also can be connected. Nevertheless, Virilio's ideas contain conclusions that are actually worth considering.

1. He rates architecture with the "formal logic of the image." Obviously, spatial structures for Virilio can also have pictorial qualities; i.e. a certain deviation from the planocentric discourse exists.[66]
2. He avoids subsuming holography among photography—meaning the series of geometrical optics—or cinema—the geometrical-physiological hybrid, as Bryson and Williams did. He recognizes that holography no longer belongs in these series.
3. Even though his classification of holography and infography with virtuality (see again the striking back cover in Figure 9.10) is not precise, it nevertheless is not completely wrong (see Chapter 10).

Summarizing, the discussion of Bryson's, Williams', and Virilio's texts shows that the holographic image was not a proper object of art-historical or philosophical discourse. There is probably no media technology that is so marginalized in *theory* while it has long since become quite indispensable in different *practices*. This difference seems to be constitutive for holography. In the following section, I want to discuss some of the currently relevant practices.

9.2 The spatial knowledge of holo-interferometry

The following section will deal with the "most widespread and commercially important application" (Johnston 2006a, 191) of holography, namely *holographic interferometry*. Similarly to the basic principles of holography itself, this method was 'discovered' more or less simultaneously by different groups of scientists in different forms together with the emergence of three-dimensional holographic images, i.e. since the use of the laser. We are dealing with a set of methods that were not predicted by anyone, but which to a certain extent were unavoidable insofar as they are dependent on the extreme susceptibility of the holographic process to breakdowns. As Geimer has observed, "every new photographic method has created its own specific disruptions and accidents. The photographic process released unforeseen and often at first unexplainable developments" (Geimer 2002, 321).

These at first "unexplainable developments" can again be the starting point for new methods—they are the place at which the epistemological margin between simple disturbance and unknown phenomena appears that generate new knowledge.[67] But this knowledge does not simply appear by itself, as the early experimenter Matt Lehmann writes:

> One of our very first holograms was of a business card with a few coins laid on it. When it was reconstructed the card had a series of black bands across it. We realized that these were caused because the card had moved during exposure but gave no thought to the fact that we had discovered a technique of non-destructive testing.[68] Our only thought was that the hologram was spoiled by the card movement. (Lehmann 1982, 5)

Some may overlook the possible new forms of knowledge that can emerge from a disturbance; they treat a disturbance only as a disturbance. But others make a disturbance productive although it is not clear in the actual moment whether the disturbance is even *able* to generate new knowledge. Emmett Leith retrospectively talks about the creation of a hologram around 1963 that took place in a similarly disturbed way:

> One of the objects we used was a sheet from a paper calendar, measuring about five inches on a side. To give stability, we pasted the calendar sheet to a block of aluminium. The resulting holographic image was good except for a circular black spot about half-inch or less in diameter, which covered up one of the numbers on the calendar. We made another hologram and yet another. It was always the same story – just one defect, and always in the same place. Examination of the object revealed that the aluminium block had a circular hole in it, just at the place where the image defect occurred. Juris remarked that this would be a good method to measure object motion. (Quoted in Johnston 2006a, 191)

This means an 'image defect'—a disturbance—occurs. But there is a significant difference. In the quote Lehman only talks of *one* disturbed attempt, whereas Leith reports a *series* of experiments: The defect occurs always in the same spot, i.e. it shows a certain regularity—and only if a disturbance seems to obey some sort of rule can it be the starting point for new knowledge and thus of a possible new technological sedimentation. Repetition thus may unsheathe a still unknown knowledge in a disturbance (see Leith 1996, 23). Retrospectively—quite swiftly, as usual—this new knowledge appears in the last sentence of the quote above: Juris (Upatnieks) draws a conclusion that does not immediately make sense. Why is the "defect" a sign for a good method for measuring the movement of objects? Because the gentle movements of the paper across the small hole had led to a change in the interference pattern: "When reconstructed, this time-averaged exposure reconstructs a bright image where the motion was a multiple of a full wavelength, and dimmer for intermediate motions" (Johnston 2006a, 192). Retrospectively it is easy for Leith to believe in having invented—and not 'found'—a sort of interferometer, i.e. a measuring device working with interferences.[69]

Interferometry is a science going back to the nineteenth century. Albert A. Michelson and Edward W. Morley were already using interference patterns in 1887 in order to measure lengths with the same apparatuses "used in the experiments on the relative motion of the earth and the luminiferous aether."[70] But until the early 1960s the main problem was the absence of sufficiently coherent light. However, when working with laser light from *c.* 1963 onward, it became unavoidable to meet with 'defects' or specific interference patterns sooner or later. Each speck of dust, each small flaw in a lens and each small roughness of surfaces diffracts a percentage of the light that then interferes with the rest of the light and thus creates light and dark rings and speckles.[71] Thus, shortly after the introduction of the laser around 1964, different forms of holo-interferometry were 'discovered' in different international laboratories. "[H]ologram interferometry only needed the laser and the hologram for nearly anyone to discover it" (Stetson 1991, 18).

Since Leith and Upatnieks had to deal with movements *during the period of exposure* (which can be quite long for hologram recordings because of the low sensitivity of the high-resolution plates), a good name for the method they were using might have been "time average holographic interferometry." But Leith and Upatnieks did not really analyze it systematically; this was done almost at the same time by Robert L. Powell and Karl Stetson instead, who published a first important paper on the subject in 1965—and a little later themselves coined the term "time average holographic interferometry" for their method.[72]

They examined the vibrations of a small tin can that was made to vibrate with an electromagnet, controlling its vibrations accurately regarding frequency and amplitude and the developed holograms showed streaks of interferences (see Figure 9.12). Parts of the can moved towards the emulsion or away from it, while other parts remained relatively static. The white zones in the holo-interferograms show parts in which constructive interference was taking place. The dark parts on the other hand show those vibrating areas in which destructive interference occurred.

They demonstrated in their paper how it is conversely possible to deduce the amplitude and frequency of the vibrations. They underlined that the method could be used for analyzing the vibrations of complex structures, in particular because of the important advantage of the holographic interferometry in comparison with the conventional one:

> Any system which operates by mechanical vibrations may be studied with the detailed analysis made possible by this technique.

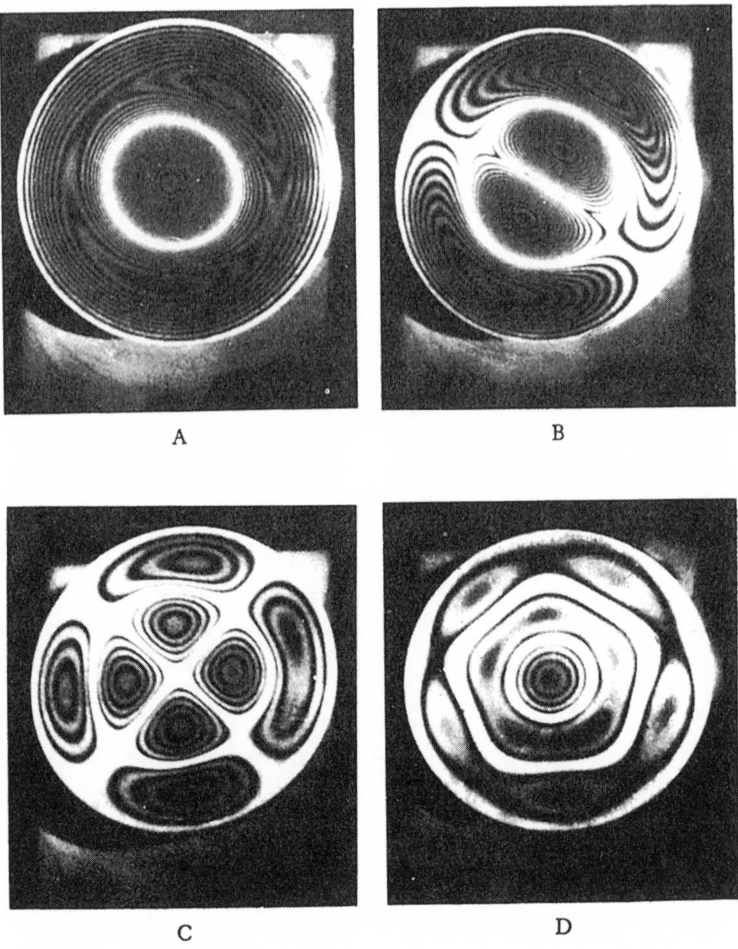

FIGURE 9.12 *Interference patterns on a tin can brought to vibration by Powell and Stetson (1965), in Klein (1970, 136).*

Examples of such systems are audiospeaker diaphragms, musical instruments such as percussion or stringed instruments, or audio transducers of many sorts. Also the technique may be applicable to models of larger systems where vibrations are undesirable, such as bridges, architectural structures, aerodynamic, or hydrofoil structures. The chief advantage is that the structure

> under analysis need not be modified. No fibers need be attached, no sensing mechanisms need to touch the vibrating structure, measurements may be made in vacuum or under water or any such transparent medium; in general, the vibration detection is independent of the physical system under measurement. The subject surfaces do not have to be polished or optically coated, and no mirrors have to be attached to the structure under analysis. Yet the precision of measurements may be to within fractions of a micron. (Powell and Stetson 1965, 1597)

The great advantage of holo-interferometry, then, is that it can also be done on non-mirroring surfaces, which of course immensely widens the field of possible objects (see Klein 1970, 142). The analysis of the vibration can be used for the analysis of the spatial structure of objects insofar as the behavior of the vibration can indicate the inner tensions of the object. However, Powell and Stetson's time-averaged method was not used, and for a good reason:

> The detection cannot be carried out in real time using visual persistence, and thus the hologram recording gives only after-the-fact information about what *has* happened, rather than an indication of what is happening. (Powell and Stetson 1965, 1597)

And so, the method of real time holographic interferometry was progressively established instead. This means that initially a hologram of an object is recorded. After developing it, the hologram is brought back exactly to the place at which it was recorded. There it is again illuminated with the object ray, i.e. with the coherent laser light reflected by the object. In the process the object undergoes modifications—for example, with a different temperature or certain pressures. The differences—even the smallest ones—between the actual object ray (i.e. the actual form of the wavefront imprinted on the light by the object) and the stored form of the wavefront (i.e. the hologram of the object before the modification) again lead to interference patterns. Since the object can be changed in real time and since each of these modifications can be directly compared with the reference hologram, we speak of real-time holographic interferometry. The following figures show an early industrial example for the use of this method at the beginning of the 1970s, namely the *GC Optronics Holographic Tire Analyzer*. Figure 9.13 is a photograph of the facility; Figure 9.14 shows its schematic arrangement.

The diagram may look complicated, but in principle it is nothing other than a usage of the principle of the double ray or off-axis holography already developed by Leith and Upatnieks shown in Figure 9.6. Figure 9.15 shows an example for such a holo-interferogram of a tire.

As can be seen from the diagram in Figure 9.14, mirrors are installed to the left and the right of the tire so that the tire can be seen not only from the front but also from the side. The arrows in Figure 9.15 show spots at which conspicuous interference fringes can be seen. These point out inner tensions of the tire, for example because some of the bonding of the laminations is not perfect and the tire is deformed unevenly by the pressure applied. The spatial knowledge produced by the transplane holographic image then refers also to the *inner space* of objects and the tensions to be found

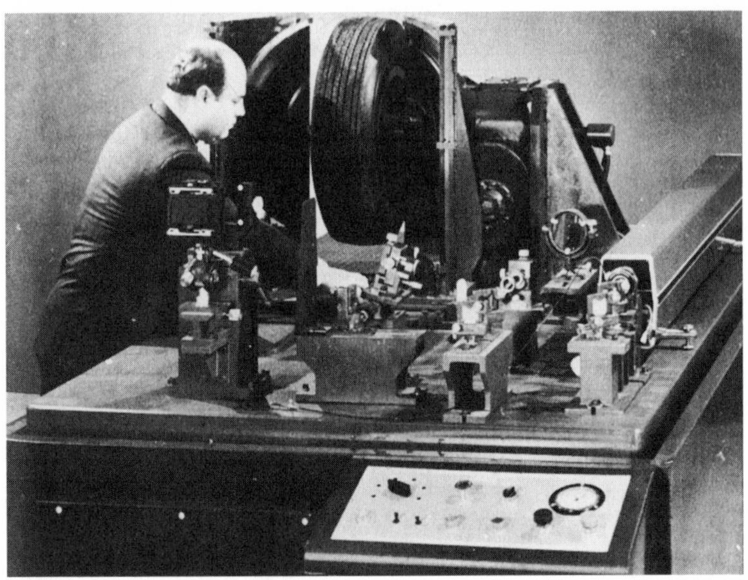

FIGURE 9.13 GC Optronics Holographic Tire Analyzer, *photograph of the facility, in Klein (1970, 143).*

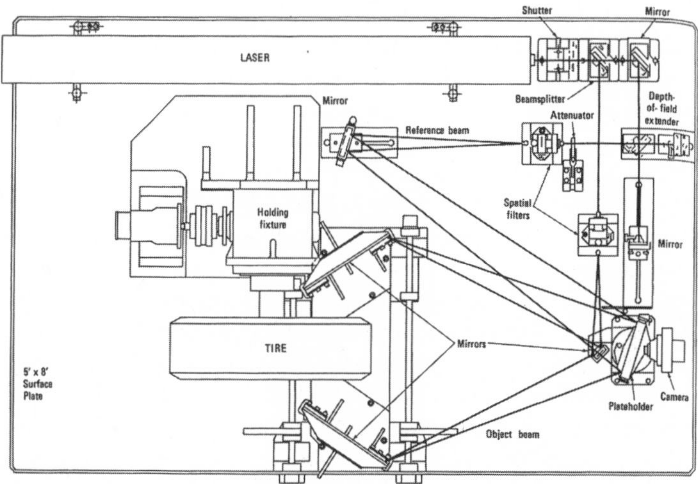

FIGURE 9.14 GC Optronics Holographic Tire Analyzer, *schematic arrangement, in Klein (1970, 144).*

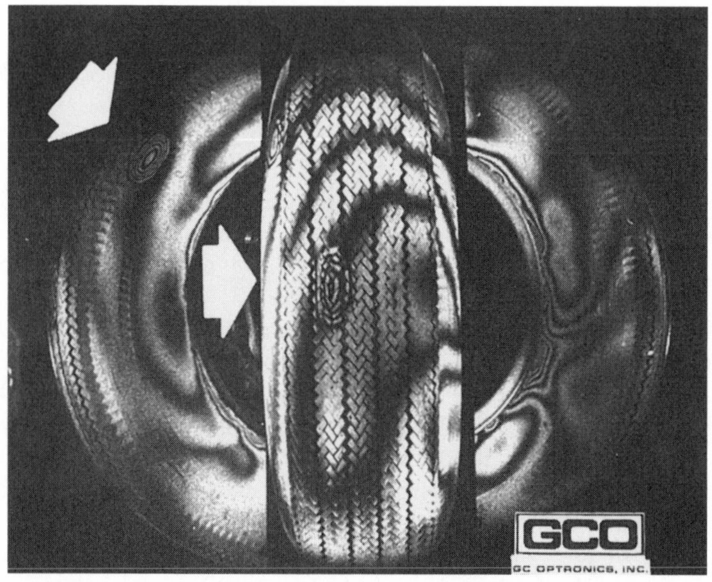

FIGURE 9.15 *Image of a tire in the holographic tire analyzer, in Klein (1970, 145). The arrows mark the spots which reveal the defects in the tire by way of interference fringes.*

in them. One could say that holo-interferometry makes those states visible that in principle remain invisible for every 'normal' photographic medium: the *inner off of the objects*. In photographs and film, the off denotes the exterior of the image, static in photographs, dynamic in film. It is rarely made a subject of discussion that the interior of all depicted objects also belongs to the off, even though—especially in horror films—the opening of the body can be seen as becoming the on of the inner off. Also x-rays, which are also recorded photographically, transfer the inner off into partial visibility. Even though x-ray photographs show the more solid inner parts of bodies, they do not show their *states* regarding inner tensions. Using the effects of the wave-optical series for controlling objects very quickly became an important industrial practice labeled *holographic nondestructive testing*:

> Any deformation of the object surface, down to a few microinches can be measured without difficulty. Since each fringe relates to the deformation of the surface, variation in the geometry of a fringe is directly relatable to the topology or shape of the surface.[73]

The example in Figure 9.15 shows that the spatial knowledge made possible by holography does not necessarily have to be referred back to the three-dimensional impression of holographic images[74] since the disturbance in the spatial structure of the objects becomes visible also in the reproductions that can be shown here only two-dimensionally. The spatial information made available by an *optical* medium does not necessarily have to correspond with a *visual* spatial aspect, or, as Johnston has observed regarding holo-interferometry: "These early applications of holography had little to do . . . with three-dimensional displays" (2006b, 199). I will discuss this difference between optical and visual media below. It also shows in that a simply *visual* interpretation of the interference fringes created only by the human eye was soon regarded as an unreliable method, thus this task was relegated to electronic sensors connected to digital computers.[75]

Another form of holo-interferometry should be mentioned here, namely the method of *holographic contouring*, which provides "precisely measurable depth information about three-dimensional scenes" (Johnston 2006a, 195). This form of holographic spatial knowledge deals less with the inner off of objects or their states; it deals with the spatial structure of a scene. In the process, an object or a scene is illuminated with two lasers whose frequencies lie close to each other (or with one laser that is capable of creating two frequencies lying close to each other). These two holograms are recorded onto one plate and then reconstructed again with a single frequency laser light. The result is two reconstructions of a slightly different size interfering with each other, thereby creating interference fringes. "If the object was motionless during the original exposure, those fringes mapped out spatial steps corresponding to the wavelength difference between the two laser emissions" (Johnston 2006a, 195).

To a certain extent, this method recalls the acquisition of spatial information by distorting projected grids as I have discussed in connection with photo sculpture (see Chapter 3). As it had been possible there to infer the spatial structure of the scene from the distortion of the grid, one can also draw conclusions here from the interference fringes. However, despite all visual similarities, both methods belong to different optical series. When projecting the grid to the scene, the logic of projection—i.e. the logic of geometrical optics—is being used insofar as to a certain extent we are dealing with an inversion of Alberti's idea of projecting the object by way of a grid onto the plane. Holographic contouring, on the other hand, does not project. The interference pattern only appears in the reconstruction when using the wave effects of the light.

Nevertheless the comparison is interesting because it leads us back to the analysis and reproduction of *sculptural* structures. Figure 9.16 shows a somewhat surrealistic arrangement of objects that does not follow any kind of iconology; it only serves to demonstrate the contouring method. In view of Brewster's attempts to use stereoscopy for taking photographs of sculptures (as described in Chapter 2), the obvious question arises whether holography could not also be a storage medium for spatial information of sculptures and whether holo-interferometry could not also be a means of analyzing sculptural objects.

And indeed, probably the earliest attempts along those lines were initiated in 1971 by the increasingly catastrophic condition of sculptural and architectonic artworks in Venice.[76] Air pollution and inundation were threatening terrible losses:

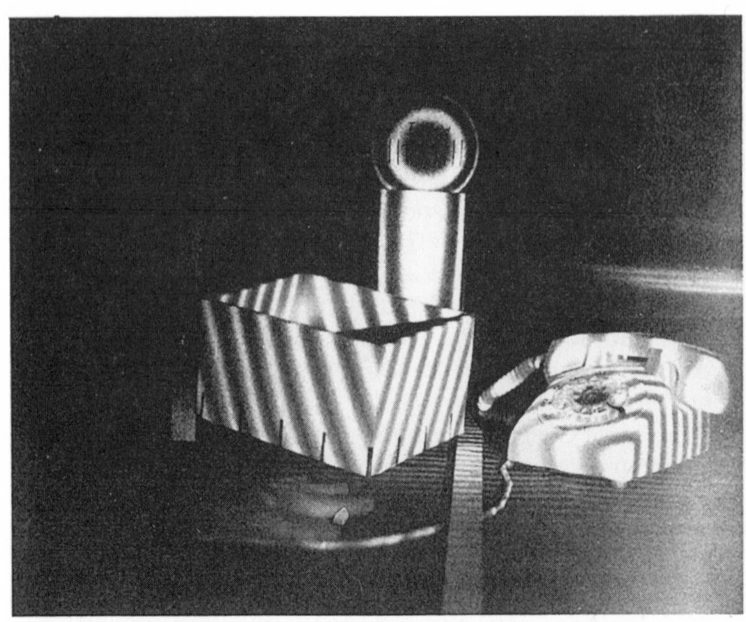

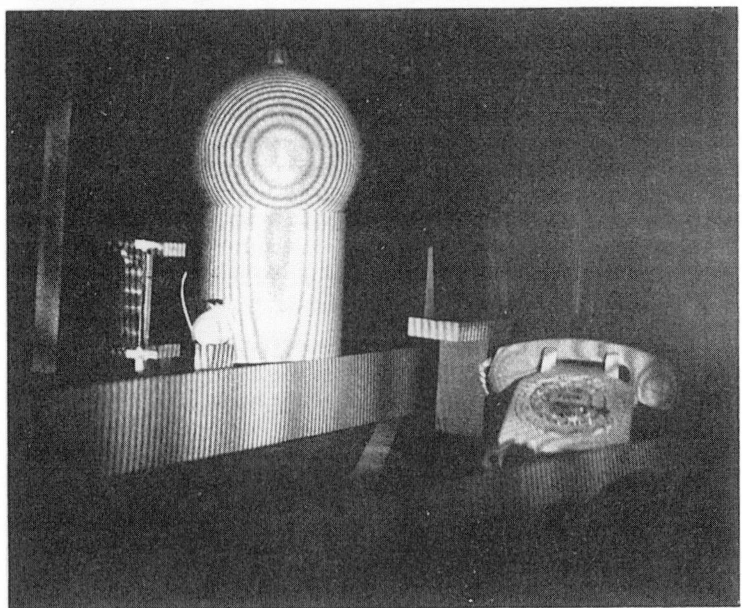

FIGURE 9.16 *Holographic contouring of a scene, in Heflinger and Wuerker (1969, 29).*

> If a rapidly deteriorating object cannot be conserved, the next move (admittedly desperate) is to conserve information about the object. The information needs to be reasonably complete and conveniently retrievable. Recent developments in holography are of potential significance in this context. (Munk and Munk 1972, 439)

Similar to Brewster's suggestion, the idea of a "museum of three-dimensional images"[77] obviously took center stage. Figure 9.17 shows one of the biggest holograms of sculpture. Scientists who had been inspired by the problems in Venice in cooperation with the Louvre were able to create a hologram of the *Venus de Milo* in real size: "The 2.20 meters high image is roughly 2 meters behind the hologram plate" (Fournier, Tribillon and Vienot 1977, 120).

The potential that the high-resolution holographic images offered not only for conservation but also for the analysis of artworks was soon discovered.[78] Holograms could

> be invaluable in comparative analysis determining damages sustained by art treasures. . . . The detection of fissures, peeling areas or slow disintegrations could be accomplished through periodic checking of the original piece against its holographic image.[79]

Obviously, the authors are alluding to the method of real time holographic interferometry. However, a use of this method requires a direct comparison of the artwork with its hologram. But as a rule this is somewhat difficult because many of the artworks are physically bound to their location. Therefore, instead one uses a method in which two holograms are recorded one after the other onto the same plate, while between the two recordings perhaps, as an example, the temperature of the object is changed. During the reconstruction, the two slightly different holograms overlap showing patterns of interference. Figure 9.18 shows four interferograms of Pier Francesco Fiorentino's painting *Santa Caterina* from the fifteenth century.

As one can very clearly see from the interferograms, which were created by way of the thermal drift method (i.e. the cautious use of warming), there are interference fringes that are pointing at tensions in the structure of the painting—the materiality of painting is made visible in a very special way, quite outside of reflexive aesthetic

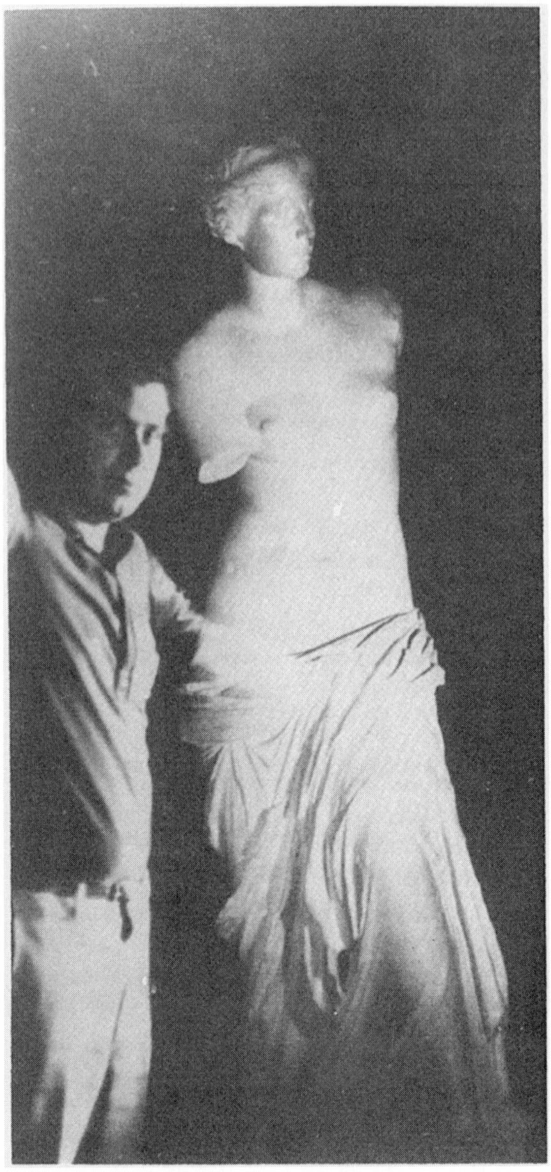

FIGURE 9.17 *Holographic image of the* Venus de Milo, *in Fournier, Tribillon and Vienot (1977, 120). The effect of the holographic image cannot be reproduced here.*

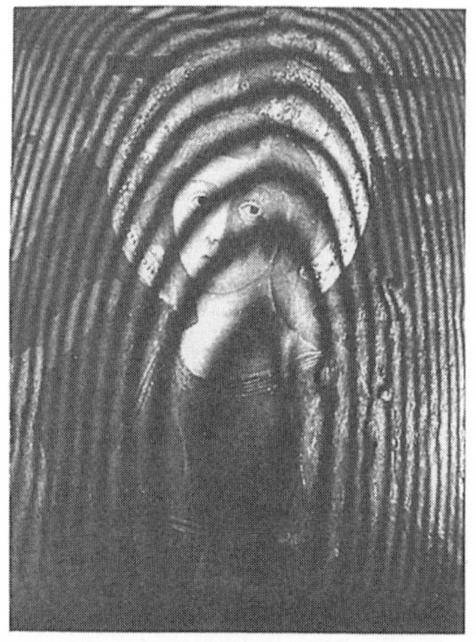

Fig. 4. Detached regions revealed through the ambient-drift method.

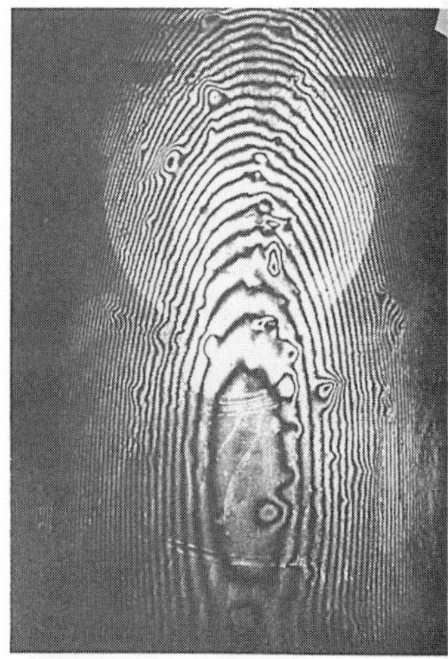

Fig. 6. Detached regions revealed through the thermal-drift method.

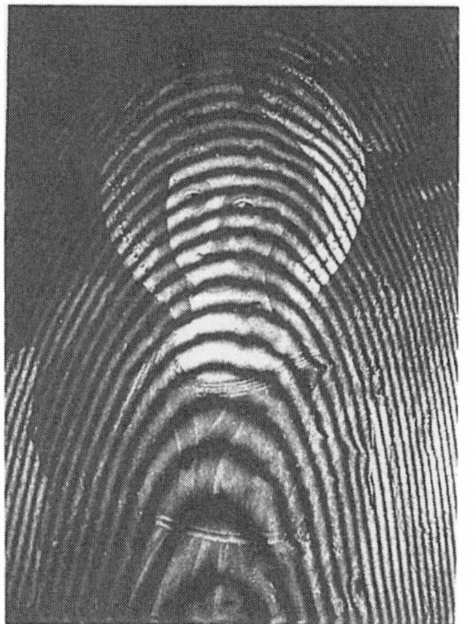

Fig. 5. Same as Fig. 4, except that the time interval between the two exposures has been doubled.

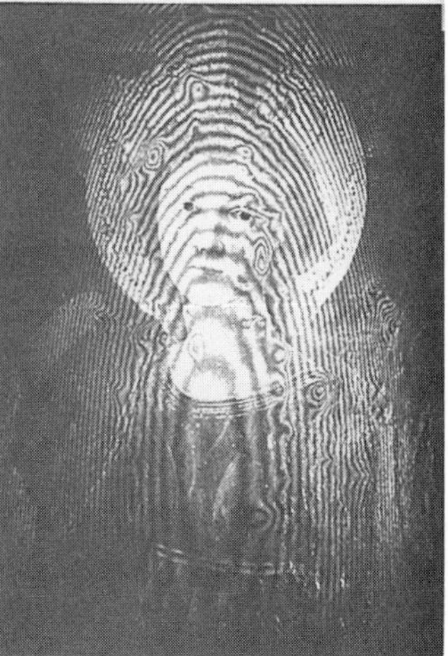

Fig. 7. Same as Fig. 6, except that the fringe contrast has been reduced.

FIGURE 9.18 *Four holo-interferograms of a painting from the fifteenth century, in Amadesi et al. (1974, 2012).*

discourses. In Venice, interferometric images were made in similar studies, for example of Donatello statues revealing inner tensions in one of the statues, which disclosed hitherto unknown mistakes of a repair from more than one hundred years ago (see Asmus et al. 1973, 59; Westlake, Wuerker and Asmus 1976, 86–8). Once more the *inner space of the objects* is made visible by way of the transplane images, thereby making it controllable.

But what are the drawbacks of holographic-transplane reproductions of sculptural objects? A first problem is that holography, as a lensless image, can only show objects that—depending on the distance between object and plate—match the size of the plates since no enlargement or reduction is possible without a lens. The recording of large sculptural objects then demands large photo plates: "[I]t is very cumbersome to process such heavy and bulky pieces."[80] But, of course, it is no coincidence that the first pictorial hologram shows a toy train and not a real one, simply because it is *small* enough.[81] Secondly, one could assume that sculptures would have to be taken out of their architectonic context in order to be recorded in the dark without stray light.[82] But with the help of pulse lasers that are able to create very bright and extremely short laser flashes (10^{-7} sec.) in the so-called Q-switched mode, "outdoor holograms"[83] are made possible. Thirdly, one can probably get over the—not mandatory—absence of color because of the use of monochromatic light since (in the widest sense of the word classicist) sculptural objects are almost white in most cases; also, art history has been using only black and white photographs for a long time. Since it is not quite as limited, holography then can be regarded as a step into the direction of transplane reproductions of sculptures.

As Figure 9.19 from one of the essays on the use of holography for safeguarding artworks demonstrates, the holographic image indeed facilitates movement with regard to the "illuminated points"[84] of the sculptural object as if it were a real object: "For instance by moving his head from one side of the plate to the other, he can vary the parallax and look at different sides of the object. He can also focus on different planes of the object, thus verifying the depth of field" (Munk and Munk 1972, 439). Nevertheless, the sculptural object is always only illuminated from one side, i.e. it *is not reproduced in toto*.[85] Even though it is not possible to move completely around the sculpture, one has certain degrees of freedom (unlike with stereoscopic images);[86] one can choose views and thus

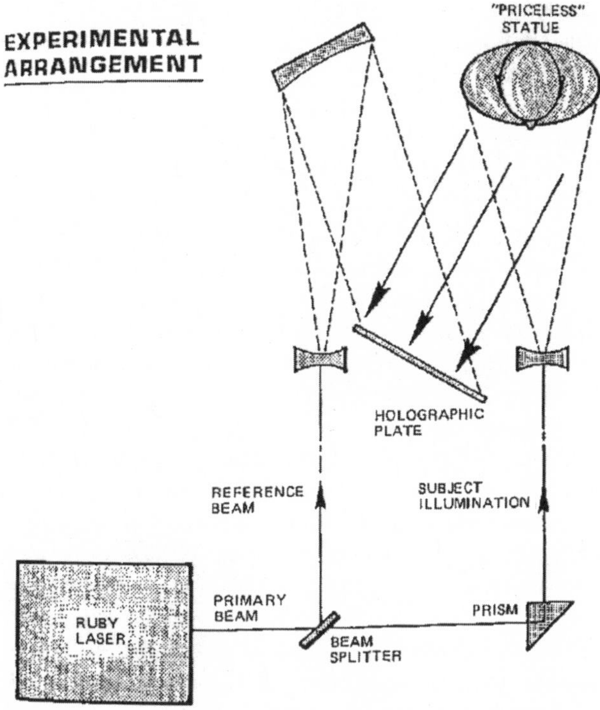

FIGURE 9.19 *Experimental arrangement, in Westlake, Wuerker and Asmus (1976, 85).*

one can, to a certain extent, perform Wölfflin's experiment (see Chapter 2) at least partially oneself, with the media-specific joy of trying to find the best view.

The fact that holography as a method of reproducing sculptures in the realm of art history or art criticism has not been established might be attributed mainly to the technical demands of its creation and reproduction (good transmission holograms need laser light for reconstructing the wave front), which increase quickly into exorbitant realms when dealing with larger objects. One has to add that almost parallel with the development of holography another development already began to emerge that is ultimately more flexible and moreover is able to include the potentials of the hologram (and of stereoscopy), at least in principle. That is the development of virtualization, i.e. simulation based on digital computers. We will deal with these and with the potentials of transplane imaging later.[87]

9.3 Wave optics and the 'simulation' of geometrical optics: Holographic-optical elements, optical vs. visual media

Holography was also 'discovered' somewhere else independently from Dennis Gabor and Emmett Leith. This led to a particularly interesting application of holography, the so-called holographic optical elements (HOEs), that demonstrate concretely to what extent the series of wave optics can include the series of geometrical optics. These are a good example for an omnipresent and hardly thought about use of transplane pictorial technologies.[88] The genealogy of this method in a way starts in a surprising area—in literature.

Moscow 1944: Ivan Yefremov, an important Soviet paleontologist, had just completed a science-fiction story that would be published one year later. Its English title became *Shadows of the Past* (trans. 1954) and it contains autobiographical elements since its main character is a paleontologist, Sergej Pavlovich Nikitin, who together with other scientists is searching for traces of the past (skeletons of dinosaurs). The protagonists find some, but they also encounter curious black mirror plates that could be sedimentations of tree resin hardened over thousands of years.

> On one angle of the cube there blazed a huge black mirror. The paleontologist gazed at it all in wonder. 'This is the asphalt deposit' said Miriam quietly, 'or rather the deposit of solidified rosin. It runs in even layers through hardened ironbearing sandstone, probably of aeolian origin'. (Yefremov 2001, 24)

One evening, the group of scientists meet by accident close to one of these mirror plates. Nikitin gives an extended speech on paleontology and it is noticeable how Yefremov—very much in the tradition of good science-fiction literature—attempts to convey knowledge in a didactic way, when something very peculiar happens:

> A muffled cry came from Marusya. Nikitin paused and looked round. The next instant his heart stood still and every nerve of his body was petrified. Against the bluish-black slab of fossilized rosin, as from a yawning abyss there appeared a gigantic grey-green ghost. A huge dinosaur was hanging motionless in the air, above the upper edge of a craggy precipice, rearing 30 feet over the heads of the stupefied little group below. . . . The dark cliffs were peeping through the ghost, but every little detail of the dinosaur's body was plainly to be seen. . . . The vision was intensely life-like. . . . Several minutes flew by. And as the sunlight began to fade, the motionless image melted away and finally disappeared altogether. In its place there remained only the black mirror, which had lost its bluish sheen and was now shining dully like copper. (Yefremov 2001, 28–9)

The scientists become witnesses of a quite extraordinary, three-dimensional, colored and high-resolution manifestation that obviously has something to do with the incidence of light onto the mysterious black mirror. Later in the story most of the participants in the expedition will believe that they had had a hallucination under the influence of the heat. But not the protagonist Sergej Pavlovich Nikitin. In the years to come he will attempt to find an explanation while his colleagues increasingly believe that he has turned mad. But he continues to reflect on the phenomenon and one day he finds the answer:

> Wait! Nikitin jumped up and walked up and down the room. The reflection had been a coloured one! The one thing to do was to dig into the theory of colour photography! . . . He had gone through the theory . . . when he came across a letter written by Joseph Niepce [*sic*] to Louis Daguerre in the thirties of the last century . . . 'And it turned out that the emulsion (asphalt rosin) of the plate changed under the action of light, which gave in passing light something akin to the image on a slide and all the shades of colour were plainly visible,' wrote Joseph Niepce [*sic*]. . . . Reading on, Nikitin discovered that the structure of the smooth surface of photographic plates changes under the action of stationary light waves and that these waves produce definite colour images, as distinct from the usual black and white images produced by the chemical action of light on photographic plates

> covered with silver bromide. These imprints of complex reflections of light waves, which remain invisible even when strongly magnified, have one peculiarity – they reflect light of only a definite colour and when the prototype is lighted under a strictly definite angle. The sum total of these imprints produces a marvellous image in natural colours. Nikitin knew now that in natural conditions light may have direct action on certain materials and produce images without necessarily disintegrating combinations of silver. This was just the link that was missing from his chain of thought. (Yefremov 2001, 34–5)

Even though Yefremov attributes the invention of the interference color photography to Joseph Nicéphore Niépce and Louis Jacques Mandé Daguerre, it was actually discovered by Gabriel Lippmann in 1891.[89] The main point is, however, that the pictorial phenomenon that he describes and connects to 'light waves' furnishes *spatial information* that goes beyond the geometrical-perspectival projection onto the plane ("a huge dinosaur was hanging motionless in the air")—not even Lippmann's interference color photography was able to do that. Already in 1944, several years before Dennis Gabor and even twenty years before Emmett Leith and Juris Upatnieks created the first pictorial hologram, the paleontologist speculated on *three-dimensional images* based on wave optical knowledge.

Some time later, Yefremov wrote another short science-fiction story entitled "Star Ships." Again, it deals with paleontologists who this time are unearthing some dinosaur fossils containing very fine, razor sharp holes indicating highly developed fire arms—millions of years before mankind. The scientists come to the—as improbable as unavoidable—conclusion that extraterrestrial beings must have visited earth. And while they continue digging they indeed find the skull of an alien humanoid and a mysterious, dark, semi-transparent plate. At first it is quite unclear what this is all about. One of the protagonists starts examining it:

> He placed the mysterious instrument, or part of an instrument, beneath the glare of a special microscopic bulb and turned it about, trying to detect some detail of construction that had so far escaped detection. Suddenly, in the circle of the reverse side of the disc, he caught a glimpse of something that showed faintly under the opaque film. With bated breath, he strained his eyes to see what

> that something was, changing the angle of the disc. And then, through the cloudy film which time had imprinted on the transparent substance of the circle, he saw, or imagined he saw, a pair of eyes that looked straight up at him. With a muffled cry the Professor dropped the heavy disc. . . . 'And on this side there's a picture!' cried Shatrov. 'I saw a pair of eyes! Eyes! And I'm sure it's a portrait of a star-man, of the one, perhaps, whose skull we have here! Perhaps it's a sort of identification on the apparatus. . . . Look at the circle's form . . . it's an optical lens.' . . . From the deep bottom of the absolute transparent layer, magnified by some mysterious optical device to its natural proportions, there looked out at them a strange but an undoubtedly human face. (Yefremov 2001, 258–9)

An image that is at the same time a lens. An image that dependent on the angle of vision can be viewed more or less well. An image in "natural proportions" can be seen (although it is not quite clear whether Yefremov thereby really means a three-dimensional image). An image that could also have been used for "identification." One does not have to praise the imaginative faculties of science-fiction literature in order to realize that certain characteristics and usages of holography have been anticipated in an astounding way.

According to Yuri Denisyuk's own statement (1992, 376), "Star Ships" influenced him; he was a scientist who started working on interference patterns around 1958, searching for three-dimensional images. Possibly he was inspired by Yefremov's at least indirect mentioning of Lippmann's interference color photography and thus he attempted to record the interference pattern that a convex spherical mirror creates: "He conceived his first experimental objects as a generalized version of Lippmann's liquid mercury mirror. . . . As he initially conceived his new method, Denisyuk concluded that it would create a structure in the emulsion that was identical to the optical properties of the original object."[90] The experiment succeeded after many difficulties with ameliorating the necessary emulsions around 1959 (see Denisyuk and Protas 1963): "In accordance with the theory, the wave photographs of such mirrors were equal in optical strength to the optical strength of the original mirror."[91] At the time Denisyuk still did not have laser light available, only the light of a mercury arc lamp as had been the case for Gabor twelve years earlier. Unlike Gabor's holograms or Leith's and Upatnieks' transmission-light holograms shortly afterwards, they are visible in white light—a white light of the sun as it had been described by Yefremov. In Denisyuk's method, during the recording object rays and reference rays hit the holographic plate from different sides. The object is placed behind the holographic plate and reflects the light onto the irradiated plate. In this process, standing waves are formed. These, then, are not only stored as a two-dimensional intensity distribution on the surface of the hologram, as in Leith's and Upatnieks' method, but *also* as a laminar structure with a lamellar distance in the emulsion layer of half a wave length (it is in this regard that Denisyuk is following Lippmann).[92] When it is reproduced, one looks at the side of the hologram that during the recording was hit by the reference wave. In the course of this, the individual lamellas in the depth of the developed photographic layer have the effect of an interference filter: The hologram reflects an almost monochromatic light from the white light and the original wave front is reconstructed by way of this monochromatic light. Therefore, Denisyuk holograms can be seen in white light. These white light holograms then are reflection holograms (see Figure 9.20).

Denisyuk created a hologram of a mirror that then acts like the mirror (reminding us directly of Yefremov's black mirror).

A procedure of geometrical optics (the reflecting mirror)[93] can be reproduced by the wave optical hologram in a similar way as wave optics epistemologically can include geometrical optics as a specific case. Therefore, an artistic hologram, e.g. a self portrait by Edwina

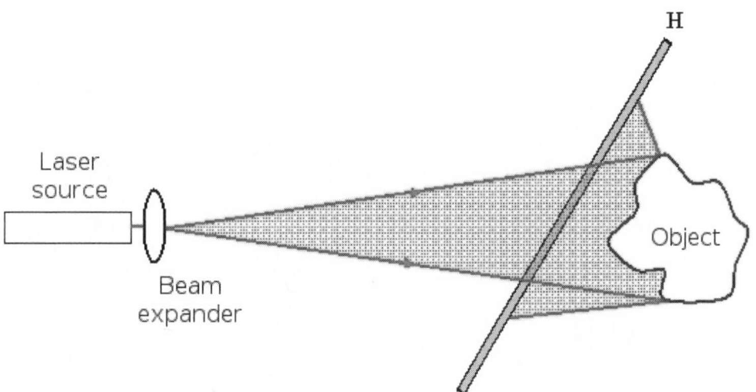

FIGURE 9.20 *Recording of a Denisyuk hologram.*[94]

Orr (1982, 30×40 cm) which is part of Matthias Lauk's impressive collection of holograms in the DASA in Dortmund (Germany),[95] is able to include an enlargement lens that enlarges just like a magnifying glass (Figure 9.21).

As a self-referential art object (and therefore potentially with a media-aesthetic function), this hologram shows first of all that the lensless image can include all lens-supported images. However, secondly and inversely no hologram (and no Lippmann interference

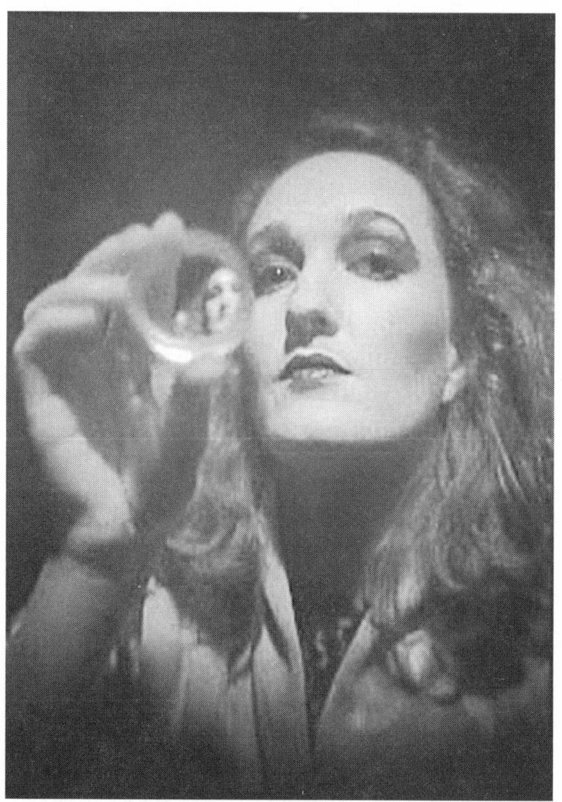

FIGURE 9.21 *Edwina Orr,* Self Portrait *(1982), 30×40 cm, white light reflection hologram; http://www.jrholocollection.com/collection/orr.html* [last accessed September 2, 2013]. *By representing a lens that still enlarges even as an image, this hologram illustrates the inclusion of geometrical optics. However, this phenomenon cannot be reproduced here.*

color photography) can be represented with a visual method based on a lens, i.e. with a geometrical-optical visual method. Therefore—unfortunately—commercially available catalogues of holography exhibitions are so tiring.[96] This last observation leads to the insight already discussed in Chapter 4, namely that visual technologies based on the series of wave optics can possibly be used for securing the authenticity of documents (see Schröter 2009).

But the first observation still needs a bit more clarification since it points to the epistemological inclusion of the series of geometrical optics by wave optics already mentioned in the introduction.[97] It permits the production of holographic-optical elements, HOEs for short. HOEs are holograms that contain the characteristics of, for example, a mirror (as in Denisyuk), a lens or other—even complex—geometrical-optical appliances.[98] As far as holograms can be understood as a kind of lens anyway; as I have said before, this use—not as the condition for a reconstruction of a three-dimensional image but as optical instrument—is not astonishing. The great advantage of HOEs lies in that the most complicated lens systems can be 'simulated,' if you will, with a minimum of cost and particularly space.[99]

A quite common and not at all curious or marginal use of HOEs is in scanner discs within systems with which one reads the barcode on goods (see Figure 9.22). The disc rotates and contains several holographic 'lenses.' "By continuously providing many angles of laser scanning, the product code can be identified even when the item is passed casually over the scanner."[100] This explains the puzzling mystery taking place with each supermarket visit, of how a cash register can deal with the crumpled up label on the plastic bag (to be sure, there are also scanning systems not based on holography). Again, holography in the form of holographic-optical elements is not a *visual* medium directed at the eyes of viewers but an optical one serving to acquire information (the barcode) in a spatially undefined situation (crumpled up bag, non-directed scanning). Both the deskilling of sales-representatives as the acceleration of turnover and the better control of stock turnover depend on the utilization of the holographic-transplane image: "The objective . . . was to minimize the constraints on the operator so that throughput and productivity could be increased."[101] In this application, holography is used to maximize the efficiency of workers, although it is not based on physiological optics.

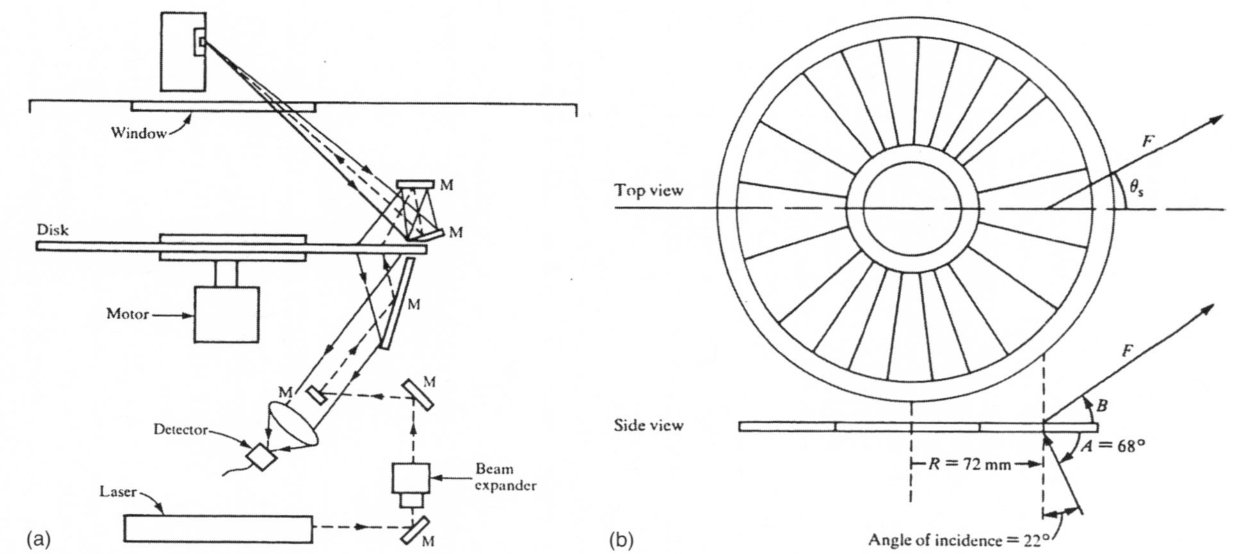

FIGURES 9.22 *(a)* Scanning system of a cash register in a supermarket, *and (b)* respective scanning disc, *in Dickson et al. (1982, 230–1).*

Holography is based on optical knowledge but is not necessarily a visual medium in the sense that it would be directed at human senses. It is therefore necessary to register that *optical* media *do not have to be visual* media. The concepts of a history of vision and a history of optical media that are often confounded in the discussions in visual studies have to be clearly divided. The latter refers to media that operate by using different optical series; the former refers to the way in which the images that are *also* created with such media are manifested for human perception (their phenomenology and its discursivation). However, the history of vision should not be discarded as anthropocentric—for example, by invoking some kind of poststructuralist critique of the subject. But it shows that physiological optics should not be elevated into the only valid series, as Crary did. It is not the manifestation for the viewers alone that should be gauged—but not its contrary either. Both, the focus on the optical and on the visual, are relevant and irreducible perspectives.

The examples delineated last—the use of holography in everyday scanning cash registers, ordinary banknotes, credit cards and documents (see Chapter 4)—show that Yefremov's grandiose vision that in *Shadows of the Past* dreamt of a colored, three-dimensional gigantic image did not really have the micrological use of transplane images in mind. A critical analysis of the uses of holography, then, would not have to search for their object in the three-dimensional and illusionistic effects taking us by surprise—especially since this kind of usage is rather marginal.[102] In the current "dispositives of power" (Foucault), holographic elements are more likely being used for control, analysis or non-reproducibility. Therefore, holography cannot be positioned solely within a history of vision.

9.4 Media aesthetics of the transplane image 8—artistic holography: Illusionism, light and achrony

Nevertheless, holography is also not satisfactorily explained as part of a history of optical media alone. The great excitement provoked by the first presentation of pictorial holography by Leith and Upatnieks shows to what extent an impact was made by the spatial impression of holographic images—and still is making today. The term holography, particularly in the popular imaginary, is often and in a rather unclear way representative for hyperrealist, three-dimensional images (see Johnston 2006a, 393–414).

A popular example for a three-dimensional image can be seen in a famous scene in *Star Wars* (USA 1977, Dir. George Lukas). One of the characters, Luke Skywalker (Mark Hammill), is repairing the droid R2-D2 and in doing so activates a sculptural projection showing the beautiful and politically persecuted princess Leia (Carrie Fischer) who is crying for help. This representation[103] does not much resemble a hologram since it shows a colored, moving, miniaturized figure that moreover is somehow being projected in mid-air. Even though the virtual or real images of holography also seem to be hovering in front of or behind the plate, nevertheless there is of course no projection ray as is being hinted at in the scene. Maybe only some type of volumetric, solid state display could create such images floating in mid-air (see Chapter 8). Nevertheless this sequence is automatically associated with holography in the respective commentaries.[104]

Another quite well-known example for the popular discourse on holography can be found in the television series *Star Trek—The Next Generation* (USA 1987ff.). There is a so-called holodeck, obviously named after holography. The holodeck is a room on board the space ships (and space stations) in which a situation can be created into which one can enter that is audio-visually absolutely realistic and can be haptically touched, and olfactorily as well as gustatorily experienced. The room is being used for recreation, for (even sexual) pleasure or in order to train different sports. Since this fiction associates real colors, tactility and interactivity with holography, i.e. characteristics that as a rule cannot (or in a very limited way) be attributed to holographic images,[105] the term holography in *Star Trek* is used synonymously with realistic, three-dimensional and even object-like images.[106] The images in the holodeck are so realistic that they cannot be distinguished from real objects any longer[107] whereas the holographic image in *Star Wars* still gave a certain flickering, translucent, glaring, and video-like impression.

An element in the phantasm of the holodeck becomes particularly clear, one that already had surfaced during the discussion of photo sculpture (see Chapter 3), namely that one is dealing with images that are so illusionist that tendentially they suspend the difference between object and image, a notion often connected with the different types of 3D images. Emmett Leith once called holography a "method of making the most realistic . . . photographic images in the world" (Leith 1983, 1). Already Rudolf Arnheim talked about holography in a similar sense:

> As holography is perfected, it begins to exhibit the terrifying rigor mortis of all new advances toward illusion. I look at the life-size portrait of the inventor, Dennis Gabor. He stands before me in full volume. As I move from the left to the right, I see a part of his shirt that was hidden before by his jacket, and the reflections on his eye-glasses change. I see his head first from the left, then from the right. So complete is the illusion of the man's three-dimensional presence that his immobility makes him a frightening corpse. The strength of the spell makes me ungratefully aware of what is missing. Instead of an image of a live man, I see a real ghost faking life. It will take a while before this new advance toward realism loses the power of seeming to be reality. It happened before with the motion picture, the stereoscope, the sound film.[108]

This means that holography is a new, uneasy example of illusionist deception in which a 'real ghost' is faking life to us. The bizarre, paradoxical figure that it is the *consummate* illusion which would make us experience a lack (of a 'feeling of life') is discursively necessary since a truly consummate illusionist image could not even be recognized *as* an illusionist image; it would simply be a repetition of the object. When the images of things become as threatening as the things themselves—which is exactly the plot of many episodes of the television series centered on the fictitious holodeck—it no longer makes sense to talk at all of 'images.' An image of a gangster that can shoot me simply *is* a gangster. A truly accomplished portrait of Dennis Gabor would be Dennis Gabor himself. Arnheim then has to underline the difference in order to still speak about a holographic *image*. Reading the last two sentences of the quote, nevertheless, the illusion obviously is still too *big* for him—otherwise holography would not first have to lose the impression of being reality in order to be acceptable.[109] The further examples given by Arnheim for this process are the moving image, stereoscopy(!), and the sound film. Only when a new type of image or audio-visual presentation is no longer confused with the presented events so that it can be perceived *as* an image or an audio-visual presentation can one ask for the specific media-aesthetic potentials. “Self-referential appearing” (Seel 1993a, 781) obviously presupposes that not all attention is drawn to the appearance of something.

Initially, this argumentation has the problem that there is never this extreme identity of the image with the object—the fright of the viewers when seeing the incoming train of the Lumières is (mostly) a myth (see Loiperdinger 2004; in more detail Bottomore 1999). The reason might be that new media are normally experienced at special places designed for them (one ‘goes to the movies’) and not somewhere at a train station where one might assume at all that a train suddenly appears. Therefore, the early reception of a new medium is distinguished as a rule by a stunned surprise when faced with the never before seen (or heard) achievements of new technologies. And this simply does not imply the repression of the specific potentials *and limitations* but, on the contrary, their attentive consideration. At places like fairs where, for example, a new medium like film was presented for the first time, the carnies were mainly concerned with attracting a public with sensational new effects. People therefore knew that a new experience was waiting for them and that they were supposed to judge it. Once more recalling the early example of Leith and Upatnieks: In order to experience and judge the advertised sensational phenomenon of the first pictorial holograms, the physicists and other visitors came in the special context of a conference and so the differences instantly become apparent: the early holograms were monochrome. *At the beginning of its history, the medium is more the message than at any later date.* Contrary to Arnheim’s claim, it is rather the getting used to ‘new media’ that eclipses the observation of their specific limitations so that they can become the unproblematic mediators of narrations or of a ‘reality’ behind the frequently invoked window. Only later, in a third step and on the background of such stabilized ways of reception can artistic, media-aesthetic strategies experiment again with effects of defamiliarization (and something like self-referential appearing). Media are at first new, then they are normal and only later they make room for media-aesthetic experiments.[110]

But even if we were to follow Arnheim’s argument, the problem remains that he wrote his commentary in 1972, i.e. not even ten years after the first pictorial holography had been created (1963).

Today, however, fifty years have passed and holography is still no part of the mainstream art scene (unlike video that has been spreading since about the same time in the 1960s).[111] In 1971 the first school for artistic holography was founded (see Johnston 2006a, 287–324). In 1975 a big exhibition[112] of holograms, including artistic ones, was held at the *International Center of Photography* in New York that was much criticized. Hilton Kramer in particular wrote a scathing review in the *New York Times* in which he attacked the "juke-box color" and the "peep-show realism" (1975, D1). Apart from the technological expenditure necessary for the creation of transmission light holograms,[113] how can the difficulties that artistic holography has had until the present time[114] be explained?

(a) As Hilton Kramer's merciless remarks on "illusionistic tricks"[115] suggest, one of the reasons could still be the gimmicky illusionism of figurative holograms, even though many artists like Margaret Benyon, Harriet Casdin-Silver and others have been attempting for a long time to create surreal and poetic works with holographic images. Also, avowed advocates of holograms observed the illusionism, criticizing it sharply as "photographic fallacy." Eduardo Kac for example writes:

> One of the most common misconceptions about holography is the notion that the medium's primary visual property is that of producing 'illusionistic' three-dimensional pictures—a kind of spatial photograph, with an added dimension. The 'naturalistic' misconception is usually grounded on unfulfilled expectations and unproductive comparisons with other media, [if] not [on] poor or inexistent research. I will go as far as to suggest that those who think of holography in these simplistic terms are just unaware of some of its most significant features and directions. (1995a, 48)

Kac rejects the notion that holograms are three-dimensional, 'improved' photographs since according to him the reproduced objects were often only meant to underline just this effect but were otherwise quite banal (as was the 'hologenic' toy-train in the first pictorial hologram by Leith and Upatnieks, see Maline 1991, 216–18). He maintains that by being fixated on an object to be represented, the media-aesthetic specifics of holography are not met. Artists, unlike "advertisers," should break with "several visual and cultural conventions."[116] This is where the difference to Leith and Upatnieks lies. They first had to find out what holograms can do; Kac is already fighting against an established repertoire of usage. Not without good reason, he is arguing that a hologram is not an image but a storage medium that allows for the reconstruction of a light wave; he illustrates this optical—but not necessarily visual—character with the use of holograms for scanning cash registers as discussed above.[117] The author points at artistic works by Viro Orazem, in which HOEs (holographic-optical elements) are explicitly not used as images but rather for modulating light (see Kac 1995a, 50–4; see Orazem 1992). A similar difference "between the hologram and the holographic image" is made by Peter Zec (1989, 426). "Zec's primary objective is to free holography from a photographic paradigm" (Maline 1995, 104). Viewed in this light it is, for example, wrong to hang a framed white light hologram on the wall, since it awakens conventional expectations for its viewing. A laser transmission light hologram in mid-air would certainly already be better—but of course it is quite difficult to install.

Different authors, moreover, underline that the holographic image is *iridescent*, i.e. its appearance is dependent on the movement of the viewers and changes with this movement. Therefore the holographic image supposedly has a central temporal and performative component that disappears when three-dimensionality is underlined.[118] Multiplex holograms, in which a filmed scene is transferred, one image after another, onto strip-type holograms, especially deconstruct the contrast between unmoving and moving images in a curious manner (see Johnston 2006a, 212–16; Schröter 2011) (Figure 9.23). While in the former case—the non-moving images—the represented scene never changes independent of whether the viewers are moving or not, in the latter—the moving images—independent of whether the viewers are moving or not, the scene is constantly changing.[119] In multiplex holograms, on the other hand, the scene changes depending on whether the viewers are moving or not. The multiplex image is *at the same time still and moving*.[120]

Some of the authors discussed here are connecting the notion that "[t]he holographic image, as optical information, is ultimately spatio-temporal and not volumetric or 'in-relief'" (Kac 1993, 128) with the thought that the hologram is a storage realm for light and not an image. This means that in the end they are able to envision

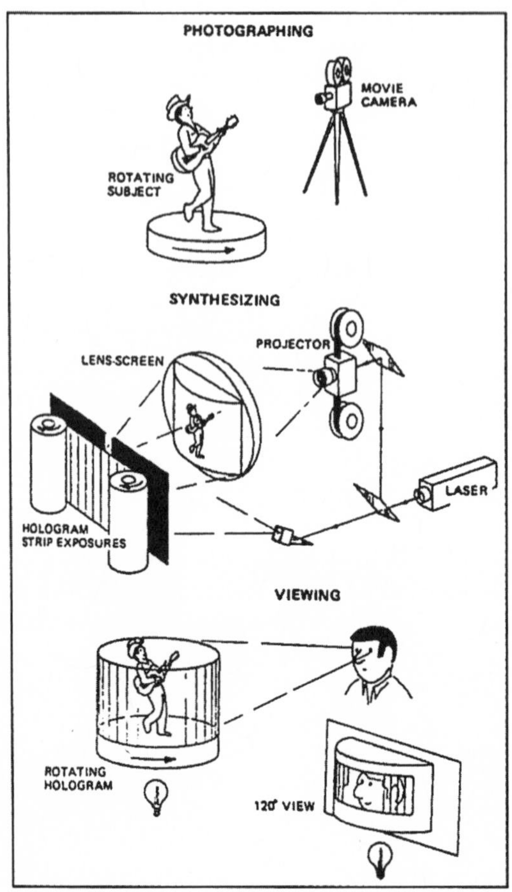

FIGURE 9.23 *Multiplex hologram recording geometry, in Johnston (2006a, 215).*

an abstract, pure modulation of light that changes with the movement of the viewer as the goal for holographic art. Quite in accordance with modernist demands of reducing the medium to its own characteristics and of assessing these characteristics self-reflexively,[121] the changing light becomes the privileged object of more or less abstract holography. In this way, holography can be classified with the tradition of art working with light—like, for example, Zero, Jesus-Raphael Soto or James Turrell.[122] Zec considers the "self-reference of light" an "essential form for the articulation of the holographic message."[123]

Obvious examples for this notion are the abstract holograms by Dieter Jung at whose center lie the surfaces of light and color that are changing and moving with the movement of the viewers (see Figure 9.24). The subject is 'colored light' in its pure self-referentiality.

Eduardo Kac has created artistic works himself, which he calls a form of holopoetry (see Kac 1989). Here, as well, an artist renounces an illusionist representation of identifiable objects in favor of moving and flowing letters and their lyrical interaction. Depending on the movements of the viewers, ephemeral poems are forming and sometimes they are only fragments of words (see Figure 9.25). The viewers are encouraged to constantly move since they want to find out whether the letters will form certain texts or not. The conventional posture and attitude of reading—sitting still—is questioned and defamiliarized.[124]

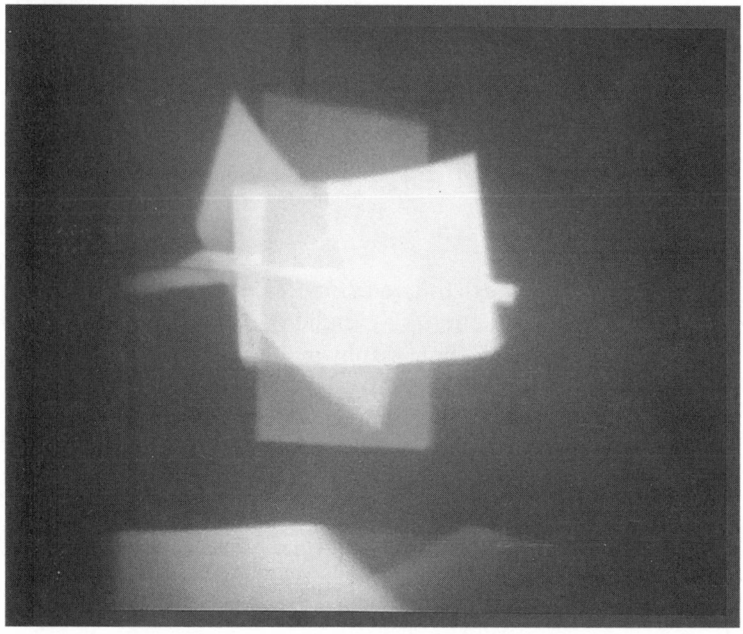

FIGURE 9.24 *A view of Dieter Jung's work* Light-Mill *(1998); computer generated holographic stereogram, 120×140 cm, in Jung (2003, 33). The effect of the holographic image cannot be represented here.*

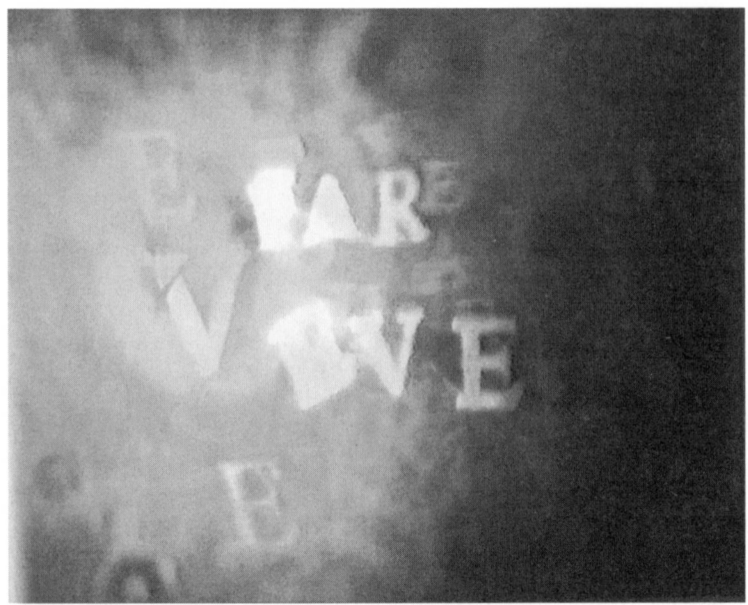

FIGURE 9.25 *A view of Eduardo Kac,* ADHUC, *© Eduardo Kac, 12 × 16 in. (30 × 40 cm), digital holopoem (1991), edition of three. Collection Jonathan Ross, London; collection Karas, Madrid; collection Vito Orazem and Söke Dinkla, Essen (Germany). The effect of the holographic image cannot be represented here.*

The viewpoint discussed here maintains that holography is still in its juvenile state without having found the way to its own specific media aesthetics. Just as photography in the nineteenth century had imitated painting (pictorialism) in order to establish itself as worthy of being called art—and by doing so instead achieved exactly the opposite result—now artistic holography relied too much on photography.[125] Just as pictorialism was kitschy, also illusionist holography was "holokitsch."[126] The authors discussed here consistently repeat *this* history of photography:

> By trying to address some of the key issues of holography today we are putting ourselves in the position of the essayist who, around 1869, tried to encompass the cultural meaning of photography. (Kac 1993, 138)

But this comparison is problematic not only because it re-invokes the repudiated paradigm on the level of the historical discourse, but also because new media have been accepted much faster since photography was invented—video again being the best example. But that does not seem to have helped holography; somehow it is still unaccepted and not considered contemporary (I will discuss this in a moment) so that the hope that it would finally arrive in *its own modernism* in order to be accepted by the art scene today—2013—gradually seems more and more hopeless.

But Zec has presented an additional argument, one also taken up in a similar way by Andrew Pepper who addresses the problem from a more fundamental point of view. Instead of viewing the 'illusionism' of holography as a photographic disguise of a dynamics of holography that in reality is temporal, performative and luminous, the term 'illusionism' is rejected completely: "The essence of the holographic message is to overcome illusion as well as to distinguish between the holographic image and reality" (Zec 1989, 427). He maintains that it is a radically new form of image. He believes that the term 'illusion' itself comes from a traditional discourse oriented on perspectival painting and photography and therefore is not appropriate to the matter at hand. In the terms proposed here, the thesis would be: Holography is not (or hardly) accepted as a form of art because so far it is the only type of image that fundamentally breaks with the planocentric regime of geometrical optics[127]—unlike even video that remains a specific materialization of geometrical optics.[128] "Holography offers an entirely new organization of space."[129] Planocentrism is not only simply a question of visual theory or media-historical discourse; it is also a conventionalized form of perception.

> What is disturbing is that the qualities inherent in holographic space are often confused and diluted because of our familiarity with traditional picture representations on a flat surface. . . . We are surrounded by flat representations of the three-dimensional world. When we approach a flat image, a photograph for example, we know that it is flat. . . . A hologram is, most often, a flat surface, and even though we know that the important characteristic of a hologram is that it displays a truly three-dimensional image, its flat appearance will induce us to bring to

> bear all that we naturally expect from a flat surface. . . . It is the combination of a flat surface, the ability to look at a displayed three-dimensional image from many different angles and the parameters of the holographic viewing zone that combine to make holographic space fundamentally different from the space provided by other media. (Pepper 1989, 295–6; see Figure 9.26)

According to Pepper, the only spatial experience coming close to it is that of sculpture. And yet, the holographic image is not an object

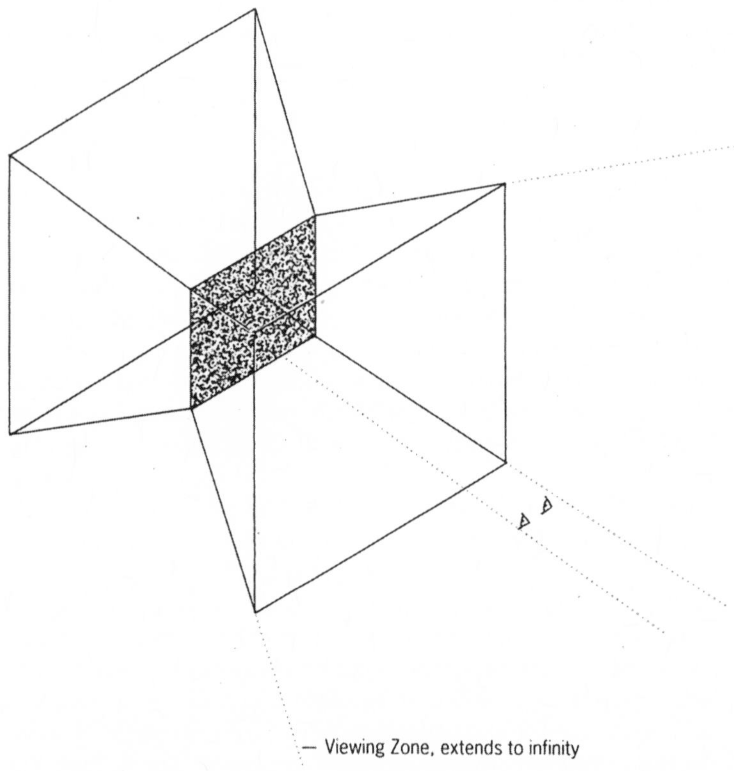

FIGURE 9.26 *Diagram of holographic space, in Pepper (1989, 298). The holographic object can appear before or behind the plate or even pass through the plate. Especially the last transgression of the plane is a viewing experience unknown prior to holography. See Pepper (1989, 297).*

in space; in a quite unsettling way it represents something between image and object (as Fahle 2009b observes very lucidly; see also Fahle 2009a). Within the framework of traditional art historical terminology, it becomes difficult to analyze holographic images using the conventional terms associated with two dimensional images, since holographic images require either taking into account pairs like formal logic of the plane vs. illusionary depth (or rather surveying the image area vs. the image's interior events)[130] *or*—regarding sculpture—terms like viewpoints, direction vectors, surface and volume. A hologram should not be regarded "as a picture, but rather as a map or a recording of space. In this respect, holography is a sculptural medium."[131] The holographic image is three-dimensional like a sculpture but—often—appears on a wall that makes it look like a painting.

The term 'illusionism' is thus already insufficient because the spatiality of the holographic image does not run contrary to the plane with its own planimetric logic, thereby denying it 'illusionistically.' The surface area of the hologram itself does not show anything; it is not governed by a planimetric regime. Therefore, an illusionistic denial of the plane does not exist; rather, the surface area of the holographically represented object is, as one could say, itself the surface of light (see Fahle 2009b). This becomes quite clear in the case where the real image hovers before the plane (in case of the virtual image behind the plane one might be tempted to talk of a modification of the paradigm of the *finestra aperta*). Thus, the connection to notions regarding the 'surface' that are so prominent in the discussions on sculpture seems natural (see for example Boehm 1977, 26–30). However, unlike sculpture the surface of the holographic object does not have any tactile values in the more narrow sense. Accounts of viewers who are confronted with a (good) hologram for the first time are said to attempt touching the object and are then amazed that it has no materiality. Conversely, very often sculptures—despite their sometimes strong tactile values—are not supposed to be touched for conservatory reasons; when confronted with holograms one grasps at nothing anyway. Holograms generate a tension between the presence and the absence of the object *without taking recourse to the plane*—this may be its "iconic difference" and not the "paradox of the 'flat depth"' (Boehm 1994c, 33) by which the dialectics of presence and absence in 'illusionistic,' central perspectival (and also in stereoscopic) images are governed. As a rule, viewers attempt to examine the represented object from different sides; their animated movement in holographic exhibitions is striking in comparison to other exhibitions.[132] People move around in order to see different *views* of the represented object, similarly as one does with sculptures. Doesn't this physical activity of the viewers then underline Crary's assumption that modernism is characterized by a somatocentric, physiological-optical regime? No, because Crary is talking about the physiology of viewing, the knowledge of which (regarding the series of physiological optics) is a prerequisite of the cinema for example. However, for the creation of holograms this knowledge is irrelevant; the corporeality of viewing, as in characteristics of the eye or the cognitive processing of visual stimuli, plays no role in wave optics. Even with just one eye one would be able to perceive the plasticity of the holographic image by taking up different locations in space. Unlike stereoscopy, binocular vision is not mandatory for holography. It is rather the body of the viewers that is spatially mobilized. As a rule, however, one cannot see a hologram from all sides.[133] Upon leaving the viewing zone, the image suddenly disappears and only an empty space remains in its place (iridescence). As Zec has criticized, holograms are often hung on the wall so that the movement all around is barred, making the transplane character of these images stand out. Characteristically, they are leaving the planocentric regime, but without becoming spatial as in the case of sculpture (or installation).[134] Viewed in this light, also figurative holograms could pursue media-aesthetic strategies; for example, by referring the viewers back to their own mobility. This could be achieved by presenting them in forms of installation that would allow a kind of communicative parcours, directing the viewers to move around in certain ways.[135]

One could then deduce that it is not necessary to differentiate holography from the paradigm of the photographic image, directing it towards modernism in order to make holography more acceptable. This modernist narrative is still based on the paradigm of photography (and its historical development). Perhaps one should insist that holography itself is completely different even in its figurative, three-dimensional manifestations. It is not holography that should change (and how could it?) but the continued hegemonial types of perception oriented on the plane and on projection that should (and contrary to Crary's claim obviously have not disappeared). They continue to be more or less stable even after almost fifty years of pictorial holography. One cannot even say that holography as a materialization of the series of wave optics is somehow marking the end of the series of geometrical optics and that geometrical optics only continues to exist 'ideologically.'[136] In fact, newer forms of images have emerged in the meantime that can still—over and over again into the future—be understood as heterogeneous materializations of the series of geometrical optics, like for example photorealistic computer graphics operating, among others, with ray tracing. The series of geometrical optics—often connected with that of physiological optics—simply continues to process, turning its back on holography.[137] This is where the difference between a history of optical and a history of visual media surfaces once again. While in the former, the series of wave optics includes geometrical optics as a case of approximation so that for example HOEs can substitute lenses and mirrors; in the latter, the series of geometrical optics remains dominant.

It is therefore not surprising that in 1998 the art historian Norman Bryson, discussed above, concluded that holography contains a particular historical *achrony*: "[H]olography is the one reproductive medium that seems to have never fully arrived" (Bryson 1998a, 10). Significantly, by taking recourse to the popular phantasms already mentioned, he first responds to the 'illusionistic' promises of holography:

> At least in popular imagination, faith in holography's promise was for a long time unshakable. When, in *Star Wars*, the beleaguered Princess sent out her inter-galactic call of distress ('Obi Won Kanobe [*sic*], you're our only hope'), her message was, of course, encrypted in holographic form. When, later on, the denizens of *Star Trek: The Next Generation* felt the need for some advanced kendo lessons, or a walk in a rainforest, naturally they repaired to the holodeck. (Bryson 1998a, 10–11)

But the promise of perfect illusion[138] at some point has moved on to new digital media—the catchword is *virtual reality* (VR).[139] Holography lagged behind as a strange phenomenon in comparison to the more advanced computer-technological methods of virtual reality, connecting the departed promise of a utopian future with photographic methods that seem dated and technically demanding:

"There is something about holography that is essentially untimely; it was born too late, or too soon; in a sense its time has never come" (Bryson 1998a, 12). Above all, even the methods of immersive computer graphics restitute the paradigm of linear perspective again. Even if the viewers do not face the image as a plane but are supposed to be 'immersively' and interactively drawn 'into' the image (which is really only a gradual difference), this is only successful by using the perspectival projection.[140] In an early text on so-called *head mounted displays*, i.e. what at the beginning of the 1990s for some time was known as (stereoscopic) data glasses (see Figure 1.2), the developer Ivan E. Sutherland writes:

> The fundamental idea behind the three-dimensional display is to present the user with a *perspective image which changes as he moves*. . . . The image presented by the three-dimensional display must change in exactly the way that the image of a real object would change for similar motions of the user's head. . . . Our objective in this project has been to surround the user with displayed three-dimensional information.[141]

Even the most immersive images of virtual reality belong to the series of geometrical optics.[142] But holography never belonged to that story; this is what makes it so strange. But at the same time—according to Bryson—this could be its strength:

> Yet this quality of temporal homelessness, of never fully arriving on the scene of history, is in fact one of holography's most intriguing properties. . . . [H]olography is able to challenge and dislocate our normally secure conceptions of time, of progress, and of history itself. . . . To be in culture is to move among many different times and spaces, within a present that is more like a palimpsest than it is like a fresh page, more like a nexus than a point on a line. (Bryson 1998a, 12)

And indeed, in holography (and also in Lippmann photography) one could at least realize that the history of the optical and the visual media are a palimpsest of different series that cannot be derived from each other and that neither successively displaces the other. The achronical quality of holography therefore permitted other artistic applications to develop that did not have to apologetically dissolve the holographic space into an abstract light. It could far better be used as a sort of spatial archive that counters the successionistic reductionism by foregrounding irreducible complexity (already by being able to present different optical series together). Bryson demonstrates this with Susan Gamble's and Michael Wenyon's holographic installation *Bibliomancy* (1998). By holographing an idiosyncratic choice of books, each of which represent an "unrepeatable historical moment," this collection of books transverses historical time. "Indeed, the titles have clearly been chosen so as to dramatize to the greatest possible degree the local contexts and circumstances of their production" (Bryson 1998a, 13; see Figure 9.27).

With the hologram of a book shelf, Wenyon and Gamble seem to quote a well-known photograph by Henry Fox Talbot (see Figure 9.28).

Henry Fox Talbot included this photograph of a section of his book shelves in his early book of photographs *The Pencil of Nature*—one of the first-ever published photo books. In this work, which appeared from 1844 to 1846 in six installments of four photographs each, Henry Fox Talbot wanted to present the spirit and purpose of the new medium photography, and so each of the altogether twenty-four plates, which demonstrated different implementations, was accompanied by a textual commentary. Plate III, *Articles of China*, for example, shows a shelf with cups, vases and tureens. The commentary says: "And should a thief afterwards purloin the treasures – if the mute testimony of the picture were to be produced against him in court – it would certainly be evidence of

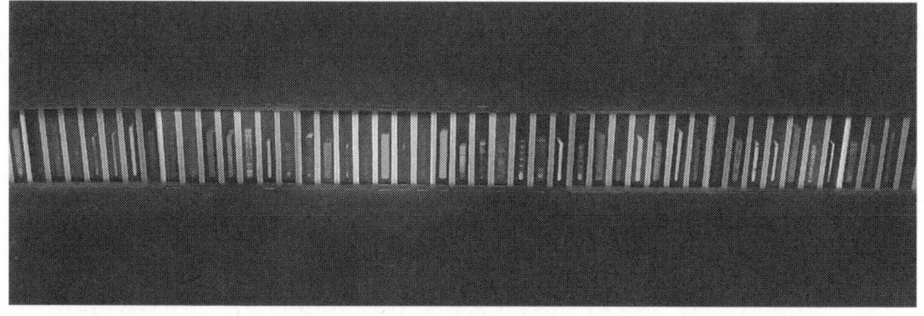

FIGURE 9.27 *Susan Gamble and Michael Wenyon,* Bibliomancy *(1998, holographic installation). The effect of the holographic image cannot be represented here.*

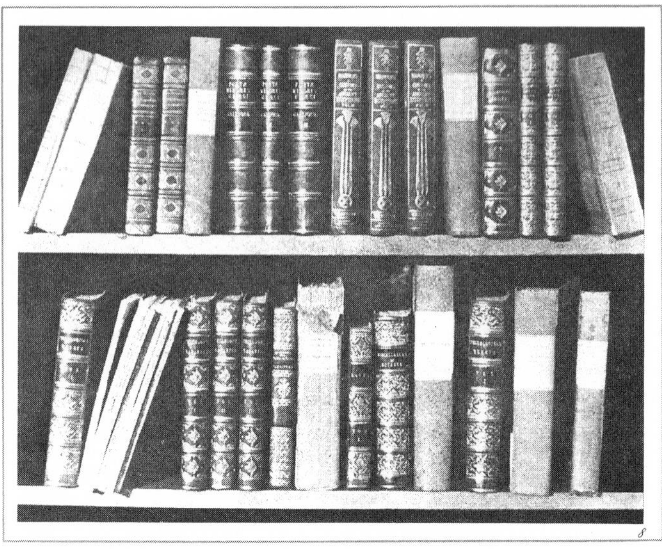

FIGURE 9.28 *Henry Fox Talbot, Plate VIII,* A Scene in a Library, *in Talbot (1969, n.p.).*

a novel kind" (Talbot 1969, n.p.). Plate VIII, *A Scene in a Library*, however, is accompanied by a strange commentary:

> Among the many novel ideas which the discovery of Photography [*sic*] has suggested, is the following rather curious experiment or speculation. I have never tried it, indeed, nor am I aware that any one else has either tried or proposed it, yet I think it is one, which, if properly managed, must inevitably succeed. When a ray of solar light is refracted by a prism and thrown upon a screen, it forms there the very beautiful coloured band known by the name of the solar spectrum. Experimenters have found that if this spectrum is thrown upon a sheet of sensitive paper, the violet end of it produces the principal effect: and, what is truly remarkable, a similar effect is produced by certain *invisible rays* which lie beyond the violet, and beyond the limits of the spectrum, and whose existence is only revealed to us by this action which they exert. Now I, would propose to separate the invisible rays from

> the rest, by suffering them to pass into an adjoining apartment through an aperture in a wall or screen of partition. This apartment would thus become filled (we must not call it *illuminated*) with invisible rays, which might be scattered in all directions by a convex lens placed behind the aperture. If there were a number of persons in the room, no one would see the other: and yet nevertheless if a *camera* were so placed as to point in the direction in which any one [*sic*] were standing, it would take his portrait, and reveal his actions. For to use a metaphor we have already employed, the eye of the camera would see plainly where the human eye would find nothing but darkness. Alas! that [*sic*] this speculation is somewhat too refined to be introduced with effect into a modern novel or romance; for what a *dénouement* we should have, if we could suppose the secrets of the darkened chamber to be revealed by the testimony of the imprinted paper. (Talbot 1969, n.p.)

Initially, then, Talbot is describing a (by now well-known) situation, a dark room with an opening through which the (invisible) rays are entering. The scene is a metaphor of that camera that itself is supposed to take a picture of the room and the people in it. At the same time, nobody in the room can see anything, simply because it is dark—this means that the series of physiological optics is excluded. The series of geometrical optics dominates the scene—at a time in which according to Crary the regime of physiological optics is already ruling. But Talbot is at least implicitly pointing at wave optics (that in his time was already slowly beginning to gain ground) by pointing to the "invisible light rays" outside of the spectrum, a phenomenon that has to be described with the concept of different wave lengths in continuity to the visible light. But how does this strange text fit with the image that is showing a book shelf? In her commentary on the scene, Carol Armstrong initially observes that of course the photograph of the book shelf also shows the content of a "dark chamber," namely simply itself as a photograph. Thus the text is self-referentially reflecting the act of taking a photograph (see Armstrong 1998, 128). She adds that it is maybe the goal of this strange constellation—a photograph of books and the description of a dark room precisely in which one cannot read—to underline the difference between image and text. After all,

> the image of the shelved volumes figures an old world of the text into which a new kind of image intrudes to make a new, scarcely imaginable world of the book. 'A Scene in a library' is 'the testimony of the imprinted paper', which, with its authenticating yet barely readable trace of two shelves of books, *verifies in advance the future possibilities of that new world*, its new set of speculative relations between text and image, and its new relay of visibility and invisibility. (Armstrong 1998, 129; my emphasis)

With this in mind, Talbot's image is looking ahead into a future in which *numerous photo-illustrated volumes will be placed in shelves*—volumes like *The Pencil of Nature*. But Armstrong's descriptions can still be expanded. Talbot is indeed experimenting with ideas on the future use of photographic media. The image then does not only reflectively refer to photography, to the "change of cognitive and semiological focus" (Armstrong 1998, 129) between (photographic) image and writing. It is also referring to the optical (and other) knowledge that will in the future allow for the development of optical methods since the reports by experimenters also have to be published. Thus, the image/text constellation on the one hand seems to hold a position that is optimistic about progress regarding the technological development, while on the other hand it (inadvertently) impedes this optimism insofar as the situation described by Talbot seems to predict technologies of spatial control through imperceptible rays in an almost uncanny way (examples being radar or the use of infrared cameras). Talbot is joyfully speculating on technological developments that establish a totalitarian regime of visibility. Even darkness does not offer protection any longer.

Talbot's different predictions correlate with the meaning of the unusual word 'bibliomancy,' i.e. the soothsaying by randomly opening books, in particular the bible. The *OED* defines bibliomancy according to a source from 1864 in the following way:

> Bibliomancy or Divination by Books, was known to the ancients under the appellation of Sortes Homericæ and Sortes Virgilianæ. The practice was to take up the works of Homer and Virgil, and to consider the first verse that presented itself as a prognostication of future events. (OED Online 2013)

In this respect one could infer that Wenyon and Gamble are referring to the complex temporal structure of Talbot's photo/text-constellation. Bryson writes:

> The books in the installation exist in a complex, recursive, jubilantly non-linear relation to history. Photographs of books confine them to the past tense, that of the fully accomplished action. *Bibliomancy* restores its books to a present tense which, nevertheless, travels in time and space to points past, present, and future. (1998a, 16)

It seems to me that the reference to a mere past tense for photography simplifies the issue.[143] The question is not merely the *contrast* between photography that leaves the books in a closed past on the one hand and holography on the other, which moves them by the pressurizing effect of its spatial appearance that is directly affecting the viewer into a present that is referring both to past and future. I would underline that the connection between these different temporalities is the point. The additional dimension of presence is opened up to past and future when Wenyon and Gamble are quoting Talbot's photograph because it is first of all from the *past*, but secondly standing at the beginning of the history of photography whose *future* just began in 1844. Thirdly, it is reflexively foreshadowing its own *future* in connection with a text and its motif of books as a storehouse of knowledge. This 'anterior future' (Barthes) of a future past in a medium—holography—that never had 'its time' but that—because of its haunting presence—at the same time always seems to be from the past and connotes the future constitutes the complex temporality of this holographic installation. Or, as Bryson has observed:

> The truly fascinating dimension of holography, and of this installation, is its overcoming of historical fixity, or temporal closure: because the hologram exists always and only in the present, it can never be captured and confined within linear time. Its inability to arrive on the scene of history in any definitive or final sense is precisely what is magical about it. (Bryson 1998a, 16)

However, if holography never really arrives at the scene of history then it can also never become a part of the history of art.

In this sense it must be underlined that it can hardly be the break with the series of geometrical optics alone that is responsible for the lack of acceptance of holography. In modernism, where painting had decidedly broken with central perspective, this could have been thoroughly appreciated. But of course one could also argue that in modernism a sort of division of labor had established itself. Painting (tendentially) turns away from geometrical optics (central perspective) leaving this field to technological media (photography, video) that since the 1960s have been able to blow open the flaccid modernist paradigm of self-reference by again taking recourse to the 'real' (in the sense of Hal Foster's *Return of the Real*, see Foster 1996), i.e. to external reference. After all, nobody less than Clement Greenberg, the mastermind of modernism, had already acknowledged in 1946 that photography was allowed to be the only medium that could be "naturalistic" (Greenberg 1988a, 61). Photography and video were able to bring to art the "look of non-art" (Greenberg 1993, 252) giving rise to its conceptual self-analysis. As Bryson has observed,[144] on the other hand, holography was pointedly tied down to a technical, laborious procedure. It seemed as if the anachronistic ideas of the artist as someone who was gifted with unique skills were associated with it[145]—an unfavorable association at a time (1960s) when the conventional notion of art was massively attacked by a decided "amateurism."[146] One might say that regarding the media-aesthetic discourse of the times, holography was to a certain extent oriented too much on handicrafts. Besides, if one is dealing with the qualitatively more interesting laser transmission light holograms, holography requires a lot of expenditure for a presentation.

There is a quite telling anecdote. In 2005 I went to an exhibition in Geneva because of the promised presentation of Bruce Nauman's holographic works from 1969.[147] That only two of many more holograms were presented would have been fairly easy to cope with, but what made it much worse was that they were transmission light holograms that should have been illuminated with a red laser in order to see the images (strange poses adopted by Nauman).[148] Instead they were illuminated by normal white light and one could not see anything. Another example: In a more recent catalogue from an exhibition, two of Nauman's holographic works were pictured for which the material indicated was "Hologram, Glass, Infrared light." It is above all significant that the light source indicated is "infrared light." Of course it was not infrared light (deeply red light to invisible heat radiation) that was needed for the presentation of Nauman's holograms. Instead red laser light was required.[149]

Bruce Nauman
Hologram E (aus der zweiten
Hologramm-Serie:
Full Figure Poses A–J), 1969
Hologramm, Glas, Infrarotlicht
25,4 × 20,3 cm

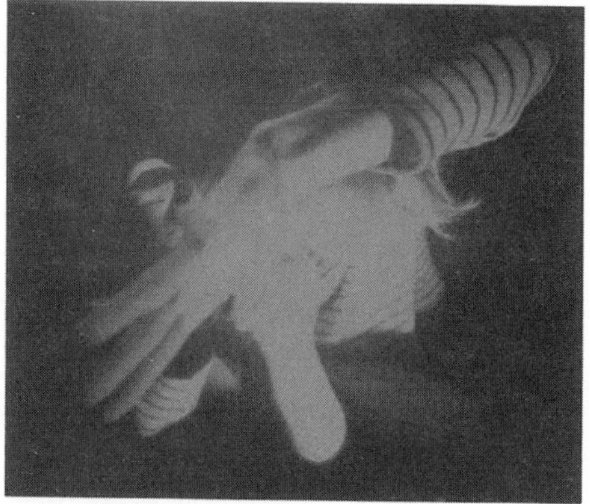

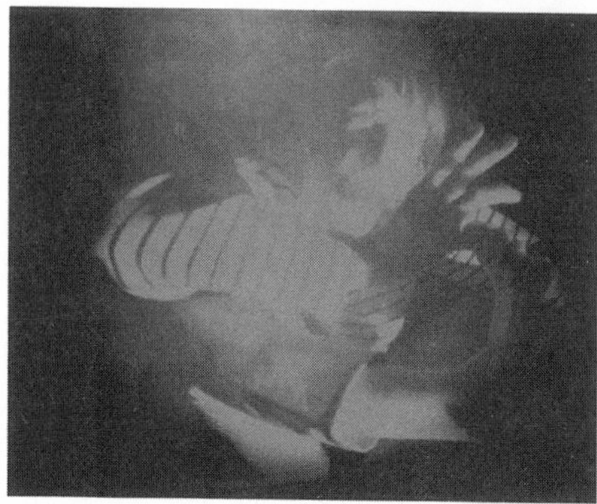

Bruce Nauman
Hologram J (aus der zweiten
Hologramm-Serie:
Full Figure Poses A–J), 1969
Hologramm, Glas, Infrarotlicht
25,4 × 20,3 cm

FIGURE 9.29 Two Holographs *by Bruce Nauman with commentary, in Curiger (2006, 147). The effect of the holographic image cannot be represented here.*

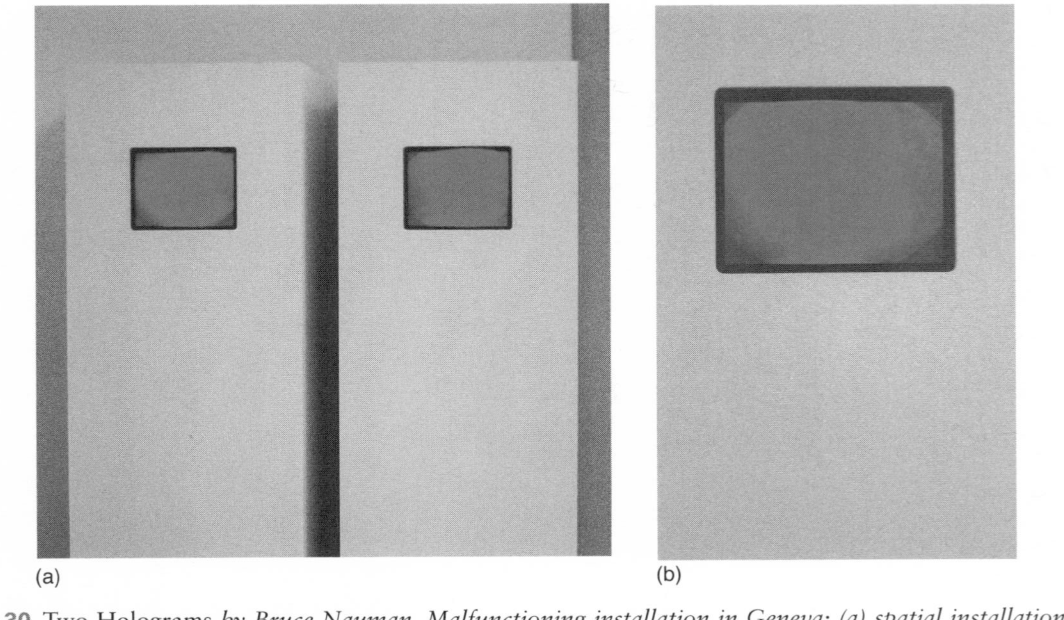

(a) (b)

FIGURE 9.30 Two Holograms *by Bruce Nauman. Malfunctioning installation in Geneva: (a) spatial installation; (b) detail showing that the holograms cannot be seen because of the faulty illumination (photos by Jens Schröter).*

Both examples underline once more to what extent holography is foreign to the art system that least of all seems to understand the specifics of *this* medium in particular, despite all its insistence on 'media specifics' and 'media reflection' (what is again underlined by the reproach of 'illusionism' discussed above).

Taking together all these factors—alleged illusionism, its orientation on handicraft, but also its mostly monochromatic coloring,[150] and finally the largely missing movement[151] (the later spreading multiplex-holography excepted)—give reasons for the defeat of holography by video as a new artistic medium. Video by contrast fits in with the regime of geometrical (and physiological) optics; it finally permitted artists to incorporate moving images into their works (since it is much cheaper and easier to handle than film), it can be black and white and it can have 'amateurish' effects. All these factors explain why video as a new medium could be established quickly in the art system and why holography could not.[152]

9.5 Conclusion

To sum up, holography is without doubt the most complex and literally the most enigmatic phenomenon in the field of technical transplane images. It is not only the only 'pure' materialization in the series of wave optics; it has also been sedimented in a whole series of heterogeneous forms through which new ways of producing spatial knowledge were possible. At the same time, dealing with holography illustrates the enormous difficulties that theoretical discourse or the art system experience when attempting to fit some of its phenomena into successionistic and homogenizing histories of optical or visual media. It also exemplifies that this is not readily possible since to reflect on holography also forces a reflection on the basic question of media historiography. Instead of displacing regimes one has to take one's point of departure from parallel, overlapping series of optical knowledge. This can be seen once again in holography itself: It is a materialization of the series of wave optics, but simultaneously it can also include procedures of geometrical optics. Before this could be determined, the individual characteristics of holography had to be unearthed from this superposition in the first place.

Holography, apart from this, also reveals the difference between optical and visual media. Not all media operations on the basis of optical knowledge have to be addressed to the human senses. Holography can operate as an 'image' for the human eye; it can, however, also be an optical instrument or a tool. Generally speaking, a given technological method is not a visual medium from the beginning—nor does it have to remain one even if it has been established as such before.[153] Whether something is a visual medium is obviously crucially dependent on the discursive practice in which an optical technology operates. The strangeness of the technical-transplane images thus also estranges us from the self-understood habit of classifying certain phenomena as 'visual media.'

Notes

1 Kittler (1999, xl). With his reference to moirés at "the sectional plane of two optical media," he seems to allude to the patterns of interference emerging when two identical and coherent light waves overlap. These are central for the concept of holography.

2 Goethe (2000, 16). See Crary (1990, 67–71).

3 See Chapter 4 for my critique of Crary's one-sided reading of the *Theory of Colors* underlining only the series of physiological optics.

4 When waves interfere, 'crest' or 'valley' are amplified where crests meet crests and valleys meet valleys; when crest meets valley the wave is eliminated.

5 See Grimaldi (1665, 2): "Nobis alius Quartus [*sic*] modus illuxit, quem nunc proponimus, vocamu[s]q; Diffractionem."

6 See Huygens (1912, 3–4) in particular on the comparison of sound and light.

7 See Frankel (1976). See also Buchwald (1989, xiv) who underlines that it is not the transition from a particle theory to a wave theory which is the real radical point in the wave theory of light. Rather, the break lies in the rejection of the idea of the bundle of linear rays (whether they consist of particles or of individual waves) in favor of the concept of a transversal wavefront consisting of interfering spheric waves starting from each point of the object and each point of the wavefront at a given point in time ("Huygens' principle," see Huygens 1912, 16–22). Interestingly enough in 1787 in the *Physicalisches Wörterbuch by* J. S. T. Gehler: http://archimedes.mpiwg-berlin.mpg.de/cgi-bin/archim/dict/hw?lemma=Beugung%20

des%20Lichts&step= entry&id=d008 [last accessed August 13, 2013] one can find the following remark on diffraction: "One can see that Newton is inclined to regard diffraction as an effect of the attraction of solids by light. Smith (*Lehrbegrif* [*sic*] *der Optik*, vol. 1 § 186) shows that such an attracting power must be infinitely stronger than gravity. Other scientists, for example von Mairan, dü [*sic*] Tour, dü [*sic*] Sejour (Mém. De Paris 1775) explain diffraction by way of the atmospheres that they take on around the solids consisting of compacted matter and that are supposed to refract the passing light rays." Not a single word is mentioned about the fact that diffraction could be based on the wave character of light!

8 See section 1.2.3. In 1802, Thomas Young addressed physiological optics and specifically trichromatic vision. This again shows that the different series of optics in reality often intermingle; therefore, they had to be taken apart heuristically in this present study.

9 Apart from the fact that starting with a seminal essay by Einstein from 1905 (1967) that was awarded the Nobel Prize for physics in 1921, light is described as a dualism of *waves and particles*. This is the point at which the series of quantum optics appears as I have mentioned above; a series that itself includes the series of wave optics, see Fox (2006); Saleh and Teich (1991, 385).

10 Already Huygens had assumed that it should spread in an 'ether,' an assumption that was considered superfluous only since Einstein's special theory of relativity of 1905 (see Einstein 1923)—even though Einstein himself came back to the ether numerous times; on the ether see Kümmel-Schnur and Schröter (2008).

11 Kittler (1999, xli) enigmatically continues to talk about the "[p]atterns and moirés of a situation that has forgotten us." See Kittler (2010, 124): "This concept of waves . . . allowed researchers like Fresnel and Faraday to study light interference and its moiré-type pattern around 1830, which would be important for fundamental film effects." It is striking that regarding moirés, Kittler only refers to "fundamental film effects" and not to the more significant holography. See on moirés from a physical point of view McCurry (1966) and Meyer-Arendt (1984, 255–7).

12 Cotton (1901b, 9, italics in the original: "In the experiments, of whose first results Mr. Cotton gives an account, he suggests obtaining webs by photographing interference patterns—this time, however, *without using a lens*. . . . A screen or a photographic plate with a *plane surface* is apparently covered with a series of straight and equidistant interference fringes in the form of a web whose value of intervals can be determined beforehand."). See also Cotton (1901a)

referring to Gabriel Lippmann and Otto Wiener. To this day research is done on holography at the *Laboratoire Aimé Cotton* (Paris), see http://www.lac.u-psud.fr [last accessed September 2, 2013]. Regarding Cotton see Hutley (1999, 791): "[In] 1901 A. Cotton described making gratings by photographing standing waves using a Daguerre process. Furthermore, he also considered the case when the mirror used to generate the standing waves was of arbitrary shape, and I think comes very close to describing a Denisyuk hologram at a time when Gabor was one year old and Denisyuk was not yet born." I will come back to Gabor and Denisyuk later.

13 See Johnston (2006a) and his detailed history of the different forms of holography that includes a large amount of material. See also Okoshi (1976, 186–294) and Zec (1987, 63–90).

14 Electron microscopes do not use glass lenses but certain electromagnetic fields with the same function: "electron objectives."

15 See also Gabor's patent specifications (1949a, col. 1): "A principal advantage realized by this invention resides in the fact that it is unnecessary to employ the conventional imaging electron lens . . . It is well-known that the resolving power of electron microscopes cannot be improved beyond a certain limit, because of the uncorrected spherical aberration of electron objectives."

16 Gabor (1949b, 456). See Klein (1970, 69–71). On the other hand, the terms holograph, holography and holographic can be traced back to the seventeenth century, indicating a handwritten document by only one author; see Pepper (1982).

17 For a succinct definition of coherence see http://en.wikipedia.org/wiki/Coherence_(physics) [last accessed August 13, 2013]: "Two waves are said to be coherent if they have a constant relative phase. The degree of coherence is measured by the interference visibility, a measure of how perfectly the waves can cancel due to destructive interference."

18 The only exception is a group of certain experimental combinations of integral photography (Chapter 5) and holography; see Pole (1967) and Okoshi (1980, 554–5).

19 There are holographic methods where the diffraction is not created by the contrast of light and dark spots but by the contrast of different refraction indexes of the emulsion ("bleached holograms"). These holograms look like transparent plates, see Upatnieks and Leonard (1969). On holograms on the basis of fine structures like reliefs see the literature in Smith (1968).

20 There are holograms in color, see Eichler and Ackermann (1993, 176–98; Bjelkhagen, Jeong and Vukičević (1996). As a current example in which color holography and Lippman photography are

compared see Bjelkhagen (2002). Since three lasers in different colors are being used in order to create color holography, color holography is a hybrid of physiological and wave optics. *Zebra Imaging* probably makes the currently most perfect holograms in the commercial sector. See their website http://www.zebraimaging.com [last accessed September 2, 2013].

21 As far as I can see, in doing this Gabor neither referred back to Lippmann nor to Cotton.

22 Rays of electrons are also subject to the wave-particle-dualism; this means they also have wavelengths, even though these are quite small.

23 Concerning this, in a mail dated June 14, 2007 Sean Johnston wrote to me: "To answer your question, in optical holography it is normal to use the same wavelength for recording and reconstructing. However, Gabor . . . used dramatically different recording [and] reconstructing wavelengths. [E]lectrons have a wavelength about 10,000 times shorter than visible light, and this means that there will be a magnification when visible light is diffracted from an electron hologram. . . . This magnification/demagnification is unfortunately different in the 'depth' dimension, so it creates a distortion of depth for three-dimensional images, but . . . Gabor . . . [did not try] to reconstruct 3D images in this way. Gabor never actually did the experiment to reconstruct an electron hologram, because the electron holograms made by his collaborators were too poor. . . . And in any case, the electron microscope samples . . . were essentially 'flat' and had no significant depth anyway." On the magnification obtained by using different wavelengths see also Gabor's respective patent (Gabor 1949a). See Denisyuk (1984, 99–105) for a lucid presentation of this magnifying process.

24 Gabor (1948, 778). Notably in 1940, Gabor filed several patents concerning the creation of three-dimensional images for cinema and television by way of stereoscopic techniques. However, he never connected them to his research on the "interference diagram." Tanner and Allibone (1997) have compiled a survey of Gabor's patents; they observe, "In considering this series of inventions in stereo[scopy], it is possible to detect a train of thought that was to lead later to the flash of insight that resulted in the discovery of holography" (109). This is a conclusion that does not seem to be correct since it ignores the epistemological break between the series of physiological and wave optics by perfunctorily basing the argument on the spatial appearance of the stereoscopic and the holographic image (which, first of all, is completely different and which, secondly, was hardly existent in Gabor's works). In his patents nothing points to an argument concerning wave optics (see e.g. Gabor 1944).

25 See section 9.2 on the difference between optical and visual media.

26 See Johnston (2005b). See also Johnston (2006a, 30) on Gabor's language in his first important paper: "The paper was aimed at electron microscopists and framed in language and orientation that made it unlikely to be noticed by other scientists."

27 Another independent 'invention' of holography took place in the Soviet Union by Yuri Denisyuk, see section 9.3.

28 Jensen et al. (1977) give a lucid explanation. See also Johnston (2006a, 78–95).

29 The reason is that coherence of signals is very important for radar from the beginning, see Klein (1970, 81). See Leith (1996, 2–7).

30 Creating a synthetic aperture in the appropriate type of radar requires that the "return signals must contain phase information which is preserved in the recording" (Cutrona et al. 1961, 128; Leith had worked on this paper as well)—this means that the phase has to be kept, which is what differentiates holography from photography. The authors continue: "It was evident that the radar would have to have excellent transmitter frequency stability and a stable *frequency reference* for use in comparing the phase of the return signals with the phase of the transmitted pulses" (my emphasis). This is where the reference beam of the later double beam method of holography by Leith and Upatnieks already begins to appear. See also Anonymous (1963, 12); Klein (1970, 82–3); Leith (1978, 97–103); (1996, 10); Stetson (1991, 16). The use of two interfering beams, by the way, is one of the oldest techniques of interferometry and was already used by Albert A. Michelson and Edward W. Morley in their famous experiment of 1887 with which they showed that there exists probably no light ether.

31 I will use this word in analogy to the word 'to photograph,' that is, 'to holograph' means recording a hologram of something.

32 See Denisyuk (1984, 58–64); Zec (1987, 56–62) and Johnston (2006a, 95–9). On the difference of the 'real' and the 'virtual' image see principally Hecht (1987, 131).

33 As in many other cases, a different knowledge and technology emerges from the 'disturbance' by the real image: the "phase conjugation"; see Leith (1996, 22–3). On current research on a doubled virtual image see Cao et al. (1996).

34 Some of these early holograms portrayed, as in Gabor's work, the names Huygens, Young, Fresnel, i.e. the pioneers of wave optics; see Johnston (2006a, 96n).

35 See the rather popularized text "Photography by Laser" in the *Scientific American* by Leith and Upatnieks (1965). It details the contrast of holography (and thus the comparison) with conventional photography. In early press coverages on holography it is often called "lensless photography," i.e. it is therefore described quite traditionally using photographic terms; see Anonymous (1963, 12) where the author talks for example of a "camera-like device" and the like. Leith (1983, 2) underlines that together with Upatnieks he had been looking for a photographic approach in order to be able to explain the new method in an understandable way.

36 On the history and method of laser see Carroll (1964) and Bromberg (1991).

37 See Leith and Upatnieks (1963b, 1381). They were using one of the first commercially available Helium-Neon lasers.

38 See Leith and Upatnieks (1963a, 522): "Reconstructions of continuous tone transparencies are comparable in quality to pictures printed by a conventional half-tone process."

39 See Anonymous (1963, 12). See also Leith's (1983, 2) remark: "Why had they chosen this course? I suspect our account seemed a bit wild and improbable, and perhaps they were skeptical."

40 See Leith and Upatnieks (1963a; 1963b). Conspicuously the first essay is still called "Wavefront Reconstruction with Continuous-Tone *Transparencies*" while the second one is named "Wavefront Reconstruction with Continuous-Tone *Objects*" (my emphasis).

41 In some illustrations showing the recording process there are lenses in the way of the object- and the reference beam. These lenses are not in contradiction with the notion of holography as 'lensless'. See Klein (1970, 114): "Though two lenses are at work here, neither is an imaging lens, like the lens in any camera." The lenses only serve to widen the laser light—convex mirrors are able to do this as well. See fundamentally Meyer-Arendt (1984, 92): "Mirrors can do the same things that lenses can. In many cases mirrors may be exchanged for lenses."

42 Apart from the fact that both the brothers Lumière as well as Leith and Upatnieks had to presuppose the existence of trains and therefore possible train images—but that is not the same as to say they were reflexively thematizing train images.

43 See section 9.4 for the example of holography.

44 See section 1.3. If the first holographic image were not the result of tinkering but a planned, purposeful invention then quoting Lumière would have been possible and even probable.

45 Even the diffraction of light, which is one of the central conditions of holography, is nothing but a disturbance for geometrical-optical lens optics.

46 On this notion see Glaubitz et al. (2011, 26–34).

47 See Johnston (2004; 2005a; 2006a, 229–446). Gates (1971) even talks of a "rebirth" of optics as a result of the laser, and of holography particular to industrial contexts.

48 See Heerden (1963a; 1963b). However, Coy (2007) is pointing out that holography had already been seen since the 1960s as the "storage technology of the next decade." Up to today a functioning holographic storage system has not been brought to the market. See the current discussions at http://en.wikipedia.org/wiki/Holographic_Versatile_Disc [last accessed August 13, 2013].

49 On the metaphorics of three-dimensional photography see Johnston (2006b).

50 Apart from the elaborate, costly and therefore rare fully colored holograms that I have mentioned before, the so-called rainbow holograms are an exception (see Zec 1987, 78–82; Johnston 2006a, 209–12). They iridescently show objects in all spectral colors while doing without the vertical parallax but clearly do not depict the object in the natural colors.

51 Similar to integral photography discussed in Chapter 5.

52 As I have already mentioned in the introduction to this study, see for example Potmesil and Chakravarty (1982).

53 See—strange to a lesser degree—Westlake (1970) and—in part even stranger—the contributions in Wilber (1982). Because of this characteristic, holography is valued as a metaphor also in recent sociology for the complex world society, see Urry (2003, 50–1). See also Rieger (2009), who rather underlines that holography should not be seen as anthropomorphous because of its strange characteristics; see on this question also the short remarks in Chapter 11. In theoretical physics holography is also invoked, see Bousso (2002).

54 See Anonymous (1963, 12)—in this early newspaper article on holography it is called 'lensless photography.' However, there is at least one special method that combines cinematography and holography (so-called multiplex holograms, see Zec 1987, 82–6), in which lenses are being used. But here as well they are not used for recording the holographic pattern. See also Eichler and Ackermann (1993, 36) on so-called lensless Fourier holograms.

55 Therefore, it was soon used for the imaging of volumes; for example, in particle physics where the processes had to be depicted in detectors;

for example, in bubble chambers, see Henderson (1970, 55–9). If one were to simply photograph the content of such a detector, all events from the different depths would come together on one plane—namely the image plane. This would completely obscure the processes in the chamber. Therefore, from early on stereoscopic methods of recording were used. C.R.T. Wilson, who had developed the first cloud chamber around 1911, had already been using stereoscopy since 1914, see Chaloner (1997, 371); on bubble chambers see Bassi et al. (1957) and Galison (1997, 379). Stereoscopic methods, however, continue to have problems with depth of field in greater volumes so that later ones used holographic recording methods, see among others Bjelkhagen et al. (1984). These authors explicitly underline that the limiting of the depth of field in geometrical-optical projections (and even if they are stereoscopically doubled) is the real impulse for the use of holography in bigger bubble chambers; see also Herve et al. (1982, 417). Interestingly (or more precisely—significantly) Galison's (1997) otherwise so-elaborate history of the material culture of particle physics *does not say a single word about* holographic detectors. Authors like Hagen (2002, 196, n. 4) then conclude from reading Galison's study that photographic technology disappears from the practice of particle physics in the middle of the 1980s, even though in 1989 holographic detectors for bubble chambers were still being installed, see Kitagaki et al. (1989, 81 in particular): "It was therefore logical to apply the technique of holographic photography to the Tohoku 1.4 m bubble chamber." However, the depiction of a volume by way of holographic methods is limited by the coherence length of the light used. The reason for the fact that the white light holograms that are better known in public as a rule still contain blurred areas can be attributed to the fact that they are holographic images of *only one level* of a three-dimensional laser-transmission-light master hologram that in reality reaches to a much greater depth.

56 Unless, of course, one changes the wave length of the reconstruction beam as Gabor has suggested; but this method of enlargement creates strong distortions of the depth of field.

57 Along these lines Leith and Upatnieks underline (1965, 24): "Unlike ordinary photography, however, no lens or other image-forming device is used and consequently no image is formed."

58 Kittler (2010, 71) points out that "all optical media even today [require] the development of usable lens systems"—with such a premise the lensless imaging of holography cannot become a part of the history of optical media. But see Rieger and Schröter (2009), which is the first book on holography from the standpoint of media studies.

59 Maybe Bryson wanted to write "cinematography" instead of "holography"—at least two pages previously (1983, 87) cinema (and not holography) is mentioned together with photography.

60 Several years later, however, Bryson (1998a) returns to holography. I will discuss this text in connection with the question of the media aesthetics of holographic imaging in section 9.4.

61 See the presentation of this debate in Winkler (1992, 19–76).

62 I want to disregard the difference between hologram as the carrier of the interference pattern and holography as the general name for all methods of recording transplane interference patterns or wave front reconstructions here.

63 Especially since holograms, like Lippmann photographs (see Chapter 4), are iridescent—i.e. the image seems to be dependent on the movement and position of the viewer.

64 See Chapter 10. It is interesting to note that Kittler (2004, 193) also only speaks *en passant* about holography when discussing a "history of the computed image."

65 Somewhere else Virilio (2000, 10) mentions that "*[d]igital optics* will then succeed analogue optics, as the latter once cleverly complemented the ocular optics of the human gaze." Again we see the concept of a succession even though it would make more sense to posit the continued coexistence of the digital (here: virtual), ocular (here: referring to the human eye, i.e. physiological), and analog optics. Apart from that, it is not quite clear what Virilio means by analog optics. In the terminology used here, it would have to be at least differentiated into geometrical and wave optics—terms that Virilio uses later without, however, making reference to the triad mentioned above. On geometrical and wave optics he writes enigmatic sentences like: "[T]he speed of rays of light (geometrical optics) is the name for the shadow of the speed of light of electro-magnetic waves (wave optics)" (Virilio 2000, 45). See Virilio (1990, 91): "[L]a vitesse de la lumière des rayons (optique géometrique) se nomme l'ombre de la lumière de la vitesse des ondes (optique ondulatoire) électro-magnétiques." Virilio actually writes "de la lumière de la vitesse," although one would expect "vitesse de la lumière."

66 See similarly Kittler (2010, 54): "The word 'image' here should not be misunderstood to refer solely to the strange two-dimensional pictures on the walls of churches, palaces, and later museums, but rather also to such abstract yet brutally effective things as fortresses or church domes."

67 Along these lines Kittler (2010, 119–20; emphasis in the original) already maintained that photography emerged through a disturbance

in painting: "In case of photography, the historical step amounts rather to a painting mistake or offence that became the foundation of a new scientific media technology through the re-evaluation of all values, as Nietzsche would have said. . . . But it never occurred to any of the painters who had discovered perspective and the *camera obscura* to turn this handicap into an asset by taking advantage of the whitening or darkening effect itself." See also Eder (1978, 6–14).

68 What is meant by "non-destructive testing" will become clear below.

69 See Rheinberger (1997, 74–5). The participating scientists sometimes know themselves how problematic the triumphal history of an invention written retrospectively can be, see Stetson (1991, 18): "Is there any lesson to be learned from the events I have recounted about the discovery of hologram interferometry? Quite possibly. I think that it makes a case against taking management by objective too seriously when you are trying to manage research. Discoveries are mostly made when the right people are at the right place at the right time. But some discoveries are much more selective about their time and place than others. The laser was quite selective about its discovery; it could have happened by accident. The hologram was discovered by accident, but not recognized for what it really was."

70 Michelson and Morley (1887, 464). Conversely, one could retrospectively describe the early interferograms of the nineteenth century as a type of hologram since these are accounts of interference patterns, see Bryngdahl and Lohmann (1968).

71 As I have said before, with the earliest use of laser light these disturbances were so strong that the advantage of the laser was not immediately evident, see also Stetson (1991, 16) and Johnston (2006a, 108).

72 See Powell and Stetson (1965). At the end of their text (1598) they thank Upatnieks for the idea, but Leith later underlined that Powell and Stetson had had the idea independently; see Johnston (2006a, 193). In Stetson (1969, 386) the term "time average hologram" is used.

73 Grant and Brown (1969, 80). In an anthology published in 1970 compiling the results of the first congress in 1969 on "Engineering Uses of Holography" in Glasgow, holo-interferometic methods receive a lot of attention, see Robertson and Harvey (1970). On some problems of holographic interferometry see also Stetson (1999).

74 This is the example of a phenomenon similar to the one we experience in stereo-photogrammetry, see Pulfrich (1923). There, information in two (or more) different images is geometrically related to each other without necessarily giving the impression to the viewer

that the image is spatial. But in many stereo-photogrammetrical methods a visual coordination and an adjustment is necessary, which need exactly this spatial impression in order to measure the congruence, see Burkhardt (1989).

75 See an example from the field of conservatory use of holo-interferometrical methods discussed more extensively below, Carelli et al. (1991, 1294): "Acceptance of holographic testing methods by the art and restauration [*sic*] communities has hardly been swift, mainly because the early nondestructive tests in artifact conservation relied on a subjective, *visual* evaluation of the fringe patterns" (my emphasis).

76 See Asmus et al. (1973) where the beginning of research in holographing sculptures is dated 1971.

77 Westlake, Wuerker and Asmus (1976, 84) where even the idea can be found (89) to send holographic images to the exhibitions instead of the valuable sculptures. See also a text from 1975 written in collaboration with Juris Upatnieks attempting to promote the collection of a "holographic library of objects" since the photographs of three-dimensional objects like sculptures can only be reproduced two-dimensionally, see Upatnieks, Leonard and Martilla (1975, 108).

78 See Amadesi et al. (1974, 2009 in particular): "As far as the conservation of art is concerned, it is of utmost importance to intervene before irreparable damage is done. This in turn calls for nondestructive testing methods that can detect internal damage."

79 Westlake, Wuerker and Asmus (1976, 86). See also Amadesi, D'Altorio and Paoletti (1982) and extensively Paoletti and Spagnolo (1996).

80 Fournier, Tribillon and Vienot (1977, 118). Westlake, Wuerker and Asmus (1976, 84) state that by now objects of up to nine meters in size can be holographed if the correct distance to the holographic plate is chosen.

81 Interestingly, this brings to mind Talbot's stereoscopic views of sculptures for which he had to use diminished copies of sculptures as well, see Chapter 2. These are examples for the limitations of transplane pictoriality.

82 See for example Fournier, Tribillon and Vienot (1977, 119) where the authors state that they 'borrowed' the Venus de Milo in order to take the recording in their laboratory.

83 Munk and Munk (1972, 441). Regarding pulse lasers and holography see also Johnston (2006a, 206–9).

84 Munk and Munk (1972, 439). By using more beam splitters (and thus object rays) one can minimize shadowing, see Fournier, Tribillon and Vienot (1977, 117).

85 There were also experiments on 360° holography but it was only able to reproduce very small objects and did not gain acceptance, see Jeong, Rudolf and Luckett (1966). Indeed in 1967 a 360° hologram of a Buddha statue was produced, see Johnston (2006a, 205): "None of these variants of the 360° hologram . . . were commercially useful, because a special lighting arrangement was needed, and the enclosure was even bulkier than the object that it reconstructed. But such holograms proved unexpectedly popular with scientists and the general public, probably because they once again accentuated the difference between holography and photography. Holography was not merely three-dimensional, but potentially all-encompassing—both figuratively and literally—in ways that photography was not." The 360° hologram then underlines again to what extent transplane images are able to fascinate with spatial aspects. Today, it is volumetry that is being developed and that becomes more and more important as a type of omnidirectional/360° picture, see Chapter 8.

86 See Gabor, Kock and Stroke (1971, 15): "[T]he viewer can inspect the three-dimensional scene not just from one direction, as in stereo photography, but from many directions and with the ability of focusing sharply on all planes."

87 See Chapter 10. On 'virtualizing sculptures' see Schröter (2006b, 260–73).

88 I will discuss only one specific use here. One can find a good (even if not fully up-to-date) overview on HOEs in Marwitz (1990, 445–62) See also Lin (1996), the first volume of a series of proceedings summarizing the results of conferences in Beijing especially devoted to HOEs.

89 See Chapter 4. As I mentioned there, Niépce (1839, 43–4) had indeed made similar observations.

90 Johnston (2006a, 69). The reference to Lippmann can already be found in Denisyuk (1962); see also Denisyuk (1978a; 1978b and 1978c).

91 Denisyuk (1963, 279 and see also 282). See an email by Sean Johnston to me, dated March 20, 2007: "To answer your question: yes, a hologram of mirror acts like a mirror (if suitably recorded to form a reflective hologram, as Denisyuk did). Denisyuk in fact demonstrated that his 'wave photographs' or holograms focused light just like the original mirror did; the only difference was that it would have a focal length that varied with the wavelength of monochromatic light used. . . . This was also true of the very earliest holograms of Dennis Gabor: as he realised a few years later, a so-called 'zone plate' acts precisely like a lens with a precise focal

length." See also the general introduction into the particularly clearly phrased book by Denisyuk (1984, 73) on holography: "In terms of the mechanism of action, a hologram may be defined as an optical equivalent of the object, i.e. a structure which acts upon the given light in the same way as the object does." See also pages 74–5 in the same book where he again deals with the example of the hologram of a mirror.

92 Indeed, because this lamellar structure lies deep down in the emulsion, Lippmann photographs and Denisyuk holograms are more difficult to reproduce than holograms of the Leith and Upatnieks type where the interference pattern is found on the surface of the plate. Lippmann photographs and Denisyuk holograms are then transplane in this regard also.

93 On mirrors in the series of geometrical optics see among others Meyer-Arendt (1984, 92–103); Hecht (1987, 153–63).

94 Here also a lens is used in the recording arrangement, but this lens has again only the function of expanding the beam and not of recording the scene. Image taken from http://www.optique-ingenieur.org/en/courses/OPI_ang_M02_C10/co/Contenu.html [last accessed September 2, 2013].

95 DASA stands for "Deutsche Arbeitsschutzausstellung." It is a Museum in Dortmund (Germany) focusing on the history of working conditions (see http://www.dasa-dortmund.de [last accessed September 2, 2013]). A huge archive of technologies can be found there—including the big collection of holograms by Matthias Lauck.

96 Gabriele Schmid (see her resulting text 2009) has demonstrated an intelligent solution to this problem in an interesting lecture in 2007. She had filmed the artistic holograms about which she was talking with a video camera thereby dissolving their spatial, iridescent manifestation that in some cases implied sequences of movement themselves into temporal sequences.

97 See section 1.2.3. This inclusion becomes noticeable on a different level as well because the holo-interferometrical methods discussed above are also utilized industrially in order to control the production of lenses, see Collier (1968, 57).

98 There seems to be only one exception, see this email from Sean Johnston to me, dated March 20, 2007: "There is only one exception that I know of: the hologram of the so-called 'cube corner reflector' (the combination of three perpendicular flat mirrors to form a corner) does not behave like [the] original cube corner. This is because a single (flat) hologram cannot record the optical characteristics of the three original mirrors at a large angle."

99 Space that is scarce, for example, in satellites or, as I will discuss directly, scanning cash registers; on the endeavor made regarding 'compact optics' see Friesem and Amitai (1996).

100 Pedrotti et al. (1993, 277). See Woodcock (1986, 204), Rallison et al. (1987) and Dickson and Sincerbox (1991).

101 Dickson et al. (1982, 228). The first text in which the concept of a holographic scanner is discussed is Cindrich (1967).

102 Winston (1996, 109–18) discusses the question why holography has not yet gained acceptance in cinema or television. First of all, the technical difficulties are enormous. It is, for example, not at all clear how the huge information content of holography should allow transmission. Winston observes that some of the difficulties could certainly be solved with extensive research but "no supervening social necessity is accelerating such a development" (Winston 1996, 116). Unlike industry that had quickly discovered the usefulness of the holo-interferometric method and that therefore also developed the respective technology, there is no social pressure for the development of 3D holographic movies (principally, as I have mentioned several times, movies are a narrative medium so that the increased spatial information seems hardly necessary). Moreover, the television industry is pushing for the spreading of HDTV and flat screen monitors (probably even more so at the time of writing this study than at the time when Winston was writing his own): "New display technologies (flat screens) are also being heavily developed and will obviously mesh with digital HDTV. Not until all this is diffused, a matter for more than one decade, will an industrial and commercial window open up for holographic television" (Winston 1996, 117). In contrast, in the era of the Xerox machine the pressure existed to protect documents like banknotes and official papers against copying—and for this, holography was being used.

103 Unfortunately I cannot represent the images from *Star Wars* in this book, because of the problematic politics of *Lucasfilms*. They not only demanded simply surreal prices for the reproduction of the images—*Lucasfilms* also insisted on censoring the text.

104 See two completely random examples from the net: http://www.guardian.co.uk/science/2010/nov/03/holographic-communication-telepresence: "In Star Wars, Princess Leia records a 3D hologram of herself appealing for help from the Rebel Alliance in her epic battle against the Empire. The Emperor himself projects holographic messages to his henchman, Darth Vader. And, very soon, you too will be able to transmit messages in a similar way, whether or not you are involved in a galactic battle between good and evil" and

http://www.factmonster.com/cig/theories-universe/universe-as-hologram.html: "Have you ever seen a hologram? They are those eerie, ghostly, two-dimensional images that appear to be three-dimensional. The first time I saw one was in Star Wars, when Princess Leia's holographic image was projected by R2D2 to Luke Skywalker. They've become quite popular over the last twenty years or so." [Both links in this note last accessed September 2, 2013]

105 A sort of 'interactivity' can only be imagined regarding computer generated holograms and it is just this that supposedly is the case regarding the fictitious holodeck. Generating holograms in real time can of course be imagined but because of the enormous size of information needed for generating patterns of interference it is a process that necessitates gigantic resources of data processing. With ingenious data compression, however, one can get good results; see the new developments of SeeReal: http://www.seereal.com/download/press/Pro-Physik_07-07-30.pdf. "SeeReal has developed new paths using the advantages of holography with reasonable processing power and modest demands of the monitor. SeeReal does this by limiting the three-dimensionally represented scenes of a film to the viewers' line of vision, combining it with a camera that tracks the movements of the eyes so that only a fraction of the holographic data has to be calculated." See http://www.seereal.com [last accessed September 2, 2013]. See also Chapter 10 for computer generated holograms.

106 Pizzanelli (1992) briefly describes the evolution of this "mythical hologram" in the history of cinema and television.

107 Besides, for the creators of the series the fictitious hyperrealism of the images in the holodeck has the advantage that one can have the alleged computer simulation acted out by completely normal actors in quite normal stage settings.

108 Arnheim (1989, 157). He wrote this commentary on May 2, 1972. See the important commentary on this in Kac (1995b, 131–2).

109 In particular, since the illusionism of holography can be easily connected with prejudiced cultural criticism as in Eco: "Holography could prosper only in America, a country obsessed with realism where, if a reconstruction is to be credible, it must be absolutely iconic, a perfect likeness, a 'real' copy of the reality being represented" (Eco 1986b, 4). Only, the strange thing is that the holograms of which Eco is talking in his essay do not at all provide a "full-color photographic representation that is more than three-dimensional" (Eco 1986b, 3). Pizzanelli (1992, 430–1), therefore, rightfully observes that Eco's criticism in reality mirrors his secret

wishes for holography rather than the reality of this technical-transplane image.

110 Indeed, media technologies often become objects of the art scene once they are hardly being used any more (Krauss 2002 has made this into an aesthetic program). By anticipating the discussion awaiting us, one could maybe say that holography never became an art because it has never been really normal.

111 See the instructive—even though not current—but not exactly encouraging assessment of discussions with different New York gallery owners and curators, in Lightfoot (1989). However, in 1977 at the *Documenta* 6 in Kassel (Germany), at least some holograms by Harriet Casdin-Silver were also exhibited within the group installation *Centerbeam*.

112 There were quite a series of large holography exhibitions at a later time (e.g. *Light Fantastic* 1977 in London; *Light Years Ahead* 1980 in London); but they were aimed less at artistic goals.

113 Therefore, in the realm of artistic approaches holograms are used that can more easily be reconstructed with white light—only a few artists, like, for example, Paula Dawson, continued using laser light.

114 Not even such beautiful and informative catalogues as published by Jung (2003) will basically change anything. Numerous other catalogues, essays and monographs present an overview on the various approaches to artistic holography, see Claus (1985, 72–82); Coyle (1990) and Dawson (1996).

115 Kramer (1975, D1). McCauley (2000) observed that this criticism of illusionism had also weighed heavily on stereoscopy.

116 Kac (1993, 124). The examples of popular representations of holography in *Star Wars* or *Star Trek* mentioned above would then be ideological representations that prolong a photographic-illusionistic concept of holography.

117 Kac (1993, 125–8). And thus we experience an almost surrealistic meeting between both the scanning cash register and art.

118 This is also underlined by Kac. He is referring to the influential book by Youngblood (1970) on *Expanded Cinema* in which the future possibilities of holographic films also play a role (399–419). Holography, here, is already moving close to cinematography. This connection between holography and film naturally heralds the question whether 'holographic cinema' would not be the obvious conclusion to Kac's considerations. He discusses this possibility himself (1995a, 54–6); but for three reasons holographic cinema seems not to be a useful option. First, it is technically extremely

difficult to realize holographic films (particularly in true colors); attempts in this area have developed furthest in the former USSR (see Komar 1977; Winston 1996, 109–18). Secondly, films as a rule are based on their narration that hardly necessitates additional spatial information—apart from the sensational effect that quite quickly wears off. In light of the first point, this second point carries considerable weight. Thirdly, a too close connection between holography and the cinema would again make holography comparable to another medium, and Kac can hardly criticize the subsumption of holography under photography in order to demand subsuming it under cinema at the same time.

119 Apart from the special case of the freeze-frame where as a rule the movement of the image can be seen from the disturbance of the image.

120 Kac (1995a, 48). This curious characteristic can be found outside of holography at most in certain forms of op-art and later in so-called interactive images created by computers, i.e. those that with their mutability dependent on the viewers are hardly as new as their apologists maintain; see Hünnekens (2003).

121 Zec (1989, 425): "[A]ny truly useful analysis of the unique aesthetic message of holography has to first deal with the medium itself and the investigation of its inherent autonomous structure."

122 From the mid-nineties Turrell started working with holography (and stereoscopy) himself, see Jung (2003, 152–5). On the classification within the tradition of light art, see also Claus (1985, 43–82).

123 Zec (1989, 429). Maline (1995) criticizes Zec for evidently following formalist and modernist art concepts (like, for example, those by Greenberg 1978). She accuses him of insisting on a too narrow concept of medium specificity, thereby narrowing down the field of possible aesthetic strategies for holography. In a similar way, Zec is criticized by Fahle (2009b). Fahle also underlines that light in holography constitutes the carrier—and not only the object—of the image. He sums up: "The image cannot be grasped as a whole outside of visibility; the light illuminates but only by becoming apparent in its illuminating appearance."

124 On comparable attempts in electronic literature and their implications for the understanding of text and reading attitudes see the contributions in Gendolla and Schäfer (2007). To a certain extent one could maintain that here in part the difference between the visual arts and literature is dissolved; in other words, with these uses of holography the traditional genre labels are beginning to disintegrate.

125 As I have shown above, Leith's and Upatnieks' experiments indeed began with the reproduction of photographic images and in the earliest newspaper reports holography was only regarded as a new form of photography—it was not even mentioned that it is three-dimensional (see Deschin 1963; Osmundsen 1963).

126 Zec (1989, 429)—but Zec is fundamentally against this term.

127 Indeed holography is much more fundamentally different from geometrical optics than stereoscopy. See Zec (1989, 427): "The existence of holography is primarily due to the development of a totally different perception of the physical world, which has made a radical break with geometric optics." See also Layer (1989).

128 See Pepper (1989, 295): "Since the impact of perspective during the Renaissance, we now take for granted the ability to 'capture' a three-dimensional image and present it convincingly on a flat surface. That surface might be paper for a drawing, canvas for a painting, light-sensitive emulsion for photography, phosphorescent screen for video [!] or the flat white screen for the reflected light of cinema."

129 Haran (1980, 7). Thereby she is referring (among other things) to the almost prophetical end of Edgerton's study (1975, 165) that seems to suggest the emergence of transplane images beyond geometrical optics: "Surely in some future century, when artists are among those journeying throughout the universe, they will be encountering and endeavoring to depict experiences impossible to understand, let alone render, by the application of a suddenly obsolete linear perspective."

130 Terms that can be used for videos without problems, see Maline (1991, 217).

131 Claus (1985, 81). Denisyuk (1984, 75) observed: "As it happens, a hologram is a unique copy of the object, and it may be regarded as a certain trend in the development of the technique of sculpture." This "analogy between holography and sculpture" has recently shown in another way as well. In recent artistic sculptures, positions can be found that themselves seem to come close to the media aesthetics of the holographic image; for example, in works of the hyperrealist sculptor Evan Penny. In his new series *No One in Particular*, he sculpts detail-perfect non-existing persons in the form of portrait busts, or more precisely in the form of bust-like wall-reliefs. These relief-like sculptures are somewhat bigger than a real person and when seen from the front they seem alarmingly realistic, but as a whole they are very flat. Thus, they combine sculptural and planar elements: "The closest photographic analog to one of Penny's fully three-dimensional figures is the hologram. In fact, this three-

dimensional photographic image is invoked in the first overt reference to photography in Penny's oeuvre. It originates in the three-dimensional negative images created as optical illusions by the concave interiors of works like *Mask* (1990) and *Screen* (1994–98), in which moulds themselves are cast into sculptures that take the form of fragments of monumental heads" (Tousley 2004, 42). The examples are chosen by the author because these are sculptures turned inside-out, similar to the pseudoscopic, real images of holography. See also Dyens (1989).

132 As De Montebello (1977, 79) has observed with the example of integral photography (see Chapter 5): "[T]he observer rarely remains completely still in the presence of a three-dimensional image; he wants to see more, and his motion unveils more points of information." Of course female observers are included in this.

133 Apart from the rare case of the 360° holograms that I have briefly mentioned earlier.

134 Fahle (2009b) relates the holographic image with the aesthetics of installation. However, in following the differentiation between sculpture and installation, as Potts (2001) is suggesting, the comparison with sculpture seems to be more fitting since the installation is a space within space with frames created by markings of all kinds, often empty at the center and thereby inviting the viewers to explore. Sculpture, on the other hand, is an object that one approaches and to which one seeks a specific distance, a description that seems to fit better with holograms.

135 See for example Schmid (2009) on a holographic installation by Philippe Boissonnet.

136 Maybe in a similar argument with which Crary (1988a, 43) had claimed that the paradigm of the camera obscura had collapsed at the beginning of the nineteenth century, only to be surprisingly resurrected at its end as its own "mirage."

137 This relatively historical isolation of holography is perhaps a reason why so many artists working in this realm accompany their own works with a sometimes excessive discourse of self-interpretation, see for example Benyon (1995, 89): " 'Eddie Coloured' is a reflection hologram of a young black man . . . framed in a rectangle of wood, with a gouache underpainting including the written message 'Do not frame'. This refers both to the unacceptability of frames in current art, and the possibility that those with black skin may be adversely set up, 'framed', in British Culture. . . . 'Penetrate the surface' is a version of 'Wrapped flowers' which has marks and the text 'penetrate the . . . surface of the emulsion' written with silver pen on

the surface of the glass. . . . Small silver pen markings tie the three dimensional image to the two dimensional surface of the hologram, so that both interact. The instruction to the viewer to 'penetrate the surface of the emulsion' alludes both to the physical act of viewing, the hologram beyond the image plane, and the metaphysical act of penetrating superficial appearances. . . . An underlying reason why I am making holograms now, rather than paintings, is because they are a purer way of connecting up with those really early, pre-verbal memories that are experiences of light. . . . My early student explorations of my female psyche were so misunderstand [*sic*] by my male tutors that I was asked whether there was anything the matter with me."

138 Still, Youngblood (1970, 399) was quite sure: "It is certain that holographic cinema and television will be common by the year 2000; but more probably this will take place within fifteen years from now." Or, as none other than Andy Warhol (1975, 158) said: "Holograms are going to be exciting, I think. You can really, finally, with holograms, pick your own atmosphere. They'll be televising a party, and you want to be there, and with holograms, you will be there. You'll be able to have this 3-D party in your house, you'll be able to pretend you're there and walk in with the people. You can even rent a party. You can have anybody famous that you want sitting right next to you." See also the pioneer in computers Vannevar Bush (1967, 89).

139 Actually, the 'holodeck' is the phantasmatic figuration of a perfect virtual reality; see Schröter (2004c, 221–34).

140 See Panofsky (1991, 60) mentioning that the central perspective in painting already has the tendency "to extend forward across the picture plane; indeed, because of the short perpendicular distance it appears to include the beholder standing before the panel" by way of its isotropy. This phantasm also existed in the discussions on early film; see Bottomore (1999, 191–6).

141 Sutherland (1968, 757; my emphasis). On Sutherland see Schröter (2007b). See Chapter 10.

142 And, provided they are animated, the series of physiological optics.

143 Roland Barthes (1982, 96) had already pointed out that one can also attribute a kind of past future to photography: "But the *punctum* is: *he is going to die*. I read at the same time: *This will be* and *this has been*; I observe . . . an anterior future of which death is the stake. By giving me the absolute past . . . the photograph tells me death in the future. What *pricks* me is the discovery of this equivalence. In front of the photograph of my mother as a child, I

tell myself: she is going to die: I shudder . . . *over a catastrophe which has already occurred*. . . . every photograph is this catastrophe."

144 See Bryson (1998a, 11): "Aside from its use of the laser, almost everything about holography suggests the nineteenth century photographer's studio: the careful painting of emulsions on glass . . . the painstaking trimming of glass plates by hand – even its use in 'fine art' settings, to simulate traditional art objects, or to record the kind of artifacts that belong in the museum."

145 Kramer (1975, D1) had already accused many artists working with holography of provinciality.

146 To this effect see Wall (1995, 258–66) on the role of photography in conceptual art. Buchloh's critique from 1997 of Becher's approach stressing craftsmanship has been mentioned before (see Chapter 6).

147 Nauman is one of the first and without doubt the most well known artist who was involved with holography—a fact that certainly was made easier because he had studied physics.

148 On the role of the body in Nauman's work see recently Wagner (2007).

149 This clearly follows from Nauman (1994, 236). In the same catalog (Nauman 1994, 222) it is made clear that Nauman has assumed similar poses on infrared photos made by Jack Fulton that led to five works entitled *Studies for Holograms (A–E)* (1970). But those are not the works shown here.

150 See Hagen (1991) who criticizes the lack of color flexibility in holography. Holograms cannot be black and white; they have to be either monochrome (most often green or red), iridescently shimmering in all colors of the rainbow, or—and this is much more difficult—fully colored. At the time when the first artists attempted to be successful with holography, not even color photographs were fully accepted by museums; this only began to emerge slowly with William Eggleston's controversial exhibition at the MoMA. This exhibition, by the way, was torn to pieces by the same Hilton Kramer of the *New York Times*, who had already sharply attacked the large holography exhibition in New York in 1975 where he had criticized the holograms and their mainly rainbow colors: "Their color, moreover, is atrocious" (Kramer 1975, D1).

151 See Bryson (1998a, 11) once again: "What was required of the media of the future was that they reproduce motion, like cinema: yet this was precisely what holography could not deliver. The viewer of a hologram might move about, but the objects stonily stayed put."

152 In the aforementioned catalog with the beautiful title *The Expanded Eye*, the hologram is referred to as a "playful 'magician's medium' " (Curiger 2006, 21).

153 This thesis is supported by the statistical evaluations of the literature on holography that Johnston (2003) has made. Notably, it is striking that the number of exhibitions on holography (both artistic and of a different kind) have significantly decreased since the 1980s (457 and 461, fig. 1D). Obviously, holography has partially lost the status of a visual medium again, which it had gained in the 1970s.

CHAPTER TEN

Since 1960: Repetition and difference: The interactive-transplane image

The Series of Virtual Optics 3

After 1945 the *series of virtual optics* appeared and developed only gradually at first and then faster and faster, as mentioned in my introduction, binding together more or less all the previously developed optical series and making new connections that had been impossible up to that point. Since about 1945 digital computer technology had been on the rise[1] and had been increasingly used since the 1960s for the creation of images. In as far as the three optical series—geometrical optics, wave optics and physiological optics—can be formulated mathematically, they can also in principle be computed.

Geometrical optics, for example, knows the law of refraction and the rules of linear perspective; in the 1960s these rules were already being translated into algorithms for computers as evidenced by computer scientists who took recourse to old treatises at the outset of computer graphics. As Lawrence Roberts observed at a panel in 1989: "Well, the mathematics for the three-dimensional display [meaning here 'perspective'] was done pretty much . . . going back to the eighteen hundreds in terms of when they did a lot of perspective geometry."[2] One of the most widespread methods of computer graphics is ray tracing: "Ray tracing utilizes the principles of geometrical optics . . . where propagation is assumed along discrete ray paths from transmitter to receiver" (Remley, Anderson and Weisshaar 2000, 2350). Taking recourse to that prototypical lute that Dürer, Holbein and others liked so much to represent perspectivally foreshortened, and by drawing on the tile floor, which since the Renaissance has been favored for demonstrating linear perspectival foreshortening,[3] the figure from one book on computer graphics (Figure 10.1) shows that the plane continues to play the central role in its capacity as a *projection plane*—as it already did in Alberti (1972a, 49; 2011, 34)—also in the virtual repetition of geometrical optics.

As far as, for example, perspective as an algorithm is nowadays "poured . . . into hardware" (Kittler 2001, 34–5) in the form of graphic cards and thereby accelerated, one can say—contradicting Crary's assertion that it disappeared—that geometrical optics continues to exist in store-bought PCs, even though in a different

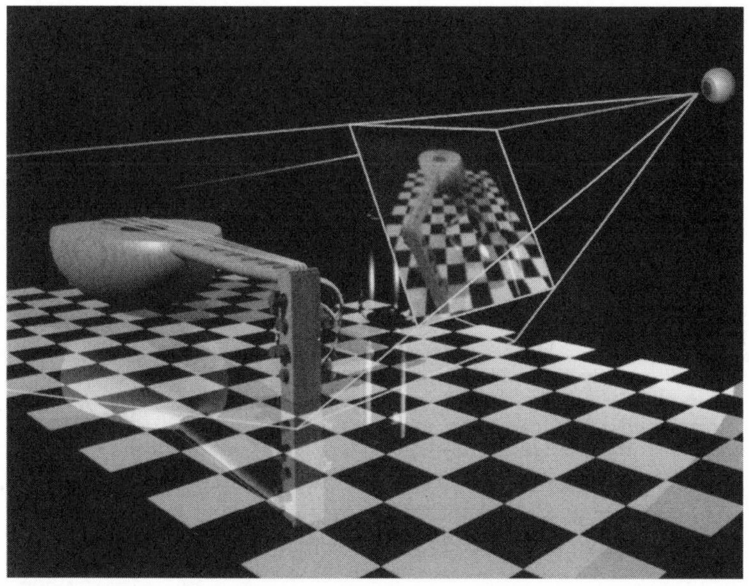

FIGURE 10.1 *Illustration of ray tracing, in Mitchell (1992, 155). The "intersection of the visual pyramid" (Alberti 2011, 34) can be clearly recognized.*

material sedimentation than in the painterly linear perspective or in photo optics (see Vollmer 2007).

The laws of *wave optics*, according to which, for example, patterns of interference form between two coherent light rays, can also be formulated mathematically even though in a more complicated manner.[4] As soon as the first experiments with holography emerged in the 1960s, different scholars had the idea that it should be possible to calculate interference patterns. If one prints the calculated patterns onto suitable materials, it should be possible to artificially create holograms.[5] (See Figure 10.2.)

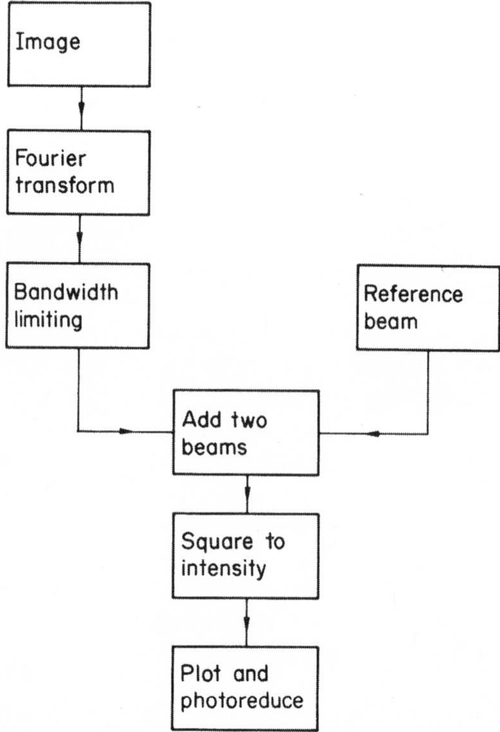

FIGURE 10.2 *Diagram of computer generated holography, in Firth (1972, 49). On the left the virtual 'object beam' is generated via Fourier-Transformation. It is then superposed with the virtual 'reference beam' and then the pattern is printed.*

Physiological optics may be more difficult to formalize insofar as it describes not physical facts, but the characteristics of the human body.[6] Nevertheless, since the 1960s there had been attempts made to use, for example, the insights gleaned about the binocular difference necessary for creating a stereoscopic effect in order to generate stereoscopic images by way of computers.[7]

Below, I cannot and will not trace the whole history of computer graphics, i.e. including all attempts in which the three optical series were repeated in a shifted way in the fourth series of virtual optics.[8] I only want to address two aspects:

1 How can we define 'virtual'—i.e. the series of virtual optics—regarding digital computers? What then does the virtual repetition of optical series mean?

2 In what way is the virtual repetition also repetition *and* difference? And in what way does this simultaneity of repetition and difference open up a new type of the transplane image, namely the *interactive-transplane image*?

The Virtual: In this book, I am using the term 'virtual' with two different meanings. First of all, it signifies the 'virtual' image, differentiated from the 'real' one as it is defined by optics, as an image that—different from a real image—cannot be captured on a screen (e.g. the mirror image).[9] Secondly, it refers to the series of virtual optics, i.e. the mathematical formalization of the previous three optical series and the algorithmic processing of these formalizations in computers. These two meanings have to be differentiated clearly—and here the second meaning is at the center. What then does 'virtual' mean more precisely in the discursive field of computer sciences? (See Schröter 2004c, 166–8). Primarily 'virtual' is being used with reference to *virtual memories*. The term 'virtual memory' has taken on its current meaning since 1962. The main problem of the electronic computers of that time was that storage with a fast access time was hardly affordable. Therefore it was necessary to export the information on the main memory that was not currently needed to the auxiliary memory. 'Memory allocation' refers to the process that decides which data are currently needed in the main memory and which can be exported to the auxiliary one. In the first years of computer programming, the allocation had to be accomplished manually by programmers using appropriate programming routines to accomplish this task. When during the middle of the 1950s more advanced programming languages were being used and therefore the programs became more complex, this method was a hindrance. A series of solutions were suggested of which in the end the virtual memory gained general acceptance, so that the computer system could allocate the real addresses to the virtual addresses in the memory space with the help of an address translation function, indiscernible to the programmer. Only the currently needed parts of programs and data are loaded into the central memory. Virtual memory then operates on the basis of separating the logical memory space from the material one. *This separation of logical structure/form*[10] *and material substrate lies at the core of the concept of the virtual.*[11] Depending on the question, the computer simulation of a real object or process used by the sciences, by medicine or by the military[12] consists in detaching formalized structures mathematically from the materiality of the object[13] in order to have them serve as the basis of an approximative model that then can be performatively put to the test. A computer simulated entity is a virtual entity.

Obviously, Brewster's term 'virtually' from the year 1851 that I quoted in Chapter 2 can be compared insofar as he talks about the future sculptor who "virtually . . . carr[ies] in his portfolio the mighty lions and bulls of Nineveh,—the gigantic Sphinxes of Egypt,—the Apollos and Venuses of Grecian art," i.e. transports the statues (structurally) but in reality without their matter, which had made them non-transportable (in Wade 1983, 221). Eight years after Brewster, Sir Oliver Wendell Holmes will also write with reference to the stereoscopic photography:

> Form is henceforth divorced from matter. In fact, matter as a visible object is of no great use any longer, except as the mould on which form is shaped. Give us a few negatives of a thing worth seeing, taken from different points of view, and that is all we want of it. Pull it down or burn it up, if you please . . . Matter in large masses must always be fixed and dear; form is cheap and transportable. (1859, 747)[14]

Even though at the time the point could not have been to subject the detached forms to a mathematical formalization, the basic idea of virtualization already exists, i.e. the idea of dissociating form and matter and transferring that form to another matter (here: the stereogram). With the passage quoted above, Kittler credits Holmes even with the beginning of the history of the modern concept of information: "According to Holmes, therefore, modern information conceals itself under the ancient philosophical concept of form" (Kittler 2010, 41). If this is true, then the transplane image of stereoscopy is the beginning of virtualization—one more reason to finally take the history of transplane images seriously.

Be that as it may, one can apply the detachment of matter and form and the operative processing of this form in computers also to the materialities of the previous optical series; for example, to the lenses of geometrical optics. Starting from empirical measuring that also include the limitations of the lenses, one can mathematically describe their performance and then create a *virtual lens* from this description in the computer. With such a lens one would be able to create images that ideally would look like photographs (see Potmesil and Chakravarty 1982). Such a *simulated* lens can of course also be altered beyond all that is physically possible since it is a mathematical structure without matter. And it is precisely this which epitomizes the simultaneity of repetition and difference in the "virtualization of optics" (Kittler 2001, 35).

But these simulations are limited. Not only can we not calculate everything[15] but also those facts that could in principle be calculated can drive computers to their limits.

> Conversely, computer graphics, because it is software, consists of algorithms and only of algorithms. The optical algorithm for automatic image synthesis can be determined just as easily as non-algorithmic image synthesis. It would merely have to calculate all optical, i.e. electromagnetic, equivalencies that quantum electrodynamics recognizes for measurable spaces, for virtual spaces as well; or, to put it more simply, it would have to convert Richard Feynman's three-volume *Lectures on Physics* into software. Then a cat's fur, because it creates anisotropic surfaces, would shimmer like cat's fur; then streaks in a wine glass, because they change their refraction index at each point, would turn the lights and things behind them into complete color spectra. Theoretically, nothing stands in the way of such miracles.

> Universal discrete machines, which is to say, computers, can do anything so long as it is programmable. But it is not just in Rilke's *Malte Laurids Brigge* but also in quantum electro-dynamics that 'realities are slow and indescribably detailed.' The perfect optics could be programmed just barely within a finite time, but, because of infinite monitor waiting times, would have to put off rendering the perfect image. (Kittler 2001, 36)

With his reference to Richard Feynman and quantum electrodynamics, Kittler is referring to the knowledge of quantum optics (which can be described as a special case of quantum electrodynamics) encompassing wave optics and thus geometrical optics (see Saleh and Teich 1991, 385). A complete and general simulation of quantum optics would comprise all geometrical-optical and wave-optical phenomena. But such a simulation surpasses the capacity of current computers in many concrete cases. For example, the computing of interference patterns for "synthetic holography" (Crary 1990, 1) is already a considerably elaborate endeavor: "Synthetic holography imposes high requirements on computational power and storage capacities. The reduction of effort is therefore a common goal" (Ritter et al. 1997, 273). The continuing development in the series of virtual optics as a rule depends less on the changes of basic optical knowledge than on finding effective algorithms and data-reductions that allow for computing virtual optics with acceptable operational and temporal efforts,[16] not to mention the problems with the peripheral devices on which the images are supposed to be shown (which is also a problem in generated holography). I should add that computers are in no way limited to repeat the previous optical/visual media via *simulation* (in an altered way); photographs, for example, can also be transferred into digital data by way of *sampling*[17] and sampled and simulated data can be connected with each other.[18]

Repetition and Difference: The example of a (mathematically) simulated virtual lens that can be altered into forms unlike anything physically possible illustrates a fundamental option of all virtual simulation.[19] One can, for example, attempt simulating the process of creating photographs as accurately as possible (for example, in order to insert generated special effects seamlessly into an otherwise photographic film, see Schröter 2003). Nevertheless, simulations as a rule do not serve the purpose of unerringly duplicating the phenomenon to be simulated—even if it were possible regardless of the limits of calculability, of resources or of peripheries. And why should it? The phenomenon to be simulated already exists; therefore the simulation only makes sense when first of all only certain *aspects* of the phenomenon concerning *operative* questions and aims are simulated. For example, during military or civil aviation training, a flight simulator should simulate the relevant reactions of a real airplane as closely as possible. But of course the real airplane should not be duplicated 1:1—because in the case of a simulated crash this would mean possible death, but it is exactly this that is to be prevented with the help of the simulators. A truly illusionist flight simulator would be quite meaningless.[20] It is for this very reason that the complaints about the disappearance of reality in simulation are missing their point. Secondly, one of the aims of simulation (and therefore also of the virtual objects created by them, e.g. in particular in the realm of natural sciences) is being able to modify certain parameters and constraints. For example, it can be tested whether certain phenomena, simulated according to mathematical models, behave according to the experimental data (see Galison 1997, 689–780; Gramelsberger 2010). One can also attempt to find out how certain phenomena would react under different conditions. Since the simultaneity of repetition and difference is the constitutive factor for the virtuality of computer simulation, it is not only the series of geometrical optics that is possibly repeated *in a modified way*. The same is true of course for the other optical series and for this reason also for the transplane images that can be created by them. This means that in the field of virtual optics new kinds of transplane images can be created.

A first example: As I argued above one can use holograms in order to record complex geometrical-optical lens arrangements, thereby reproducing them with minimum spatial requirements.[21] But it is also possible to create virtual models of geometrical arrangements modified beyond all physical possibilities. These models can be translated into virtual holography, thereby creating an interference pattern which can be printed. This is how holographic-optical elements are obtained that have hitherto completely unknown characteristics: "Geometries of representation can be created that even with great expenditure cannot be produced as glass optics" (Marwitz 1990, 445). These kinds of elements with peculiar optical characteristics are being used in manifold applications today (particularly in the natural sciences, in astronautics, but also in the scanning cash registers already discussed).

A second example: In 1960 Béla Julesz published a paper in which he discussed the mechanisms of depth perception from a physiological-optical point of view. The introduction begins with the following sentences:

> The perception of depth involves monocular and binocular depth cues. The latter seem simpler and more suitable for investigation. Particularly important is the problem of finding binocular parallax, which involves matching patterns of the left and right visual fields. Stereo pictures of familiar objects or line drawings preclude the separation of interacting cues, and thus this pattern-matching process is difficult to investigate. More insight into the process can be gained by using unfamiliar picture material devoid of all cues except binocular parallax. To this end, artificial stereo picture pairs were generated on a digital computer. When viewed monocularly, they appear completely random, but if viewed binocularly, certain correlated point domains are seen in depth. (Julesz 1960, 1125)

The point then is to generate images that do not have any other depth cues than the binocular difference—and such images can only be produced with computers. Clearly in terms of the constitutive simultaneity of repetition and difference discussed above, stereoscopy is being simulated—*but only in one of its aspects* (*the image represents binocularity but no objects*). The essay contains some of the *random-dot-stereograms* developed from this (see Figure 10.3).

This method was of little importance apart from the significant role it played for the exploration of vision, i.e. for the development of the series of physiological optics.[22] The crucial fact is that with computers synthetic stereoscopic views can be created that cannot be obtained in any other way.

A third example deals with the virtual repetition/shift of stereoscopy as well. As I have said in Chapter 1, the pattern of

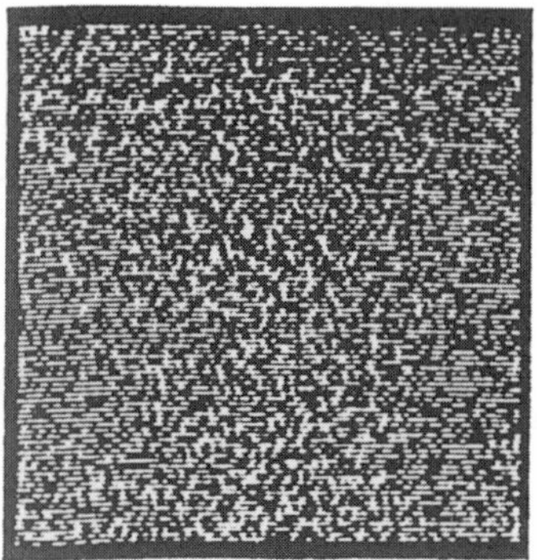
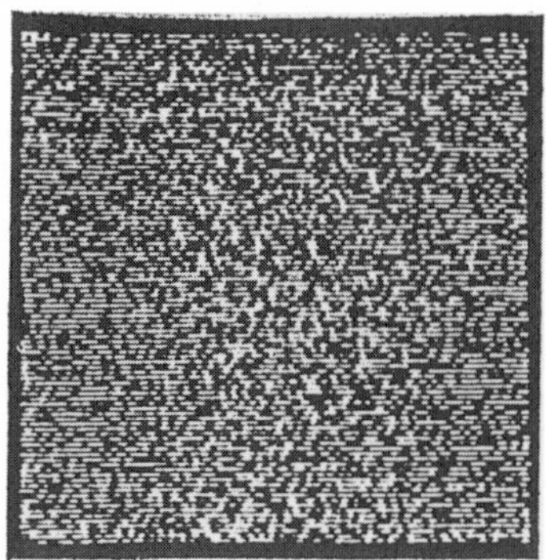

FIGURE 10.3 Random-Dot-Stereogram *showing a square above the background when viewed stereoscopically, in Julesz (1960, 1129).*

stereoscopy—which according to Crary disappeared around 1900—re-emerged around 1990 with the so-called data-glasses that received much attention (see Figure 1.2). The development of these head-mounted displays (HMDs) had been driven forward since the mid 1960s mainly by Ivan Sutherland.[23] In 1968 a first publication appeared on this subject, which in the opening paragraphs sketches the basic idea:

> The fundamental idea behind the three-dimensional display [HMD] is to present the user with a perspective image which changes as he moves. . . . Although stereo presentation is important to the three-dimensional illusion, it is less important than the change that takes place in the image when the observer moves his head. The image presented by the three-dimensional display must change in exactly the way that the image of a real object would change for similar motions of the user's head. . . . Our objective in this project has been to surround the user with displayed three-dimensional information.[24]

The intended three-dimensional image is supposed to connect two elements. First of all it aims at a stereoscopic presentation of perspectival images, as in traditional stereoscopy. Secondly, and more importantly, the image is supposed to change with the movement of the head in order *to surround* the user with an image.

Therefore, the HMD connects the stereoscopic image with the 360° panorama.[25] This connection is historically new. It becomes possible only because the image changes with the movement of the viewing subject's head. It is not an accident that in Sutherland's text on HMDs the word 'virtual' appears (see Sutherland 1968, 757, 759 and 763). The three-dimensional space that surrounds the viewer is a virtual one. Here lies the important difference with the 360° view of the traditional panorama. The panorama is real, it continues to exist also 'behind the back' of the viewing subject.[26] In the virtual environment, however, only the section at which the viewer is looking at the moment is being displayed—Sutherland therefore is talking of a "virtual screen position" (1968, 757). The virtual environment is primarily only a mathematical description of a space. This structure is set off against the data that the viewing subject conveys with its head-movements (scanned by head-tracking),[27] thereby creating the image for the display. The virtual environment is *actualized* performatively in the process of interaction. James J. Gibson, the American psychologist who specialized in psychology of perception, wrote: "It is the writer's opinion, however, that there are basic discrepancies . . . between the stereoscopic and the panoramic [images], which will make it impossible to use them simultaneously in one grand effort to achieve 'complete realism'" (Gibson 1954, 21). Gibson obviously did not yet know the HMDs and their virtual synthesis of panorama and stereoscope. In their virtual repetition, stereoscopy is thus connected to the panorama in a hitherto quite impossible way.

Sutherland's HMD was semi-permeable and thus permitted superposing the computer images with those of real space:

> Half-silvered mirrors in the prisms through which the user looks allow him to see both the images from the cathode ray tubes and objects in the room simultaneously. Thus displayed material can be made either to hang disembodied in space or to coincide with maps, desk tops, walls, or the keys of a typewriter. (Sutherland 1968, 759)

Hence, when he developed the HMD Sutherland did not even have the goal to create an *illusionist* space that would isolate the viewer. The HMD was conceived as an interface to enable the presentation of information (for example, for scientific visualization or for military purposes—see the maps named by Sutherland). In terms of today's increasingly discussed *augmented reality*, real space is supposed to be superposed with its virtual (and therefore not identical) double. The aim of these interactive-transplane images is also taking spatial control through operative visualization. To date, HMDs are boosting the efficiency of fighter pilots, for example. However, the early HMDs for fighter pilots used were not semi-permeable since the pilot had to be isolated from all disruptive external influences by closing off the visual field. A first functional prototype, the VCASS (Visually Coupled Airborne Systems Simulator), was introduced as data-glasses simulating fighter planes in 1982. The project was continued with the name *Super Cockpit* from 1986 onward; in the process, the representation was reduced to the crucial information.[28] It would be plainly absurd to squeeze the pilot into an HMD that would then illusionistically show him exactly that which he also could see *without* the HMD. Functional uses of images are by no means necessarily illusionistic ones. The total illusion or its approximation can lead to disorientation and paralysis, as can be seen from simulation sickness in CAVEs and similar environments (see Biocca 1992). Subtly organized multimedial interactive-transplane images on the other hand could possibly address the user in an optimal way even—or especially—if the individual elements do not combine into illusionism. As I have shown repeatedly, the question of the interactive-transplane image cannot be answered with the term illusionism, which is much too unrefined.

Even without the HMD, among other things the currently much discussed topic of 'interactive' (see Manovich 1996b; Schröter and Spies 2006) digital images developed thanks to Sutherland's early attempts. They are interactively transplane in the sense that they present virtual space on monitors in a geometrical-optical way, i.e. they project them in a linear-perspectival manner, yet they also enable navigation (see Manovich 2001, 244–85 in detail) through this space (see Venus 2009) via their performative actualization.

Currently they are a commonly used type of imaging; for example, in computer games (see Beil 2010). Sutherland's stereoscopy, while still in use, is not always applied although in principle it still remains an option. In the transplane reproduction of complex sculptural structures (as has been repeatedly discussed in this book), the imaging methods based on interactive-transplane images are increasingly being used as due to their virtual character they are much more flexible than stereoscopic or holographic methods, which they, in principle, could include if necessary (see Schröter 2006b, 260–73). Such miracles are made possible precisely because the series of virtual optics "make[s] optic modes optional at all" (Kittler 2001, 35).

Notes

1 See Ceruzzi 1998.

2 Siggraph (1989, 72). On the algorithmic character of linear perspective see Kittler (1997b, 10–13).

3 See Panofsky (1991, 40–1 and 57–9; illustration of the tile floor on p. 167).

4 For a detailed mathematical presentation of geometrical and wave optics see Hecht (1987). As I have mentioned before, the mathematically elegant Lippmann photography (see Chapter 4) can be quite easily modeled virtually.

5 See Johnston (2006a, 216–20). Probably the first paper on computer generated holograms is Lohmann and Paris (1967). See also Firth (1972), Tricoles (1987), and Stuart (1990).

6 Nevertheless, see already Helmholtz (1985, § 31) as an example for the detailed attempt at mathematically formulating "Binocular Double Vision," an element of physiological optics.

7 See for example Julesz (1960).

8 On these procedures see inter alia Foley et. al. (1997) and Watt (2000). On the history see inter alia Mitchell (1992), Kittler (2001), Berz (2009), and Schröter (2004c, 194–205).

9 See Hecht (1987, 131)—a difference that is particularly relevant for integral photography (Chapter 5) and holography (Chapter 9).

10 I am using these terms synonymously.

11 My term 'virtual' is clearly a more narrow one than that of Rieger (2003, 33) who says: "Formations and their media are neither limited nor can they be limited; they are valid always and everywhere, they are the allotope and allochrone human condition—and that is what makes them so uncanny. When we transfer this to virtuality we have to concede that human beings are perpetuated events of just this

virtuality. Whatever human beings are doing, they are doing it under the banner of some images." Moreover, Rieger seems to identify virtuality with images.

12 On the history and function of computer simulation see Schröter (2004e). See also Gramelsberger (2010; 2011) on the usage of computer simulation in the natural sciences.

13 For example, by measuring experimental regularities that can be mathematically described.

14 See also Schröter (2007a).

15 See Frey (1967, 94–134) on the external and internal limitations of calculation. See also Harel (2000).

16 Giving as examples ray tracing and the radiosity method (which has passed somewhat out of use by now), Kittler (2001) is pointing out that as a rule different rendering methods solve different aspects dissimilarly; therefore, for all practical purposes different combinations of a variety of methods are usually the best approach.

17 Photo sculpture (Chapter 3) can be placed at the beginning of the series of virtual optics on the level of sampling. One cannot sample holograms easily since the interference patterns are much too complex for most scanners.

18 See in more detail Schröter (2004a).

19 See Tholen (2002, 19–60) for a fundamental consideration of 'shifted repetition' in the area of digital simulation.

20 See Esposito (1998, 287) who has suggested the following: "The term 'virtual' actually has nothing to do with fiction. It originated in optics and refers to images reflected in mirrors. The mirror does not 'represent' an alternative reality for observers (which can be attributed to other observers); it 'presents' to them 'real' reality from a different point of view, thereby widening their field of observation. In the same way, virtual reality does not 'represent' fictional reality; it rather 'presents' the reality of fiction to the observer, in other words an alternative possibility of constructing a possibility [of viewing], thereby widening the observers' area of contingency irrespective of the perspective of the producer of the fiction. Like the mirror image, [this alternative possibility] does not refer to the distinction reality/fiction but to the observational conditions; in this case it is the differentiation of actual and potential possibilities, i.e. the self-reference of the observation." Esposito then suggests using the optical definition of 'virtual' (which in optics, however, is defined by referring to the screen, a fact that does not play any role in Esposito's definition) as

the basis for understanding 'virtual reality'—by which she is probably referring to computer-based and interactive areas. In other words, Esposito is connecting what to my mind should be separated. Her approach is problematic because she equates the mirror image that in principle is identical with the real situation—the mirror reflects all that can be seen in the real scene, that is to say, all the visual information and could thus be regarded as the only genuinely 'illusionistic image' (Eco 1984 for this reason goes on to dismiss the term 'mirror image' itself as incorrect and misleading)—with virtual reality which to all intents is never 100 percent identical with the (perceived) real situation (for example, in flight simulators). The decidedly *operative* aspect of simulation that originates from its genealogy is thus obscured (and it is not by accident that Esposito starts her text on page 270 directly after differentiating virtuality and simulation). See also Esposito (1995).

21 See section 9.3. A question is: How does the digital simulatability of mathematically formulated (geometrical, physiological, wave) optics relate to the epistemic inclusion of geometrical optics in wave optics? Can the capability of holography of representing geometrical-optical devices without their materiality (for example, in holographic-optical elements—HOEs) not be compared with a virtual modeling in the computer? The following statement seems to point in that direction: "The holographic object is an exact replica of the original except that it lacks inertia" (Bringolf 1979, 3). One can assume that the informational detachment of information from form (which Holmes 1859, 747 had already described and which continues in HOEs) is a kind of an analog precursor of the digital virtuality described here. Therefore Virilio's classifying holography with 'infography' within the one category 'virtuality,' which I have criticized in Chapter 9, also contains a grain of truth.

22 With the emergence of low-priced PCs around 1990 the method became temporarily popular as "Magic Eye"; see Baccei (1993). See also http://www.magiceye.com [last accessed September 2, 2013].

23 On Sutherland see Schröter (2007b).

24 Sutherland (1968, 757). Thielmann (2007, 64) is pointing out that in the history of computers the development of transplane image(spaces) was at least equiprimordial with the development of plane displays. Certainly the plane image *does not* come *before* the transplane one.

25 See Sutherland (1968, 757): "We can display objects beside the user or behind him which will become visible to him if he turns around."

26 See Hick (1999, 235–63) on the 360° view of the panorama during the nineteenth century. The panorama is not a transplane image; it is only a very big and curved linear-perspectival image, i.e. a geometrical-optical one.

27 Meyer et al. (1992) have published a study on different procedures of head-tracking and other position-tracking systems.

28 See Furness (1986, 48), who underlines that "screening and filtering information for the display and . . . for enhancing mission performance" is one of the main tasks of the display. See also http://www.hitl.washington.edu/publications/m-86-1/ [last accessed September 2, 2013].

PART THREE
Conclusions

CHAPTER ELEVEN

2013: Resume

In 1966 Charlotte Posenenske started the set of works called *Three-dimensional Images* (see Figure 11.1). Posenenske's works have become known only recently; today she is named among the minimalists, those artists who radicalized and thus surmounted high modernism with its emphasis on two-dimensionality.[1] They moved away from the plane to the 'specific object'—into spatiality. Posenenske's three-dimensional images are especially enlightening for this process. The plane still exists—white lacquered aluminum, a reference to the empty canvas—but this illusion is promptly shattered by being folded like a piece of paper; parts of the image seem lighter or darker depending on the angle from which the viewers are looking according to the incidence of light. It seems as if they were metaphors for the technical-transplane image that became more and more important in the 1960s—a fact that probably was unknown to Posenenske. In the genealogy of the volumetric image from 1961 onwards, different and important steps were taken; pictorial holography emerged in 1963 through the lucky encounter of wave front reconstruction and laser-light; around 1968 the model of stereoscopy again surfaced in Ivan Sutherland's first data-glasses and in 1970 De Montebello would have his ameliorated integral photography patented. Certainly no causal connection can be constructed here—only the coincidence of the technical and artistic tendencies into the direction of the transplane image is indeed very striking.

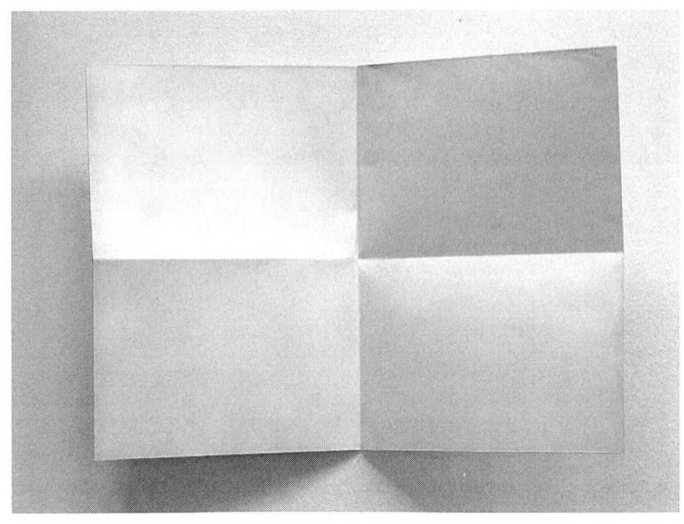

FIGURE 11.1 *Charlotte Posenenske,* Three-Dimensional Image *(1966).*

This coincidence is at least a symptom for the rising importance of questions and problems that were connected with planes, the role they played for visual concepts, their limitations of representation and operationalization of information related to space (and therefore possibly itself spatially structured).

As I have attempted to show in this study, the development of different types of transplane images—i.e. those images that transcend the linear-perspectival projection onto the plane according to the laws of geometrical optics—is a genuine phenomenon of modernity. In modernity parallel to the development and expansion of the first technological-transplane images of stereoscopy, a break with linear perspective in visual arts can also be recorded. However, while painting was taking its own planar materiality into consideration (see Foucault 2009 on Manet), stereoscopy had to deal with the analysis and the control of space as well as with the commercialization of space in the emerging society of the spectacle.

The theoretical and methodological point of departure for this book was Jonathan Crary's *Techniques of the Observer*, describing stereoscopy not just in a positivist-historical way, but striving to classify it within a media-historical model related to optics. As I hope to have shown, especially Crary's attempt at relating photography and stereoscopy both systematically and historically is charged with profound problems. It is in particular his notion of a successive and exclusive sequence of relatively homogeneous 'regimes of vision' that leads to massive problems.

11.1 First conclusion: Layering and not succession in media history

By way of contrast to Crary I have suggested that different optical series exist parallel to each other. This is the first conclusion of this book. One of the very marks of modernity concerning optical or visual media is the co-existence of the series of geometrical, wave, and physiological optics. This neither means that individual series cannot be more important in certain historical phases than others, nor does it mean that the series coexist without contact—one example being the epistemic inclusion of geometrical optics by wave optics, even though the series have been developing relatively autonomously. Added to this from the 1960s onwards is the displaced repetition and recombination of these three series in virtual optics. This means that the connections and reciprocal shifts of the different series are in fact the rule. The knowledge of the three (or four) optical series makes it possible to think of many different types of optical or visual technologies. Indeed, an entire host of possible methods have been tested at least experimentally. The most important effect—apart from movement—of the technologies based on the series of wave and physiological optics is the fact that more *information on space* can be stored and presented in images. However, the often very difficult path of materializing and sedimenting technological knowledge does not always quickly lead to expedient results; often it needs an enormous amount of technological and financial expenditure.

11.2 Second conclusion: The importance of the seemingly marginal transplane images for the production of space

Many transplane technologies are therefore employed in areas that are not accessible to public view; areas in which information on space is required *at any cost* like natural sciences, military, and medicine. Contrarily, in mass media narration or events (for example, sport) are being favored and therefore moving images and sound are central issues, realms in which additional information on space will hardly ever be required, especially not if the financial or other expenditures are high—this may be one of the reasons for the repeated failures of the attempts at establishing 3D movies or television as popular mass media.

Almost all previous historiographies of mass media have one problem, namely that they are either oriented exclusively on the system of mass media[2] and/or on that of the arts. However, transplane visual technologies are seldom found as mass media and—as I have shown with some cases—only rarely in the arts. Also, Crary's assessment that the stereoscope became obsolete around 1900 attests to the fact that many of these technologies are rated as peripheral or having disappeared, although many of these seemingly failed or marginalized peripherals and indirect routes of media history are not quite as marginal as it seems at first glance. In different institutional contexts, different transplane visual methods have been used for different purposes thereby changing the institutional contexts themselves. Photo sculpture resurfaces in rapid prototyping of quite ordinary industrial processes; Lippmann photography can be found on high security credentials; stereoscopy is present in data glasses of fighter pilots, in medical visualization, in bubble chambers, computer games and virtual realities; holography is used in scanner cash registers, in bubble chambers, on banknotes or in materials testing; volumetric displays (soon?) may be adopted in traffic control units, medical visualization or in radar analysis; recently, integral photography has been made applicable for the acquisition of spatial data for computers and is used in so-called light field cameras or as a new display technology. Very significantly in connection with the spreading of computers, transplane methods have often been once again utilized in virtually shifted ways.

Constricting the field of optical media to the conspicuous cases not only limits it quantitatively but also qualitatively. As one may say, despite the (according to Lefebvre and, considering the history of transplane images, quite obvious) increased production of space in modernity, the histories of optical media are curiously centered on time and movement—maybe precisely *because* they are histories. These histories thus also lack the *political* dimension of the production of space by way of the increased use of transplane images in different spatial and/or physical practices of control—as is ideologically manifested in the most bizarre way in the utilization of the 'Raumbild' in the Third Reich.

11.3 Third conclusion: the difference of optical and visual media. Anthropomorphic vs. non-anthropomorphic media models

These historiographies could not formulate a clear picture of the differentiation of visual and optical media simply because they only involved the publicly visible optical media intended for visual consumption, be it by the 'masses' or by isolated 'connoisseurs.' All optical technologies as a matter of course seemed to be addressed to the eyes of viewers—and in this sense they were visual. But it becomes quite clear when dealing with holography that optical media, i.e. those that transfer and/or store and/or process optical information, do not necessarily have to be visual media that are addressed to the eye and its conventions of viewing.[3] Considering this necessary differentiation something else becomes clear. In his review of Ulrike Hick's study *Geschichte der optischen Medien* (history of optical media), Peter Geimer has asked the following question:

> Do we consider technical media in Marshall McLuhan's sense anthropologically, e.g., as an extension and externalization of the human senses? Or do we conversely maintain in Friedrich Kittler's sense that the development of technical

> media is following its own genealogy that cannot be grasped by anthropomorphisms? (Geimer 2000. See Kittler 2010, 29–31)

The question then would be which methodological design would make sense for describing optical media. One would have to choose one and then courageously structure the material according to it. However, to the same degree as the model introduced here repudiates the reciprocal exclusion of different and epochal paradigms or regimes supporting the coexistence of parallel and frequently cross-linked optical series, the opposition between the anthropomorphic and non-anthropomorphic descriptions of technical media (see Winkler 2000) will also lose its exclusive poignancy. Technologies like stereoscopy that historically rest on the knowledge of the specificities of human vision—namely the series of physiological optics—can be described indeed as 'externalizations' to the extent that the knowledge (for example, on binocular difference) of human bodies is presupposed by their construction. Regarding a method like Lippmann photography—based on a detailed and mathematically formalized knowledge about the wave characteristics of light but which does not at all presuppose any knowledge of the characteristics of human perception[4]—one can conversely talk of a non-anthropomorphic genesis. This is not meant to say that no person has contributed to the creation of this technology (humans were part of it in Kittler's model of media-historical escalation as well—even if only in the form of the military; see Schröter 2004g) but in the sense that no knowledge about the "Man-form" (Deleuze 2011, 102) was necessary to conceptualize this technology. This means that instead of deciding a priori whether *all* technologies are externalizations *or* whether they have a non-anthropomorphic genealogy, we would need to analyze which knowledge in a concrete historical manner—of the prevailing optical series as well as chemical, technological and electronic knowledge—has sedimented into which technologies pressured by which concrete and "urgent" historical "needs" (Foucault 1980, 195).[5] From this point of view, optical media—and a fortiori all media technologies—have to be located in a *continuum* of possible links between anthropomorphic and non-anthropomorphic forms of knowledge and materials.[6]

11.4 Fourth conclusion: Critique of the planocentric notion of the image

"In any case, revising the notion of the image also means revising the notion of sculpture. If the notion of sculpture was finally reflected upon, different from and relating to the notion of the image, it could convey new impulses for determining what an image is," Elisabeth von Samsonow (2007, 282) has recently argued. It is not my claim having revised the notion of the image and in addition that of sculpture. However, it is my fourth contribution to the discussion to attempt drawing these terms closer to each other since transplane images (as is suggested by the label "three dimensional images" or "3D" for short) cannot be seamlessly subsumed under a notion of the image that is mostly characterized by the plane. As Charlotte Posenenske has shown, it is necessary to understand also in the theory of images that the boundaries of the plane have to be transgressed without completely abandoning them.

It would be necessary to dissolve the strict opposition between image and space[7] in favor of a continuum between the most planar, monochrome and the most sculptural images (up to sculpture itself). Along this axis the different configurations of planar arrangement and spatiality could be analyzed regarding their media aesthetic and functional implications. Thus, Boehm's "paradox of the planar depth" (1994c, 33) that he called an exemplary case in point for iconic difference could be differentiated and would not remain a simple conflict between planimetric and linear perspectival organization.

This differentiation would also force us to differentiate the 'observer' (or 'viewer'), so much heralded in the scholarly debates of art history and the theory of images. In planocentric discourses the viewer continues to be a static, monocular eye, even if it is being guided by the organization of the picture plane to move along the surface. Herein one can recognize the parentage of the planocentric discourse from the pictorial forms of the Renaissance as well as from modernist discourse (see Glaubitz and Schröter 2004). The modernist revolution against perspectival images even underlined the importance of the plane. Looking at the historical development, it is no surprise that currently the much-discussed 'image' continues to be connected pivotally with the notion of the plane.

In 2003, Stefan Majetschak wrote a paper in which he attempted bringing together several considerations concerning a transdisciplinary notion of the image. He expressly urges that such a concept would need to be neutral first with regard to functional and artistic images and secondly with regard to certain media.[8] But in *one* respect his targeted general notion of the image is not neutral. He maintains:

> If in this paper I have been asking for a general concept that is able to encompass all the various phenomena of pictoriality, then here the term in the more narrow sense refers to *usually planar* visual shapes throughout the complete range of their appearances—from fresco or classical panel painting to digitally encoded computer graphics. (2003, 27, n. 16; my emphasis)

Even though variety should be considered, the image is nevertheless only related "in the more narrow sense" to the 'ordinary'—and in the end this means "*planar*"—phenomena. The "general concept" is defined from the start as the "sacrosanct plane" (Boehm 1994b, 332). That the image is something that can only be understood as a continuum *between* plane and space—between 2D and 3D—is being repressed and that Majetschak is relegating this stipulation to a footnote only underlines this.

But we also have to take the mobility of the viewers' eyes and therefore their corporeality into consideration. This is not only a criticism that is made from feminist points of view;[9] it also becomes essential in order to understand the specificities of visibility of transplane images. Here already the long tradition of sculptural theory—but also the debate on minimalism—offers terms like 'intended viewpoints,' 'volume,' 'surface' or 'spatial orientation' that could at least be applied to holographic and volumetric images.[10] Yuri Denisyuk had already noted an "analogy between holography and sculpture" (1984, 75) in 1978. And Rosalind Krauss (1982, 314) has pointed to the analogy between the movements of the eye feeling its way into the depth of the different levels of the image in stereoscopy and the movements when walking. In the case of multiplex holography discussed before, the image is moving when the viewers are moving. Depending on the movement of the viewers even the difference between static and moving image is becoming permeable (see Schröter 2011). Here as well a differentiated continuum between images that indeed imply a static monocular viewer (like certain linear perspectival constructions) to those that imply a mobile, binocular viewer (like, for example, sculptures or holograms) would ultimately have to be taken as a basis.

Crary's argument that the observer in modernity is an embodied observer and therefore becomes the object of certain disciplinary procedures (in the sense of Foucault) making him or her an effective consumer of the spectacle of mass media is convincing. But it has to be taken into account that there is not only the series of physiological optics examining the bodily functions regarding their subsequent functionalization for media consumption. The observer implied in the set-up of the camera obscura—geometrical optics—still coexists. And furthermore, there are types of images like holography that seem to imply an embodied observer unlike the type of embodied observer implied by physiological optics. The least one can say is that in modernity there are several different types of observers—with varying and perhaps often contradictory politics. But contrary to Crary's insistence on the disappearance of the paradigm of the camera obscura, there remains the plane as the central discursive figure. Only by analyzing and criticizing planocentric discourse does the plurality of different forms of images become visible.

Majetschak has presented a quite conclusive definition for 'image':

> An image . . . is a texture of markers inserted into the latent forms of any arbitrary medium; this texture contains internal differentiations that in certain contextual conditions can be viewed *as* an analog notation for one option of ordering visual reality among other possible realizations of visuality. (Majetschak 2003, 43)

Contrary to his own self-limitation of the selection of pictorial phenomena quoted above, this proposal in no way implies centering the concept of 'image' on the plane. Even if one cannot bring oneself to the conclusion that "the manipulation of space [could], as a title . . . well replace the threadbare concept of image" (Kittler 2001, 43) I suggest that any planocentric limitation of the concept of 'image' should be avoided by every future scholarly discussion in the theory of images.

Notes

1 See in detail De Duve (1996, 199–280).

2 As the subtitle of their book specifies, the impressive study by Rusch, Schanze and Schwering (2007) remains bound to "Film—Radio—TV—Computer," i.e. to mass media. Not even photography is included.

3 This is not only true for optical/visual media, but also for those operating with sound (see Volmar 2007); a similar differentiation would also have to be made here—for example sonic/auditive. An example of a medium operating with sound not being addressed to human ears was the mercury-delay-storage of very early computers, see Coy (2007).

4 See Connes (1987, 158) on Lippmann photography: "The vagaries of human vision . . . are not even considered." One general remark has to be made which I made already in Chapter 1: Of course all images are in a sense related to human perception because they are made to be viewed (in photography, for example, the chemical emulsions are made to be sensitive to visible light). But insofar as this is true for every image it is a useless truism. One can still differentiate between images which are based on physical knowledge about light and those which are based on knowledge of perception in the strict sense.

5 Crary (1990, 136) could not decide between a "fully embodied viewer" simultaneously with a "denial of the body." But perhaps there is no need to make this decision at all.

6 See Latour (1991), Akrich (1992), and Law (1992).

7 Of course perspective is a way of connecting image and space – but it's just *one* way and the whole field of transplane images shows that there are a lot more ways to connect image and space.

8 See Majetschak (2003, 30). On the difference between functional and artistic images see also Majetschak (2005).

9 See Williams (1995); Hentschel (2001).

10 Regarding virtual pictorial spaces these considerations can be found in some of the contributions in Winter, Schröter and Spies (2006).

BIBLIOGRAPHY

Adam, Peter. 1992. *Art of the Third Reich*. New York: H.N Abrams.

Adcock, Craig E. 1983. *Marcel Duchamp's Notes from the "Large Glass": An N-dimensional Analysis*. Ann Arbor, MI: UMI Research Press.

Adelmann, Ralf. 2003. "Friedrich Kittler: Optische Medien. Berliner Vorlesung 1999." *Sehepunkte. Rezensionsjournal für die Geschichtswissenschaften* 11 (3). http://www.sehepunkte.de/2003/11/pdf/2705.pdf [last accessed August 14, 2013].

Adorno, Theodor W. 1990. "The Form of the Phonograph Record." Translated by Thomas Y. Levin. *October* 55: 56–61.

Aggarwal, J. K. and H. C. Chien. 1989. "3-D Structures from 2-D Images." In *Advances in Machine Vision*, edited by Jorge L. C. Sanz, 64–121. New York: Springer.

Aitken, Jane Andrews. 1986. *Renaissance Perspective: Its Mathematical Source and Sanction* (Phd dissertation). Harvard University.

Akrich, Madeleine. 1992. "The De-Scription of Technical Objects." In *Shaping Technology/Building Society: Studies in Sociotechnical Change*, edited by Wiebe E. Bijker and John Law, 205–24. Cambridge, MA: MIT Press.

Alberti, Leon Battista. 1972a. "De Pictura: On Painting." In *On Painting and On Sculpture*, edited by Cecil Grayson, 31–116. London: Phaidon Press.

—— 1972b. "De Statua: On Sculpture." In *On Painting and On Sculpture*, edited by Cecil Grayson, 117–42. London: Phaidon Press.

—— 2000. *Das Standbild. Die Malkunst. Grundlagen der Malerei*, edited by Oskar Bätschmann, Christoph Schäublin and Kristine Patz. Darmstadt: Wiss. Buchges.

—— 2011. *On Painting: A New Translation and Critical Edition*, translated by Rocco Sinisgalli. Cambridge: Cambridge University Press.

Alpers, Svetlana. 1983. *The Art of Describing: Dutch Art in the Seventeenth Century*. Chicago: University Press.

Alscher, Ludger, Günter Feist, Peter H. Feist and Peter Junghanns. 1983. *Lexikon der Kunst: Architektur, Bildende Kunst, Angewandte Kunst,*

Industrieformgestaltung, Kunsttheorie. Vol. 4 of 5 vols. Westberlin: Das europäische Buch.

Amadesi, S., A. D'Altorio and D. Paoletti. 1982. "Sandwich Holography for Painting Diagnostics." *Applied Optics* 21 (11): 1889–90.

Amadesi, S., F. Gori, R. Grella and G. Guattari. 1974. "Holographic Methods for Painting Diagnostics." *Applied Optics* 13 (9): 2009–13.

Andersen, Kirstin. 1992. *Brook Taylor's Work on Linear Perspective*. New York: Springer.

Anonymous. 1870. "Das Stereoscop." *Licht. Zeitschrift für Photographie* 2: 209–12.

—— 1908. "La photographie en relief est trouvée! 'Je sais tout' interviewe le Professeur Lippmann." *Je sais tout: La revue de la découverte* 4 (43): 545–8.

—— 1935. "Für das Raumbild werben – aber wie?" *Das Raumbild: Monatszeitschrift für die gesamte Stereoskopie und ihre Grenzgebiete* 1 (8): 173–175.

—— 1948. "Raumfilmarbeit in der Sowjetunion." *Bild und Ton. Fachzeitschrift für das gesamte Gebiet der Filmtechnik* 1 (1): 10–12.

—— 1963. "Lensless Photography Uses Laser Beams to Enlarge Negatives, Microscope Slides." *The Wall Street Journal*, December 5.

—— 1984. "Marcel Duchamp." In *The Société Anonyme and the Dreier Bequest at Yale University: A Catalogue Raisonné*, edited by Robert L. Herbert, Eleanor S. Apter and Elise K. Kenney, 225–45. New Haven and London: Yale University Press.

Apel, Friedmar. 2002. "Erobert das Unsichtbare! Für Jonathan Crary ist Aufmerksamkeit ein Mittel zur Repression." *Frankfurter Allgemeine Zeitung*, August 9.

Arago, François. 1839. *Das Daguerreotyp oder die Erfindung des Daguerre, die mittelst der Camera obscura und des Sonnenmikroskops auf Flächen dargestellten Lichtbilder zu fixieren*. Stuttgart: Scheible.

Arai, Jun, Makoto Okui, Masaki Kobayashi and Fumio Okano. 2004. "Geometrical Effects of Positional Errors in Integral Photography." *Journal of the Optical Society of America* 21 (6): 951–8.

Armstrong, Carol. 1998. *Scenes in a Library: Reading the Photograph in the Book, 1843–1875*. Cambridge, MA: MIT Press.

Arnheim, Rudolf. 1933. *Film*. London: Faber & Faber.

—— 1948. "The Holes of Henry Moore: On the Function of Space in Sculpture." *The Journal of Aesthetics and Art Criticism* 7 (1): 29–38.

—— 1989. *Parables of Sun Light: Observations on Psychology, the Arts, and the Rest*. Berkeley: University of California Press.

Aschenbrenner, Claus. 1952a. "A Review of Facts and Terms Concerning the Stereoscopic Effect." *Photogrammetric Engineering* 18 (5): 818–23.

—— 1952b. "The Interpretation of Tridimensional Form from Stereo Pictures." *Photogrammetric Engineering* 18 (3): 469–72.

Asmus, J. F., G. Guattari, L. Lazzarini, G. Musumeci and R. F. Wuerker. 1973. "Holography in the Conservation of Statuary." *Studies in Conservation* 18 (2): 49–63.

Atherton, Margaret. 1997. "How to Write the History of Vision: Understanding the Relationship Between Berkeley and Descartes." In *Sites of Vision: The Discursive Construction of Sight in the History of Philosophy*, edited by David Michael Levin, 135–65. Cambridge, MA: MIT Press.

Athineos, Spyros, Nicholas P. Sgouros, Panagiotis G. Papageorgas, Dimitris E. Maroulis, Manolis S. Sangriotis and Nikiforos G. Theofanous. 2006. "Photorealistic Integral Photography Using a Ray-traced Model of Capturing Optics." *Journal of Electronic Imaging* 15 (4): 043007–1–043007–8 [*sic*].

Aufschnaiter, Paul von. 1935. "Bewegtheit und Raumbild." *Das Raumbild: Monatszeitschrift für die gesamte Stereoskopie und ihre Grenzgebiete* 1 (4): 78–9.

Aumont, Jacques. 1992. "Projektor und Pinsel. Zum Verhältnis von Malerei und Film." *Montage/av* 1 (1): 77–89.

Babington-Smith, Constance. 1985. *Air Spy. The Story of Photo Intelligence in World War II*. Falls Church, VA: American Society for Photogrammetry Foundation.

Baccei, Tom. 1993. *Magic Eye: A New Way of Looking at the World*. Vol. I. Kansas City, MO: Andrews McMeel Publishing.

Balke, Friedrich. 2002. "Der Raum der modernen Gesellschaft und die Grenzen seiner Kontrolle." In *Raum – Wissen – Macht*, edited by Rudolf Maresch and Niels Werber, 117–34. Frankfurt/M.: Suhrkamp.

Barkan, Elazar and Ronald Bush, eds. 1995. *Prehistories of the Future. The Primitivist Project and the Culture of Modernism*. Stanford, CA: Stanford University Press.

Barsy, Andor von. 1943. *Raumbild-Fotografie: Technik und Gestaltung der Stereoaufnahme*. Halle: Knapp.

Barthes, Roland. 1982. *Camera Ludica: Reflections on Photography*, translated by Richard Howard. New York: Hill and Wang.

Bassi, P., A. Loria, J. A. Meyer, P. Mittner and I. Scotoni. 1957. "Stereoscopy in Bubble Chambers." *Il Nuovo Cimento* 5 (6): 1729–38.

Batchen, Geoffrey. 1991. "Seeing Things: Vision and Modernity." *Afterimage* (September): 5–7.

—— 1993. "Enslaved Sovereign, Observed Spectator: On Jonathan Crary, Techniques of the Observer." *Continuum: The Australian Journal of Media and Culture* 6 (2): 80–94.

—— 1997. *Burning with Desire: The Conception of Photography*. Cambridge, MA: MIT Press.

Batchko, Robert G. 1992. "Volumetric Displays." *Information Display* 8 (9): 8.

Bätschmann, Oskar and Christoph Schäublin. 2000. "Einleitung: Leon Battista Alberti über das Standbild, die Malkunst und die Grundlagen der Malerei." In *Das Standbild – Die Malkunst – Grundlagen der Malerei*, by Leon Battista Alberti, edited by Oskar Bätschmann and Christoph Schäublin, 13–140. Darmstadt: Wiss. Buchges.

Bätzner, Nike, Werner Nekes and Eva Schmidt, eds. 2008. *Blickmaschinen*. Köln: DuMont.

Bauch, Kurt. 1994. "Imago." In *Was ist ein Bild?*, edited by Gottfried Boehm, 275–99. München: Fink.

Baumgartner, Hans Michael. 1972. *Kontinuität und Geschichte: Zur Kritik und Metakritik der historischen Vernunft*. Frankfurt/M.: Suhrkamp.

Becker, Andreas. 2004. *Perspektiven einer anderen Natur. Zur Geschichte und Theorie der filmischen Zeitraffung und Zeitdehnung*. Bielefeld: transcript.

Beckmann, Angelika. 1991. "Fotoskulptur. Überlegungen zu einem Bildmedium des 19. Jahrhunderts." *Fotogeschichte* 39: 3–16.

Becquerel, Edmond. 1848a. "De l'image photochromatique du spectre solaire, et des images colorées obtenues dans la chambre obscure." *Compte rendus hebdomadaires des séances de l'académie des sciences* 27: 483.

—— 1848b. "De l'image photographique colorée du spectre solaire." *Compte rendus hebdomadaires des séances de l'académie des sciences* 26: 181–3.

Beil, Benjamin. 2010. *First Person Perspectives: Point of View und figurenzentrierte Erzählformen im Film und im Computerspiel*. Münster: Lit.

Beil, Benjamin and Jens Schröter. 2011. "Die Parallelperspektive im digitalen Bild." *Zeitschrift für Medienwissenschaft* 4: 127–38.

Belloc, M. A. 1858. "The Future of Photography." *The Photographic News* 1 (2): 13–14.

Bellone, Roger and Luc Fellot. 1981. *Histoire mondiale de la photographie en couleurs*. Paris: Hachette.

Belting, Hans. 2008. *Florenz und Bagdad. Eine westöstliche Geschichte des Blicks*. München: C.H. Beck.

Benjamin, Walter. 1978. "The Work of Art in the Age of Mechanical Reproduction." In *Illuminations: Essays and Reflections*, edited by Hannah Arendt, translated by Harry Zohn, 217–52. 5th edn. New York: Schocken Books.

—— 2006. *Berlin Childhood Around 1900*, translated by Howard Eiland. Cambridge, MA: Harvard University Press.

Bensmann, Burkhard. 1989. *Raum- und Bewegungsdarstellung bei Marcel Duchamp*. (Phd dissertation) University of Kassel.

Benton, Stephen A., ed. 2001a. *Selected Papers on Three-Dimensional Displays*. Bellingham, WA: SPIE Optical Engineering Press.

—— 2001b. "Introduction." In *Selected Papers on Three-Dimensional Displays*, edited by Stephen A. Benton, xv–xxiv. Bellingham, WA: SPIE Optical Engineering Press.

Benton, Stephen A., Thomas E. Slowe, Adam B. Kropp and Steven L. Smith. 1999. "Micropolarizer-Based Multiple-Viewer Autostereoscopic Display". http://www.media.mit.edu/spi/SPIPapers/sab/upol-3D.pdf [last accessed August 14, 2013].

Benyon, Margaret. 1973. "Holography as an Art Medium." *Leonardo* 6 (1): 1–9.

—— 1995. "Holography as Art: Cornucopia." *SPIE Proceedings* 2333: 88–93.

Berchtold, Maike. 1987. *Gipsabguß und Original*. (Phd dissertation) University of Stuttgart.

Berz, Peter. 2001. *08/15 – ein Standard des 20. Jahrhunderts*. München: Fink.

—— 2009. "Bitmapped Graphics." In *Zeitkritische Medien*, edited by Axel Volmar, 127–54. Berlin: Kadmos.

Besl, Paul J. 1989. "Active Optical Range Imaging Sensors." In *Advances in Machine Vision*, edited by Jorge L. C. Sanz, 1–63. New York: Springer.

Bijker, Wiebe Eco. 1990. *The Social Construction of Technology*. (Phd dissertation) University of Twente.

Biocca, Frank. 1992. "Will Simulation Sickness Slow Down the Diffusion of Virtual Environment Technology." *Presence: Teleoperators and Virtual Environments* 1 (3): 334–43.

Bith, Fritz. 1938. "Banknotenfälscher und Raumbild." *Das Raumbild: Stereoskopisches Magazin für Zeit und Raum* 5: 113.

Bjelkhagen, Hans I. 1999a. "Lippmann Photography: Reviving an Early Colour Process." *History of Photography* 23 (3): 274–80.

—— 1999b. "New Optical Security Device Based on One-Hundred-Year-Old Photographic Technique." *Optical Engineering* 38 (1): 55–61.

—— 2002. "Super-Realistic-Looking Images Based on Colour Holography and Lippmann Photography." http://holography.co.uk/archives/Bjelkhagen/Belkhagen.pdf [last accessed August 14, 2013].

Bjelkhagen, Hans I., Tung H. Jeong and Dalibor Vukičević. 1996. "Color Reflection Holograms Recorded in a Panchromatic Ultrahigh-Resolution Single-Layer Silver Halide Emulsion." *The Journal of Imaging Science and Technology* 40 (2): 134–46.

Bjelkhagen, Hans I., Tung H. Jeong and Raymond J. Ro. 1998. "Old and Modern Lippmann Photography." *SPIE Proceedings* 3358: 72–83.

Bjelkhagen, Hans I., F. Pouyat, P. Kasper, E. E. Miranda, R. L. Sekulin, W. Venus and L. Walton. 1984. "Test of High Resolution Two-Beam Holography in a Model of the Big European Bubble Chamber, BEBC." *Nuclear Instruments and Methods in Physics Research* 220 (2–3): 300–8.

Blunck, Lars. 2008. *Duchamps Präzisionsoptik*. München: Schreiber.

Blundell, Barry G., Adam J. Schwarz and Damon K. Horrell. 1994. "Cathode Ray Sphere: A Prototype System to Display Volumetric Three-Dimensional Images." *Optical Engineering* 33 (1): 180–6.

Blundell, Barry and Adam Schwarz. 1994. "Regions of Extreme Image Distortion in Rotating-Screen Volumetric Display Systems." *Computers & Graphics* 18 (5): 643–52.

—— 2000. *Volumetric Three-Dimensional Display Systems*. New York: Wiley.

—— 2002. "The Classification of Volumetric Display Systems: Characteristics and Predictability of the Image Space." *IEEE Transactions on Visualization and Computer Graphics* 8 (1): 66–75.

Boehm, Gottfried. 1969. *Studien zur Perspektivität: Philosophie und Kunst in der Frühen Neuzeit*. Heidelberg: Winter.

—— 1977. "Plastik und plastischer Raum." In *Skulptur: Ausstellung in Münster*, 23–44. Münster: Westfälisches Landesmuseum für Kunst.

—— 1980. "Bildsinn und Sinnesorgane in Anschauung als ästhetische Kategorie." *Neue Hefte für Philosophie* (18–19): 118–32.

—— 1992. "Bilder jenseits der Bilder. Transformationen in der Kunst des 20. Jahrhunderts." In *Transform. BildObjektSkulptur im 20. Jahrhundert, Kunstmuseum und Kunsthalle Basel*, edited by Theodora Vischer, 15–21. Basel: Kunstmuseum.

—— ed. 1994a. *Was ist ein Bild?* München: Fink.

—— 1994b. "Die Bilderfrage." In *Was ist ein Bild?*, edited by Gottfried Boehm, 325–43. München: Fink.

—— 1994c. "Die Wiederkehr der Bilder." In *Was ist ein Bild?*, edited by Gottfried Boehm, 11–38. München: Fink.

—— 2004. "Jenseits der Sprache? Anmerkungen zur Logik der Bilder." In *Iconic Turn: Die neue Macht der Bilder*, edited by Christa Maar and Hubert Burda, 28–43. Köln: DuMont.

—— 2005. "Das spezifische Gewicht des Raums: Temporalität und Skulptur." In *Topos Raum: Die Aktualität des Raums in den Künsten der Gegenwart*, edited by Angela Lammert, Michael Diers, Robert Kudielka and Gert Mattenklott, 31–41. Nürnberg: Verlag für moderne Kunst.

Boehm, Gottfried and Helmut Pfotenhauer, eds. 1995. *Beschreibungskunst – Kunstbeschreibung: Ekphrasis von der Antike bis zur Gegenwart.* München: Fink.

Bogart, Michele. 1981. "Photosculpture." *Art History* 4 (1): 54–65.

Bois, Yves-Alain. 1981. "Metamorphosen der Axonometrie/ Metamorphoses of Axonometry." *Daidalos* 1: 40–58.

—— 1990. *Painting as Model.* Cambridge, MA: MIT Press.

Booker, Jeffrey. 1963. *A History of Engineering Drawing.* London: Chatto & Windus.

Bordwell, David. 1985. *Narration in the Fiction Film.* Madison, WI: University of Wisconsin Press.

Bormann, Sven. 1994. *Virtuelle Realität: Genese und Evaluation.* Bonn: Addison-Wesley.

Bosse, Abraham. 1987. *Manière universelle de Monsieur Desargues.* Alburgh: Archival Facsimiles.

Bossel, Hugo. 1909. "Herstellung von Skulpturen mit Hilfe der Kinematographie." *Die Photographische Industrie*: 376–7.

Bottomore, Stephen. 1999. "The Panicking Audience? Early Cinema and the 'Train Effect'." *Historical Journal of Film, Radio and Television* 19 (2): 177–216.

Bousso, Raphael. 2002. "The Holographic Principle." *Reviews of Modern Physics* 74: 825–74.

Braunfels-Esche, Sigrid. 1981. "Reliefs und Reliefauffassung von Adolf von Hildebrand." In *Reliefs: Formproblem zwischen Malerei und Skulptur im 20. Jahrhundert*, edited by Ernst Güse, 23–34. Bern: Benteli.

Bressa, Birgit. 2001. *Nach-Leben der Antike: Klassische Bilder des Körpers in der NS-Skulptur Arno Brekers.* (Phd dissertation) University of Tübingen. http://w210.ub.uni-tuebingen.de/dbt/volltexte/2001/234/ pdf/promotion.pdf [last accessed August 14, 2013].

Brewster, David. 1971. *The Stereoscope: Its History, Theory, and Construction, with Its Application to the Fine and Useful Arts and to Education.* New York: Morgan and Morgan.

Bringolf, Peter. 1979. "Holography and the Mass Media." *Canadian Journal of Communication* 6 (1): 3–9.

Brinkmann, Uwe. 1983. "A Laser-Based Three-Dimensional Display: This Elegant Device May Find Numerous Applications." *Lasers & Applications* (March): 55–6.

Bromberg, Joan Lisa. 1991. *The Laser in America 1950–70.* Cambridge, MA: MIT Press.

Brosch, Renate. 2000. *Krisen des Sehens: Henry James und die Veränderung der Wahrnehmung im 19. Jahrhundert.* Tübingen: Stauffenburg.

Broude, Norma. 1978. "New Light on Seurat's 'Dot': Its Relation to Photo-Mechanical Color Printing in France in the 1880's." In *Seurat in Perspective*, edited by Norma Broude, 163–75. Englewood Cliffs: Prentice-Hall.

Brunette, Peter and David Wills. 1994. "The Spatial Arts: An Interview with Jacques Derrida." In *Deconstruction and the Visual Arts: Art, Media, Architecture*, edited by Peter Brunette and David Wills, 9–32. Cambridge: Cambridge University Press.

Bryngdahl, O. and A. W. Lohmann. 1968. "Interferograms Are Image Holograms." *Journal of the Optical Society of America* 58 (1): 141–2.

Bryson, Norman. 1983. *Vision and Painting. The Logic of the Gaze*. New Haven: Yale University Press.

—— 1998a. "Books, Too, Have Their Destinies: Wenyon and Gamble's Bibliomancy." In *Bibliomancy: An Exhibition of Holograms*, edited by Susan Gamble and Michael Wenyon, 10–16. Boston: Boston Athenaeum.

—— 1998b. "Cute Futures: Mariko Mori's Techno-Enlightenment." *Parkett* 54: 76–91.

Buchloh, Benjamin. 1998. "Warburg's Paragon? The End of Collage and Photomontage in Postwar Europe." In *Deep Storage: Collecting, Storing, and Archiving in Art*, edited by Ingrid Schaffner and Geoffrey Batchen, 50–60. Munich: Prestel.

Buchwald, Jed Z. 1989. *The Rise of the Wave Theory of Light: Optical Theory and Experiment in the Early Nineteenth Century*. Chicago: University of Chicago Press.

Bunn, James H. 1981. *The Dimensionality of Signs, Tools, and Models*. Bloomington, IN: Indiana University Press.

Burkhardt, Rudolf. 1989. "Photographie und Stereoskopie als Grundlagen der Photogrammetrie." In *Stereoskopie. Technik, Wissenschaft, Kunst und Hobby*, edited by Gerhard Kemner, 33–42. Berlin: Museum für Verkehr u. Technik.

Burri, Regula Valérie. 2008. "Doing Distinctions: Boundary Work and Symbolic Capital in Radiology." *Social Studies of Science* 38 (1): 35–62.

Bush, Vannevar. 1967. *Science Is Not Enough*. New York: Morrow.

Bushart, Magdalena. 1983. *Skulptur und Macht: Figurative Plastik im Deutschland der 30er und 40er Jahre*. Berlin: Akademie der Künste.

Bussmann, Georg. 1974. "Plastik." In *Kunst im 3. Reich: Dokumente der Unterwerfung. Ausstellungskatalog*, 110–20. Frankfurt/M.: Frankfurter Kunstverein.

Cabanne, Pierre. 1971. *Dialogues with Marcel Duchamp*, translated by Ron Padgett. London: Thames and Hudson.

Cahen, Olivier. 1990. *L'image en relief: de la photographie stéréoscopique à la video 3D*. Paris: Presses de l'école des Mines.

Cao, Junqing, Yinmei Shao, Yiping Sun, Xiangning Li and Ye Ding. 1996. "Two New Phenomena of Holographic Imaging." *SPIE Proceedings* 2885: 182–8.

Carelli, Pasquale, Domenica Paoletti, Giuseppe Schirripa Spagnolo and Alfonso D'Altorio. 1991. "Holographic Contouring Method: Application to Automatic Measurements of Surface Defects in Artwork." *Optical Engineering* 30 (9): 1294–8.

Carey Lea, Matthew. 1887. "On Red and Purple Chloride, Bromide and Iodide of Silver; on Heliochromy and on the Latent Photographic Image." *The American Journal of Science* 33 (197): 349–64.

Carroll, John Millar. 1964. *The Story of the Laser*. London: Souvenir Press.

Carter, B. A. R. 1970. "Perspective." In *The Oxford Companion to Art*, edited by Harold Osborne, 840–61. Oxford: Clarendon Press.

Ceruzzi, Paul E. 1998. *A History of Modern Computing*. Cambridge, MA: MIT Press.

Chaloner, Clinton. 1997. "The Most Wonderful Experiment in the World: A History of the Cloud Chamber." *The British Journal for the History of Science* 30 (3): 357–74.

Chevalier, Charles. 1839. *Die Camera lucida: eine gründliche Anweisung über den Gebrauch dieses neuen optischen Instruments*. Quedlinburg, Leipzig: Basse.

Cindrich, Ivan. 1967. "Image Scanning by Rotation of a Hologram." *Applied Optics* 6 (9): 1531–4.

Clair, Jean. 1978a. "Duchamp and the Classical Perspectivists." *Art Forum* 16: 40–9.

—— 1978b. "Opticeries." *October* 5: 101–12.

Claus, Jürgen. 1985. *ChipppKunst. Computer, Holographie, Kybernetik, Laser*. Frankfurt/M., Berlin: Ullstein.

Clausberg, Karl. 1999. *Neuronale Kunstgeschichte: Selbstdarstellung als Gestaltungsprinzip*. Wien: Springer.

Coddington, J. L. and R. J. Schipper. 1962. "Practical Solid State Three Dimensional (3-D) Display." *IRE International Convention Record* 10 (3): 177–84.

Coe, Brian. 1979. *Farbphotographie und ihre Verfahren: Die ersten hundert Jahre in natürlichen Farben 1840–1940*. München: Laterna Magica.

Colgate, G. 1994. "Document Protection by Holograms." In *Optical Document Security*, edited by Rudolf L. Renesse, 149–67. Norwood, MA: Artech House.

Collier, Peter. 2002. "The Impact on Topographic Mapping of Developments in Land and Air Survey: 1900–1939." *Cartography and Geographic Information Science* 29 (3): 155–74.

Collier, Robert J. 1968. "Holography and Integral Photography." *Physics Today* 21 (7): 54–63.

Connes, P. 1987. "Silver Salts and Standing Waves: The History of Interference Colour Photography." *Journal of Optics (Paris)* 18 (4): 147–66.
Cotter, Holland. 1994. "Art in Review. 'Lustmord' Jenny Holzer Barbara Gladstone Gallery 99 Greene Street (near Broome Street) SoHo Through June 30." *The New York Times*, May 13.
Cotton, Aimé. 1901a. "Réseaux obtenus par la photographie des ondes stationnaires." *(Séances de la) Société Française de Physique*, Séance du 5 Juillet: 70–3.
—— 1901b. "Réseaux obtenus par la photographie des franges d'interférence." *Bulletin bimensuel de la Société Française de Physique* 164: 9–11.
Coy, Wolfgang. 2007. "Optische Digitalspeicher . . . im Kontext" presented at Das holographische Wissen, DASA Dortmund.
Coyle, Rebecca. 1990. "Holography – Art in the Space of Technology: Margaret Benyon, Paula Dawson and the Development of Holographic Arts Practice." In *Culture, Technology and Creativity in the Late Twentieth Century*, edited by Philip Hayward, 65–88. London: Libbey.
Crary, Jonathan. 1977. "Marcel Duchamp's 'The Passage from Virgin to Bride'." *Arts Magazine* 51: 96–9.
—— 1985. "Notes on the Kaleidoscope and Stereoscope." *Journal: A Contemporary Arts Magazine* 5 (Autumn): 38–41.
—— 1988a. "Modernizing Vision." In *Vision and Visuality*, edited by Hal Foster, 29–49. Seattle: Bay Press.
—— 1988b. "Techniques of the Observer." *October* 45: 3–35.
—— 1990. *Techniques of the Observer: On Vision and Modernity in the Nineteenth Century*. Cambridge, MA: MIT Press.
—— 1991. "Capital Effects." *October* 56: 121–31.
—— 1997. "Olafur Eliasson: Visionary Events." In *Olafur Eliasson*, edited by Kunsthalle Basel, n.p. Basel, Berlin: Kunsthalle Basel.
—— 1999. *Suspensions of Perception: Attention, Spectacle, and Modern Culture*. Cambridge, MA: MIT Press.
—— 2005. "Your Colour Memory: Illuminations of the Unforeseen." In *Olafur Eliasson – Minding the World*, edited by Gitte Ørskou and Olafur Eliasson, 209–25. Aarhus: ARoS Aarhus Kunstmuseum.
Curiger, Bice, ed. 2006. *The Expanded Eye: Stalking the Unseen. Kunsthaus Zürich, 6/16/2006–9/3/2006*. Ostfildern-Ruit: Hatje Cantz.
Cutrona, L. J., W. E. Vivian, E. N. Leith and G. O. Hall. 1961. "A High-Resolution Radar Combat-Surveillance System." *IRE Transactions on Military Electronics* MIL-5 (2): 127–31.
Daley, Raymond C., Laurence G. Hassebrook, Jr. Tungate, John M. Jones, Hadley T. Reisig, Timothy A. Reed, Bryan K. Williams, Jerry S.

Daugherty and Mark Bond. 1995. "Topographical Analysis with Time-Modulated Structured Light." *SPIE Proceedings* 2488: 396–407.

Damisch, Hubert. 1987. *The Origin of Perspective*. Cambridge, MA: MIT Press.

—— 2001. *La Dénivelée: à l'épreuve de la photographie*. Paris: Éd. du Seuil.

Damus, Martin. 1981. *Sozialistischer Realismus und Kunst im Nationalsozialismus*. Frankfurt/M.: Fischer-Taschenbuch-Verlag.

Daston, Lorraine and Peter Galison. 1992. "The Image of Objectivity." *Representations* 40 (Autumn): 81–128.

Dawson, Paula. 1996. *The Concrete Holographic Image: An Examination of Spatial and Temporal Properties and Their Application in a Religious Art Work*. College of Fine Arts, University of New South Wales. http://unsworks.unsw.edu.au/fapi/datastream/unsworks:484/SOURCE01 [last accessed August 14, 2013].

De Chapeaurouge, Donat. 1975. "Der Konflikt zwischen Zentralperspektive und Bedeutungsmaßstab." In *Festschrift für Georg Scheja: Zum 70. Geburtstag*, edited by Albrecht Leuteritz, 108–18. Sigmaringen: Thorbecke.

De Duve, Thierry. 1977. "A propos du Readymade." *Parachute* 7: 19–22.

—— 1991. *Pictorial Nominalism: On Marcel Duchamp's Passage from Painting to the Readymade*. Minneapolis/Oxford: University of Minnesota Press.

—— 1996. *Kant after Duchamp*. Cambridge, MA: MIT Press.

De Montebello, Roger Lannes. 1977. "Wide-Angle Integral Photography – The Integram System." In *Three Dimensional Imaging*, edited by Stephen Benton, 73–91. Bellingham, WA: SPIE Optical Engineering Press.

De Montebello, Roger Lannes. 2001. "Integral Photography (U.S.-Patent 3.503.315)." In *Selected Papers on Three-Dimensional Displays*, edited by Stephen Benton 317–21. Bellingham, WA: SPIE Optical Engineering Press.

De Saint Victor, Niépce. 1855. "Mémoire sur la gravure héliographique obtenue directement dans la chambre noire et sur quelques expériences scientifiques." *Comptes rendus hebdomadaires des séances de l'académie des sciences* 41: 549–53.

Debord, Guy. 2006. *The Society of the Spectacle*, translated by Ken Knabb. London: Rebel Press.

Decordova, Richard. 1990. "From Lumière to Pathé: The Break-Up of Perspectival Space." In *Early Cinema: Space, Frame, Narrative*, edited by Thomas Elsaesser, 76–85. London: British Film Institute.

Deecke, Thomas. 1981. "Skulptur und Fläche." In *Reliefs: Formprobleme zwischen Malerei und Skulptur im 20. Jahrhundert*, edited by Ernst-Gerhard Güse and LWL-Landesmuseum für Kunst und Kulturgeschichte Münster, 93–8. Bern: Benteli.

Deleuze, Gilles. 2011. *Foucault*, translated and edited by Séan Hand. New York: Continuum.

Deleuze, Gilles and Félix Guattari. 2004. *A Thousand Plateaus*, translated by Brian Massumi. London, New York: Continuum.

Denis, Maurice. 1996. "Definition of Neo-Traditionism." In *Theories of Modern Art. A Source of Books by Artists and Critics*, edited by Herschel Browning Chipp, 94–9. California Studies in the History of Art. Berkeley: University of California Press.

Denisyuk, Yuri. 1962. "Photographic Reconstruction of the Optical Properties of an Object in Its Own Scattered Radiation Field." *Soviet Physics Doklady* 7 (6): 543–5.

—— 1963. "On the Reproduction of the Optical Properties of an Object by the Wave Field of Its Scattered Radiation." *Optics and Spectroscopy* 14: 279–84.

—— 1978a. "Holography for Artistic Purposes with Three-dimensional Recording and Lippmann Plates." *Sov. Phys. Tech. Phys.* 23: 954–7.

—— 1978b. "Holographic Art with Recording in Three-Dimensional Media on the Basis of Lippmann Photographic Plates." *Optica Applicata* 8: 49–53.

—— 1978c. "Holographic Art with Recording in Three-Dimensional Media on the Basis of Lippmann Photographic Plates." *SPIE Proceedings* 136: 365–8.

—— 1984. *Fundamentals of Holography*. Moscow: Mir Publications.

—— 1992. "Certain Features of the Development of Display Holography in the USSR." *SPIE Proceedings* 1600: 376–86.

Denisyuk, Yuri and I. R. Protas. 1963. "Improved Lippmann Photographic Plates for Recording Stationary Light Waves." *Optics and Spectroscopy* 14: 381–3.

DePiero, Fred W. and Mohan M. Trivedi. 1996. "3-D Computer Vision Using Structured Light: Design, Calibration, and Implementation Issues." *Advances in Computers* 43: 243–78.

Derrida, Jacques. 1976. *Of Grammatology*, translated by Gayatri Chakravorti Spivak. Baltimore and London: The Johns Hopkins University Press.

Deschin, Jacob. 1963. "No-Lens Pictures: Photographic Technique Employs Light Alone." *The New York Times*, December 15.

Dickinson, H.W. 1929. *The Garreth Workshop of James Watt*. London: HMSO.

Dickson, LeRoy, G.T. Sincerbox and A.D. Wolfheimer. 1982. "Holography in the IBM 3687 Supermarket Scanner." *IBM Journal of Research and Development* 26 (2): 228–34.

Dickson, LeRoy and Glenn T. Sincerbox. 1991. “Holographic Scanners for Bar Code Readers.” In *Optical Scanning*, edited by Gerald F. Marshall, 159–211. New York: Dekker.

Didi-Huberman, Georges. 1999. *Was wir sehen blickt uns an. Zur Metapsychologie des Bildes*. München: Fink.

Dobbe, Martina. 2000a. “Bildwerke im Bild: Zur Mediatisierung von Plastik im Fernsehen.” In *Die Kunstsendung im Fernsehen der Bundesrepublik Deutschland (1953–1985). Geschichte – Typologie – Ästhetik*, edited by Gundolf Winter, Martina Dobbe and Gerd Steinmüller, 1: 335–77. Potsdam: Verlag für Berlin-Brandenburg.

—— 2000b. “Wie man Skulpturen aufnehmen soll: Konzepte und Kategorien der kunstreproduzierenden Photographie.” In *Die Kunstsendung im Fernsehen der Bundesrepublik Deutschland (1953–1985). Geschichte – Typologie – Ästhetik*, edited by Gundolf Winter, Martina Dobbe and Gerd Steinmüller, 1: 29–67. Potsdam: Verlag für Berlin-Brandenburg.

—— 2003. “Das verkörperte Auge. Einige bildwissenschaftliche Fragen an das Medium Plastik.” In *Winter-Bilder. Zwischen Motiv und Medium. Festschrift für Gundolf Winter zum 60. Geburtstag*, edited by Martina Dobbe and Peter Gendolla, 258–74. Siegen: Universitätsverlag.

Döring, Jörg. 2009. “Raumbilder 1930. Siegfried Kracauers spatiale Hermeneutik für die Frankfurter Zeitung.” In *Das Raumbild: Bilder jenseits ihrer Flächen*, edited by Gundolf Winter, Jens Schröter and Joanna Barck, 331–50. München: Fink.

Döring, Jörg and Tristan Thielmann, ed. 2008. *Spatial Turn: Das Raumparadigma in den Kultur- und Sozialwissenschaften*. Bielefeld: transcript.

Drost, Wolfgang. 1986. “Die Herausforderung des Fortschritts an die Kunst: Von der ‘technischen’ zur ‘kreativen’ Photoskulptur (Willème, Pötschke, Reissig, Selke – Kammerichs, Ceroli).” In *Fortschrittsglaube und Dekadenzbewußtsein im Europa des 19. Jahrhunderts. Literatur – Kunst – Kulturgeschichte*, edited by Wolfgang Drost, 327–46. Heidelberg: Winter.

—— 2005. “Die Photoskulptur zwischen Kunst und Industrie.” In *Recherchen eines Dilettanten zur Kunst und Literatur: Vom Manierismus bis zum ‘Fin de Siècle’*, 371–89. Siegen: Universitätsverlag.

Dubois, Philippe. 1998. *Der fotografische Akt. Versuch über ein theoretisches Dispositiv*. Amsterdam: Verlag der Kunst.

Duchamp, Marcel. 2002. *Marcel Duchamp: Museum Jean Tinguely Basel, 03/20/2002–06/30/2002*. Ostfildern-Ruit: Hatje Cantz.

Dyens, Georges M. 1989. "Holosculpture: Holography and Sculpture, Spirit and Matter." *Leonardo* 22 (3/4): 383–8.
Eco, Umberto. 1984. "Mirrors." In *Semiotics and the Philosophy of Language*, 202–26. Bloomington, IN: Indiana University Press.
—— 1986a. "Language, Power, Force." In *Travels in Hyperreality: Essays*, translated by William Weaver, 239–56. New York: Harcourt-Brace.
—— 1986b. "Travels in Hyperreality." In *Travels in Hyperreality: Essays*, translated by William Weaver, 1–58. New York: Harcourt-Brace.
Edelman, Bernard. 1979. *Ownership of the Image: Elements for a Marxist Theory of Law*. London: Routledge & Kegan Paul.
Eder, Josef Maria. 1880. "The Reactions of Chromic Acid and Chromates Upon Substances of Organic Origin, Considered with Reference to Their Uses in Photography." *Anthony's Photographic Bulletin* 11 (38): 38–42; 71–5; 111–14; 143–7; 174–9.
—— 1905. *Geschichte der Photographie*. Halle a. S.: Knapp.
—— 1978. *History of Photography*, translated by Edward Epstean. New York: Dover Publications.
—— 1979. *Geschichte der Photographie*. New York: Arno Press.
Eder, Josef Maria and G. Pizzighelli. 1881. "Beiträge zur Photochemie des Chlorsilbers." *Monatshefte für Chemie und verwandte Teile anderer Wissenschaften (Wien)* 2 (1): 33–49.
Edgerton, Samuel Y. 1975. *The Renaissance Rediscovery of Linear Perspective*. New York: Basic Books.
—— 1993. *The Heritage of Giotto's Geometry: Art and Science on the Eve of Scientific Revolution*. Ithaca and London: Cornell University Press.
Editorial. 1936. "Rückblick und Vorschau." *Das Raumbild: Monatszeitschrift für die gesamte Stereoskopie und ihre Grenzgebiete* 2 (12): 265–6.
Eichler, Jürgen and Gerhard Ackermann. 1993. *Holographie*. Berlin: Springer.
Einstein, Albert. 1923. "On the Electrodynamics of Moving Bodies." In *The Principle of Relativity: A Collection of Original Memoirs on the Special and General Theory of Relativity*, 35–65. Courier Dover Publications.
—— 1967. "On a Heuristic Point of View about the Creation and Conversion of Light." In *The Old Quantum Theory*, edited by Dirk Ter Haar, 91–107. Oxford and Braunschweig: Pergamon Press.
Eisenstein, Sergeij. 1949. "About Stereoscopic Cinema." *Penguin Film Review* 8: 35–45.
Elkins, James. 1994. *The Poetics of Perspective*. Ithaca, NY: Cornell University Press.
Engell, Lorenz. 2001. "Die genetische Funktion des Historischen in der Geschichte der Bildmedien." *Archiv für Mediengeschichte* 1: 33–56.

Engelmann, William F. 1956. "Photogrammetry Applied to Making Sculpted Portraits." *Archives internationales de photogrammétrie / International Archives of Photogrammetry* 12 (4): GV–84–GV–94.

Esposito, Elena. 1995. "Illusion und Virtualität: Kommunikative Veränderungen der Fiktion." In *Soziologie und künstliche Intelligenz: Produkte und Probleme einer Hochtechnologie*, edited by Werner Rammert, 187–216. Frankfurt/M. and New York: Campus.

—— 1998. "Fiktion und Virtualität." In *Medien, Computer, Realität. Wirklichkeitsvorstellungen und Neue Medien*, edited by Sybille Krämer, 269–96. Frankfurt/M.: Suhrkamp.

Estanave, M.E. 1906. "Dispositif de stéréophotographie et stéréoscopie à l'aide des réseaux." French Patent 371.487, filed January 24, 1906.

—— 1908a. "Dispositif de stéréophotographie et stéréoscopie à l'aide des réseaux. 2E addition au brevet d'invention No 371.487." French Patent 8.860, filed January 30, 1908.

—— 1908b. "Plaque photographique pour relief à vision directe ou plaque 'autostéréoscopique'." French Patent 392.871, filed August 1, 1908.

—— 1930. "Photographies intégrales obtenues sans objectifs." *Comptes Rendus hebdomadaires des séances de l'académie des sciences* 190: 1405–6.

Evans, R. M. 1961. "Some Notes on Maxwell's Colour Photograph." *The Journal of Photographic Science* 9: 243–6.

Evans, Robin. 1989. "Architectural Projection." In *Architecture and Its Image: Four Centuries of Architectural Representation. Works from the Collection of the Canadian Centre for Architecture*, edited by Eve Blau and Edward Kaufman, 18–35. Montréal: Centre Canadien d'Architecture.

Fahle, Oliver. 2009a. "In einem Raum: Bildtheoretische Bestimmungen der Holographie." In *Das Raumbild: Bilder jenseits ihrer Flächen*, edited by Gundolf Winter, Jens Schröter and Joanna Barck, 315–29. München: Fink.

—— 2009b. "Zwischen Bild und Ding: Holographie und die Grenze der Bildtheorie." In *Das holographische Wissen*, edited by Stefan Rieger and Jens Schröter, 123–36. Zürich: Diaphanes.

Fajans, Jack. 1992. "Xyzscope: A New Option in 3-D Display Technology." *SPIE Proceedings* 1668: 25–6.

Farinelli, Franco. 1996. "Von der Natur der Moderne: Eine Kritik der kartographischen Vernunft." In *Räumliches Denken*, edited by Dagmar Reichert, 267–300. Zürich: vdf.

Favalora, G. E. 2005. "Volumetric 3D Displays and Application Infrastructure." *Computer* 38 (8): 37–44.

Fawcett, Trevor. 1986. "Graphic versus Photographic in the 19th Century Reproduction." *Art History* 9 (2): 185–212.

—— 1987. "Plane Surfaces and Solid Bodies: Reproducing Three-Dimensional Art in the Nineteenth Century." *Visual Resources* 4 (1): 1–23.

Fink, Daniel A. 1971. "Vermeer's Use of the Camera Obscura – A Comparative Study." *The Art Bulletin* 53 (4): 493–505.

Fink-Eitel, Hinrich. 1989. *Foucault zur Einführung*. Hamburg: Junius.

Fiorentini, Erna. 2004. "Subjective Objective: The Camera Lucida and Protomodern Observers." *Bildwelten des Wissens. Kunsthistorisches Jahrbuch für Bildkritik* 2 (2): 58–66.

Firth, Ian Mason. 1972. *Holography and Computer Generated Holograms*. London: Mills and Boon.

Fitzner, Sebastian. 2008. "'Raumrausch und Raumsehnsucht'. Zur Inszenierung der Stereofotografie im Dritten Reich." *Fotogeschichte* 28 (109): 25–37.

Flusser, Vilém. 1993. *Gesten. Versuch einer Phänomenologie*. Frankfurt/M.: Fischer.

—— 2000. *Towards a Philosophy of Photography*, translated by Anthony Mathews. London: Reaktion Books.

Fohrmann, Jürgen. 2001. "Medien der Präsenz – Einleitung." In *Medien der Präsenz: Museum, Bildung und Wissenschaft im 19. Jahrhundert*, edited by Jürgen Fohrmann, Andrea Schütte and Wilhelm Vosskamp, 7–10. Köln: DuMont.

Foley, James D., Andries van Dam and Steven K. Feiner. 1997. *Computer Graphics: Principles and Practice*. Boston: Addison-Wesley.

Foster, Hal. 1996. *The Return of the Real: The Avant-Garde at the End of the Century*. Cambridge, MA: MIT Press.

Foucault, Michel. 1966. *Les mots et les choses*. Paris: Gallimard.

—— 1969. *L'archéologie du savoir*. Paris: Gallimard.

—— 1972. *The Archaeology of Knowledge and the Discourse on Language*, translated by A. M. Sheridan Smith. New York: Pantheon Books.

—— 1975. *The Birth of the Clinic: An Archaeology of Medical Perception*, translated by A. M. Sheridan Smith. New York: Vintage.

—— 1980. "The Confession of the Flesh." In *Power/Knowledge: Selected Interviews and Other Writings 1972–1977*, edited by Colin Gordon, translated by Colin Gordon, Leo Marshall, John Mepham and Kate Soper, 194–228. New York: Pantheon Books.

—— 1984. "Nietzsche, Genealogy, History." In *The Foucault Reader*, edited by Paul Rabinow, 76–100. New York: Pantheon Books.

—— 1994. *The Order of Things: An Archaeology of the Human Sciences*. New York: Random House.

—— 1998. "Different Spaces." In *Aesthetics, Method, and Epistemology*, edited by James D. Faubion, 175–86. New York: The New Press.

—— 2009. *Manet and the Object of Painting*, translated by Matthew Barr. London: Tate Publishing.

Fournier, Jean-Marc and P. L. Burnett. 1994. "Color Rendition and Archival Properties of Lippmann Photographs." *The Journal of Imaging Science and Technology* 38 (6): 507–12.

Fournier, Jean-Marc, Gilbert Tribillon and Jean-Charles Vienot. 1977. "Recording of Large Size Holograms in Photographic Emulsion; Image Reconstruction." In *Three Dimensional Imaging*, edited by Stephen Benton, 116–21. Bellingham, WA: SPIE Optical Engineering Press.

Fox, Mark. 2006. *Quantum Optics: An Introduction*. Oxford: Oxford University Press.

Francastel, Pierre. 1952. *Peinture et société: Naissance et destruction d'un espace plastique de la Renaissance au Cubisme*. Lyon: Audin.

Françon, Maurice. 1974. *Holography*. New York and London: Academic Press.

Frank, Manfred. 1989. *What Is Neostructuralism?*, translated by Sabine Wilke and Richard Gray. Minneapolis: University of Minnesota Press.

Frankel, Eugene. 1976. "Corpuscular Optics and the Wave Theory of Light: The Science and Politics of a Revolution in Physics." *Social Studies of Science* 6 (2): 141–84.

Freitag, Ulrich. 1992. "Semiotik und Kartographie." In *Kartographische Konzeptionen: Beiträge zur theoretischen und praktischen Kartographie*, 1–19. Berlin: self-published. Fachbereich Geowissenschaften, Freie Universität Berlin.

Frey, Gerhard. 1967. *Die Mathematisierung unserer Welt*. Stuttgart: Kohlhammer.

Fried, Michael. 1968. "Art and Objecthood." In *Minimal Art: A Critical Anthology*, edited by Gregory Battcock, 116–47. New York: E. P. Dutton.

Friesem, A. A. and Yaakov Amitai. 1996. "Planar Diffractive Elements and Compact Optics." In *Trends in Optics: Research, Developments and Applications*, edited by Anna Consortini, 125–44. San Diego, CA: Academic Press.

Frieß, Peter. 1993. *Kunst und Maschine: 500 Jahre Maschinenlinien in Bild und Skulptur*. München: Deutscher. Kunstverlag.

Frizot, Michel, ed. 1998. *A New History of Photography*. London: Könemann.

—— 2000a. "Lenticular Screen Systems and Michel Bonnet's Process." In *Paris in 3D*, edited by Françoise Reynaud, Catherine Tambrun and Kim Timby, 170–91. London: Booth-Clibborn Editions.

—— 2000b. "Line Screen Systems." In *Paris in 3D*, edited by Françoise Reynaud, Catherine Tambrun and Kim Timby, 153–8. London: Booth-Clibborn Editions.

—— 2000c. "Photostéréosynthèse: A New Approach to 3-D Photography." In *Paris in 3D*, edited by Françoise Reynaud, Catherine Tambrun and Kim Timby, 145–9. London: Booth-Clibborn Editions.

Furness, Thomas A. 1986. "The Super Cockpit and Its Human Factors Challenges." *Proceedings of the Human Factors and Ergonomics Society Annual Meeting* 30 (1): 48–52.

Gabor, Dennis. 1944. "System of Photography and Projection in Relief." US Patent 2351032, filed June 13, 1944.

—— 1948. "A New Microscopic Principle." *Nature* 161 (4098): 777–8.

—— 1949a. "Method of Obtaining Enlarged Images." US Patent 2492738, filed December 27, 1949.

—— 1949b. "Microscopy by Reconstructed Wave-Fronts." *Proceedings of the Royal Society of London, Series A. Mathematical and Physical Science* 197: 454–87.

Gabor, Dennis, Winston Kock and George Stroke. 1971. "Holography: The Fundamentals, Properties and Applications of Holograms Are Reviewed." *Science* 173 (3991): 11–23.

Gaedicke, Johannes. 1900. "Über das Selke'sche Photoskulptur-Verfahren unter Vorführung von Experimenten." *Verhandlungen des Vereins zur Beförderung des Gewerb[e]fleißes* 79: 61–7.

Galison, Peter. 1997. *Image and Logic: A Material Culture of Microphysics*. Chicago: University of Chicago Press.

—— 1998. "Judgment Against Objectivity." In *Picturing Science, Producing Art*, edited by Caroline A. Jones and Peter Galison, 327–59. New York: Routledge.

Gall, Jean-Luc. 1997. "Photo/sculpture: L'invention de François Willème." *Études photographiques* (3). http://etudesphotographiques.revues.org/index95.html [last accessed August 14, 2013].

Ganis, William V. 2004. "Digital Sculpture: Ars Ex Machina." *Sculpture: A Publication of the International Sculpture Center* 23 (8). http://www.sculpture.org/documents/scmag04/sept04/rapidproto/sept04_rapidproto.shtml [last accessed August 27, 2013].

Gates, J. W. C. 1971. "Holography, Industry and the Rebirth of Optics." *Review of Physics in Technology* 2 (3): 173–91.

Geimer, Peter. 2000. "Ulrike Hick: Eine Geschichte der optischen Medien". Review. http://swbplus.bsz-bw.de/bsz070847231rez.html [last accessed August 14, 2013].

—— 2001. "Photographie und was sie nicht gewesen ist." In *Wahrnehmung der Natur. Natur der Wahrnehmung. Studien zur Geschichte visueller Kultur um 1800*, edited by Gabriele Dürbeck and Bettina Gockel, 135–49. Dresden: Verlag der Kunst.

—— 2002. "Was ist kein Bild? Zur 'Störung der Verweisung'." In *Ordnungen der Sichtbarkeit. Fotografie in Wissenschaft, Kunst und Technologie*, edited by Peter Geimer, 313–41. Frankfurt/M: Suhrkamp.

Gendolla, Peter and Jörgen Schäfer, eds. 2007. *The Aesthetics of Net Literature: Writing, Reading and Playing in Programmable Media*. Bielefeld: transcript.

Georgiev, Todor and Chintan Intwala. 2003. "Light Field Camera Design for Integral View Photography." http://www.tgeorgiev.net/IntegralView.pdf [last accessed August 14, 2013].

Gern, Pitter. 1939. "Der Führer besucht den Raumbild-Verlag." *Das Raumbild: Stereoskopisches Magazin für Zeit und Raum* 7: 145–9.

Gershenfeld, Neil. 2005. *FAB: The Coming Revolution on Your Desktop – from Personal Computers to Personal Fabrication*. New York: Basic Books.

Gerstner, Karl. 2003. *Marcel Duchamp: Tu m'. Rätsel über Rätsel*. Ostfildern-Ruit: Hatje Cantz.

Getty Museum. 2002. *William Henry Fox Talbot: Photographs from the J. Paul Getty Museum*. Los Angeles: The J. Paul Getty Museum.

Gibson, James J. 1954. "A Theory of Pictorial Perception." *Educational Technology Research and Development* 2 (1): 3–23.

Gierloff-Emden, Hans Günter. 1957. "Bedeutung und Anwendung der Stereophotogrammetrie." In *Photographie und Kinematographie: Grundlagen und Anwendung in der Wissenschaft*, edited by Herbert Schober, 210–16. Hamburg: Wesemeyer.

Glaubitz, Nicola and Jens Schröter. 2004. "Quälende Kuben und beruhigende Tableaus: Fragmente einer Diskursgeschichte des Flächen- und des Raumbildes." *Sprache+Literatur* 35 (1): 33–63.

Glaubitz, Nicola, Henning Groscurth, Katja Hoffmann, Jörgen Schäfer, Jens Schröter, Gregor Schwering and Jochen Venus. 2011. *Eine Theorie der Medienumbrüche 1900/2000*. Siegen: Universitätsverlag.

Goethe, Johann Wolfgang von. 1989. *Sämtliche Werke nach Epochen seines Schaffens*, edited by Karl Richter and Peter Schmidt. Vol. 10: Zur Farbenlehre (1810). München: Hanser.

—— 2000. *Theory of Colours*, translated by Charles Lock Eastlake. 13th edn. Cambridge, MA and London: MIT Press.

Gombrich, Ernst H. 1960. *Art and Illusion: A Study in the Psychology of Pictorial Representation*. New York: Pantheon Books.

—— 1973. "Illusion and Art." In *Illusion in Nature and Art*, edited by R. L. Gregory and Ernst H. Gombrich, 193–244. London: Duckworth.

—— 1982. *The Image and the Eye: Further Studies in the Psychology of Pictorial Representation*. Oxford: Phaidon.

Gosser, H. Mark. 1977. *Selected Attempts at Stereoscopic Moving Pictures and Their Relationship to the Development of Motion Picture Technology, 1852–1903*. New York: Arno Press.

Gottdiener, M. 1987. "Space as a Force of Production: Contribution to the Debate on Realism, Capitalism and Space." *International Journal of Urban and Regional Research* 11 (3): 405–16.

Goussot, M. 1923. "La photographie aérienne." *Revue militaire française*: 27–36; 168–88.

Goux, Jean-Joseph. 1985. "Descartes et la perspective." *L'esprit créateur* 25 (1): 10–29.

Grab, Christoph. 1993. "Event Display." In *Raum und Verfahren*, edited by Jörg Huber and Alois Martin Müller, 189–204. Basel: Stroemfeld/ Roter Stern.

Gramelsberger, Gabriele. 2010. *Computerexperimente: Zum Wandel der Wissenschaft im Zeitalter des Computers*. Bielefeld: transcript.

Gramelsberger, Gabriele, ed. 2011. *From Science to Computational Science: Studies in the History of Computing and its Influence on Today's Sciences*. Zürich: Diaphanes.

Grant, R. M. and G. M. Brown. 1969. "Holographic Nondestructive Testing (HNDT)." *Materials Evaluation* 27: 79–84.

Greenberg, Clement. 1978. "Modernist Painting." In *Esthetics Contemporary*, edited by Richard Kostelanetz, 198–206. Buffalo, NY: Prometheus Books.

—— 1988a. "The Camera's Glass Eye: Review of an Exhibition of Edward Weston." In *The Collected Essays and Criticism, Volume 2: Arrogant Purpose, 1945–1949*, 60–3. Chicago: University of Chicago Press.

—— 1988b. "Review of the Exhibition Collage." In *The Collected Essays and Criticism, Volume 2: Arrogant Purpose, 1945–1949*, 259–62. Chicago: University of Chicago Press.

—— 1992. "Towards a Newer Laocoon." In *The Collected Essays and Criticism, Volume 1: Perceptions and Judgments, 1939–1944*, by Clement Greenberg, 23–37. Chicago: University of Chicago Press.

—— 1993. "Recentness of Sculpture." In *The Collected Essays and Criticism, Volume 4: Modernism with a Vengeance, 1957–1969*, by Clement Greenberg, 250–6. Chicago: University of Chicago Press.

Grimaldi, Francesco Maria. 1665. *Physico-Mathesis de Lvmine, coloribvs et iride, aliisqve adnexis libri duo, in quorum primo asseruntur noua experimenta . . . In secunda autem dissoluuntur argumenta in prima adducta* . . . Bononiæ: Benatius.

Gronemeyer, Nicole. 2004. *Optische Magie: Zur Geschichte der visuellen Medien in der Frühen Neuzeit*. Bielefeld: transcript.

Grynsztejn, Madeleine, Daniel Birnbaum and Michael Speaks, ed. 2004. *Olafur Eliasson*. Contemporary Artists. London: Phaidon.

Guerlac, Henry E. 1987. *Radar in World War II*. 2 vols. Los Angeles: Tomash.

Günzel, Stephan. 2007. "Raum – Topographie – Topologie." In *Topologie. Zur Raumbeschreibung in den Kultur- und Medienwissenschaften*, edited by Stephan Günzel, 13–29. Bielefeld: transcript.

Hagen, Charles. 1991. "Holograms: The Defense Resumes. A Commercial and Technical Success, but Is It Art?" *The New York Times*, November 30.

Hagen, Wolfgang. 2002. "Die Entropie der Fotografie: Skizzen zu einer Genealogie der digital-elektronischen Bildaufzeichnung." In *Paradigma Fotografie: Fotokritik am Ende des fotografischen Zeitalters 1*, edited by Herta Wolf, 195–235. Frankfurt/M.: Suhrkamp.

—— 2005. "Das dritte Bild: Kontingenzen und Zäsuren in der Genealogie des Fernsehens." In *SchnittStellen – Basler Beiträge zur Medienwissenschaft*, edited by Sigrid Schade, Thomas Sieber and Georg Christoph Tholen, 617–32. Basel: Schwabe.

Haines, K. and B. P. Hildebrand. 1965. "Contour Generation by Wavefront Reconstruction." *Physics Letters* 19 (1): 10–11.

Halle, Michael. 1997. "Autostereoscopic Displays and Computer Graphics." *Computer Graphics* 31 (2): 58–62.

Hammond, John H. 1981. *The Camera Obscura: A Chronicle*. Bristol: Hilger.

Hammond, John H. and Jill Austin. 1987. *The Camera Lucida in Art and Science*. Bristol: IOP Publications

Hansen, Fritz. 1937. "Die Stereoskopie im Dienste der Volksbildung." *Das Raumbild: Monatszeitschrift für die gesamte Stereoskopie und ihre Grenzgebiete* 3 (9): 161–3.

Haran, Kalina. 1980. "Cultural Implications of Holographic Space." *Holosphere* 9 (9): 7.

Harel, David. 2000. *Computers Ltd. What They Really Can't Do*. Oxford: Oxford University Press.

Harris, L. D., J. J. Camp, E. L. Ritman and R. A. Robb. 1986. "Three-Dimensional Display and Analysis of Tomographic Volumetric Images Utilizing a Varifocal Mirror." *IEEE Transactions on Medical Imaging* MI-5 (2): 67–72.

Hauck, Guido. 1885. *Die Grenzen zwischen Malerei und Plastik und die Gesetze des Reliefs*. Berlin: Reimer.

Haugeland, John. 1981. "Analog and Analog." *Philosophical Topics* 12 (1): 213–26.

Hayes, R. M. 1989. *3-D Movies: A History and Filmography of Stereoscopic Cinema*. Jefferson, NC: McFarland & Co Inc.

Hecht, Eugene. 1987. *Optics*. 2nd edn. Reading, MA: Addison-Wesley.

Heerden, Pieter J. van. 1963a. "Theory of Optical Information Storage in Solids." *Applied Optics* 2 (4): 393–400.

—— 1963b. "A New Optical Method of Storing and Retrieving Information." *Applied Optics* 2 (4): 387–92.

Heflinger, L. O. and R. F. Wuerker. 1969. "Holographic Contouring via Multifrequency Lasers." *Applied Physics Letters* 15 (1): 28–30.

Heidegger, Martin. 1993. "The Origin of the Work of Art." In *Basic Writings: From Being and Time (1927) to the Task of Thinking (1964)*, 139–212, edited by David Farrell Krell. San Francisco: HarperSanFrancisco.

—— 2009. "Art and Space." In *The Heidegger Reader*, edited by Günter Figal, translated by Jerome Veith, 305–9. Bloomington, IN: Indiana University Press.

Helmholtz, Hermann von. 1985. *Helmholtz's Treatise on Physiological Optics*, translated from the Third German Edition, edited by James P. C. Southall. Vol. III. The Perception of Visions. Birmingham, AL: Leslie B. Adams.

Henderson, Cyril. 1970. *Cloud and Bubble Chambers*. London: Methuen.

Henderson, Linda Dalrymple. 1983. *The Fourth Dimension and Non-Euclidean Geometry in Modern Art*. Princeton, NJ: Princeton University Press.

—— 1998. *Duchamp in Context: Science and Technology in the Large Glass and Related Works*. Princeton, NJ: Princeton University Press.

Hentschel, Linda. 2001. *Pornotopische Techniken des Betrachters: Raumwahrnehmung und Geschlechterordnung in visuellen Apparaten der Moderne*. Marburg: Jonas.

Herschel, John F. W. 1840. "On the Chemical Action of the Rays of the Solar Spectrum on Preparations of Silver and Other Substances, both Metallic and Non-Metallic, and on Some Photographic Processes." *Philosophical Transactions of the Royal Society of London* 130: 1–59.

Herve, A., K. E. Johansson, P. Lecoq, P. Olivier, J. Pothier, L. Veillet, G. Waurick and S. Tavernier. 1982. "Performance of the Holographic Bubble Chamber HOBC." *Nuclear Instruments and Methods in Physics Research* 202 (3): 417–26.

Herz, Rudolf. 1994. *Hoffmann & Hitler. Fotografie als Medium des Führer-Mythos*. München: Klinkhardt & Biermann.

Hess[e?] [sic], Walter. 2001. "Stereoscopic Picture." In *Selected Papers on Three-Dimensional Displays*, edited by Stephen A. Benton, 291–4. Bellingham, WA: SPIE Optical Engineering Press.

Hesse, Walter. 1939. "Der vollkommene plastische Film." *Kinotechnik. Zeitschrift für die Technik im Film* 21 (3): 61–7.

—— 1954. "Der stereo-parallaktoskopische Film." *Filmtechnikum: Die Fachzeitschrift für Film-, Kino- und Fernsehpraxis* 5: 114–17; 141–4.

Hick, Ulrike. 1994. "Die optische Apparatur als Wirklichkeitsgarant: Beitrag zur Geschichte der medialen Wahrnehmung." *Montage/av* 3 (1): 83–96.

—— 1999. *Geschichte der optischen Medien*. München: Fink.

Hildebrand, Adolf von. 1907. *The Problem of Form in Painting and Sculpture*. New York: G. E. Stechert & Co.

Hildebrandt, Thankmar. 1959. *Stereobilder zeichnende Geräte: Ein Leitfaden für Bauingenieure, Architekten, Maschinenbauer sowie alle Fachkreise, die mit der räumlichen Darstellung technischer Gegenstände zu tun haben*. Baden-Baden: Verlag für Angewandte Wissenschaften.

Himstedt, August. 1884. *Über Lissajous'sche Curven*. Freiburg: Lehmann.

Hiort, Tina Corinna. 2000. *X-Ray Fluorescence Holography and Multiple Energy X-Ray Holography: A Comparative Study*. Hamburg: DESY.

Hochberg, Julian. 1989. "The Perception of Moving Images." *IRIS* 5 (2): 41–68.

Hochberg, Julian and Virginia Brooks. 1996. "Movies in the Mind's Eye." In *Post-Theory: Reconstructing Film Studies*, edited by David Bordwell and Noël Carroll, 368–87. Madison, WI: University of Wisconsin Press.

Hoffmann, Christoph. 2001. "φ-Phänomen-Film: Der Kinematograph als Ereignis experimenteller Psychologie um 1900." In *Die Adresse des Mediums*, edited by Stefan Andriopoulos, Gabriele Schabacher and Eckhard Schumacher, 236–52. Köln: DuMont.

Holmes, Sir Oliver Wendell. 1859. "The Stereoscope and the Stereograph." *Atlantic Monthly* 3: 738–48.

—— 1861. "Sun-Painting and Sun Sculpture." *Atlantic Monthly* 8: 13–29.

Holzer, Jenny. 1996. *Lustmord*. Ostfildern-Ruit: Cantz.

Hünnekens, Annette. 2003. "Expanded Picture." In *Holographic Network*, edited by Dieter Jung, 56–83. Bramsche: Rasch.

Husserl, Edmund. 2005. "Modes of Reproducing and Phantasy; Image Consciousness." In *Phantasy, Image Consciousness, and Memory (1898–1925)*, translated by John B. Brough, 401–52. Dordrecht: Springer.

Hutley, M. C. 1999. "Back to the Future in Optics." *Journal of Optics A: Pure and Applied Optics* 1: 790–3.

Huygens, Christian. 1912. *Treatise on Light In Which Are Explained the Causes of That Which Occurs in Reflexion, and in Refraction and Particularly in the Strange Refraction of Iceland Crystal*, translated by Silvanus P. Thompson. London: Macmillan and Co.

Igarashi, Yutaka, Hiroshi Murata and Mitsuhiro Ueda. 1978. "3-D Display System Using a Computer Generated Integral Photograph." *Japanese Journal of Applied Physics* 17 (9): 1683–4.

Inboden, Gudrun. 2002. "'um der kunst willen jn [*sic*] heimlicher perspectiua': Karin Sanders Verräumlichungen." In *Karin Sander. Staatsgalerie Stuttgart*, 12–40. Ostfildern-Ruit: Hatje Cantz.

Innis, Harold A. 1991. "The Problem of Space." In *The Bias of Communication*, 92–131. Toronto: University of Toronto Press.

Ives, Herbert E. 1902. "A Novel Stereogram." *Journal of the Franklin Institute* 153 (1): 51–2.

—— 1908. "An Experimental Study of the Lippmann Color Photograph . . ." *The Astrophysical Journal* 27: 325–52.
—— 1930. "Parallax Panoramagrams Made with a Large Diameter Concave Mirror." *Journal of the Optical Society of America* 20: 597–600.
—— 1931. "The Projection of Parallax Panoramagrams." *Journal of the Optical Society of America* 21: 397–409.
—— 1932. "A Method of Projection in Relief and Color." *Journal of the Optical Society of America* 22 (4): 191–8.
—— 2001. "Optical Properties of a Lippmann Lenticulated Sheet." In *Selected Papers on Three-Dimensional Displays*, edited by Stephen A. Benton, 311–16. Bellingham, WA: SPIE Optical Engineering Press.
Ivins, William M. 1975. *On the Rationalization of Sight: With an Examination of Three Renaissance Texts on Perspective*. New York: Da Capo Press.
Iwanow, S. P. 1954. *Die dreidimensionale Farbfotografie*. Berlin: Aufbau.
Jacobsen, Chris Johnson. 1990. "X-Ray Holography: A History." In *X-ray Microscopy in Biology and Medicine*, edited by K. Shinohara, 167–77. Berlin: Springer.
Janin, Jules. 1839. "Le Daguérotype." [*sic*] *L'artiste* 147 (4): 145–8.
Jansson, Erik, Nils Erik Molin and Harry Sundin. 1970. "Resonances of a Violin Body Studied by Hologram Interferometry and Acoustical Methods." *Physica Scripta* 2 (6): 243–56.
Jantzen, Hans. 1938. *Über den kunstgeschichtlichen Raumbegriff*. München: Verlag der Bayerischen Akademie der Wissenschaften
Jay, Martin. 1988. "Scopic Regimes of Modernity." In *Vision and Visuality*, edited by Hal Foster, 3–27. Seattle: Bay Press.
Jensen, Homer, L. C. Graham, Leonard J. Porcello and Emmett N. Leith. 1977. "Side-Looking Airborne Radar." *Scientific American* 237 (4): 84–95.
Jensen, Julius. 1871. "Der stereoskopisch-geometrische Zeichenapparat." *Archiv für Anthropologie* 4: 233–9.
Jeong, Tung H., Paul Rudolf and Arleigh Luckett. 1966. "360° Holography." *Journal of the Optical Society of America* 56 (9): 1263–4.
Johnson, Geraldine A. 1995. *The Very Impress of the Object: Photographing Sculpture from Fox Talbot to the Present Day*. London: University College London.
Johnston, Sean. 2003. "Reconstructing the History of Holography." *SPIE Proceedings* 5005: 455–64.
—— 2004. "Holography: From Science to Subcultures." *Optics and Photonics News* 15 (7): 36–41.
—— 2005a. "Shifting Perspectives: Holography and the Emergence of Technical Communities." *Technology and Culture* 46 (1): 77–103.

—— 2005b. "From White Elephant to Nobel Prize: Dennis Gabor's Wavefront Reconstruction." *Historical Studies in the Physical and Biological Sciences* 36 (1): 35–70.

—— 2006a. *Holographic Visions: A History of New Science*. Oxford: Oxford University Press.

—— 2006b. "Absorbing New Subjects: Holography as an Analog of Photography." *Physics in Perspective* 8 (2): 164–88.

Jones, Ronald. 2001. "A Thousand Words: Thomas Ruff Talks About 'L.M.V.D.R.' " http://www.thefreelibrary.com/A+thousand+words:+Thomas+Ruff+Talks+about+%22L.M.V.D.R.%22-a080485036 [last accessed August 14, 2013].

Joseph, Stephen F. 1984. "Wheatstone's Double Vision." *History of Photography* 8 (4): 329–32.

Joyce, James. 1992. *Ulysses*. London: Penguin Books.

Joyce, Kelly. 2005. "Appealing Images: Magnetic Resonance Imaging and the Production of Authoritative Knowledge." *Social Studies of Science* 35 (3): 437–62.

Judd, Donald. 1987. "Specific Objects." In *Complete Writings 1975–1986*, 115–24. Eindhoven: Van Abbemuseum.

Judge, Arthur William. 1926. *Stereoscopic Photography: Its Application to Science, Industry and Education*. London: Chapman & Hall.

Julesz, Bela. 1960. "Binocular Depth Perception of Computer-Generated Patterns." *Bell System Technical Journal* 39 (5): 1125–62.

Jung, Dieter, ed. 2003. *Holographic Network*. Bramsche: Rasch.

Kac, Eduardo. 1989. "Holopoetry and Fractal Holopoetry: Digital Holography as an Art Medium." *Leonardo* 22 (3/4): 397–402.

—— 1993. "On Holography." In *New Media Technologies*, edited by Ross Harley, 122–39. North Ryde, NSW: Australian Film, Television and Radio School.

—— 1995a. "Beyond the Spatial Paradigm: Time and Cinematic Form in Holographic Art." *Blimp* Spring: 48–57.

—— 1995b. "Aesthetics and Representation in Holography." *SPIE Proceedings* 2333: 123–37.

Kahlau, Rudolf. 1936. "Raumbild und Schule." *Das Raumbild: Monatszeitschrift für die gesamte Stereoskopie und ihre Grenzgebiete* 2 (10): 217–18.

Kailer, Katja and Anja Bierbaum. 2002. *Girlism: Feminismus zwischen Subversion und Ausverkauf*. Berlin: Logos.

Kanolt, Clarence W. 2001. "Photographic Method and Apparatus." In *Selected Papers on Three-Dimensional Displays*, edited by Stephen Benton, 295–302. Bellingham, WA: SPIE Optical Engineering Press.

Kaplan, Sam H. 1952. "Theory of Parallax Barriers." *Journal of the Society of Motion Picture and Television Engineers* 59 (1): 11–21.

Katz, Amrom. 1948. "Aerial Photographic Equipment and Applications to Reconnaissance." *Journal of the Optical Society of America* 38 (7): 604–10.

Kelsall, Malcolm. 1983. "The Iconography of Stourhead." *Journal of the Warburg and Courtauld Institutes* 46: 133–43.

Kemp, Wolfgang. 1978. "Perspektive als Problem der Malerei des 19. Jahrhunderts." In *Kunst als Bedeutungsträger: Gedenkschrift für Günther Bandmann*, edited by Werner Busch, 405–16. Berlin: Mann.

—— 1980. "Vorwort." In *Theorie der Fotografie I. 1839–1912*, edited by Wolfgang Kemp, 9–45. München: Schirmer Mosel.

Kern, Stephen. 1983. *The Culture of Time and Space 1880–1918*. Cambridge, MA: Harvard University Press.

Ketchpel, R. D. 1963. "Direct-View Three-Dimensional Display Tube." *IEEE Transactions on Electron Devices* 10 (5): 324–8.

Kipnis, Nahum. 1991. *History of the Principle of Interference of Light*. Science Networks / Historical Studies. Basel: Birkhäuser.

Kirkpatrick, Paul and Hussein El-Sum. 1956. "Image Formation by Reconstructed Wavefronts. I. Physical Principles and Methods of Refinement." *Journal of the Optical Society of America* 46 (10): 825–31.

Kirsch, Scott. 1995. "The Incredible Shrinking World? Technology and the Production of Space." *Environment and Planning D: Society and Space* 13: 529–59.

Kitagaki, T., K. Abe, T. Akagi, Y. Chiba, K. Furuno, M. Gunji, H. Hanada, K. Hasegawa, H. Hayano and T. Hayashino. 1989. "A High Resolution Holographic Freon Bubble Chamber for the Fermilab High Energy Neutrino Experiment." *Nuclear Instruments and Methods in Physics Research Section A: Accelerators, Spectrometers, Detectors and Associated Equipment* 281 (1): 81–92.

Kittler, Friedrich A. 1990. "Real Time Analysis, Time Axis Manipulation." In *Zeit-Zeichen. Aufschübe und Interferenzen zwischen Endzeit und Echtzeit*, edited by Georg Christoph Tholen and Michael O. Scholl, 363–77. Weinheim: VCH, Acta Humaniora.

—— 1993. "Vorwort." In *Draculas Vermächtnis. Technische Schriften*, 8–10. Leipzig: Reclam.

—— 1996. "The History of Communication Media." http://www.ctheory.net/articles.aspx?id=45 [last accessed August 14, 2013].

—— 1997a. "Farben und/oder Maschinen denken." In *HyperKult: Geschichte, Theorie und Kontext digitaler Medien*, edited by Martin Warnke, Hubertus von Amelunxen, Wolfgang Coy and Georg Christoph Tholen, 83–98. Basel: Stroemfeld/Nexus.

—— 1997b. *Kunst und Technik*. Basel; Frankfurt/M.: Stroemfeld.

—— 1999. *Gramophone, Film, Typewriter*. Stanford, CA: Stanford University Press.

—— 2000. *Eine Kulturgeschichte der Kulturwissenschaft*. München: Fink.

—— 2001. "Computer Graphics: A Semi-Technical Introduction." *Grey Room* 2: 30–45.

—— 2004. "Schrift und Zahl: Die Geschichte des errechneten Bildes." In *Iconic Turn: Die neue Macht der Bilder*, edited by Hans Burda and Christa Maar, 186–203. Köln: DuMont.

—— 2010. *Optical Media: Berlin Lectures*, translated by Anthony Enns. Cambridge: Polity Press.

Klein, H. Arthur. 1970. *Holography: With an Introduction to the Optics of Diffraction, Interference, and Phase Differences*. Philadelphia: Lippincott.

Knodt, Robert. 1999. *Verfahren der Fotografie: Bilder der fotografischen Sammlung im Museum Folkwang Essen*. 2nd edn. Essen: Museum Folkwang Essen.

Koch, Wolfgang Günther. 1998. "Zum Wesen der Begriffe Zeichen, Signatur und Symbol in der Kartographie." *Kartographische Nachrichten* 48: 89–96.

Koenderink, Jan J. 1998. "Pictorial Relief." *Philosophical Transactions of the Royal Society of London. Series A: Mathematical, Physical and Engineering Sciences* 356 (1740): 1071–86.

Kofman, Sarah. 1973. *Caméra obscura de l'idéologie*. Paris: Éd. Galilée.

Kohlepp, Klaus G. 2005. "Wachstum im Wandel der Zeiten – Entwicklungsgeschichte der Kunststoffe." *Kunststoffe* (5): 22–32.

Köhnen, Ralph. 2009. *Das optische Wissen: mediologische Studien zu einer Geschichte des Sehens*. München: Fink.

Komar, Victor. 1977. "Progress on the Holographic Movie Process in the USSR." *SPIE Proceedings* 120: 127–44.

Konecny, Gottfried. 1985. "Keynote Address: The International Society for Photogrammetry and Remote Sensing – 75 Years Old, 75 Years Young." *Photogrammetric Engineering & Remote Sensing* 51 (7): 919–34.

Korn, Arthur. 1923. *Bildtelegraphie*. Sammlung Göschen. Berlin and Leipzig: de Gruyter.

Koselleck, Reinhart. 1971. "Wozu noch Historie?" *Historische Zeitschrift* 212 (1): 1–18.

—— 2003. "Raum und Geschichte." In *Zeitschichten. Studien zur Historik*, 78–96. Frankfurt/M.: Suhrkamp.

Kosenina, Alexander. 2001. "Das bewaffnete Auge. Zur poetischen Metaphorik von Mikroskop und Guckkasten." In *"Das Schöne soll sein": Aisthesis in der deutschen Literatur*, edited by Peter Heßelmann, 101–27. Bielefeld: Aisthesis.

Köster, Werner. 2002. *Die Rede über den "Raum": Zur semantischen Karriere eines deutschen Konzepts*. Heidelberg: Synchron.

Kowanda, Andreas. 1997. "Zur Gliederung des kartographischen Zeichensystems." *Kartographische Nachrichten; Organ der Deutschen Gesellschaft für Kartographie e. V., der Schweizerischen Gesellschaft für Kartographie und der österreichischen Kartographischen Kommission in der österreichischen geographischen Gesellschaft* [= *Cartography and Geographic Information News*] 47 (1): 1–6.

Kramer, Hilton. 1975. "Holography – a Technical Stunt." *The New York Times* (July 20): D1 [*sic*].

Krauss, Rosalind E. 1982. "Photography's Discursive Spaces. Landscape/View." *Art Journal* 42 (4): 311–19.

—— 1985a. "Notes on the Index: Part 1." In *The Originality of the Avant-Garde and Other Modernist Myths*, 196–209. Cambridge, MA: MIT Press.

—— 1985b. "The Originality of the Avant-Garde." In *The Originality of the Avant-Garde and Other Modernist Myths*, 151–70. 2nd edn. Cambridge, MA: MIT Press.

—— 1986. "Antivision." *October* 36: 147–54.

—— 1987. "Theories of Art after Minimalism and Pop." In *Discussions in Contemporary Culture 1*, edited by Hal Foster, 59–64. Seattle: Bay Press.

—— 1988. "The Impulse to See." In *Vision and Visuality*, edited by Hal Foster, 50–78. Seattle: Bay Press.

—— 1990. "The Blink of an Eye." In *The States of "Theory": History, Art, and Critical Discourse*, edited by David Carroll, 175–99. New York: Columbia University Press.

—— 1991. "Where Is Poppa?" In *The Definitely Unfinished Marcel Duchamp*, edited by Thierry de Duve, 433–62. Cambridge, MA: MIT Press.

—— 1993. *The Optical Unconscious*. Cambridge, MA: MIT Press.

—— 1998. "Marcel Duchamp oder das Feld des Imaginären." In *Das Photographische: Eine Theorie der Abstände*, 73–89. München: Fink.

—— 2002. "Reinventing the Medium: Introduction to Photograph." In *James Coleman*, edited by George Baker, 185–210. Cambridge, MA: MIT Press.

Kricke-Güse, Sabine and Ernst-Gerhard Güse. 1981. "Einleitung." In *Reliefs: Formprobleme zwischen Malerei und Skulptur im 20. Jahrhundert*, edited by Ernst-Gerhard Güse, 13–18. Münster: Benteli.

Krikke, Jan. 2000. "Axonometry: A Matter of Perspective." *Computer Graphics and Applications, IEEE* 20 (4): 7–11.

Krüger, Matthias. 2007. *Das Relief der Farbe. Pastose Malerei in der französischen Kunstkritik 1850–1890*. München: Deutscher Kunstverlag.

Kuchinka, Eduard. 1926. *Die Photoplastik*. Halle (Saale): Knapp.

Kümmel, Albert. 2006. "Körperkopiermaschinen. François Willèmes technomagisches Skulpturentheater (1859–1867)." In *Skulptur: zwischen Realität und Virtualität*, edited by Gundolf Winter, Jens Schröter and Christian Spies, 191–212. München: Fink.

Kümmel, Albert and Erhard Schüttpelz, eds. 2003. *Signale der Störung*. München: Fink.

Kümmel-Schnur, Albert and Jens Schröter, eds. 2008. *Äther. Ein Medium der Moderne*. Medienumbrüche. Bielefeld: transcript.

Laber, Hans. 1937. "Von Gutenberg zu Schönstein . . . Bücher, die den Raum erleben lassen: Das 'Raumbild-Werk', eine Neuerscheinung auf dem Büchermarkt." *Das Raumbild: Monatszeitschrift für die gesamte Stereoskopie und ihre Grenzgebiete* 3: 22–23.

Lacan, Jacques. 1978. *The Four Fundamental Concepts of Psychoanalysis*, translated by A. M. Sheridan Smith. New York: Norton.

Lalvani, Suren. 1996. *Photography, Vision, and the Production of Modern Bodies*. Albany: State University of New York Press.

Lange, Sigrid. 2001. "Einleitung: Die Aisthesis des Raums in der Moderne." In *Raumkonstruktionen in der Moderne: Kultur – Literatur – Film*, edited by Sigrid Lange, 7–22. Bielefeld: Aisthesis.

Larfouilloux, Jacques. 1999. *Sculpture et philosophies: perspectives philosophiques occidentales sur la sculpture et ses techniques de Socrate à Hegel*. Paris: Éd. Arguments.

Larsson, Lars Olof. 1974. *Von allen Seiten gleich schön: Studien zum Begriff der Vielansichtigkeit in der europäischen Plastik von der Renaissance bis zum Klassizismus*. Stockholm: Almqvist & Wiksell International.

Latour, Bruno. 1986. "Visualization and Cognition: Thinking with Eyes and Hands." *Knowledge and Society. Studies in the Sociology of Culture Past and Present* 6: 1–40.

—— 1991. "Technology Is Society Made Durable." In *A Sociology of Monsters: Essays on Power, Technology and Domination*, edited by John Law, 103–31. London: Routledge.

—— 1996. "Foreword: The Flat-earthers of Social Theory." In *Accounting and Science: Natural Inquiry and Commercial Reason*, edited by Michael Power, xi–xvii. Cambridge: Cambridge University Press.

—— 2005. *Reassembling the Social: An Introduction to Actor-Network-Theory*. Oxford: Oxford University Press.

Lattmann. 1969. "Raum als Traum: Hans Grimm und seine Saga von der Volkheit." In *Propheten des Nationalismus*, edited by Karl Schwedhelm, 243–63. München: List.

Law, John. 1992. "Notes on the Theory of the Actor-Network: Ordering, Strategy, and Heterogeneity." *Systems Practice* 5 (4): 379–93.

Layer, Harold A. 1979. "Stereoscopy: Where Did It Come From? Where Will It Lead?" *Exposure* 17 (3): 34–48.

—— 1989. "Holographic and Stereoscopic Space: New Research Directions." *Leonardo* 22 (3/4): 411–13.

Lefebvre, Henri. 1978. *Le mode de production étatique. De l'État* III. Paris: Union Générale d'Éditions.

—— 1991. *The Production of Space*. Oxford: Blackwell.

Lehmann, Anette Jael. 2004. "Mediated Motion: Installationsräume und performative Aisthetik am Beispiel von Olafur Eliasson." In *Performativität und Medialität*, edited by Sybille Krämer, 347–69. München: Fink.

Lehmann, Hans. 1907. "Über eine neue kornlose Platte für die Lippmann-Photographie." *Zeitschrift für wissenschaftliche Photographie* 5: 279–83.

—— 1908. "Über die Abstimmung der Lippmannplatten." *Eder's Jahrbuch für Photographie und Reproductionstechnik* 22: 157–64.

Lehmann, Matt. 1982. "Holography's Early Days at Stanford University." *Holosphere: The News Letter of Holographic Science and Technology* 11 (9): 1, 4–5.

Leith, Emmett. 1978. "Synthetic Aperture Radar." In *Optical Data Processing: Applications*, edited by David P. Casasent, 89–117. Berlin: Springer.

—— 1983. "Some Highlights in the History of Display Holography." In *Proceedings of the International Symposium on Display Holography* 1, edited by Tung H. Jeong, 1–4. Lake Forest: Holography Workshops, Lake Forest College.

—— 1996. "A Short History of the Optics Group of the Willow Run Laboratories." In *Trends in Optics: Research, Developments and Applications*, edited by Anna Consortini, 1–26. San Diego, CA: Academic Press.

—— 2003. "Reflections on the Origin and Subsequent Course of Holography." *SPIE Proceedings* 5005: 431–8.

Leith, Emmett and Juris Upatnieks. 1961. "New Techniques in Wavefront Reconstruction." *Journal of the Optical Society of America* 51 (12): 1469.

—— 1962. "Reconstructed Wavefronts and Communication Theory." *Journal of the Optical Society of America* 52 (10): 1123–30.

—— 1963a. "Wavefront Reconstruction with Continuous-Tone Transparencies." *Journal of the Optical Society of America* 53 (4): 522.

—— 1963b. "Wavefront Reconstruction with Continuous-Tone Objects." *Journal of the Optical Society of America* 53 (12): 1377–81.

—— 1964. "Wavefront Reconstruction with Diffused Illumination and Three-Dimensional Objects." *Journal of the Optical Society of America* 54 (11): 1295–301.

—— 1965. "Photography by Laser." *Scientific American* 212 (6): 24–35.
Lemke, Sieglinde. 1998. *Primitivist Modernism: Black Culture and the Origins of Transatlantic Modernism*. Oxford: Oxford University Press.
Liandrat-Guigues, Suzanne. 2002. *Cinéma et sculpture: Un aspect de la modernité des années soixante*. Paris: Harmattan.
Lightfoot, D. Tulla. 1989. "Contemporary Art-World Bias in Regard to Display Holography: New York City." *Leonardo* 22 (3/4): 419–23.
Lin, Freddie Shing-Hong, ed. 1996. *Holographic Optical Elements and Displays*. Bellingham, WA: SPIE Optical Engineering Press.
Lindberg, David C. 1981. *Theories of Vision from Al-Kindi to Kepler*. Chicago: University of Chicago Press.
Lippmann, Gabriel. 1891. "La photographie des couleurs." *Comptes rendus hebdomadaires des séances de l'académie des sciences* 112: 274–5.
—— 1894. "Sur la théorie de la photographie des couleurs simples et composées par la méthode interférentielle." *Journal de Physique* 3 (3): 97–107.
—— 1908. "Epreuves réversibles donnant la sensation du relief." *Journal de Physique théorique et appliquée* 7 (1): 821–4.
—— 1911. "Expériences sur la photographie intégrale." *Procès-verbaux et résumés de communications. Société Française de Physique*: 69.
—— 2001. "Épreuves réversibles: Photographies intégrales." In *Selected Papers on Three-Dimensional Displays*, edited by Stephen Benton, 305–10. Bellingham, WA: SPIE Optical Engineering Press.
Littfeld, Richard J., Randy Heiland and Christian R. Macedonia. 1996. "Virtual Reality Volumetric Display Techniques for Three-Dimensional Medical Ultrasound." In *Health Care in the Information Age: Medicine Meets Virtual Reality*, edited by Suzanne J. Weghorst, Hans B. Sieburg and Karen S. Morgan, 498–510. Amsterdam: IOS Press.
Lohmann, Adolf. and D. P. Paris. 1967. "Binary Fraunhofer Holograms, Generated by Computer." *Applied Optics* 6 (10): 1739–48.
Loiperdinger, Martin. 2004. "Lumiere's Arrival of the Train: Cinema's Founding Myth." *The Moving Image* 4 (1): 89–118.
Lorenz, Dieter. 1983. "Der Raumbild-Verlag Otto Schönstein: Zur Geschichte der Stereoskopie." *Kultur und Technik* 4: 210–20.
—— 1987. *Das Stereobild in Wissenschaft und Technik: Ein dreidimensionales Bilderbuch*. Köln: DFVLR.
—— 1989. "Die Stereobild- und Stereomesstechnik in der Meteorologie." In *Stereoskopie: Technik, Wissenschaft, Kunst und Hobby*, edited by Gerhard Kemner, 61–70. Berlin: Museum für Verkehr und Technik.
—— 2001. *Der Raumbild-Verlag Otto Schönstein: Zur Geschichte der Stereoskopie*. Berlin: DHM.

Lüdemann, Susanne. 1999. "Beobachtungsverhältnisse. Zur (Kunst-) Geschichte der Beobachtung zweiter Ordnung." In *Widerstände der Systemtheorie: Kulturtheoretische Analysen zum Werk von Niklas Luhmann*, edited by Albrecht Koschorke and Cornelia Vismann, 63–75. Berlin: Akademie Verlag.

Luhmann, Niklas. 1976. "Evolution und Geschichte." *Geschichte und Gesellschaft: Zeitschrift für Historische Sozialwissenschaft* 2: 284–305.

Lumière, Auguste and Louis Lumière. 1893. "Sur les procédés pour la photographie des couleurs d'après la méthode de M. Lippmann." *Bull. Soc. Franç. Phot.* 2 (9): 249–51.

Lumière, Louis. 1920. "Représentation photographique d'un solide dans l'espace Photo-stéréo-synthèse." *Comptes rendus hebdomadaires des séances de l'académie des sciences* 171: 891–6.

Lummerding, Susanne. 1998. "Darüber im Bild sein, im Bild zu sein." *Camera Austria* 62/63: 53–60.

Lüscher, [?] 1936. "Mehr Raum dem Raumbild!" *Das Raumbild: Monatszeitschrift für die gesamte Stereoskopie und ihre Grenzgebiete* 2 (2): 43.

Luzy, Émile and Charles Dupuis. 1912. "Procédé pour obtenir projections en relief." French Patent 461.600, filed October 31, 1912.

Mach, Ernst. 1896. "On the Stereoscopic Application of Roentgen's Rays." *The Monist* 6 (3): 321–3.

—— 1986. "Why Has Man Two Eyes?" In *Popular Scientific Lectures*, translated by Thomas J. McCormack; with an Introduction by Jeremy Bernstein La Salle, 66–88. Chicago: Open Court.

Mader, H. 1938. "Über Luftbildmessung: Betrachtung zu einem Senkrecht-Luftbildpaar." *Das Raumbild: Stereoskopisches Magazin für Zeit und Raum* 1 (April): 9–10.

Magnan, Kathleen F. 1996. "The Cyber-Chic of Mariko Mori." *ART Asia Pacific* 3 (2): 66–7.

Mahler, Josef. 1954. "Modern Stereo Techniques." *Photographic Science and Technique* 2 (1): 84–7.

—— 2001. "Stereoscopic Apparatus." In *Selected Papers on Three-Dimensional Displays*, edited by Stephen Benton, 232–234. Bellingham, WA: SPIE Optical Engineering Press.

Majetschak, Stefan. 2003. "Bild und Sichtbarkeit: Überlegungen zu einem transdisziplinären Bildbegriff." *Zeitschrift für Ästhetik und allgemeine Kunstwissenschaft* 48 (1): 27–45.

—— 2005. "Sichtvermerke. Über Unterschiede zwischen Kunst- und Gebrauchsbildern." In *Bild-Zeichen. Perspektiven einer Wissenschaft vom Bild*, edited by Stefan Majetschak, 97–121. München: Fink.

Maline, Sarah. 1991. "Eluding the Aegis of Science: Art Holography on Its Own." *SPIE Proceedings* 1600: 215–19.

—— 1995. "A Stranger in a Strange Land: Holography, Aesthetics and Criticism 1968–1993." *SPIE Proceedings* 2333: 103–9.

Malraux, André. 1978. *The Voices of Silence*. Princeton, NJ: Princeton University Press.

Mann, Heinz Herbert. 2000. "Optische Instrumente." In *Erkenntnis, Erfindung, Konstruktion: Studien zur Bildgeschichte von Naturwissenschaften und Technik vom 16. bis zum 19. Jahrhundert*, edited by Hans Holländer, 357–408. Berlin: Mann.

Manovich, Lev. 1996a. "The Automation of Sight: From Photography to Computer Vision." In *Electronic Culture: Technology and Visual Representation*, edited by Timothy Druckrey, 229–40. New York: Aperture.

—— 1996b. "On Totalitarian Interactivity." http://manovich.net/TEXT/totalitarian.html [last accessed August 14, 2013].

—— 2001. *The Language of New Media*. Cambridge, MA: MIT Press.

Martin, F. David. 1976. "The Autonomy of Sculpture." *The Journal of Aesthetics and Art Criticism* 34 (3): 273–86.

Marwitz, Hartmut, ed. 1990. *Praxis der Holografie: Grundlagen, Standard- und Spezialverfahren*. Ehningen bei Böblingen: Expert.

Marx, Karl. 1901. *Value, Price, and Profit: Addressed to Working Men*, edited by Eleanor Marx Aveling. New York: Labor News Company.

—— 1981. *Grundrisse: Foundations of the Critique of Political Economy*, translated by Martin Nicolaus. Harmondsworth: Penguin Books.

Maxwell, James Clerk. 1861. "On the Theory of Three Primary Colours." *Proceedings of the Royal Institution* 3 (1858–1862): 370–4.

McAllister, David F., ed. 1993. *Stereo Computer Graphics and Other True 3D Technologies*. Princeton, NJ: Princeton University Press.

McCauley, Anne. 2000. "Realism and Its Detractors." In *Paris in 3D*, edited by Françoise Reynaud, Catherine Tambrun and Kim Timby, 23–9. London: Booth-Clibborn Editions.

McCrickerd, J. T. 1972. "Comparison of Stereograms: Pinhole, Fly's Eye, and Holographic Types." *Journal of the Optical Society of America* 62 (1): 64–70.

McCrickerd, J. T. and Nicholas George. 1968. "Holographic Stereogram from Sequential Component Photographs." *Applied Physics Letters* 12 (1): 10–12.

McCurry, R. E. 1966. "Multiple Source Moiré Patterns." *Journal of Applied Physics* 37 (2): 467–72.

McKay, Herbert C. 1944. "Notes from a Laboratory." *American Photography* (September): 36–8; 44; 45; 52.

McLuhan, Marshall. 1965. *Understanding Media: The Extension of Man*. New York: McGraw-Hill.

Mehrtens, Herbert. 2003. "Bilder der Bewegung – Bewegung der Bilder. Frank B. Gilbreth und die Visualisierungstechniken des Bewegungsstudiums." *Bildwelten des Wissens. Kunsthistorisches Jahrbuch für Bildkritik* 1 (1): 44–53.

Merritt, John O. 1984. "Visual Tasks Requiring 3-D Stereoscopic Displays." *SPIE Proceedings* 462: 56–63.

Meschede, Friedrich. 2002. "1:1 vs. 1:10 oder wie Werner Meyer einer Veränderung im Werk von Karin Sander Modell stand." In *Karin Sander: Staatsgalerie Stuttgart 2002*, edited by Gudrun Inboden, 68–78. Ostfildern-Ruit: Hatje Cantz Publishers.

Metzner, [?]. 1936. "Das Raumbild im Unterricht." *Das Raumbild: Monatszeitschrift für die gesamte Stereoskopie und ihre Grenzgebiete* 2 (8): 169–71.

Meyer, Kenneth, Hugh L. Applewhite and Frank A. Biocca. 1992. "A Survey of Position Trackers." *Presence: Teleoperators and Virtual Environments* 1 (2): 173–200.

Meyer-Arendt, Jürgen R. 1984. *Introduction to Classical and Modern Optics*. Englewood Cliffs, NJ: Prentice Hall.

Michelson, Albert A. and Edward W. Morley. 1887. "On a Method of Making the Wavelength of Sodium Light the Actual and Practical Standard of Length." *The London, Edinburgh, and Dublin Philosophical Magazine and Journal of Science* (24): 463–6.

Michelson, Annette. 1973. "Anemic Cinema: Reflections on an Emblematic Work." *Artforum* 12 (2): 64–9.

Milner, Max. 2006. "Camera obscura: Im Dunkeln sehen." In *Das Unsichtbare sehen: Bildzauber, optische Medien und Literatur*, edited by Sabine Haupt and Ulrich Stadler, 19–36. Wien and New York: Ed. Voldemeer.

Mitchell, William J. T. 1994. "The Pictorial Turn." In *Picture Theory: Essays on Verbal and Visual Representation*, 11–34. Chicago: University of Chicago Press.

Mitchell, William John. 1992. *The Reconfigured Eye: Visual Truth in the Post-Photographic Era*. Cambridge, MA: MIT Press.

Mollon, J. D. 2002. "The Origins of the Concept of Interference." *Philosophical Transactions of the Royal Society of London. Series A: Mathematical, Physical and Engineering Sciences* 360 (1794): 807–19.

Mori, Mariko. 2000. "À la recherche du paradis perdu/In Search of Paradise Lost. Interview par Eleanor Heartney." *Art Press (English Edition)* 256 (April): 36–40.

Mort, Joseph. 1989. *The Anatomy of Xerography: Its Invention and Evolution*. Jefferson, NC: McFarland.

Muirhead, J. C. 1961. "Variable Focal Length Mirrors." *Review of Scientific Instruments* 32 (2): 210–11.

Müller, Axel. 1997. *Die ikonische Differenz: Das Kunstwerk als Augenblick*. München: Fink.
Müller-Tamm, Jutta. 2005. *Abstraktion als Einfühlung: Zur Denkfigur der Projektion in Psychophysiologie, Kulturtheorie, Ästhetik und Literatur der frühen Moderne*. Freiburg im Breisgau: Rombach.
Munk, Judith and Walter Munk. 1972. "Venice Hologram." *Proceedings of the American Philosophical Society Held at Philadelphia for Promoting Useful Knowledge* 116 (5): 415–42.
Musatti, C. L. 1924. "Sui Fenomeni Stereokinetici." *Archiv. Hal. Di Psicologia* 3: 105–20.
Mussman, Toby. 1967. "Marcel Duchamp's Anemic Cinema." In *The New American Cinema: A Critical Anthology*, edited by Gregory Battcock, 147–55. New York: Dutton.
Nankivell, J. F. 1963. "The Theory of Electron Stereo Microscopy." *Optik. Zeitschrift für das gesamte Gebiet der Licht- und Elektronenoptik* 20 (4): 171–98.
Nareid, Helge. 1988. "A Review of the Lippmann Colour Process." *Journal of Photographic Science* 36 (4): 140–7.
Nareid, Helge and Hans M. Pedersen. 1991. "Modeling of the Lippmann Color Process." *Journal of the Optical Society of America* 8 (2): 257–65.
Nassenstein, H., H. T. Buschmann, H. Dedden and E. Klein. 1970. "An Investigation of the Properties of Photographic Materials for Holography." In *The Engineering Uses of Holography*, edited by Elliott R. Robertson and James M. Harvey, 25–38. Cambridge: Cambridge University Press.
Nauman, Bruce. 1994. *Bruce Nauman: Exhibition Catalogue and Catalogue Raisonné*. Basel: Wiese.
Neef, Andreas, Klaus Burmeister and Stefan Krempl. 2005. *Vom Personal-Computer zum Personal-Fabricator: Points of Fab, Fabbing Society, Homo Fabber*. Hamburg: Murmann.
Neurath, Otto. 1915. "Prinzipielles zur Geschichte der Optik." *Archiv für die Geschichte der Naturwissenschaften und der Technik* 5 (1): 371–89.
Newhall, Beaumont. 1969. *Airborne Camera: The World from the Air and Outer Space*. New York: Hastings House.
Nichols, Bill and Susan J. Lederman. 1980. "Flicker and Motion in Film." In *The Cinematic Apparatus*, edited by Teresa DeLauretis and Stephen Heath, 96–105. London: Macmillan.
Nielsen, Keld. 1989. "Another Kind of Light: The Work of T. J. Seebeck and His Collaboration with Goethe. Part I." *Historical Studies in the Physical and Biological Sciences* 20 (1): 107–78.
—— 1990. "Another Kind of Light: The Work of T. J. Seebeck and His Collaboration with Goethe, Part 2." *Historical Studies in the Physical and Biological Sciences* 21 (2): 317–97.

Niépce, Nicéphore. 1839. "Notice sur l'héliographie." In *Historique et description des procédés du Daguerréotype et du Diorama*, edited by Louis Jacques Mandé Daguerre, 39–46. Paris: Giroux.

Ninio, Jacques. 2000. "Three-Dimensional Perception." In *Paris in 3D*, edited by Françoise Reynaud and Catherine Tam, 17–21. London: Booth-Clibborn Editions.

Nöth, Winfried. 1998. "Kartensemiotik und das kartographische Zeichen." *Zeitschrift für Semiotik* 20 (1/2): 25–39.

Novotny, Fritz. 2000. "Passages from Cézanne and the End of Scientific Perspective (1938)." In *The Vienna School Reader. Politics and Art Historical Method in the 1930s*, edited by Christopher S. Wood, 379–433. New York: Zone Books.

OED Online. 2013. Oxford University Press. http://www.oed.com [last accessed August 14, 2013].

Okano, Fumio, Haruo Hoshino, Jun Arai and Ichiro Yuyama. 1997. "Real-Time Pickup Method for a Three-Dimensional Image Based on Integral Photography." *Applied Optics* 36 (7): 1598–603.

Okoshi, Takanori. 1976. *Three-Dimensional Imaging Techniques*. New York: Academic Press.

—— 1980. "Three-Dimensional Displays." *Proceedings of the IEEE* 68 (5): 548–64.

Orazem, Vito. 1992. "Holography as a Material for Light: Radical Holography." *SPIE Proceedings* 1600: 160–5.

Osmundsen, Knut. 1963. "Scientist Camera Has No Lens, It Records the Photo Pattern Directly on Photographic Film." *The New York Times*, December 5.

Oster, Gerald. 1959. "Optical Art." *Applied Optics* 4 (11): 1359–69.

Otsuka, Rieko, Takeshi Hoshino and Youichi Horry. 2004. "Transpost: All-Around Display System for 3D Solid Image." *Proceedings of the ACM Symposium on Virtual Reality Software and Technology*, 187–94. New York: ACM.

Paech, Joachim. 1988. *Literatur und Film*. Stuttgart: Metzler.

—— ed. 1994. *Film, Fernsehen, Video und die Künste. Strategien der Intermedialität*. Stuttgart: Metzler.

—— 1998. "Intermedialität: Mediales Differenzial und transformative Figurationen." In *Intermedialität: Theorie und Praxis eines interdisziplinären Forschungsgebiets*, edited by Jörg Helbig, 14–30. Berlin: E. Schmidt.

—— 2003. "Überlegungen zum Dispositiv als Theorie medialer Topik." In *Der kinematographische Apparat. Geschichte und Gegenwart einer interdisziplinären Debatte*, edited by Robert F. Riesinger, 175–94. Münster: Nodus-Publ.

—— 2005. "Medienwissenschaft." In *Bildwissenschaft. Disziplinen, Themen, Methoden*, edited by Klaus Sachs-Hombach, 79–96. Frankfurt/M.: Suhrkamp.

Païni, Dominique. 2004. "Should We Put an End to Projection?", translated by Rosalind E. Krauss. *October* 110: 23–48.

Panofsky, Erwin. 1991. *Perspective as Symbolic Form*. New York: Zone Books.

Paoletti, Domenica and Giuseppe Schirripa Spagnolo. 1996. "Interferometric Methods for Artwork Diagnostics." *Progress in Optics* 35: 197–255.

Pápay, Gyula. 2005. "Kartographie." In *Bildwissenschaft. Disziplinen, Themen, Methoden*, edited by Klaus Sachs-Hombach, 281–95. Frankfurt/M.: Suhrkamp.

Parker, E. and P. R. Wallis. 1948. "Three-Dimensional Cathode-Ray Tube Displays." *Journal of the Institution of Electrical Engineers – Part III: Radio and Communication Engineering* 95 (37): 371–87.

Paul, William. 1993. "The Aesthetics of Emergence." *Film History* 5 (3): 321–55.

Pedrotti, Frank L., Leno S. Pedrotti and Leno M. Pedrotti. 1993. *Introduction to Optics*. 2nd edn. Englewood Cliffs, NJ: Prentice Hall.

Peirce, Charles S. 1998. "The Basis of Pragmatism in the Normative Science." In *The Essential Peirce: Selected Philosophical Writings. Volume 2 (1893–1913)*, edited by Peirce Edition Project, 371–97. Bloomington: Indiana University Press.

Pellerin, Denis. 1995. *La photographie stéréoscopique sous le second empire*. Paris: Bibliothèque Nationale de France.

Pennington, K. S. and P. M. Will. 1970. "A Grid-Coded Technique for Recording 3-dimensional Scenes Illuminated with Ambient Light." *Optics Communications* 2 (4): 167–9.

Pepper, Andrew. 1982. "Holography: The History of the Word." *Holosphere* 14 (1): 11.

—— 1989. "Holographic Space: A Generalised Graphic Definition." *Leonardo* 22 (3/4): 295–8.

Perkins, D. W. 1962. "Spherical Spiral Display." *Space Aeronautics* (September): 64–7.

Phillips, David. 1993. "Modern Vision." *Oxford Art Journal* 16 (1): 129–38.

Phillips, N. J., H. Heyworth and T. Hare. 1984. "On Lippmann's Photography." *The Journal of Photographic Science* 32: 158–69.

Pirenne, Maurice. 1970. *Optics, Painting and Photography*. Cambridge: Cambridge University Press.

Pizzanelli, David J. 1992. "Evolution of the Mythical Hologram." *SPIE Proceedings* 1732: 430–7.

—— 1998. "Counterfeit Holograms and Simulations." *SPIE Proceedings* 3314: 86–96.

Pole, R. V. 1967. "Three-dimensional Imagery and Holograms of Objects Illuminated in White Light." *Applied Physics Letters* 10 (1): 20–2.

Potmesil, Michael and Indranil Chakravarty. 1982. "Synthetic Image Generation with a Lens and Aperture Camera Model." *ACM Transactions on Graphics* 1 (2): 85–108.

Potts, Alex. 1998. "The Minimalist Object and the Photographic Image." In *Sculpture and Photography: Envisioning the Third Dimension*, edited by Géraldine A. Johnson, 181–98. Cambridge: Cambridge University Press.

—— 2000. *The Sculptural Imagination: Figurative, Modernist, Minimalist*. New Haven, CT: Yale University Press.

—— 2001. "Installation and Sculpture." *Oxford Art Journal* 24 (2): 5–23.

Powell, Robert L. 1970. "Discussion." In *The Engineering Uses of Holography*, edited by Elliott R. Robertson and James M. Harvey, 128–9. Cambridge: Cambridge University Press.

Powell, Robert L. and Karl A. Stetson. 1965. "Interferometric Vibration Analysis by Wavefront Reconstruction." *Journal of the Optical Society of America* 55 (12): 1593–8.

Prasad, Amit. 2007. "The (Amorphous) Anatomy of an Invention: The Case of Magnetic Resonance Imaging (MRI)." *Social Studies of Science* 37 (4): 533–60.

Prümm, Karl. 2004. "Gefährliche Augenblicke: Ernst Jünger als Medientheoretiker." In *Ernst Jünger: Politik – Mythos – Kunst*, edited by Lutz Hagestedt, 349–70. Berlin: de Gruyter.

Pulfrich, Carl. 1923. *Die Stereoskopie im Dienste der Photometrie und Pyrometrie*. Berlin: Springer.

Rallison, R. D., G. L. Heidt and Tung H. Jeong. 1987. "Holographic Scanners for Machine Vision, Printing, and Bar Code Applications." *SPIE Proceedings* 747: 17–24.

Rawson, Eric G. 1969. "Vibrating Varifocal Mirrors for 3-D Imaging." *IEEE Spectrum* 6 (9): 37–43.

Real, R. R. 1972. "Concept of 3-D Map Display with Stereo-Orthophoto." *Applied Optics* 11 (6): 1427–9.

Regener, Susanne. 1999. *Fotografische Erfassung: Zur Geschichte medialer Konstruktionen des Kriminellen*. München: Fink.

Rehkämper, Klaus. 2002. *Bilder, Ähnlichkeit und Perspektive: Auf dem Weg zu einer neuen Theorie der bildhaften Repräsentation*. Wiesbaden: Deutscher Universitäts Verlag.

Reissig, W. 1893. "Verfahren zur Herstellung von Reliefs nach plastischen Gegenständen mit Hilfe der Photographie: Patentirt [*sic*] im Deutschen Reiche vom 26. September 1893 ab." German Patent 74622, filed September 26, 1893, and issued April 14, 1894.

Remley, Kate A., Harry R. Anderson and Andreas Weisshaar. 2000. "Improving the Accuracy of Ray-tracing Techniques for Indoor Propagation Modeling." *IEEE Transactions on Vehicular Technology* 49 (6): 2350–8.

Reuscher, Günter and Dirk Holtmannspötter. 2004. *Quantenoptik: Anwendung nichtklassischen Lichts. Technologieanalyse*. Düsseldorf: Zukünftige Technologien Consulting der VDI Technologiezentrum GmbH.

Reynaud, Françoise, Catherine Tambrun and Kim Timby, ed. 2000. *Paris in 3D*. London: Booth-Clibborn Editions.

Rheinberger, Hans-Jörg. 1997. *Toward a History of Epistemic Things: Synthesizing Proteins in the Test Tube*. Stanford: Stanford University Press.

Richardson, Dorothy. 1979. "The Tunnel." In *Pilgrimage 2*, 9–288. London: Virago.

Richter, Steffen. 1980. "Die 'Deutsche Physik'." In *Naturwissenschaft, Technik und NS-Ideologie. Beiträge zur Wissenschaftsgeschichte des Dritten Reichs*, edited by Herbert Mehrtens, 116–41. Frankfurt/M.: Suhrkamp.

Rieger, Stefan. 2001. *Die Individualität der Medien: Eine Geschichte der Wissenschaften vom Menschen*. Frankfurt/M.: Suhrkamp.

—— 2002. *Die Ästhetik des Menschen. Über das Technische in Leben und Kunst*. Frankfurt/M.: Suhrkamp.

—— 2003. *Kybernetische Anthropologie: Eine Geschichte der Virtualität*. Frankfurt/M.: Suhrkamp.

—— 2009. "Holographie: Das Versprechen der Ganzheit." In *Das holographische Wissen*, edited by Stefan Rieger and Jens Schröter, 87–106. Zürich: Diaphanes.

Rieger, Stefan and Schröter, Jens, ed. 2009. *Das holographische Wissen*. Zürich: Diaphanes.

Ritter, A., O. Deussen, H. Wagener and T. Strothotte. 1997. "Holographic Imaging of Lines: A Texture Based Approach." In *IEEE Conference on Information Visualization, 1997. Proceedings*, 272–8.

Roberts, David E. 2003. "History of Lenticular and Related Autostereoscopic Methods". http://microlens.com/pdfs/history_of_lenticular.pdf [last accessed August 14, 2013].

Roberts, David E. and Trebor Smith. n.d. "The History of Integral Print Methods." ftp://ftp.umiacs.umd.edu/pub/aagrawal/HistoryOfIntegralImaging/Integral_History.pdf [last accessed August 14, 2013].

Robertson, Elliott R. and James M. Harvey, ed. 1970. *The Engineering Uses of Holography*. Cambridge: Cambridge University Press.

Robinson, Arthur Howard and Barbara Petchenik, ed. 1976. *The Nature of Maps: Essays Toward Understanding Maps and Mapping*. Chicago: University of Chicago Press.

Roetting, Petra. 2000. " 'Das verwilderte Auge': Über Fotografie und Bildarchive in der Kunstwissenschaft." In *Darstellung und Deutung: Abbilder der Kunstgeschichte*, edited by Matthias Bruhn, 61–88. Weimar: VDG.

Rohr, Moritz von. 1920. *Die binokularen Instrumente: Nach Quellen und bis zum Ausgang von 1910*. Berlin: Springer.

—— 1925. *Zur Entwicklung der dunklen Kammer (camera obscura)*. Berlin: Verlag der Central-Zeitung für Optik und Mechanik.

Rohwaldt, Karl. 2002. "Photoskulptur." In *Medientheorie 1888–1933: Texte und Kommentare*, edited by Albert Kümmel and Petra Löffler, 57–62. Frankfurt/M.: Suhrkamp.

Rood, Ogden N. 1880. *Die moderne Farbenlehre*. Leipzig: Brockhaus.

Rood, Ogden N. 1973. *Modern Chromatics: Students' Text-Book of Color with Applications to Art and Industry*. New York: Van Nostrand.

Root, Nile. 1985. "Light Scanning Photomacrography: A Brief History and Its Current Status." *Journal of Biological Photography* 53 (2): 69–77.

Rowell, Margit. 1975. "Kupka, Duchamp, and Marey." *Studio International* 189 (973): 48–51.

—— 1979a. "The Planar Dimension 1912–1932: From Surface to Space." In *The Planar Dimension, Europe 1912–1932*, 9–31. New York: Solomon R. Guggenheim Foundation.

—— ed. 1979b. *The Planar Dimension, Europe 1912–1932*. New York: Solomon R. Guggenheim Foundation.

Rubin, William S. ed. 1984. *Primitivismus in der Kunst des 20. Jahrhunderts*. München: Prestel.

Rusch, Gebhard. 2007. "Mediendynamik: Explorationen zur Theorie des Medienwandels." In *Mediendynamik*, edited by Gebhard Rusch, Helmut Schanze and Gregor Schwering, 13–95. Marburg: Schüren.

Rusch, Gebhard, Helmut Schanze and Gregor Schwering, ed. 2007. *Theorien der neuen Medien. Kino – Radio – Fernsehen – Computer*. Paderborn: Fink.

Ryder, Richard C. 1988. " 'Blitzkrieg' in the West: The Fateful Spring of 1940." *Stereo World* 15 (2): 20–6.

—— 1990. "Anschluss!" *Stereo World* 17 (1): 22–9.

Sachs-Hombach, Klaus and Klaus Rehkämper. 1999. "Aspekte und Probleme der bildwissenschaftlichen Forschung – eine Standortbestimmung." In *Bildgrammatik: Interdisziplinäre Forschungen zur Syntax bildlicher Darstellungsformen*, edited by Klaus Sachs-Hombach and Klaus Rehkämper, 9–22. Magdeburg: Scriptum.

Saleh, Bahaa E. A. and Malvin Carl Teich. 1991. *Fundamentals of Photonics*. New York: John Wiley & Sons.

Samsonow, Elisabeth von. 2007. "Bilder und Codes von Plastizität." In *Bilderfragen: Die Bildwissenschaften im Aufbruch*, edited by Hans Belting, 271–84. München: Fink.

Schaaf, Larry John. 2000. *The Photographic Art of William Henry Fox Talbot*. Princeton, NJ: Princeton University Press.

Schapiro, Meyer. 1972. "On Some Problems in the Semiotics of Visual Art: Field and Vehicle in Image-Signs." *Simiolus: Netherlands Quarterly for the History of Art* 6 (1): 9–19.

Scharf, Aaron. 1975. *Art and Photography*. Reprint. Harmondsworth: Penguin Books.

Schiavo, Laura Burd. 2003. "From Phantom Image to Perfect Vision: Physiological Optics, Commercial Photography and the Popularization of the Stereoscope." In *New Media, 1740–1915*, edited by Lisa Gitelman and Geoffrey B. Pingree, 113–38. Cambridge, MA: MIT Press.

Schlör, Walter. 1926. "Photoskulptur." *Die Umschau: Illustrierte Wochenschrift über die Fortschritte in Wissenschaft und Technik* 30: 718–22.

Schmaltz, Gustav. 1932. "Eine Methode zur Darstellung der Profilkurven rauher Oberflächen." *Die Naturwissenschaften* 20 (18): 315–16.

Schmauks, Dagmar. 1998. "Landkarten als synoptisches Medium." *Zeitschrift für Semiotik* 20 (1/2): 18–24.

Schmid, Christian. 2003. *Stadt, Raum und Gesellschaft. Henri Lefebvre und die Theorie der Produktion des Raumes*. (Phd dissertation) University of Jena.

Schmid, Gabriele. 2009. "Zwischen Bildern: Die holographische Installation als Handlungsfeld." In *Das Holographische Wissen*, edited by Stefan Rieger and Jens Schröter, 161–80. Zürich: Diaphanes.

Schmidt, Gunnar. 2002. "Zeit des Ereignisses – Zeit der Geschichte: Am Beispiel der Multiperspektivität." In *Ephemer – Temporär – Provisorisch*, edited by Immanuel Chi, Susanne Düchting and Jens Schröter, 175–96. Essen: Klartext.

Schmidt, Johann Karl. 2001. "Body-Scan." In *Ornament und Versprechen*, edited by Johann Karl Schmidt, 112–19. Stuttgart: Quantum Books.

Schnapka, [?]. 1936. "Dem Flachbildner zum Nachdenken." *Das Raumbild: Monatszeitschrift für die gesamte Stereoskopie und ihre Grenzgebiete* 2 (3): 49–50.

Schneider, Birgit and Peter Berz. 2002. "Bildtexturen. Punkte, Zeilen, Spalten. I. Textile Processing/II. Bildtelegraphie." In *Mimetische Differenzen: Der Spielraum der Medien zwischen Abbildung und Nachbildung*, edited by Sabine Flach and Georg Christoph Tholen, 181–220. Kassel: University Press.

Schoepf, Herrmann. 1937. "Das Raumbild als Anschauungsmittel." *Das Raumbild: Monatszeitschrift für die gesamte Stereoskopie und ihre Grenzgebiete* 3: 5–6.

Scholz, Oliver R. 1991. *Bild, Darstellung, Zeichen. Philosophische Theorien bildhafter Darstellung*. Freiburg: Alber.

Schröter, Jens. 1996. "Dilemma des Schweigens: Einige Bemerkungen zu MTV Unplugged." In *FFK 8. Dokumentation des 8. Film- und Fernsehwissenschaftlichen Kolloquiums an der Universität Hildesheim*, edited by Johannes von Moltke, Elke Sudmann and Volker Wortmann, 190–201. Hildesheim: Inst. für Theater- und Medienwiss. der Universität.

—— 2000. "Die Form der Farbe: Über ein Parergon in Kants Kritik der Urteilskraft." In *Kants Schlüssel zur Kritik des Geschmacks: Ästhetische Erfahrung heute – Studien zur Aktualität von Kants "Kritik der Urteilskraft"*, edited by Ursula Franke, 135–54. Hamburg: Meiner.

—— 2003. "Virtuelle Kamera: Zum Fortbestand fotografischer Medien in computergenerierten Bildern." *Fotogeschichte* 23 (88): 3–16.

—— 2004a. "Das Ende der Welt: Analoge und digitale Bilder – mehr und weniger Realität?" In *Analog/Digital – Opposition oder Kontinuum. Beiträge zu Theorie und Geschichte einer Unterscheidung*, edited by Jens Schröter and Alexander Böhnke, 335–54. Bielefeld: transcript.

—— 2004b. "Analog/Digital – Opposition oder Kontinuum." In *Analog/ Digital – Opposition oder Kontinuum? Zur Theorie und Geschichte einer Unterscheidung*, edited by Jens Schröter and Böhnke, 7–30. Bielefeld: transcript.

—— 2004c. *Das Netz und die virtuelle Realität: Zur Selbstprogrammierung der Gesellschaft durch die universelle Maschine*. Bielefeld: transcript.

—— 2004d. "Intermedialität, Medienspezifik und die universelle Maschine." In *Performativität und Medialität*, edited by Sybille Krämer, 385–411. München: Fink.

—— 2004e. "Computer/Simulation: Kopie ohne Original oder das Original kontrollierende Kopie." In *OriginalKopie: Praktiken des Sekundären*, edited by Gisela Fehrmann, Erika Linz, Eckhard Schumacher and Brigitte Weingart, 139–55. Köln: DuMont.

—— 2004f. "Technik und Krieg: Fragen und Überlegungen zur militärischen Herkunft von Computertechnologien am Beispiel des Internets." In *Die Medien und ihre Technik*, edited by Harro Segeberg, 356–70. Marburg: Schüren.

—— 2004g. "1948 – die Holographie. Zu einem verwirrenden Phänomen in der Geschichte der technologischen Bilder." *Archiv für Mediengeschichte* 4: 105–16.

—— 2005a. "World Brain – Electronic Brain – Global Brain. Plädoyer für De-Sedimentierung." *Paragrana. Zeitschrift für historische Anthropologie* 14 (2): 283–303.

—— 2005b. "Der Pilz im nationalsozialistischen Raumbild. Anmerkungen zu einem Fund aus der Zeit des Dritten Reichs." *Der Tintling. Die Pilzzeitschrift* 10 (3): 33–9.

—— 2006a. "Fragmentierung und Rekonstruktion: Notizen zu einer Geschichte des Löschens 2." In *Fragment und Schnipsel*, edited by Jens Schröter and Gregor Schwering, 33–7. Marburg: Schüren.

—— 2006b. "Wie man Skulpturen rendern soll. Zur Geschichte der transplanen Reproduktion." In *Skulptur – Zwischen Realität und Virtualität*, edited by Gundolf Winter, Jens Schröter and Christian Spies, 231–74. München: Fink.

—— 2006c. "Archive – post/photographic." http://www.medienkunstnetz.de/themes/photo_byte/archive_post_photographic/textsummary/ [last accessed August 14, 2013].

—— 2007a. "Banknoten der Natur: Überlegungen zum Verhältnis von Fotografie und Geld: Marx, Holmes, Benjamin, Sekula." *Fotogeschichte* 27 (105): 51–8.

—— 2007b. "Von grafischen, multimedialen, ultimativen und operativen Displays: Zur Arbeit Ivan E. Sutherlands." In *Display II: Digital*, edited by Tristan Thielmann and Jens Schröter, 33–48. Marburg: Schüren.

—— 2009. "Das holographische Wissen und die Nicht-Reproduzierbarkeit." In *Das holographische Wissen*, edited by Stefan Rieger and Jens Schröter, 77–86. Zürich: Diaphanes.

—— 2011. "Technologies Beyond the Still and the Moving Image: The Case of the Multiplex Hologram." *History of Photography* 35 (1): 23–32.

—— 2012. "Four Models of Intermediality." In *Travels in Intermedia[lity]*, edited by Bernd Herzogenrath, 15–36. Hanover: Dartmouth College Press.

Schröter, Jens and Christian Spies. 2006. "INTERFACE: Analoger Close-Circuit vs. digitale Interaktivität?" In *Das Spiel mit dem Medium: Partizipation – Immersion – Interaktion*, edited by Britta Neitzel and Rolf Nohr, 104–16. Marburg: Schüren.

Schudeisky, Albrecht. 1918. *Projektionslehre: Die rechtwinklige Parallelprojektion und ihre Anwendung auf die Darstellung technischer Gebilde nebst einem Anhang . . . Für Selbstunterricht und Schulgebrauch*. Leipzig and Berlin: Teubner.

Schug, Albert. 1997. "Über die Bedeutung der neo-impressionistischen Theorie Seurats." In *Pointillismus. Auf den Spuren von Georges Seurat*, edited by Rainer Budde, 10–38. München: Prestel.

Schulz, Martin. 2007. "Ent-Larvung der Bilder: Zum Anachronismus der TV-Gesichter." In *Bilderfragen: Die Bildwissenschaften im Aufbruch*, edited by Hans Belting, 285–306. München: Fink.

Schüttpelz, Erhard. 2006. "Die medienanthropologische Kehre der Kulturtechniken." *Archiv für Mediengeschichte* 6: 87–110.

Schwarte, Ludger. 2004. "Raumbildungsprozesse. Zur Logik des dynamischen Bildraums bei Goodman, Boehm und Foucault. Mit einem Exkurs über den Fetischcharakter der Dingwahrnehmung." In *Raum-Dynamik/dynamique de l'espace. Beiträge zu einer Praxis des Raums/contributions aux pratiques de l'espace*, edited by Franck Hofmann, Jens E. Sennewald and Stavros Lazaris, 73–96. Bielefeld: transcript.

Schwarz, Heinrich. 1966. "Vermeer and the Camera Obscura." *Pantheon* 24: 170–180.

Schwerzel, Robert, Van E. Wood, Vincent D. McGinniss and Carl M. Verber. 1984. "Three-Dimensional Photomechanical Machining with Lasers." *SPIE Proceedings* 458: 90–7.

Seel, Martin. 1993a. "Vor dem Schein kommt das Erscheinen: Bemerkungen zu einer Ästhetik der Medien." *Merkur* 9/10: 770–83.

—— 1993b. "Zur ästhetischen Praxis der Kunst." *Deutsche Zeitschrift für Philosophie* 41 (1): 31–43.

—— 1997. "Ästhetik und Aisthetik: Über einige Besonderheiten ästhetischer Wahrnehmung." In *Bild und Reflexion. Paradigmen und Perspektiven gegenwärtiger Ästhetik*, edited by Birgit Recki and Lambert Wiesing, 17–38. München: Fink.

—— 2005. *Aesthetics of Appearing*, translated by John Farrell. Stanford: Stanford University Press.

Seiling, Albrecht. 1935. "Flieger-Stereoskopie (Weltkrieg 1914–1918)." *Das Raumbild: Monatszeitschrift für die gesamte Stereoskopie und ihre Grenzgebiete* 1 (6): 127–8.

Sekula, Allan. 1975. "The Instrumental Image: Steichen at War." *Artforum* 14: 26–35.

—— 1989. "The Body and the Archive." In *The Contest of Meaning: Critical Histories of Photography*, edited by Richard Bolton, 343–89. Cambridge, MA: MIT Press.

—— 2004. "The Traffic in Photographs." In *Modernism and Modernity. The Vancouver Conference Papers*, edited by H.D. Buchloh, Serge Guilbaut and David Solkin, 121–54. Halifax, Nova Scotia: The Press of the Nova Scotia College of Art and Design.

Selke, Willy. 1897. "Verfahren zur plastischen Nachbildung körperlicher Gebilde in beliebiger Reliefhöhe mit Hilfe der Photographie. Patentirt [*sic*] im Deutschen Reiche vom 2. Juli 1897 ab." German Patent 102005, filed July 2, 1897, and issued March 18, 1899.

—— 1898a. "Photosculpture Apparatus." US Patent 675417, filed January 20, 1898.

—— 1898b. "Verfahren zur photographischen Aufnahme von Lichtschnitten für die plastische Nachbildung von körperlichen Gegenständen. Patentirt [*sic*] im Deutschen Reiche vom 28. Juni 1898 ab." German Patent 110918, filed June 28, 1898, and issued May 25, 1900.

—— 1899. "Verfahren zur plastischen Nachbildung körperlicher Gebilde mit Hilfe der Photographie. Zusatz zum Patente 102005 vom 2. Juli 1897. Patentirt [*sic*] im Deutschen Reiche vom 7. Januar 1899 ab." German Patent 107608, filed January 7, 1899, and issued November 15, 1899.
—— 1901. "Verfahren zur Herstellung von photographischen Lichtschnittaufnahmen für die plastische Nachbildung körperlicher Objekte. Patentirt [*sic*] im Deutschen Reiche vom 6. Januar 1901 ab." German Patent 138388, filed January 6, 1901, and issued February 6, 1903.
—— 1907. "Verfahren zur Nachbildung körperlicher Gebilde mit Hilfe von photographischen Aufnahmen und einem Punktierverfahren. Patentiert [*sic*] im Deutschen Reiche vom 22. März 1907 ab." German Patent 242710, filed March 22, 1907, and issued January 15, 1912.
—— 1909. "Verfahren und Vorrichtung zur plastischen Wiedergabe eines Objekts nach zwei photographischen Meßbildern. Patentiert [*sic*] im Deutschen Reiche vom 17. Dezember 1909 ab." German Patent 261959, filed December 17, 1909, and issued July 4, 1913.
Selle, Walter. 1952a. "Das VIEWMASTER-Stereo-Kleinstbildsystem." *Photo-Technik und -Wirtschaft* 6: 238–9.
—— 1952b. "Der Ursprung der Viewmaster-Stereoskopie." *Photo-Technik und -Wirtschaft* 9: 360–1.
—— 1953a. "Третье Измерение – 'Die 3. Dimension' im Sowjetfilm." *Kinotechnik* 10: 293–5.
—— 1953b. "Третье Измерение – 'Die 3. Dimension' im Sowjetfilm." *Kinotechnik* 12: 344–7.
—— 1971. *3D im Bücherspiegel: Zur Bibliographie der Stereoskopie 1939–1970 nebst Einführungen in die Holographie sowie einem Anhang Dt. Norm-Entwürfe DIN 4531, Stereoskopie*. Berlin: Deutsche Gesellschaft für Stereoskopie.
Shannon, Claude Elwood. 1938. "A Symbolic Analysis of Relay and Switching Circuits." *Transactions of the American Institute of Electrical Engineers* 57: 713–23.
Sher, Lawrence D. 1993. "The Oscillating-Mirror Technique for Realizing True 3D." In *Stereo Computer Graphics and Other True 3D Technologies*, edited by David F. McAllister, 96–213. Princeton, NJ: Princeton University Press.
Siegert, Bernhard. 2004. "Too High Fidelity." In *Die Medien der Kunst – die Kunst der Medien*, edited by Gerhard Johann Lischka and Peter Weibel, 66–89. Wabern/Bern: Benteli.
Siggraph. 1989. "Retrospectives II. Siggraph Panel Proceedings." *Computer Graphics* 23 (5).
Silliman, Robert H. 1974. "Fresnel and the Emergence of Physics as a Discipline." *Historical Studies in the Physical Sciences* 4 (January): 137–62.

Simon, Gérard. 1992. *Der Blick, das Sein und die Erscheinung in der antiken Optik*. München: Fink.

Simon, William. 1969. "A Method of Producing a Three-Dimensional Cathode Ray Tube Display." *Behavior Research Methods & Instrumentation* 1 (5): 179–80.

Simons, Oliver. 2007. *Raumgeschichten. Topographien der Moderne in Philosophie, Wissenschaft und Literatur*. München: Fink.

Smith, Graham. 1990. *Disciples of Light: Photographs in the Brewster Album*. Malibu, CA: J. Paul Getty Museum.

Smith, Howard M. 1968. "Photographic Relief Images." *Journal of the Optical Society of America* 58 (4): 533–8.

Smith, Peter H. 1998. "Imager for Mars Pathfinder (IMP): A Multispectral Stereo Imaging System." *SPIE Proceedings* 3295: 4–9.

Snyder, Joel. 1980. "Picturing Vision." *Critical Inquiry* 6: 499–526.

—— 1998a. "Nineteenth-Century Photography of Sculpture and the Rhetoric of Substitution." In *Sculpture and Photography: Envisioning the Third Dimension*, edited by Géraldine A. Johnson, 21–34. Cambridge: Cambridge University Press.

—— 1998b. "Visualization and Visibility." In *Picturing Science/Producing Art*, edited by Peter Galison and Caroline A. Jones, 379–97. New York: Routledge.

Sobieszek, Robert A. 1980. "Sculpture as the Sum of Its Profiles: Francois Willème and Photosculpture in France 1859–1868." *The Art Bulletin* 62 (4): 617–30.

Soltan, Parviz, John A. Trias, Waldo R. Robinson and Weldon J. Dahlke. 1995. "Laser-Based 3D Volumetric Display System." In *Interactive Technology and the New Paradigm for Healthcare: Medicine Meets Virtual Reality III Proceedings, San Diego, January 19–22, 1995*, edited by Richard M. Satava et al., 349–58. Amsterdam: IOS Press.

Soltan, Parviz, John A. Trias, Weldon Dahlke, Mark Lasher and Malvyn McDonald. 1996. "Laser-Based 3-D Volumetric Display System (The Improved Second Generation)." http://handle.dtic.mil/100.2/ADA306215 [last accessed August 14, 2013].

Sorel, Philippe. 2000. "Photosculpture: the Fortunes of a Sculptural Process Based on Photography." In *Paris in 3D*, edited by Françoise Reynaud, Catherine Tambrun and Kim Timby, 81–90. London: Booth-Clibborn Editions.

Soulas, J. 1978. "Realism in Stereoscopic Photography." In *Stereophotography: A Monograph. Comprising Publications of the Royal Photographic Society from 1953–1977 on the Subject of Stereophotography*, edited by Maurice Baker, 5–7. London: R.P.S. Publications.

Spengler, Oswald. 1926. *The Decline of the West*, translated by Charles Francis Atkinson. London: Allen & Unwin.

Stanke, Karl. 1938. "Betrachtungen über das Raumbild." *Das Raumbild: Stereoskopisches Magazin für Zeit und Raum* 1 (April): 20–2.

Stauffer, Serge. 1992. *Marcel Duchamp: Interviews und Statements*. Stuttgart: Cantz.

Steadman, Philip. 2001. *Vermeer's Camera: Uncovering the Truth Behind the Masterpieces*. Oxford: Oxford University Press.

Steichen, Edward Major. 1919. "American Aerial Photography at the Front." *The Camera* 23: 359–66.

Steigerwald, Jörn. 2000. "Das göttliche Vergnügen des Sehens: Barthold Hinrich Brockes' Techniken des Betrachters." *Convivium. Germanistisches Jahrbuch Polen*: 9–43.

Steiner, George. 1992. "The Mandarin of the Hour." In *Critical Essays on Michel Foucault*, edited by Peter Burke, 84–9. Aldershot: Scolar Press.

Stenger, Erich. 1937. "Zur Geschichte der Stereokamera." *Das Raumbild: Monatszeitschrift für die gesamte Stereoskopie und ihre Grenzgebiete* 3 (6/7): 102–7; 122–7.

—— 1950. *Siegeszug der Photographie in Kultur, Wissenschaft, Technik*. Seebruck a. Chiemsee: Heering.

—— 1958. *The March of Photography*. London and New York: Focal Press.

Stern, Adrian and Bahram Javidi. 2006. "Three-Dimensional Image Sensing, Visualization, and Processing Using Integral Imaging." *Proceedings of the IEEE* 94 (3): 591–607.

Stetson, Karl A. 1969. "A Rigorous Treatment of the Fringes of Hologram Interferometry." *Optik* 29 (4): 386–400.

—— 1991. "The Origins of Hologram Interferometry." *Experimental Techniques* March/April: 15–18.

—— 1999. "The Problems of Hologram Interferometry." *Experimental Mechanics* 39 (4): 249–55.

Stiegler, Bernd. 2001. *Philologie des Auges: Die photographische Entdeckung der Welt im 19. Jahrhundert*. München: Fink.

—— 2003. "Friedrich A. Kittler: Optische Medien, Berliner Vorlesung 1999." (Review) *Fotogeschichte* 87: 70–1.

—— 2004. "Michel Foucault und die Fotografie." In *Foucault und die Künste*, edited by Peter Gente, 277–97. Frankfurt/M.: Suhrkamp.

—— 2006. "Das Sichtbare und das Unsichtbare. Kleine Wahrnehmungsgeschichte der Photographie." In *Das Unsichtbare sehen: Bildzauber, optische Medien und Literatur*, edited by Sabine Haupt and Ulrich Stadler, 141–60. Wien and New York: Ed. Voldemeer.

Stoichita, Victor I. 1997. *The Self-Aware Image: An Insight into Early Modern Meta-Painting*. Cambridge: Cambridge University Press.

Straub, Erik. 2005. "Inter-Face. Zum Verfahren der Fotoskulptur." *Bildwelten des Wissens. Kunsthistorisches Jahrbuch für Bildkritik* 3 (2): 61–3.

Stuart, B. L. 1990. *Computer Generated Holography as a Three-Dimensional Display Medium*. Ohio: Wright Patterson Airforce Base.

Sutherland, Ivan E. 1968. "A Head-Mounted Three Dimensional Display." *Proceedings of the December 9–11, 1968, Fall Joint Computer Conference, Part I*: 757–64.

Szilard, J. 1974. "An Improved Three-Dimensional Display System." *Ultrasonics* 12 (6): 273–6.

Takada, Hideaki, Shiro Suyama and Munekazu Date. 2006. "Evaluation of the Fusional Limit Between the Front and Rear Images in Depth-Fused 3-D Visual Illusion." *IEICE Transactions on Electronics* E89-C (3): 429–33.

Talbot, Henry Fox. 1851. "Sur la production des images photographiques instantanées." *Comptes rendus hebdomadaires des séances de l'académie des sciences* 33: 623–7.

—— 1969. *The Pencil of Nature*. New York: Da Capo Press.

—— 1980. "Some Account of the Art of Photogenic Drawing, or, The Process by Which Natural Objects May Be Made to Delineate Themselves without the Aid of the Artist's Pencil." In *Photography: Essays and Images: Illustrated Readings in the History of Photography*, edited by Beaumont Newhall, 23–31. New York: Museum of Modern Art.

Tank, Kurt Lothar. 1935a. "Baukunst im Raumbild." *Das Raumbild: Monatszeitschrift für die gesamte Stereoskopie und ihre Grenzgebiete* 1 (5): 101–3.

—— 1935b. "Zur Ästhetik des Raumbildes." *Das Raumbild: Monatszeitschrift für die gesamte Stereoskopie und ihre Grenzgebiete* 1 (1): 8–12.

—— 1942. *Deutsche Plastik unserer Zeit*, edited by Wilfrid [*sic*] Bade. München: Raumbild-Verlag Schönstein.

Tanner, P. G. and T. E. Allibone. 1997. "The Patent Literature of Nobel Laureate Dennis Gabor (1900–1979)." *Notes and Records of the Royal Society of London* 51 (1): 105–20.

Thielmann, Tristan. 2007. " 'You Have Reached Your Destination!' Position, Positioning and Superpositioning of Space Through Car Navigation Systems." *Social Geography* 2: 63–75.

Thinius, Carl. 1937. "Der Wert der plastischen Bildbetrachtung." *Das Raumbild: Monatszeitschrift für die gesamte Stereoskopie und ihre Grenzgebiete* 3 (3): 41–5.

Tholen, Georg Christoph. 2002. *Die Zäsur der Medien: Kulturphilosophische Konturen*. Frankfurt/M.: Suhrkamp.

—— 2007. "Der Ort des Raums: Zur Heterotopie der Einbildungskraft im 'digitalen' Zeitalter." In *Topologie: Zur Raumbeschreibung in den Kultur- und Medienwissenschaften*, edited by Stephan Günzel, 99–114. Bielefeld: transcript.

Thompson, Kristin. 1980. "Implications of the Cel Animation Technique." In *The Cinematic Apparatus*, edited by Theresa De Lauretis and Stephen Heath, 106–20. London: Macmillan.

Thomson, E. 1896. "Stereoscopic Roentgen Pictures." *The Electrical Engineer* 21: 256.

Timby, Kim. 2000. "The Inventors of 3-D Photography in France: Patents 1852–1922." In *Paris in 3D*, edited by Françoise Reynaud, Catherine Tambrun and Kim Timby, 159–64. London: Booth-Clibborn Editions.

Tortual, Caspar Theobald. 1842. *Dimension der Tiefe im freien Sehen und im stereoskopischen Bilde*. Münster: Verlag der Coppenrath'schen Buch- und Kunsthandlung.

Tousley, Nancy. 2004. "Absolutely Unreal: The Sculpture and Photography of Evan Penny." In *Evan Penny: Absolutely Unreal*, 29–55. London: Museum London.

Traub, Alan C. 1967. "Stereoscopic Display Using Rapid Varifocal Mirror Oscillations." *Applied Optics* 6 (6): 1085–7.

Treece, Walter A. 1955. "Estimation of Vertical Exaggeration in Stereoscopic Viewing of Aerial Photographs." *Photogrammetric Engineering* 21 (4): 518–27.

Tricoles, G. 1987. "Computer Generated Holograms: An Historical Review." *Applied Optics* 26 (20): 4351–60.

Trotter, David. 2004. "Stereoscopy: Modernism and the 'Haptic'." *Critical Quarterly* 46 (4): 38–58.

Tsuji, Shigeru. 1990. "Brunelleschi and the Camera Obscura: The Discovery of Pictorial Perspective." *Art History* 13 (3): 276–92.

Ulmann, Arnulf. 1984. *Bildhauertechnik des Spätmittelalters und der Frührenaissance*. Darmstadt: Wissenschaftliche Buchgesellschaft.

Upatnieks, Juris and Carl Leonard. 1969. "Diffraction Efficiency of Bleached, Photographically Recorded Interference Patterns." *Applied Optics* 8 (1): 885–9.

Upatnieks, Juris, Carl Leonard and E. J. Martilla. 1975. "Archival Storage of Three-Dimensional Images." *Proceedings International Optical Computing Conference* 1975: 108–11.

Urban, Annette. 2000. "Versuchsanordnung über Photographie: Die Nachtbilder und Stereoaufnahmen von Thomas Ruff." In *Ansicht Aussicht Einsicht: Architekturphotographie, Ausstellungskatalog*, edited by Monika Steinhauser, 106–13. Düsseldorf: Richter.

Urry, John. 2003. *Global Complexity*. Cambridge: Polity.

Valenta, Eduard. 1894. *Die Photographie in natürlichen Farben unter besonderer Berücksichtigung des Lippmann'schen Verfahrens*. Halle: Wilhelm Knapp.
Van Tiggelen, R. 2002. "In Search for the Third Dimension: From Radiostereoscopy to Three-Dimensional Imaging." *Journal Belge de Radiologie – Belgisch Tijdschrift voor Radiologi* 85: 266–70.
Veltman, Kim. 1979. "Military Surveying and Topography: The Practical Dimension of Renaissance Linear Perspective." *Revista da Universidade de Coimbra* XXVII: 263–79.
—— 1995. "Elektronische Medien, die Wiedergeburt der Perspektive und die Fragmentierung der Illusion." In *Illusion und Simulation: Begegnung mit der Realität*, edited by Stefan Iglhaut, Florian Rötzer and Elisabeth Schweeger, 229–39. Ostfildern-Ruit: Cantz.
Venus, Jochen. 2009. "Raumbild und Tätigkeitssimulation. Video- und Computerspiele als Darstellungsmedien des Tätigkeitsempfindens." In *Das Raumbild: Bilder jenseits ihrer Flächen*, edited by Gundolf Winter, Jens Schröter and Joanna Barck, 259–79. München: Fink.
Virilio, Paul. 1988. *La machine de vision*. Paris: Édition Galilée.
—— 1989. *Die Sehmaschine*. Berlin: Merve
—— 1990. *L'inertie polaire*. Paris: Bourgois.
—— 1991. *Lost Dimension*. New York: Semiotext(e).
—— 1995. *The Vision Machine*, translated by Julie Rose. Bloomington, IN: Indiana University Press.
—— 1998. "Critical Space." In *The Virilio Reader*, edited by James Der Derian, 58–73. Malden, MA: Blackwell.
—— 2000. *Polar Inertia*, translated by Patrick Camiller. London: SAGE.
Vogel, Hermann. 1892. *The Chemistry of Light and Photography in Their Application to Art, Science, and Industry*. London: Kegan Paul, Trench, Trübner & Co.
Volkmann, Ludwig. 1903. *Grenzen der Künste. Auch eine Stillehre*. Dresden: Kühtmann.
Vollmer, Dennis Ray. 2007. "Does It Have to Be 3D? Zum Phänomen der 3D-Technologie in Computerspielen." In *Display II. Digital*, edited by Tristan Thielmann and Jens Schröter, 87–104. Marburg: Schüren.
Volmar, Axel. 2007. "Die Anrufung des Wissens: Eine Medienepistemologie auditorischer Displays und auditiver Wissensproduktion." In *Display II. Digital*, edited by Tristan Thielmann and Jens Schröter, 105–16. Marburg: Schüren.
Wade, Nicholas J., ed. 1983. *Brewster and Wheatstone on Vision*. London: Academic Press.
—— 2003. "The Chimenti Controversy." *Perception* 32 (2): 185–200.
Wagner, Anne M. 2007. "Nauman's Body of Sculpture." *October* 120: 53–70.

Wagner, Hans-Ulrich. 1992. " 'Volk ohne Raum'. Zur Geschichte eines Schlagwortes." *Sprachwissenschaft* 17 (1): 68–109.

Waldenfels, Bernhard. 1994. "Ordnungen des Sichtbaren." In *Was ist ein Bild?*, edited by Gottfried Boehm, 233–52. München: Fink.

—— 1995. *Deutsch-französische Gedankengänge*. Frankfurt/M.: Suhrkamp.

—— 1999. *Sinnesschwellen: Studien zur Phänomenologie des Fremden*. Vol. 3. Frankfurt/M.: Suhrkamp.

Wall, Jeff. 1995. "Marks of Indifference: Aspects of Photography in, or as, Conceptual Art." In *Reconsidering the Object of Art: 1965–1975*, edited by Ann Goldstein and Anne Rorimer, 246–67. Cambridge, MA: MIT Press.

Wallach, Hans and D. N. O'Connell. 1953. "The Kinetic Depth Effect." *Journal of Experimental Psychology* 45 (4): 205–17.

Wallburger, Walter. 1937. "Das Raumbild im Dienste des Schulunterrichts." *Das Raumbild: Monatszeitschrift für die gesamte Stereoskopie und ihre Grenzgebiete* 3: 24–5.

Warhol, Andy. 1975. *The Philosophy of Andy Warhol: From A to B and Back Again*. London: Cassell.

Watt, Alan H. 2000. *3D Computer Graphics*. 3rd edn. Wokingham: Addison-Wesley.

Wedel, Michael. 2007. "Sculpting with Light: Early Film Style, Stereoscopic Vision and the Idea of a 'Plastic Art in Motion'." In *Lo stile cinematografico: XIII convegno internazionale di studi sul cinema, XIII International Film Studies Conference, University of Udine*, edited by Enrico Biasin, Giulio Bursi and Leonardo Quaresima, 483–97. Udine: Forum.

Wedgwood, Thomas and Humphry Sir Davy. 1980. "An Account of a Method of Copying Paintings Upon Glass, and of Making Profiles, by the Agency of Light Upon Nitrate of Silver." In *Photography: Essays and Images. Illustrated Readings in the History of Photography*, edited by Beaumont Newhall, 15–16. New York: Museum of Modern Art.

Weiss, Thomas. 2007. "Die Zukunft der Fotografie: Adobe gewährt einen Blick ins Labor." http://www.macwelt.de/news/software/34966 2/ [last accessed August 14, 2013].

Wellmann, Marc. 2005. *Die Entdeckung der Unschärfe in Optik und Malerei: Zum Verhältnis von Kunst und Wissenschaft zwischen dem 15. und dem 19. Jahrhundert*. Frankfurt/M.: Lang.

Westlake, Darrell, Ralph F. Wuerker and John F. Asmus. 1976. "The Use of Holography in the Conservation, Preservation and Historical Recording of Art." *SMPTE Journal* 85 (2): 84–9.

Westlake, Philip R. 1970. "The Possibilities of Neural Holographic Processes Within the Brain." *Kybernetik* 7 (4): 129–53.

Wheatstone, Charles. 1983. "Contributions to the Physiology of Vision – Part the First: On Some Remarkable, and Hitherto Unobserved Phenomena of Binocular Vision." In *Brewster and Wheatstone on Vision*, edited by Nicholas J. Wade, 65–93. London: Academic Press.

Wheelock, Arthur K. 1995. *Vermeer and the Art of Painting*. New Haven: Yale University Press.

White, John. 1987. *The Birth and Rebirth of Pictorial Space*. London: Faber.

Whitman, Robert. 2003. *Playback*. New York: Dia Art Foundation.

Wiener, Otto. 1890. "Stehende Lichtwellen und die Schwingungsrichtung polarisirten [*sic*] Lichtes." *Annalen der Physik und Chemie* N. F. 40 (6): 203–43.

—— 1895. "Farbenphotographie durch Körperfarben und mechanische Farbenanpassung in der Natur." *Annalen der Physik und Chemie* N. F. 55 (6): 225–81.

Wiesing, Lambert. 1997. *Die Sichtbarkeit des Bildes: Geschichte und Perspektiven der formalen Ästhetik*. Reinbek bei Hamburg: Rowohlt.

Wilber, Ken, ed. 1982. *The Holographic Paradigm and Other Paradoxes*. Boulder, CO: Shambhala.

Will, P. M. and K. S. Pennington. 1971. "Grid Coding: A Preprocessing Technique for Robot and Machine Vision." *Artificial Intelligence* 2 (3–4): 319–29.

Willème, François. 1861. "La sculpture photographique." *Le moniteur de la photographie* 15: 34.

Williams, Linda. 1995. "Corporealized Observers: Visual Pornographies and the 'Carnal Density of Vision'." In *Fugitive Images: From Photography to Video*, edited by Patrice Petro, 3–41. Bloomington, IN: Indiana University Press.

Williams, Rodney Don and Felix Garcia. 1989. "Volume Visualization Displays." *Information Display* 5 (4): 8–10.

Winkler, Hartmut. 1992. *Der filmische Raum und der Zuschauer. 'Apparatus' – Semantik – 'Ideology'*. Heidelberg: Winter.

—— 2000. "Die prekäre Rolle der Technik." In *Über Bilder sprechen: Positionen und Perspektiven der Medienwissenschaft*, edited by Heinz B. Heller, 9–22. Marburg: Schüren.

—— 2004a. "Mediendefinition." *Medienwissenschaft* (1): 9–27.

—— 2004b. *Diskursökonomie: Versuch über die innere Ökonomie der Medien*. Frankfurt/M.: Suhrkamp.

Winston, Brian. 1996. *Technologies of Seeing: Photography, Cinematography and Television*. London: British Film Institute.

—— 2003. *Media Technology and Society: A History from the Telegraph to the Internet*. London: Routledge.

Winter, Gundolf. 1985. "Distanz: Zu einer medialen Grundbedingung der Skulptur." In *Modernität und Tradition: Festschrift für Max Imdahl zum 60. Geburtstag*, edited by Gottfried Boehm, Karlheinz Stierle and Gundolf Winter, 271–87. München: Fink.

—— 1999. "Das Bild zwischen Medium und Kunst." In *Bild – Medium – Kunst*, edited by Yvonne Spielmann and Gundolf Winter, 15–30. München: Fink.

—— 2006. "Medium Skulptur: Zwischen Körper und Bild." In *Skulptur – Zwischen Realität und Virtualität*, edited by Gundolf Winter, Jens Schröter and Joanna Spies, 11–29. München: Fink.

Winter, Gundolf, Jens Schröter and Joanna Barck, eds. 2009. *Das Raumbild: Bilder jenseits ihrer Flächen*. München: Fink.

Winter, Gundolf, Jens Schröter and Christian Spies, eds. 2006. *Skulptur – zwischen Realität und Virtualität*. München: Fink.

Winzen, Matthias. 2001. *Thomas Ruff 1979 to the Present*. Köln: König.

Witte, I. M. 1921. *Kritik des Zeitstudienverfahrens: Eine Untersuchung der Ursachen, die zu einem Misserfolg des Zeitstudiums führen*. Berlin: Springer.

Wittgenstein, Ludwig. 1955. *Tractatus Logico-philosophicus*. With an Introduction by Bertrand Russell. 6th edn. London: Routledge & Kegan Paul, Trench, Trubner & Co.

Wolf, Herta. 1998. "Galton mit Mach." In *BildKörper: Verwandlungen des Menschen zwischen Medium und Medizin*, edited by Marianne Schuller, Claudia Reiche and Gunnar Schmidt, 77–120. Hamburg: Lit.

—— 2000. "Vorwort." In *Die Originalität der Avantgarde und andere Mythen der Moderne*, by Rosalind E. Krauss, 9–38. Amsterdam and Dresden: Verlag der Kunst.

Wolf-Czapek, Karl Wilhelm. 1911. *Angewandte Photographie in Wissenschaft und Technik: In vier Teilen*. Berlin: Union Deutsche Verlags Gesellschaft.

Wölfflin, Heinrich. 1946a. "Adolf Hildebrand's Problem der Form." In *Kleine Schriften*, edited by Joseph Gantner, 104–6. Basel: Schwabe.

—— 1946b. "Adolf von Hildebrand zu seinem siebenzigsten Geburtstag am 6. Oktober." In *Kleine Schriften*, edited by Joseph Gantner, 89–99. Basel: Schwabe.

—— 1950. *Principles of Art History: The Problem of the Development of Style in Later Art*. New York: Dover Publication.

—— 2013. "How One Should Photograph Sculpture." *Art History* 36 (1): 52–71.

Woodcock, B. H. 1986. "Holographic Optics." *Physics in Technology: A Journal of Reviews, Reports and Comment* 17: 200–11.

Wright, Fred E. Major. 1919. "War-Time Development of the Optical Industry." *Journal of the Optical Society of America* 2/3 (1/2): 1–7.

Wyss, Beat. 1996. *Der Wille zur Kunst: Zur ästhetischen Mentalität der Moderne*. Köln: DuMont.

Yefremov, Ivan. 2001. *Stories*. Hawaii: Intl Law & Taxation Publications.

Young, Thomas. 1802. "On the Theory of Light and Colours." *Philosophical Transactions of the Royal Society* 92: 12–48.

—— 1804. "Experiments and Calculations Relative to Physical Optics." *Philosophical Transactions of the Royal Society* 94: 1–16.

—— 1807. *A Course of Lectures on Natural Philosophy and the Mechanical Arts*. Vol. 1. London: Johnson.

Youngblood, Gene. 1970. *Expanded Cinema*. London: Studio Vista.

Zec, Peter. 1987. *Holographie: Geschichte, Technik, Kunst*. Köln: DuMont.

—— 1989. "The Aesthetic Message of Holography." *Leonardo* 22 (3/4): 425–30.

Zeidler, Sebastian. 2004. "Totality Against a Subject: Carl Einstein's Negerplastik." *October* 107: 14–46.

Zenker, Wilhelm. 1867. "Versuch einer Theorie der Farben-Perception." *Archiv für mikroskopische Anatomie* 3 (1): 248–61.

—— 1868. *Lehrbuch der Photochromie (Photographie der natürlichen Farben) nach den wichtigen Entdeckungen von E. Becquerel, Niépce de St. Victor, Poitevin u. a.* Berlin: Self-published.

Zimmermann, Peter. 1976. "Kampf um den Lebensraum. Ein Mythos der Kolonial- und der Blut-und-Boden-Literatur." In *Die Deutsche Literatur im Dritten Reich: Themen, Traditionen, Wirkungen*, edited by Horst Denkler and Karl Prümm, 165–82. Stuttgart: Reclam.

TABLE OF IMAGE RIGHTS

Every effort has been made to trace copyright holders and we apologize in advance for any unintentional omission. We would be pleased to insert the appropriate acknowledgment in any subsequent edition.

If there are any complaints please contact me under: schroeter@medienwissenschaft.uni-siegen.de

	Artist/title	Specific copyright information
1. 1	Living room with stereoscope (on the armchair), in Crary (1990, 117)	Courtesy of The MIT Press
1. 2	Return of stereoscopy in the data glasses of virtual reality, in Bormann (1994, 80)	NASA/Wade Sisler
1. 3	Henry Fox Talbot, *Buckler Fern* (1839), Photogram, Negative, 22,1 × 17,7 cm, in Getty Museum (2002, 25)	The J. Paul Getty Museum, Los Angeles William Henry Fox Talbot, Buckler Fern, 1839, Photogenic drawing negative, Image: 22.1 × 17.8 cm (8 11/16 × 7 in.)
1. 4	Stereoscopic drawings, in Wheatstone (1983, 73)	© The Royal Society
1. 5	Section of the visual pyramid composed of lines (Taylor 1715), in Andersen (1992, 231)	

1. 6	Tony Smith, *DIE* (1962). One can see how the cube projected in Figure 1.5 now returns as a real object	© VG Bild-Kunst, Bonn 2013
1. 7	Equivalent but different configurations from a certain point of view, in Gombrich (1982, 192)	
1. 8	Stereoscopic aerial photograph, in Judge (1926, 211 opposite page)	
1. 9	Patents for 3D-Processes (dominantly stereoscopy) in France. In Timby (2000, 159). A marked upsurge around 1900 is obvious	
1. 10	Pablo Picasso, *Les Demoiselles D'Avignon* (1907).	© Succession Picasso / VG Bild-Kunst, Bonn 2013
2.1a	Henry Fox Talbot, *Bust of Patroclus*. Plate V, in Talbot (1969)	The J. Paul Getty Museum, Los Angeles William Henry Fox Talbot, Bust of Patroclus, before February 7, 1846, Salted paper print, Image: 17.8 × 16 cm (7 × 6 5/16 in.) Sheet: 22.5 × 18.6 cm (8 7/8 × 7 5/16 in.)
2.1b	Henry Fox Talbot, *Bust of Patroclus*. Plate XVII, in Talbot (1969)	The J. Paul Getty Museum, Los Angeles William Henry Fox Talbot, The Bust of Patroclus, August 9, 1843, Salted paper print from a Calotype negative print, Image: 14.9 × 14.5 cm (5 7/8 × 5 11/16 in.) Sheet: 21.8 × 17.4 cm (8 9/16 × 6 7/8 in.)
2.2	Stereoscopic image of a sculpture, Brewster's *Account*, in Wade (1983, 223)	

2.3	William Henry Fox Talbot, Statuette of *The Rape of the Sabines* (Brewster's copy of a Talbot print), in Smith (1990, 129)	The J. Paul Getty Museum, Los Angeles William Henry Fox Talbot, Statuette of *The Rape of the Sabines* (Brewster's copy of a Talbot print), probably 1841–1843, medium, Image: 15.2 × 9.5 cm (6 × 3 3/4 in.) Sheet: 17.5 × 11.4 cm (6 7/8 × 4 1/2 in.)
2.4	Casts on Three Shelves, in the Courtyard of Lacock Abbey, in Smith (1990, 148)	The J. Paul Getty Museum, Los Angeles William Henry Fox Talbot, Casts on Three Shelves, in the Courtyard of Lacock Abbey, probably 1842–1844, Salted paper print from a Calotype negative print, Image: 13.5 × 14 cm (5 5/16 × 5 1/2 in.) Sheet: 18 × 17.9 cm (7 1/16 × 7 1/16 in.)
3.1	Willème's photo-sculpture studio, in Kümmel (2006, 194)	
3.2	Not yet touched up photo sculpture (Sorel 2000, 81)	
3.3	Drawing showing W. Reissig's method from his patent, in Reissig (1893, 4)	Source: Kaiserliches Patentamt, Patentschrift Nr. 74622
3.4	Alberti: Implementation of *Exempeda, Finitiorum* and *Norma*, in Alberti 2000, 43	With permission from Oskar Bätschmann
3.5	Schematic representation of Willy Selke's early method: Construction of the photo sculpture apparatus, in Selke (1898a)	United States Patent and Trademark Office, US675417
3.6	Rough state of a photo sculpture by Selke, in Straub (2005, 61)	

3.7	Schematized representation of Selke's method of photo sculpture: Advancing shadow; in Rohwaldt (2002, 60)	With permission from Suhrkamp Verlag GmbH & Co. KG
3.8a,b	Fig. 1, 2, in Schlör (1926, 718)	With kind permission of the Umschau Zeitschriftenverlag, Sulzbach
3.9	Detail, back of head of Gianlorenzo Bernini's *David*, with grid, structured light-method of reconstruction	
3.10	Karin Sander, *Persons 1:10*, 1997–1999, Galería Helga de Alvear, Madrid, 01.12.1999–22.01.2000, 3D body scans of living persons, FDM (fused deposition modeling), ABS (acrylonitrile-butadiene-styrene), airbrush Scale 1:10; height: each ca. 18 cm. Photo: Studio Karin Sander. Courtesy Galería Helga de Alvear, Madrid.	© VG Bild-Kunst, Bonn 2013 © Karin Sander
4.1	Sir John F. W. Herschel, Table correlating colored light and coloring of a paper soaked with AgCl, in Herschel (1840, 18). By 'extreme red' he means infrared	© The Royal Society
4.2	Facsimile reproduction of a direct chemical color photograph on a chlorinated silver plate by Niépce de Saint Victor (exhibited at the world fair in 1867), in Eder 1905: plate XII. See color plate 1	With permission from SPEOS

4.3	Diagram of Lippmann photography, in Bjelkhagen (1999b, 56)	With permission from Hans I. Bjelkhagen and SPIE
4.4	Lippmann's Integral, in Lippmann (1894, 104)	With permission from EDP Sciences
4.5	A Lippmann photograph of a parrot, in Coe (1979, 27). It is not possible to reproduce the appearance of a Lippmann photograph here. See color plate 2	Photograph: Dr. Neuhauss (1899); National Media Museum / Science & Society Picture Library
4.6	First three-color photograph by Maxwell (1861) in Bellone and Fellot (1981, 88). See color plate 3	
4.7	Extract of the author's credit card, on the right the security hologram. The effects of a hologram cannot be reproduced here. Instead of the script 'Mastercard' that appears in all colors depending on the light angle and that seems to lie behind the slightly convex image of a double terrestrial globe oscillating in the colors of the rainbow, one can only see spatially flat and blurred streaks	
5.1	Lippmann inspects an integral photo plate with a microscope; an assistant exposes the plate without another camera, in Anonymous (1908, 547)	

5.2	Diagram of integral photography, in Lippmann (1908, 823)	With permission from EDP Sciences
5.3	Drawing from a patent for lenticular images. The lenticular grid can be seen as planar view and as sectional view, in Hess (2001, 294)	United States Patent and Trademark Office, US1128979
5.4	Mariko Mori, *Birth of a Star* (1995), 3-D duratrans, acrylic, light box, and audio CD; 70³/16 × 45¼ × 4¼ in. (178.3 × 114.9 × 10.8 cm), Museum of Contemporary Art, Chicago. (Unfortunately, the effect of the lenticular image cannot be shown here). See color plate 4	© Mariko Mori 2009. All Rights Reserved. Photo courtesy of Mariko Mori / Art Resource, NY. © Mariko Mori, Member Artists Rights Society (ARS), New York/VG Bild-Kunst, Bonn 2013
6.1	Stereoscopy: Otto Schönstein, founder of Raumbild publishers, in his office, in Lorenz (2001, 2)	
6.2	Stereoscopy of Leni Riefenstahl while filming the Olympic Games in 1936. Photographer Hugo Jäger, in Lorenz (2001, 35)	With permission from Stiftung Deutsches Historisches Museum
6.3	Report of the "Reichsstelle zur Förderung des deutschen Schrifttums" of June 8, 1938 on the support of the stereoscopic image album Deutsche Gaue, in Lorenz (2001, 4)	
6.4	Stereoscopic image of the Reichsparteitag NSDAP in Nuremberg in 1937. Photographer Hugo Jäger, in Lorenz (2001, 33)	With permission from Stiftung Deutsches Historisches Museum

6.5	Technique of the Photoplasticon, in Benton et al. (1999, 2)	
6.6	Advertising for the Photoplasticon, in Benton (2001a, 235)	With permission from American Optical Corporation
6.7	Hitler viewing images through a stereo viewer, one section can be found in Gern (1939, 147). The whole image can be seen here; Heinrich Hoffmann at the left foreground (from the back), to Hitler's right baldheaded Otto Schönstein. Source: Bayerische Staatsbibliothek München/Fotoarchiv Hoffmann (Image No.: hoff-26107). With my thanks to Angelika Betz.	Source: Bayerische Staatsbibliothek München/Fotoarchiv Hoffmann
6.8	Cover of *Deutsche Plastik unserer Zeit*, Tank (1942)	
6.9a,b	User's Manual for the Use of the Stereo viewer. Front and Back Cover. Supplement to Tank (1942)	
6.10a,b	Stereoscopic image: Arno Breker's sculpture *Die Wehrmacht* in front of the former *Neue Reichskanzlei* (Architect Albert Speer) in Berlin; view of the back of the stereoscopic picture	
6.11	Thomas Ruff, *Ruhrgebiet I* (1996), in Bätzner, Nekes and Schmidt (2008: 142)	© VG Bild-Kunst, Bonn 2013

7.1	Kurt Schwitters, *Merzbild mit gelbem Block* (1926), Painted Wood, 65 × 56 cm, View from the side, in Rowell (1979b, 113).	© VG Bild-Kunst, Bonn 2013
7.2	Marcel Duchamp *Tu m'* (1918), 70 × 313 cm, in Gerstner (2003, 6). See color plate 5	© Succession Marcel Duchamp / VG Bild-Kunst, Bonn 2013
7.3	*Tu m'* seen from the side, in Gerstner (2003, 22)	© Succession Marcel Duchamp / VG Bild-Kunst, Bonn 2013
7.4	Marcel Duchamp, *Dust Breeding*, (1920; Photography by Man Ray), from http://www.metmuseum.org/toah/works-of-art/69.521 [last accessed September 2, 2013]	© Succession Marcel Duchamp / VG Bild-Kunst, Bonn 2013
7.5	Marcel Duchamp *Handmade Stereopticon Slide* (1918/1919), in Krauss (1993, 131)	© Succession Marcel Duchamp / VG Bild-Kunst, Bonn 2013
7.6	Marcel Duchamp: *The Bride Stripped Bare By Her Bachelors, Even*, aka *The Large Glass* (1915–1923), in Krauss (1993, 121)	© Succession Marcel Duchamp / VG Bild-Kunst, Bonn 2013
7.7	From the "Essay on Perspective," in Bosse (1987, 175)	With permission from The Erskine Press
7.8	Marcel Duchamp, *Rotary Demisphere (Precision Optics)* (1925), in Krauss (1993, 129)	© Succession Marcel Duchamp / VG Bild-Kunst, Bonn 2013
7.9	Marcel Duchamp, *Rotoreliefs* (1935), in Duchamp (2002, 117).	© Succession Marcel Duchamp / VG Bild-Kunst, Bonn 2013

7.10	Fig. 2, in Musatti (1924, 109)	
7.11a,b	Marcel Duchamp, *Rotorelief Spiral Blanche* and *Testing Disc*, in Rood (1973, 139)	© Succession Marcel Duchamp / VG Bild-Kunst, Bonn 2013
7.12a,b	Marcel Duchamp: *Rotorelief Corolle* and *Spiral Scan Pattern*, in Parker and Wallis (1948, 372)	© Succession Marcel Duchamp / VG Bild-Kunst, Bonn 2013
8.1a,b	Early Diagrams for a "Moving Screen" and a "Moving Mirror" Display, two fundamental forms of volumetric display of the "swept volume"-type (see below), in Parker and Wallis (1948, 373)	
8.2	Overview of the different types of volumetric displays, at: http://www.blohm.onlinehome.de/files/paper_pw_98.pdf [last accessed September 2, 2013]	The Felix 3D-Display uses the Helix 3D-method that was patented by its inventor Prof. Rüdiger Hartwig in 1976. With this method, laser beams are projected onto a quickly rotating helix (= screw, spiral) in a transparent tube, which generates light spots that as a whole produce a three-dimensional image. In his patent specifications, Prof. Hartwig cited, among other things, air traffic control as a possible area of application where the three-dimensional representation would be able to indicate the height and distance of the aircraft.
8.3	Fictitious volumetric display used in a sort of traffic control system, in Wiliams and Garcia (1989, 9)	With permission from Society for Information Display
8.4	Volumetric Display, in Soltan et al. (1995, 352.1)	Reprinted from Publication (see column "title"), with permission from IOS Press

8.5	Usage of a (fictitious) volumetric display for underwater control, in Soltan et al. (1996, 16)	
8.6	Usage of a (fictitious) volumetric display for a command-and-control situation, in Soltan et al. (1996, 18)	
8.7	Usage of a (fictitious) volumetric display for the control of a female body during birth, in Soltan et al. (1996, 20)	
8.8a,b	Volumetric Display in Jenny Holzer's *Lustmord* (1993–1996), left: installed at the Bergen Museum of Art, Bergen (1994); right: Detail from Holzer (1996, 99, 102)	© VG Bild-Kunst, Bonn 2013
8.9	Olafur Eliasson, *Your Blue Afterimage Exposed* (2000), Private collection, © Olafur Eliasson	With permission from Olafur Eliasson
8.10	Olafur Eliasson, *Camera Obscura* (1999), installation View: Dundee Contemporary Arts, Scotland (1999), Photo: Colin Ruscoe, © Olafur Eliasson and Dundee Contemporary Arts	With permission from Olafur Eliasson
8.11a,b	Olafur Eliasson, *Convex/Concave* (1995/2000), installation View: ZKM, Karlsruhe, Germany, Photo: Franz Wamhof, © Olafur Eliasson	With permission from Olafur Eliasson

8.12	Principle of varifocal mirror imaging, in Rawson (1969, 39)	© [2013] IEEE. Reprinted, with permission, from Rawson, Eric G. (1969): "Vibrating Varifocal Mirrors for 3-D Imaging", in: IEEE Spectrum, September 1969, p. 39
8.13	Louis Lumière: *Portraits of Pierre Bellingard*, 6 plates component of a photo-stéréo-synthèse (c. 1921), Collection Institut Lumière / Fonds Lumière © Institut Lumière	Collection Institut Lumière / Fonds Lumière © Institut Lumière
9.1	Double slit experiment according to Young. Interference of light waves into an interference pattern, http://en.wikipedia.org/wiki/File:Doubleslit.svg [last accessed September 2, 2013]	CC-by-sa-3.0-migrated, GFDL; User: *Lacatosias,* Stigmatella aurantiaca, Stannered
9.2	Enlarged illustration of the interference pattern in a hologram, in Johnston (2006a, 102)	
9.3	Gabor's in-line arrangement, in Johnston (2006a, 28)	
9.4	Off-axis hologram; early arrangement for recording a slide, in Leith and Upatnieks (1963b, 1377). It is evident that the object to be holographed has to be diaphanous	With permission from The Optical Society
9.5	Hologram of a photograph with the corresponding reconstruction, in Leith and Upatnieks (1963b, 1380)	With permission from The Optical Society

9.6	Off-axis hologram scheme of generating images as per Leith and Upatnieks, http://upload.wikimedia.org/wikipedia/commons/thumb/7/77/Holograph-record.svg/2000px-Holograph-record.svg.png [last accessed September 2, 2013]. This somewhat changed arrangement can not only 'transilluminate' at least partially or half transparent objects but can also illuminate solid ones	CC Attribution-Share Alike 3.0 Unported, User: Bob Mellish
9.7	View of a hologram as per Leith and Upatnieks; http://upload.wikimedia.org/wikipedia/commons/thumb/a/a0/Holography-reconstruct.svg/2000px-Holography-reconstruct.svg.png [last accessed September 2, 2013]	CC Attribution-Share Alike 3.0 Unported, User: Bob Mellish
9.8	One of the first holographic images by Leith and Upatnieks, in Johnston (2006a, 114). The holographic image cannot be reproduced here	With permission from Juris Upatnieks
9.9	Still from *L'arrivée d'un train à La Ciotat* (F 1895)	Arrivée d'un train à la Ciotat (Cat. Lumière N°653) Louis Lumière, 1897 © Association frères Lumière
9.10	Back cover of Virilio (1989)	With permission from Merve Verlag
9.11	Listing of Virilio (1989) at the university library Siegen. Third tag: holography	

9.12	Interference patterns on a tin can brought to vibration by Powell and Stetson (1965), in Klein (1970, 136)	With permission from Lippincott Williams & Wilkins
9.13	*GC Optronics Holographic Tire Analyzer*, photograph of the facility, in Klein (1970, 143)	With permission from Lippincott Williams & Wilkins
9.14	*GC Optronics Holographic Tire Analyzer*, schematic arrangement, in Klein (1970, 144)	With permission from Lippincott Williams & Wilkins
9.15	Image of a tire in the holographic tire analyzer, in Klein (1970, 145). The arrows mark the spots which reveal the defects in the tire by way of interference fringes	With permission from Lippincott Williams & Wilkins
9.16	Holographic contouring of a scene, in Heflinger and Wuerker (1969, 29)	Reprinted with permission from [HEFLINGER, L. O./WUERKER, R. F. (1969): "Holographic Contouring via Multifrequency Lasers", in: Applied Physics Letters, Vol. 15, No. 1, 1969, S. 28–30.]. Copyright 1969, American Institute of Physics
9.17	Holographic image of the *Venus de Milo*, in Fournier, Tribillon and Vienot (1977, 120). The effect of the holographic image cannot be reproduced here	
9.18	Four holo-interferograms of a painting from the fifteenth century, in Amadesi et al. (1974, 2012)	With permission from The Optical Society
9.19	Experimental arrangement, in Westlake, Wuerker and Asmus (1976, 85)	With permission from SMPTE

9.20	Recording of a Denisyuk hologram, at http://www.optique-ingenieur.org/en/courses/OPI_ang_M02_C10/co/Contenu.html [last accessed September 2, 2013]	CC-PD, Pascal Picart
9.21	Edwina Orr, *Self Portrait* (1982), 30×40 cm, white light reflection hologram, at: http://www.jrholocollection.com/collection/orr.html [last accessed September 2, 2013]. By representing a lens that still enlarges even as an image, this hologram illustrates the inclusion of geometrical optics. However, this phenomenon cannot be reproduced here	White light Reflection Hologram: Self portrait: Made by Edwina Orr. Copyright Edwina Orr and Richmond Holographic Studios Ltd.
9.22a,b	Scanning system of a cash register in a supermarket and respective scanning disc, in Dickson et al. (1982, 230–231)	With permission from IBM Technical Journals
9.23	'Multiplex' hologram recording geometry	Courtesy MIT Museum
9.24	A view of Dieter Jung's work *Light-Mill* (1998); computer generated holographic stereogram, 120×140 cm, in Jung (2003, 33). The effect of the holographic image cannot be represented here	© archivjung

9.25	A view of Eduardo Kac, *ADHUC*, © Eduardo Kac, 12×16 IN. (30×40 cm), digital holopoem (1991), edition of three. Collection Jonathan Ross, London; collection Karas, Madrid; collection Vito Orazem and Söke Dinkla, Essen (Germany). The effect of the holographic image cannot be represented here	© Eduardo Kac
9.26	Diagram of holographic space, in Pepper (1989, 298). The holographic object can appear before or behind the plate or even pass through the plate. Especially the last transgression of the plane is a viewing experience unknown prior to holography. See Pepper (1989, 297)	With permission from Andrew Pepper
9.27	Susan Gamble and Michael Wenyon, *Bibliomancy* (1998, holographic installation). (The effect of the holographic image cannot be represented here)	© Susan Gamble & Michael Wenyon
9.28	Henry Fox Talbot, Plate VIII, *A Scene in a Library*, in Talbot (1969, n.p.)	The J. Paul Getty Museum, Los Angeles William Henry Fox Talbot, *A Scene in a Library*, before January 1845, Salted paper print print, Image: 12.9 × 17.8 cm (5 1/16 × 7 in.)
9.29	Two holographs by Bruce Nauman with commentary, in Curiger (2006, 147). (The effect of the holographic image cannot be represented here)	© VG Bild-Kunst, Bonn 2013

9.30	Two Holograms by Bruce Nauman. Malfunctioning installation in Geneva, spatial installation on the left, detail on the right showing that the holograms cannot be discernible because of the faulty illumination (photos by Jens Schröter)	© VG Bild-Kunst, Bonn 2013
10.1	Illustration of ray tracing, in Mitchell (1992, 155). The "intersection of the visual pyramid" (Alberti 2011, 34) can be clearly recognized	Mitchell, William J., The Reconfigured Eye: Visual Truth in the Post-Photographic Era, figure 7.19, © 1992 Massachusetts Institute of Technology, by permission of The MIT Press
10.2	Diagram of computer generated holography, in Firth (1972, 49). On the left the virtual 'object beam' is generated via Fourier-Transformation. It is then superposed with the virtual 'reference beam' and then the pattern is printed	
10.3	*Random-Dot-Stereogram* showing a square above the background when viewed stereoscopically, in Julesz (1960, 1129)	Reprinted with permission of Alcatel-Lucent USA Inc.
11.1	Charlotte Posenenske, *Three-Dimensional Image* (1966)	With permission from Burkhard Brunn

INDEX

Page numbers in italics refer to figures and illustrations.